HUMANISM AND EDUCATION IN MEDIEVAL AND RENAISSANCE ITALY

This is the first comprehensive study of the school curriculum in medieval and Renaissance Italy. Robert Black's analysis finds that the real innovators in the history of Latin education in Italy were the thirteenth-century schoolmasters who introduced a new method of teaching grammar based on logic, and their early fourteenth-century successors, who first began to rely on the vernacular as a tool to teach Latin grammar. Thereafter, in the later fourteenth and for most of the fifteenth century, conservatism, not innovation, characterized the earlier stages of education. The study of classical texts in medieval Italian schools reached a highpoint in the twelfth century but then collapsed as universities rose in importance during the thirteenth century, a sharp decline only gradually reversed in the two centuries that followed. Robert Black demonstrates that the famous humanist educators did not introduce the revolution in the classroom that is usually assumed, and that humanism did not make a significant impact on school teaching until the later fifteenth century.

Humanism and Education is a major contribution to Renaissance studies, to Italian history and to the history of European education, the fruit of sustained manuscript research over many years.

' publications include *Benedetto Accolti and the Florentine Renaissance* ( ), *Romance and Aretine Humanism in Sienese Comedy* (with Louise George Clubb,), *Studio e Scuola in Arezzo durante il medioevo e Rinascimento* ( ) and *Boethius's* Consolation of Philosophy *in Italian Medieval and Renaissance Education* (with Gabriella Pomaro,).

A woodcut from Niccolò Perotti's *Rudimenta grammatices*, published by Christophorus Pesis at Venice in . Copyright: The British Library. The woodcut illustrates the full grammar curriculum of an Italian Renaissance school. Elementary education is represented by the child on the right holding an alphabet table / psalter (reproduced here with a typical handle). On the left is a slightly more advanced pupil who has moved beyond the psalter to the parts of speech (Donatus); his own psalter is shown cast aside on the floor. Beyond him is a disciplinary whip. The pupils on the right appear younger than those facing them; the former seem to represent the level of secondary Latin grammar while the latter are possibly beginning the study of rhetoric and letter writing. It is significant that the pupils in the school have their own textbooks, illustrating pupil ownership of schoolbooks in Italian education, a practice documented as far back as the thirteenth century. This illustration may constitute an advertisement for Perotti's own textbook, published here, which covered the whole range of Latin grammatical education, from the alphabet and parts of speech, through secondary grammar (syntax), up to elementary rhetoric and letter writing.

HUMANISM AND EDUCATION IN MEDIEVAL AND RENAISSANCE ITALY

Tradition and Innovation in Latin Schools from the Twelfth to the Fifteenth Century

ROBERT BLACK

CAMBRIDGE UNIVERSITY PRESS
Cambridge, New York, Melbourne, Madrid, Cape Town, Singapore, São Paulo

Cambridge University Press
The Edinburgh Building, Cambridge CB2 8RU, UK

Published in the United States of America by Cambridge University Press, New York

www.cambridge.org
Information on this title: www.cambridge.org/9780521401920

First published 2001
This digitally printed version 2007

A catalogue record for this publication is available from the British Library

Library of Congress Cataloguing in Publication data

Black, Robert, Ph.D.
Humanism and education in medieval and Renaissance Italy : tradition and innovation in Latin schools from the twelfth to the fifteenth century / Robert Black.
p. cm.
Includes bibliographical references and index.
ISBN 0 521 40192 5 (HB)
1. Latin language – Study and teaching – Italy – History – To 1500. 2. Latin language, Medieval and modern – Study and teaching – Italy. 3. Latin philology – Study and teaching – Italy – History – To 1500. 4. Educational innovations – Italy – History – To 1500. 5. Education, Humanistic – Italy – History – To 1500. 6. Humanism – Italy – History – To 1500. 7. Education, Medieval – Italy. 8. Humanists – Italy. I. Title.

PA2065.17 B58 2001
488′.0071′245 – dc21 00–050236

ISBN 978-0-521-40192-0 hardback
ISBN 978-0-521-03612-2 paperback

Contents

Acknowledgements

I have accrued numerous debts of gratitude over the many years of working on this book, and it is a great pleasure to acknowledge the liberal support and help which I have been fortunate enough to enjoy. I have received generous financial assistance from the British Academy, the Harvard University Center for Italian Renaissance Studies (Villa I Tatti), the Leverhulme Trust, the National Endowment for the Humanities and the University of Leeds. I should also like to thank the sta of the Biblioteche Medicea Laurenziana, Nazionale Centrale and Riccardiana for their patience and indulgence in putting up with the excessive requests for manuscripts which my collaborators and I have had to make in the many years of preparation involved in this study; I am also particularly grateful to the directors of the Laurenziana and Riccardiana for repeatedly allowing us to see original manuscripts, rather than microfilm copies, from their reserve and excluded collections, as well as for the facility of inspecting manuscripts with ultraviolet light when necessary. I am also extremely grateful for assistance from Gian Carlo Alessio, Rino Avesani, James Banker, Alison Brown, Virginia Brown, Alan Bullock, Geo rey Bursill-Hall, Angela Bussi Dillon, Francis Cairns, Maurizio Camaiti, Teresa D'Alessandro, Jonathan Davies, Albinia de la Mare, Teresa De Robertis, Claudio de' Stefani, Consuelo Dutschke, Vincenzo Fera, Arthur Field, Carla Frova, Luciano Gargan, Paul Gehl, Sebastiano Gentile, James Ginther, Peter Godman, Richard Goldthwaite, Paul Grendler, Jacqueline Hamesse, James Hankins, John Henderson, George Holmes, Kristian Jensen, Gavin Kelly, F. W. Kent, Christiane Klapisch, Jill Kraye, Vivien Law, Claudio Leonardi, David Lines, Alastair Minnis, Reinhold Müller, Birger Munk Olsen, Anna Maria Nada Patrone, Lodi Nauta, W. Keith Percival, the late Alessandro Perosa, Olaf Plauta, Malcolm Polfreman, Michael Reeve, Brian Richardson, Richard Rouse, Nicolai Rubinstein, David Rutherford, Federico Sanguineti, Franco-Lucio Schiavetto, Vito Sivo, Quentin

Skinner, Claudia Villa, Ronald Witt, Marjorie Curry Woods and Jan Ziolkowski. I also wish to pay tribute to the example, and express my gratitude for the enthusiastic encouragement, of the late Paul Oskar Kristeller. I owe a special debt to my wife Jane, not only for her moral support and editorial assistance, but also for her work as my research assistant during the academic year – . I am extremely grateful to Silvia Rizzo for reading the entire typescript and for pointing out a number of significant errors, especially in Latin. But my greatest academic and scholarly debt is to the palaeographer, Gabriella Pomaro, without whom, it is no exaggeration to say, this book could not have been written. Finally, I should like to express my deep gratitude to Cambridge University Press for their indulgence over repeated delays in the delivery of this book, and I am especially grateful in this regard to my editor, Richard Fisher. I should also like to thank my copy-editor, Jean Field, for her meticulous reading of the text.

This book is dedicated to my wife, Jane, and my two daughters, Emily and Alison.

School of History
University of Leeds
January

Abbreviations

Aesop	*Fabulae*, tr. Walter the Englishman	
Ambros.	Milan Biblioteca Ambrosiana	
ASA	Arezzo Archivio di Stato	
	Provv.	Deliberazioni del Consiglio Generale
ASF	Florence Archivio di Stato	
	CStrozz.	Carte Strozziane
	MAP	Mediceo avanti il Principato
ASI	*Archivio storico italiano*	
ASPCD	Prato Archivio di Stato Comune Diurni	
ASPistoia	Pistoia Archivio di Stato	
	Provv.	Consigli Provvisioni
ASSColle	Siena Archivio di Stato Comune di Colle Valdelsa	
ASSG	San Gimignano Archivio storico comunale	
	NN	Serie NN
ASU	Udine Archivio di Stato	
Avianus	*Fabulae*	
BAV	Vatican City Biblioteca Apostolica Vaticana	
	Arch. S. Pietro	Archivio San Pietro
	Barb. Lat.	Barberiniano Latino
	Ott. Lat.	Ottoboniano Latino
	Pal. Lat.	Palatino Latino
	Urb. Lat.	Urbinate Latino
	Reg. Lat.	Reginense Latino
	Vat. Lat.	Vaticano Latino
BL	London British Library	
	Add.	Additional manuscripts
	Royal	Royal manuscripts
BML	Florence Biblioteca Medicea Laurenziana	
	AD	Acquisti e doni
	Ashb.	Ashburnham
	Ashb. Append.	Ashburnham Appendice
	CS	Conventi Soppressi
	dxt.	destro

	Edili	Edili
	Med. Fies.	Mediceo Fiesolano
	Med. Pal.	Mediceo Palatino
	Pl.	Plutei
	sup.	superiore
	sin.	sinistro
BNCF	Florence Biblioteca Nazionale Centrale	
	CS	Fondo Conventi Soppressi
	Landau Fin.	Fondo Landau Finaly
	Magl.	Fondo Magliabechiano
	Magl. Append.	Magliabechiano Appendice
	NA	Nuove accessioni
	Pal.	Fondo Palatino
	Panciat.	Fondo Panciatichiano
BNP	Paris Bibliothèque Nationale	
	N. Acq.	Nouvelles Acquisitions
	Sorb.	Sorbonne
Bodley	Oxford Bodleian Library	
	Can. lat.	Canonici classici latini
	Can. misc.	Canonici miscellanei
	Lat. class.	Latini classici
	Lat. misc.	Latin miscellaneous
	Laud Lat.	Laudenses latini
	Rawl.	Rawlinson manuscripts
Boethius	*Consolatio philosophiae*	
Bonvesin	Bonvesin da la Riva *Vita scolastica*	
BRF	Florence Biblioteca Riccardiana	
Cato	pseudo-Cato *Disticha*	
Cicero	*O* = *De o ciis*, *A* = *De amicitia*, *S* = *De senectute*, *SS* = *Somnium Scipionis*, *P* = *Paradoxa stoicorum*, *DT* = *Disputationes tusculanae*	
Claudian	*De raptu Proserpinae*	
DBI	*Dizionario biografico degli italiani*, Rome –	
Geo rey	Geo rey of Vinsauf *Poetria nova*	
GSLI	*Giornale storico della letteratura italiana*	
GW	*Gesamtkatalog der Wiegendrucke*, Leipzig –	
Hain	Ludwig Hain, *Repertorium bibliographicum*, Stuttgart –	
Henry	Henry of Settimello *Elegia*	
Horace	*AP* = *Ars poetica*, *S* = *Sermones*, *E* = *Epistolae*, *CS* = *Carmen saeculare*, *Epo.* = *Epodes*, *O* = *Carmina*	
IGI	*Indice generale degli incunaboli delle biblioteche d'Italia*, ed. T. M. Guarnaschelli and D. Valenziani, Rome –	

IMU	*Italia medievale e umanistica*
JHI	*Journal of the History of Ideas*
John the Abbot	John the Abbot *De septem viciis et septem virtutibus*
JWCI	*Journal of the Warburg and Courtauld Institutes*
MSV	*Miscellanea storica della Valdelsa*
n.n.	not numbered
Ovid	*Met.* = *Metamorphoses*, *Her.* = *Heroides*, *AA* = *Ars amatoria*, *RA* = *Remedia amoris*
PL	*Patrologia latina* ed. J. Migne, Paris,
Plimpton	New York Columbia University Plimpton manuscripts
Prosper	*Epigrammata* (ed. *PL*, . –) and *Poema coniugis ad uxorem* (ed. *PL*, . –); these texts are normally presented as one work without a break (see below, n.)
Prudentius	*D* = Prudentius *Dittochaeon*, *P* = *Psychomachia*
Pseudo-Boethius	*De disciplina scolarium*
RPL	*Res publica litterarum*
Sallust	*BC* = *Bellum Catilinae*, *BJ* = *Bellum Iugurthinum*
Seneca	*Tragoediae*
Silk	Edmund T. Silk, ed., *Nicholas Trevet on Boethius. Exposicio Fratris Nicolai Trevethi Anglici Ordinis Predicatorum super Boecio De Consolacione*, unpublished typescript in New Haven Yale University Library
SM	*Studi medievali*
sn.	*signum*
Statius	*A* = *Achilleis*, *T* = *Thebias*
STC	*Short-Title Catalogue of Books Printed in Italy and of Italian Books Printed in Other Countries from to now in the British Museum*, London
Val. Max.	Valerius Maximus *Facta et dicta*
Vergil	*A* =*Aeneid*, *E* = *Eclogues*, *G* = *Georgics*
WOM	Word-order marks

Editorial note regarding citations from manuscripts and publications

Vernacular glosses are indicated in italics.

[ ] means that letters or words enclosed appear in the manuscript but are thought to be erroneous; they are also used to enclose editorial comments such as [*sic*] [MS:] [space].

< > means that letters or words have been added for the sake of coherence; their omission may have been due to scribal error, or they may no longer be legible.

Letters or words enclosed in round brackets ( ) indicate an uncertain expansion of an abbreviation.

Question marks immediately following letters or words indicate an uncertain reading.

Italicized words indicate a lemma.

= is used to indicate an interlinear gloss. What appears on the left of the sign is the word or phrase being glossed; on the right, the gloss itself.

{} occasionally enclose an interlinear gloss which is supplying an understood word: e.g. {ego} inquam.

In the case of Boethius's *Consolation of Philosophy*, (, p. ,) or (, m. ,) and so on refer to the relevant prose passage or metre line of the Bieler edition.

The orthography and latinity of the manuscripts have been retained, although the punctuation and capitalization have been modernized. *Sic* has been indicated where there is a notable or gross divergence from correct grammatical or classical usage.

Folios will normally be indicated without the abbreviations fol., fo., f., or .

Normally manuscripts from the Plutei series in the Biblioteca Medicea Laurenziana will be cited without Pl. Thus Biblioteca Medicea Laurenziana Pluteo . will be cited as BML . . When a number of manuscripts from the Plutei are listed in

sequence (for example in ch. or in Appendices and), the manuscripts will be listed in numerical order, not in the order they appear in Bandini's catalogues and in the card indices of the library (where manuscripts from Santa Croce with Plutei numbers including sin. or dxt. follow higher numbers from the principal collection, e.g. sin. after . and so on).
/ = new verse or new line.
// = new folio.
Unless otherwise indicated, all dates have been modernized.

A note on chronological terminology

I have used a number of chronological terms in a conventionalized manner; no interpretation or greater significance is meant to be implied thereby.

later antiquity	–
early middle ages	–
Dark Ages	–
high middle ages	–
later middle ages	–
middle ages/medieval	–
Renaissance	–
pre-humanist	–
humanist	–
Duecento	thirteenth century
Trecento	fourteenth century
Quattrocento	fifteenth century
Cinquecento	sixteenth century

In discussing manuscript glosses, the term 'contemporaneous' is used to described a writer working at about the same time as the copyist.

Dates according to centuries are indicated by Roman numerals (XVc.). XV^1: first half of the fifteenth century; $XV^{1/4}$: first quarter of fifteenth century; XVmid: mid fifteenth century; XIV/XVc: turn of the fifteenth century; XVex.: – ; XVin.: – ; and so on.

Introduction

Latin education was the foundation stone of medieval and Renaissance Italian culture. The learning of the Latin language and the introduction to Latin literature were the principal preoccupations of schools throughout the middle ages and Renaissance: indeed, until the rise of abacus or commercial arithmetic schools in the thirteenth and especially fourteenth centuries, and before the introduction of Greek into the school curriculum in the fifteenth century, no subject other than Latin was studied at the lower stages of the educational hierarchy.

Given the fundamental importance of the subject, it may seem puzzling that there has been no comprehensive historical study of the Latin curriculum in medieval and Renaissance Italy. This has perhaps been due to the fact that the Latin syllabus has been shared among several modern academic disciplines. The most important work has been done by philologists, such as Remigio Sabbadini and Vittorio Rossi and their more recent Italian successors, for example, Gian Carlo Alessio, Rino Avesani, Giuseppe Billanovich or Silvia Rizzo. Their principal concern has, of course, been philological rather than historical: focusing on individual works and individual teachers, they have gone far in building up a picture of pre-humanist and humanist education; but because their discipline ultimately concentrates on the particular rather than the general, philologists have not aimed to reconstruct the story of the curriculum's development over a long period. Work of great importance has also been undertaken by students of linguistics, and in particular by Keith Percival, who has laid the foundations for a critical study of medieval and Renaissance theoretical grammar. But again, because a scholar such as Percival is concerned fundamentally with the theory and development of Latin language and grammar rather than with the history of Latin education, he has not been interested in reconstructing the multi-faceted story of the evolution of the elementary and secondary grammar curriculum from its foundations in the twelfth century through to the Renaissance.

The Italian educational syllabus has also been considered by philosophers and historians. In the earlier years of the twentieth century, it tended to be subject to current academic fashions, especially those of positivism and neo-Crocean idealism. Giuseppe Manacorda's classic survey of Italian education in the middle ages, a work which extends into the fifteenth century, deals in a typically positivist fashion with the curriculum: there is detail in abundance but no overall historical picture. Quite the opposite is true of the preeminent Italian historian of Renaissance philosophy, Eugenio Garin. He brilliantly succeeded in replacing the positivism of Sabbadini and Manacorda with an overarching scheme of historical development; the di culty was that his vision of medieval and Renaissance education was thoroughly permeated with preconceptions derived from Hegelian/Crocean/Gentilian idealist philosophy and philosophical history. Among recent historians there has been renewed interest in school-level education, but in the work of scholars such as Giovanna Petti Balbi, Carla Frova, Giovanni Ortalli or Anna Maria Nada Patrone the curriculum has remained a secondary concern, overshadowed by the institutional and social dimensions of education; Paul Grendler has discussed the curriculum at greater length, but manuscript textbooks hardly enter his treatment,[1] which remains a synthesis of secondary sources (most importantly, the work of Garin) and published primary material, mainly writings of famous Italian humanists. Another limitation has been that, even for assiduous archival scholars, the documentary sources for the history of the curriculum are limited. Despite years of research in the Aretine and Florentine archives, for example, I have been able to find only a tiny cluster of documents relating to the curriculum (in contrast to the institutions and personnel of education); moreover, the archival curriculum documents, such as they are, almost invariably relate to the elementary, rather than the more advanced, levels of school education.[2]

One discipline largely absent from the study of educational history has been palaeography. Despite the fact that Italy can perhaps boast of the most sophisticated tradition of palaeographical manuscript study among all Western countries, this expertise has rarely been focused on the educational dimensions of manuscripts and particularly of schoolbooks. Notably absent has been the attempt to employ the tools of palaeography to date and localize manuscript schoolbooks, and then to use

[1] He considers four manuscripts of school authors (all of the *Disticha Catonis*), and a total of nineteen manuscripts: see Grendler ( ), – . [2] Black (d).

these results to develop a history of the canon of Latin authors read at school over a number of centuries.[3]

Another problem with modern scholarship on Italian curriculum history is that it tends to look from the top down. Dominant in previous writings have been the names of humanist luminaries such as Vergerio,[4] Barzizza, Guarino, Perotti, Valla and Poliziano. This has no doubt been due to the prominence in this field of philologists, who are justifiably concerned with outstanding and innovatory individuals. The humdrum anonymous school grammarians, glossators or pupils have scarcely interested the students of humanist philology. I remember vividly a conversation with the late Alessandro Perosa in the Biblioteca Riccardiana at the end of . That luminary of Italian philology declared that too much e ort had been spent on the *éminences* of humanism; it was now time to turn to the lower strata of culture in order to see how more than per cent of the population actually learned Latin.

This book is an attempt to fill these gaps in modern scholarship. I have attempted to use the tools of palaeography and philology to amass the data required for an historical picture of the evolution of the Italian school curriculum. Here, I am the first to acknowledge the technical di culties of the task undertaken. I began working in the later s on the curriculum and in particular on schoolbooks as a source for the history of the educational curriculum. After nearly five years of what I readily acknowledge to be haphazard and amateurish research, I had the great good fortune to encounter one of today's leading Italian palaeographers: Gabriella Pomaro, who first became my research assistant and co-worker in January . This collaboration revolutionized the possibilities for this study. On the basis of an examination together of , manuscripts in and , besides a subsequent detailed study of a group of more than codices (mainly Boethius, pseudo-Boethius, Ovid, Henry of Settimello and Statius) – work which has led to the joint publication of a book on Boethius's *Consolation of Philosophy* in Italian medieval and Renaissance education[5] – I hope to have been able to reconstruct a history of the Latin literary canon in Italian schools from the twelfth to the fifteenth century.

This book is o ered as an account of the curriculum throughout medieval and Renaissance Italy. In fact, there was no such thing as a

[3] Paul Gehl's recent attempts (and) to use palaeography to study a limited time period (the Trecento) have technical and interpretative problems.

[4] For a recent treatment of his *De ingenuis moribus*, see McManamon ( ), – .

[5] Black and Pomaro ( ).

regionalized Italian curriculum in the middle ages and the Renaissance. Although there were great variations with regard to educational preferences, both in terms of institutions and individual types of teaching employed throughout the Italian peninsula, it is clear that the middle ages and Renaissance witnessed the emergence of a general Italian syllabus. A main reason for this overall uniformity was the great mobility of teachers throughout Italy. Thus, to give just a few examples, in fourteenth-century Ravenna grammar masters from Cremona, Forlì, Pratovecchio, Fregnano, Camerino, Parma, Trent and Castrocaro are to be found;[6] Bassano wanted to appoint a teacher from Padua in but in the end had to settle for one from Bologna;[7] there was a strong prevalence of non-Genoese and non-Ligurian teachers in Genoa in the thirteenth and fourteenth centuries;[8] in Venice teachers came not only from North Italy (Parma, Mantua, Milan, Ferrara, the Trentino) and even from the South (Calabria, Sicily, Puglia) but also from all over Europe (Albania, Bavaria, Germany, France, Portugal, Prague).[9] In Tre- and Quattrocento Piedmont there were teachers not only from Lombardy (Tortona, Cremona, Brescia, Pavia, Bergamo, Milan) but also from elsewhere in North Italy (Verona, Bologna, Trent) besides from France nearby (the Dauphiné, Embrun, Nice) and even faraway (Moulins (in Central France) and Paris).[10] In my own documentary history of Aretine education, there are teachers from Milan, Parma, Tolentino and Cittaducale, not to mention Picardy, Toledo, Bourges and Bohemia.[11] During his long teaching career, Giovanni Conversini da Ravenna (–) taught in Bologna, Florence, Ferrara, Treviso, Conegliano, Belluno, Venice, Udine and Muggia.[12] In his autobiography, Conversini eloquently summed up the reasons for teachers' itinerancy:

> I speak for a common cause, not just my own. The teachers of children who are hired by the people, must on no account place their trust in the present: they must beware of the fickleness of the populace. They should always keep their ears open for new invitations and for favours from abroad; for when they stay too long in one place, their authority declines and they are considered worthless and are despised, because the populace despises what it is accustomed to and what is too easy.[13]

A second underlying reason for this general uniformity was the fact that the entire European grammatical curriculum was overwhelmingly traditional, the heritage of the Roman world as gradually modified from

[6] Bernicoli ( ), – . [7] Chiuppani ( ), .
[8] See Gorrini ( ), – for a wide-ranging list, including a number of non-Italians.
[9] Ortalli ( ), – . [10] Nada Patrone ( ), – . [11] Black (d).
[12] Kohl ( ), – . [13] Sabbadini ( ), , tr. Rubinstein ( ), .

the fifth to the fourteenth century not so much by regional variations as by generalized European religious, political, institutional and social developments, leading first to the prevalence of monastic schools and then of those run by the secular clergy. It is no accident that the kind of curriculum evident in Italy at the beginning of the twelfth century, with its emphasis on taxonomic grammar and on immersion in the study of the Latin authors, is largely indistinguishable from that found in Northern Europe at the same time. When the Italian grammatical syllabus began to diverge from the Northern European pattern at the beginning of the thirteenth century, this was due to changes in the structure of higher education with the emergence of the professional universities weighted heavily in favour of medicine, law and notarial studies, as well as to pressures from the forces of secularization and urbanization which were increasingly coming to dominate Italian society. These were peninsular rather than merely regional developments, and it is therefore not surprising that the grammar curriculum evolved generally as a single entity in Italy: it is hardly remarkable to find, as a result, that a textbook such as *Ianua* developed in a uniform way throughout the peninsula in the later fourteenth and fifteenth centuries, and that the grammar of a Tuscan master such as Francesco da Buti became a best-seller all over Italy at the turn of the fifteenth century.

The findings here are based on an intensive study of manuscripts now found in Florentine libraries: from a census of , possible literary manuscripts actually examined (not to mention many more eliminated on the basis of catalogue entries) manuscripts have been selected to form a handlist of school Latin authors now found in Florentine libraries. An examination of this handlist will provide the reader with a third and decisive reason why this book is published as a study of the Italian curriculum in general. Little more than a third of the manuscripts have been localized to Florence or Tuscany. The majority are either from other regions of Italy or are books that o er no clue as to their provenance but merely can, with security, be identified as Italian.

Locality	Number of codicological units[14]
Florence	
Tuscany	
Italy	
Central Italy	
Northern Italy	
Southern Italy	

[14] Counting each part of a composite manuscript as a separate unit.

For the study of theoretical grammar, the conclusions have been based on all the grammatical manuscripts of a school level which it has been possible to identify in Florentine libraries. A number of these (e.g. the grammars of Pietro da Isolella da Cremona, Pietro da Asolo, Gaspare Veronese or Pomponio Leto) have nothing to do with Tuscany, and, of course, other non-Tuscan published grammatical authors (most famously Guarino and Perotti) have been studied. Any work of history must of course be selective, but it seems to me that, from an historical viewpoint, systematic work through the manuscript collections of Florence as one preeminent Italian cultural centre may be preferable, or at least of equal value, to examination of individual manuscripts in a variety of collections which have characterized previous work on this subject. Florentine libraries o er an ideal opportunity for such a census: not only do the collections there o er a vast range of pre-Trecento literary manuscripts (not just in the Laurenziana but also, to a surprising extent, in the Riccardiana and Nazionale), but the huge spectrum of codices in the Laurenziana not only derives from fifteenth-century patrons and humanists (concentrated largely in the Laurenziana's Plutei, which include an enormous range of non-Florentine and non-humanist manuscripts as well) but also conventual (e.g. Fondi Conventi Soppressi, S. Marco, S. Croce), ecclesiastical (e.g. Fondo Edili) and later Florentine (e.g. Fondo Strozzi) and non-Florentine collections (e.g. Fondo Ashburnham); moreover, both the Laurenziana and Nazionale have large recent series of new acquisitions (Fondi Acquisti e Doni and Nuove Accessioni), where, of course, purchases have extended far beyond Florentine or Tuscan sources.

The first chapter of this book focuses on the historiographical perspectives which have shaped previous studies of the Latin curriculum. In particular, an attempt has been made to emphasize the advantages, as well as drawbacks, of both the positivist and the neo-Hegelian idealist approaches. I have also tried to suggest the merits and disadvantages of another study of humanist education by Anthony Grafton and Lisa Jardine (   ), a work which has been extensively criticized for its anti-humanist polemics but whose insight into the philological rather than moral nature of humanist teaching has not been fully appreciated; the main shortcoming of Grafton and Jardine's study is that they did not consider the medieval background to humanist philological teaching: here I hope to show that, not just in the Renaissance but also in the Italian middle ages, teaching was overridingly philological rather than moral.

In chapter , I examine the development of the elementary curriculum, showing how traditional methods of learning to read, developed in the middle ages (and in antiquity) before pupils had their own books, persisted into the fifteenth century, when pupil ownership of reading manuals gradually modified the reliance on memory in learning to read Latin in favour of translation. In this chapter I also deal in detail with the development of the fundamental Italian textbook of elementary education, the so-called *Ianua*, not only publishing for the first time a detailed analysis of the earliest known manuscript of this work but also showing how the nature of the text changed in response to evolving social and economic needs in later medieval and early Renaissance Italy.

In chapter , I focus on the fundamental changes which occurred in Latin education as a result of the emergence of a new philosophy of language in twelfth-century France. This innovative approach to language made possible the development of a comprehensive theory of syntax, enabling masters to work out a digestible system of teaching sentence structure and prose composition for the first time. This new theory and teaching method was popularized throughout Europe by one of the most significant textbooks of all time: Alexander of Villedieu's *Doctrinale*, published in , a work just as influential in Italy as in Northern Europe. Alexander invented the secondary grammar manual – a work which presupposes the knowledge of Latin forms already learned at the elementary level. This new secondary grammar syllabus as defined by Alexander became widespread in Italy during the thirteenth century, not only through the circulation of his own work but also by means of the Italian prose textbook or *Summa* of secondary grammar, a genre which followed Alexander's syllabus closely. However, Italian grammar was already diverging from transalpine patterns in the sense that, whereas in Northern Europe grammar was taught by memorizing verse treatises such as *Doctrinale*, in Italy pupils tended to own their own copies of prose textbooks. In the fourteenth century, these prose *summe* were given a more systematic format; even more important was the introduction of the vernacular as a tool of Latin teaching in the Trecento. In contrast to all the rapid developments in secondary grammar from the twelfth to the fourteenth centuries, the Quattrocento was a period of conservatism. The traditional character of the most widely circulated humanist treatises by Guarino and Perotti is well known through the fundamental work of Percival.[15] In this book I confirm that the vast majority of the

[15] Rizzo ( ) and ( ) has concurred in this view, adding that her study of humanist school grammars confirms that their terminology was little changed from medieval precedents.

lesser known and anonymous fifteenth-century secondary grammars were equally conservative.

The fourth chapter deals with the canon of Latin authors, divided since the twelfth century into minor (e.g. *Disticha Catonis*, *Ilias latina*, Prudentius, Prosper of Aquitaine, Henry of Settimello or Bonvesin da la Riva) and major (i.e. the Roman poetic and prose classics) authors. Based on the survey of schoolbooks in Florentine libraries, the findings here have been that the burgeoning study of the Roman classics at school in Italy during the twelfth century collapsed in the thirteenth century. This result confirms the hypothesis originally put forward by Louis Paetow in of the downfall of the classics in thirteenth-century Europe and Italy as a result of the rise of the univerisities; this view, founded on contemporary witnesses, was dismissed, on the basis of impressionistic evidence, by E. K. Rand ( ) and Helene Wieruszowski ( ) but has recently been revived by Francesco Bruni ( ), only to be once more questioned by Gian Carlo Alessio and Claudia Villa ( ). The debate hitherto has had to rely on sporadic and impressionistic evidence, but the new positive and systematic data provided by this book will, it is hoped, raise the question to a new level of scholarly discussion. The fourteenth century witnessed an extensive revival of the school classics, as well as the continuation of the study of the texts (such as the minor authors and Boethius's *Consolation*) which had been substituted for the classics in the thirteenth century. Fifteenth-century humanism, in this context, represents a continuation of the Trecento revival, in which some authors such as Cicero and Vergil attained a level of popularity unprecedented in the middle ages. Throughout the first half of the century there was also continued study of the minor authors and of Boethius's *Consolation* on a level commensurate with Trecento activity on these texts. This mixture of innovation and tradition, characteristic of the school canon in the earlier fifteenth century, was not put aside until the last decades of the century, when the humanists, in their role as education censors, finally began to have success in purging texts such as Boethius's *Consolation* and many of the minor authors from the curriculum.

Chapter considers how the Latin authors were read at school. Some recent studies have tended to equate the contents of modern printed editions with what medieval and Renaissance schoolboys read and understood in these texts.[16] This assumption can disregard the overriding importance of glossing in the process of reading before the advent of

[16] Grendler ( ); Gehl ( ).

printing. This book takes another approach, basing its findings on a study of manuscript glosses of the Florentine schoolbooks, besides a consideration of the school copies of Boethius's *Consolation* in the Bodleian Library, Oxford. The conclusion is that the glossing and teaching of these authors throughout the middle ages and Renaissance in the Italian schoolroom was overwhelmingly philological; the few moral or philosophical glosses are invariably lost in a vast sea of philological detail. Teachers made use of the great medieval commentary tradition on an author such as Boethius, but they did so selectively and always with their rudimentary philological concerns at the forefront. Thus a basic schoolbook such as Boethius's *Consolation*, far from being used as a text of moral philosophy, appears to have been read in the thirteenth, fourteenth and fifteenth centuries as a convenient anthology of Latin prose and poetry, filled with valuable grammatical, mythological, geographical, lexical and metrical material. In this chapter the approach is topical rather than chronological: although there were a few developments in teaching literary texts in the Italian schoolroom, nevertheless the overwhelming conclusion of my study of manuscript glosses has been the continuity of educational methods and interests in the period from to .

Chapter deals with the question of how pupils were taught to refine their prose writing style. It is clear that they first learned Latin according to the word order and syntax of the modern Romance languages: in other words, they were first taught what we should now call medieval Latin. In the middle ages this type of language was given the name *ordo naturalis*. Once they had fully mastered this basic Latin syntax, they moved on to what was called *ordo artificialis*. This involved an ornamented prose style, one, however, which presupposed a command of the grammatical rules of syntax involved in *ordo naturalis*. In Italian schools from the beginning of the thirteenth up to the earlier fifteenth century, the key textbook for learning this style was Geo rey of Vinsauf's *Poetria nova*, a work generally misunderstood as teaching poetic composition; in fact, the glosses to the text make it clear that the work, regardless of the author's intention, was used to teach prose style. Geo rey taught what amounted to an abstract system of stylistics, based ultimately on Cicero and Roman rhetorical theory but distorted through the prism of medieval rhetoric, the *ars dictaminis*. Under the influence of humanism in the fifteenth century, this type of stylistic ornamentation became unpalatable; teachers such as Perotti and particularly Agostino Dati substituted an easy route to Ciceronianism in their best-selling abbreviated manuals of style. Nevertheless, the basic division of teaching Latin into two stages, one grammatical, the other stylistic or rhetorical, remained. In the Renaissance, just as in the middle ages, pupils first learned *ordo naturalis* (or medieval Latin); they then gradually purified this language primarily through study of stylistic manuals, whether Geo rey of Vinsauf's *Poetria nova* or Agostino Dati's *Elegantiolae.*

Some definition of a few key terms may help to clarify the scope of this book. In England, the word school is strictly limited to pre-university education; pupils attend school, whereas universities admit students. In the United States, usage of these terms is more fluid: there are students at elementary (grammar) schools, just as there are at high schools; moreover, even great universities can be called schools. In Italy, *scuola* as an institution normally corresponds to the English usage of school, but one can speak of a preeminent university professor such as Bartolus of Sassoferrato and his *scuola,* meaning either the locality in which he taught or his pupils. In Italian, the term *scuola* tends to be broader than the English school, but not quite as wide as in American usage. In this book, I shall use the term school in the English sense. There is some contemporary justification for this. In the Catasto (tax declarations) of Florentines and their subjects, for example, there was a linguistic distinction between pupils who went to school (*scuola*) and students who went to university (*studio*),[17] as there was between school (*scholae*) and university (*studium*) in the statutes of Forlì from the second half of the fourteenth century.[18] For Italian readers of this book, the usage adopted for school here corresponds to the term *scuola di base* encountered in recent literature on the history of education; I should like to convey the point that in this book pre-university education is being discussed. These distinctions between school and university, of course, are relevant only to the thirteenth century and thereafter, when universities began to emerge. Nevertheless, even in the high middle ages there were curricular distinctions between lower and upper levels of study: it was generally recognized that youth was devoted to the pagan classics, whereas mature years should be dedicated to higher subjects (such as the Scriptures).[19] The focus of this book will be on these lower levels of the educational hierarchy, both before and after the rise of the universities. The picture which emerges from this study may seem conservative but it should be stressed that, when entering the Quattrocento, this book does not deal with the humanist school as a whole (an institution on

[17] See e.g. Black (d), – , – . [18] See Frova ( ), n. .
[19] See e.g. texts by Lanfranc of Pavia and Gerald of Wales, cited by Munk Olsen ( ), .

which more research based on surviving schoolbooks is needed), but only with its lower strata (in Guarino's case, the so-called elementary and grammatical, but not the final rhetorical, levels).[20] There can be little doubt that, as the pupil reached the upper rhetorical levels and even the end of the grammatical syllabus treated in this book (see ch. below), humanist teaching was ever more innovative; conversely, Quattrocento grammar instruction tended to be conservative, all the more so the lower the educational ladder was descended, and therefore it is little wonder that the humanists strove to free themselves as much as possible from the subordinate strata of the educational world (see ch. below,).

[20] Sabbadini ( ), – . Some students began their studies with humanists at an advanced age, for example, Giorgio Valagussa, who first went to Guarino's *scuola* (in modern Italian) but not school (in English) at about the age of nineteen (Resta ( ),).

Italian Renaissance education: an historiographical perspective

The history of education is particularly susceptible to influence from wider intellectual, philosophical and political movements; scholars have been tempted to justify their own intellectual formation by applauding or condemning the educational attitudes and assumptions of previous epochs. Historians have normally been university teachers and involvement in present-day educational issues has encouraged a tendency to see their own situation and ideals in past structures of learning. Justifications and critiques derived from contemporary educational preoccupations have frequently been imposed onto the remote past. It is necessary to begin this study of Italian pre-university education with these truisms in mind, because so much of what has been written about medieval and Renaissance education has been a ected by contemporary agendas. An e ort, however imperfect, must be made to identify modern preoccupations.[1] This is particularly important because current polemics have often had positive e ects, leading to new insights into the past, but these genuine perceptions must be distinguished from the mass of anachronistic distortion. Historical fashions have often had beneficial results: automatic scepticism in the face of innovation can be mistaken for trenchant criticism; here too one must weigh up fashion's advantages and limitations.

A case in point comes from the great age of Italian positivism, which at the turn of the twentieth century encouraged widespread research in local archives and led to the publication of numerous fundamental documentary studies, including Bellemo on Chioggia; Cecchetti, Bertanza

1 The purpose of this chapter is to bring into focus some of the major issues in the history of Italian school education and its curriculum which developed in scholarly literature in the course of the twentieth century and which will be explored in this book; its aim is historiographical, not bibliographical. Therefore, many notable studies will not be mentioned here. Further bibliography for the medieval and Renaissance Latin school curriculum will be found at the end of the volume. Recent bibliographical surveys can be found in Petti Balbi ( ); Ortalli ( ); Frova ( ); Nada Patrone ( ), a preliminary version of Nada Patrone ( ).

and Della Santa and Segarizzi on Venice; Barsanti on Lucca; Debenedetti on Florence; Gabotto on Piedmont; Massa on Genoa; Zanelli on Pistoia and Battistini on Volterra.[2] Archival work was complemented by the study of manuscripts and early printed editions, particularly focusing on the contribution of prominent teachers, including for example Rossi on Travesio, but most notable here was of course Sabbadini with his work on Giovanni da Ravenna, Barzizza and especially Guarino.[3] Such studies formed the basis of Manacorda's *Storia della scuola in Italia. Il medio evo*,[4] which, although primarily concerned with the earlier middle ages, nevertheless extended its scope into the fourteenth and fifteenth centuries.

All these works, including Manacorda's survey, enjoyed the advantages as well as the limitations of other studies influenced by positivist fashions. The contents and the problems were usually determined by the documentary evidence uncovered. Little need was felt to go beyond empirical discussion to form a broader or more analytical view of the development of schools and education in Italy. Much important material was brought to light, but no overall synthesis or general picture emerged. There was, for example, almost no assessment of the impact of humanism and the Renaissance on education; not even Sabbadini came up with a coherent evaluation of Guarino's place in the overall history of schools and teaching.

When Eugenio Garin turned to the study of Renaissance education after the Second World War,[5] Italian intellectual fashions had changed: positivism had been discredited and the dominant current was neo-Hegelian and often Crocean or Gentilian idealism. Garin's reaction to Sabbadini's work on Guarino shows how much the climate had changed:

On closer inspection, the fact that several decades of tireless and constant work, conducted with great rigour and over a vast horizon, did not even lead to an attempt at [genuine] history is not without good reason. The material, at times chaotically assembled, was too much and too little […] Whoever looks at Sabbadini's notes and at his attempts at synthesis will be almost dumbfounded: the contours are dulled; all is lost in a uniform grey. The discussion of particular points does not always meet the need for a comprehensive judgement; all historical perspective is diminished.[6]

[2] Bellemo ( ); Cecchetti ( ); Segarizzi (– b); Bertanza and Dalla Santa ( ); Barsanti ( ); Debenedetti (–); Gabotto ( ); Massa ( ); Zanelli ( ); Battistini ( ).

[3] Rossi ( ); Sabbadini ( ) ( ) ( ) ( ) and ( ).

[4] Manacorda ( ).

[5] Garin ( ) ( ) ( ) ( ).

[6] Garin ( ), – .

Garin here revealed the impatience of a new generation with the outdated ways of their predecessors.

Garin, unlike his positivist predecessors, did not see his principal purpose as an intellectual historian in bringing to light new evidence or information which then of itself would lead to greater knowledge; although he examined and even edited a number of unpublished sources for Renaissance education,[7] most of his work consisted of reinterpreting published texts and secondary material. Indeed, his major contribution was to have developed a highly focused, yet broad-ranging view of Renaissance education and particularly of the impact of humanism on schools and teaching.

Garin's interpretation was based on a sharply drawn contrast between the middle ages and the Renaissance. He painted a gloomy picture of late medieval scholastic methods, aims and curriculum. He suggested that barbarous discipline was the norm in medieval Italian schools.[8] The mainstays of the curriculum were manuals such as *Ianua*, Alexander of Villedieu's *Doctrinale*, Evrard de Béthune's *Graecismus*, Giovanni da Genova's *Catholicon*, Papias and Hugutio of Pisa's *Derivationes*; these were, he continued, read mainly in conjunction not usually with the Roman classics but with the traditional school authors such as pseudo-Cato's *Distichs*, *Ecloga Theoduli*, *Facetus*, Matthew of Vendôme's *Thobias*, *Liber parabolarum*, Aesop's fables (translated by Walter the Englishman), *Floretus*, Prudentius's *Dittochaeum*, Prosper of Aquitaine's *Epigrams* and *Physiologus*.[9] From such a curriculum boys were taught contempt for the secular world; indeed, all medieval education – even at its most classicizing – was directed, according to Garin, to religious, theological and spiritual goals.[10] When the Roman classics were occasionally brought into the schoolroom, they were a means to an end, not an end in themselves.[11] Indeed, for Garin, it had been the fundamental antipathy of the middle ages to classical culture more than the barbarian invasions which had destroyed the ancient world.[12] When secular learning was cultivated in the later middle ages, it was for technical, professional training, to allow each individual to fit into his appropriate level in the social hierarchy.[13] Scholastic education was fundamentally antipathetic to the empirical study of nature or to any real content in education; texts, not genuine subjects in themselves, were the objects of learning.[14]

For Garin, Renaissance humanism represented a revolutionary

[7] See especially Garin ( ), , . [8] Garin ( ), .
[9] Garin ( ), ; Garin ( ), – . [10] Garin ( ), – . [11] Garin ( ), – .
[12] Garin ( ), . [13] Garin ( ), , . [14] Garin ( ), .

change in European cultural history, and this dramatic new force was particularly powerful and e ective in the classroom. Most important were new aims for education:

> The school created in fifteenth-century Italy was [...] an educator of man, capable of shaping a child's moral character so as not to be preconditioned but free, open in the future to every possible specialization, but before all else humane and whole, with social links to all mankind and endowed with the pre-requisities for the mastery of all techniques but in full self-control [...] and not liable to run the risk of becoming a tool itself.[15]

In this new process of the liberal education of the whole man, Garin emphasized the role of the classics – 'the discovery of the antique accomplished by the humanists, their discovery of man as an individual entity, historically concrete and determinable'.[16] The study of the ancients represented the

> acquisition of historical consciousness and critical consciousness, of awareness of self and others, of an understanding of the fullness of the human world and its development [...] The revived study of the ancients, rediscovered as such, came to signify the discovery of a sense of human colloquium and collaboration, the initiation to the world of men. Educating youth in the classics truly thus helped to provide the beginning of an awareness of the human community in its development and its unity.[17]

Garin's view was that objective self-knowledge is developed only through knowledge of others; to know himself, an individual must be able to take someone else's perspective. This is what Garin believed humanist educators accomplished with their revival of antiquity. Through their philological, critical, historical understanding of the ancients, they enabled their pupils to know the great, exemplary figures of antiquity and hence to know themselves. This could not have occurred in the middle ages because antiquity was not then studied historically for its own sake but subjectively and uncritically, and so medieval classical studies – in so far as they existed – could not lead to the development of the whole man.

New aims meant a new curriculum and so Garin pointed to 'the abrupt change of textbooks. The *auctores octo* tend to disappear rapidly from Italian schools [...] In their place are substituted manuals and adaptations by Guarino and the direct reading of the classics.'[18] New aims also meant new types of institutions. The humanist schools were identical neither to the elementary schools nor to the universities of medieval Italy:

[15] Garin ( ), . [16] Garin ( ), . [17] Garin ( ), . [18] Garin ( ), xxii.

a new school, intermediate between elementary and university, is on the one hand formed as a renovation and unification of elementary teaching, while on the other it encroaches on the teaching of [university-level] disciplines.[19]

Educators such as Guarino Veronese or Vittorino da Feltre, as well as their humbler imitators among communal teachers, developed broader institutions of secondary instruction, which provided a wide general education, taking pupils from elementary Latin up to the threshold of professional university study. According to Garin, they were not mere grammar schools but provided teaching in all the subjects of the trivium and quadrivium, as well as in philosophy in its widest sense. They minimized the study of formal grammar, emphasizing instead the direct reading of the classics; moreover, they used texts not as ends in themselves as in the middle ages but as genuine gateways to real subjects. They were not guardians of the social hierarchy, giving technical training for narrow professions or occupations, but they educated all men equally before the choice of a career. True to their concern with the development of the whole man, humanist educators abandoned the cruel and barbarous discipline of the medieval schoolmasters in favour of persuasion, example and reason.[20] To underline the importance of these new humanist schools, Garin suggested that there was a shift in the centres of cultural gravity from traditional universities to 'private schools, individual courses, academies'.[21] From Italy, this educational revolution engulfed Northern Europe: a Parisian master, if he had reawakened after 'a century's sleep, in the Cinquecento, would not have recognized the world of learning, would have found nothing with which he had been familiar. In Italy, the phenomenon occurred first, almost a hundred years before.'[22]

Garin's formulation quickly established itself as the orthodox interpretation, and it was only in that a significant challenge was mounted by Anthony Grafton and Lisa Jardine with their article on the school of Guarino,[23] which was then incorporated into their book, *From Humanism to the Humanities: Education and the Liberal Arts in Fifteenth- and Sixteenth-Century Europe.*[24] While Garin lacked sympathy with scholasti-

19 Garin ( ), xix.

20 See especially Garin ( ), ; Garin ( ), – ; Garin ( ), xi–xiii, xix–xxi; Garin ( ), , , , , , , –, , . 21 Garin ( ), – . 22 Garin ( ), .

23 Grafton and Jardine ( ).

24 Grafton and Jardine ( ). An earlier, more limited critique of Garin's work on humanist education had been made by Robey ( ), where he argued that Vergerio's treatise *De ingenuis moribus* is more concerned with learning for its own sake than with inculcating civic virtue in pupils.

cism and deeply identified with humanism, the opposite is true of Grafton and Jardine: they see humanism as the foundation of the modern liberal arts movement in education, whose values they reject. In essence they renounce the equation between character building and the study of a canon of texts, a link which is fundamentally assumed in all systems of liberal education, whether by Cicero and Quintilian or the Renaissance humanists, Gentile and Garin, or Eliot and Leavis. On the other hand, they champion the merits of scholasticism on intellectual as well as utilitarian grounds.[25]

Each of these phases in historiographical development has yielded beneficial results. Without positivists such as Sabbadini or Manacorda there would have been far less evidence for Garin to analyse; without Garin it would have been less obvious that all the undigested research of the positivists failed to constitute a coherent historical view; without Grafton and Jardine, Garin's picture of humanist achievement would still seem all too persuasive. Yet the studies of Garin, on the one hand, and of Grafton and Jardine, on the other, are not necessarily the balanced reflections of uncontroversial authorities; their works need to be approached as contributions which have set the terms of a heated debate. Indeed, both camps have felt that more was at stake than simple historical investigation and analysis. Grafton and Jardine openly acknowledge that they have been influenced by the climate of modern educational polemics; Garin was equally a ected by twentieth-century educational currents. Grafton and Jardine may reflect the resentment of the New Left at the élitism of an establishment whose status has been guaranteed by a mystique surrounding the classical, liberal arts education provided by the public schools and Oxford and Cambridge, while Garin's works are redolent of Italian educational preoccupations before and after the Second World War.

In the idealist philosopher, Giovanni Gentile, as minister of education, reorganized Italian secondary schooling, shifting the emphasis from a technical to a broader non-specialized curriculum. After primary school, *scuole complementari* were established, furnishing the majority with a general academic education and replacing the old technical schools, which were abolished; the remaining technical institutes were downgraded, providing for only about half as many pupils as formerly. Gentile reorganized the syllabus, too, putting more stress on humanities such as Italian literature and history; Latin, previously limited to the *licei*, was

[25] Grafton and Jardine ( ), xii–xiii.

introduced into technical institutes, teacher-training schools (*istituti magistrali*) and scientific and girls' *licei*. Philosophy was to be taught not only in *licei classici* but even in *istituti magistrali* and *licei scientifici*, becoming the key, unifying subject of the curriculum. Even when these reforms were watered down throughout the s, the humanist tone of Italian secondary education remained, and Latin became the core subject of the curriculum at the new *scuole medie* established as junior secondary schools for most of the population.[26]

Of course these reforms, introduced by and identified with the Fascist regime, came under attack in the political atmosphere of post-war Italy. As Gentile's protégé, Garin entered the fray to safeguard what many Italian intellectuals considered to be a principal achievement of the Fascists under his mentor's guidance – the establishment of a national humanist, liberal arts education not just for an élite but for a wide segment of the population. Hence, Garin's impassioned defence of the humanist school in the foreword to *L'educazione in Europa*; indeed, he explicitly related his forthcoming historical treatment of Renaissance education to contemporary 'debates, ever more intense, on the reform of Italian schools'.[27] For him, humanist education was not the study of dead languages but a moral formation in contact with exemplary human experience, shaping the critical historical consciousness. Humanist education gave freedom from tyranny, whether of bosses, institutions, machines, organizing groups, church, or state. The association with heroic individuals of the past led to critical and tolerant understanding and a concrete sense of humanity. He rejected a type of schooling in which each person was given a technical training according to his social station and function, thus perpetuating class di erences. Instead, youth should be brought by general education to the point of professional choice, so that they could think, direct and control the political leaders themselves.[28] Garin might just as well have been speaking of the dispute between humanists and scholastics during the Renaissance as of the debate between Gentilian theorists and technocrats in the twentieth century. He identified the educational issues of contemporary Italy with those of the fourteenth and fifteenth centuries.

Moreover, Garin's thesis was not only the product of educational politics but also of the intellectual world of neo-Hegelian idealist philosophy, which had a profound influence on twentieth-century Italian

[26] Clark ( ), . Minio-Paluello ( ) contains a clear outline of educational reforms in Italy under the Fascists, besides a lucid explanation of Gentile's educational theory and its close parallels to Croce's ideas on – . [27] Garin ( ), . [28] Garin ( ), – .

thought, especially in the field of Renaissance intellectual history. Bertrando Spaventa introduced Hegel into Italian philosophical circles during the s,[29] and his approach was a determining influence on the two giants of Italian philosophy in the early twentieth century – Croce and Gentile. Benedetto Croce gave little attention to humanism, but his support for the Hegelian literary historian De Sanctis and criticisms of the pro-Catholic revisionist To anin added weight to this tradition in Italy.[30] It was above all Giovanni Gentile who developed an Hegelian/idealist interpretation of Renaissance humanism in Italy: the middle ages had devalued man and life in this world; Italian humanism, by contrast, restored the dignity of man, the potential of the human mind and the value of earthly existence.[31] This Hegelian approach continued to find powerful support in contemporary Italian philosophical circles, and Garin, as Gentile's protégé, gave particular emphasis to this view of Renaissance humanism as a new philosophy of man, in contrast to the medieval devaluation of humanity.[32]

Garin, moreover, also embraced the other colossus of Italian neo-Hegelian idealism. In emphasizing freedom as the end result of a humanist education and maintaining that liberal studies created the free man, he recalled Croce's central tenet that the history of mankind represented an instinctive striving for freedom, that history was the story of liberty. Croce's stress on the development of the human spirit through history was reflected in Garin's view that through the historical study of the ancients the whole man was formed. Croce's rejection of materialism in favour of idealism was seen in Garin's view that a humanist education gave men ideals, not material benefits gained through vocational competence; similarly, this Crocean emphasis on the historical development of ideas rather than things was found in Garin's view that the di erence between the middle ages and the Renaissance was not so much a material distinction in the level of classical culture as a new intellectual attitude towards the classics. Garin was a true Crocean historicist: historicism's axiom that there are no absolute standards and that everything is contingent on its historical position is found in Garin's emphasis on the humanists' discovery, through their liberal education, of the diversity of man and his development: they acquire an almost Crocean enlightened relativism, realizing there is no unique truth, that 'knowledge [*scienza*] in cannot be the same as [it was] in , that

29 Spaventa ( ); Ferguson ( ), .
30 De Sanctis ( ); Croce ( ); Ferguson ( ), – , .
31 Ferguson ( ), – , Gentile ( ) ( ) and ( ).
32 Garin ( ).

it is organic and the rational result of precise data'.[33] For Garin, through philology and liberal education, pupils in the Renaissance became aware of the individuality of all human societies and of the entire historical process; his view that true classical learning resulted only from historical understanding reflected historicism's postulate that genuine knowledge could be obtained only through history.

Particularly historicist were Garin's tendency to see events in terms of a larger historical process and his suggestions that only through comprehending these greater historical abstractions could concrete events be understood. Thus the succession of Barzizza to Travesio as the communal grammarian of Verona represented a profound 'change of times'.[34] Gregory the Great's and Peter Damian's criticisms of secular learning were not mere polemical positions, specific to particular controversies (the suppression of paganism or the encouragement of purer monasticism), but for Garin they became signs of the profoundly anti-classical *Weltanschauung* of the middle ages.[35] Cicero was revived by earlier humanist teachers not because of their greater enthusiasm for antiquity but because of their new focus on man, with whom Cicero had been completely preoccupied.[36] Poliziano's rejection of Cicero as a model and his stress on self-expression represented the growth of historicist individualism, not merely a preference for Quintilian (who stressed *ingenium*) over Cicero (who emphasized *imitatio*). Valla's revival of Latin was not the result of his Roman patriotism but of his recognition of the universal human community and of a general human, not just Roman, renaissance.[37]

As has been seen above, the roots of twentieth-century Italian idealism are in Hegel, and so it is not surprising that Garin voiced a number of Hegelian commonplaces. The notion of the essential interrelation of di erent aspects of life in a given period – central to the Hegelian concept of the spirit of the age[38] – is seen in Garin's vision of a new poetry, linked to a new education, to a new political and social equality, liberty, humanity, secularism.[39] The Hegelian view of the Reformation as the religious embodiment of the Renaissance is apparent in Garin's assertion that humanism led to a religious reform because it freed man's critical spirit.[40] The Hegelian historian with whom Garin particularly sympathized was Burckhardt,[41] whose famous motto, 'the discovery of man and the world', he repeated and paraphrased.[42] Indeed, Garin's view that objective self-knowledge was accomplished by the revival of

[33] Garin ( ), . [34] Garin ( ), . [35] Garin ( ), . [36] Garin ( ), .
[37] Garin ( ), – . [38] Gombrich ( ). [39] Garin ( ), .
[40] Garin ( ), . [41] Gombrich ( ). [42] Garin ( ), , – .

antiquity was foreshadowed by Burckhardt;[43] in fact, Garin explicitly acknowledged his a nity with Burckhardt.[44] Characteristic of the Hegelian/Burckhardtian approach to historical periodization were Garin's chronological ambiguities. Just as Burckhardt had to push the beginnings of the Renaissance back to the court of Frederick II, so Garin had to allow for the appearance of typically Ciceronian (and Renaissance) attitudes to language, eloquence, character formation and education under the Carolingians and in the twelfth century.[45] Similarly, in order to find concern with subjects apart from texts he seemed to make Descartes appear as a Renaissance philosopher.[46]

A recent approach to this philosophical and political/ideological penetration of scholarship on Renaissance education has been an inclination to reinforce historical orthodoxy.[47] Paul Grendler tends to accept Garin's view of the influence of humanism on Renaissance education, while discounting the critique of Grafton and Jardine. He adopts the Burckhardtian strains in Garin's work, painting a negative picture of late medieval Italian school education: he plays down the teaching of the Roman classics and a rms the predominance, until the arrival of the humanists, of the traditional medieval school authors,[48] while emphasizing the wider limitations of medieval thought.[49] The coming of the *studia humanitatis*, on the other hand, represented 'a curriculum revolution, one of the few in the history of Western education, in the relatively short time of about fifty years – to '.[50] There was a decisive rejection of the medieval syllabus: 'The humanists of the fifteenth century changed the Latin curriculum, a major academic revolution. They discarded the late medieval Latin curriculum of verse grammars and glossaries, morality poems, a handful of ancient poetical texts, and *ars dictaminis*.'[51] Grendler accepts that there was some teaching of classical Latin poetry in the medieval classroom,[52] but sees a new approach in the introduction by humanist teachers of Cicero's letters into the grammar syllabus.[53] Grendler defends Garin's orthodoxy against the heterodox blasts of Grafton and Jardine, suggesting that their critique is anachronistic.[54]

More profitable than adherence to one or the other side of this debate would perhaps be an attempt to identify the major issues which this

[43] Burckhardt ( ), . [44] Garin ( ), . [45] Garin ( ), – .
[46] Garin ( ), . [47] Grendler ( ). [48] Grendler ( ), – .
[49] Grendler ( ), . [50] Grendler ( ), – . [51] Grendler ( ), .
[52] Grendler ( ), – . See Garin ( ), . [53] Grendler ( ), .
[54] Grendler ( ), .

dialogue has raised. One of these is obviously the question of the contrast between medieval and humanist education. Here adversarial polemics have tended to reinforce the assumption that schools and curriculum in the middle ages and Renaissance were radically divergent. Indeed, one feature shared by Garin's, Grafton's and Jardine's and Grendler's work is an emphasis on the gulf separating medieval and humanist education: while Garin and Grendler highlight the limitations of the medieval Italian school in comparison with its Renaissance successor, Grafton and Jardine reinforce precisely the same historical mould by insisting on the vitality of scholastic education in contrast to the rigidity of humanist teaching. Nevertheless, by sustaining the view that the coming of humanism at the turn of the fifteenth century signalled, whether for better or worse, an educational revolution, these approaches tend to obscure significant elements of continuity before and after ; moreover, by focusing on the advent of humanism as the decisive turning point in the history of late medieval and early modern education, such perspectives sometimes overlooked other significant moments of change.

Grafton and Jardine, as well as Garin, highlight the contrast between humanism and scholasticism when comparing medieval and Renaissance education at the school level. And yet this point of view disregards one fundamental fact: scholastic subjects were rarely studied before university. Logic, philosophy, medicine, law and theology were the almost exclusive preserve of the Italian *studia.* To contrast scholasticism with humanism is to set university-level instruction against pre-university learning; humanist teachers are comparable with thirteenth- or fourteenth-century grammar and/or rhetoric masters rather than with dialecticians, philosophers or theologians. The assumption of a sharp contrast between middle ages and Renaissance in terms of the dispute between humanism and scholasticism has diverted historical study from a systematic comparison between medieval and Renaissance elementary and grammar teaching. When such an analysis is undertaken – whether in terms of theoretical textbooks,[55] or of practical teaching techniques[56] – then it will be seen that tradition is at least as striking as innovation with regard to a number developments in Italian education during the fifteenth century. Even with regard to the canon of authors read at the grammar school level, it will become clear that the Quattrocento presented a complex picture of tradition and innovation

[55] See below, chs. , .   [56] See below, ch. .

in the study of Latin literature in the Italian schoolroom.[57] The most novel feature of the school curriculum in the fifteenth century was the teaching of Latin prose writing: it will be seen that Ciceronian style was introduced into the classroom in the course of the Quattrocento. And yet even at this level, the overall curricular structure remained, as it had been in the earlier period, based on a progression from natural and simple language to artificial and ornate style; pupils continued to learn two kinds of prose at school, with medieval Latin remaining the point of departure for stylistic ornament and artifice.[58]

Moreover, the preoccupation of scholarship with the educational changes brought in the wake of the fifteenth-century Renaissance has tended to put into the shade the possible e ects on pre-university education of other major intellectual upheavals. It is well known that the rise of the universities and of scholasticism after the turn of the thirteenth century constituted one of the major turning points in the history of Western learning. As Italian universities concentrated on and gained a monopoly of higher professional education particularly in law and medicine but also in philosophy (the so-called arts), it will be seen that the preliminary grammar or Latin curriculum also became compartmentalized, entrusted to specialist grammar teachers. The e ect of this new specialization of education is well known at the university level: Italian scholasticism became ever more preoccupied with the philosophical, scientific and, eventually, theological disciplines. However, there has been little attention devoted to the collateral e ects of these developments on the grammar schools. It must be asked whether broader philosophical studies and questions (especially moral philosophical issues and topics) continued to be pursued at the school level, or whether they were now relegated to the universities. The rise of scholasticism brought new authors into vogue: not just Aristotle and the Arabs but also new grammatical texts such as *Magnae derivationes*, *Doctrinale*, *Graecismus* and *Catholicon*; it must be wondered whether the old stalwarts of the classroom, such as Vergil or Cicero's shorter moral treatises (*De amicitia*, *De senectute*, *Somnium Scipionis*, *Paradoxa stoicorum* and *De o ciis*) su ered a corresponding loss of popularity. Another major intellectual change in the thirteenth century was the rise of the Italian vernacular. Although it may have remained theoretically inconceivable to teach elementary reading and writing in the *volgare*, nevertheless increasing use of the vernacular in literary, commercial, religious and political life will be seen to have

[57] See below, ch. . [58] See below, ch. .

exerted profound e ects on educational practice; indeed, it needs to be considered to what extent the *volgare* was used in the actual teaching of Latin.[59] Moreover, the end of the thirteenth century saw the rise of pre-humanism, with the introduction of new texts previously little read in the middle ages, such as Seneca's tragedies or Valerius Maximus's *Facta et dicta*; it must be asked to what extent such works began to enter the grammar curriculum during the fourteenth century, well before the advent of the humanist educators.[60] Overall, it will become clear that curriculum change at the pre-university level was a complex development from the thirteenth to the fifteenth centuries in Italy: spotlighting Renaissance humanism as the only or even the paramount influence in the history of education over these three centuries is to oversimplify a complex and many-sided historical process.

Another important issue arising out of the debate over humanist education is the moral content of grammar teaching, a question forcefully raised on a concrete level by Grafton and Jardine, who examine Guarino's actual classroom practice on the basis primarily of four commentaries apparently deriving from his school. These seem to show that, whether Guarino was teaching his own lexical *Carmina di erentialia*, Vergil's *Georgics, Rhetorica ad Herennium* or Cicero's *De amicitia*, his focus was on language, grammar and philology (in its broad sense including historical, mythological and geographical exegesis), not on moral philosophy;[61] in other words, despite Guarino's own claims that he shaped his pupils' characters, equipping them for the active life in order to benefit state and society, he in fact o ered little explicit training in morals. Grafton and Jardine therefore conclude that the product provided by humanist teachers did not live up to the claims of their advertising.[62]

Why then did parents, civic governments, rulers or the church employ these self-important and dubious educators? Grafton and Jardine answer that humanist education was not successful or appealing because it created better men but rather because its tedious philological and mnemonic methods, with their emphasis on rote learning rather than analysis and logical argument, trained pupils to be docile – hence the potentially malleable bureaucrats in the emerging absolutist regimes of early modern Europe; scholasticism, on the other hand, was unsuited for this new social and political function of education because it trained men to think and argue for themselves.[63]

59 See below, and .
60 See below, .
61 Grafton and Jardine ( ), – , – , .
62 Grafton and Jardine ( ), – , , , .
63 Grafton and Jardine ( ), xiii–xiv.

Grendler rejects Grafton's and Jardine's conclusion that the content of humanist teaching did not live up to its pretentious claims of moral improvement. They have objected, he declares,

> that Italian Renaissance Latin education failed to inculcate the values of the citizen-orator, partly because of a preoccupation with the minutiae of learning Vergil, Cicero, and others. Obviously, schools devoted a great deal of e ort to minutiae, particularly at the primary and secondary levels. But there seems no reason to doubt that teachers and theorists who asked students to compile notebooks of moral and civic *sententiae* tried to teach these values. And the reading, from the *Disticha Catonis* to Cicero's letters, was full of moral and social commonplaces.[64]

Such a point of view, however, presumes that the medieval and early Renaissance reader approached the text in the same way as the modern reader, but this assumption can overlook the essential contribution of the commentary and glossing tradition. Indeed, such were the technical hurdles in the period before printing that one must assume that what the medieval reader took from a classic text is what appears in the glosses, not in the original text. In the middle ages and early Renaissance, there were no readily accessible, easily used editions of literary texts such as began to appear in print from the end of the fifteenth century. The manuscript copies which readers had to cope with were highly corrupt, often di cult or impossible to decipher; moreover, pupils were working with a language which was not their mother tongue and of which they usually had a far from competent knowledge. Even more significant was the di culty of the Latin literary canon itself: these were not works to be easily comprehended, like now, in accessible translations. They were composed in a deliberately elevated and even obscure style; thorough comprehension of this canon was more than a life's work for the greatest scholars. Pupils (and readers in general) coped with these immense di culties through glossing and commentary. It will be seen that they used a wide range of interlinear and marginal techniques in order to begin to climb the mountain of textual understanding.[65] It is clear that they were able to extract far less, not more, from these texts than was o ered by the glossing and commentary tradition; the fact is that whatever their glosses reveal constitutes the limit, not the minimum, of their comprehension and understanding. Glossing was an inherent and essential aspect of reading in the middle ages, as witnessed by the proliferation of commentaries on such texts as Boethius's *Consolation*. As Egbert of Liège declared,

[64] Grendler ( ), . [65] See below, .

You who rummage in the writings of Vergil without glossing them pick only at the shell without tasting the nut.[66]

Similar had been the experience of a ninth-century Italian teacher, who complained that lack of an adequate commentary had prevented him from coming to terms with Juvenal's last two satires.[67] The reliance placed by medieval and Renaissance readers on glossing is further demonstrated by Boccaccio, who found that, without them, he could not do justice to Statius's *Thebais.*[68] Indeed, it is no accident that the medieval method of reading, involving copious interlinear and marginal glossing, not to mention the entire handwritten commentary tradition, eventually waned with the progress of the printed book; stable texts, published translations and printed commentaries eventually obviated the need for painfully gradual comprehension based on interlinear and marginal glossing.

Further investigation and study of school glossing is called for, all the more so in view of suggestive remarks regarding manuscript schoolbooks before the age of humanism made by Paul Gehl, who observes that the glosses on these characteristic school texts were philological, not moral.[69] Grendler too finds that the methods of sixteenth-century teachers similarly resembled the practices of their fourteenth- and fifteenth-century forerunners: indeed, one of the most interesting patterns to emerge from his discussion of sixteenth-century teaching is the general absence of morals as a topic in school-level commentaries: 'Despite the barrage of humanistic assertions that Terence taught virtue, printed commentaries did not draw out moral lessons but confined themselves to expository paraphrase, grammatical analysis, and explanation of unfamiliar persons and terms';[70] 'Renaissance commentators on Horace confined themselves to grammatical, rhetorical, and poetical analysis';[71] the 'commentary tradition of Caesar consisted almost exclusively of geographical and historical information', nor 'did the commentaries draw moral lessons from Caesar's works';[72] a 'teacher who paraphrased the text and explained Sallust's meaning did not have to develop moral lessons from historical behavior, because Sallust did it for him';[73]

66 'Qui sine commento rimaris scripta Maronis, / Inmunis nuclei solo de cortice rodis': Egbert von Lüttich ( ), , vv. – : see Riché ( ), ; Alessio ( ), .

67 'Mox pariter primo Iuvenale [...] / cuius nempe duos extremos carpere libros / egestas commentorum nos distulit egre': cited by Villa ( ), , ; see Alessio ( ), – .

68 Billanovich ( ), : 'Nam cum pridem casu fortuito pervenisset ad manus meas liber pulcerrimus [...] emi pro pretio competenti: sed cum sine magistro vel glosis intellectum debitum non attingam [...]'

69 Gehl ( ), – .

70 Grendler ( ), .

71 Grendler ( ), .

72 Grendler ( ), , .

73 Grendler ( ), .

'Valerius Maximus might be seen as a moral philosopher, but Renaissance schools treated him as a historian.'[74] All these suggestive hypotheses by Grafton and Jardine, Gehl and Grendler have inspired the further study of manuscript glosses contained in this book, whose findings, as will be seen below, have been to confirm the view that glossing and commentary at the school level in medieval and Renaissance Italy was philological, not moral.[75]

A close study of school glosses, therefore, will tell a di erent story from the one detailed in Gehl's own work on Trecento Tuscan education, where he relies on the contents of modern printed texts rather than on accompanying manuscript glosses as a guide to the lessons which might have been learned in the medieval and Renaissance schoolroom. His justification for this procedure is signalled in the title *A Moral Art*: Latin was a moral, not just a philological and grammatical subject in the middle ages. The implication is that the study of glosses is less than imperative, because morality was being taught anyway through the very nature of the subject. What this approach tends to overlook is that Latin's status as a morally inspiring study has been a commonplace taken for granted throughout the history of Western education since antiquity. Roman educational theorists such as Cicero and Quintilian had stressed the moral aims of education and yet when the actual educational practices of grammarians such as Donatus, Servius or Priscian are examined, one finds only grammar and philology, not morals; indeed, despite emphasizing the moral utility of the classics,[76] Quintilian's own description of how they should be commented upon in the schoolroom focuses exclusively on philological details.[77] The logical consequence of all this is not that actual teaching was in fact moral because the Latin language was assumed to be an ethical subject but the very opposite: because it was taken for granted that Latin was a moral discipline, teachers did not have to inculcate moral lessons in the classroom. For the very reason that Latin was assumed to be a moral art, teaching in the schoolroom did not have to focus on lessons for good behaviour but could concentrate on technicalities of grammar and philology.

Like Grafton and Jardine, Grendler produces evidence that among sixteenth-century Italian teachers too there is evidently the same tacit assumption that close reading itself engendered morality: although their commentaries on Terence contained no moral lessons, some 'instructors developed the moral lessons orally. The editor of a new Aldine printing

[74] Grendler ( ), . [75] See ch. below. [76] *Institutio oratoria*, .viii. – .
[77] *Institutio oratoria*, .viii. – .

( ) of the *Comoediae*, who claimed to have spent years teaching Venetian youths, made this point. One must explain orally to boys that Terence develops virtue. His ingenious artifices and situations engender delight and teach good habits to the young, he wrote.'[78] Similarly, despite the solely literary and rhetorical character of Horace commentaries, 'Giovanni Fabrini in summarized the view that moral philosophy could be taught through Horace: "Horace's intention is to bring man to perfection, filling him with those moral virtues that make him perfect, in e ect rational and, as a consequence, blessed."'[79] These Italian teachers asserted that there was a connection between reading classical literature and the development of good character, but their classroom practice (not surprisingly, given the dubious morality of so much Roman poetry and drama), as revealed by their commentaries, did not develop the links explicitly or concretely.

The determination to refute Grafton's and Jardine's thesis that grammar was not a moral art has tended to divert attention from a pressing historical question: why was this moral content so egregiously absent in school education particularly during the fourteenth and fifteenth centuries? Here further study of the commentary tradition is essential. Indeed, if one considers earlier medieval teachers such as Remigius of Auxerre, William of Conches or Nicholas Trevet, who have left, for example, fundamental commentaries on a canonical educational text such as Boethius's *Consolation*, it will be found that their teaching was not only philological and grammatical but also embraced a wide range of philosophical topics (including morals), not to mention natural science and theology.[80] On the other hand, the commentaries by Italian teachers of Boethius, such as Pietro da Moglio and Giovanni Travesio, have been found to be almost entirely grammatical and philological.[81] Discounting or overlooking the glossing tradition shifts the focus away from this fundamental problem of educational history: why were medieval and scholastic teachers so much more concerned with philosophical (including moral) questions than their Italian successors in the fourteenth and fifteenth centuries?

This question demands more detailed consideration than has been o ered by historians of schools and teaching: if medieval education is identified with Aristotelian scholasticism, then the possibility of a comparative examination of the glossing of similar school texts over a chron-

[78] Grendler ( ), . [79] Grendler ( ), . [80] Silk ( ); Silk; Nauta ( ).
[81] Black and Pomaro ( ), esp. – ; Federici Vescovini ( ); Frati ( ).

ological range embracing both the middle ages and Renaissance does not arise. Once, however, it is realized that similar texts were read and glossed at school throughout the medieval and Renaissance periods, then there arises the problem of why humanist educators and their medieval forerunners, the Italian schoolmasters of the thirteenth and fourteenth centuries, eliminated the rich moral and philosophical content of the commentary tradition emanating from earlier medieval schools.

When the question is posed in this way, it is not di cult to find the answer. Indeed, the crux of the issue is the specialization of education which occurred in the course of the later twelfth and thirteenth centuries in the wake of the emergence of the universities. In earlier medieval schools, on the one hand, there had been a unitary curriculum, beginning with elementary reading and grammar and terminating with philosophy/theology, all of which was taught within one institution;[82] on the other hand, with the new specialized educational system which emerged at the turn of the thirteenth century, higher studies such as law, medicine, philosophy and theology became the preserve of universities and *studia*, whether secular or conventual. Their counterparts were similarly emerging specialized institutions of lower education, both primary and secondary: elementary schools for reading and writing, grammar schools for Latin and abacus schools for mercantile studies. Corresponding to these specialized institutions were specialist teachers: *doctores puerorum* for reading and writing, *maestri di abaco* for commercial arithmetic and *magistri grammatice* for Latin. The horizons of elementary teachers hardly extended further than the most rudimentary knowledge of Latin; the culture of abacus masters was firmly rooted in the vernacular, which was the language of their textbooks and curriculum; Latin was the province of the grammar masters, whose interests and preparation were limited to Latin language, literature and basic philology.

[82] There had been precedents for an institutional division between elementary and secondary education, for example, the Roman distinction between teachers of reading and writing, on the one hand, and grammar on the other (Quintilian, .iv.); with the contraction of education in the earlier middle ages, however, the tendency had been to see the school, whether monastic or cathedral, as a single institution: Charlemagne's *Admonitio generalis* of , providing for 'scholae legentium puerorum [...] psalmos, notas, cantus, compotum, grammaticam per singula monestaria vel episcopia' (cited by Riché ( ), n.), seems to imply single schools encompassing both the trivium and the quadrivium. Carolingian external schools were little developed and even so did not imply a hierarchy of learning: Hildebrandt ( ). The document describing the division of Milanese cathedral schools in the earlier XIc. into two groups, one 'ad docendos pueros', the other 'philosophorum vero scholae diversarum artium peritiam habentium, ubi urbani et extranei clerici philosophiae doctrinis studiose imbuebantur' (Sasse Tateo ( ), and n.), seems to imply an institutional division between schools for boys and study at a higher level, not one between elementary and secondary schools.

There is all the di erence in the world between a teacher such as William of Conches, whose interests and knowledge ranged from grammar to philosophy, science and theology, and his later Trecento Italian counterpart, Pietro da Moglio, grammarian at Bologna, with horizons scarcely reaching beyond Latin grammar, philology and rhetoric. The humanist successors of these medieval Italian grammarians, of course, took the linguistic and philological interests of their predecessors to new and previously unimagined depths, but they fundamentally remained within the context of the same specialized educational system which had developed in the course of the thirteenth and fourteenth centuries: it will hardly come as a surprise to find that, like their humbler medieval Italian predecessors, they too focused on grammar and philology, not on philosophy, in their school-level glosses and commentaries. This demotion of grammar to a school-level subject was peculiar to later medieval Italy; in Northern Europe the study of grammar continued to extend into higher education, closely associated with logic and philosophy: hence speculative and modistic grammar – a subject to which Italians made almost no contribution – was a university, not a school-level discipline north of the Alps.[83]

However, the specialization of education in the later middle ages and early Renaissance did not stop with the division between elementary and grammar teaching. A further type of specialist master emerged in the fourteenth century: the *auctorista*, who developed his particular expert knowledge in lecturing and commenting on the classical authors. Earlier in the middle ages, teachers such as Remigius of Auxerre or William of Conches had covered an enormous spectrum, as is revealed by their commentaries, which ranged from treatments of relatively simple grammarians such as Donatus and of typical school authors such as Cato or Prudentius, to the Roman classics such as Ovid or Vergil and rhetorical texts by Cicero, not to mention their expositions of philosophy and theology. In the fourteenth century, however, there emerged a new type of specialist master who gave particular attention to the authors and to rhetoric. Famous examples of such teachers were Giovanni del Virgilio in the early Trecento, Nofri di Giovanni at Colle Valdelsa in ,[84] and Gasparino Barzizza at the turn of the fifteenth century. Of course, there continued to be an overlap between *auctoristi* and *grammatici*. Towns such as Arezzo, especially in the later Tre- and

[83] For the division of grammar into two streams during the XIIc. and XIIIc., one directed at school-level education, the other towards higher levels of study (especially logic and philosophy), see Kessler ( ), ; Gardenal (b), , who cites further bibliography, nn. – .

[84] See Bacci ( ), and below, .

earlier Quattrocento, expected their *maestri di grammatica* to cover both grammar and the classical authors: it is no accident that from this broad Aretine environment there emerged a teacher such as Domenico di Bandino, who taught not only basic and secondary grammar, but also lectured on classical authors such as Cicero and Statius in Bologna. But at the same time there were clear signs of specialization, as in the case of Giovanni Travesio, who after was exempted from teaching basic grammar to boys ('doctrina puerorum et gramatice positive'), and promoted now 'ad legendum auctores magnos, rethoricam et grammaticam speculativam'.[85] Similar indications of specialization also found expression in the contrast between *auctorista* and *grammaticus* which was articulated with clarity at Fano in , when the citizenry expressed the desire to have a grammarian, not an *auctorista*.[86] It is well known that the *auctoristi* of the later middle ages became the *umanisti* of the Renaissance.[87] Of course, some humanists continued to wear two hats in the Quattrocento: renowned examples were Guarino Veronese or even Lorenzo Valla. But the growing division between the two areas of the curriculum is unmistakable. Petrarch, of course, was, as in so many other things, a harbinger of future developments: not only did he resist becoming a grammar teacher all his life but he wrote famously to a prominent grammarian and friend, Zanobi da Strada, upbraiding him for his ignoble profession.[88] Even a master who loved teaching such as Giovanni Conversini could bitterly refer to 'pedagogii sordidum munus', 'infestum fedumque negocium discipulare' and 'sordida et humilis grammatice veritatis catedra'; Conversini himself was reproved by a friend for his 'fedissimum exercitium'.[89] These attitudes and trends were given concrete expression in countless university *rotuli* of the fifteenth century, where teachers of grammar were distinguished both in terms of title and of salary from professors of rhetoric and poetry.[90] It is no accident that Suetonius's distinction between the *grammaticus* and

85 Rossi ( ), .

86 Bartoccetti ( ), : 'uno maestro che sia bono gramaticho senza esser auctorista o poeta, sperando che i loro figlioli imparено gramaticha e non più, e chi volesse che imparassero più, gli mande a studiare altrove'.

87 See Billanovich ( ), – . A transitional moment is noticeable in , when a grammarian in Modena bought a house from his earnings 'ex exercitio legendi in scolis et docendi gramaticam, poetas, rethoricam et humanitatis auctores': Vicini ( ), .

88 Petrarca (–), , – . See Rubinstein ( ), n. ; Grendler ( ), .

89 Sabbadini ( ), – , where similar examples from Vergerio, besides from Ferrara and Naples, are cited. See Rubinstein ( ), n. , who rightly points out that this view of the grammar schoolmaster was not just a topos.

90 Park ( ); Davies ( ); Verde (–), , – *passim*; Dorati da Empoli ( ), – , – ; Chambers ( ). For the same kind of curriculum divisions operating in Venice, see Ross ( ), – , – .

grammatista[91] came back into vogue in the later Quattrocento.[92] In terms of the school curriculum, the *studia humanitatis* were becoming separate from mere *grammatica*, each emerging as the preserve of its own particular class of teachers, *grammatisti* as distinct from *umanisti*.[93]

This further specialization had significant curriculum implications. Humble and limited in their preparation and knowledge, the horizons of Italian grammar teachers in the fifteenth century hardly extended beyond the Latin language: it is no accident that their glosses on the authors rarely ranged further than simple philology, with little sign of moral or other philosophical interests. The pretensions and scope of the humanists, in their role as professors not so much of grammar but of rhetoric and moral philosophy, sometimes extended further, as can be seen in the commentaries of a figure such as Barzizza.[94] But the curriculum division is still evident in humanist teachers who remained firmly

91 *De grammaticis*, : 'Sunt qui litteratum a litteratore ita distinguunt, ut Graeci grammaticum a grammatista, et illum quidem absolute, hunc mediocriter doctum existimant.' See *De grammaticis*, .

92 See Pico's famous letter to Ermolao Barbaro: 'movent mihi stomachum grammatistae quidam, qui cum duas tenuerint vocabulorum origines, ita se ostentant, ita venditant, ita circumferunt iactabundi [...]' (ed. Garin ( ),). See also ibid. : 'Viximus celebres, o Hermolae, et posthac vivemus, non in scholis grammaticorum et paedagogiis, sed in philosophorum coronis, in conventibus sapientum [...]' See also Poliziano's distinction: 'Grammaticorum enim sunt haec partes, ut omne scriptorum genus [...] ennarent. Nostra aetas, parum perita rerum veterum, nimis brevi gyro grammaticum sepsit [...] Nec enim aliud grammaticus graece, quam latine litteratus: nos autem nomen hoc in ludum trivialem detrusimus, tanquam in pistrinum [...] Caeterum apud graecos hoc genus non grammatici sed grammatistae, non litterati apud latinos sed litteratores, vocabantur' (Poliziano ( ), – : see Billanovich ( ), ; Scaglione ( ), –). See Poliziano ( ), , – : 'odio omni fastidioque dignissimos, qui quamquam semper elementarii sunt, vindicare tamen inter doctos fautores audent sibi censuram litterarum'. See citations from Francesco Baldelli and Agostino Mascardi dating from the late XVIc. and earlier XVIIc., in Battaglia (–), s.v. *grammatista*.

93 See Grendler ( ), – ; Campana ( ), , – ; Kristeller (b), , ; Avesani ( ), – ; Grendler ( ); Billanovich ( ), . From , a specialized appointment was regularly made in Modena 'pro doctore publico humanitatis': see Vicini ( ), , and Bertoni and Vicini (–), – , , ; for 'maestri di humanità' in XVIc. Lucca, see Berengo ( ), n. , , cited by Billanovich ( ), . In XVImid. Vicenza, no one could be admitted as a physician who himself or whose father or brother had during the previous ten years exercised an 'artem mecanicam et ruralem', including 'ludum litterarium, scilicet docendo grammaticam': Zanazzo ( ), . The distinction between humanists and humble grammarians was drawn forcefully in the edition of Tommaso Garzoni's *Piazza universale*, as cited by Avesani ( ), and Grendler ( ), – : 'si scuopre manifesto l'errore, e la prosontione d'alcuni, che quando a pena sono tinti de' primi elementi di grammatica, & insegnano que' principij per non dir pedantarie si arrogano questo nome, & vogliono esser chiamati Humanisti, profanando con la loro prosontione questo nome honoratissimo [...]' Similar was the distinction drawn by Marco Antonio Mariago in his commentary on *De oratore*, also published in : 'Hinc satis apparet, quam imperite faciunt ii, qui humanitatem pro grammatica tantum accipiant et professores humanitatis appellent eos, qui grammaticam docent' (cited by Avesani ( ),).

94 See e.g. Panizza ( ), – .

committed to the grammar school: it is no accident that moral philosophy is almost entirely absent from the commentaries of Guarino.[95] Here he was wearing the hat of his grammatical colleagues, in whose glosses, as will be seen below (ch.), the occasional superficial reference to moral philosophy is almost invariably lost in a vast sea of basic philological detail.

[95] See e.g. his commentaries on Terence and Valerius Maximus in BRF , where, following the pattern established in the earlier middle ages (see below,), Guarino announces a high moral purpose in the *accessus* (v) but in the body of the commentary o ers only philological comments.

The elementary school curriculum in medieval and Renaissance Italy: traditional methods and developing texts

DOCTORES PUERORUM

By the end of the thirteenth century, a new class of specialist elementary teacher was emerging. These were the *doctores puerorum*, who have been noted as early as in Florence and were numerous there by the turn of the fourteenth century.[1] With their appearance a marked distinction had arisen between Italian elementary and secondary education; this new specialization is evident in the many outlines of school curricula which first began to appear in the fourteenth century. Such syllabuses were laid out by the communes, usually because teachers were allowed to charge higher fees to more advanced pupils. In Arezzo during the s and s, for example, there were three levels of teaching: the most elementary class was for pupils not yet reading Donatus; the second was for the Donatists; the third and most advanced was for the study of the Latin language (*lactinare*) and literature (*auctores*).[2] This kind of division was typical throughout fourteenth- and fifteenth-century Italy,[3] and it held true for private tutors as well as public elementary and grammar schools.[4] There was usually a clear division between elementary and grammar or Latin education, towns often employing one type of teacher

[1] Debenedetti (–), – ; for five *magistri puerorum* in Florentine *estimo* of , see Gorrini (–), , n. .

[2] Black (d), , . For similar tripartite division into 'maiori, mediocri, infimo gradu' in Recanati in , see Borracini Verducci ( ), . For other similar examples, see Manacorda, ( ), , – ; Rossi ( ), – , – ; Avesani ( ), – ; Gargan ( ), – ; Sabbadini ( ), – ; Cipolla ( ), ; Colini-Baldeschi ( ), ; Colini-Baldeschi ( ), .

[3] A few examples are Barsanti ( ), , ; Battistini ( ), – ; Manacorda ( ), , – ; Gabotto ( ), , – ; Rossi ( ), – ; Nada Patrone ( ), – ; for Recanati, see Borracini Verducci ( ), – ; for Bologna, see Zaccagnini (b), – ; for Milan see Ortalli ( ), – .

[4] The Sienese notary Cristofano di Gano was taught to read at home in Rigomagno by Manno Piccolomini, his grandfather, who 'cominciò a insegnare a leggiare infine al Donato e anco el Donato'. Afterwards he sent him to Siena 'et posemi con maestro Petro dell'Ochio, che stava da la Misericordia', and from him the boy learned Latin ('gramatica'). See Cherubini ( ), ; Milanesi ( ), – . The same distinction between *Donatus* and *grammatica* also held true for Machiavelli's education; see new edition of educational passages in Bernardo Machiavelli's diary: Black (c), – .

for reading and writing and a real grammarian for Latin.[5] The *doctores puerorum* of the fourteenth century became the *maestri di leggere e scrivere* or *maestri di fanciulli* of the fifteenth:[6] men (or very occasionally women) of little education, drawn from the artisan class,[7] who seem to have known little or no Latin. As distinct from grammar teachers, who almost always corresponded in Latin, these elementary teachers usually wrote their letters and submitted their petitions in the vernacular.[8] Their tax returns were written in mercantile script, in contrast to grammar teachers,[9] who tended to write in notarial or later in the fifteenth century sometimes in humanist italic script.[10] As is clear from a letter of one elementary teacher in Prato in , he had turned to elementary teaching not as a desirable profession but as a last resort, because he was too infirm and feeble to earn his living otherwise.[11] This particular *maestro di fanciulli* had been a notary but had fallen on hard times and so had had to turn to the teaching of reading, which he was still doing in .[12] These elementary teachers usually took boys from their ABCs through the psalter and finished with Donatus: as our Pratese *maestro* says, he taught boys to 'legere la tavola, il saltero e il donatello'.[13] *Tavola*, *salterio* and *donadello* –

[5] Black (d), , ; ASPCD , r (January); ASSColle , xli verso (March) and , xlii verso (September); ASSG NN , lxxvi recto (June); Zanelli ( ), n. ; Rossi ( ), . Bonvesin da la Riva ( ), , distinguished between the eight grammar masters ('professores artis grammatice') and the more than seventy teachers of reading ('inicialium [...] literarum pedagogii') in Milan at end of Duecento. See Manacorda ( ), , – ; Frova ( ), .

[6] ASF Catasto , r; , r; , r; , v; , r; , r. For *magistri puerorum*, see Borracini Verducci ( ), ; Colini-Baldeschi ( ), – ; Zaccagnini ( ), .

[7] See below, n. .

[8] Black (d), ; ASPCD , r (January); , v– r (February); , v– r (January).

[9] ASF Catasto , r; , r; , r, , v; , r. An exception is Maestro Piero di Lorenzo Malamma, who 'insegna a fanciulli legiere' and wrote in a formal Gothic hand: ASF Catasto , r.

[10] ASF Catasto , r– r (Portata of Maestro Giovanni d'Ubertino da Asti, grammar teacher in Pistoia); , r (Portata of Ser Federigo di Giovanni, schoolmaster in Castelfiorentino); , r–v (Portata of Ser Guido d'Antonio da Isola Maggiore, near Perugia, grammar teacher in Cortona); Black (d), – (Portata of Maestro Francesco di Ser Feo di Nigi da Arezzo, grammar teacher there). For a selection of autograph letters by XVc. grammar masters, see ASF MAP . (Girolamo di Marco, grammar teacher in San Miniato, before); . . . , . . . , . . , . . . , . (Giovanni di Niccolò Peregrini da Volterra, grammar teacher in Poggibonsi, Livorno, Colle Valdelsa, Grosseto and Massa Marittima, –); . (Jacopo da Pistoia, grammar teacher in Prato,); . (Cantalicio, grammar teacher in San Gimignano,).

[11] ASPCD , r: non essere sano et forte della sua persona per modo che esso si possa faticare et essa sua persona exercitare come che egli vorebbe per lo migliore, s'è dato ad insegnare a fanciugli [...] legere et scrivere per non cadere in miseria.

[12] ASF Catasto , r, r: Questa è la famiglia del sopradecto Ser Martino et le loro etadi, poverecti i quali esso allieva et notrica con gram faticha [...] Ser Martino di Martino predecto va a griccie, perch'è perduto dell'uno lato e non si può aiutare et però s'è dato a 'segnare legiere a fanciulli.

[13] ASPCD , r.

these were the basic textbooks of elementary education in medieval and Renaissance Italy.[14]

TABULA, CARTA, SALTERIUM

Tabula or *carta* was a sheet of parchment or paper which began with the alphabet and concluded with syllables to sound out;[15] it was fixed on a

14 Pistoia: (June) qui magister etiam percipere possit […] pro legente et studente in donato xl S. D. et pro quolibet discente sive studente <in> psalterio et huiusmodi voluminibus xx S. et pro quolibet infante aut puero elementario aut qui legit tabulam decem S. et non ultra (ASPistoia Provv. , v– r). (March) [Ser Federigus] qui docet pueris legere tabulam, salterium et donatum ac etiam abbacum (ASPistoia Provv. , v); Zanelli ( ), – . Prato: (January) Martino di Martino […] s'è dato ad insegnare a fanciugli legere la tavola, il saltero et il donatello (ASPCD , r). San Gimignano: (June) quod ipse Ser Dore [Ser Johannis de Sancto Geminiano] doceat […] omnes et singulos pueros ab eo audire et discere volentes legere videlicet tabulam psalterium donatum (ASSG NN , lxxviiii verso–lxxx recto). (August) quod magistro […] liceat accipere a scolaribus suis infrascripta salaria et ab eis [et] quolibet ipsorum e ectualiter habere, videlicet: […] A legentibus donatum licteras et similiter S. triginta in anno ab eis percipiendos de mense in mensem. A legentibus salterium tabulam et similiter S. viginti quactuor in anno ab eis percipiendos de mense in mensem etc. (ASSG NN , v). (February) A legentibus donatum […] pro quolibet — l. S. x. A legentibus tabulam et psalterium anno quolibet et pro quolibet L. unam et S. quattuor — l. S. iiii° (ASSG NN , r– v). (October) Salaria que dicto comuni solvere debent scolares qui cum dicto Ser Ma o [Lupi] studebunt singulis in mensibus […] Legentes donatum et regulas S. quindecim. Legentes psalterium et tabulam s. duodecim. (ASSG NN , v– v). (March) A legentibus donatum, […] S. triginta, a legentibus salterium et simila soldos viginti quattuor, a legentibus tabulam S. duodecim quo libet anno ut prefertur (ASSG NN v– v). (December) A scolaribus legentibus donatum […] soldos triginta in anno pro quolibet, a scolaribus legentibus psalterium soldos viginti quatuor in anno pro quolibet, a scolaribus legentibus tabulam soldos duodecim. (ASSG NN , r– r). (October) A scolaribus legentibus donatum literas et similia soldos triginta in anno pro quolibet, a scolaribus legentibus psalterium soldos viginti quatuor in anno pro quolibet, a scolaribus legentibus tabulam soldos duodecim in anno pro quolibet (ASSG NN , r– r). Colle Valdelsa: (November) a legentibus donatum, salterum vel libricciolum proquolibet et quolibet mense S. duo, a legentibus cartam tabulam vel collum pro quolibet et quolibet mense S. unum et D. vi (ASSColle , ci recto). (March) A legentibus donatum, salterium vel libricciolum pro quolibet quolibet mense – S. duos; a legentibus cartam, tabulam vel collum pro quolibet quolibet mense – S. unum D. sex. (ASSColle , lxxxxii verso–lxxxxiii recto) (January) A legente cartam —S. decem in totum, a legente quaternum sive salterium — S. viginti in totum, a legente donatum testualiter — S. quadraginta in totum — a legente donatum sensualiter — S. quinquaginta in totum (ASSColle , lxiii verso–lxiiii recto). Arezzo: (April) 'de uno coiaiutore, qui […] debeat […] adoctrinare scolares legentes Donatum, Salterum et Tabulam' (Black (d),). For Lucca, see Barsanti ( ), , ; for Volterra, see Battistini ( ), – . For the rest of Italy, see Manacorda ( ), , – ; Gabotto ( ), , – ; Rossi ( ), – ; Borracini Verducci ( ), – ; Chiuppani ( ), – . An early document with the same division between elementary and secondary education after Donatus is found at Bassano in : 'quod scolaris de gramatica audiens catum et a cato superius teneatur solvere dicto magistro pro quolibet . denarios. parvorum pro mense […] Et scolaris audiens donatum. et ab inde inferius solvat eidem magistro. duos soldos. denariorum venetorum pro quolibet mense': Chiuppani ( ), .

15 Lucchi ( ), ; Grendler ( ) – ; Black (b), ; Gehl ( ), – ; Alexandre-Bidon ( ), – .

wooden board and took its name either from the parchment or paper (*carta*) or from the board (*tabula*). There were large versions for the teacher to use or small models for the pupil to hold.[16] They are also called *cedula* or *pagina*.[17] There are references to their being called *collum*[18] or neck, but this possibly refers not to a neck in the sense of a handle but conceivably to the type of parchment used, since the necks of the skins provided the cheapest vellum.[19] The introduction to reading by learning the alphabet and then syllables[20] was a technique going back to Greek and Roman antiquity;[21] the smallest Roman schoolboys were known as *abecedarii* or *syllabarii*.[22] In the earlier middle ages, too, children began with the alphabet and proceeded to syllables: as Remigius of Auxerre wrote in the ninth century, 'the instruction of small children normally involves first the study of letters, then of syllables';[23] similar was Peter Damian's scheme articulated in the eleventh century.[24]

As Peter Damian implies, the next stage was reading words and phrases: in late Roman antiquity this was accomplished by reading and learning by heart the collection of aphorisms known as Cato's *Distichs*, a text going back to perhaps the third century .[25] In the early middle ages, however, a significant change of curriculum occurred: the *Disticha Catonis* were replaced as the first reading text by the Psalter.[26] This change of reading matter began first in monastic schools and soon spread to parish and ecclesiastical schools, as well as to lay education.[27] Throughout the middle ages, being *psalteratus* was synonymous with literacy.[28] In the early middle ages, novice monks had had to learn all psalms, a process which could take up to three years for normal pupils, whereas the gifted might accomplish the feat in as little as five months.[29] Even in the early middle ages it seems that this task was considered too onerous for the whole of literate society;[30] by the later middle ages it is

[16] Lucchi ( ), ; Grendler ( ), – . [17] Gabotto ( ), , .

[18] Colle Valdelsa: (August) alii legentes donatum libricciolum tabulam collum vel cartam solvant in anno pro quolibet S. xii (ASSColle , xviii verso–lviiii recto). (August) A legentibus libricciolum donatum cartam tabulam vel collum S. xii. (ASSColle , lxvi recto). (November) A legentibus cartam tabulam vel collum pro quolibet et quolibet mense S. unum et D. vi (ASSColle , ci recto). (March) A legentibus cartam, tabulam vel collum pro quolibet quolibet mense – S. unum D. sex (ASSColle , lxxxxii verso–lxxxxiii recto).

[19] Lucchi ( ), .

[20] In Recanati in , beginning readers were called 'abecedaristis': Borracini Verducci ( ), .

[21] Marrou ( ), – , . [22] Marrou ( ), .

[23] Riché ( ), .

[24] PL . : 'In litterario quippe ludo, ubi pueri prima articulatae vocis elementa suscipiunt, alii quidem abecedarii, alii syllabarii, quidam vero nominarii [...] appellantur.'

[25] Marrou ( ), . [26] Riché ( ), – ; Riché ( ), .

[27] Riché ( ), – ; Riché ( ), . [28] Riché ( ), .

[29] Riché ( ), , n. . [30] Riché ( ), .

clear that the entire psalter was no longer serving as the introductory reading text.[31] This is not only suggested by the diminutive nomenclature in wide use (*salteruzzo, saltero piccolo, psalteriolus*)[32] but also by the famous story recounted by Boccaccio, who was appalled on his visit to Montecassino to find the writing being erased from ancient codices in order to make psalters for boys.[33] It is obvious that several entire psalters could hardly be created out of the eight folios constituting a quaternion.

On the evidence of curriculum outlines, it is clear that in later medieval and early Renaissance Italy, the elementary pupil, having learned the alphabet from the *tavola* or *carta*, still went on to the *salterio*. However, the contents of the fourteenth- or fifteenth-century Italian psalter are not immediately obvious. It is known from library and book-sellers' inventories that vast numbers of *salteri da fanciullo* or *da putto*, *salteruzzi* or *psalteri piccoli* existed,[34] but there seem to be no surviving Italian fourteenth- or fifteenth-century introductory reading texts explicitly identified as *salteri.*[35] One surviving elementary reading text, made for Massimiliano Sforza in (Milan Biblioteca Trivulziana MS),[36] was not actually entitled *salterio* or psalter but *Liber Iesus.* Grendler's examples show that in the sixteenth century *salterio* had come to mean a beginning reading book consisting of various prayers and religious texts, often preceded by an alphabet and a selection of syllables;[37] but liturgically psalter still meant psalms and in the fifteenth century *salterio* could still mean a collection of psalms – or more specifically the seven penitential psalms – used as a first reading text. In most outlines of curricula, the elementary syllabus consisted of *tavola/carta, salterio, donato/donatello*, but in Piedmont, *salterio* was sometimes replaced by *septem psalmi*, so that the syllabus was *carta/tabula, septem psalmi, donatus.*[38] Nevertheless, in Tuscany it seems that prayers and devotional texts had definitively replaced psalms in the *salterio.* In a letter about her daughter Tina to her husband Francesco Datini in , Margherita Datini wrote: 'La Tina àne letto il saltero; arebe di bisogno di qualche libricuolo che

31 The partial reading of the psalter by future clerks learning to read may have been occurring already in the early XIIc. See Pasqui ( ), : 'Presbiter Petrus de Monte Gerlone [...] dixit: Citulus eram et iam legebam in psalterium [...]'; : 'Presbiter Pepo prepositus de Avegnone [...] dixit: Puer eram et legebam in psalterio in plebe de Saturnino tempore Gualfredi episcopi senensis.' 32 See below, nn. , .

33 Cited by Lucchi ( ), : 'aliqui monachi volentes lucrari duos vel quinque solidos, radebant unum quaternum et faciebant psalteriolos quos vendebant pueris'.

34 Lucchi ( ), , , , , , ; Grendler ( ), ; Verde ( ), , , , , , ; Bec ( ), , , , , , , , , , ; Novati ( ), – ; Martini ( ); de la Mare (a), – . 35 Grendler ( ), .

36 Facsimile and transcription of this manuscript published by Bologna ( ); manuscript discussed by Lucchi ( ), – , and Grendler ( ), – .

37 Grendler ( ), . 38 Gabotto ( ), , , , , .

vi fosse suso i sette salmi e l'u cio della Donna ch'avesse buona lettera.'[39] In translation, this passage reads: 'Tina has read the psalter; she needs a book containing the seven psalms and the o ce of our lady which needs to be well-written [i.e. easily readable].'[40] The significant point about this passage is that it shows that, by the turn of the fifteenth century in Tuscany, the psalter no longer consisted of the seven penitential psalms, but must already have contained various prayers and miscellaneous devotional texts, such as are found in Massimiliano Sforza's *Liber Iesus.* Further evidence comes from the final folio of a secondary Trevisan grammatical textbook by Pietro da Asolo, once grammar teacher in Treviso,[41] compiled by a Frater G. in and .[42] It was common practice for schoolboys to practise writing the alphabet at the beginning or end of their manuscripts; these *probationes* also served to indicate that texts were schoolbooks. In this case Frater G. went further, giving the alphabet, abbreviation signs and two prayers, the *Ave Maria* and the *Pater Noster.*[43] This material resembles Milan Biblioteca Trivulziana MS , and probably constituted a skeletal psalter, placed here, like the usual alphabets, to indicate the close of a schoolbook. What is significant again is that this introductory reading text or skeletal psalter no longer contains psalms. Moreover, other titles are sometimes given for first reading texts – *libricciolus,*[44] *libretto,*[45] *quaternus,*[46] vespers[47] –

39 Pampaloni ( ), n. .

40 The phrase 'che vi fosse suso' is an archaic way of saying 'nel quale ci sono'. I should like to correct an error of interpretation in Black (b), – . I suggested a regrouping of letters in this text, but after discussions with Silvia Rizzo, Teresa De Robertis and Alan Bullock, I realize that this was philologically impossible and that the original transcription must be correct.

41 Pietro da Asolo (*c.* / –) was grammar teacher in Treviso (– , –) and Conegliano (–). For a well-documented and careful account of his career, see Gargan ( ), – , .

42 BML Ashb. , v. This manuscript is described in *I codici ashburnhamiani* ( ), – and discussed by Gargan ( ), – . For dates, see r, v.

43 A.b.c.d.e.f.g.h.i.k.l.m.n.o.p.q.r.f.s.t.u.x.y.ç. (et). (cum/con).(rum).

Ave Maria gratia plena dominus tecum, benedicta tu in mulieribus et benedictus fructus ventris tuy Iesus. Sancta Maria mater dei. Ora pro nobis nunc et in hora mortis. Amen.

Pater noster qui es in cellis, sanctificetur nomen tuum. Adveniat regnum tuum. Fiat voluntas tua sicut in cello et in terra. Panem nostrum quotidianum da nobis hodie et dimitte nobis debita nostra, sicut et nos dimitimus debitoribus nostris et ne nos inducas in temptationem sed libera nos a malo. Amen.

Virgo dei genitris, quem totus non capit orbis,
In tua se clausunt viscera satus homo [*sic*].

44 See n. above. 45 Grendler ( ), n. .

46 Grendler ( ), – ; Gabotto ( ), , , , , . This text is also called *caternetus* or *caternus*: see Gabotto ( ), , , . These Piedmontese texts make it clear that *quaternus* was some sort of alternative to the psalter (Gabotto ( ), : 'quaternum sive septemsalpmos'), not another name for *carta* or *tabula,* as implied by Grendler ( ), – . This is also suggested in a document from Colle Valdelsa: quaternum sive salterium (ASSColle , lxiii recto).

47 Gabotto ( ), , , , . There is a correspondence between the term *vesperaliis* in Piedmont and *vesperistis* in Recanati (Borracini Verducci ( ), ,).

indicating a variety of contents in the religious texts used. Some regional variation even in the fifteenth century is suggested by the above Piedmontese evidence: the seven penitential psalms were the basic medieval devotional texts and hence eminently suitable as introductory reading material. Nevertheless, the direction of the Italian curriculum here is clear: the psalms were being replaced by common prayers and devotional texts, a process which was completed by the sixteenth century.[48]

In the middle ages, a pupil acquired the skills of basic reading by subjecting the psalter to a two-stage process. The first focused on a written text: the pupil had a psalm written on his waxed tablet and read it over and over again. The second involved memory: by reading the psalm from his tablet many times, the pupil eventually learned the text by heart and so was able to dispense with the written text. After appropriate examination by his teacher, he was then assigned another psalm, and the whole process was repeated. This procedure, involving first reading from a written text and secondly recitation from memory without the written text, is described in the sixth-century monastic *Regula magistri*.[49] The process changed little throughout the middle ages; indeed, boys were still reading the psalter on the basis of a written text copied onto their waxed tablets in the fifteenth century, as is clear from a gloss, describing the use of the stylus (*graphium* or *pezelo*) to read the psalter, in contrast to the quill

[48] A curriculum history of the education of two Venetian boys from to was published by Cecchetti ( ), , and has recently been re-examined by Ortalli ( ), and n. . The schoolbooks that these boys used were entirely conventional (*salterio*, Donatus (*Ianua*), *Disticha Catonis*, Prosper's *Epigrammata*, Prudentius's *Dittochaeon*, *Facetus*) apart from a 'Sallustio', bought together with a *salterio* at the beginning of their education. The 'Sallustio' cost *grossi*, in contrast to *grossi* for the *salterio*. Unfortunately, the original document has been mislaid in the Venetian archives (see Ortalli ( ), n.). However, it seems unlikely that a text of Sallust could have cost less than a brief collection of prayers or psalms. In the original transcription (Cecchetti ( ),) three dots appear before the Roman numeral ' ': perhaps there was another letter or letters in front (such as). It was common for several copies of the psalter to be bought for the same pupils or household: see e.g. ASF Carte Gherardi – Piccolomini d'Aragona (Ricordanza of Gherardo di Bartolomeo Gherardi), left (July) Gherardo di Bartolomeo Gherardi [...] de' dare S. . Paghò Piero de' Pechori e compagnia [...] a Agnolo d'Antonio chartolaio per II salteri per miei fanciulli — S. .

[49] *La règle du maître* ( ), – : 'alii legant, alii audiant, alii litteras discant et doceant, alii psalmos, quos habent superpositos, meditentur. Nam cum eos maturaverint et memoria perfecte tenuerint, adducti a praepositis suis ipsum psalmum aut canticum seu quamvis lectionem memoriter abbati restituant. Et cum perreddiderit, mox petat pro se debere orari. Et cum pro eo a circumadstantibus oratum fuerit, conplenti abbati genua osculetur qui reddidit. Cui mox aut ab ipso novus [psalmus] aut a praepositis iubetur superponi, et postquam superpositum fuerit quodvis, antequam se meditet, item a circumadstantibus petat pro se orari et sic incoent meditare.' French translation cited by Riché ( ), – .

pen with which books were copied.[50] Indeed, the procedure of learning the psalter verse by verse and reciting it back piecemeal to the teacher was still used in Bolognese schools in the mid-Trecento.[51] The main technical development in the course of the thirteenth, fourteenth and fifteenth centuries was the substitution of ready-made psalters, such as those described by Boccaccio,[52] for versions copied onto waxed tablets, but the basic approach of first reading from a written text followed by memorization without the text remained unchanged.[53]

A curious fact in the history of Italian pre-university education in the thirteenth and fourteenth centuries is that the vernacular was not used at what must seem to us the most obvious point in the curriculum: the elementary stages of learning to read. There are no surviving texts entitled psalter before the sixteenth century, and yet indirect evidence suggests that these first reading texts were in Latin. An early surviving manuscript belonging to the psalter genre (although entitled simply *Liber Iesu*) consisted of Latin devotional texts.[54] Earlier evidence comes from the Trevisan skeletal psalter mentioned above and consisting of the alphabet, abbreviation signs and two prayers, the *Ave Maria* and the *Pater Noster*.[55] What is significant about this text for understanding the teaching of elementary reading is that the two prayers are in Latin. More

[50] BRF , r (gloss to *Graecismus*, XV[1]): Notandum quod stilus dictus a sto stas. Assumitur dupliciter, scilicet proprie et improp[r]ie. Prop[r]ie assumitur pro graphio, id est pezelo quo pueri utuntur in legendo donatum psalterium. Improp[r]ie dupliciter asumitur primo modo pro pena qua libri scribentur, secundo modo assumitur tripliciter a poietis.

[51] See Giovanni Conversini da Ravenna's account of a schoolmate's failure to learn the psalter in this way: 'cum semel nescisset psalterii versum reddere […]' (Sabbadini ( ), ; Garin [ ],) *Redere* here means recite from memory: see the subsequent passage ((Sabbadini [ ], ; Garin [ ], : '[…] complecti mente ac reddere compellebat' (cited in full below in ch. , , n.).

[52] Italian pupils were already owning their own psalters in XIIIc.: see document dating from to in Venice, where at least one psalter (and possibly two: see n. above) was purchased for the sons of Marco Zambon (Cecchetti ( ), ; Ortalli ( ),). By the end of XIVc. teachers seem to have been distributing psalters among their pupils: see the inventory dated February of the recently deceased 'Magister Lodisius Calvus de Vicheria regens scolas grammaticales in hac civitate Ianuensi', which includes 'salteria parva pro pueris' (Gorrini (–), ,). His other books consisted largely of standard grammar school fare for the end of the Trecento: Vergil's *Georgics*, 'travetum' (=Nicholas Trevet's commentary on Boethius's *Consolation*), Boethius [*Consolation*], copies of Lucan, 'Priscianus unus maior' [= books to of *Institutiones grammaticae*], Ovid's *Heroides*, two copies of Geo rey of Vinsauf's *Poetria nova*, Henry of Settimello's *Elegia*, Seneca's *Tragedies*, Ovid's *Metamorphoses*. He also had copies of Seneca's letters to Lucilius, which were not normally read at grammar school: see ch. below, .

[53] See below, , for vocabulary *al testo* (reading from a written text) and *al senno* (memorization) in use during XIVc. and XVc.

[54] Milan Biblioteca Trivulziana MS , prepared for Massimiliano Sforza in s: ed. Bologna ( ). See above, . [55] BML Ashb. , v. See above, .

evidence comes from the research of Danièle Alexandre-Bidon, who has identified texts depicted in illustrations of children learning to read; these point to Latin, not to vernacular texts.[56] It may have been educationally problematic, if not impossible, to teach basic reading technique in a language without any fixed orthography, such as the Italian *volgare* before the sixteenth century. Indeed, in the middle ages and early Renaissance, Latin was regarded as an artificial, created, unchanging language, an *ars* suitable for teaching, whereas the vulgar languages were regarded as changeable, unstable, and literally as forms of babble,[57] learnt naturally but formally unteachable; only with the triumph of the humanist view of Latin as itself a natural, historically changing language in the sixteenth century could it become conceivable to teach fundamental language skills in the vernacular medium. It is important to remember the close association, even identification, of *ars* and teaching in the middle ages; Latin was teachable precisely because it was considered an artificial language, whereas teaching the vernacular was inconceivable because it was natural, not artificial, not an *ars*. A particularly significant indication of exclusively Latinate elementary education, moreover, is the progressive structure of the elementary curriculum. Curriculum outlines throughout Italy specify a similar syllabus progressing from table to psalter to Donatus.[58] The text used in Italy as *Donato* or *Donadello*, the so-called *Ianua*, was always in Latin; dual language *Ianue* – the so-called *Donato al Senno* – do not appear before the advent of printing.[59] The elementary curriculum would make little sense if vernacular devotional texts, for example, the seven penitential psalms, had been inserted as a preparation to read a demanding elementary Latin work such as *Ianua*. The fact that vernacular prayers and psalms exist in manuscript in no way indicates[60] that these were texts used to learn reading: an accurate reading of Margherita Datini's letter, cited above ( ), showing that the seven psalms were no longer synonymous with the psalter by the turn of the fifteenth century, is concrete evidence that collections of the seven psalms,

[56] Alexandre-Bidon ( ), – .

[57] On changing conceptions of Latin and vernacular in the middle ages and Renaissance, see the important study by Rizzo ( ), – , who cites a wide range of texts and bibliography.

[58] See above, n. .

[59] Grendler ( ), – . Latin morphologies very rarely appeared with vernacular translations in Italy during the middle ages. One has been published by Sabbadini ( ), – , but the text was not *Ianua*, and it is not clear that it was intended or used to teach elementary reading.

[60] As suggested by Gehl ( ), : 'penitential psalms in Tuscan *volgare*, for example, are known in many manuscripts and would be among the first popular products of Italian printing presses in the s. Reading and writing masters would surely have thought it useful for beginners to learn to read such texts in the vernacular.'

whether in the vernacular or in Latin, were not used as psalters to teach reading. Many elementary teachers in the fourteenth century – the so-called *doctores puerorum* or *maestri di fanciulli*[61] – were often (as mentioned above,) recruited from the artisan class[62] and so scarcely literate in Latin. The divergence in salary sometimes provided for teachers in the fourteenth century who were or were not able to teach Latin resulted from the di erential between employing a lowly *doctor puerorum* and a proper *magister grammatice*, rather than from the teaching of elementary reading in the vernacular.[63] Teaching alphabet sheets (*tabula/carta*), simple Latin prayers, and *Ianua* phonetically[64] did not require active use of Latin, which was needed only at the later stages of the curriculum, when Latin syntax, composition and authors were studied.[65] The

[61] See above, n. .

[62] The sons of 'Bartolo di Lorenzo, maestro d'insegniare legere e scrivere a fancugli' in were leather workers: ASF Catasto , r; 'Maestro Giuglielmo di Messer Vechio da Bolognia insegnia legere a fanculli' in had a wife who 'fila a rocha' (wound bobbins): ASF Catasto , r.

[63] In San Gimignano in , the reading and writing teacher was paid lire a year (ASSG NN , lxviii verso–lxxx recto) whereas in the grammar teacher was paid florins a year (ASSG NN , lxxiiii verso–lxxv verso). In Colle Valdelsa in the reading and writing teacher was paid lire a year (ASSColle , xxix verso), whereas the grammar teacher in the same year was paid lire a year (ASSColle , cxlii verso–cxliiii recto).

[64] For *donato al testo e al senno*, see below, .

[65] Lucchi ( ), , put forward an interesting hypothesis for the development of an alternative vernacular reading syllabus, based on an introductory reading manual with the title *Libro utilissimo da imparare presto a leggere et proferrire tutte le syllabe, chiamato el Babuino.* The only surviving copy, published at Perugia in and preserved in Bologna Biblioteca Universitaria (Raro A), consists of an alphabet and abbreviation signs, followed by vernacular definitions of vowels and consonants; lists of syllables, proper names of men and women as well as geographical localities, all in alphabetical order and introduced by vernacular titles; and finally a group of the most common Latin prayers. Lucchi also pointed to a few other such vernacular reading manuals, all dating between and . Such works were obviously meant to be vernacular alternatives to the Latin school psalter; Lucchi gives evidence that these texts were primarily meant for self-teaching outside school, and points out that some of their authors were abacus teachers. This evidence shows that, in the XVIc., there was a little learning of reading in the vernacular, especially outside formal reading or grammar schools and possibly associated with abacus teaching.

The question remaining is whether these kinds of vernacular alternative elementary reading manuals were also in use before the XVIc. Here there is virtually no evidence. The same teachers sometimes taught abacus and reading in the XIVc., XVc. and XVIc. (Colle Valdelsa: (April) Cum pueri de Colle devientur et nichil discant, provisum est per o tium priorum dicte terre quod Magister Johannes Naldi de Abaco eligatur [...] in magistrum ad docendum legere pueros ac etiam artem arismetrice (ASSColle , xlv verso); he is elected for one year beginning on April 'ad docendum legere pueros et artem arismetrice' (ibid. xlvi verso). On November the commune elected 'Magistrum Johannem Naldi de Colle magistrum del abbacho in magistrum [...] ad docendum pueros legere et eos in arte arismetrice instruere' (ASSColle , liii recto). (January) Magister Johannes Naldi de Colle dicit et exponit quod ipse est paratus et paratum se o ert docere pueros de Colle [...] et omnes alios volentes discere legere et scribere abbachum et geometriam (ASSColle , v). Prato: (February) Petitio Antonii Filippi Salvii de Prato petentis eligi ad docendum abacum pueros in terra Prati et etiam legere et scribere (ASPCD v). Arezzo: Black (d), (May),

evidence for an entirely latinate reading syllabus in fourteenth- and fifteenth-century Italy, therefore, seems conclusive.[66]

IANUA

The final stages of elementary education in medieval and Renaissance Europe were presided over by Donatus.[67] But it has long been recog-

footnote (*cont.*)
(November)). However, when reference is made to the textbooks used by these abacus/elementary reading teachers, it is to the standard reading syllabus of *carta/tabula*, psalter and Donatus; e.g. Pistoia: (March) 'electio [...] Ser Federigi [...] qui docet pueros legere tabulam, salterium et donatum ac etiam abbacum' (Zanelli ( ), , n.); Arezzo: (November) 'obligandosi insegnare la carta, il salterio ai fanciulli ve andranno, et l'abocho et scrivere' (Black (d),).

The only possible evidence from before the XVIc. cited by Lucchi is a poem by a Venetian calligrapher, Fra Filippo della Strada, who lived from *c.* to ('son fatto in breve amastrato / solo il babovino aveva io emparato / quando me posi in stampe ad studiare') (Lucchi ( ), ; Nada Patrone ( ),). The meaning of *babovino* here is unclear: the word in the title from seems to derive from the ape-like movements of the lips made by learner readers as they sounded out their first syllables (Lucchi ( ),), and here it could mean simply 'I had only just learned to sound out syllables'; rather than an actual textbook, as inferred by Lucchi, the word *babovino* could refer to a technique of sounding out or *compitare.* Indeed, the existence of such a pedagogical method may have induced the author in to adopt the word *babuino* as his title; there is no need to hypothesize the existence of a lost series of *Babuini* to account for the adoption of *el babuino* as a title in . Moreover, the mere fact that the textbook was in the vernacular does not mean that the method suggested here by Fra Filippo with the term *babovino* was also in the vernacular. The evidence, such as it is, merely suggests that a few abacus teachers in the earlier XVIc. attempted to launch reading courses in the vernacular. Moreover, in some cases the vocabulary *babbuinos*, *baboias*, *babinbabo*, *baboi*, etc. may have referred to more advanced learning activities, such as school-level dramatic performances: see Nada Patrone ( ), – . For similar doubts about Lucchi's hypotheses for the pre-sixteenth century, see Frova ( ), – ; Nada Patrone ( ), – .

66 Nevertheless, Gehl ( ), , says that, for the fourteenth century, the 'evidence that some schooling was entirely in the vernacular is sketchy but incontrovertible', citing as evidence a document published by Witt ( ), , n. regarding the communal schoolmaster in Buggiano in : '[the commune] possit pro eius salario sibi stantiare, si docebit gramaticam, libros quinquaginta et, si non doceret gramaticam, libros vigintiquinque'). Witt ( ), , takes this passage to mean that 'local schoolmasters employed by these rural communes often did not know Latin'. Gehl's interpretation ( ), – , is: '[...] in the case of the Buggiano statutes [...] the city fathers provided for a stipend of lire for a schoolmaster who could teach *grammatica* and lire if the only one available could not o er such instruction [...] The master who could not teach *grammatica* but who could teach reading and writing was surely not teaching in Latin.' A more accurate translation of the Latin text is: [the commune] can authorize payment to him [namely, the teacher], if he will teach grammar, of lire, and if he were not teaching grammar, of lire. Gehl takes the passage to mean that a teacher would be paid according to his abilities: more if he knew Latin, less if not. But since the text is not about whether the teacher can, but whether he will, teach *grammatica* (Latin), the subject of the passage is the level at which he will be teaching, not his linguistic capacities. For the views of Witt ( ), see n. , below.

67 The fundamental importance of Donatus, even in XVIc. Italy, is illustrated by a vernacular annotation, in the hand of a (non-Tuscan) Cinquecento schoolboy, on a copy of Terence (BML . , v): Poiché non volete imprare donato e le regole se<n>sa le quali non i<m>pareresti mai cosa alchuna [...] The *regole* here referred to correspond to the grammar rules of teachers

nized that in Italy during the high and late middle ages the principal textbook in elementary schools was not Aelius Donatus's *Ars minor*[68] but the manual spuriously attributed to Donatus which Sabbadini christened *Ianua* after the first word of its verse prologue and which, as a parsing grammar, dominated the Italian manuscript tradition and early printing.[69]

Ianua*: its origins and early character*

Ianua owed its birth to dissatisfaction in the early middle ages with Donatus's *Ars minor.* Indeed, Donatus's genuine elementary grammar, written for native speakers, was unsuited to the needs of medieval pupils who were learning Latin as a second language. On the one hand, medieval teachers responded by supplementing the *Ars minor* with additional grammatical material, including paradigms, declensions and conjugations omitted by Donatus as well as rules for the recognition of declensions unnecessary for native Latin speakers[70] but developed in the East by teachers such as Priscian for their native Greek-speaking pupils. On the other hand, medieval grammarians also composed their own elementary treatises to replace the *Ars minor.* One particular new type to emerge was the parsing grammar. This was based on a traditional Roman teaching method preserved for posterity by Priscian in his *Partitiones*, where the first verse of each book of the *Aeneid* is parsed minutely. This work began to be copied assiduously in the ninth century, and its influence can be seen in parsing grammars which first appear at about this time. This type of treatise takes the broad outline of Donatus's *Ars minor* as its starting point, divided as it is into sections on each of the eight parts of speech and cast in catechetical form. However, instead of general questions on the parts of speech as in the *Ars minor*, one word is

such as Francesco da Buti and Guarino Veronese: the term was generic for a secondary grammar manual in the XIVc. and XVc.

68 In Carolingian Italy, the genuine *Ars minor* of Donatus was still being used as the basic text of elementary education, as suggested by the *Ars Donati* by Paul the Deacon, which was a reproduction of Donatus's text, with the interpolation of largely additional declensions and conjugations as normal in medieval versions of the *Ars minor* (for this practice, see the next paragraph below in the text). On Paul's *Ars Donati*, ed. Amelli ( ) from the unique version in BAV Pal. Lat. , see also Lentini ( ), – , – , who points out that this work was an elementary treatise for beginners.

69 Sabbadini ( ), , – ; Schmitt ( ), , – ; Garin ( ), ; Grendler ( ), – ; Black (a), – ; Black (b), – ; Gehl ( ), – ; Black (e), – ; Pinborg ( ), – ; Rizzo ( ), ; Law (b), – .

70 This important point about the supplementing of the *Ars minor* for non-native Latin speakers was current in the later nineteenth century: see Reichling ( ), xiii; Specht ( ), .

chosen to represent each part of speech and questions are asked about it in particular, providing a full exercise in parsing; general grammatical definitions are introduced in explanation of particular questions about an individual example. This type of grammar sometimes employed Donatus's grammatical definitions and terminology, but increasingly theoretical material tended to be taken from Priscian's *Institutiones*.[71]

Jan Pinborg suggested that the kernel of *Ianua* was provided by one such Priscianic parsing grammar, *Dominus quae pars*. Having dated the two earliest manuscripts of this latter grammar to the twelfth century, Pinborg speculated that one of these, Paris Bibliothèque Nationale MS lat. , provided the kernel for the two most important medieval parsing grammars, the so-called *Remigius*, in which the exemplary noun is *Dominus*, and *Ianua*, in which it is *Poeta*.[72] Schmitt too had considered the relation between *Remigius* and *Ianua*, but he concluded that their relationship was ambiguous, since *Ianua* could just as well have been the source for *Remigius* as vice versa.[73] However, Schmitt's scepticism was based on a comparison of *Ianua* with fifteenth-century versions of *Remigius*, in which the similarities are diluted by many di erences characteristic of later, highly embellished *Remigius* texts.[74] The parallels between *Ianua*'s basic parsing catechism and the skeletal text of the early Paris Remigius published by Pinborg are ostensibly striking.[75]

However, there has recently emerged new evidence which seems to rule out Pinborg's hypothesis of a kernel text for both *Remigius* and *Ianua*. The two earliest skeletal manuscripts of *Remigius*, Douai Bibliothèque Municipale MS , r– v and Paris Bibliothèque Nationale MS lat. , r– v, both are Northern European, probably French, dating from the second half of the twelfth century.[76] And yet at the same time a full version of *Ianua* was already in circulation. This is clear from my discovery of *Ianua* in a British Library manuscript, Harley .[77] *Ianua* was in fact a text in Italian use well before the earliest known manuscript versions of the skeletal *Remigius* texts.

Harley represents the earliest known text of *Ianua*, pre-dating other versions by at least a century. Like all *Ianua* versions, this manuscript is divided into eight sections, each treating a part of speech in catechetical form. The core of each section is made up of an analysis of a

71 Law ( ), – ; ( ), – ; (a), – ; (b), – .
72 Pinborg ( ), – . 73 Schmitt ( ), . 74 Pinborg ( ), – .
75 Pinborg ( ), – .
76 I have examined both these manuscripts on microfilm; this dating and provenance have been confirmed by Gabriella Pomaro. 77 See Appendix .

particular example of one of the parts of speech, beginning with the question 'Poeta que pars est?' for the noun, and using *amo*, *legens*, *ego*, *ad*, *bene*, *heu* and *et* as the basic examples for the questions about the other part of speech.[78] After identifying the various parts of speech, each section then proceeds to a definition, as, for example, 'Nomen. Quare? Quia significat substantiam et qualitatem.' The core of each of the eight sections of the treatise consists of questions and answers about accidence, for example, gender, case, tense, signification, number and figure for participles. Accidence – discussed through question, answer and example – is the only topic treated in the sections devoted to the four indeclinable parts of speech, but for the four declinable parts the text gives extensive paradigms, declensions and conjugations in characteristic fashion.[79]

It is unknown who made the original adaptation of Priscian into *Ianua* or when this took place, and yet a number of features of this text in its early days are significant. In the first place, it was an elementary schoolbook. This is clear from its inclusion of extensive paradigms of nouns, verbs, participles and pronouns, as well as its concentration on simple rules for their formation. Far from taking the basic generation of Latin forms for granted, the treatise made Latin morphology its central focus. In contrast, Priscian's aim in the *Institutiones grammaticae* had been taxonomic: like other ancient grammarians, he wanted to provide the tools whereby native speakers and advanced Latin readers, who already were fully in command of Latin morphology, could analyse and classify grammatical forms when commenting on literary texts. This taxonomic vocabulary and approach was handed down to all medieval grammarians, including the author of *Ianua*, but the overridingly elementary focus of the latter's work is clear not only from the extensive and numerous paradigms but also from the inclusion of elementary definitions of categories of Latin accidence which, as has been seen, were added to the material drawn from Priscian, in order to ensure that its users would not be confused by unexplained technical terminology. The second important feature of the *Ianua* text in its early incarnation (such as is found in Harley) is that the grounding in Latin forms which it o ered its users was by no means summarial or abbreviated but rather copious and

[78] BL Harley , r– v (noun), v– v (verb), v– v (participle), v– v (pronoun), v– r (preposition), r– r (adverb), r– v (interjection), v– r (conjunction).

[79] Gardenal (a) seems to misunderstand the contents of *Ianua*, calling it '*Ianua Donati* (che si fermava ai verbi attivi), riduzione medioevale dell'*Ars minor* di Donato' and suggesting here that this work did not cover the indeclinable parts of speech; it was also not a reduction of Donatus's *Ars minor* but rather a reworking of material mainly from Priscian.

thorough. Not only were there full declensions and conjugations of regular inflected parts of speech, but numerous irregularities were also considered; moreover, general rules for the formation of nouns and verbs were included, as well as many exceptions to these principles. It is clear that the purpose of *Ianua* in its early form was to provide a solid grounding for pupils who, it was assumed, would progress further in the study of Latin language and literature. Just as early medieval pupils had to memorize numerous psalms and other basic devotional texts to gain the basic skills of reading, so it was taken for granted in the early days of *Ianua* that they would possibly spend years memorizing a long text on the parts of speech to give them a thorough grounding in Latin morphology and in the terminology necessary for later literary comment and analysis. The early text of *Ianua* was not a quick route to Latinity. Indeed, an indication of the links of early *Ianua* with a wider Latin curriculum is the retention in Harley of quotations of classical authors taken from Priscian.[80]

Ianua*'s early prevalence in Italy*

It must be wondered why *Ianua* came to prevail in Italy. One reason is that a parsing grammar beginning with *poeta* as the exemplary word for nouns seems to have reflected a particular and time-honoured Italian educational practice. Paolo da Camaldoli's *Donatus* began with the question 'Poeta quae pars est?'[81] Moreover, *Ianua* manuscripts, all containing a text originally beginning with 'Poeta quae pars est?', are primarily Italian (thirty-four in all, of which at least twenty-nine are Italian).[82] In contrast, manuscripts of parsing grammars with the incipit 'Dominus que pars est', a tradition which ultimately coalesced into the later medieval text known as *Remigius*,[83] are almost entirely Northern European, the majority being from Germany.[84] Another significant point is that *Ianua*'s Priscianic ordering of the parts of speech,[85] in contrast to the order of the *Ars minor* followed in *Remigius*,[86] may reflect the particular attachment to Priscian in Italy, where, alone in Europe, there had been a continuous manuscript tradition of his works since antiquity.[87] It is also

80 See v, r, v, r, v. 81 Ed. Sivo (a), . 82 See Appendix .

83 Ed. Pinborg ( ).

84 Bursill-Hall ( ) gives thirty-nine in total, twenty-one from German, eight from British and eight from French libraries, but one only from a Flemish and an Italian collection.

85 Schmitt ( ), . 86 Pinborg ( ), – .

87 Passalacqua ( ); Law ( ), . Italian propensity for Priscian can be seen in the analysis of manuscript provenance for Donatus's *Ars grammatica* and Priscian's *Institutiones* made by Cervani

noteworthy that the grammatical rules found in the eleventh-century Italian *Ars grammatica* by Papias[88] are a reworking of Priscian,[89] as was acknowledged by the author: 'Sed quia multorum maximeque ipsius Prisciani habeamus auctoritatem'.[90] A similar Italian preference for Priscian is clear in a twelfth-century Italian morphological fragment, found in BML CS , r– v. This is an elementary treatise, since it provides full paradigms of third-, fourth- and fifth-declension nouns, as well as of pronouns. At the very beginning of the fragment, there are clear links to Priscian, who is explicitly cited.[91] This is a reference to *Institutiones*, . – (Keil (–), . –), where the endings of third-declension nouns are classified as long or short. Nevertheless, there was still possibly a lingering attachment here to Donatus, whose order of the parts of speech (noun, pronoun, verb, etc.) seems to be preferred to Priscian's (noun, verb, pronoun, etc.); a similar a nity for Donatus may have persisted in the later twelfth century, when Paolo da Camaldoli's *Donatus* provided an elementary morphology consisting of alternating Priscianic and Donatist material, with the parts of speech presented in Donatus's order.[92]

( ), – : the former o ers no example of known Italian provenance, whereas for the latter there are twenty-two cases of Italian origin (although there is an overwhelming North European provenance for both texts).

88 On Papias, see now the new critical edition of the *Ars grammatica* by Cervani ( ), who says 'più comunemente lo si ritiene italiano, ma anche questa ipotesi appare infondata' (iii). However, she also says that there is a tradition going back to Ptolemy of Lucca that he was a Lombard (iii and n.). According to de Angelis ( ), iv–v, the presence of geographical place names is insu - cient proof of Italian provenance, but Cervani ( ), v–vi, points out that these are given a prominent place in the treatise. Cervani also says (vi, n.): 'Problematica, ma interessante [...] la presenza di un fiume detto Caterona nella maggioranza dei codici (il nome non si trova nei repertori geografici [...])'. However, in Graesse ( ), , , there is the following entry: 'Caterona (fluvius), Catrona: Carona (Corona), Fl. in Italien'. According to Amati (– ?), , : 'Carona' is a 'Piccolo torrente che ha principio a Corano, attraversa la via Emilia a levante da Castel S. Giovanni, nella prov. di Piacenza, e sbocca nella Lora sotto il nome di Boriacco.' This reference to a tiny stream near Piacenza is a strong indication that Papias was an Italian, and indeed from Lombardy too. I read the text originally in BML Ashb. [2], r– r; on this MS see now Cervani ( ), xxvi–xxvii. On Papias's *Ars grammatica*, see Manacorda ( ), , ; Percival ( ), and n. ; Garin ( ), ; Grendler ( ), , and especially Cervani ( ), who cites further recent bibliography. Recent scholars no longer take seriously Mercati's hypothesis that Papias was the name of the title, not of the author: see Cervani ( ), v, n. .

89 Hagen, in Keil (–), , clxxxiv–clxxxvi; Cervani ( ), iv, lxxxvii .

90 Cervani ( ), ; BML Ashb. [2], r.

91 r: Tertia declinatio terminales habet litteras , id est, a e o l n r s x c t. Terminationes vero nominativi duas, licet a Prisciano suo loco producte seu correpte enumerentur.

92 Ed. Sivo (a).

Other early manuscripts of Ianua*: the character and development of the text before the fifteenth century*

In terms of chronology, the next *Ianua* manuscript dates from the later thirteenth century. This is BNP lat. , a manuscript which formed part of the legacy of Pierre of Limoges (d.) to the Sorbonne.[93] According to Richard Rouse, 'B.N.lat. is of north French origin, most likely Paris, and was probably written ca. – .'[94] Not much later is BML Strozzi , r– v, a manuscript which, until my study appeared in , had not been identified as containing a version of this text. Before that time this text had variously been described as 'Anon, *De octo partibus orationis* + prologue',[95] as 'Pseudo-Donatus, *De octo partibus*'[96] or *Donati prima grammaticae rudimenta, seu de octo partibus orationis*,[97] but now this identification appears to be standard.[98] This manuscript has been studied palaeographically by Teresa De Robertis, Gabriella Pomaro and Albinia de la Mare. The consensus of their views is that it is an Italian hand, dating to the first quarter of the fourteenth century.[99]

BNP lat. and BML Strozzi o er a *Ianua* text which in several important respects resembles BL Harley . Catechisms regarding how many species, genders, numbers, figures and cases of nouns,[100] and how many genders, tenses, modes, persons and conjugations of verbs[101] seem to appear particularly in these three versions. All three manuscripts have numerous exemplary paradigms for the third nominal declension,[102] and all three texts have additional material on feminine nouns declined only in the singular,[103] and of masculine nouns in the singular changing to neuter in the plural.[104] But most striking is the inclusion of definitions of the parts of speech and their 'property', based on Priscian; in other versions of *Ianua*, if such general material is included it is usually

93 On this manuscript, see Fierville ( ), – ; Bursill-Hall ( ), ; Delisle ( ), ; Thurot ( ), ; Pellegrin ( ), note . 94 Private communication.

95 Bursill-Hall ( ), 96 Gehl ( ), . 97 Bandini (–), . .

98 See Gehl ( ), , where *Ianua* now replaces 'Pseudo-Donatus, *De octo partibus*' in Gehl ( ), .

99 I no longer accept my dating of this manuscript to the XIIIc., as suggested in Black (a). I am happy to accept the unanimous views of these three professional palaeographers, who have been kind enough to give me their opinion of this manuscript.

100 BML Strozzi , v– r; BNP lat. , r–v (see Schmitt, , n.); BL Harley , v, v, r.

101 BML Strozzi , v– r; BNP lat. , v– r; BL Harley , r, v, r–v, v.

102 BML Strozzi , r– v; BNP lat. , r– v; BL Harley , v– r.

103 See Harley r, BML Strozzi r, BNP lat. r.

104 Harley v– r, BML Strozzi v, BNP lat. r.

relegated to an appendix,[105] but in these three versions this material is interspersed throughout the text.[106]

It is clear, therefore, that both BNP lat. and BML Strozzi have continued to follow the textual style represented earliest in Harley by o ering a copious version of *Ianua*, one which contrasts with the jejune summaries typical of the fifteenth century. Although BNP and BML Strozzi have eliminated some detailed grammatical material found once in Harley, they have now compensated by adding new material of their own, not previously found in Harley; in this way, in fact, both BNP and BML Strozzi, while making some new selections with regard to particular grammatical content, have maintained the overall copious style of Harley. Notable is the inclusion of digressions on the vocative in each of these former manuscripts,[107] but most striking is the inclusion of numerous mnemonic verses in each of these two versions, a frequent feature of many grammatical works but apparently not otherwise found in *Ianua*.

Some of these changes to *Ianua* represent the influence of new pedagogic fashions in the thirteenth century. Priscian had long been considered too unwieldy for direct classroom use. This is clear not only from the emergence no later than the early twelfth century of *Ianua*, itself a compendium of parts of Priscian, but also from Papias's *Ars grammatica*. These last-mentioned grammar rules, based heavily on Priscian, were written because the *Institutiones grammaticae* were too long to use as a textbook: hence the author's declaration that he would extract the essence of Priscian ('Prisciani dispositionem summamque'), that he would be as brief as possible ('quam brevius potero'), that his work would o er a useful short cut ('utile [...] et compendiosum'). The problem was how to memorize the essential grammatical material o ered by Priscian: the *Institutiones grammaticae* were too long, but the compendium contained in Papias's *Ars grammatica* could, according to its author, be firmly memorized and retained ('Ista vos ergo memorie commendetis mentisque receptaculo quam firmiter teneatis').[108] Priscian continued to be criticized, with ever-increasing vehemence, in successive centuries: one thirteenth-century grammarian wrote that Priscian's lengthy volumes were so di use and confused that they could be assimilated only with the greatest e ort and with totally undisturbed concentration.[109]

105 Schmitt ( ), – .

106 E.g. see Harley r, BML Strozzi r, BNP lat. r. Cf. Priscian *Institutiones*, , and (Keil (–), , –). 107 BML Strozzi , r; BNP lat. , v.

108 Cervani ( ), . Cf. BML Ashb. ², r.

109 Thurot ( ), n. : 'Illa enim Prisciani spaciosa volumina gramaticam artem ita di use et confuse pertractant, ut non nisi omni cura et ab omni negotio expeditis illa sit replicare consilium.'

The publication and circulation in the thirteenth century of the two great verse grammars by Alexander of Villedieu and Evrard of Béthune further inspired grammarians to rethink their teaching methods and materials. In comparison to the confusion, disorder, prolixity and incomprehensibility of Priscian, these works now seemed clear, brief, orderly and accessible.[110] Moreover, the greatest advantage was their use of verse, a medium which represented a just concord between terseness and copious eloquence, a perfect harmony between words and content, an ideal balance between excessive length and over-conciseness.[111] Most important, the verse of Alexander and Evrard o ered a pedagogic advantage over Priscian's prose: not only was it easier to take in, more agreeable and briefer, but it was also easier to memorize.[112] Similar was the sentiment expressed by a glossator recounting the origins of the *Doctrinale*.[113]

In this new climate of the thirteenth century, when the verse grammars of Alexander and Evrard were circulating with ever-increasing appeal in Italy,[114] the *Ianua* of Harley seemed distinctly out of date: not only was it based almost entirely on a no longer fashionable author (Priscian), but it was also entirely in prose. It is not surprising, therefore, that, in the two *Ianua* versions representing the thirteenth-century reworking of the text (BNP and BML Strozzi), a number of long grammatical explanations taken from Priscian[115] were now excised, to be replaced by numerous mnemonic verses.[116] In fact one of the most

[110] Thurot ( ), : 'Non est igitur mirum, si legitur liber iste [sc. *Doctrinale*], in quo compendiose traditur quod erat primitus dispendiosum et confusum, in quo ordinate traditur quod erat primitus inordinatum, in quo sub luce traditur quod erat primitus nubilosum, in quo potest capi de facili quod nonnulli capere desperabant.'

[111] Thurot ( ), : 'versus est metrica oratio, succincte et clausulatim progrediens, venusto verborum matrimonio et sententiarum flosculis pitturata, nichil in se superfluum nichilque continens diminutum.'

[112] Thurot ( ), : 'Sermo metricus, quem sequitur actor iste [sc. Alexander de Villadei], ad plura se habet quam prosaycus, quem sequitur Priscianus; et hoc ita probatur: sermo metricus utilis factus ad faciliorem acceptionem, ad venustam et lucidam brevitatem, et ad memoriam firmiorem.' See Manacorda ( ), , ; Wrobel, in Evrard de Béthune ( ), ix. The spelling of *auctor* as *actor* became common in manuscripts beginning in the XIIIc.: see Thurot ( ), , n. .

[113] Thurot ( ), : 'Magister Alexander arripuit viam Parisius, et ibi vocatus fuit ab episcopo Dolensi ad introducendum nepotes suos [...] Et magister Alexander videns quod isti nepotes non possent bene retinere regulas Prisciani prosaicas, cum non essent adhuc provecti, edocebat eos regulas Prisciani metricas.'

[114] Reichling ( ), cxxi ; Manacorda ( ), , , . [115] See Appendix .

[116] See Fierville ( ), ; other mnemonic verses are found in BNP lat. on v, r, v: the two examples published by Fierville are from v. See also BML Strozzi , v, v, v, r, v, v. The set of verses on v (Quinque, puer, numero neutra passiva tibi do / Guadeo cum fio soleo, simul audeo fido) appears too in the *Catholicon* of Giovanni da Genoa (completed in

prominent verse additions to the text of *Ianua*, in conformity with the new fashion for grammatical poems in the thirteenth century, was the introductory poem from which the text draws its name, absent in the twelfth-century Harley but first present in BNP lat. .[117] In fact, BML Strozzi has yet another five-verse prologue preceding the usual *Ianua sum rudibus*.[118] These verses indeed are the reason why this manuscript of *Ianua* lay undiscovered until : in his catalogue of the library, Bandini gave only the first four of these verses, omitting entirely the 'Ianua sum rudibus' prologue.[119] The first preface of this manuscript, with its rhyming Leonine verses, in fact provides a link to the poetic fashions of thirteenth-century grammars, recalling as it does the Leonine verses of this thirteenth-century prologue to Evrard's *Graecismus*.[120]

: see Manacorda ( ), , ; Percival ( ), – ; Garin ( ), ; Marigo ( ). However, it is impossible to know whether the *Catholicon* was quoting this version of *Ianua* or vice versa, or whether both were drawing on a common source (possibly a version of Alexander of Villadei's *Doctrinale*). See Percival ( ), . For other mnemonic verses in this manuscript, see v, v– r, r, v, r, r, r, v, v, r, r, v, v, r.

117 BNP lat. , r:

Ianua sum rudibus primam cupientibus artem
Nec sine me quisquam rite peritus [ms.: paritus] erit.
Nam genus et casum speciem numerumque figuram
Hiis que flectuntur partibus insinuo.
Pono modum reliquis quid competat optime pandens
Et quam non doceam dictio nulla manet.
Ergo legas studiumque, rudis, deduc tibi, lector;
Namque iugi studio discere multa potes.

It is improbable that this verse prologue was inspired by the twelve-hexameter preface to Phocas's *Ars de nomine et verbo*, a work which was almost unknown in Italy before Poggio's recovery of the text in : see below, .

118 Incipiunt partes per quas properamus ad artes,
Has quisquis nescit, piger in levitate quiescit.
Harum Donatus fuit auctor in arte probatus,
Quas tradens turbe, Romana scripsit in urbe.
Monstrans dificile m , pueri, cito carpere callem.

I am grateful to Silvia Rizzo for the emendation to the last line.

119 Bandini (–), . .

120 Thurot ( ), :

'Hoc excusetur, quod materiale tenetur,
Si quid longatur contra metra vel breviatur.
Intima scruteris, vocum sensus imiteris.
Utilis est brevitas mentes factura peritas.'

Mayfredo di Belmonte introduced his *Doctrinale* of with the following set of Leonine verses, thus giving further testimony to the strength of the tradition influencing Strozzi :

'Quiquis amat letam subito contingere metam,
Se non absentet, pocius nostra scripta frequentet.
Dicor Donatus, doctrinam tradere natus,
Nam propere lumen nostrum dat in arte volumen.
Annis millenis viginti quinque ducentis
Transactis factus, Manfredo sum peractus.' (Gasca Queirazza ( ),)

What is noteworthy about the chronology of *Ianua* manuscripts is that the earliest versions of the text – particularly Harley and BML Strozzi but also BNP lat. – are considerably fuller grammatical treatises on the parts of speech than the summaries typical of later *Ianua* versions, whether in manuscript or incunabular format; indeed, suggestions can be o ered about the intellectual climate which favoured this fuller style of elementary introduction to Latin morphology during the twelfth and thirteenth centuries. It is usually acknowledged that grammar had languished in Italy[121] during the early middle ages,[122] but the publication of Papias's vocabulary (entitled *Elementarium*) and *Ars grammatica* in the eleventh century and the composition of *Ianua* at about the same time or shortly thereafter laid the foundations for a renaissance of Italian grammatical activity.[123] The parsing grammar had begun to appear with regularity in Northern Europe from the ninth century onwards, but the earliest Italian manuscript of a parsing grammar is from the twelfth century,[124] and it is a sign of renewed Italian grammatical interest that this genre quickly became the favourite Italian beginning Latin textbook. Moreover, the late twelfth and early thirteenth century saw a marked increase of Italian interest in Northern European grammatical texts and vocabulary. Distinctive terms such as supine, gerund and governance (*regere*) – first popularized in Northern Europe[125] – appear with increasing frequency in Italian grammatical works of the thirteenth century;[126] moreover, this was the period in which Northern European grammars such as *Doctrinale* and *Graecismus* became increasingly fashionable in Italy.[127] The thirteenth century saw the culmination of this revival of Italian grammatical studies, initiated by the *Magnae*

121 Apart perhaps from the Carolingian activity primarily in the area of Montecassino and Benevento, inaugurated by Paul the Deacon and continued by Hilderic of Montecassino and Bishop Ursus of Benevento: see Amelli ( ); Morelli ( ); Lentini ( ); Cervani ( ), ; Sivo ( ), – . See also above, n. and below, .

122 Manacorda ( ), , , ; Hunt ( ), – ; Percival ( ), – . Another interesting indication of the weak state of grammatical study in earlier medieval Italy, in contrast to France, is the manuscript circulation of Papias's *Ars grammatica*. Although probably composed by an Italian (see above, n.), there are only three pre-Trecento manuscripts of possible Italian provenance, in contrast to more than thirty from France. See Cervani ( ).

123 Testimony of the Italian grammatical renaissance in the later XIIc. and early XIIIc. are the descriptions of Bologna in as 'in litteralibus studiis prae ceteris Italiae civitatibus' and by Boncompagno da Signa (*c.* –*c.*) as 'caput exercitii litteralis': Zaccagnini ( ), . Here *litteralis* refers to studies based on Latin.

124 Bursill-Hall ( ) lists no parsing grammar in an Italian library dating earlier than XIIIc., and so Harley is, in the present state of knowledge, the earliest manuscript of an Italian text of a parsing grammar.

125 Thurot ( ), , , ; Heinimann ( ), – .

126 Fierville ( ), , ; Marchesi ( ), .

127 Reichling ( ), cxxi ; Manacorda ( ), , , . See below, .

derivationes of Hugutio of Pisa.[128] Noteworthy participants in this renaissance of Italian grammar were Paolo da Camaldoli,[129] Bene da Firenze,[130] Mayfredo di Belmonte,[131] Giovanni da Pigna,[132] Pietro da Isolella,[133] Sion da Vercelli[134] and the century's work culminated in with the completion of Giovanni da Genova's *Catholicon*,[135] which became a standard Latin-to-Latin lexicon over the next two centuries.[136] In this educational environment, a lengthy text of *Ianua*, such as is provided by Harley or BML Strozzi , could have served the aims of ambitious grammar masters anxious to furnish a broad foundation in their subject.

The later development of Ianua

However, by the fifteenth century *Ianua* had been abbreviated: only condensed versions appear among later manuscript copies and early printed editions. It may have taken as long as a century for the condensed version of *Ianua* to establish itself and prevail over the longer traditional versions of the text; in fact, there is apparently a gap of as much as a hundred years between the copying of Strozzi (itself probably representing a text dating from the later thirteenth century) and the date of remaining full *Ianua* manuscripts.[137]

The shortening of *Ianua* in the fourteenth century may suggest the work's changing function in the classroom; its abbreviation coincides with new educational aims and the new class of teachers discussed above, the specialist elementary masters, or *doctores puerorum*.[138] Their aims were not to teach grammar but only elementary reading and

128 Manacorda ( ), , ; Percival ( ), and n. ; Marigo ( ); Garin ( ), – .

129 See Sivo (a) and below, – .

130 Marchesi ( ). See below, , .

131 Mayfredo di Belmonte, teacher in Vercelli in , composed a grammar entitled *Doctrinale* or *Donatus* in . This text, focusing on orthography and etymology and organized according to the eight parts of speech, had many of the normal features of XIIIc. Italian grammatical texts: catechetical format, mnemonic verses often borrowed from Alexander and Evrard, Priscianic content, scholastic grammatical terminology. The work survives in two manuscripts: cod. of the Biblioteca Capitolare di Ivrea (XIVex.) and MS . . of Seville Biblioteca Colombina (XVc.), probably used in the schools of Biella (Piedmont). See Capello ( ), – ; Gasca Queirazza ( ), – nn. and ; Professione and Vignono ( ), ; Gasca Queirazza ( ), – ; Cappellino ( ), , .

132 Gardenal (a); Avesani (b), n. ; Percival (a), , n. . See below, .

133 Schmitt ( ), n. ; Percival ( ), ; Hunt ( ), n. ; Novati ( ), n. ; Schia ni ( ), n. ; Fierville ( ); Thurot ( ), – . See below, .

134 See below, .

135 Manacorda ( ), , ; Percival ( ), – ; Garin ( ), ; Marigo ( ).

136 Manacorda ( ), , ; Marigo ( ).

137 See Appendix .

138 See above, .

writing, as is clear from the contract which Lippo Casini of the Florentine parish of San Lorenzo signed in with 'd. Clementia doctrix puerorum' of the parish of Santa Maria Maggiore, who, for the fee of soldi, 'promisit ... eidem ... tenere, docere et instruere Andream, fratrem ipsius ..., legere et scribere, ita quod convenienter sciat legere Psalterium, Donatum et instrumenta, et scribere, sine aliquo alio pretio';[139] similar was the Genoese contract of , whereby a teacher promised to teach a boy called Simone 'artem gramatice ita ut sciat comode legere et scribere rationes suas'.[140] Such practical educational aims did not require the grammatical excursuses, mnemonic verses, prolonged definitions and numerous paradigms of Harley , BML Strozzi or BNP lat. , but rather the streamlined format of a text such as BNCF Magl. . .[141] It is hardly surprising that the abbreviated *Ianua* became the standard version of 'Donatus' used in elementary education in Florence and throughout Italy in the fourteenth and fifteenth centuries.

The 'Donatus' of Harley , BNP lat. and BML Strozzi , with their extensive paradigms, examples, mnemonics, rules and excursuses, o ered texts to form the basis of an active knowledge of Latin, but the condensed *Ianua* of the fourteenth and fifteenth centuries was used, not primarily as a manual for learning the rudiments of Latin grammar, but rather as a reading text. In the first place, this is suggested by book inventories, which make it clear that innumerable *Ianue* (called *donadelli*) were copied and owned in the fifteenth century.[142] On the other hand, statistics from such sources as the Florentine Catasto of , where only out of , boys mentioned at school were said to be learning grammar, suggest that Latin had become a minority school subject by the fifteenth century.[143] This strong predominance of reading over grammar had already been clear in Giovanni Villani's famous statistics

139 Debenedetti (–), .

140 Gorrini (–), . Similar were Genoese contracts in which Latin was taught only ('donec ita et tamen') insofar as it pertained to merchants ('quod pertinet ad mercatores') ( ); there was to be teaching of reading, writing and 'latinari secundum quod pertinet ad o cium mercatoris' or 'facere epistolas sive breves bene et su cienter ad modum mercatorum Januensium' ( ): Gorrini (–), – .

141 The contrast Gehl ( ), , draws between a 'heavily abbreviated' BML Strozzi and a 'little abbreviated' BNCF Magl. . is problematic: an examination of the roughly corresponding folios reproduced in Black (a), between and , will show that both texts contain the same degree of abbreviation. Another di culty with Gehl's discussion of Magl. . is that he dates the part of the manuscript containing *Ianua* and *Cato* ( ) to XIIIc., instead of XVc.

142 Novati ( ), – ; Martini ( ), , , ; de la Mare (a), – ; Verde ( ), , , , , , , , , , , , , , ; Bec ( ), – , – , – , – , , – , – , – , – , .

143 Grendler ( ), .

about school attendance in Florence *c.* .[144] A similar picture emerges for the first half of the fifteenth century: according to the Catasto of , boys are recorded as attending some kind of school. Of these, are said to be at reading schools; at abacus schools; at an unspecified type of school; and only one at grammar school. Of the unidentified pupils, are twelve years of age or older and so could be attending a grammar school; on the other hand, are eleven years old or younger and so were probably at reading schools.[145] It is di cult to reconcile these contrasting patterns without concluding that *Ianua* must have been mainly used outside the grammar curriculum.

Positive evidence that *Ianua* was principally a reading text is provided by appointment documents, for it is clear that the specialist teachers of the *donadello* were elementary reading masters such as Ser Dore di Ser Giovanni, who was elected 'magister ad docendum pueros legere et scribere' in San Gimignano in and whose duties included teaching 'omnes et sigulos pueros ab eo audire et discere volentes vz. tabulam, psalterium, donatum';[146] indeed, in the Lucchese grammar teacher was forbidden to instruct anyone who had not already mastered Donatus,[147] while in the commune of Pistoia laid down an explicit division of labour: in his school the grammarian could not teach Donatus, which was to be the exclusive preserve of 'uno o dua maestri che debano insegnare a fanciulli'.[148] Donatus was not part of the grammar syllabus: in fourteenth-century Colle Valdelsa a distinction was drawn between schooling 'in grammaticalibus' on the one hand and 'lettera seu doctrina donati, libricioli, carte' on the other,[149] while fifteenth-century Bucine di erentiated 'gramaticha' from 'el saltero o donadello',[150] as did Bassano as early as ;[151] indeed, in Piedmont Donatus was distinguished even from 'primum latinum',[152] while in Trecento Arezzo it was declared that elementary reading, including Donatus, was taught before the pupil was

[144] G. Villani (–), , (ch.).

[145] ASF Catasto , r–v; , r–v; , v, r, r; , r; , r; , r, r; , r; , r; , v, r, v, r, r, v; , r, r; , r (r), r–v; , v (v); , r–v, v; , v, v; , v– r; , v; , v; , r, v; , r, – r r, r; , r, v; , r, r, v; , r, r, r, r, – r, r, r; , r, v, r; , r, v, r, v– r; , r; , v; , r; , r, r, r, r, r; , r; , r; , r; , v; , r.

[146] ACSG NN , lxxviiii verso–lxxx recto (June). [147] Barsanti ( ), .

[148] Zanelli ( ), – .

[149] ASSColle , v (March): tam in gramaticalibus quam in lettura seu doctrina donati, libbricioli, carte et aliis pertinentibus ad dictum ministerium seu artem.

[150] Mazzi ( ), . [151] See n. above. [152] Gabotto ( ), , – .

introduced to grammar.[153] Donatus was *read*, Latin was *done*: 'facientes latinum', 'legentes Donatum' (Colle Valdelsa,[154] San Gimignano[155]); 'lactinare', 'legere Donatum' (Pistoia,[156] San Gimignano);[157] 'legentes Donatellum', 'lactinantes in latino' (Volterra).[158] This vocabulary is making a point: *Ianua* was being used not so much as a manual to learn Latin but as a reading text.

How *Ianua* was actually taught to boys who did not yet know Latin is suggested by the distinction frequently made between two stages of reading this text: 'Donato per lo testo et per lo senno.'[159] *Per lo testo* was sometimes rendered as *a veduta*,[160] *testualiter*,[161] *cum textu*,[162] whereas *per lo senno* was often translated *cum sensu*[163] or *sensualiter*.[164] 'Per lo testo' means reading with the aid of a written text, whereas *cum sensu*, *sensualiter*, *per lo senno* or *per l'insenno*[165] signifies by intellect (*cum sensu*), i.e. by heart. At first these *maestri di fanciulli* had their pupils simply sound out and read the words of *Ianua* directly from a written text, either copied onto a waxed tablet[166] or, beginning in the thirteenth century, from a copy of the text owned by the pupil;[167] the emphasis at this stage was phonetic reading: hence, the

153 ASA Provv. , r (January): Cum videatur et sit utile ac necessarium habere in civitate Aretii unum magistrum qui instruat pueros in primis litteris ac etiam doceat Donatum et Catonem et alios libros antequam inttroducantur ad gramaticam [...]

154 ASSColle , lviiii recto (August), lxvi recto (August); ci verso (November); , lxxxxiii recto (March). 155 ASSG NN , cxiii verso (April).

156 ASPistoia Provv. , v– r (June).

157 ASSG NN, , r (February), v– v (October : see Pecori ( ),); , v– v (March); , r– r (December); , r– r (October).

158 Battistini ( ), – . In view of the evidence linking *Ianua* with the beginning reading texts (*tavola/carta, salterio*) and separating it from the grammar syllabus, Gehl's statement ( ), , seems puzzling: 'In the trecento the Donatus was used almost exclusively as a propaedeutic to further Latin study. It was not given to students for whom the further Latin course was not planned.' 159 Zanelli ( ), . 160 Klapisch-Zuber ( ), .

161 ASSColle , lxiiii recto (January).

162 Lucchi ( ), ; Borracini Verducci ( ), , .

163 Lucchi ( ), ; Colini-Baldeschi ( ), ; Borracini Verducci ( ), , .

164 ASSColle , lxiiii recto (January). 165 Black (c), – . See below, .

166 See BRF , r: graphio id est pezelo quo pueri utuntur in legendo donatum.

167 As early as midXIIIc., schoolboys were owning their own copies of *Ianua*: see document published by Cecchetti ( ), (cf. Ortalli ( ),) where *donatus* was purchased for the sons of Marco Zambon *c.* . There is substantial documentary evidence of *donadelli* purchased for schoolboys in Florence in XIV². ASF Carte del Bene , r: Amerigho di Borghognione [del Bene] dì XIIII de febraio ' per uno donadello per se – L. S. . CStrozz. . , v: deono dare dì III di gennaio [...] sono per uno donadello et catto che si comperò per Checcho; v: Messer Pazino di Messer Franciescho delgli Strozzi de' avere a dì di gennaio [...] sono per uno donadello che ssi conperò a Checcho di Messer Palla – L. S. D. . De' avere dì XVIII di gennaio [...] per conperare uno donadello per Nani di Misser Palla [...] – L. S. D. ; r: E deono dare detto dì [December] L. S.quindici [...] sono per uno donadello che ssi conperò per Simone [...] – L. S. D. ; v: E de' avere detto dì [December] L. S. quindici [...] sono per uno donadello per Simone di Misser Palla [...] – L. S. D. ; v [February]: E deono dare dì VII di febraio [...] L. due S. quindici

rendering sometimes of *per lo testo* as *donatum legens syllabicandum* and *donatum legens syllabicando.*[168] At this textual stage, pupils were hardly yet learning Latin; here the emphasis was on phonetic technique, on *sillibicare* and *compitare,*[169] on reading skills, rather than on the Latin language itself.[170]

Nevertheless, *Ianua* could also serve the small numbers of Italian boys who went beyond elementary reading and writing to the actual learning of Latin. If pupils went on to the next level, *per lo senno*, the emphasis was on memory. There was a phrase *per lo senno a mente* signifying a knowledge so thorough as to know something by memory,[171] and so *Donato per lo senno* meant learning *Ianua* so well as to know the text by memory and without the written text. It is clear that *Ianua* must have been memorized at this stage by boys about to learn Latin, because there was no other manual in the grammar curriculum which included full declensions of nouns and pronouns and complete conjugations of regular and irregular verbs.[172] Guarino's *Regule* and its medieval forerunners such as Goro d'Arezzo's *Regule parve* or Francesco da Buti's *Regule* included only partial paradigms and assumed a knowledge of declensions and conjugations.[173]

[...] demmo per conperare uno donadello – L. S. D. ; r: E de' avere dì VII di febraio [ ] [...] L. due e S. quindici [...] sono per conperare uno donadello per Simone [...] L. . S. . D. . [168] Massa ( ), .

[169] For *sillibicare* in Bonaventura's scheme of learning to read, see Manacorda ( ), , ; see also Lucchi ( ), . For *compito* and *compitare* (meaning 'sounding out'), see Lucchi ( ), ; Klapisch ( ), . The first seven years of the education of the Pavian clerk Opicinus de Canistris from to were divided into two stages: first three years for 'legere vel sillabicare', the next four 'in studio grammatice' (i.e. Latin) (Sasse Tateo ( ), –).

[170] This type of phonetic reading without meaning often remained with Italians in later life: hence Peter Damian's accusation of those who babble syllable by syllable without understanding ('syllabatim [...] balbutiant'), cited by S. Reynolds (b), .

[171] Tommaseo and Bellini (–), pt. , , s.v. senno: '† Saper per lo senno a mente, *Aver piena e indubitata contezza, Saper benissimo, minutamente, Avere esattamente a memoria. Varch. Stor.* . . *(C)* In Firenze vivono ancora, se non più, diecimila persone, le quali le sanno . . . per lo senno a mente. *Galil. Sist.* . Ci sono molti, che sanno per lo senno a mente tutta la Poetica, e sono poi infelici nel compor quattro versi solamente.' This is the phrase used by Bernardo Machiavelli in his *Libro di ricordi*, r: 'R° q° dì detto di sopra chome insino a dì del presente cominciò Nicholò mio andare a imparare da Ser Baptista di Filippo da Poppi. Insegnagli il donadello per lo insenno a mente.' See Black (c), . Also significant is the phrase 'Donao a seno et a mente' transcribed by Grendler ( ), , n. , from the Venetian Professioni di fede of .

[172] Gehl's statement ('Full mastery of grammatical terms and paradigms could not have been learned from the *Ianua* alone. For that the student needed to work carefully through some of the Latin reading texts': ( ),) needs amendment. Full mastery of the paradigms is what *Ianua* did o er; before the appearance of Perotti's *Rudimenta*, there was no other manual o ering all the paradigms. As for grammatical terminology, there was much of this in *Ianua*, but it had to be complemented by secondary study of a text such as Francesco da Buti's or Guarino's *Regule*. Literary texts from the minor or major authors (see below, ch.) obviously contained no theoretical grammatical terminology. [173] See below, .

However, the emphasis on memorization for pupils learning 'Donato al senno' may have been on the wane in the fifteenth century. This may be suggested by the contrast between Guarino's *Regule*, first mentioned in , [174] and Perotti's *Rudimenta*, finished in . [175] Whereas Guarino, as well as his predecessors such as Goro and Francesco da Buti, excluded full paradigms, these are included by Perotti; [176] the elementary Latin teacher may no longer have been able to assume that his pupils, having completed the study of *Donato al senno*, knew the paradigms by heart. The later profusion of interlinear and interverbal translations of *Ianua*, called *Donato al senno*, [177] indicates a shift of emphasis from memorization to translation for the class learning *per lo senno*, *cum sensu* or *sensualiter*; by the later fifteenth century the sense of *al senno* was changing from 'by memory' to 'with translation'. Indeed, the ability to translate a few words of Latin was the minimum expected of Donatists by the early sixteenth century, as is clear from Nicolò Liburnio's vernacular grammar, *Le tre fontane*, published in Venice in . [178] This text describes precisely the level of Latin attained by pupils after having studied *Donato al senno* with its interlinear of interverbal paraphrases: translation, not memorization. Indeed, the benefits of memorizing *Ianua* were probably fewer in the fifteenth than they had been in the thirteenth century. A long text of *Ianua*, typical of the early manuscripts, would, when memorized, have served the aims of ambitious grammar masters anxious to establish a broad basis for their subject. On the other hand, the streamlined text, typical of later manuscript copies and early printed editions, was more suitable

174 Grendler ( ), . 175 Grendler ( ), .

176 Guarino, *Grammaticales regulae*, Venice (Bodley shelfmark Auct. O. infra. .); Marchesi ( ), – , for the text of Goro's *Regule parve*; Francesco da Buti, *Regule gramatice*, Bodley Lat. misc. e. ; Perotti, *Regulae Syppontinae*, Venice (Bodley shelfmark Auct. , Q. .).

177 Grendler ( ), – , – . Latin morphologies rarely appeared with vernacular translations in Italy during the middle ages. As mentioned above (see n.), one has been published by Sabbadini ( ) but the text was not *Ianua*, and it is not clear that it was intended or used to teach elementary reading. I have examined a microfilm of the manuscript published by Sabbadini (Milan, Biblioteca Ambrosiana S. sup.) and his dating of XIII/XIVc. appears reasonable, in view of the few Caroline elements remaining in the script; I am grateful to Arthur Field for providing me with these photocopies from Notre Dame University Library during the Ambrosiana's closure. Another example, with vernacular from Piedmont, was published by Manacorda ( ). Again the text was not *Ianua* and there is no compelling reason to believe that it was used to teach elementary reading. Manacorda dated the MS to XIIc. or XIIIc., but he provided an illustration in (–), , where the hand seems to be N. Italian, XIV[1].

178 v: è di mestieri non punto allargarmi dalle saggie ammonitioni di Fabio Quintiliano: Percio che lasciando gli huomini gia dottrinati da parte, bisognami dell'imparanti l'ingegno considerare: acciò che ogni persona meggianamente accorta tenendo qualche prattica del Donato grammaticale, co gli esempi delle Tre nostre fontane, possa convenevolmente addottrinarsi. Il perche qual fanciulletto è in Italia da si povero padre procreato; il quale al meno secondo l'idioma, dove è nasciuto non impari dar il volgar (qual che si sia) al Nome, et al Verbo latino.

I am grateful to Brian Richardson for showing me this text.

as an elementary reading book than as a foundation for a thorough and lasting training in Latin. Another point about memorization is that mnemonic verses seem to appear only in the earlier manuscripts of *Ianua*, i.e., BML Strozzi and BNP lat. . This particular change in the contents of versions of *Ianua* in the course of the fourteenth and fifteenth centuries is further evidence that *al senno* was ceasing to mean memorization and coming to mean translation.[179]

Ianua came to dominate the final stages of the elementary curriculum in Italy; although Italians may have been slow to succumb to the attractions of parsing grammars, their eventual conversion was more whole-hearted than in Northern Europe. Indeed, Italy is the only European country in which manuscripts of parsing grammars significantly outnumber manuscripts of the *Ars minor*. The figures, based on Bursill-Hall ( ), are:

	Parsing grammars	*Ars minor*
Germany		
France		
Britain		
Italy		

Parsing grammars seem to have been particularly popular among German-speaking pupils and teachers, among whom *Remigius* ('Dominus quae pars') achieved a remarkable following; however, even in Germany, the *Ars minor* managed to compete e ectively.

This contrast between Northern and Southern European elementary

[179] This interpretation of the reading of *Ianua* in two stages *per lo testo e per lo senno* has been questioned by Gehl ( ), , who has suggested that *per lo testo* as well as *per lo senno* referred to memorization, the first of a visual type, the second of a more internalized kind; in this connection he cites a passage from Augustine's *De doctrina christiana* (,): 'The first care [...] is to know these books. Although we may not yet understand them, nevertheless, by reading them we can either memorize them or become somewhat acquainted with them. Then, those things that are clearly asserted in them as rules, governing either life or belief, should be studied more intelligently and attentively.' However, the Augustinian text makes no suggestion of a 'visual and aural' (Gehl ( ),) type of memorization. What Augustine is referring to here is the two-staged reading process described above ( ) in the *Regula magistri*: at first reading on the basis of the written text, secondly internalized reading achieved through complete memorization. Some memorization was bound to occur at the initial textual stage as a result of constant phonetic reading and re-reading of texts, as Augustine suggests when he says that 'by reading them we can either memorize them or become somewhat acquainted with them', but memorization was not the overriding aim of this first stage, as is clear from the Augustinian passage, where two alternative outcomes are described: either memory or mere familiarity. In fact, the VIc. monks mentioned above as learning to read the psalter in two stages made a clear distinction between initial reading from a written text on their tablets ('alii psalmos, quos habent superpositos, meditentur') and subsequent memorization ('nam cum eos maturaverint et memoria perfecte tenuerint'): *Règle du maître* ( ), , – . Even in the age of Augustine, there was a basic reading stage from written material, followed by a separate memory stage.

textbooks is arguably due to the di ering structure of the educational curriculum on either side of the Alps. In the north, elementary grammars – whether parsing or the *Ars minor* – remained an integral part of the grammar syllabus: of the thirty-eight northern manuscripts of 'Dominus quae pars', all but one form part of anthologies of other grammatical works; similarly, of the ninety-nine non-Italian manuscripts of the *Ars minor*, eighty-two give the text as part of an anthology together with other grammatical texts.[180] The transmission of *Ianua*, on the other hand, tells an entirely di erent story. (See Appendix II.) Of the twenty-nine Italian manuscripts of *Ianua*, at least seventeen are not preserved together with other grammatical works,[181] and overall at least nineteen of the thirty-four surviving *Ianua* manuscripts are not part of grammatical anthologies.[182] This suggests a di erent context for *Ianua* in the fourteenth and fifteenth centuries from that of other parsing grammars, which were tied to the grammatical curriculum.

By now *Ianua* was primarily associated with the literary, not the grammatical tradition, as is suggested by its eventual almost indissoluble link to another great standby of the medieval classroom: Donatus's connection with Cato's *Distichs* seems to have been a traditional association, to judge from Conrad of Hirsau's remarks in the twelfth century.[183] But it was in Italy that this curriculum progression became a real marriage. Most surviving texts of *Ianua* from the beginning of the fourteenth century form a pair with Cato's *Distichs*.[184] The *Distichs* had provided simple reading material for pupils throughout the middle ages, and its manuscript coupling with *Ianua* confirms that this one-time grammar manual was seen primarily as an introductory reading text. The inclusion of *Ianua* in two Italian school anthologies, BML Strozzi and BNCF Magl. . , further suggests that *Ianua* was becoming part of the cycle of school reading material in Italy. However, *Ianua* more usually appeared separately with Cato, and this indicates that in Italy there was normally a distinction between elementary reading material and reading material studied in a grammar school. On the other hand, Cato seems not to have been paired with the *Ars minor* or other elementary

[180] The figures in this paragraph are based on Bursill-Hall ( ).

[181] These are Marston, Vienna and , Oxford , Paris , El Escorial, Plimpton, Venice , Ott. Lat., Este , Trivulziano, Med. Pal., Berlin, BRF , Brescia, Magl. . , Padua Universitaria. It is impossible to know whether or not the five fragmentary manuscripts of *Ianua* published by Scalon ( ) originally came from codices containing other grammatical works.

[182] The two non-Italian manuscripts without other grammatical texts are Harley and Casanatense.

[183] Conrad of Hirsau ( ), : 'Catonem igitur iunge Donato quasi sillabarium abecedario: sicut enim literam sillabae vel dictionis cognitio, sic Cato Donatum in parvulorum studio subsequitur.'

[184] See Appendix .

grammars, and this contrast also confirms that Donatus's genuine treatise, as well as northern parsing grammars, retained their traditional status as primarily grammar textbooks.

Ianua's success in Italy seems therefore to have been due to its peculiar place in the curriculum. Late medieval and Renaissance Italians wanted a textbook with literary associations, one which could provide terminal reading material for children who would not usually continue their Latin studies. *Ianua* was less attractive in Northern Europe because it was not normally connected with the grammatical tradition. In Northern Europe, elementary education seems to have been firmly part of a fuller grammatical curriculum, as is suggested for example by the manuscript associations of *Remigius* and the *Ars minor*; *Ianua*, with its literary connections, was therefore less attractive north of the Alps. These literary a liations, however, were exactly what parents and teachers in Italy were seeking for elementary education: hence, *Ianua*'s success there in supplanting the *Ars minor* or other elementary grammars traditionally associated with the grammatical curriculum. 'The Italian Renaissance learned from *Ianua*'[185] precisely because it had become, for most pupils, a beginning reading text, and no longer a grammar manual.

185 Grendler ( ), .

ADDENDUM: The meaning of the terms *per lo senno, per l'insenno, cum sensu* or *sensualiter* is problematic. In my earlier articles (Black (a) , (b) , (c) , (e)) I interpreted this terminology to mean 'with meaning' or 'with comprehension'. While writing this present book, I have come to the view that this translation is not correct, and that the terminology meant 'by intellect', i.e. 'by memory'. The word 'senno' is ambiguous: on the one hand it can mean 'sense', but on the other it can also signify wits, as in the phrases 'perdere il senno' ('to lose one's wits') or 'senno naturale' ('mother wit') (see Reynolds ed. ( ),). Similarly, the word 'sensus' in classical Latin normally meant 'sense', 'understanding' or 'meaning', but in medieval Latin it came also to have the further meaning of 'intellectus' (see Du Cange s.v.) or 'mind' (as in the phrases 'sensus divinitatis' or 'sensus divinus' meaning 'divine mind': see Souter ( ),). If interpreted in this latter way, this terminology would mean 'with one's wits or intellect', that is, without the written text and by heart.

What has particularly convinced me of the latter meaning is the broader philological context. I am perplexed to understand what 'comprehension' could signify at the level *per lo senno*. It seems clear that the first stage in reading was sounding out from a written text (*al testo*) (see above). If the next stage signified 'with meaning', then one would expect to find glossed manuscript copies of *Ianua*: in the middle ages and Renaissance, comprehension was synonymous with glossing, particularly interlinear word-for-word equivalents. However, it is a fact that manuscript copies of *Ianua* were not glossed. (See below, .) If on the one hand comprehension and understanding were not involved at the level *cum sensu* or *per lo senno*, then on the other memorization had to be paramount here. When the pupil passed from *Ianua* to the level of *Regule grammaticales* (for example by Francesco da Buti or Guarino), a knowledge of the paradigms was taken for granted, since verb conjugations and noun, participle and pronoun declensions were not included in these texts. (See below, *passim.*) Memorization of the paradigms had to have taken place at the earlier level of *donato per lo senno.*

The secondary grammar curriculum

The concept of a general secondary textbook of Latin grammar did not exist in antiquity. Once pupils had finished learning an elementary manual such as Donatus's *Ars minor*, the only comprehensive grammatical textbooks were sophisticated and advanced works such as Priscian's *Institutiones grammaticae.*[1] Other secondary textbooks tended to be specialized, such as Donatus's *Ars maior*[2] (which dealt with only phonetics, the parts of speech and figures), Priscian's *Institutio de nomine pronomine et verbo*[3] or Phocas's *Ars de nomine et verbo.*[4] The methods of teaching Latin had been developed for native speakers. Once the parts of speech had been mastered through a simple morphology such as the *Ars minor*, what was required for further Latin study was a more sophisticated taxonomic system, such as that o ered by Donatus's *Ars maior* or books to of Priscian's *Institutiones.*[5] This would provide the pupil with an ever more sophisticated terminology and framework for the reading and analysis of literary authors. As far as Latin sentence composition was concerned, basic syntax did not have to be taught to native speakers; sophisticated syntactical problems were handled through the doctrine of the figures (treated extensively for example in book of Donatus's *Ars maior*), which discussed exceptions and permitted lapses of correct grammatical usage.[6] The absence of basic or systematic syntactical instruction in the Roman grammatical syllabus is demonstrated by the fact that only one early Roman grammarian, Varro, in the lost books to of his *De lingua latina*, is thought to have treated syntax.[7] Stylistic refinement was primarily the province of rhetoric and not grammar; it was also assumed that pupils would gradually assimilate an adequate writing style by immersion in the reading of the good authors.

[1] See Keil (–), ed., – and supplement. [2] Ed. Holtz ( ); Keil (–), .
[3] Keil (–), . [4] Keil (–), . [5] Keil (–), – .
[6] Keil (–), . [7] Percival ( ), .

Of course, the situation was di erent in the Greek-speaking East, especially after the bilingual culture of the Mediterranean world dissolved in later antiquity. It is no accident that many of the fundamental textbooks for advanced grammatical study were the work of Priscian, a native Latin speaker from North Africa who taught in Constantinople during the early sixth century. But by then Latin was already an advanced optional subject, mainly necessary for diplomats, administrators and especially lawyers, who had to cope with the Roman legal corpus and tradition. So Priscian's students tended to be sophisticated linguists, already thoroughly grounded in the Greek grammatical and rhetorical tradition. This explains the erudite character of Priscian's grammatical writings. The level at which he lectured on the classical authors was detailed and recondite, as is clear from the *Partitiones duodecim versuum Aeneidos principalium*, where the first verse of each of the twelve books of the *Aeneid* is given a learned and minute philological and grammatical commentary.[8] The same is true for his theoretical grammatical works, and in particular for his *Institutionum grammaticae libri XVIII.*[9] This was a work for advanced linguists who had already mastered one highly inflected and literary classical language. Ostensibly the work is systematically organized, divided as it is into eighteen books, dealing in apparently logical progression with phonetics (books –), the eight parts of speech (noun ( ), verb ( ), participle ( ), pronoun ( ), preposition ( ), adverb and interjection ( ), and conjunction ( )) and finally syntax ( ). But each section is soon swamped by innumerable citations and analyses of classical Latin texts, by constant and lengthy comparisons with Greek examples and by continual erudite digressions: philological learning engulfs logical presentation and extinguishes hope of accessibility for all but the most advanced and sophisticated students and scholars. The overpowering character of the work is nowhere more evident than in the two last books on syntax.[10] These must have seemed particularly desirable in a non-Latin culture such as the Greek East, but, although on the face of it Priscian's treatment is systematic and logical (first he discusses construction in general and then focuses on verbal syntax, moving in order through impersonals, indicatives, imperatives, optatives, subjunctives, cases, passives and absolutes), it nevertheless rapidly degenerates into countless excursuses and myriad citations of Greek and Roman authors. These two books

[8] Keil (–), . [9] Keil (–), .

[10] Keil (–), . Priscian's treatment of syntax was based on the only significant surviving Greek syntactical treatise, Apollonius Dyscolus's Suntãsiw

(running to some pages in the Keil edition) could not serve as an introductory manual to Latin syntax for medieval non-Latin speakers; although they were sometimes copied separately from the rest of the *Institutiones*, forming the so-called *Priscianus minor*, they served mainly as works of reference or as the starting point for learned commentaries on syntax. Books and did not inaugurate a new genre of medieval Latin syntactical manuals; on the contrary, they evidently put o imitators and followers, remaining the only works on Latin construction to be handed down to the middle ages, and comprising a unique heritage until the twelfth century. Their unsatisfactory content and presentation are clear from the fact that *Priscianus minor* survives in notably fewer manuscripts than the first sixteen books: the material that they provided was far from suitable for a school-level course on syntax.[11]

How then did early medieval Italian children, after mastering the *Ars minor* or its equivalent, continue their Latin studies and in particular cope with syntax? The answer is that they simply carried on with the methods developed in late Roman antiquity. This meant further study of the parts of speech, using treatises such as Donatus's *Ars maior* or Priscian's *Institutiones*, or newly composed works such as the ninth-century *Ars grammatica* by Hilderic of Montecassino or the *Adbreviatio artis grammaticae* by his contemporary Ursus of Benevento.[12] These latter works were written with an educational context in mind: Hilderic continued to use the dialogue format of Donatus's *Ars minor*[13] and made direct reference to his pupils,[14] while Ursus's reference to abbreviation in his title suggested an attempt to bring down the voluminous grammatical heritage of antiquity to the school level.[15] However, the result was two weighty and learned works: Hilderic's *Ars* occupies more than folios (and perhaps for that reason remains still only in small part edited) and draws on many grammatical sources besides Donatus and Priscian,[16] whereas Ursus's text, filling double-columned quarto folios (and likewise still unpublished),[17] even frequently supplements Priscian himself, especially by reference to Donatus but also to other grammarians such as pseudo-

[11] Reichling ( ), xiv; Percival ( ), .

[12] See Lentini ( ); Morelli ( ). Hilderic's work was deliberately post-elementary, as revealed by lack of paradigms: Lentini ( ), ; the same was true for Ursus's compendium: see Morelli ( ), *passim*. [13] Lentini ( ), – *passim*, .

[14] Lentini ( ), . For further educational features of the text, see Lentini ( ), .

[15] See Morelli ( ), : 'sono eliminate totalmente, o quasi, le citazioni, che dovevano in gran parte riuscir oscure agli scolari cui Ursus si dirigeva'.

[16] Lentini ( ), – . It presumed some acquaintance with Greek and possibly Hebrew, besides direct knowledge of Priscian: Lentini ( ), – , .

[17] Lentini ( ), ; Morelli ( ), .

Vergil.[18] In early medieval Italy, the school was a unitary institution, going from elementary to advanced education, and works of such erudition and detail had a wider scope than o ering easily digestible secondary instruction for children. Hilderic's treatise was still limited, like the first two books of the *Ars maior*, to phonetics and the parts of speech,[19] while Ursus, together perhaps with a less able follower, added to these topics a treatment of figures, so covering the whole range of Donatus's longer theoretical grammar.[20] This meant that syntax had to be assimilated by total immersion in Latin authors, complemented by gradual acquaintance with exceptional constructions learnt through studying the figures[21] or by scattered syntactical references in a text such as Hilderic's *Ars*[22] or by struggling with Priscian's inaccessible treatment, either in the original version or in a compendium.[23] Nevertheless, this system seems to have worked without much problem in the culture of early medieval Europe. Latinity – and in particular the ability to write fluently in the language – was a skill demanded of a tiny proportion of society: a minute handful of the laity and only the clerical élite.

But this *status quo* began rapidly to change in the eleventh and twelfth centuries, with the vast expansion of education, both in terms of student numbers and institutions. The burgeoning administrative, clerical, notarial, legal and academic classes could not be satisfied with the painfully slow methods of artificial immersion in the authors; these were aspiring professionals with careers to pursue and quicker progress was needed. Moreover, with their wider and more specialized academic and professional ambitions, these men of the new millennium wanted greater theoretical depth in Latin than was o ered by a work such as Donatus's *Ars maior.* It is no accident that it was in the eleventh century and in Italy – a particularly intensive moment and focal point for educational, cultural and social expansion – that the question of Priscian reasserted itself. It has been seen above that *Ianua* and Papias's *Ars grammatica*, both works dating from before the mid-twelfth century, were conceived as partial substitutes for Priscian. *Ianua* was intended for this purpose at the elementary level,[24] while Papias's *Ars grammatica* had the

[18] Morelli ( ), ; Lentini ( ), . Ursus presumes, like Hilderic, minimal acquaintance with Greek: Morelli ( ), . [19] Lentini ( ), – .

[20] Morelli ( ), – . [21] E.g. Morelli ( ), – .

[22] Lentini ( ), : 'Regole di sintassi Ilderico ne dà qui e lì incidentalmente, quando gli si presenta l'occasione.' See Lentini ( ), – .

[23] Ursus's *Adbreviatio* perhaps originally included the last two books of *Institutiones* on syntax, but the relevant fascicles may have been lost from the only MS: see Morelli ( ), .

[24] See above, .

same aim at the secondary level.[25] The latter was not an elementary treatise, since no declensions or conjugations were given: a knowledge of *Ianua* (or its equivalent) was presumed. The problem was how to memorize the essential secondary grammatical material o ered by Priscian: the *Institutiones grammaticae* were too long, but it was hoped that the compendium o ered by Papias could be readily memorized and retained.[26] Nevertheless, Papias's *Ars grammatica* posed only a partial solution to the problem: it was entirely a treatise on phonetics and the parts of speech. Its attraction was that it abridged and summarized the first sixteen books of the *Institutiones* of Priscian,[27] an authority whose material could not continue to be neglected by secondary Latin pupils, evidently no longer satisfied with the much more limited scope of Donatus's treatment in books and of the *Ars maior*; as such Papias's *Ars grammatica* achieved a notable circulation, preserved as it is in more than forty manuscripts.[28]

As a treatise only on phonetics and the parts of speech, the *Ars grammatica* of Papias remained within the conventional limitations of secondary grammatical study: there was yet no treatment at all of syntax. This traditional secondary syllabus was still prevalent in Italy a hundred years later, during the later twelfth century, when Paolo da Camaldoli composed his grammatical and rhetorical works, now found in a single manuscript (BNP lat.). These consisted of a treatise on the parts of speech;[29] an introductory treatise on versification; a florilegium of prosody (not actually by Paolo but an older work by an anonymous author, probably of the eleventh century); an *ars dictaminis*; and a collection of model letters. The treatise on the parts of speech was an elementary work, as is clear from title, where Paolo says that it is written for everyone and therefore entitled *Donatus*, the name given to all versions both of the *Ars minor* and of *Ianua*: 'quoniam ad utilitatem omnium est datus, ideo Donatus est vocatus'.[30] Indeed, the work draws heavily on *Ianua*,[31] and it is obvious that Paolo intended it as a contribution to the genre of the copious versions of *Ianua* which constituted the first stage of learning Latin morphology in Italian schools in his day. Most compilators of *Ianua* tended to overlook the fact that the grammatical material presented by Donatus and Priscian di ered not only in order of the parts

[25] Cervani ( ), lxxxvii: 'un testo destinato alla scuola'.

[26] See above, .

[27] Priscian had been condensed earlier by Rabanus Maurus in *Excerptio de arte grammatica Prisciani*: see Hertz, x in Keil (–), ; Keil (–), , xxxii; Reichling ( ), xiv.

[28] Cervani ( ), iv. For Papias's procedure in condensing Priscian, see Cervani ( ), – .

[29] Ed. Sivo (a).

[30] Ed. Sivo (a), , ; see Sivo (a), .

[31] See Sivo (a), – .

of speech but also in terms of grammatical doctrine; while other organizers of *Ianua* simply followed Priscian, Paolo actually drew on both ancient authorities, presenting first material from Priscian and then from Donatus on each part of speech in explicitly labelled sections.[32] From the point of view of secondary grammar, what is significant about this manuscript of Paolo's works is that it appears to constitute a complete foundation course in grammar and rhetoric. The pupil would pass from the parts of speech to versification, prosody and then *dictamen*. What is important to note here is that Paolo's foundation course entirely omits any consideration of secondary syntax: in traditional fashion, the pupil progressed from a detailed consideration of the parts of speech to advanced grammatical topics such as versification and prosody and then moved on to rhetoric in the form of *dictamen* and model letters. In twelfth-century Italy Latin prose composition seems apparently still to have been an untaught subject: the pupil went from the parts of speech directly on to advanced grammar and introductory rhetoric; the assumption still seems to have been that prose composition could be assimilated through detailed study of morphology followed by immersion in the authors.

What made possible the emergence of a coherent secondary Latin grammar course, and especially of a full and systematic treatment of syntax, were the developments in language theory and logic which took place in French schools, and particularly in Paris, during the twelfth century. Again dissatisfaction with Priscian was a fundamental stimulus to change, as was made clear by William of Conches.[33] William criticized Priscian's failure to give clear definitions and his neglect of what he called causes. It may seem paradoxical to expect a consideration of causation in a work on grammar, but French schools were, even in the early twelfth century, coming under the growing influence of logic (even

32 'De nomine secundum Priscianum', 'De nomine secundum Donatum', 'De pronomine secundum Priscianum', 'De pronomine secundum Donatum', etc.: ed. Sivo (a), *passim*.

33 Thurot ( ), : 'Quoniam in omni doctrina gramatica precedit, de ea dicere proposuimus, quoniam, etsi Priscianus inde satis dicat, tamen obscuras dat definitiones nec exponit, causas vero inventionis diversarum partium et diversorum accidentium in unaquaque pretermittit [...] Quod ergo ab istis minus dictum est, dicere proposuimus, quod obscure, exponere, ut ex nostro opere aliquis causas inventionis predictorum querat et di nitionum Prisciani expositiones [...]' For William's influence on the leading figure of the new French school of language philosophy, Petrus Helias, see Fredborg ( ).

before the assimilation of the full Aristotelian logical corpus) and so it is only to be expected that a master such as William would be looking for a more logical approach to language than was to be found in Priscian's undigested, confusing and disordered treatment.[34] Priscian's omission of causes became a stock criticism in the northern schools; indeed, the logical shortcomings of his work were sometimes ascribed to his excessive reliance on the ancient authors: the masters of the twelfth and thirteenth centuries were all too aware that Priscian's approach to grammar was philological, not logical.[35]

The lack of an overall logical framework and structure for language in Priscian served as a spur to twelfth-century grammarians. For example, Priscian had no concept of subject and predicate.[36] Merely recognizing the need for various parts of speech is not the same as the categorical logical proposition that every sentence consists of two essential building-blocks. It was only when the categories of *subiectum* and *praedicatum* were developed for logical propositions that a corresponding grammatical terminology emerged, first perhaps evident in the teachings of Petrus Helias, who used the terms *supponi* and *apponi* to signify the grammatical units 'subject' and 'predicate':

> a noun is never in the predicate unless it complements a substantive verb [namely e.g. to be or to become], nor does a verb appear in the subject unless to complement a substantive noun; but any noun in itself can be the subject, and any verb in itself can be the predicate.[37]

Soon the uniquely medieval terminology *suppositum* and *appositum* emerged.[38]

A logical approach to language thus generated a coherent syntactical theory of subject and predicate, and similarly grammatical logic was responsible for the emergence of comprehensive theory of Latin word

[34] See Thurot ( ), ; Reichling ( ), xiv.

[35] Thurot ( ), : 'Cum Priscianus non docuerit gramaticam per omnem modum sciendi possibilem, in eo sua doctrina est valde diminuta. Unde constructiones multas dicit, quarum tamen causas non assignat, sed solum eas declarat per auctoritates antiquorum grammaticorum. Propter quod non docet, quia illi tantum docent qui causas suorum dictorum assignant.'

[36] He declares that 'si tollas nomen aut verbum, deficiet oratio, desiderans vel nomen vel verbum [...] non tamen dico, quod non etiam ex pronomine et verbo perfecta constat oratio' (,). See Percival ( ), .

[37] Thurot ( ), : 'nomen nunquam apponitur nisi auxilio verbi substantivi, nec verbum supponitur nisi auxilio nominis substantivi; sed quodlibet nomen per se supponitur, et verbum per se apponitur'.

[38] Thurot ( ), : 'Ad perfectionem locutionis duo sunt necessaria, scilicet suppositum et appositum. Suppositum est illud de quo fit sermo [...] Appositum est illud quod dicitur de supposito. Casualia fuerunt inventa ad significandum suppositum ... Verba fuerunt inventa ad significandum appositum.'

order. The subject logically precedes the predicate, as is explained by Petrus Helias.[39] This logical structure generated a necessary grammatical sequence of words: because the subject precedes the verb in logic, it followed that grammatically the subject preceded the verb in the order in which the words were spoken or written.[40] This came to be known as 'debita et communis forma constructionis', 'communis modus in contextu partium orationis'[41] or 'ordo naturalis';[42] what this meant was the naturally logical order of words.[43] This order had a place for all potential elements of a sentence.[44] Word order is thus conceived of as a logical structure: the terminology *a parte ante* and *a parte post* appears first in twelfth- and thirteenth-century grammatical writings to express a logical relationship.[45] Logically, motion comes first, then the destination or source of the motion: hence *ante se*. But grammatically this then becomes a formula for word order and, indeed, a convenient pattern for basic sentence structure: a supine, whether ending in -um or -u, requires in front of itself a verb of motion.

What the medieval grammarians called 'ordo naturalis' had been termed 'recta ordinatio' by Priscian (,).[46] But for Priscian this does not constitute the cornerstone of a comprehensive syntactical

[39] Thurot ( ), : 'Cum enim dico currit, actum quidem per verbum significo; sed actus non potest esse, nisi alicui insit; ideoque non potest illius verbi determinari significatio, nisi ostendatur de quo dicitur.' The idea that external reality determines linguistic order is also found in Priscian (.), but his treatment is philological rather than logical: see below, .

[40] Thurot ( ), : 'Suppositum est illud quicquid precedit principale verbum vel intelligur precedere.' [41] Thurot ( ), .

[42] For further discussion of this terminology, which has a huge bibliography, see Rizzo ( ), – ; Scaglione ( ), – , – ; Mengaldo ( ), – ; S. Reynolds ( ), – ; Mariotti ( ), – .

[43] Thurot ( ), : 'Naturalis ordo est, quando nominativus cum determinatione sua precedit et verbum sequitur cum sua, ut *ego amo te*.' For William of Conches's treatment of 'naturalis ordo dictionum', see Kneepkens ( ), – .

[44] Thurot ( ), – : 'Nominativus et vocativus precedunt verbum … quia nominativus et vocativus significant substantiam … et verbum significat agere vel pati … et quia substantia precedit quoslibet actus di nitione, cogitatione, tempore … Quia vocativus dicit et significat substantiam excitate, nominativus dicit et significat substantiam agentem, et quia aliquis prius excitatur ad agendum, quam agat, ideo vocativus precedit nominativum … Dativus et accusativus postponuntur suis verbis … quia illud quod determinat dependentiam alicuius, sequitur illud … Quia determinatio sequitur suum determinabile, et quia adverbium est determinatio verbi et verbum est determinabile, ideo verbum sequitur ipsum … Genitivus ponitur post istam partem a qua regitur …'

[45] Thurot ( ), : 'Primum supinum, quod est accusativi casus, exigit verbum ante se poni, quod significat motum ad quem, ut *vado lectum*. Sed supinum ablativi casus ante se appetit poni verbum significans motum a quo, ut *venio lectu*.'

[46] , : 'Sciendum tamen, quod recta ordinatio exigit, ut pronomen vel nomen praeponatur verbo, ut "ego et tu legimus, Virgilius et Cicero scripserunt", quippe cum substantia et persona ipsius agentis vel patientis, quae per pronomen vel nomen significatur, prior esse debet naturaliter quam ipse actus, qui accidens est substantiae.'

theory, but rather a philological observation about normal linguistic practice among the authors. The contrast between his philological approach and the logical approach of the twelfth-century grammarians is clear from his next sentence, where he observes that contravention of this normal order of noun/pronoun followed by verb is sanctioned by the usage of the authors.[47] The practice of the authors, not the demands of logic, determine word order for Priscian.[48]

Another concept to be developed as part of a comprehensive linguistic theory in the twelfth century was the notion of governance. The idea that the verb possessed a power or force constraining another part of speech to be in one case rather than in another was present in Priscian.[49] But Priscian had no one technical term to describe this relationship, using a number of di erent words such as *adiungi*, *coniungi*, *sociari* as well as *exigere*.[50] Among medieval grammarians the verb *regere* assumed the status of agreed grammatical jargon, as was recognized by Petrus Helias.[51] But this new technical language was not the only novel feature of the treatment of governance among twelfth-century grammarians. Priscian had treated governance as only one more philological characteristic of the Latin language: he viewed the phenomenon in an entirely empirical fashion, limiting governance to the command exercised by verbs over nouns or pronouns in the oblique cases only. For medieval grammarians, on the other hand, governance was extended beyond the oblique cases to the nominative as well; the verb was now thought to govern all elements of the sentence, including not only its object but also its subject.[52] For Petrus, governance by the verb included of course not

47 'licet tamen et praepostere ea proferre auctorum usurpatione fretum' (,).

48 See Thurot ( ), for an early example (XIc.) of normative treatment of word order, where there is apparent no consideration of exceptional usage as sanctioned by ancient authors, and yet where the overriding logical framework apparent in XIIc. is not yet evident; this passage also mentioned by Kneepkens ( ), .

49 See Thurot ( ), . With regard to the verb *possidet*, for example, he declared: 'Verbi huius [possidet] natura hoc exigente, ut intransitive quidem nominativum, transitive vero accusativum exigat' (,).

50 Percival ( ), . For further Priscianic synonyms, see Rizzo ( ), .

51 Thurot ( ), – : 'Ubi gramatici huius temporis dicunt "dictio regit dictionem", ibi Priscianus dicit "dictio exigit dictionem", et quod alii dicunt regimen, ipse dicit exigentiam apertiori utens locutione.' Rizzo ( ) points out ( ) that *regere* was not first used in the middle ages, Sabbadini having indicated two occurrences in Servius's commentary on the *Aeneid*, and Thurot its occurrence in the ancient grammarian Consentius. As this passage makes clear, nevertheless, it was well known from XIIc. onwards that *regere* was characteristic modern (i.e. medieval in our terms), not ancient, usage.

52 As Petrus Helias declared: 'dictionem regere aliam dictionem nil aliud est, quam trahere secum eam in constructione ad constructionis perfectionem [...] Unde verbum exigit nominativum, quia ad perfectionem constructionis trahit secum nominativum in constructione; ut cum dico *lego*, actum legendi designo alicui inesse, itaque significo sermonem fieri de aliquo. Nominativus

only the nominative but also the oblique cases.[53] Moreover, governance was extended by Petrus beyond the verb to include all parts of speech, including the preposition,[54] the participle[55] and even the noun.[56] Priscian's approach to governance had been inconsistent and incomplete,[57] but in the hands of Petrus Helias it became a general theory of syntax, stipulating the way in which all words of a sentence were related.[58]

A final feature of the new logically underpinned language theory to emerge in the twelfth century was the idea of the syntactical figure, the *figura constructionis*. For ancient grammarians there had been a clear distinction between figures associated with rhetoric and those connected with grammar.[59] This idea was followed by medieval grammarians.[60] But for Donatus the distinction was between figures of speech (*figurae verborum*) and of thought (*sensuum*); the idea of syntax did not enter into his discussion.[61] The same is true for Priscian, who had introduced the term *figura* into his chapters on syntax (,), but, like Donatus, he does not distinguish between figures of construction (*figurae constructionis*) and

autem significat id de quo fit sermo. Quare illud verbum trahit secum nominativum in constructione ad perfectionem constructionis, quia aliter non erit perfecta constructio' (Thurot ( ), –).

53 Thurot ( ), : 'Verbum autem non tantum regit nominativum, sed etiam oblicos. Quum enim verbum significat actum transeuntem ab uno in aliud, tunc verbum in constructione trahit oblicum. Ut cum dico *Socrates legit*, ostendo actum transire a Socrate. Sed semper pendet animus auditoris ex re ut significatur per oblicum. Querit enim semper quid legit. Et ideo ad maiorem constructionis perfectionem trahit hoc verbum secum accusativum, ut *Socrates legit Virgilium*.'

54 Thurot ( ), : 'prepositio trahit oblicum in constructione. Cum enim dico *averto faciem meam ab illo*, ibi *ab* significat separationem. Quia prepositio significat separationem, sed non determinat cuius rei separationem, ideo necessario secum trahit oblicum, per quem separatio illa certificetur. Unde prepositio illa habet oblicum regere.'

55 Thurot ( ), : 'Eodem modo etiam participium regit obliqum casum.'

56 Thurot ( ), : 'Nomen etiam exigit oblicum casum, quia quoddam nomen significat rem ut pendet ex re significata per oblicum, ut *pater* ex vi relativa significat rem ut pendet ex re significata per genitivum. Unde auditor semper expectat cuius pater. Ideo iste nominativus trahit secum genitivum in constructione, ut *pater filii*.'

57 For Priscian the mutual relationship among nouns, pronouns, adjectives and participles was not handled, as with verbs, from the point of view of the governing but rather from that of the governed word and its case: e.g. possessive genitive, genitive of quality, etc.; moreover, his inconsistent approach extended mainly to verbs and nouns. (See Percival ( ), – .) Medieval grammarians developed a uniform and universal theory of governance in which the keystone was always the governor, not sometimes the governor, at other times the governed.

58 Petrus Helias's theory of syntax was apparently indebted to William of Conches, and both seem to have drawn on an earlier Magister Guido: see Kneepkens ( ), citing further bibliography.

59 As Donatus declared: 'Schemata lexeos sunt et dianoeas, id est figurae verborum et sensuum. sed schemata dianoeas ad oratores pertinent, ad grammaticos lexeos' (Keil (–), iv,).

60 Thurot ( ), , n. : 'Figura ... locutionis ad oratores pertinet, ut dicit Donatus.' Thurot ( ), : 'Gramatice vicium sepe figura notat.'

61 See Thurot ( ), – , n. .

rhetorical figures (*figurae locutionis*). In contrast, there was no such reluctance on the part of Petrus Helias, for whom the idea of figure became a fundamental building-block of syntactical theory.[62]

This systematic and logical approach to language, as created by the twelfth-century French grammarians, did not remain an esoteric branch of higher learning in the middle ages; on the contrary, it was brought down to the humbler levels of the educational hierarchy in the most decisive manner imaginable at the very turn of the thirteenth century. In ,[63] Alexander of Villedieu composed what must be one of the most influential and innovatory works in the history of education: *Doctrinale*. It was the first comprehensive and systematic grammar textbook (including syntax) to be composed explicitly for the secondary level; it was a book which took on board the innovations in linguistic theory and particularly in the realm of syntax which had been developed in the twelfth century; it decisively put to one side Priscian's discursive and philological format in favour of a systematic and logical presentation. Although not the first grammatical work to be composed in verse in the middle ages[64] or antiquity,[65] nevertheless there can be no doubt that *Doctrinale* established the genre and was responsible for the vogue of verse grammars composed throughout Europe in the thirteenth century. It is no wonder that *Doctrinale* became an immediate best-seller throughout Europe, and continued to occupy the pedagogical forefront for more than three centuries; indeed, this was a period in which a particular premium was placed on an ordered presentation in teaching, as was recognized by the great late fourteenth-century Italian lawyer, Baldus de Ubaldis.[66]

Doctrinale shared one aim with works of the preceding two centuries, such as *Ianua* or Papias's grammatical compendium: to provide a prac-

62 Thurot ( ), : 'Non est idem figurativam esse constructionem et locutionem [...] Figurativa locutio est ubi voces de propria significatione ad aliam significationem transferuntur convenienter, ut *prata rident* [...] Propria vero constructio est ubi voces in eisdem accidentibus intransitive construuntur, ut *Sor legit*. Figurativa est quando voces diversorum accidentium aliqua rationabili causa intransitive construuntur, ut *ego Priscianus lego*.'

63 Reichling ( ), xxxvi .

64 Possibly *Liber pauperum* by Jean de Beauvais, a little-known XIIc. grammarian, some of whose verses Alexander possibly borrowed for *Doctrinale*: see Sivo (b), . For an earlier verse treatise on prosody used by Alexander, see Hurlbut ( ).

65 For Terentianus Maurus, who composed a grammatical monograph, not a grammatical textbook, in verse in the second century , see below, .

66 *In primam Digesti Veteris partem commentaria*, Venetiis , Prooemium, v. Quoniam, nn. – , : Omnia doctrinarum omnium fere principia a voce habentur magistra et sine ordine tradi non possunt. Est enim ordo principia mediis et media suis finibus iungens, et scire quid facias et nescire quo ordine facias, teste Ambrosio, non est perfectae cognitionis [...] Ordo enim est modus entium, unde memorialis cedula ex ordine vel ex spiritu colligato e cacior redditur.

tical substitute for Priscian's *Institutiones*. Alexander was seen as a reviser of Priscian, as is clear from another work of his, the (now lost) *Alphabetum maius*, which was entitled *Correptio Prisciani* by a thirteenth-century glossator';[67] he himself implied that he saw *Doctrinale* too as a revision of Priscian.[68] In fact, this was the interpretation of these lines given by the same thirteenth-century glossator.[69]

Doctrinale also had a further purpose in common with a number of other works composed at the turn of the thirteenth century: the displacement of the Roman classics from the school curriculum.[70] This was not only an explicit objective of *Doctrinale*[71] but also of Alexander's *Ecclesiale*, where he emerged as a declared opponent of the school of Orléans, famous for its classicism.[72] Alexander's anti-classicism not only indicated a new direction for the literary side of the curriculum but also a new approach to the teaching of syntax in the classroom: the traditional method of immersion in the authors was to be put to one side, and replaced by grammar based on logic and philosophy. Alexander emerges not only as the arch-enemy of Orléans but also as the champion of the new philosophy's home, Paris, where he himself had studied.[73]

Alexander's antipathy to the Roman classics and his frustration with Priscian represented a well-trodden path at the turn of the thirteenth century,[74] but *Doctrinale*'s verse format was more novel.[75] Ancient grammars had been prose works, apart from Terentianus Maurus's *De litteris syllabis et metris Horatii*, a work discovered at Bobbio only in ;[76] the place for verse in classical grammatical compositions had been in the many citations included from the Roman poets. The unconventionality of Alexander's medium has long been recognized, albeit pejoratively, by critics, one of whom declared it to be 'a monstrous idea to squeeze an

[67] Thurot ( ), – .

[68] Thurot ( ), : 'Que de gramatica sunt visa michi magis apta [sc. than in Priscian],/In doctrinali pro magna parte locavi.'

[69] Thurot ( ), – : 'Quod fere tota gramatica traditur in hoc libro [sc. *Doctrinale*] videtur actor innuere in quodam libro quem composuit, qui dicitur *Correptio Prisciani*, quia correxit Priscianum in multis locis in illo libro supra dicto, ubi dixit istos versus: *Que de gramatica sunt visa michi magis apta / In doctrinali pro magna parte novavi* [*sic pro locavi*].'

[70] See Thurot ( ), – , ; see below, .

[71] See Reichling ( ), xx, xxxvii, vv. – , – (Reichling ( ), –).

[72] Thurot ( ), ; see – for prologue of *Ecclesiale*, where Alexander elaborates hostility to Orléans classicism. See Reichling ( ), xxvii; Delisle ( ), . *Ecclesiale* was intended to replace Ovid's *Fasti* as the true calendar: (Reichling ( ), .

[73] Reichling ( ), xxi , xxvi; Thurot ( ), .

[74] See above, and below, .

[75] It is possible, although not proven, that Alexander knew of Jean de Beauvais's *Liber pauperum*, since both works share a few of the same verses: Sivo (b), ; mnemonic verses circulated independently of texts and sporadic adoption of the same verses does not necessarily indicate textual dependence. See Percival ( ).

[76] Keil (–), , .

entire grammar into verses'.[77] The use of invented verses to expound grammatical points in prose grammars was also rare before Alexander: there are, for example, a few of these in Petrus Helias,[78] as there are similarly in Paolo da Camaldoli.[79] In fact, the practice may have experienced an early development in the medieval Italian tradition, given that a few such mnemonic verses are found in Papias's *Ars grammatica*.[80]

According to the glossators of *Doctrinale*, the work's verse format came about by accident. Employed by the bishop of Dol to teach his nephews, Alexander noticed that the boys could not remember Priscian in prose, and so he turned some Priscianic rules into verse for them. One day when he was away, the bishop asked his nephews a grammatical question, to which they responded with the metric rules provided by their teacher. This astounded the bishop, who asked for the source of these grammatical verses; their reply was that they had learned them from their teacher. He then persuaded Alexander to compile an entire book of these verse rules for his nephews: the result was *Doctrinale*, which he then published at the behest of the bishop.[81]

The importance of Alexander's innovation was immediately recognized by successive grammarians: Evrard de Béthune composed his verse grammar, *Graecismus*, only thirteen years later in ,[82] while Alexander's harshest medieval critic, John of Garland, a die-hard Orléanist,[83] wrote many grammatical treatises in verse;[84] an Italian imitator of Alexander was Maestro Sion or Simon di Vercelli (d.), whose own partly verse *Novum Doctrinale*, possibly datable between and ,[85] was transcribed by a pupil in , the year of his teacher's death.[86] From the mid-thirteenth century, there was scarcely a grammat-

[77] Neudecker ( ), , cited by Reichling ( ), lxxv.
[78] Thurot ( ), n. ; Sivo ( ), , – ; Gardenal (b), .
[79] See Sivo (b), ; Sivo (a), – , .
[80] Reichling ( ), lxxxii–lxxxiii, n. ; Cervani ( ), xcv–xcvi, . Mnemonic verses can occasionally be detected in ancient grammarians such as Caper, but interestingly an orthographer such as Bede, who borrowed from Caper, converted his metres into prose (Sabbadini ( ), –), a fact suggesting the disuse into which this teaching technique had fallen during the early middle ages. [81] Thurot ( ), ; Reichling ( ), xxiii.
[82] Date established definitively by Reichling ( ), lxxx–lxxxiii.
[83] See Reichling ( ), xxviii, liv . [84] Reichling ( ), lxxv.
[85] Alessio ( ), lxix n. ; Gardenal (a), n. .
[86] Contained in only one MS (Biblioteca Capitolare di Novara, MS : see Mazzatinti (–), , – ; Bursill-Hall ( ) gives an incorrect shelf-mark). It purports to be a full Latin course, treating 'latinandi metrificandi dictandi', that is grammar, metrics and style. The strictly grammatical first section deals primarily with parts of speech (in Priscianic order), syntax and figures. For its contents summarized, see Capello ( ), – ; Bersano ( ), – ; Mazzatinti (–), , ; Gardenal (a), – , who further discusses its treatment of prepositions (including extracts), – , – . It has more than mnemonic verses, included to

ical work composed without at least the principal rules commemorated in verse.[87] In fact, the tradition of using verse to fix grammatical rules in the memory of pupils continued as a central feature of Latin pedagogy from the time of Alexander up to and beyond the nineteenth[88] and even into the twentieth century, where it was still being used in English schools in the s and s.[89] With *Doctrinale*, indeed, there emerged a new type of verse: not just didactic poetry whose purpose was moral or religious improvement and sometimes aesthetic pleasure, but also technical verse, whose primary aim was to fix grammatical rules in the memory of pupils.[90]

Doctrinale was the first grammar textbook embracing the entire syllabus as defined by Priscian and Donatus to be expressly composed for the secondary level: Papias and Paolo da Camaldoli, for example, had excluded syntax.[91] Alexander explains that he is not writing for beginners by saying that he intends the book for 'clericulis [...] novellis'.[92] This line was explicitly expounded in the thirteenth-century *Admirantes* gloss as referring to secondary pupils.[93] *Doctrinale*, unlike Donatus's *Ars minor* or *Ianua*, provides no definitions, conjugations or declensions. The book explicitly presumes a knowledge of *Donatus*, to which the reader is referred for the declension of pronouns and for the conjugation of regular verbs.[94]

The systematic character of the book is immediately clear from the preface, where Alexander announces the topics that he will cover (vv. –). This division, given as it is in verse, was intended to be memorized, like the rest of the text, so providing the pupil with a table of contents to carry with him in his head and enabling him to orient himself within the text. Soon glossators divided the book into twelve chapters, corresponding to the above verse division;[95] by the early fourteenth

obviate Priscian's prolixity and aid memory: Bersano ( ), . For his orthography, see below, . [87] Reichling ( ), lxxv; Thurot ( ), .

[88] Reichling ( ), lxxv.

[89] The method formed an important element in B. H. Kennedy's legendary Latin Primer, where macaronic verses combined Latin and English; this textbook, published under various titles such as *The Public School Latin Primer*, *The Child's Latin Primer* and *The Revised Latin Primer*, first appeared in mid XIXc.; republished as late as . [90] Reichling ( ), lxxiv–lxxv.

[91] See above, .

[92] 'Scribere clericulis paro Doctrinale novellis' (v. ; Reichling ( ),).

[93] Thurot ( ), , n. : 'Causa finalis tangitur, cum dicit *clericulis*, id est ad utilitatem clericorum, nec multum in scientia provectorum. Sed quoniam in predicto vocabulo diminutio declaratur, ne per illam diminutionem videatur scribere improvectis, eandem diminutionem temperat, cum dicit *novellis*. Nam isto vocabulo mediocribus scribere designat ... novellis id est parum de novitate habentibus.' [94] Vv. , , ; Reichling ( ), , , .

[95] Reichling ( ), lxxi.

century the chapters had been grouped into three larger sections in some manuscripts, with the first seven chapters forming the section on the parts of speech (the so-called etymological division), the eighth and ninth constituting the syntactical part, and the last part made up of the final three chapters on versification and figures.[96]

In terms of the traditional grammar curriculum, the most conventional part of *Doctrinale* was the section on the parts of speech: most of this material had previously been covered in works such as the grammatical compendium by Papias.[97] This section is mainly based on Priscian,[98] although it is selective: it deals with only declinable parts of speech;[99] the focus is entirely on the generation of regular and especially irregular forms,[100] and so the material from Priscian's books to , dealing with prepositions, adverbs, interjections and conjunctions,[101] is omitted. These indeclinable parts of speech had been learned while reading the *Ars minor* or *Ianua*, and so it was evidently felt that this treatment was adequate to justify exclusion from a verse grammar whose purpose was to fix rules and irregularities in the pupil's memory, especially in the case of parts of speech which, by definition, were neither regular nor irregular.

The section dealing with prosody was not new to the secondary grammar syllabus, having been included, for example, in Paolo da Camaldoli's grammatical anthology;[102] similarly, figures had been treated coherently and digestibly since antiquity in the form of Donatus's *Barbarismus*, which served as the source of the corresponding section by Papias and would do the same for Alexander.[103] But the section on syntax was entirely novel in the secondary syllabus. Alexander's syntactical treatment shows a generic resemblance to *Priscianus minor* but in detail it is little based on Priscian,[104] being either an independent composition or derived from an unknown predecessor;[105] Alexander in fact broke away from Priscian's organization (or lack of it), supplying the first systematic exposition of syntax in a secondary context, based on the principles and terminology established by the Parisian language philosophers of the twelfth century.[106]

There had, of course, been earlier studies of syntax and construction in the middle ages; the twelfth-century French schools, with their growing interest in the connections between logic and language, had provided fertile ground for such works. Perhaps the most notable of

[96] Reichling ( ), lxxi–lxxii. [97] See above, . [98] Reichling ( ), lxxviii.
[99] Reichling ( ), lxxii–lxxiii. [100] Reichling ( ), lxxiii. [101] Keil (–), , – .
[102] See above, . [103] Reichling ( ), lxxix. [104] Reichling ( ), xxxi.
[105] Reichling ( ), lxxviii. [106] Reichling ( ), xv.

these had been Petrus Helias's *Summa super Priscianum*,[107] a book dating from the mid-twelfth century.[108] Although Petrus's *Summa* shared a broad academic and educational context with Alexander's *Doctrinale*, the resemblance between the two works goes no further. In the first place, unlike Alexander's textbook, Petrus's *Summa* remains within the genre of a commentary on Priscian, following the topical order of the last two books of the *Institutiones*.[109] Secondly, Alexander excludes vast amounts of material treated by Priscian, focusing only on two main themes: governance of cases and word order.[110] In contrast, Petrus's work had developed into a further expansion of the subject, with major changes of content and structure; it was clearly Petrus's aim to replace Priscian with a more logical, systematic and comprehensible treatment. Although he thereby eliminated a number of Priscian's countless literary examples, he did not reduce the number of general topics treated; on the contrary, these were often augmented, as for example when he created, out of Priscian's confused, rambling and inadequate initial discussion,[111] nine general precepts applicable to all forms of construction.[112] Petrus's work was conceived for the upper strata of the academic curriculum, o ering a new vision and treatment of the entire topic of Latin syntax; Alexander, in contrast, was providing a clear and systematic textbook for the lower levels of the school hierarchy, albeit not for absolute novices.

The syntactical part of *Doctrinale* is divided into two sections, the first of which treats governance (ch.). Here the organizing principle is case: parts of speech and constructions governing the nominative (vv. –), genitive (–), dative (–), accusative (–) and ablative (–) cases are handled in order.[113] The chapter ends

[107] Reilly ( ). Earlier edition of *Summa* on Priscianus Minor (i.e. books and on construction) in Tolson ( ). [108] Gibson, in Tolson ( ), .

[109] As stated at very start of *Liber Constructionum*: 'quo ordine tractet Priscianus de constructione. Eodem enim ordine et nos tractabimus de ea': ed. Reilly, , (cf. Tolson ( ),). See also 'Tabula Capitum', + – + in Tolson ( ), where he demonstrates running correspondence between Priscian and Petrus. [110] See below, – .

[111] . – ; Keil (–), , – . [112] Reilly ( ) ed., – ; Tolson ( ), – .

[113] The organization of syntax according to case was an unusual departure for Alexander. Priscian had considered various types of case construction but only with nouns: e.g. genitive of possession, quality, etc.; dative of possession, with adjectives, etc.; accusative of relation; ablative of instrument, of quality, absolute, etc. Alexander extended this approach to other parts of speech. Alexander's source for this presentation is unknown: obviously not from the only two Latin grammarians who used it (Carisius and Diomedes). See Sabbadini ( ), – . This approach was adopted by Evrard de Béthune in *Graecismus* (see below,), and also by Tebaldo (see below,), besides in a short treatise on case governance by one Maestro Uguccione, preserved in Ambrosian manuscript E inf. (XIVc.): see Sabbadini ( ), . Sabbadini seems to assume that this Maestro Uguccione is identical with author of *Magnae derivationes*, dating the

with a discussion of participles (vv. –). While this part of the work treats the way words are linked together when one determines or governs the case of the other, the second section in chapter considers other aspects of the relationship among words in sentences. It begins with a discussion of transitive and intransitive constructions (vv. –) and their various subdivisions. Then Alexander gives the natural or logical word order of the sentence, a concept of central importance in twelfth-century Parisian language theory (vv. –): vocative, nominative, personal verb, adverb, dative, accusative; gentive and other oblique cases follow the governing verb; accusative and ablative follow the preposition. Alexander follows this pivotal discussion by giving exceptions to this natural word order (vv. –). The next subsection of the chapter on construction concerns agreement (vv. –), the discussion of construction concluding by considering the implications for syntax of negatives (–), impersonals (–), supines and gerunds/gerundives (–), prepositions (–) and conjunctions (– , –); inserted (vv. –) is a brief discussion of words constructed as words and not as part of the meaning of the sentence and so indeclinable (e.g. *homo dictio dissyllaba*).[114]

The other great medieval verse grammar, Evrard de Béthune's *Graecismus*, was a less innovatory work than *Doctrinale*: not only did Evrard imitate Alexander in the work's verse format, but *Graecismus*'s scope was more in line with the traditional grammar syllabus.[115] Moreover, it imitates *Doctrinale*'s overall coherence, which is clear from an analysis of its contents found in a copy of the *editio princeps* (*c.*).[116] Here the book is divided into three major sections: *permissiva*, covering figures (i.e. permitted grammatical lapses) and corresponding to chapter in the Wrobel edition; *prohibitiva*, comprising grammatical errors (*vitia*) and consisting of chapter in Wrobel; and *preceptiva*, that is, recommended correct grammatical practices, which occupy the remaining

footnote (*cont.*)
treatise therefore to *c.* , although there is no evidence other than similar Christian names. This approach to syntax, proceeding according to case, did not find favour among subsequent Italian grammarians. In the XIVc. syntax was organized according to parts of speech (see e.g. treatment by Francesco da Buti below ( )) and this approach was also followed by XVc. humanist grammarians such as Guarino.

114 See Reichling ( ), n.

115 Evrard intended to lay out the work's contents in his prose preface (Wrobel ( ), –), but, as has been pointed out (Thurot ( ), –), there apparently was a problem in the transmission of the text here, since the table of contents has no grammatical connection with the preceding paragraph; moreover, the preface gives an order of material not followed by the text as transmitted by the manuscripts, and some subject matter treated in the work is omitted from the preface (e.g. chapter on syntax).

116 See Wrobel ( ), xi–xii.

twenty-five chapters. *Preceptiva* is broken down into four parts: prosody, orthography, etymology and syntax. The first twenty-six chapters of the book, treating as they do figures, prosody and the parts of speech, represent the traditional secondary syllabus, as encountered in Papias and Paolo da Camaldoli.

Within this traditional structure Evrard diverges from Alexander in that his emphasis comes to be on vocabulary and on lexical questions, especially in the chapters grouped together under the subtitle of etymology. In this section Evrard presents what amounts to a metrical lexicon, in contrast to Alexander's metrical grammar: the core of *Graecismus* consists of lexicography whereas the focus of *Doctrinale* is on rules.[117] Evrard o ers a metrical textbook deliberately complementary to Alexander's: the latter recast in a metrical format more accessible to the schoolroom the theoretical innovations of the twelfth-century French grammarians, while the former made the lexical achievements of Papias and Hugutio available to pupils in the form of mnemonic verses. The great medieval lexicons of the eleventh and twelfth centuries were huge works of reference, too large to memorize in a classroom where pupils did not have copies of their own textbooks; *Graecismus*, on the other hand, brought this encyclopedic learning down to the grammar-school level, its verse format enabling pupils to commit to memory lexical material which the copious prose of Papias's *Elementarium* and *Magnae derivationes* had confined to reference only. Again for obviously pedagogic reasons, Evrard abandoned the great medieval dictionaries' alphabetic order, organizing his work in terms of topics, for example, devoting an entire chapter to the nomenclature of the muses[118] and other classical figures, or providing long lists of synonyms for words such as *navis*.[119]

The other aspect of the *Graecismus* which di ers from older educational patterns is found in the final chapter entitled 'De diasyntastica', consisting of a mere sixty-one lines;[120] Evrard manages to pack a remarkable number of essential syntactical rules into this brief space, demonstrating a skill in compression and synthesis which goes some way to explaining this work's remarkable circulation in the three centuries following its composition in . The syntactical chapter is divided into four main sections: constructions with impersonal verbs, agreement of nouns and adjectives, constructions with the nominative case and constructions with the oblique cases. With regard to nominative

[117] See Percival ( ), .

[118] Ch. ('De nominibus Musarum et gentilium'), ed. Wrobel ( ), – . See Percival ( ), .

[119] Ed. Wrobel ( ), . See Percival ( ), .

[120] Wrobel ( ), – .

constructions he makes use of the concept of natural word order, so important in twelfth-century language philosophy, to o er the simplest possible explanation: if the nominative precedes the verb, then it is a personal verb; if it follows the verb, then the verb is a vocative (e.g. *vocor*), substantive (e.g. *sum*) or similar. He concludes this section with a one-line rule laying down that *quam* governs the nominative in the case of a comparative. Constructions with oblique cases receive an equally succinct treatment and the handling of verbal construction is similarly concise. Evrard concludes *Graecismus* with a one-line epilogue pointing out that verbs of motion take supines ending in either *tum* or *tu*. This work's brief syntactical chapter shows how far grammar in the classroom had moved from the discursive and seemingly endless treatment of Priscian's last two books: Evrard had learned well his lessons in organization and systematic exposition from Alexander, not to mention the logical underpinning of grammar which was the legacy of the twelfth-century Parisian school. Possibly because of its more restricted syllabus, nevertheless, *Graecismus* always ran a clear second behind *Doctrinale*, preserved as the latter is in more than manuscripts (in contrast to *Graecismus*'s just over).[121]

Although *Doctrinale* and *Graecismus* were both northern French works, they reached Italian schools rapidly in the thirteenth century, when, indeed, there was continued dissatisfaction with Priscian.[122] In the first place, this di usion is suggested by the surviving manuscripts. Of the thirty thirteenth-century manuscripts listed by Reichling,[123] five are now preserved in Italian libraries (BML . , BAV Pal. Lat. , Marciana . , Montecassino T.T. , BML sin.) and although two of these are definitely northern European (BML . , BAV Pal. Lat.), at least one other is certainly Italian in origin (Marciana .). Similarly, of the twenty-nine *Graecismus* manuscripts now in Italian libraries, seven are datable to the thirteenth century (Bologna Universitaria cod. ( ), BML sin. , BML CS , Milan Ambros. Cod. E. inf.,

[121] Bursill-Hall ( ), .

[122] XIIIc. Italian *dictator* provided this eulogy for recently deceased grammarian: 'Nam ipse solus de tenebrosis et confusis Prisciani tractatibus educens lucem, purgavit tenebras [...]': cited by Corradi ( ), .

[123] BNCF Magl. . and BRF , attributed by Reichling to XIIIc., are actually XIV^2 manuscripts: see below, .

Milan Ambros. Cod. O. sup., Modena Biblioteca Estense Cod. Alpha W. . (Lat.)), and of these only two (BML . sin. : French, dated ;[124] BML CS : French[125]) have been eliminated as non-Italian. More conclusive evidence comes from Italian grammars written in the thirteenth century. Pietro da Isolella's *Summa*,[126] datable to the thirteenth century,[127] contains material taken from *Doctrinale* and *Graecismus*,[128] as does Giovanni da Genoa's *Catholicon*, completed in .[129] Most important, however, is the testimony of the Piedmontese grammarian

124 v:

Finitus est liber. Qui scripsit, il eut nom Lambert.
Natus fuit de Castro qui vocatur Virgeio.
Explicit Grecismus—[*deletum*]
Anno Domini M°CC°LXX°quinto. Fuit actum
Prima die mense februarii.

Castrum Virgeium is Vergy, in Côte-d'Or, near Gevry-Chambertin.

125 BML CS (S.ma Annunziata), XIII², French: scribes frequently use long final 's'; 't' is largely of the Caroline lower style (like 'c'); French style of abbreviation for 'qui' ('i' suprascript, rather than horizontal stroke below line).

126 Published anonymously by Fierville ( ); actual authorship discovered by Novati ( ), n. . See Hunt ( ), ; Avesani (a), n. ; Gardenal (a), and nn. , , ; Alessio ( ), lxxiv–lxxvii. This work, generally entitled *Summa* (see e.g. Hunt ( ), n. and below for BML . and BRF), was apparently the most widely circulated grammar in Italy with that title (see Bursill-Hall ( ), , for list of about fifty manuscripts). As such, it is the best candidate for anonymous *Summa* in a well-known curriculum of the communal school of Moncalieri dating from (Gabotto ( ), , republished by Nada Patrone ( ), , n.), whose identification has puzzled scholars: see Frova ( ), , n. ; *Summa* appears anonymously in similar curricula from Genoa in (Petti Balbi ( ),) and from Turin in (Gabotto ( ), , republished by Nada Patrone ( ), n.). Rizzo ( ), n. , points out that this Genoese *Summa* is not Rolandino de' Passeggeri's notarial textbook (see Petti Balbi ( )) but rather one of many secondary grammars using that title. The standing achieved by Pietro's *Summa* even in the thirteenth century is demonstrated by the Statutes of Parma, redacted between and , which laid down that 'quilibet doctor artis grammaticae teneatur legere scholaribus suis Sommam cremonensem': Ronchini ( ), . Ronchini was evidently unfamiliar with Pietro da Isolella da Cremona's widely circulated *Summa*, so that his attempt to refer this passage to a lesser grammarian from Cremona, Gherardo da Belloria, possibly the author of grammatical texts and other works (( ), xi), is unconvincing.

127 Hunt ( ) points out that the work is preserved in several XIIIc. manuscripts: n. . More specifically, the text was apparently composed between , the date of the composition of Sponcius of Provence's *Summa de constructione*, used extensively by Pietro (see Fierville ( ), xvi–xix, , , and (for dated colophon)), and , the date of publication of Giovanni da Genova's *Catholicon*, which borrowed an entire chapter from Pietro da Isolella (see Sivo ( ), –). This *terminus post quem*, suggested by Paetow ( ), n. , has been doubted by Gardenal (a), n. and n. , pointing out that there are also references in the text to the pontificate of Innocent (presumably III) and Bishop Sicardus (–). As will be seen below, Pietro's *Summa* is a pastiche, so that these references may come from earlier borrowed material, just like the passages from Sponcius. An hypothesis putting the composition of Pietro's *Summa* back to the pontificate of Innocent III would require the further unlikely hypotheses that the work was either revised by the author forty years later, or that the original text lay dorment for forty years, only to be given additions from Sponcius after .

128 Fierville ( ), n. , n. , n. , – , , , (*Doctrinale*, vv. –), , .

129 Percival ( ), .

Mayfredo di Belmonte, who in composed a grammar in Vercelli, giving it the title of *Doctrinale*, in imitation of and homage to Alexander of Villedieu.[130]

Until the turn of the thirteenth century, there appears to have been relatively little di erence between the secondary curricula in Northern Europe and in Italy: it is hardly surprising to find a traditional secondary Italian textbook such as Papias's *Ars grammatica* circulating on both sides of the Alps.[131] However, the emergence of the two great verse grammars, and especially *Doctrinale*, proved to be a decisive point of divergence for the secondary curriculum. How were teachers to employ these works in the classroom? Their verse format implied memorization by pupils, but teachers on either side of the Alps took di erent approaches to this problem. In Northern Europe, it is clear that these verse grammars were treated in the traditional way: that is, like the psalter and Donatus (whether the *Ars minor* or some kind of parsing grammar such as *Dominus quae pars est?*),[132] they were memorized by pupils in their entirety. This is clear from two simple facts. In the first place, *Doctrinale* and *Graecismus* remained the main two secondary grammars in wide circulation in Northern Europe from the thirteenth to the fifteenth centuries; their only rivals, Ludolphus de Lucho's *Flores grammaticae*,[133] and pseudo-Petrus Helias's *Priscianus metricus*,[134] were also verse grammars and similarly would have been intended for memorization. Secondly, pupils in Northern Europe seem not to have owned their own schoolbooks: it was only with the arrival of printing that prose secondary grammar manuals began to circulate widely in Northern Europe. The German *Exercitium puerorum grammaticale* of greeted printing as an innovation which would allow boys to have their own textbooks and so save their teachers from having to read out everything to their pupils; the inference is that before printing schoolbooks had to be dictated by teachers and memorized by pupils.[135] The elementary and secondary medi-

[130] On this work, its manuscripts and contents, see above, , n. . Sivo ( ) put forward an hypothesis regarding the existence of a now lost compendium of Priscian which served as common source for parts of Petrus Helias's *Summa*, *Doctrinale*, Paolo da Camaldoli's *Donatus*, Pietro da Isolella and *Catholicon*, but this philological argument has no relevance for analysing the historical e ect exercised by works of enormous circulation such as *Doctrinale* and *Graecismus*.

[131] Cervani ( ), vii–lx; Bursill-Hall ( ), – . [132] See above, .

[133] Bursill-Hall ( ), – : verse treatise dealing almost exclusively with syntax, dating from XIIIc. (mentioned by Radulphus Brito, late XIIIc.): see Percival ( ), n. .

[134] Bursill-Hall ( ), .

[135] Jensen ( ), , and n. : 'Pro pueris nostris instituendis in hoc opusculo non opus est lectione pervia, quoniam res ipsa clarissime atque facillime ante oculos est depicta. Scolarum igitur rectores, preceptores atque lectores non sua capita frangant legendo, vociferendo, clamando,

eval curriculum in Northern Europe was based on memory: pupils learned the psalter, Donatus and *Doctrinale* by heart; their theoretical grammatical knowledge was based on their book of memory.

In Italy, on the other hand, the secondary curriculum developed along di erent lines: memory, while still important, did not remain the paramount teaching technique at this level. In the first place, this is clear from the number of surviving manuscripts in Italy of *Doctrinale* and *Graecismus*: only thirty-one manuscripts of the former[136] and twenty-nine of the latter[137] are preserved in Italian libraries, amounting to just about per cent of the total number of manuscripts. Secondly, there rapidly emerged a series of alternative secondary grammars by Italian masters: in the thirteenth century, the major competitors to Alexander and Evrard were Bene da Firenze, Tebaldo, Pietro da Isolella da Cremona and Giovanni Balbi da Genova, the latter two of whom wrote secondary grammar textbooks whose manuscript circulation in Italy[138] exceeded the distribution achieved there by the two great Northern verse grammars. What is significant about these alternative Italian textbooks from the point of view of the secondary curriculum and its use is that they were all prose works. This of course implies that they were not memorized by the pupils. There then immediately arises the further question of how pupils learned from these Italian prose textbooks; the answer is simple: they bought or wrote their own copies.[139] It is significant that several of these works (e.g. those by Bene da Firenze, Giovanni da Pigna and Pietro da Isolella) were normally known as *Summe*, the standard university term for textbook. In the thirteenth century, with the rise of the *Studia generalia*, practices arose for the rapid copying of texts for students, known as the *pecia* (piece) or *reportatio* systems.[140] Although much grammar teaching in Italy took place away from the *studio* context, there

sed maiore vel minore lectione discipulis data pro eorum qualitate, conditione et etate, qui legant, relegant, resumant, repetant.' [136] See above, . [137] See above, .

[138] For these grammars and their circulation, see above, n. , and below, , .

[139] The evidence that Italian secondary grammar pupils owned their own grammatical textbooks in XIIIc. is compelling. Firstly, schoolboys owned their own copies of more elementary textbooks such as psalter and *Ianua* by XIIImid: see document published by Cecchetti ( ), (see Ortalli ( ),), where the succession of schoolbooks from psalter and *Ianua* through *Disticha Catonis*, Prosper, Prudentius and *Facetus* were purchased for the sons of Marco Zambon between and . Secondly, Bonvesin da la Riva, in *Vita scolastica*, dating from later Duecento, assumes that pupils owned their own books (Vidmanová-Schmidtová ( ), vv. –). Thirdly, Bonvesin (vv. –) admonished silent reading by individual pupils in a class, so suggesting that they had their own books. Finally, Bonvesin not only authorized teachers to accept schoolbooks in pawn from pupils, but also mentioned in his own will of that he had himself engaged in this practice. See Sasse Tateo ( ), – , – .

[140] See *Cambridge History of Renaissance Philosophy* ( ), ; Alessio ( ), – .

is little doubt that the practices in great university cities such as Bologna and Padua or even in smaller university towns such as Arezzo, where grammar was taught in close connection with the Studio and often under its supervision,[141] came to exercise a powerful influence in Italian education. An early stage in the development of the grammatical textbook in prose is represented by the *Summa* of Bene da Firenze, who came to Bologna by [142] and taught grammar and rhetoric there for an unknown period (dying before).[143] It is not surprising that the prose textbook filtered down to the grammar-school level in the course of the thirteenth century; indeed, a work such as Pietro da Isolella's *Summa* was intended for boys, as is clear from the opening of the third chapter: 'ad instructionem rudium sub compendio doceamus'.[144] With a rapidly expanding legal, notarial and medical class in the Italian cities, it was only to be expected that the educational practices used to train professionals at universities would also come to prevail in the preparatory schools run by grammar teachers. In Northern Europe, universities tended to remain the preserve of a clerical élite, without the same pressure from lay society to turn out ever growing numbers of professionals. Northern grammar schoolboys, often destined for some kind of ecclesiastical career, were not subject to the constraints and influences exercised by secular Italian society in order rapidly to produce large numbers of basically educated latinists to pass through universities and then to

141 See Black (d).

142 The suggestion by Alessio ( ), xxviii, putting the beginning of Bene's career at Bologna back to end of XIIc., on the basis of a passage in which he is associated with 'magistro Ottone' at Bologna, seems unconvincing, since the argument depends on the unlikely identification of a grammarian called Otto with a professor of canon law there between and . Bene himself distinguishes between these disciplines: see Alessio ( ), . On the basis of this hypothesis, Alessio then further suggests that 'diverrebbe possibile proiettare il suo magistero grammaticale avanti il ed attrarre, di conseguenza, attorna a tale data quello di Bene', so putting the date of composition of Bene's *Summa grammatice* to *c.* . The chain of hypotheses is too long here: it is just as likely (indeed more so) that there were two Ottos teaching in Bologna: one a grammarian (otherwise unknown), the other a canonist. According to Alessio's suggested date for Bene's *Summa*, it would antedate *Doctrinale*; however, this hypothesis would make it di - cult to explain the strong presence of Northern French grammatical concepts and preoccupations in Bene's *Summa*. A simpler solution is to assume that Bene's teaching in Bologna began about the time of the first documentary reference to him ( ) and to see his *Summa grammatice* as a response to influence of *Doctrinale* in Italy in the earlier XIIIc. Alessio's dating is accepted without further evidence by Gardenal (a), and n. .

143 On Bene's biography, most recent discussion is by Alessio ( ), xxvii–xxxi; see also Gaudenzi ( ), – ; Bene da Firenze ( ), – . On his *Summa grammatice*, see Marchesi ( ), – ; C. Frati, in Gaudenzi ( ), ; Alessio ( ), xxx–xxxi; Gardenal (a), – , – .

144 Fierville ( ), . The corresponding passage in Pietro da Isolella's source, Sponcius of Provence's *Summa*, suggests that the phrase 'rudium sub compendio' meant secondary pupils: 'ego Magister Sponcius, Provincialis [...] ad utilitatem meorum scolarium novellorum, trado Summam [...] levissimam et perfectam' (Fierville ( ),).

swell the ranks of the Italian notarial, medical and legal professions; Northerners were in a position to exercise the greater patience involved in memorizing the entire text of a work such as *Doctrinale* to serve as the basis for further Latin study. In the increasingly secularized and urbanized society of thirteenth-century Italy, on the other hand, there was an ever growing demand for rapid educational results: hence, the emergence of the pupil-owned prose *summa*.[145]

Nevertheless, there is also no question that the Northern verse grammars were widely used in Italy, beginning in the thirteenth century, albeit without the monopoly which they enjoyed beyond the Alps. How then were these texts used? The answer is provided by their rival *Summe* themselves. Pietro da Isolella, for example, constantly cited mnemonic verses, many of which he drew from *Graecismus* and *Doctrinale*;[146] Tebaldo and Giovanni Balbi did the same,[147] as did Bene da Firenze, Giovanni da Pigna and Sion da Vercelli.[148] It has been seen that early manuscripts of *Ianua* also included many mnemonic verses, sometimes from these northern verse grammars too.[149] It is clear that, in Italy, *Doctrinale* and *Graecismus* fundamentally operated as storehouses of mnemonics to be selectively used by teachers to fix essential grammatical points in their pupils' memories; this kind of role is consistent with the lower manuscript numbers of these works (see above,). Indeed, this selective role for the northern verse grammars seems to have persisted in Italy into the Quattrocento, when, for example, Battista Guarini recommended chapters , , and of *Doctrinale* in particular.[150]

However, the metric grammars from Northern Europe, and in particular *Doctrinale*, had a more significant overall influence in Italy than this selective mnemonic use. In fact, *Doctrinale* defined the parameters of the secondary grammar curriculum both north and south of the Alps. Alexander's work made such an impact on grammar education that, even when Italian teachers moved away from the direct use of his textbook as the basic manual for the secondary level in the course of the thirteenth century, they continued to follow the syllabus which he was the

[145] Manacorda ( ), , noticed the contrast in XIIIc. between prose grammar treatises in Italy and verse textbooks north of Alps, but did not infer from this a di erence in pupil ownership of books nor in teaching methods. In view of all the evidence for pupil ownership of textbooks in Italy beginning in XIIIc. (see throughout the present book for ownership notes, etc.), the illustration cited by Jensen ( ), n. (see frontispiece of this book) in the Venetian version of Perotti's *Rudimenta grammatices* of , showing a teacher with the word *silentium* behind him and young and older pupils all reading their own books, would seem to represent normal later medieval Italian classroom practice: silent reading of pupil-owned copies.

[146] See Fierville's ( ) notes, *passim*. [147] See below, , .

[148] Gardenal (a), – , – *passim*. [149] See above, . [150] See Garin ( ), .

first to lay out. This syllabus, broadly consisting of the parts of speech, syntax, metrics, accent and figures, corresponds, for example, to the grammatical works of the Bolognese master, Bene da Firenze, whose grammar textbooks include a *Summa*[151] (covering gerunds/supines/infinitives, phonetics, and the parts of speech, emphasizing syntax),[152] a supplementary treatise on construction,[153] a tractate *De accentu*[154] and a set of *Regulae de metris*.[155] Particular features of *Doctrinale* are also preoccupations of Bene da Firenze: gerunds[156] and supines;[157] derivative verbs;[158] construction with prepositions[159] and conjunctions;[160] heteroclyte nouns;[161] impersonal verbs.[162] Moreover, the treatise also contains numerous mnemonic verses in the manner of *Doctrinale*.[163]

Alexander's formative influence is also clear if a comparison is made between the content of *Doctrinale* and that found in the most important of these Italian secondary prose *Summe*.

Alexander	Pietro da Isolella, *Summa grammaticae*, ed. Fierville ( )
Ch. : Nouns, declensions	Ch. (Definitiones, De nomine), (De declinationibus)
Ch. : Heteroclyte nouns	Ch. (De nominibus),

151 Preserved in seven MSS: see list in Alessio ( ), xxx–xxxi, including BNCF CS B. . , r– r, the version I used. I collated this text with published passages in Marchesi ( ), based on MS of Biblioteca S. Caterina di Pisa (Bursill-Hall ( ), , gives the wrong shelf-mark), and there is an almost exact correspondence. Although in BNCF CS B. . , text is attributed to Maestro Bonfiglio by the copyist/organizer of the MS on r (Hanc summam gramatice inveni intitulatam sub nomine cuiusdam Magistri Bonfigli et non ponebat aliquod pronomen aliud agnomen), it must be assumed that this is an erroneous attribution in a late manuscript (subscripsi et prosecutus in script(is) fui usque ad finem ego Johanes Ser Jacobi de Ceuli pisanus civis et [...] finivi die XIII iunii more pisano); indeed, another hand added 'id est Magistrum Bene' as a gloss on r over words 'secundum magistrum nostrum', apparently thus correcting Giovanni's erroneous attribution. See Alessio (a), n. ; Alessio ( ), xxxi.

152 Marchesi ( ), – ; Frati, in Gaudenzi ( ), – : Pisa Biblioteca di S. Caterina MS , r– r; Venice Biblioteca Marciana Lat. . , r– r.

153 Marchesi ( ), – : Pisa Biblioteca di S. Caterina MS , r– r.

154 Marchesi ( ), ; Gaudenzi ( ), – : BNP N. Acq. , r– r.

155 Marchesi ( ), ; Gaudenzi ( ), : BNP N. Acq. , v .

156 Marchesi ( ), . Cf. *Doctrinale*, ed. Reichling ( ), vv. , , , , – .

157 Marchesi ( ), . Cf. *Doctrinale*, ed. Reichling ( ), ch. .

158 Marchesi ( ), . Cf. *Doctrinale*, ed. Reichling ( ), ch. .

159 Marchesi ( ), – . Cf. *Doctrinale*, ed. Reichling ( ), vv. – .

160 Marchesi ( ), – . Cf. *Doctrinale*, ed. Reichling ( ), vv. – .

161 Marchesi ( ), – . Cf. *Doctrinale*, ed. Reichling ( ), ch. .

162 Marchesi ( ), . Cf. *Doctrinale*, ed. Reichling ( ), vv. – .

163 See Marchesi ( ), – for two examples; *c.* sets of mnemonic verses in the version preserved in BNCF CS B. . .

Ch. : Comparison	Ch. (De nomine), – , ch. (De comparativis),
Ch. : Nouns: gender	Ch. (De generibus nominum)
Ch. : Verbs: perfects and supines	Ch. (De verbo; de praeterito et supino)
Ch. : Verbs: defective and anomalous	Ch. (De verbis)
Ch. : Verbs: derivative	Ch. (De verborum speciebus)
Ch. , : Governance, construction	Ch. (De constructione), v (De oratione; de supposito et apposito), (De relativis), (De constructione), n. (governance of comparatives), , (governance of comparatives, superlatives, miscellaneous points of governance and construction)
Ch. : Metre	Ch. (De re metrica)
Ch. : Accent	Ch. (De accentibus)
Ch. : Figures	, (figures)

Pietro da Isolella's *Summa* became the most widely circulated of the thirteenth-century Italian secondary prose grammar manuals, preserved as it is in more than fifty manuscripts;[164] despite uncertainty regarding the order of the material in this work, owing to the lack of a critical edition,[165] it is clear that the overall contents of the text were shaped by Alexander. For example, one of the major divergences between Alexander's treatment of the secondary syllabus and that of previous grammars such as Papias's *Ars grammatica* was his almost complete omission of the indeclinable parts of speech and their accidence, and similarly Pietro da Isolella treats them minimally. Moreover, Alexander's lead in omitting definitions of the parts of speech was followed by Pietro, who includes only this material for nouns.[166] Of the five topics omitted by Alexander and treated by Pietro (pronouns, rhyming verse, prose dictamen, suppletions and adverbs), two (pronouns and adverbs) are discussed

[164] Bursill-Hall ( ), .

[165] Fierville ( ), xv, who published text of this work anonymously on basis of only two manuscripts (Laon and BNP lat.), observed that the order of chapters seemed scarcely logical.

[166] Fierville ( ), ; he points to omission of definitions for pronoun and verb (,), without realizing that Pietro was conforming to generic conventions of secondary grammar, as defined by Alexander, whereby it was assumed that definitions of parts of speech had been already treated at elementary level through Donatus or *Ianua*.

at length in *Graecismus* (ch. and), showing the influence which that verse grammar also exercised on the development of the Italian secondary syllabus in the thirteenth century. In fact, Pietro da Isolella's chapter on construction shows a significant resemblance in conception to the last chapter of *Graecismus* on the same subject, both dividing the topic into, first, governance of nominal cases and then of verbs, while his chapter on pronouns has several passages closely related to sections of *Graecismus.*[167]

Despite their fundamental importance for secondary grammar, *Doctrinale* and *Graecismus* were not conceived as entirely self-su cient textbooks. Their verse format by its very nature precluded definition and explanation, and indeed the need for further elucidation was foreseen by Alexander himself.[168] Throughout Europe this explication took the form of an important commentary tradition, beginning in the thirteenth century itself, soon after the publication of *Doctrinale.* Because of the more exclusive concentration on this text in Northern Europe, it is not surprising that the glossing tradition there developed more significantly, with one commentary emerging as particularly authoritative. This was the gloss with the incipit 'Admirantes quondam philosophi, cum viderent rerum mirabiles bonitates';[169] in the thirteenth century this commentary appears in seven manuscripts,[170] all preserved in French and German libraries. The identified commentators from the thirteenth century are also found in manuscripts from French libraries,[171] and overall there are only a handful of unglossed thirteenth-century manuscripts.[172] Some of the glossed ones are in Italian libraries, and several of these can be confirmed as Italian; nevertheless it is clear that the early commentary tradition of *Doctrinale* was weaker in Italy than in Northern Europe. One explanation for this fact is the less intensive study of the text as a whole in Italy, as mentioned above; another is the existence of the secondary *Summe*, which themselves served as a kind of explanation and reworking of the grammatical material found in *Doctrinale* and *Graecismus.*

A work such as Pietro da Isolella's *Summa* served as an explication, elaboration and complement to *Doctrinale* and, to a lesser extent, to *Graecismus.* It is largely self-explanatory, o ering the definitions and comments not found in *Doctrinale*, as is clear, for example, from comparing the respective treatments of first-declension nouns.[173] Alexander's formulation is suc-

167 Pointed out by Fierville ( ), – .
168 Vv. – .
169 Reichling ( ), lxii; Thurot ( ), – .
170 Reichling ( ), n. , , , , *, , *.
171 Reichling ( ), n. *, *.
172 Reichling ( ), n. , *, , , ; cf. ccxciv.
173 Cf. *Doctrinale*, ed. Reichling ( ), vv. – with Pietro da Isolella, ed. Fierville ( ), – .

cinct but leaves much to be explained by the teacher: e.g., that there are five declensions; that *rectus* means the nominative case; that *primus, secundus, tertius, quartus, quintus, sextus* mean the nominative, genitive, dative, accusative, vocative and ablative cases respectively. All this is elucidated in Pietro's prose, which also clarifies the meaning of the figure *syncopa* or *apocopa* by giving the example of '*Trojugenum* pro *Trojugenarum*'.[174]

Even when Pietro da Isolella disagreed with Alexander, he still tended to remain within the latter's framework of discussion. This is clear, for example, in the chapter dealing with metre (ch. : De re metrica). Alexander had recognized six metric feet: dactyl, spondee, trochee, anapaest, iambus and tribrach (vv. –). Pietro, possibly following medieval Italian traditions,[175] acknowledged only three: dactyl, spondee and trochee ( ). Similarly, Alexander had excluded the possibility of elision (vv. –), which, in contrast, was recognized by Pietro ( ). Nevertheless, Pietro's chapter on metrics is still developed along lines laid down by Alexander. Not only does his classification of vowels and consonants resemble Alexander's (cf. with vv. –), but his extended discussion of the quantities of first, middle and final syllables is directly related to Alexander's treatment.[176]

The overall shape of Pietro da Isolella's *Summa* was thus largely determined by *Doctrinale*, while in addition, there were also numerous instances when individual passages in *Graecismus* (especially in chapter on pronouns but also elsewhere) were explicated.[177] But since these two works were partly intended, as has been seen, to o er practical alternatives to Priscian's *Institutiones*, it is not surprising to find that Pietro da Isolella, in his attempt to provide the kind of definitions and explanations lacking in the verse grammars, returned frequently to Priscian himself.[178]

There is no doubt that Pietro da Isolella was following the path established by Alexander and Evrard when he included sections on syntax in his *Summa*, but in the event he did not have to rewrite in prose the relevant chapters of either *Doctrinale* or *Graecismus*, having found a treatise on

[174] Similarly, Pietro gives self-explanatory treatment of the syllabus laid out by Alexander with regard to other nominal declensions (ch. ; cf. *Doctrinale*, ch.) and genders (ch. ; cf. *Doctrinale*, ch.); heteroclyte nouns (ch. ; cf. *Doctrinale*, ch.); anomalous and defective verbs, gerunds, supines and participles (ch. ; cf. *Doctrinale*, ch.); and figures (chs. , – , , – ; cf. *Doctrinale*, ch.).

[175] Paolo da Camaldoli declared, 'Moderni tamen non utuntur nisi tribus pedibus, dactilo, spondeo et trocheo': Fierville ( ), n. .

[176] Cf. – , ed. Fierville ( ) with *Doctrinale*, ed. Reichling ( ), vv. , , and .

[177] See Fierville's ( ) notes, *passim*.

[178] See Fierville's ( ) notes, *passim*.

construction, written in by a Provençal grammarian and *dictator*, Sponcius.[179] More than a century ago Fierville showed that Pietro's sections on construction, relatives and interrogative adverbs were taken almost entirely from Sponcius's *Summa de constructione*.[180] Both Sponcius and Pietro begin with a discussion of the types of construction (transitive, intransitive, reciprocal and retransitive); then there follows a treatment of constructions with impersonal verbs; next come figures of construction; a section on construction with oblique cases follows; then there is a treatment of construction with verbs.[181] At this point the form of presentation, but not the content, diverges: Sponcius moves on to relatives and then interrogative adverbs,[182] while Pietro proceeds directly to the latter topic,[183] reserving his treatment of relatives for a subsequent chapter.[184] The only substantial di erence between the two works is that Pietro da Isolella appends to his treatment of interrogative adverbs a discussion of the cases into which nouns must be put in order to answer the corresponding interrogative adverbs.[185]

Sponcius was not a widely circulated grammarian in the middle ages: his treatise on construction seems to survive in only two manuscripts, BNP lat. and BL Arundel . It is fortunate for him that Pietro da Isolella came upon his treatise on construction, securing a far wider influence for his treatment of syntax than the text enjoyed under Sponcius's own name. Sponcius also composed a textbook on *dictamen* to which he referred at the beginning of his *Summa de constructione*.[186] It is no surprise to discover that Pietro da Isolella borrowed from this work too (ch. : 'De dictamine in soluta oratione'). It is probable that Pietro's access to Sponcius's *Summa dictaminis* was by way of a manuscript containing both of Sponcius's *Summe* (such as BNP lat.), and it is interesting that Pietro decided to include a short chapter on prose dictamen in his secondary grammatical textbook. This was not a topic treated either by Alexander or by Evrard, and its inclusion reflects the Italian ambience of Pietro's work. The *ars dictaminis* was of course one of the major subjects studied in Italian universities in the thirteenth century, and the notarial profession was one of the most important outlets for grammar pupils in thirteenth-century Italy; it therefore made perfect sense for a grammar teacher such as Pietro da Isolella to include in his *Summa grammaticae* a brief foretaste of what many of his pupils would

179 Ed. in part by Fierville ( ), – . 180 Fierville ( ), xvi–xvii, xviii–xix
181 See Fierville ( ), – and – . 182 Fierville ( ), – .
183 Fierville ( ), – . 184 Fierville ( ), – . 185 Fierville ( ), – .
186 Fierville ( ), .

soon digest in more substantial form. Pietro's treatment of the topic, following Sponcius's, began with a definition of *dictamen*, moved on to consider the faults of prose style, continued with a discussion of the parts of the letter, and concluded with various stylistic definitions (including the *coma*, period, clause, *punctus* and *cursus*).[187] Pietro also added a number of sections to his *Summa* not found in Sponcius's works, nor indeed in those of Alexander, Evrard or Priscian: the most important of these sections treated subject and predicate (*suppositum* and *appositum* in medieval grammatical terminology: ch.), rhyming verse (ch.), and suppletions (i.e. auxiliary verbs completed by participles, gerunds and supines: ch.).

One of the most important contributions of Pietro da Isolella was his use of medieval grammatical terminology as developed in the French schools of the twelfth century.[188] This included *suppositum* and *appositum* for subject and predicate, terms and concepts which never appear in Priscian[189] and which were defined and illustrated by Pietro.[190] Implicit in this definition is the notion of natural or logical sentence order, so that the subject can be defined as the part of the sentence preceding the verb, while the predicate (*appositum*) becomes the rest of the sentence. From an educational viewpoint, this was, of course, an easy way to make pupils understand the abstract concepts of subject and predicate: word order allowed the pupil to identify the subject as whatever came in front of the verb. Another Northern medieval grammatical term is *regimen*, meaning determinance by one part of speech of another's case: Pietro uses this terminology as an abstract noun ('sequitur de regimine casuum':) but more often as a verb ('ultimus illorum potest regi a suo passivo':), most frequently substituting some form of the verb *exigere* for *regere*.[191] Pietro also uses the northern medieval terminology *ante se* and *post se* to indicate the grammatical relations between parts of the sentence: thus a verb can govern in front of itself one case and another after itself.[192] Here again he is using the medieval concept of natural word order to teach the relationship among verbs and their subjects and objects: the logical relation between parts of the sentence is expressed through word order. This then becomes a convenient teaching tool: all the pupil has to know, for example, is that the accusative goes in front of certain impersonal verbs, which are then followed by the genitive.[193] A concept of linguistic philsophy became, in the hands of an Italian grammar master such as Pietro

[187] Fierville ( ), – , – . [188] For this terminology, see above, .
[189] Thurot ( ), ; Fierville ( ), n. . [190] Ed. Fierville ( ), .
[191] See Fierville ( ), – , – , – , ; 'exigere' used by Priscian: see Thurot ( ), .
[192] E.g. Fierville ( ), , , – *passim*, . [193] Fierville ( ), .

da Isolella, a way of teaching Latin almost by, so to speak, filling in the blanks. All these simplified terms and methods would become ubiquitous in Italian secondary grammars throughout the fourteenth and fifteenth centuries.[194]

When Bene da Firenze and Pietro da Isolella were writing, the secondary prose *summa* was still in its infancy, a fact which explains both works' lack of overall coherence and organization. Bene's treatise begins with a discussion of gerunds, supines, infinitives and their construction; then he returns to the normal beginning of the grammar syllabus by discussing phonetics; his handling of the parts of speech is a mixture of accidence, morphology and syntax.[195] Pietro da Isolella's treatise is even more confused in presentation: although he makes an apparently logical start, beginning with general definitions, phonetics, the parts of speech, the noun, nominal types and genders (chs. and), he interrupts the normal Priscianic pattern (namely, phonetics followed by the parts of speech) to treat construction (ch.). Not even this topic is treated systematically, since he digresses with a discussion of interrogatives (ch. , –) and nominal declensions (ch.), before returning to syntax to consider subjects and predicates (ch.) and relatives (ch.). He then turns to the pronoun (ch.) and the verb (ch.), evidently following Donatus's order of the parts of speech (noun, pronoun, verb, etc.), but this topic is also interrupted by treatments of metre (ch.), rhyme (ch.) and prose *dictamen* (ch.). He returns to verbal types (ch.), but then digresses to accents (ch.) before proceeding to auxiliary verbs and their corresponding participles, supines and gerunds (ch.). He finishes the work with five supplementary chapters (ch.), labelled 'regulae intercisae', to cover material which he had previously not included.

Not only was the secondary prose *summa* still a novelty, but a grammarian such as Pietro was drawing on a variety of sources: not just Priscian, Alexander and Evrard but also Sponcius. The approaches taken by his authorities were hardly similar: for example, Alexander's treatment of governance proceeded case by case, including all parts of speech, whereas Sponcius treated first governance by nouns and then by verbs.[196] Pietro's *Summa* was a pastiche: definitions and rules from Priscian; syntax and *dictamen* from Sponcius; declensions, heteroclytes,

[194] See below, .
[195] Marchesi ( ), – ; Gaudenzi ( ), . Marchesi ( ) seems justified speaking of 'enorme confusione' ( ); 'la materia [...] procede, fra le ripetizioni e le digressioni continue, confusissima' (–).
[196] See above, , .

anomalous and defective verbs, gerunds and supines from Alexander; pronouns from Evrard. Pietro's role as a quasi-commentator on Priscian, Alexander and Evrard could only have contributed to the eclectic and rambling structure of his *Summa.*

Despite its shortcomings, it remains a fact that Pietro da Isolella's textbook continued to be an influential work in later Duecento Italy: its wide manuscript circulation is testimony to the fact that the prose *summa* fulfilled an important educational need. Pietro da Isolella's approach was normal in the thirteenth-century Italian classroom. Other prose *Summe grammatice* dating from the thirteenth century often bear a notable resemblance to Pietro da Isolella's textbook, and extensive borrowings were even made from Pietro's text by near contemporary Italian grammarians. An example of all this is provided by the gigantic grammatical *Summa*, entitled *Catholicon* and published by Giovanni Balbi da Genova in .[197] This text is most famous as including a great alphabetical dictionary of Latin, which occupies the work's fifth and by far largest book. But this section is preceded by four other books o ering a *summa* of theoretical grammar whose scope resembles Pietro da Isolella's textbook. The contents of *Catholicon* are outlined in the work's preface.[198] By orthography, Giovanni meant phonetics, covered briefly in the first chapter of Pietro da Isolella's *Summa*; the second book on prosody corresponds to Pietro da Isolella's chapters , and ; the third book, dealing with the parts of speech and their construction, is equivalent to chapters , and of Pietro's textbook; and the fourth book on figures corresponds to Pietro's treatment in chapters and . Moreover, Giovanni Balbi actually borrows at least one entire chapter (namely ch. on nominal genders) from Pietro da Isolella's *Summa.*[199] Another thirteenth-century grammatical *summa* with similarities to Pietro's textbook was Sion da Vercelli's *Novum Doctrinale*, in which, like Pietro, syntax is highlighted[200] and amply discussed, using Northern grammatical terminology (*exigere, determinare, regere, servire, regimen, determinatio*); also like Pietro, Sion has a long discussion of relatives, as well as a

[197] For the work's wide circulation, see Bursill-Hall ( ), – .

[198] El Escorial cod. A. . , r: Divisio autem istius libri talis est. Primo, licet principaliter intendam de prosodia, tamen quia orthographia est quodam modo via ad prosodiam, agam de orthographia. Secundo de prosodia. Tercio de ethymologia et dyasintastica quasi mixtim aliqua dicam. Deinde specialiter de constructione et suis speciebus et partibus necnon de regimine subiungam. Quarto determinabo de figuris. Quinto de orthographia, prosodia, origine, significatione quarumdam dictionum, que sepe inveniuntur in biblia et in dictis sanctorum et etiam poetarum, secundum ordinem alphabeti ordinate subiungam.

[199] Sivo ( ), – ; Sivo (a), , n. .

[200] Capello ( ), : 'studium grammaticorum precipue circa constructionem versatur'.

treatment of figures, and, most strikingly, Sion, again like Pietro, includes treatments of metrics, rhythm and *dictamen.*[201] A further Duecento grammar resembling Pietro's work was the *Summa*, datable perhaps between and ,[202] by the Veronese teacher Giovanni da Pigna, whose treatment of syntax and *dictamen* especially resembled Pietro's;[203] like Pietro he also prominently included figures as well as discussions of accent, rhythm and *dictamen.*[204]

Pietro's treatment of secondary syntax also resembles in a number of ways the approach adopted by another contemporary, Tebaldo, who composed a treatise on syntax entitled simply *Regule.*[205] In teaching syntax, the overall topics covered by Tebaldo broadly corresponded to ones treated by Pietro da Isolella:

Tebaldo

v– v: adjectives and their construction with substantives
v– r: comparatives (formation (v– v) and construction (v– r))
r– v: superlatives (formation (r–v) and construction (v))
r– v: relatives and their construction
v– r: interrogatives and their construction
r– r: partitives and their construction
r: construction of nominative case with verb
r– v: genitive and its construction
v– v: dative and its construction
v– r: accusative and its construction
r: vocative and its construction
r– r: ablative and its construction[206]

Moreover, both wrote for children, the former declaring, as has been seen, that he was teaching 'ad instructionem rudium sub compendio',[207] while the latter stated, 'rudium utilitati volens intendere diligenter quedam artis gramatice introductoria breviter compillo'.[208] Moreover,

201 See Capello ( ), – . 202 Gardenal (a), – .
203 Gardenal (a), – , nn. and . Giovanni puts particular emphasis on syntax: Gardenal (b), and *passim.*
204 Gardenal (a), – , who points out that Giovanni's emphasis on indeclinable parts of speech di ers from the treatment of Pietro da Isolella (n.).
205 References to Tebaldo's *Regule* will be to BML AD . See Appendix .
206 See Fierville ( ), – , n. , – , – , – , – , – .
207 Fierville ( ), . 208 BML AD , v.

Tebaldo followed the path taken by both Bene da Firenze and Pietro da Isolella, composing his treatise as a prose *summa*, not as a verse textbook, without, like Pietro, overlooking the advantages of metrics.[209]

But Tebaldo o ered a more systematic presentation of syntax than was found in the treatises by either Pietro da Isolella or Bene da Firenze, overcoming the problems of organization which had dogged both Pietro and Bene. He achieved this by devising his own structure for the presentation of syntax. He began with the construction of nouns, but, unlike Sponcius and Pietro, he divided these not according to case but in order of nominal types (adjectives, in ancient and medieval grammatical theory, were classified as nouns) (see facing page):

This then allowed him to consider the six cases as a separate section, which he then broke down into a subdivision for each individual case and then further into a subsection for each part of speech within a case:

r: nominative case and its construction

r– v: genitive and its construction
r– r: with verb
r– v: with participle
v– v: with noun, gerund, adverb, preposition, interjection, adjective

v– v: dative and its construction
v– r: with verb
r– v: with participles, nouns, adverbs

v– r accusative and its construction
v– v: with verb
v– r: with participles, gerunds, supines, nouns
r– r: with preposition
r: with interjection

r: vocative and its construction

r– r: ablative and its construction
r– v: with noun

209 r, r.

v– v: with verb

v– r: absolutely, prepositions

Systematic, too, was his provision of numbered rules for several subsections.[210]

Tebaldo's systematic presentation of secondary grammar foreshadows the more methodical approach which would become increasingly characteristic of post-elementary grammatical textbooks in fourteenth-century Italy. The organized procedure typical of the Trecento can be illustrated in the most widely circulated and important secondary[211]

210 r: hec prepositio in modis iungitur accusativo: primo modo [...] secundo modo [...] See v– v for many more examples.

Another possible XIIIc. short school-type Italian treatise on construction is published by Percival ( ) from MS (. .) of Rome Biblioteca Angelica. Date of MS is problematic. Narducci ( ) and Sabbadini ( ) suggest turn of XIIIc., whereas Percival ( ) puts it in early XVc. Without seeing the MS or a reproduction, it is obviously impossible to come to any conclusion, although Percival's description (a blend of humanist and Gothic script) might possibly apply equally to a XIIIc. hybrid of Caroline and Gothic handwriting. From reading the text, I am inclined to XIIIc. dating (but not earlier), to judge from mnemonic verses and exclusive use of Latin. Text deals with types of construction (transitive, intransitive, reciprocal), with construction of nouns and verbs as well as of participles and prepositions (briefly), and with figures of construction.

211 There is no question but that Francesco da Buti's *Regule grammaticales* were intended as a secondary grammar text for schoolboys: he declares explicitly that he is writing for school-children in the preface (Bodley Lat. misc. e. , r: Ne rudium turba scolarium vago deduceretur errore sed recto tramite gradirentur ad metam, ego Franciscus de Bruti piscis [*sic*] civis gramatice ac rectorice profexor indignus regulas gramatice in hoc opusculo prout valui ord[in]etenus compilavi). (On the school-level meaning of *rudes*, see Frova ( ), , besides n. above). Moreover, this grammar manual is part of a progressive course for children, since his *Regule rectorice* which follow in several manuscripts (see Alessio (a),) are also written for *rudes* (Bodley Lat. misc. e. , r, cited below, , n.): this means that the entire course laid out in *Regule grammaticales* was conceived for children, forming as it does the prologue to a further text on rhetoric for *rudes.* In any case, the secondary, school-oriented nature of Francesco's grammar is clear from his overall syllabus, which, as will be seen below, follows the pattern laid out by previous secondary grammarians such as Alexander and Pietro da Isolella. Gehl's statement that Francesco's *Regule* 'include a great deal of highly advanced material in reference form' and that it could have served 'for a university-level course in grammar' (, –) is puzzling. As will be seen below, all the topics covered, even the later sections, were necessary for the most elementary Latin prose composition, which would be impossible without a knowledge of the syntax of participles, pronouns and conjunctions – topics introduced only at the end of Francesco's grammar course. Indeed, even in the last section on figures, the Latin sentences that he invents as examples are puerile, as are the kinds of vernacular phrases used for translation which permeate the work. Novati ( ), , n. , had pointed to '*Regulae grammaticales*, compilate da Francesco per o rire ai giovinetti,

grammar manual of the fourteenth century: the Pisan teacher Francesco da Buti's *Regule grammaticales*, written between and [212] and preserved in at least twenty-seven manuscripts.[213] The *Regule grammaticales* treat the following broad topics:

Preface
Nouns: accidence and concordance
Verbs: construction
Nouns: irregular and heteroclyte, derivative, adjectival, governance, comparative, superlative, partitive, numerical, interrogative, relative, infinitive, distributive, verbal
Verbs: irregular formations, meanings, derivatives, compounds
Participles: definition, formation, meaning, governance, construction
Pronouns: definition, formation, accidence, construction
Conjunctions: definition, classification, construction
Figures: definition, classification, construction

On the one hand, the *Regule* represent the culmination of Italian secondary traditions going back to the thirteenth century: like Alexander and Pietro da Isolella,[214] Francesco focuses on the declinable parts of speech, especially irregular verbs and nouns as well as on nominal types (comparatives, superlatives, relatives, etc.), and like them he gives an important place to governance and syntax, as well as to figures; as with Evrard and Pietro,[215] he devotes a section to pronouns. Although Alexander and Pietro had dealt only peripherally with conjunctions,[216] they had been treated at length by Bene da Firenze[217] and duly found their place in Francesco's *Regule*, which similarly included a section devoted to participles, a topic discussed substantially by Pietro in his chapter on suppletions.[218] Like the prose *summe* of the Duecento,

che s'avvivano allo studio del latino'; Jensen ( ), , notes that Francesco's *exordium* shows that it was a schoolbook, although not for absolute beginners.

212 Bausi ( ), .

213 For lists of manuscripts, see Percival ( ), ; Percival ( ), n. ; Percival (a), n. ; Alessio (a), – n. . Bursill-Hall ( ) cites eighteen manuscripts, all listed by Alessio, who also cites six more; further manuscript (Chicago University of Chicago Library MS) cited by Gehl ( ), n. . Of these, I used: BML Antinori ; BML Med. Pal. ; BNCF CS B. . (fragmentary); BNCF Landau Fin. (fragmentary); BRF (fragmentary); BRF ; Bodley Can. Misc. ; Bodley Lat. misc. e. . The following hitherto unidentified manuscripts are to be added:

Florence Biblioteca Moreniana Palagi , containing text without preface (XIVex.), apparently written in Siena and used in Pisa. Reused Sienese notarial parchment from XIVmid (r: civis Senarum notarius, v: civitatis Senarum, r: , r: , v: de Senis [...]).

Munich Staatsbibliothek cod. (fragmentary): see n. below.

214 See above, . 215 See above, . 216 See above, . 217 See above, .

218 See above, .

Francesco made extensive use of mnemonic verses,[219] and his grammatical terminology is thoroughly traditional, reflecting the roots of the Italian tradition in the French schools of the twelfth century: *suppositum, a parte post, a parte ante, regere, determinari, ex natura*[220] is the vocabulary constantly encountered in Francesco's textbook.

On the other hand, Francesco's work also reflects the systematic approach now characteristic of the fourteenth century: he turned away decisively from the disordered presentation typical of thirteenth-century prose *summe.* The principle of organization adopted by Francesco was not topical but rather educational: material was presented in what he considered to be the order of progressive di culty. This teaching structure is embodied in the sections of the text, which is divided into three overall levels (minor, middle and major), with the first stage of *latinum minus* further subdivided into four forms:

Latinum minus	
Prima banca	Accidence and concordance of nouns Verbal construction: active and passive
Secunda banca	Verbal construction: neutral and common
Tertia banca	Verbal construction: deponent and impersonal (beginning)
Quarta banca	Verbal construction: impersonal (end) Gerunds, supines and defective verbs
Latinum mediocre	Nouns: irregular and heteroclyte, derivative, adjectival, governance, comparative, superlative, partitive, numerical, interrogative, relative, infinitive, distributive, verbal Verbs: irregular formations, meanings, derivatives, compounds Participles: definition, formation, meaning, governance, construction Pronouns: definition, formation, accidence, construction
Latinum maiorum	Conjunctions: definition, classification, construction Figures: definition, classification (emphasis on figures of construction)

219 E.g. BRF , v, r, r, v, r, v, v– r, r, v, v, r, etc.

220 *Appositum,* in contrast to the other terms, seems to have been relatively rare in Francesco's grammatical vocabulary: for one appearance, see Bodley Lat. misc. e. , r–v.

Found as it is in several manuscripts,[221] this structure probably goes back to the original version of the text and apparently reflects how Francesco organized his own school. Indeed, as a consequence of this approach, verbs and nouns are treated at two di erent levels: the needs of teaching have finally prevailed over a rigidly topical structure dictated by the parts of speech and inherited ultimately from ancient grammarians such as Donatus and Priscian.

Another aspect of the more systematic approach taken by Trecento grammar masters is the treatment of verbal syntax found in a grammar such as Francesco's *Regule*. Pietro da Isolella, following Sponcius, had handled this topic discursively: he began with the four types of construction derived from Priscian (transitive, intransitive, reciprocal, retransitive); he then moved to constructions with infinitives and gerunds; then to the syntax of impersonal verbs; then to the tripartite classification of verbs as substantive, vocative and accidental; this third accidental subclass was then broken down into absolute and transitive verbs, the latter of which were then further subdivided into active, passive, neuter, common and deponent verbs.[222] In contrast, Francesco da Buti's presentation meets the needs of the teacher, consisting of an ever more rigorous selection, beginning with the broadest general classification and progressively narrowing to his final didactic point. Thus, he begins with definition of the verb,[223] then passes to the eight categories of verbal accidence,[224] including *genus*, which is then further subdivided into personal and impersonal verbs; he then gives three general categories of personal verbs (substantive, vocative, accidental); accidental verbs are finally further broken down into seven types (active, passive, common, deponent, *neutrum passivum* and *neutro passivum*).[225] There is no detailed discussion until he reaches this final subclass, which represents the real focus of his interest: the earlier progressive subdivisions are ultimately revealed as a mere introduction; selectivity and teaching needs have prevailed over the requirements of comprehensive coverage.

The syntactical behaviour of verbs is his chosen theme: he wants to provide his pupils with a series of simple formulae for Latin construction. He accordingly treats the individual types of verb *in extenso*,

[221] E.g. Bodley Lat. misc. e. : (r) Expliciunt regule nominum pertinentes ad scolares de prima. See r, v, r, r, v. BRF : (r) Expliciunt regule tertie bance. Incipiunt regule quarte bance. See v. Florence Biblioteca Moreniana Palagi : (r) Expliciunt regule nominum pertinentium ad scolares de prima bancha. See also v, v. BML Antinori : (r) Incipiunt regule mediocres. [222] Fierville ( ), – (Pietro da Isolella), – (Sponcius).
[223] BRF , v. [224] BRF , v– v. [225] BRF , v– r.

breaking each down into species according to syntactical function.[226] The first species is treated beginning with a summary of its verbal syntax using the *post se/ ante se* system, followed by a list of exemplary verbs and their four principal parts followed by a vernacular translation, and concluding with exemplary sentences, causal explanations and other possible additions in the predicate (ablative constructions with or without prepositions).[227] The second species of active verbs (governing the accusative and genitive) is treated similarly,[228] and Francesco's typology of verbal syntax can be exemplified in tabular form:[229]

	post se	examples
Active verbs	accusative	amo, diligo, etc.
	accusative + genitive	emo, estimo, etc.
	accusative + dative	do, facio, etc.
	two accusatives	flagito, posco, etc.
	accusative + ablative	vacuo, allevio, etc.
Passive verbs	ablative (with *a* or *ab*)	amor, diligor, etc.
	ablative (with *a* or *ab*) + genitive	vendor, emor, etc.
	ablative (with *a* or *ab*) + dative	dicor, narror, etc.
	ablative (with *a* or *ab*) + accusative	flagitor, poscor, etc.
	ablative (with *a* or *ab*) + ablative (etc.)	vacuor, impleor, etc.

With this tabular presentation, Trecento grammarians such as Francesco da Buti had arrived at a simple formulaic method of teaching Latin syntax: all that was required of the pupil was to find the correct verbal class and then the construction of the verb with the appropriate oblique cases would follow a set pattern.

226 Bodley Lat. misc. e. , r: Nota quod verborum activorum quinque sunt species: quedam volunt post se accusativum tantum. Quedam accusativum et genitivum. Quedam accusativum et dativum. Quedam duos diversos accusativos. Quedam accusativum et ablativum.

227 BRF , r–v:
Nota quod sunt quedam verba activa que ante se volunt nominativum rei agentis et post se accusativum rei patientis, scilicet:
Amo -as -vi -tum *per amare*
Diligo -is -xi -ctum per [*sic*] eodem
Honoro -as -vi -tum *per honorare* [...]
Ut in hoc exemplo 'Ego amo Petrum'. Et nota quod nominativus regitur a parte ante ex natura intransitionis et acusativus a parte post ex natura transitionis [...]

228 BRF , v. 229 Bodley Lat. misc. e. , r– r.

Another new direction taken by Trecento school-level grammarians and typified by Francesco da Buti was a predominant concern with Latin construction. For Alexander and Evrard, syntax was a novelty in the secondary grammar syllabus; in both their works, it occupied a significant but limited place. Their lead was followed by the Italian prose grammarians of the Duecento: for Bene da Firenze, Pietro da Isolella and Giovanni Balbi, construction remained one among many topics, and as such syntax was restricted to clearly defined sections of their *summe*. But for the Trecento grammarians, such individual chapters on construction tended to disappear: in Francesco da Buti's *Regule*, for example, syntax permeated every section of the work, becoming the unifying theme of the treatise as a whole. Thus at the very beginning of the text, the concept of agreement is introduced,[230] and word order is incorporated into the section first listing the nominal cases, which also introduces the syntactical concepts of *ex parte ante* and *post.*[231] When first mentioning the fundamental distinction between personal and impersonal verbs – the two categories which would form almost the entire subject matter of *latinum minus* – Francesco di erentiates among their syntactical patterns, introducing the term *suppositum* as well.[232] Just as the discussion of personal verbs (i.e. active, passive, neutral, etc.) is focused, as has been seen above, on the issue of syntactical behaviour, so too is Francesco's treatment of impersonal verbs. Thus, having distinguished between active and passive impersonal verbs (i.e. those ending in '-t' (e.g. *interest*) and those ending in '-tur' (e.g. *amatur*)), Francesco quickly returns to issues of construction.[233] Similarly, as soon as gerunds are introduced, their syntactical behaviour becomes the central concern.[234]

It is perhaps not surprising that Francesco da Buti's first stage (*latinum minus*) should thus be focused on construction, given that its central theme is the syntactical behaviour of verbs. But the middle level (*latinum mediocre*) of his secondary grammar course is for the most part concerned with exceptional noun and verb types; this topic ultimately had its roots in the first seven chapters of *Doctrinale*, where the generation of individual forms is the exclusive concern of Alexander, who delays consideration of governance and construction until the following two chapters. Here too Francesco continually introduces problems of syntax, which is thereby revealed once again as the over-arching theme of his treatise. In dealing

[230] Bodley Lat. misc. e. , v. This concept had not appeared in ancient grammarians such as Donatus and Priscian: Percival ( ), .

[231] Bodley Lat. misc. e. , r. [232] Bodley Lat. misc. e. , r.

[233] Bodley Lat. misc. e. , r. [234] Bodley Lat. misc. e. , v.

with defective nouns, for example, his concern is to demonstrate how to take account of their missing forms in constructing sentences. This process of Latin prose composition was called 'giving a theme': the aspect of this exercise involving translation from the vernacular into Latin will be considered below ( ); for the moment it is important to emphasize how many subclasses of defective nouns are treated by Francesco in terms of the syntactical problems raised.[235] This kind of approach is applied to feminine nouns without plurals,[236] neutral nouns lacking some plural oblique cases,[237] and to a whole series of other defective nouns.[238] The remaining treatment of nouns in *latinum mediocre* continues to be focused on construction: not only in the passage on governance by nouns of all cases[239] – a fundamental syntactical element, previously treated by Alexander,[240] Evrard,[241] Sponcius,[242] Pietro da Isolella[243] and Tebaldo[244] – but also in subsequent sections on other nominal types.[245] Verbal syntax had already been thoroughly covered in *latinum minus* and so the focus in *latinum mediocre* is on individual verbal forms (and particularly on irregular and defective verbs and their meanings, formation, derivatives and compounds);[246] even here Francesco manages to return to his favoured theme of syntax, treating verbal governance in all cases[247] and so recalling similar discussions by Evrard,[248] Sponcius,[249] Pietro da Isolella[250] and Tebaldo.[251] What is more unusual is Francesco's handling of the last two topics of *latinum mediocre*: participles[252] and pronouns.[253] Participial construction had been summarily treated by Alexander,[254] ignored by Evrard and Tebaldo, and touched on obliquely by Pietro in his chapter on suppletions,[255] but now in the *Regule grammaticales* it was Francesco's central preoccupation in the penultimate section of *latinum mediocre*: here he was particularly concerned with problems of thematic construction, particularly arising from Latin's shortage of participial types (e.g. active past participle).[256] Finally, construction of pronouns had not been treated at all

235 Bodley Lat. misc. e. , r–v. 236 Bodley Lat. misc. e. , v– r.
237 Bodley Lat. misc. e. , r–v. 238 Bodley Lat. misc. e. , v– r, v– v.
239 Bodley Lat. misc. e. , r– r. 240 Ed. Reichling ( ), vv. – , – .
241 Ed. Wrobel ( ), – . 242 Ed. Fierville ( ), – .
243 Ed. Fierville ( ), – . 244 BML AD , v– v *passim.*
245 Including comparative (Bodley Lat. misc. e. , v– r), superlative (v– r), partitive (v– r), numerical (v, v– v), interrogative (v– r), relative (r– v), infinite (v– v), distributive (v) and verbal (v– v) nouns.
246 Bodley Lat. misc. e. , v– v. 247 Bodley Lat. misc. e. , v– v.
248 Ed. Wrobel ( ), – 249 Ed. Fierville ( ), – .
250 Ed. Fierville ( ), – . 251 BML AD , r– v *passim.*
252 Bodley Lat. misc. e. , r– v. 253 Bodley Lat. misc. e. , v– v.
254 Ed. Reichling ( ), vv. – . 255 Ed. Fierville ( ), – .
256 Bodley Lat. misc. e. , r– v.

by previous secondary grammarians who had discussed this part of speech, such as Evrard[257] and Pietro da Isolella,[258] but again Francesco da Buti's continued interest here is apparent in the syntactical direction in which he steers his treatment. Thus, when discussing the pronoun *istic*, which is defective in all plural forms except the neuter and accusative, Francesco o ers a syntactical solution to problems of Latin composition.[259]

Of the two topics covered in the last part of Francesco da Buti's secondary Latin course (*latinum maiorum*), conjunctions had traditionally been treated in secondary grammar not only taxonomically[260] but also syntactically[261] and so it is not surprising to encounter the usual syntactical vocabulary, such as *suppositum*,[262] *regere*[263] or *a parte post*,[264] in the *Regule*'s discussion of them. But all types of figures had been covered traditionally by grammarians from Donatus[265] to Alexander[266] and Evrard,[267] and so it is particularly revealing of the syntactical direction taken in secondary grammar by the *Regule* that Francesco da Buti limits his discussion to the figures of construction alone.[268] In fact, Francesco proceeds to discuss eight figures of construction, adding *evocatio*, *appositio* and *sinodoche* as sub-types of *sintosis* to *prolempsis*, *silempsis*, *zeugma* and *antitosis*.[269] In focusing on these particular figures of construction, Francesco is following the traditional Italian path for secondary grammar, established in the thirteenth century by grammarians such as Pietro da Isolella, who discussed the same figures in his treatment of construction.[270]

257 Ed. Wrobel ( ), – . 258 Ed. Fierville ( ), – .

259 Bodley Lat. misc. e. , r: Et quando datur thema per casus quibus carent debemus recurrere ad participium ens et adverbium istic, ut *eo amo costeto homine*, ego amo hominem entem [MS: entes] istic.

260 See e.g. *Graecismus*, ed.Wrobel ( ), – ; Bene da Firenze, ed. Marchesi ( ), – .

261 See e.g. *Doctrinale*, ed. Reichling ( ), vv. – , – , .

262 Bodley Lat. misc. e. , r. 263 Bodley Lat. misc. e. , r–v.

264 Bodley Lat. misc. e. , r–v. 265 Ed. Keil (–), , – .

266 Ed. Reichling ( ), vv. – . 267 Ed. Wrobel ( ), – .

268 Bodley Lat. misc. e. , r: Nota quod figure constructionis [...] sunt quinque, scilicet prolempsis silemsis zeuma sintosis et antithosis, de quibus solum in isto tractatu est videndum, obmissis aliis de quibus non est intentio.

269 Bodley Lat. misc. e. , v– r: prolempsis (e.g. (v) nos legimus, ego Salustium et tu Lucanum); silempsis (e.g. (r) ego et Berta sumus albi); zeugma (e.g. (v) Berta et isti sunt albi); sintosis (e.g. (v) populus currunt); evocatio (e.g. (r) ego Petrus curro); appositio (e.g. (r) arma sunt gladii); sinodoche (e.g. (r) ego sum fortis bracchia); antitosis (e.g. (v) sermonem quem audistis non est meus).

270 Ed. Fierville ( ), – . Pietro, as usual in treating syntax, was following Sponcius in his choice of figures of construction: see Fierville ( ), – . Sabbadini ( ), – , was in error in seeing only Priscian's five figures of construction in Pietro da Isolella, who actually deals with the normal eight: Fierville ( ), – .

It is obvious that Francesco da Buti's highly selective, organized approach was intended to make the Latin language and especially Latin prose composition – his favoured teaching activity – accessible to a widening circle of school children. Ever greater e orts were made in the Italian Trecento Latin classroom to reach out to the growing numbers of literate pupils; teachers were no longer willing just to make Latin available but now strove to bring it down to the level of the children themselves. The most important way in which these masters popularized Latin was to use the vernacular as a learning aid, introducing it into the teaching of grammar and prose composition. It will be seen below that the *volgare* had become an important adjunct to teaching Latin literature since the turn of the thirteenth century,[271] but it seems hardly to have been used at all to teach grammar before the beginning of the Trecento.[272] It has already been seen that the *volgare* was never employed at the elementary stage where basic Latin morphology was learnt through the study of *Ianua*;[273] at the secondary level, on the other hand, it was increasingly brought into the syllabus, over the course of the fourteenth century, until extended prose composition was studied on the basis of full-scale translation exercises from the vernacular into Latin. Theoretical grammar works before the end of the thirteenth century – including lexicons such as Papias's *Elementarium*, Hugutio of Pisa's *Magnae derivationes* and Giovanni Balbi's *Catholicon*, as well as secondary grammars by Papias, Paolo da Camaldoli, Bene da Firenze,[274] Mayfredo di Belmonte,[275] Giovanni da Pigna,[276] Pietro da Isolella,[277] Sion da Vercelli[278] and Tebaldo[279] – had

271 See below, .

272 For an anonymous treatise (actually extracts from Francesco da Buti's *Regule*), mistakenly assigned to XIIIc. by Antonino de Stefano, see n. below. 273 See above, .

274 BNCF CS B. . , r– r, is an entirely Latinate text, even in the section on participles (r– v), a topic usually leading to extensive vernacular interventions in XIVc. and XVc. Thematic translations (v), not written by copyist/organizer Giovanni di Ser Jacopo *de Ceuli* but rather by a later XVc. hand, have nothing to do with Bene's *Summa* and seem to be a filler of one of several blank pages.

275 The only *volgare* found in Mayfredo's *Doctrinale* are eleven vernacular words (in a text of pages in cod. of the Biblioteca Capitolare di Ivrea) appearing as vocabulary explanations. Gasca Queirazza ( ), , , considers them integral parts of the text but, in view of this MS's date (later XIVc.) when Italian Latin grammatical teaching was thoroughly imbued with the vernacular, they may perhaps be subsequent interpolations, especially given the high degree of textual fluidity characteristic of school grammatical manuscripts. Vernacular proverbs found in margins of the Ivrean MS are not part of Mayfredo's text: Gasca Queirazza ( )) . See Gasca Queirazza ( ) for Seville manuscript. 276 Gardenal (a), .

277 This text has two one-word vernacular vocabulary explanations: Fierville ( ), x.

278 No vernacular in *Novum Doctrinale*: Bersano ( ), .

279 Text in BL Add. , BML Strozzi and BML AD is entirely Latin. Second treatise attributed to Tebaldo (inc. Cuilibet verbo impersonali: see below,) has one short vernac-

been Latinate works.[280] But the second half of the Duecento of course saw the first stages of the great burgeoning of the Italian vernacular – a development that had its e ect on the teaching of formal Latin grammar at the secondary level.

One area of Latin teaching in which the vernacular made substantial headway in the fourteenth century was lexicography. There was an increasing amount of vernacular vocabulary glossing on Latin authors from the thirteenth into the fourteenth centuries,[281] and so one finds correspondingly a number of Latin/vernacular word lists compiled by grammar teachers in this period.[282] Two such vocabularies[283] derived from the lessons of Maestro Goro d'Arezzo, a commentator on Lucan in the early fourteenth century.[284] The colophon of the Harley manuscript suggests that Goro may have used this list while teaching in Siena.[285] Unlike the earlier great Latin dictionaries, which follow alphabetical order, Goro's Harley list is organized according to vocabulary classes, beginning with God and heaven, and descending to man, eating and food, the house and so forth. Goro would have taken this topical format from *Graecismus* (see , above), but his vocabulary was even more accessible than Evrard's as a result of its macaronic format.

This same type of organization was adopted by Goro's pupil, Maestro Domenico di Bandino,[286] in a vocabulary list which he gave to one of his Florentine pupils in the late fourteenth century, under the title 'Incipiunt vocabula data a Magistro Dominicho de Aretio'.[287] Domenico di

ular explanation for future participle in BML AD , r (habet talem sensum: *che amarà che leggierà*). However, this passage does not occur in BML Strozzi , an earlier MS; so perhaps it is a XIVc. interpolation.

280 Interesting that Bonvesin da la Riva, writing in later XIIIc., still assumes that teaching will be entirely in Latin: 'quarto continuo Latinis tempore verbis / hospicio cunctos omnia coge loqui' (*Vita scolastica*, ed. Vidmanová-Schmidtová ( ), , vv. –). See Sasse Tateo ( ), .

281 See below, . 282 For general discussion of these vocabularies, see Baldelli ( ).

283 BNCF Panciat. , r– v; BL Harley ; BNCF Magl. . , v– r contains Goro's 'Regule ortographie per alphabetum'. Baldelli ( ), , cites Modena Biblioteca Estense MS alpha. . . as another example.

284 BL Harley ; Vienna Schottenkloster cod. , formerly , r– v.

285 BL Harley , v: Hic incipiunt vocabula Magistri Gori de Aretio quibus ego Johannes Bini Benedicti de Sancto Angelo in Colle multa vocabula adiunxi accepta a Jacobo Paltonio iuvene doctissimo senensi. 286 Hankey ( ), .

287 This hitherto unknown list, preserved together with other educational materials (ASF Ospedale di San Matteo) in a *ricordanza* of a Florentine hospital, was discovered and very kindly passed to me by John Henderson. For a description of the manuscript, see Black (b), . It has the following ownership note on front flyleaf: Iste liber est Bartulj Dominj Bellj de Mancinis morantis in scholis Magistrj Dominicj de Aretio, amen. (For the text of Bartolo's schoolbook, see Black (b), – .) Bartolo (or Bartolomeo) was the son of an important late Trecento Florentine political figure, Messer Bello di Niccolò Mancini (d.), knighted by the Ciompi

Bandino's vocabulary[288] is divided into sections according to subject matter like his teacher's, Goro's, but it begins with man instead of God and proceeds to parts of the body; the house including domestic items, furniture and food; the garden and plants; woods and trees; and finally the farm. A typical example of this list is the section on the parts of the body (r– r n.n.). Words are not di erentiated according to parts of speech; instead, nouns are mixed indiscriminately with verbs and adjectives. The majority of entries, as would be expected, are nouns. Another feature of the list are excursuses in the form of verses to clarify and to fix di erences of meaning for the pupil, particularly in the case of homonyms; it is likely that these verses were mnemonic, as in the case of similar verse extracts found in elementary and secondary grammar texts, which are introduced, as here, with the formula *unde versus*. On one occasion, the source of the verse digression is given as *Graecismus*.[289] In school grammatical treatises, these mnemonic verses were usually anonymous too, although when sources are cited, they were usually, as here, *Graecismus*, or sometimes *Doctrinale*. Occasionally, the list is interrupted for explanatory digressions not in verse form.[290] Goro d'Arezzo had quoted classical authors on two occasions,[291] and similarly his pupil Domenico di Bandino cited Ovid to demonstrate the unusual form *cepa* rather than *cepe*.[292] The list seems to reflect the Florentine idiom of the pupil, Bartolo, whose orthography often did not reproduce his teacher's probably more Latinate vernacular and whose Latin was often ungrammatical.

The topical Latin/vernacular lexicon, established by Goro d'Arezzo in the early fourteenth century, became a standard teaching tool in the fifteenth century. Indeed, the same bundle of Florentine hospital accounts, among which Domenico di Bandino's word list was found, contains another Latin/vernacular vocabulary, this time by the early fifteenth-century Aretine grammar teacher Maestro Niccolò di Duccio.

footnote (*cont.*)
in ; his mother, Niccolosa di Messer Giovannino Magalotti, was from a Florentine élite family. (BNCF Carte Passerini (Genealogia e storia della famiglia Mancini): for full citation, see Black (b), n. .) MS probably dates from the s, when Domenico di Bandino was teaching grammar in Florence. (Domenico di Bandino taught in Florence betwen and and not again: see Hankey ( ), .) It is less likely to derive from the s, because Messer Bello is not specified as dead in the colophon; it must come before July , when Domenico di Bandino returned to teach grammar in his native city of Arezzo, never again to live in Florence (Black (d),).

Another manuscript contains a similar type of topical vocabulary list attributed to Domenico di Bandino (BNCF Landau Fin. , dated , r– r: Domenico Bandini, Vocabula. Inc. Incipiunt vocabula gramaticalia. Hic deus, dei – iddio. Expl. hoc mattutinum, -ni – el mattutino. Expliciunt Vocabula Magistri Dominici de Aretio, deo gratias amen.) Textually, however, the two lists are remote.

288 See Black (b), – . 289 r (n.n.). 290 v (n.n.).

291 BNCF Magl. . , r (Horace), r (Sallust). 292 r (n.n.).

This latter list, which seems to have been written about the same time as Bartolo Mancini's vocabulary but by a far more expert hand, has this note of possession: 'Ista vochabula sunt mea Ser <Michaelis?>Johannis Blaxij de Monte Chastello morantis in ischolis venerabilis Magistri Nicholai de Aretio', although this pupil did not write the list. Maestro Niccolò di Duccio's list is also topically organized, and there is clearly some kind of textual relationship between his and Domenico di Bandino's vocabulary, as many of the entries and mnemonic verses are the same, although Niccolò di Duccio's list is longer, containing a number of additional topics. The topical Latin/vernacular vocabulary became a well-established feature of Florentine grammar schools in the fifteenth century: other examples are from a *ricordanza* of to by Domenico di Bono Ferravecchio, detto Valdisieve, di Firenze, containing 'Vocabula nobis tributa a Magistro Antonio'[293] and from a mid fifteenth-century grammatical/literary miscellany,[294] with such familiar topics as the parts of the body and the countryside; both these lists contain mnemonic verses, like Domenico di Bandino's and Niccolò's vocabularies. A better-known early Quattrocento example is Gasparino Barzizza's treatise, in which everyday vocabulary, as in the above three Aretine examples by Goro, Domenico and Niccolò d'Arezzo, is divided into topical categories (in this latter case, divine, celestial, atmospheric, maritime, terrestrial, inanimate and animate) and given an equivalent in the author's native Bergamask dialect.[295] A mid Quattrocento example from the Veneto is by the teacher Iacopo di Calcinia, who o ered a bilingual list of 'nomina necessaria scolaribus'.[296] A later fifteenth-century example was the work of Giovambattista Cantalicio, a prominent humanist teacher who translated Latin words into his native dialect of Rieti.[297]

It was at the beginning of the fourteenth century, when Italian school masters first used the vernacular to impart Latin vocabulary, that they also began to turn to the *volgare* for teaching secondary grammar. An early example is provided by the *Regule parve*[298] of Goro d'Arezzo, who

293 ASF Manoscritti , r. 294 BNCF CS G. . , – .

295 *Vocabularium breve magistri Gasparini Pergomensis in quo continentur omnia genera vocabulorum quae in usu frequenti et quotidiana consuetudine versantur, incipiens a rebus divinis ad res caelestes, aereas, maritimas, terrestres, inanimatas ac animatas*, printed at Brescia in and Venice in : Sabbadini ( ), . Another Bergamask example of Latin–vernacular vocabulary, dated , was published by Contini ( ), – .

296 From Venice Biblioteca Marciana lat. , cited by Baldelli ( ), .

297 Baldelli ( ). Another late Quattrocento example is a -word vocabulary of teacher Iacopo Ursello da Rocca Antica (MS Vittorio Emanuele of Rome Biblioteca Nazionale), giving lexical equivalents in dialect of Sabina: cited by Baldelli ( ), .

298 BNCF Panciat. , v– r, ed. Marchesi ( ), – .

was active in the first half of the fourteenth century and whose teaching lexicon has just been mentioned. Goro's *Regule* are fragmentary, but they still show two didactic uses of the vernacular. One is the listing of Latin verbs and their principal parts together with vernacular translations to illustrate the various categories of verbal construction.[299] These Latin/vernacular verb lists – clearly included to build vocabulary as well as to illustrate the di erent verbal constructions – became a characteristic feature of secondary-level grammars in the Renaissance, including those by Guarino[300] and Perotti,[301] but Goro's other use of the vernacular was peculiar to the *Regule parve.* This was teaching the meanings of the cases through the vernacular prepositions. Thus the genitive was explained by the vernacular *de* [*di*], the dative by *a*, and the ablative by *de* [*di*], *da, in, per, cum.*[302] Goro's rules of thumb for the Latin cases by reference to the appropriate vernacular prepositions were eminently pragmatic and obviously reflected his own teaching practice, but perhaps the numerous exceptions and qualifications – some of which he himself detailed – made this method less attractive to his fellow grammar teachers.

Nevertheless, Goro shared his use of the vernacular in the Latin classroom with a number of other early fourteenth-century grammarians, whose secondary treatises also include Latin/vernacular lists of verbs illustrating the classes of verbal constructions. One example is the widely di used treatise on construction by the Florentine grammarian, Filippo di Naddo;[303] another is o ered by the 'Regule mediocres Magistri Guillielmi de Verruscola Bosorum'.[304]

Francesco da Buti also used a similar technique in the *Regule grammaticales* for teaching irregular Latin nouns. He divided these into groups according to their type of irregularity, which he first discussed in general terms and then exemplified by a list of nouns with vernacular equivalents.[305] He then proceeded to give twenty-one lists of this type for other

[299] Marchesi ( ), – . Format of presentation here is similar to that used by Francesco da Buti and illustrated above: see n. . [300] See e.g. Percival (a), .

[301] See e.g. Percival ( ), . [302] Marchesi ( ), – .

[303] See e.g. BRF , r– r.

[304] BNCF NA , r– v. On this MS and its date and provenance, see below, .

[305] Bodley Lat. misc. e. , r–v.

Nota quod sunt quedam nomina masculini generis que non declinantur in plurali numero, que in hiis versibus continentur, scilicet:

Cum fumo fimus, <sanguis> cum pulvere limus
Aer sal pontus cum mundus viscus et ether.

Nominativo hic fumus, genitivo huius fumi	lu fummo
Nominativo hic fimus, genitivo huius fimi	lo lutame
Nominativo hic sanguis, huius sanguis	lo sangue […]

For another version of this list, in Veronese dialect, see de Stefano ( ), .

irregular nouns,[306] and he adopted the same kind of presentation for irregular verbs, first discussing the irregularity and then giving a series of nine lists with vernacular equivalents.[307]

Fourteenth-century Italian grammarians went further, illustrating various syntactical points by reference to vernacular sentences which were then provided with Latin translations. This reflects the schoolroom practice of *themata*, which were vernacular passages assigned to pupils for Latin translation. This type of exercise was established by the early fourteenth century, and is explicitly mentioned by Filippo di Naddo and Guglielmo da Verucchio. Indeed, many of the grammatical points in their treatises were specifically raised in order to solve problems of translation from vernacular to Latin, and were accordingly introduced by the phrase *si detur thema.*

The use of *themata* to teach Latin syntax can be illustrated again in Francesco da Buti's *Regule grammaticales*. The concept of the theme is first introduced without vernacular phrases at the first level of his school (*latinum minus*) when he discusses potential problems for translation raised by common verbs (i.e. those with both active and passive meanings).[308] He introduces actual phrases to translate under deponent verbs, the next verbal category of *latinum minus*,[309] giving four modes for thematic translation of deponent verbs.[310] He mentions more potential problems of translation in the rest of his treatment of verbal syntax, for example when discussing neutral passives (i.e. verbs with active forms but passive meanings)[311] or impersonal verbs.[312] One such problem comes when explaining how to translate the past tense of certain verbs lacking a preterite.[313] But the most intensive use of the vernacular in treating problems of Latin composition comes at Francesco's second level (*latinum mediocre*). Here he introduces themes for the translation of nouns lacking Latin plurals[314] or for other problematic vernacular nouns.[315] At this level themes are brought into the discussion of superlatives,[316] as well as numerals,[317] verbal nouns[318] and verbs,[319] but thematic translation is a particular preoccupation for comparatives[320] and participles.[321]

306 Bodley Lat. misc. e. , v– v. 307 Bodley Lat. misc. e. , v– v.
308 Bodley Lat. misc. e. , r. 309 Bodley Lat. misc. e. , v. 310 BRF , r.
311 Bodley Lat. misc. e. , v. 312 Bodley Lat. misc. e. , v.
313 Bodley Lat. misc. e. , r–v. 314 Bodley Lat. misc. e. , r–v.
315 Bodley Lat. misc. e. , r. 316 Bodley Lat. misc. e. , v.
317 Bodley Lat. misc. e. , v. 318 Bodley Lat. misc. e. , v.
319 Bodley Lat. misc. e. , v.
320 Bodley Lat. misc. e. , r, v. Thematic translation is a recurrent technique in intervening folios.
321 Bodley Lat. misc. e. , r; cf. also r. For some textual extracts from Francesco featuring thematic translation, see Black (b), – .

Francesco da Buti was not the first Trecento school grammarian to help his pupils with such translation di culties. There is a secondary, probably Tuscan schoolbook written in notarial script of the first half of the fourteenth century which has an entire section devoted to problems of translating vernacular words such as the definite article, prepositions, or *che.*[322] This approach seems to have been imported by the early fourteenth century into the grammar syllabus from the teaching of rhetoric, where the practice had become well established during the Duecento. An early example can be found among the writings of the renowned Bolognese *dictator*, Guido Fava, whose *Parlamenta et epistole* of *c.* – consisted of a series of models for both public and private correspondence (as well as a few speeches), where mainly vernacular themes are turned into three Latin letters (and speeches) of varying stylistic levels, one *maior*, another *minor* and a third *minima.*[323] The use of thematic translation to teach *dictamen* continued to flourish at Bologna, as is clear from the letters of the prominent early Trecento Bolognese *dictator*, Pietro de' Boattieri, dating from ,[324] where various vernacular letters are followed by Latin translations and on one occasion even introduced by the phrase 'Tema istarum IIII epistolarum.'[325] Moreover, in the list of giving all Boattieri's works, mention is made of 'formando themata quelibet dicendorum'.[326] Similar vernacular letters were written by Boattieri's fellow *dictator*, Rosso d'Ognibene.[327] The practice was not restricted to Bologna: the *Parlamenti ed epistole* in Piedmontese dialect found in BNCF Magl. . , v– v and datable to the third decade of the fourteenth century[328] suggest the spread of the practice in Northern Italy,[329] and there is evidence of thematic composition in other dialects used to teach *dictamen.*[330] It is possible that the practice originated from the need for notaries to be able to translate from the vernacular into Latin and vice versa for the benefit of their private clients and public employers, a facility already documented as early as the end of the

322 BNCF . . , v– r (n.n.).

323 Ed. Gaudenzi ( ), – . See Salvioni ( ), ; Schia ni ( ), – , n. ; Bausi ( ), .

324 Zaccagnini (a), .

325 Zaccagnini (a), , .

326 Zaccagnini (a), .

327 Zaccagnini ( ), .

328 Gabriella Pomaro and I have examined the original manuscript, and it seems to us that Bertoni's dating to beginning of XIVc. is a little too early, especially in view of the beautiful formalized *scrittura cancelleresca* employed; Gaudenzi's hypothesis of earlier dating to XIIIc. is impossible.

329 Gaudenzi ( ), – ; Salvioni ( ), ; Bertoni ( ), – ; Terracini ( ), – ; Schia ni ( ), n. .

330 Schia ni ( ), n. . For XVc. Friulian and Genoese examples, see Schia ni ( ), n. .

twelfth century and required by statute in towns as far apart as Bologna and Aosta by the mid Duecento.[331] What is significant for the history of school education is that the practice of thematic translation, well established in the teaching of *dictamen* in the thirteenth century, began to be used by grammar masters to teach elementary prose composition at the beginning of the fourteenth century. In fact, this transition can possibly be documented in the Piedmontese rendering of the *Parlamenta et epistole* mentioned above. This manuscript (BNCF Magl. .) contains Piedmontese versions of four letters evidently made by one Giovanni Beccaria; what may be significant is that he is described as 'Joanin magistre de gramaia',[332] which suggests that these letters were already being used as exercises in thematic translation for the study of grammar in the early fourteenth century. It is also interesting that this manuscript continued to be used at the secondary level, passing into the hands of a boy attending the school of one Maestro Giacomo Bocconi.[333]

Although it had been clear from grammar manuals that pupils had practised the translation of *themata* at school in the fourteenth century, few actual examples of a school exercise book have come to light. The oldest example yet to emerge is a fragment in Venetian dialect, dating from the end of the Duecento; here the pupil focused on syntactical topics central to the secondary curriculum such as impersonal verbs, verbs of cost, deponent verbs, passive verbs with the ablative, neutropassive verbs, participles and comparatives.[334] Another was published by

[331] Salvioni ( ), ; Schia ni ( ), – . [332] Bertoni ( ), – .

[333] Bertoni ( ), : Iste liber est Ferrini (?) de F<...> qui est bonus puer et vadit ad scolas Magistri Iacobi de Boconis qui est bonus (v). Bertoni was right to question Gaudenzi's reading of 'Ferrini de Fabis', on the grounds that this name is written over an earlier name and is now far from clear, although it seems that 'Fabis' is more secure than either 'Ferrini' or 'Petrini'. Another signature on v (Ego Ubertinus ca<...>is scrixit) is not mentioned by Bertoni ( ) or Gaudenzi ( ), who apparently did not notice yet another early ownership note, also datable to the earlier Trecento, written upside-down on the last page of text (v): Iste scartapacius est mei Guinforti d(e) Saltariis, qui pro podices tergendo optimus existit. Presumably *scartapacius* = *scarafacium* (s.v. in Du Cange). *Probationes* by various schoolboys (v), and on preceding folios a brief *ars dictaminis* (r– r: inc. [Q]uoniam cuilibet rei tractus certitudo sive melius per difinitionem habetur ad ipsius dictaminis sumamus difinitionem per difinitio<n>em), besides an alphabet written by a schoolboy at the top of r.

[334] Belloni and Pozza ( ), – , and corresponding plates. Belloni and Pozza ( ), – , date the MS to XIIImid, and not after . This seems too early. The hand still uses XIIIc. system, with long final 's's. But there are also more modern features: the writer consistently indicates 'i's with a slash from right to left above the letter – a practice not normal until the later XIIIc.; many of the 't's are no longer half letters like 'c's but rather cut across by a horizontal stroke below the top of the vertical stroke in modern style. Consistent use is made of 'g' formed with one diagonal line from bottom left below line to top right above the line, a graphic feature which became widely di used only in XIII^2. A transitional, hybrid script. Gabriella Pomaro has examined the plates, and her view is that it is datable to the end of XIIIc.

Schia ni in ;[335] this example, in Friulian dialect, which seems to have come from Cividale del Friuli in the second half of the fourteenth century,[336] followed the current secondary grammar syllabus closely, providing translation exercises in impersonal verbs, figures and superlatives.[337] A contemporaneous Florentine example emerged, thanks to the above-mentioned discovery by John Henderson, enabling me to identify a thematic exercise book from the school of Domenico di Bandino.[338] It will be recalled that this book bears a note of possession from the Florentine schoolboy, Bartolo di Messer Bello Mancini, attending the school of Maestro Domenico d'Arezzo. The translation exercises chosen for Bartolo Mancini all concentrate on particular grammatical features of the standard secondary syllabus. For example, the first exercise focuses on the two types of supines (r n.n.); the second concentrates on constructions with gerunds and gerundives as well as a revision of supines (v n.n.). All the topics used by Domenico di Bandino for theme translations focus on problems treated theoretically in contemporary secondary grammar manuals, such as Francesco da Buti's *Regule*, discussed above. Similarly, the translation exercises carried out by Bartolo Mancini under his other teacher, Maestro Giovanni, preserved in the same manuscript, also concentrate on one particular problem of theme translation. In this latter case, the task was translating the vernacular verb *capere*, which required rendering into Latin through the adjective *capax*, and Bartolo was given twenty-two exercises of varying di culty on this one point (r– v n.n.). Bartolo's instruction under these teachers was far from slap-dash: not only was he required to carry out interminable repetition, as seen above under Maestro Giovanni, but he even had to translate Maestro Domenico's lesson plan at the beginning of the course on supines, gerunds and infinitives (r n.n.).[339]

There are signs of *themata* exercises in other school manuscripts. In an earlier fifteenth-century secondary grammar textbook, written on reused notarial parchment dating from the s, probably Florentine, for example, a pupil wrote what seems to be a vernacular *thema* for trans-

[335] Schia ni ( ), – . The brief passages for translation are numbered to , and are divided according to morning and afternoon lessons (*in sero, in mane*).

[336] Schia ni ( ), . [337] Schia ni ( ), .

[338] These translation exercises are published in Black (b), – . See n. above.

[339] Another example of a thematic exercise book, this time dated – , is BNCF Landau Fin. , r– r, r– r, which has the same mixture of vernacular/Latin *themata* and Latin/vernacular vocabulary as Bartolo Mancini's schoolbook (see ch. , , below). This technique continued to be used in earlier XVc., e.g. in Guarino's school (see Sabbadini ( ),) besides in later XVc.: see Poliziano ( ), – ; Bracke ( ); Quaquarelli ( ), . For a XVIc. example on the last page of a Terence manuscript (BML .), see below, .

lation practice on clauses of purpose: *acciochè tu sia fatto gramaticho dal maestro.*[340] Another example appears on an early fourteenth-century manuscript of Prosper's *Epigrammata.* Here an apparently fourteenth-century pupil wrote out a full example of a *thema* in atrocious Latin.[341] Both these manuscripts are Tuscan, if not Florentine, and there are further examples in Florentine libraries demonstrating the pensinsula-wide spread of the practice in the Trecento. One is a French manuscript of Statius's *Thebais,* dating from the second half of the twelfth century, which had been brought into Italy by the first half of the fourteenth century.[342] At the end of the manuscript there is the following note of possession, also datable to the fourteenth century: Frater Laurentius de Vicentia (v). What is interesting about this codex is that it also contains various Latin sentences of the *themata* type, giving practice in composition, and focusing on various problems of construction.[343] These references to Milan and Pavia, as well as Fra Lorenzo da Vicenza's note of possession, are secure evidence that this is a schoolbook from Lombardy and the Veneto. It is clear too that fifteenth-century North Italian grammarians, such as Corradino da Potremoli[344] or Gaspare da Verona,[345] assigned exercises in theme composition from the vernacular, and that Tuscan textbooks such as Francesco da Buti's *Regule* were copied and used in Northern Italy during the fifteenth century.[346] Clearly North

[340] BNCF Magl. . , v.

[341] BRF , r:

Noi legere[m]o ogimai le regul[e] fugite overo fulgitive chiamate per due nomi, l'uno perchè ele si dimenticano subito, l'altro perchè ele fano risplendere gli scholari.

Nos legemus a modo regulas fugitivas vocastas bino nomine noncupatas, uno silicet fugitiva quia fugiunt, fulgitiva quia eos posesores faciunt fu<l>gere.

[342] BML Edili .

[343] E.g., gerunds, verbs with passive forms but active meanings, ablatives of measurement and price, accusatives of limit of motion, ablatives of source, impersonal verbs and comparatives. BML Edili v– r:

Si mihi Petro qui ivi ad tegetem Martini causa videndi unam quercum alciorem pluribus quatuor brachis tua, si non foret sucesum ab omnibus manentibus, esem comestus ab uno lupo.

A te Petro vapularit scutifer Martini que verberatio constabit carioris quam verbum tu fecisti unquam.

Ego habeo unam infulam que constitit paucorum pluribus tribus soldis tua.

Cui a [*sic*] interest servire deo nisi suorum amicorum?

Fideles chlientes fuerant secuti marchionem Mediolanio Papiam qui non reliquerunt unquam ipsum in acie quoniam confiditur in sua potentia.

A nobis scolaribus qui venimus hodie ad scolas pautiores pluribus tribus quam eramus [h]eri disederatur adisere gramaticam, fondamentum homnium liberarum artium.

[344] Thurot ( ), , .

[345] BML . , v– r. For a brief set of grammar rules with thematic translations from Bergamo or, more likely, Brescia, dated , see Contini ( ), – .

[346] Bodley Lat. misc. e. is a fifteenth-century North Italian, possibly Venetian, copy of Francesco da Buti.

Italian pupils in the fourteenth century were also using new-style treatises with their heavy reliance on the vernacular.[347] This is further confirmed by the grammatical course of the fourteenth-century Trevisan master, Pietro da Asolo (BML Ashb.), who made continual use of thematic translation,[348] as well as by the Trecento Friulian grammar course probably by Maestro Pietro di Cividale del Friuli, who goes extensively into problems of *vulgare sive thema* with regard to participles,[349] not to mention the fragmentary Piedmontese grammar datable to the later fourteenth century whose thematic passages have been published by Gasca Queirazza,[350] and the thematic translations in a signed Trecento grammar manual from Bergamo.[351]

The secondary theoretical grammar course – in the form typified by Francesco da Buti's *Regule grammaticales* – was well established early in the fourteenth century. This is clear, for example, from the work of another

347 de Stefano ( ), – , published an anonymous grammar from MS lat. of Munich Staatsbibliothek, with extensive use of vernacular. de Stefano dated the manuscript to XIIIc. (–), unaware, however, that the text here actually consisted of excerpts from Francesco da Buti's *Regule*:

de Stefano, ed.:	Francesco da Buti, in Bodley lat. misc. e. :
Nota, quod sunt quedam nomina masculini generis non declinata in plurali que in his versibus continentur:	<N>ota quod sunt quedam nomina masculini generis que non declinantur in plurali numero que in hiis versibus continentur, scilicet:
Cum fumo fimus, sanguis cum pulvere, limus,	Cum fumo fimus, cum pulvere <sanguis> limus,
Aer, sol, pontus, cum mundo visus et ether.	Aer, sal, pontus cum mundus viscus et ether.
Hic fumus, huius fumi, *lo fumo*.	Nominativo hic fumus genitivo huius fumi, *lu fummo*
Hic fimus, huius fimi, *lo fango* sive *lo leamo* […]	Nominativo hic fimus genitivo huius fimi *lo lutame* […] (r)

The entire passage published by de Stefano from – corresponds to Francesco da Buti, Bodley lat. misc. e. , r– r. Similarly, – corresponds to the same manuscript, v . This Munich manuscript, therefore, cannot be dated before the end of XIVc., and so my doubts about this dating, expressed in Black (b), , were justified.

A similar fragment was published by Manacorda (–), – , from flyleaves of Bologna Biblioteca Universitaria MS , which he dates 'estremo sec. XIII o del principio del XIV' ( ). This MS gives a conventional set of verbal syntactical classes for active and passive verbs, together with invented vernacular examples and lists of Latin verbs with vernacular translations. It does not seem to be the same text as, e.g., Francesco da Buti, but its content, format and terminology correspond to the usual XIVc. pattern and so this would appear to be a XIVc., not a XIIIc., manuscript.

348 E.g. r: si datur vobis tale thema; v: quia non esset sententia thematis; r: thema; v: thema; r: thema; v: thema; r: istud thema; v: thema; r: them; v: thema; etc. On this treatise, see below, . Further examples from Treviso, dating from XIVmid, are published by Stussi ( ).

349 Schia ni ( ), – .

350 Gasca Queirazza ( ), – .

351 Contini ( ), – .

Tuscan grammarian, the Florentine Filippo di Naddo di Filippo (d.),[352] whose textbook has the *incipit* 'Constructio est unio constructibilium' and is found in a number of manuscripts, especially in Florence.[353] This treatise encompasses a secondary syllabus notably similar in scope to that already encountered in Francesco da Buti's *Regule*.[354] Here there is, as in Francesco da Buti's *Regule*, a comprehensive structure, as well as a disavowal of the Duecento grammarians' disorganized presentation. There are minor divergences from Francesco da Buti's pattern: a few di erent verbal subclasses, participles included under verbs, di ering order of nominal types, case governance placed after figures; and yet the overall range and order of topics is the same: verbs, nouns, conjunctions, figures. There is also a similarity in focus: like Francesco da Buti's, this is a treatise on syntax. This is clear not only from

[352] For biographical information, see Debenedetti (–), , n. .

[353] I have used:

ASF Carte Bardi . , XV², not earlier than , when a previous text in the manuscript was completed (r): r– v.

BML Ashb. , XV²: r– r.

BML Gaddi , XIV²: r– v.

BNCF CS G. . , XV¹: grammatical miscellany, including pages (,) with same incipits as Filippo's *Regule*, and possibly material from his treatise on – , but without full text.

BRF , XV¹: r– r. Incomplete version of 'Regule Magistri Philippi', corresponding to r– v of BRF .

BRF , XV¹: r– v.

BRF , XIV–XVc.: r– v. Beginning of Filippo di Naddo's *Regule* (corresponding to r– v of BML Ashb.).

Columbia University Library Plimpton , XVmid., apparently complete.

I have not seen the following two manuscripts, also listed by Bursill-Hall ( ), – :

Venice Biblioteca Marciana Lat. (XIVc.).

Venice Biblioteca Marciana Lat. (XVc.).

Some considerable variations exist between Gaddi and Ashb. , the former apparently a shortened version.

Filippo di Naddo composed another grammatical treatise, entitled 'Tractatus Magistri Philippi', and found in BML Gaddi , XIV², r– r. Inc. Gramaticha est scientia recte loquendi et recte scribendi. Expl. vel determinationis regule alicuius partis posite in aliam orationem. Amen. Explicit tractatus Magistri Phylippi. Deo gratias amen. This is a general treatise on construction, focusing on sentence structure and discussing such topics as *suppositum*, *appositum*, simple and composite construction. According to Bursill-Hall ( ), , it is also found in Admont Stiftsbibliothek cod. , – r.

[354] BML Ashb. : General definition of construction. Verbs. Personal verbs: active, passive, neutral substantive, neutral possessive, neutral acquisitive, neutral e ective, neutral imperfect, neutral absolute, neutral passive, neutro-passive, common, deponent; impersonal verbs; infinitives; gerunds; supines; participles; vocative, substantial, accidental verbs; derivative verbs: inchoative, meditative, frequentative, diminutive, etc. Nouns: verbal, relative, numerical, gentile, patrial, patronymic, relatives, interrogatives, comparatives, superlatives. Conjunctions. Figures. Case governance.

the incipit and opening definition of construction, but also from the treatise's ubiquitous syntactical vocabulary (e.g. *suppositum, appositum, a parte ante, a parte post, ex natura*) and from the list of verbs with vernacular translation under each verbal subclass, together with the usual type of mnemonic verses. There are also copious themes given in the *volgare* with Latin translation, and particularly revealing is Filippo di Naddo's handling of figures. Here he rapidly passes over figures of diction and of locution, and focuses on figures of construction.[355] He then gives detailed consideration to these figures of construction,[356] in fact the same eight discussed by Francesco da Buti.[357]

Overall systematic structure, abundant use of the vernacular and focus on construction were thus the main preoccupations of Filippo di Naddo in the first half of the fourteenth century, as they would be of Francesco da Buti in the second half; given their overall coherence, it is not surprising that the textbooks by these two masters established themselves as the predominant secondary grammar courses in Trecento Tuscany. It is not di cult to explain the lack of success su ered by other Trecento secondary grammar treatises now found in Florentine libraries: although they share Francesco's and Filippo's copious use of the vernacular and their preoccupation with syntax, they fail to achieve the overall systematic presentation and control of material so evident in the above two more widely circulated textbooks. An alternative secondary manual, found in only one manuscript (BNCF NA), is by 'Magistro Guillelmo de Verrucola Boçorum' (v), written on paper with a Florentine watermark of (Briquet) and with several fourteenth- and fifteenth-century ownership marks suggesting Florentine provenance.[358] The book may also have been used by two Aretine teachers, possibly while teaching in Florence.[359] The contents of the treatise show an overall similarity to the *Regule* by Francesco da Buti and Filippo di Naddo, although the di ering order of the material betrays a less coherent overall structure.[360] There are the usual mnemonic verses and categorized lists of verbs with vernacular equivalents; the syntactical focus is apparent from the omnipresent terminology (*suppositum, appositum, deter-*

355 BML Ashb. , r–v. 356 BML Ashb. , v– r. 357 See above, .

358 v, v (Strozzi, Rondinelli families). Veruccola=? Veruculum (Verucchio, near S. Marino)

359 v: Iste liber est <...> et adhuc moratur ad legendum et ad lactinandum [MS: clatinadum] in scholis Magistr Gori [de Aretio?].
r: Magistri Nicholai de <A>riçio.

360 Verbs: active, passive, neuter, common, deponent. Participles. Relatives. Interrogatives. Verbal construction and *modi significandi*. Conjunctions. Figures. Nouns. Partitives and distributives, comparatives, superlatives.

minatio, a parte ante, a parte post, regere) as well as from the numerous thematic translations.

Another secondary grammar textbook (BNCF . .), with an evidently Tuscan provenance[361] datable to the first half of the Trecento and found in only one manuscript, reveals a similar general scope but again a less than ideal structure.[362] There are the usual mnemonic verses, and the normal syntactical preoccupation is evident from the treatise's vocabulary (*suppositum, appositum, ex natura, a parte ante, ex parte post, determinatio*) and its ubiquitous thematic translations.

The above Trecento secondary grammar courses – by the Aretine Goro, by the Florentine Filippo di Naddo, by the Pisan Francesco da Buti, as well as in BNCF NA and BNCF . . – are all of Tuscan provenance, but similar syllabuses and teaching methods were disseminated throughout Italy.[363] This is clear, for example, from a manuscript (BML Ashb.) giving part of the secondary syllabus followed by Pietro da Asolo, grammar teacher in the Veneto (especially, Treviso and Conegliano) in the second half of the fourteenth century.[364] The sections of the course on participles, relatives and figures are explicitly attributed to Pietro.[365] The sections of the course dealing with nominal species as well as with distributives and partitives are almost certainly by Pietro too, given that they cite Treviso in geographical examples;[366] two remaining tractates have further North Italian references (to the Veneto and Cremona),[367] and one of the treatise's copyists was from the Pinidello near Conegliano in the Veneto.[368] The entire work was entitled 'Constructiones' by the final copyist, and in fact in an inventory of there is mentioned a 'Constructiones magistri Petri de Asolo in uno volumine'.[369] All this suggests that the entire manuscript may represent part

361 v (n.n.): hec Florentia [...] hoc Aretium [...] hic Mons Politianus.

362 General definitions. Construction. Concordance. Adjectives. Nouns. Thematic translation. Participles. Distributives. Composites. Conjunctions. Comparatives. Superlatives. Governance (*regimen*). Adverbs. Figures. Verbs.

363 Similar XIVc. traditional secondary grammatical fragment from Friuli and containing Friulian dialect throughout, possibly written by Maestro Pietro di Cividale del Friuli, was published by Schia ni ( ), – , – . As Schia ni points out, it has strong correspondences to treatises by Filippo di Naddo and Francesco da Buti.

364 For his career, see Gargan ( ), – .

365 v: Expliciunt participia edita atque composita per reverendum doctorem Magistrum Petrum de Asilo in civitate Tarvisii olim gramaticeque professorem. Amen.
(r) Expliciunt relativa data atque edita per venerabilem ac excelentisimum doctorem Magistrum Petrum de Assilo gramaticeque pro essorem.
(r) Expliciunt figure date atque composite per Magistrum Petrum de Assillo. Deo gratias amen.

366 Gargan ( ), .

367 Gargan ( ), – .

368 See below, .

369 Gargan ( ), .

of a unified secondary grammar course coming from Pietro da Asolo's school.

The overall curriculum represented by this Ashburnham manuscript was entirely typical of Trecento grammar schools.[370] This manuscript reveals the usual syntactical vocabulary (*post se*, *ante se*, *suppositum*, *appositum*), thematic translations and mnemonic verses; there is also the normal focus on the eight figures of construction (v– r). The most interesting feature of this treatise is the frequent citation of authorities, not just Christian, late ancient, medieval and scholastic such as the Bible,[371] Donatus,[372] Boethius,[373] Priscian,[374] Hugutio,[375] *Graecismus*,[376] Aristotle[377] and Aquinas[378] but also the Roman classics, including Lucan,[379] Cato,[380] Ovid[381] (*Heroides*[382] and *Metamorphoses*[383]) and Vergil;[384] it is clear that the Latin authors of golden and silver ages were introduced as sources of grammatical examples at the secondary level before the advent of fifteenth-century humanism.[385]

Despite the wide circulation of these new-style Trecento secondary grammars, it is clear that more traditional teaching methods and materials were still in use in the fourteenth century, as is evident from surviving copies of older secondary textbooks in Florentine libraries. There are, for example, several fourteenth-century manuscripts of the great French verse grammars, especially ***Doctrinale***:

370 Participles. Nominal species. Relatives. Figures. Comparatives. Infinitives. Distributives and partitives. Superlatives. Derivative verbs (frequentative and desiderative). Heteroclytes. Orthography. Adjectival nouns. Adverbs of location. Formation of preterites and supines.

371 BML Asbh. , v. 372 BML Asbh. , r.

373 BML Asbh. , r, v, r, r. 374 BML Asbh. , v, r, r, r.

375 BML Asbh. , r, r, v. 376 BML Asbh. , r, r.

377 BML Asbh. , v. 378 BML Asbh. , v.

379 BML Asbh. , v, r, r, v, v. 380 BML Asbh. , r, v.

381 BML Asbh. , r. 382 BML Asbh. , r, v, v, r, r.

383 BML Asbh. , r. 384 BML Asbh. , r, v.

385 According to Capello ( ), , Mayfredo di Belmonte in his *Donatus* or *Doctrinale* of (for this work, see above , n.), cited Lucan, Juvenal, Horace, Ovid, Vergil, *Rhetorica ad Herennium*, besides Gospels and Priscian.

Another traditional XIVc. North Italian grammarian was Folchino dei Borfoni da Cremona, who treated syntax according to the standard scheme of verbal types: see Sabbadini ( ), – and ( ), – .

Location	Date	Provenance	Glossing/commentary/use
BML Ashb.	XIV² [386]	N. Italy[387]	Copyist gives long commentary. *Accessus* (r): usual Aristotelian type, frequently used in the late-medieval Italian schoolroom;[388] text divided into chapter headings,[389] in line with normal XIVc. practice.[390] Earliest known reader, Angelo da Mantova, used it for his Latin lessons with Maestro Paolo (XIV/XVc.).[391] Subsequent puerile marginalia indicate continued school use.[392]
BNCF Magl. . [393]	XIV²	Italy	Fully glossed by copyist and possibly by one or two other contemporaneous readers. Typical expository commentary: interlinear glosses normally consist of

386 Reichling ( ), cxxx: 'saec. XIV° ineunte' but the copyist's hand is similar in type to Salutati's.

387 Various signatures and notes of possession from Bergamo, Verona and Mantua:
r: Leonardus Veronensis, Leonardus Veronensis [unformed hand, XV²]
v: Leonardus Bergomensis [same hand, better writing] Veronensis [same hand]
r: Abcdefghiklm, abcdefg [hand unclear]
v: various *probationes*: Ego Antonius de Bergomo scripsi
Ego Franciscus de Bergomo
Ownership note: Hic liber est meus Angeli de <Man >tua qui vadit ad scolam latini Magistri Pauli [XIV²–XV¹]
v: probationes: Bergomi, ego Iacobus.

388 See below, . 389 r, v, v, r, v, v, r, r, r, r, v, v.

390 Reichling ( ), lxxi. 391 See above, n. .

392 r: vocabulary notes explaining text in vernacular: equo *el mar* unda *la unda el* mors *del caval* mare *el mar* mel *la mel* [...] aqua *l'aqua* vinum *el vino* stagna *lo staglio* [...] puteus *el pozo* [...] [XV²]
r: brief marginal note by Leonardus (see n. above for him): Ante senex iuvenis adolescens [...]
r: verbs of text repeated in margin: lavo, poto, do, sto, iuvo [...] [XV²]
r: Leonardus's poems written in margin.

393 For description of part containing *Doctrinale*, see Reichling ( ), cxxv, whose impossible dating (XIIIc.) is accepted by Garin ( ), who reproduces r in plate Gehl's ( ) date (: XIVin.) seems unlikely, too, given the prevalence of typical later Trecento features, such as ' '-shaped 'r's near the beginning of words and long, curved final 's's. MS ends with a short, glossed verse treatise on preterites and supines (v– v: inc. Incipit tractatus preteritorum et supinorum. Sunt per vi cu fri mi ne pli se do so to cre ve ne [...]) and beginning of a verse treatise on orthography (v: inc. Cor fra gas le nis [...]), unmentioned by Reichling ( ), Bursill-Hall ( ) or Gehl ( ).

Location	Date	Provenance	Glossing/commentary/use
			examples,[394] or brief explanations.[395] Marginal glosses o er running exposition of and complement to verse text.[396] Commentator o ers definitions of text's terminology,[397] or explanations of its meaning, as for example when Alexander states that vocative (e.g. *vocor*) and substantive (e.g. *sum*) verbs take the nominative case in the predicate.[398] Other grammarians sometimes cited.[399]
BRF	XIVex.	Italy	Heavily glossed by numerous school-type readers, contemporaneous with copyist. Glosses expository. Interlinear: examples/vocabulary, often vernacular,[400] or brief explanations.[401] Marginal: rubricator (not copyist) indicates main sections in red.[402] School-level annotators usually provide explicatory glosses.[403]

394 E.g.:

ut faber / ut vir / ut satur / ut scanum / ut dominus / ut Teseus

Er vel ir ur aut um vel us aut eus pone secunda. (v. , v)

395 E.g.:

id est nominativum / id est accusativo / id est vocativo / tu

Primum [MS: primo] cum quarto quintoque sono dabis uno. (v. , r)

396 Chapter on heteroclyte nouns, e.g., is introduced thus:

r: Hic in parte ista tractat autor de nominibus etherocritis. Et dicitur etherocritum ab eteron, quod est diversum, et crisis, quod est declinatio, id est, nomen diversimode declinatum. Et incipit hic secundum capitulum istius libri, sicut promisit in prohemio suo, ubi dicit *istis confinem retinent.* (v.)

397 E.g.:

vult intransitio rectum supponere verbo (v.)

Intransitiva constructio est quando idem casus reguntur a parte post qui reguntur a parte ante; transitiva quando dissimiles. (r)

398 sepe vocans verbum sibi vult apponere rectum
et substantivum vel quod vim servat eorum.
(vv. –)

scilicet, omnia verba pertinentia ad motum vel ad [e]sistentiam vel ad apparentiam sive ad reputationem possunt esse copulativa et similiter participia eorum. (r)

399 est soloecismus incongrua copula vocum

est soloecismus. Donatus ait, solicismus est vitium in contextu partium orationis contra regulas artis gramatice factum. (r; cf. *Ars maior*, . , ed. Keil (–), ,)

400 v: ut vervex, *lo montone*. cortex = id est *scorça*. forfex et forpex = id est *le forfece* et *le forfece picinini.* hec calx id est *la calcina*.

401 ut hec victrix / quia in obliquis sunt vel possunt esse neutri generis

trix tenet hec tamen obliquis neutrum superaddis (v)

402 See e.g. chapter on syntax, r– r.

403 E.g.: v: Accentus est regularis modulatio vocis facta inplatione [*sic*] significativa vel accentus est certa lex que fit per elevationem vocis.

Manuscripts of ***Graecismus*** were circulating in fourteenth-century Italy too:

BML CS	XIII²	France[404]	Possibly in hands of Italian schoolboys by later Trecento, to judge from *probationes* in a XIV/XVc. hand: (v) 'Jacob', 'Fratres'; in Florence by XV²: (r) vellese Fl. / al mancho per tutto agosto altro — [folio cut] venduto.
BNCF CS J. .	June [405]	Possibly Florence[406]	Copious, all-embracing marginal commentary by the copyist. The text and commentary have the appearance of a post-school context, with wide spacing between the few lines of text per page; there is no sign of any reading at all in the manuscript, which may have remained unused before and after its donation to S. Marco.

Besides these French verse grammars, there are also copies in Florentine libraries of the thirteenth-century Italian prose *summe*, showing the continued interest of these texts for the Trecento classroom. It has already been seen that several versions of Tebaldo's *Summa* date from the fourteenth century.[407] The same is true for **Pietro da Isolella**'s textbook:

BML . , – r[408]	XIVc.	Italy	High-quality manuscript, which may still have been intended for school purposes but little read, to judge from excellent condition and negligible glossing.[409]

404 See above, .

405 v: Anno domini M°III^c^XLVI, indictione IIII^a^, die XXVIII° mensis iunii, completus iste Grecismus.

406 (Front flyleaf:) (San Marco shelfmark:) de ° banco ex parte occidentis. (Ownership mark:) Iste liber est Conventus Sancti Marci de Florentia Ordinis Predicatorum, quem donavit dicto conventui reverendus pater Frater Benedictus Dominici de Florentia. Quicumque legerit in eo, oret deum pro eius anima. Amen.

407 See Appendix III.

408 r– r: inc. Ut ad sapientiam per gramaticam venire posimus (Fierville ( ),). expl. ut coniunctiones copulative servent in constructionem o cium copulandi adinvicem [MS: o cium adiuncte] et disiuncte servent o cium disiungendi et de aliis similiter est dicendum. r– v: (Magistri Cesaris, *Notule*) inc. Nota quod partes orationis sunt octo [...] (Fierville ( ),) expl. et non propter significationem inmutandam ut quidam. Explicit liber summe deo gratias.

409 Apart from XVc. title (r: Summa Magistri Petri de Insulella), no annotation except for two brief notabilia (XIVc.) on v– r.

BRF 410	XIV[1]	Tuscan[411]	Heavily annotated only in Trecento: at least four readers (v, – , – , r– r), some leaving vernacular glosses.

:

By introducing the vernacular and adopting a more systematic approach, fourteenth-century grammar teachers gave a definitive shape to the secondary prose *summa* – one which would last throughout the Quattrocento and beyond.[412] If historians looked only at empirical evidence, there would be little justification for dividing the fifteenth from the fourteenth century as a new period in the history of secondary theoretical Latin grammar teaching. In terms of theory and content, the two most overwhelmingly popular and influential fifteenth-century secondary grammars – by Guarino Veronese and Niccolò Perotti – are essentially indistinguishable from those of their Trecento predecessors. But the problem is that Guarino and Perotti were both famous Renaissance humanists, and so historians have felt either determined or at least obliged to discover some kind of significant innovation in their teaching of secondary grammar: since the Latin language was at the heart of the Italian Renaissance, there must have been some major upheaval associated with the approach of Quattrocento humanism to formal grammar in the schoolroom. This is yet another example of writing history backwards: because the teaching of secondary grammar underwent profound changes, under the influence of Renaissance humanism, in the sixteenth and seventeenth centuries, especially in Northern Europe, it has been assumed that this reform movement was initiated and reached a significant stage of development in humanism's cradle, Italy, during the fifteenth century. But this is no more appropriate here

410 folios. r: Inc. Ut ad sapientiam per gramaticam possimus (Fierville ( ),). r: Cum studium gramaticorum precipue circa constructionem versatur, idcirco quedam de constructione, ad instrutionem [MS: indistrutionem] rudium, sub compendio doceamus. Unde videndum est quid sit construtio (Fierville ( )). r: Explicit Summa Magistri Petri deo gratis amen. Nota quod partes orationis sunt (Fierville ( ),) v: Expliciunt notule Magistri Cesaris.

411 Similarities to Pisan-type book production. v: ownership notes, with earliest (XIV[1]) from Bartolomeo di Ser Bianchi from Gambassi near S. Andrea, both Tuscan villages near Certaldo, between S. Gimignano and Castelfiorentino (Ista Summa est Bartolomei Ser Bianci de Ga<m>bassi de campo Sancti Andree k.(?), qui moratur scolis Magistri Pauli de Pistorio, gramaticalis scientie floribus p<...> scolas apud plateam <...>).

412 E.g., thematic translation was normal fare in Lucchese schools in XVIc.: see Barsanti ( ), , . For Venetian and other Tuscan examples, see Grendler ( ), – .

than in other cases of historical development: for Renaissance grammar, as elsewhere, facts are at odds with preconceptions. If the humanists were revolutionaries in the schoolroom, it was not in their formal grammar teaching.

Guarino's *Regule grammaticales*, first mentioned by him in ,[413] fall normally[414] into three sections[415] (not distinguished in the text but useful for analytical purposes): ( ) parts of grammar and phonetics, parts of speech, introduction to nouns and verbs (including agreement); ( ) verbal syntax (personal and impersonal); ( ) more material on nouns and verbs, participles and figures. The following table gives an outline of topics in Guarino's *Regule.*

Bodley Can. misc. r– r	
Parts of speech	
Nouns	
Verbs (including concordance)	
Verbal syntax	
Personals	Passive
Active	simple
simple	possessive
possessive	acquisitive
acquisitive	transitive
transitive	e ective
e ective	absolute
absolute	

[413] Grendler ( ), .

[414] Guarino's *Regule*, like many medieval secondary grammar treatises, exist in no definitive version: in common with similar works by Pietro da Isolella or Filippo di Naddo, there are vast variations in structure and text among manuscript and printed versions. As with *Ianua*, copies or editions were prepared for practical use by teachers, who adapted them according to their own needs. This has made the preparation of a critical edition of Guarino's *Regule* virtually impossible. My impression is that Francesco da Buti's *Regule* exist in a more stable text than do the above three textbooks. I have used the following versions of Guarino's *Regule*: Bodley Can. misc. , r– v, XVmid.; Bodley Can. misc. , r– v, XV², fragmentary at beginning; ASF CStrozz. . , XVmid, r– r, acephalous; Plimpton , r– v, XVmid; Plimpton , XV². I have also examined BML Ashb. , XVmid, apparently an unattributed copy: the sections on heteroclytes, participles, relatives, patronymics and figures all correspond to Guarino's *Regule* (cf. BML Ashb. , r, r– r, r, r– r with ASF CStrozz. . – .) This manuscript has been misdated to XIIIc. by Paoli ( ), , and Sabbadini ( ), , , . On Guarino's textual instability, see Percival (a) *passim.*

[415] Percival (a), .

Neutral
- copulative
- acquisitive
- transitive
- effective
- passive
- neutropassive
- possessive
- absolute

Common
- Deponent
  - possessive
  - acquisitive
  - transitive
  - effective
  - passive
  - absolute

Impersonals
Phonetics
Interrogatives
Proper, appellative nouns
Supines
Gerunds
Participles
Comparatives
Superlatives
Relatives
Heteroclyte nouns
Derivative verbs
Patronymics
Distributives
Partitives
Figures[416]

It will be seen that this is the same overall structure already encountered in Francesco da Buti's *Regule* and other fourteenth-century *summe*. Other common features among Guarino and fourteenth-century Italian secondary grammarians are: ( ) subdivisions of verbal types, followed by lists with vernacular equivalents;[417] ( ) mnemonic verses;[418] ( ) thematic translations;[419] ( ) a concentration on the declinable parts of speech; ( ) a preoccupation with syntax, as revealed by the usual scholastic syntactical vocabulary (*post se*, *ante se*, *regere*, *antecedens*, *suppositum*)[420] and a discussion of only the normal eight figures of construction (*prolempsis*, *silempsis*, *zeugma*, *sintosis*, *antitosis*, *evocatio*, *appositio*, *sinedoche*);[421] ( ) invented

416 Plimpton and , Bodley Can. misc. , r– v, ASF CStrozz. . , r– r, include similar topics. In Plimpton , active and passive verbs are not individually named; in CStrozz. active verbs are divided according to seven *maneries* but not named individually. Can. misc. , r– v is acephalous, beginning in the middle of the section on deponent possessive verbs: inc. <pre>positione persone patientis; Bursill-Hall's version of *incipit* ( ), , is inaccurate.

417 For published example, see Percival (a), .

418 Mnemonic verses are ubiquitous in Guarino's *Regule*. E.g. ASF CStrozz. . , r:

Que dant splendorem caruere cuncta supina,
Excipias unum quidem, dat fulgeo fulsum.

Grendler ( ), , recognizes that Guarino's 'use of a mnemonic verse was, again, a typically medieval feature.' Percival notes that for 'each [verbal] subclass' there is 'a set of mnemonic verses': ( ), . For further discussion of Guarino's mnemonics, see Percival ( ), – .

419 E.g. ASF CStrozz. . , r: Si detur thema per participium quod non invenitur vel si non habeat vulgare sui verbi, fiat latinum per relativum et verbum, ut *Nicolao sbandente Piero poco scrive* dicatur 'Nicolaus a quo exulat Petrus parum scribit'. Si vero ponatur in consequentia fiat per 'dum', 'donec' et 'postquam', ut *Le gallee venute tu legi*, 'post[quam] triremes venerunt tu legis'; *Ghuerrino apreçando le virtù Francesco studia*, 'Postquam a Guerrino virtus licet Franciscus studet'.

420 Discussed at length by Percival ( ), ( ), (a).

421 ASF CStrozz. . , v– r.

examples;[422] ( ) the concept of a natural word order, presupposed by the terms *ante se, post se.*[423]

It has been stated that Guarino's work 'di ers from a grammar like that of Francesco da Buti in that it dispenses with the explanatory concepts and the modistic terminology; it also makes sparing use of the terms *suppositum* and *appositum*'.[424] This statement, although accurate, can result in a misleading impression. In the first place, not all versions of Guarino dispensed with the explanatory concepts derived from French logical philosophy of language: for example, Plimpton MS includes the following: (r) per naturam cause finalis; (v) ex natura pretii vel cause materialis; (r) per naturam acquisitionis; (r) causam materialem; (v) per naturam separationis; (r) ex natura actus illati ab altero; (r) ex natura cause materialis; (r) ex natura acquisitionis; (v) ex natura cause e cientis; (v) ex natura cause materialis; (v) ex natura cause e cientis. Secondly, although Francesco da Buti uses modistic grammatical terminology, this does not constitute the essential content, structure or approach of his secondary grammar: it was part of the baggage of French scholastic grammatical terminology which he, like other Italian Due- and Trecento grammarians, had inherited and still employed; but it did not form an inherent part of Francesco's language theory (unlike the ideas of natural word order or governance, which were essential aspects of his approach to grammar). Thirdly, the vocabulary of scholastic language theory, insofar as it was extraneous to the pedagogic purposes of fourteenth-century Italian teachers, had already been abandoned by some Trecento grammarians. For example, Goro d'Arezzo, writing a hundred years before Guarino, never used the terms *suppositum* or *appositum* (nor any modistic terminology, for that matter).[425]

Where Guarino significantly di ers from Francesco da Buti or even Filippo di Naddo, as Sabbadini[426] and Percival have correctly observed,

[422] See e.g. above, , n. .

[423] See Rizzo's latest judgement ( ) on Guarino's *Regule*: 'sono del tutto tradizionali per dottrina, terminologia, struttura, e la lingua stessa in cui sono scritte non è esente da medievalismi lessicali (per es. vocaboli come *cappa* o espressioni avverbiali come *de usu, per prius* e *per posterius*) e sintattici (per es. l'uso di *quod* invece dell'accusativo con l'infinito e di *quod* per *ut* consecutivo)' ( ). This correct view of Guarino, based on the work of Percival ( ) and ( ), ultimately goes back to Sabbadini, e.g. ( ), : 'nella distribuzione della materia e nel metodo della trattazione nulla egli [sc. Guarino] aggiunse di proprio'. See Percival ( ), .

[424] Percival ( ), . [425] Ed. Marchesi ( ), – *passim.*

[426] Sabbadini seems to have been the first to suggest that Guarino's shortening of treatment inherited from XIVc. grammarians such as Francesco da Buti constituted a grammatical reform; e.g. ( ), : 'Una riforma spetta certamente a Guarino, quella di avere il più possibile semplificato e ridotto alle minime proporzioni lo schema grammaticale e d'avere con la rinomanza della sua scuola e l'autorià del sapere imposto agli altri il suo schema.'

is in the brevity of his treatment.[427] His *Regule grammaticales* o er a basic outline of the secondary grammar course as first defined by Alexander of Villedieu and given its definitive method and shape by Trecento grammarians such as Francesco da Buti, but it does so with far greater conciseness. And yet not even here was Guarino an innovator: Goro d'Arezzo had already produced a set of *Regule parve* in the first half of the fourteenth century,[428] stripped of their inessential modistic and scholastic paraphernalia.

The significant di erence between Guarino, on the one hand, and Francesco da Buti and most of his Trecento colleagues, on the other, is in their respective relationships to *Doctrinale*. Francesco da Buti and other writers of prose *summe* in the thirteenth and fourteenth centuries intended to o er an alternative to *Doctrinale*: in general, Due- and Trecento Italian grammarians used *Doctrinale* principally as a mine of verse mnemonics to reinforce their prose precepts, which were intended to stand in place of Alexander's verse rules.[429] But for Guarino, *Doctrinale* was meant to supplement, not just to reinforce, his jejune grammar precepts, as is made clear by his son Battista.[430] Guarino's *Regule* served in his school as an introduction to the more detailed treatment found in *Doctrinale*, a work which not only repeats in greater detail topics already covered in Guarino's manual such as heteroclytes, comparatives, derivative verbs, syntax and figures but also ones not treated by Guarino, such as nominal genders and declensions, perfects and supines, and prosody. As far as textbooks are concerned, Guarino's secondary theoretical grammar course was conceived in two stages: first his *Regule* and then *Doctrinale*. It is no wonder that manuscript copies of *Doctrinale* proliferated in Quattrocento Italy.[431] In one important sense, Guarino was even

427 In supplementing Percival's fundamental analysis of Guarino's *Regule*, Grendler ( ), – , makes the following two points: 'Guarino broke with the past in several ways. The first, obvious point is that he wrote his own manual […] Guarino innovated through reorganization […] Guarino's organization of the content seems more direct and streamlined than that of his predecessors.' However, if writing one's own manual turned a grammarian into an innovator, then Bene da Firenze, Pietro da Isolella, Tebaldo, Filippo di Naddo, Goro d'Arezzo, Francesco da Buti and many other anonymous XIII and XIVc. secondary grammar masters 'broke with the past' in just the same way as Guarino did. It is also imprecise to say that Guarino reorganized the material in his *Regule*: he merely abbreviated it (in comparison with Francesco da Buti but not with Goro d'Arezzo: see below, n.).

428 Marchesi ( ) had already pointed to striking similarity between Goro's and Guarino's treatment: ( ) 'E veramente queste regole di Goro presentano grande somiglianza con le famose *regulae* guariniane'; see – for examples. 429 See above, .

430 Cited by Percival ( ), , n. : 'Ad eam sententiam [sc. numerosam orationem] non inutilis erit is liber, qui sub Alexandri nomine versibus habetur, ex quo etiam praeteritorum verbi et generum nominis et declinationum formulas percipient.' See Garin ( ), ; Sabbadini ( ), . 431 See below, .

more conservative than Francesco da Buti and his Italian predecessors and contemporaries: he reinstated *Doctrinale* as an essential stage of, not just a supplement to, the secondary grammar curriculum.[432]

Although Guarino[433] can in no way be considered a reformer of grammar education along humanist lines, the same cannot be stated quite so categorically of two of his fellow humanist teachers who left manuscript evidence of their teaching practice at the secondary level. One was Guarino's contemporary, the humanist Sozomeno da Pistoia (–), who taught many sons of the Florentine élite in the first half of the fifteenth century.[434] Much of his teaching was at the post-grammatical level, including his appointment to lecture on poetry and rhetoric at the Florentine Studio in the academic year – ;[435] nevertheless, he also taught grammar in Florence: he was asked to tutor the *nipote* of a cardinal during Eugenius IV's Florentine residence,[436] and he was employed as one of the public grammar teachers in Florence by the Studio o cials in – .[437] The only surviving document of Sozomeno's activity as a teacher of secondary theoretical grammar is Bodley Lat. misc. e. , a manuscript 'dating from some time after '.[438] This manuscript, written by Sozomeno himself, does not constitute a formal grammar treatise, like those by Francesco da Buti or Guarino, but consists of a set of notes on nearly all the usual grammatical topics covered in the secondary syllabus: although he himself refers to the manuscript once as a *tractatus*,[439] the autograph alterations and

432 Pairing of Guarino's *Regule* and *Doctrinale* in later Quattrocento Italy is highlighted in a petition of from the communal grammar teacher of Sarzana, Giovanni Meduseo, to the town council: 'più di sei volte lecte et rilecte le reguli [*sic*] de la gramatica secondo Guarino e maistro Alexandro' (Mannucci ( ),).

Another way in which Guarino was more conservative than his Trecento predecessors is that his section on heteroclyte nouns is mainly in verse (recalling the treatment in chapter of *Doctrinale*) whereas Francesco da Buti and his fellow XIII and XIVc. Italian school-level grammarians had treated topic in prose, like Priscian.

433 Another Guarinian-type grammar, with usual traditional elements (thematic translation, verb lists with vernacular equivalents, emphasis on verbal syntax, mnemonic verses), was copied by Ma eo Valaresso di Giorgio, future apostolic pronotary and archbishop of Zara (d.), at Venice as a schoolboy in : see Segarizzi (– a); however, its colophon, with ubiquitous ownership formula 'Ista regule sunt mei Mafei [...]', followed by the date of copying ('fate de otubrio [...]', is no indication of authorship, as maintained by Segarizzi (– a), . Without further evidence, these grammar rules are to be regarded as an anonymous work copied by Valaresso.

434 Vespasiano (–), , – .

435 Gherardi ( ), ; Park ( ), .

436 Vespasiano (–), , .

437 Park ( ), . On Sozomeno's teaching activities in general, see Cesarini Martinelli ( ), – .

438 According to Richard Hunt and Albinia de la Mare, as related to Keith Percival: see Percival ( ), , n. .

439 Bodley Lat. misc. e. , r: de primis syllabis quere in principio huius tractatus.

annotations suggest a working copy rather than a formal treatise; moreover, there is no evidence that the text ever circulated, nor was it mentioned by Vespasiano da Bisticci as one of his works (unlike his *Chronicon universale*, which was first copied and distributed by Vespasiano himself).[440] Nevertheless, these notes must constitute Sozomeno's teaching materials as a grammar master. By the s he was already a sophisticated humanist scholar: there is no way that he would have compiled this kind of school-level grammatical miscellany except as a teacher.[441]

Bodley Lat. misc. e. shows some signs of an attempt to reform grammar teaching along recognizeably humanist lines at the secondary level. In the first place, there are no vernacular phrases or sentences, nor any thematic translations, although he does give vernacular translations of listed verbs.[442] Secondly, there is only one example of a medieval mnemonic verse; this is an unacknowledged quotation of *Doctrinale*, vv. – .[443] Thirdly, Sozomeno even introduces a Greek etymology at one point.[444] Most importantly, although the occasional Trecento grammarian such as Pietro da Asolo had cited examples from the Roman classics, it is still indicative of humanist inclinations that Sozomeno frequently gives classical examples of various grammatical usages, citing Vergil,[445] Priscian,[446] Servius,[447] Augustine,[448] Lucan,[449] Ovid,[450] Statius,[451] Juvenal,[452] Ennius,[453] Horace[454] and Boethius.[455] Nevertheless, it must be conceded that these humanist touches do not go to the heart of Sozomeno's Latin teaching, which remains essentially traditional. In the first place, his syllabus is the conventional secondary fare, derived in direct lineage from Alexander of Villedieu and the Italian prose *summe* of the thirteenth and fourteenth centuries.[456] Secondly, his

440 Vespasiano (–), , – .

441 For Percival's changing views of this manuscript, see ( ), – ; ( ), , n. .

442 See Cesarini Martinelli ( ), – for a few examples of these translated verbs.

443 v: protesis [s]upponit caput, aferesisque recidit.
Sincopa de medio tollit quod epentesis auget.
Aufert apocopa finem quem dat paragoge.

444 r: ut perizona. Nam dicitur épÒ toË per, circum, ka¤z nh, cintura.

445 v, r, v, r, r, v, r, v, r, v, r, v, v, r, v.

446 v, r, r. 447 r, r. 448 v. 449 v, v, r.

450 r, r, v, v, v. 451 r, v. 452 r, v, v. 453 v. 454 r. 455 v.

456 Verbal syntax: active/passive verbs (divided into unnamed sub-classes); neutral verbs: copulative, possessive, acquisitive, transitive, e ective, absolute, passive; neutro-passive verbs; deponent verbs (partially divided into unnamed sub-classes): transitive, e ective, absolute. Verbal conjugations. Interrogatives. Phonetics. Nominal declensions. Preterites and supines. Nominal accidence: gender, number, figure, case. Impersonal verbs. Gerunds, supines, infinitives. Verbals. Derivative verbs. Relatives. Nominal types (possessive, adjectival, patronymic, etc.) Comparatives. Superlatives. Conjunctions. Figures (mainly of construction). Prosody. Prepositions. Adverbs. Interjections.

language theory and vocabulary are entirely traditional, making ubiquitous use of scholastic terms such as *ante se*, *post se* and *regere*. Thirdly, when treating verbal syntax, Sozomeno classifies verbs according to the usual subdivisions with the conventional nomenclature. Fourthly, in common with most secondary grammarians since Alexander of Villedieu, he concentrates on the declinable parts of speech, devoting only three pages to prepositions, adverbs and interjections (v– v). Fifthly, he provides the traditional vernacular translations for the lists of verbs in every syntactical subcategory. Finally, although he does cite classical examples, he makes much more extensive use of invented phrases and sentences to illustrate grammatical points. Sozomeno obviously wanted to steer secondary grammar in a humanist direction, but it is clear that he did not know how to do without the scholastic superstructure of grammatical theory, methodology, curriculum and terminology inherited from the French and Italian grammatical traditions of the twelfth to fourteenth centuries.

Another notable humanist teacher who wrote his own secondary grammar manual[457] was Gaspare da Verona, himself a pupil of Guarino's.[458] While the latter's famous grammar had no discernibly distinctive humanist characteristics, the same cannot fairly be said of Gaspare's *Regule*, written in Rome *c.* .[459] Whereas Guarino o ered only invented Latin examples to illustrate various grammatical points, Gaspare ubiquitously cites classical authors, including Cicero,[460] Terence,[461] Statius,[462] Horace,[463] Vergil,[464] Juvenal,[465] Lucan,[466] Ovid,[467] Plautus,[468] Sallust,[469] Aulus Gellius[470] and Quintilian,[471] as well as ancient grammarians and commentators such as Servius[472] and Priscian.[473] Moreover, the work seems to contain no mnemonic verses, and in general there is much less vernacular than in Guarino and his Trecento predecessors. In overall scope, nevertheless, Gaspare's grammar was not innovatory, covering the traditional secondary

[457] I used manuscripts BRF , XV^2; BML . , XV^2; and ASF Carte Bardi . , r– r (finished October : r). [458] Grendler ( ), .
[459] Percival ( ), – . [460] BRF , r, r, r, r, v, v, r, r, r, r, v.
[461] BRF , r, v, r, v, r, v, r, v, v, v. [462] BRF , v, r.
[463] BRF , r, r.
[464] BRF , r, v, r, r, v, r, r, v, v, r, v, v, r, r, v, v, r, v, r, v, v, r, v, r, r, v, v, v, r. [465] BRF , r, v. [466] BRF , r, r.
[467] BRF , v, r, v, v. [468] BRF , r, r, v.
[469] BRF , r, v. [470] BRF , r. [471] BRF , v.
[472] BRF , r, v, v, v, r.
[473] BRF , v, r, v, r, v, v, v, v.

grammar syllabus.[474] Other traditional features are lists of verbs provided with vernacular translations and divided into the usual subclasses, the standard syntactical vocabulary (*ante se, post se*),[475] and invented Latin sentences. Moreover, although Gaspare obviously made an e ort to exclude vernacular sentences and thematic translations, he did not entirely succeed.[476] Gaspare da Verona wanted to introduce humanist reforms into secondary grammar, but his attempt was shallow: he did not know how to dispense with the traditional curricular superstructure, nor with its terminology and conceptual framework.[477]

Sozomeno and Gaspare tried – however superficially – to introduce humanist elements into their formal grammar teaching, and the same was true of the great humanist, Niccolò Perotti, whose textbook,

474 BRF : verbal syntax (r– r), relatives (r– r), interrogatives (r– r), distributives (r–v), partitives (v); participles (v– v), patronymics (v– v), comparatives (v– r), superlatives (r– r), adverbs (r– r), figures (r– v), heteroclyte nouns (v– v).

475 The term *suppositum* seems to have been used only once; see BML . , r: pro supposito.

476 BML . : v– r: Ideo notentur hec themata: *Tu mi ralegri. Tu mi puoi ralegrare.* Gaudeo te. Possum gaudere te. *Io sono amato da te. Io posso essere amato da te* [...]; (r) Ideo notentur nonnulla themata. *Questo mancha di pentirsi de' suoi peccati.* Hunc desinit penitere suorum peccatorum [...]

477 Another grammarian with reformist tendencies who nevertheless clung to the traditional medieval format of prose *summa* was Valla's pupil, Bartolomeo da Sulmona, whose work, datable between and , most closely resembled Gaspare Veronese's grammar. See Percival (b), Percival and Pascal ( ), Rizzo ( ); both Percival and Rizzo emphasize the mixed character of Bartolomeo's grammar, with the influence of Valla's new principles of usage combined with traditional features such as invented sentences.

Another grammar by a well-known humanist, produced in the later XVc., was the so-called *Canones grammatices* by Cantalicio (Giambattista Valentini). This book, which enjoyed modest incunabular circulation (*IGI* , ; *GW* –), was advertised by the author 'ad magistros grammatices' as a work in which 'Non hic barbariem notabis ullam' (Rome edition: BL shelf-mark .d. , A iiii verso), but he in fact o ered a thoroughly traditional secondary grammar, laden with vernacular and thematic translations and following the standard Italian syllabus inherited from XIIIc. and XIVc.: phonetics, nouns, verbs, verbal construction with the usual categories and lists including vernacular equivalents, impersonal verbs, gerunds, supines, participles, relatives, interrogatives, distributives, partitives, patronymics, comparatives, superlatives, adverbs of place, heteroclytes, figures of construction. One small novel feature may perhaps have been the inclusion of additional stylistic figures at the end of the treatise, recalling Pomponio Leto's treatment (see below,). This treatise was normally accompanied by brief *Canones metrices*, also written for boys and calling to mind Perotti's similar e orts (see below,). On this work, see Morici ( ), and n. . Another grammar by an Italian humanist was written by Ognibene de' Bonisoli *c.* for the children of Ludovico Gonzaga, duke of Mantua. The first half deals with the generation of nominal and verbal forms; the second is a simple dialogue between master and pupil, treating the eight parts of speech and their accidence. Although there is no treatment of syntax, the level of the treatise is secondary, since there are no paradigms; the material is traditional, the first half recalling *Doctrinale*'s treatment of noun and verb endings, the second elaborating *Ianua*'s presentation of accidence. A further resemblance to *Doctrinale* is the inclusion of a treatise on metre at the end. The work had several incunabular printings (see *IGI*, –); BNCF CS J. . is a manuscript copy of the Padua edition (*IGI*,): see. v for the copied colophon.

Rudimenta grammatices,[478] written in ,[479] became the most popular secondary grammar since the publication of *Doctrinale* and *Graecismus* at the turn of the thirteenth century.[480] Like Sozomeno and Gaspare, Perotti evidently disliked the non-classical practice of introducing mnemonic verse into grammar teaching, and there is only one occasion on which he reverted to this practice, adding a couplet to aid the recollection of common verbs.[481] Similarly, Perotti sometimes cited ancient authors and texts to illustrate grammatical points,[482] including Horace,[483] Pliny,[484] Sallust[485] and the Bible.[486]

[478] On this work, the fundamental study is Percival ( ). I read the text in the Rome (Hain ; *IGI* n. , p.) and Naples (BRF Edizioni rare) editions.
BRF was said by Kristeller ( ), , to contain a copy of the section of the *Rudimenta* on epistolography: 'l'ultima sezione dei *Rudimenta* che si intitola *De componendis epistolis* e che fu copiata e stampata anche a parte', citing in substantiation 'Ricc. ' (n.). However, the section of this manuscript treating epistolography (v– v: Inc. Sequitur Sepuntinus. Epistola igitur cum plane vocabulum est diciturque a greco [...] Expl. Exordia et rationes et artificio confirmatione etc.) consists of brief extracts; it is not a copy of whole section on epistolography, e.g.:

BRF	Perotti (Naples) (n.n.)
v: Epistola grecum plane vocabulum est. diciturque a greco épÒ toË §pist°llein quod mittere significat. Inde apostoli. Titus Livius apostolos suos fregit in senatu id est epistolas. Tres sunt dicendi caracteres amplius medius et infimus [...]	De componendis epistolis. Quare invente sunt epistole [...] Unde dicitur epistola. Epistola grecum sane vocabulum est diciturque hoc est a mittendo quod ad absentes mittatur. Unde eciam, quod similiter significat, dicuntur apostoli. Titus Livius apostolos suos fregit in senatu hoc est epistolas et nunc libelli qui a iudicibus a quibus provocatus est [...] Quid in primis observandum est in epistolis scribendis [...] Nam ut in ceteris tres sunt dicendi caracteres amplius medius et infimus, ita eciam epistole tres suos caracteres habent ab illis tamen diversos [...]

Similarly, the other sections of this manuscript identified by the scribe as from Perotti are also extracts, not complete copies, of the corresponding parts of *Rudimenta*.

[479] Percival ( ), .

[480] On the work's rapid di usion in Florence, see BNCF Magl. VI. , text of Cicero's *De inventione* (r– r), XV² before (see rear flyleaf verso: a dì <...> di março veni a stare ad Artimino nel), containing unattributed excerpts made from Perotti's grammar on v– v (compared with Rome edition, Hain). This manuscript probably had something to do with Niccolò di Ugolino Martelli: (v) Ricordo come a dì di genaio ebi dal fatore di Nicholò Martelli cioè Francesco da Pistoia suo fatore alla botegha del batilozo Fl. larghi [...] Called 'reghole supuntine pe' fanciulli', 'regole sepontine', 'regole sepontie', 'rigole di Sepuntino' or 'reghole di Sepontino' or 'reghole serpentine', this book found its way into the hands of pupils from households of Filippo Strozzi, Niccolò Strozzi, Antonio Gondi and Alessandro Capponi between and : see ASF CStrozz. . ; ASF CStrozz. . ; ASF Carte Gondi ; ASF CStrozz. . . According to Milde ( ), there are incunabular editions and Cinquecentine. For copy owned by a probable Venetian teacher in , see Connell ( ), .

[481] Percival ( ), : only set of mnemonics in the text.

[482] See Percival ( ), [483] Percival ( ), , . [484] Percival ( ), .

[485] In the section on infinitives: Naples edition is unpaginated.

[486] In the section on relatives, he cites the Bible twice. It has also been suggested that the *Rudimenta* was 'chiefly distinguished from earlier works in the genre by its exclusion of many words and

But more arguably innovatory than these desultory nods in the direction of humanist preferences was the *Rudimenta*'s presentation: this kind of change had little to do with the revival of antiquity but rather reflected the pragmatic sense and experience of a working teacher. One such new departure was Perotti's linking together of elementary and secondary grammar.[487] Ever since the publication of Donatus's *Ars minor* in late antiquity, there had been a clear division between the early stages of grammar and more advanced study. Even when medieval grammarians significantly departed from Donatus's approach with the parsing grammar, they nevertheless maintained a distinct level for elementary Latin, consisting of an introduction to the parts of speech, their accidence and their morphology: works such as *Ianua* and *Dominus quae pars est* were normally circulated as separate texts in the middle ages.[488] Perotti, however, deviated from this practice by joining together a treatise on morphology, corresponding to *Ianua*, with a secondary grammar. Perotti does not explain why he made this innovation, but it has been suggested above that, by the second half of the fifteenth century, the study of *Ianua* had tended to be down-graded from a full-scale introduction to Latin morphology to a basic reading system, and Perotti may have felt the need to cover once again the same material to which his pupils had already been exposed in *Ianua*.[489] It is clear, however, that he intended his section on morphology not to replace but rather to supplement *Ianua*. This is evident from the fact that the first section of his treatise includes not only the material contained in *Ianua* (definitions, accidence, paradigms of the parts of speech) but also subject matter normally treated at the secondary level, such as the formation of preterites and supines.[490]

Another novelty in the *Rudimenta* was the composition of the entire

footnote (*cont.*)
types of construction which derived from medieval, as opposed to classical Latin [...] Vocabulary which had been in general use in late medieval Latin was now subjected to careful historical and philological scrutiny' (Jensen (b), ; see also Jensen ( ), – ,). Although this characterization is occasionally valid in the case of some of Perotti's verb lists, it is misleading to suggest that this feature somehow dominates the work, which is in fact overwhelmingly traditional, as demonstrated not only by Percival, but reiterated by Rizzo ( ), in her list of vocabulary, usages and construction by Perotti which have no basis in classical Latin but rather derive from medieval school grammatical practice (, ,). It was inevitable that an avant-garde humanist such as Perotti, writing in the mid-Quattrocento, would purge his verb lists of obviously unclassical vocabulary, but when it came to tackling genuinely problematic aspects of the medieval teaching tradition, such as vernacular translation, scholastic syntactical theory and invented examples not found in classical authors, Perotti opted for the path of tradition rather than innovation (see below,).

487 Percival ( ), , points out that Perotti may have been aware that Pomponio Leto was writing or had already written both a morphology and a syntactical treatise; see ibid. .

488 See ch. above.

489 See above, .

490 Percival ( ), . See above, .

treatise in terms of questions and answers.[491] This approach was familiar, of course, through the format of both Donatus's *Ars minor* and *Ianua*, but it had not normally been extended to secondary grammars in the middle ages. Perotti's reason for taking this new departure may have had to do with his abandonment of mnemonic verses. Like all grammar teachers, he was inevitably concerned with the memorization of rules and vocabulary, as is clear, for example, in one of the pedagogic norms included at the beginning of the *Rudimenta*: 'Quod est primum ingenii signum in pueris? Memoria.'[492] The path to easier memorization opened by Alexander in *Doctrinale* was now closed, and so Perotti seems to have turned, as an alternative method, to the catechetical format which pupils had already been used to memorizing in *Ianua*. This new type of presentation was, strictly speaking, unclassical for a post-elementary grammar, but at least it was closely related to an ancient text such as Donatus's *Ars minor* and so was nearer to classical practice than the entirely unclassical verse format of *Doctrinale* and its imitators.

A concern with memory is also apparent in another of Perotti's innovations. In presenting the usual grammatical material, Perotti o ered a series of numbered rules, for example eight in the case of the first nominal declension.[493] He followed the same practice for nominal genders (rules); second, third and fourth nominal declensions (rules each); fifth-declension nouns (rules); first and second verbal conjugations (rules each); preterites of the first (rules), second (rules), third (rules) and fourth (rule) conjugation; and supines (rules). With numbered rules serving as an *aide-mémoire*, Perotti illustrated how pupils were meant to determine the accusative of first-declension nouns.[494] Precepts in numerical order were not, strictly speaking, Perotti's invention: they also appear, it has been seen above, in the thirteenth-century secondary manual on construction by Tebaldo,[495] as well as in the anonymous treatise on casual syntax appended to Tebaldo's tractate in several manuscripts.[496] Nevertheless, there is no sign that Perotti knew Tebaldo's work and it was probably through Perotti's example that this practice spread in European pedagogy in the sixteenth century.[497]

[491] Percival ( ), . [492] Percival ( ), . [493] Percival ( ), .

[494] Poeta quomodo facit in accusativo singulari? Poetam. Per quam regulam? Per tertiam prime declinationis qua notatur quot accusativus singularis in -am vel in -am vel in -m terminatur ut poetam, Eneam et Enchisem. [495] See above, .

[496] Inc. Exigentia casuum tractaturi: BML AD v– r; BML Strozzi , r– r.

[497] See for example the twenty precepts or the laws of history to be observed by boys, written by Josse Badius Ascensius and published in , which have been partly edited by Renouard ( ), , – .

Although to some extent innovatory from the teaching viewpoint, Perotti's *Rudimenta grammatices* were thoroughly conservative in terms of syllabus, grammatical theory and use of the vernacular. Perotti's secondary grammatical curriculum was entirely traditional, not only recalling Guarino's syllabus[498] but also the normal secondary grammar course going back to the Italian prose *summe* of the thirteenth and fourteenth centuries and ultimately to *Doctrinale.*[499] Similarly conventional was Perotti's treatment of verbs, divided into the usual syntactical categories and accompanied by vernacular translations,[500] and he also included numerous invented sentences to illustrate grammatical points.[501] He constantly employed the normal scholastic syntactical vocabulary, including *suppositum*, *ante se*, *post se*, *res agens*, *res patiens*[502] and *regere.*[503] Particularly notable is the text's use of thematic translation, a Trecento practice entirely eschewed by Sozomeno and avoided by Gaspare but indulged in with little restraint by Perotti.[504] Although Perotti introduced a number of teaching changes, in terms of grammatical content his treatise was almost entirely traditional, not even going as far as either Sozomeno or Gaspare in bringing secondary grammar into line with current humanist trends. The tremendous success enjoyed by the *Rudimenta grammatices* was probably due mainly to the fame of their author; it is hard to believe that his limited teaching innovations, interesting though they may seem, commanded as much appeal as Perotti's reputation at a time when humanist and classical fashion were so powerful. Humanist educators had not discovered a new philosophy of language suitable to the classroom to replace the scholastic terminology and theory dominant in schools since the twelfth century, and so they simply recycled the old product in updated packaging.[505]

498 Percival ( ), , who also gives a list of Perotti's topics.

499 See above, . 500 Percival ( ), . 501 Percival ( ), , , , etc.

502 Percival ( ), – .

503 Usually Perotti uses the Priscianic term *exigere*, but in the section on comparatives he writes: Quot modis non potest comparativum regere nominativum cum quam [...]

504 E.g.: Si vero thema daretur in passiva significatione in qua hoc participium presentis et preteriti imperfecti temporis non reperitur, aut resolvendum est in verbum quod reperitur aut passiva significatio thematis in activa convertenda hoc modo: *legendosi Virgilio dal maestro el se impareia*, si legeretur a magistro Virgilius disceretur aut magistro legente Virgilium disceretur.

Perotti was not the only avant-garde humanist to employ thematic translation as a teaching tool in the later XVc.: in , Poliziano gave vernacular passages followed by Latin translations to his pupil Piero de' Medici. See Poliziano ( ), – .

505 Percival's statement that Perotti 'broke new ground by adding to his grammar a manual of epistolary style' (,) needs revision; some manuscripts of Francesco da Buti's *Regule* combine his secondary grammar rules with an epistolography: see e.g. BRF and Bodley Lat. misc. e. . Also XIIIc. *summe* by Sion da Vercelli, Giovanni di Pigna and Pietro da Isolella included treatments of *dictamen*.

Disquiet over the conventional conservativism of the secondary syllabus was already evident in the teaching and writings of Sozomeno, Gaspare and Perotti, and it was almost inevitable that a more extreme approach would emerge as humanism became more militant during the second half of the fifteenth century. Such a radical solution to the problem of secondary grammar teaching was o ered by the Roman humanist and teacher, Pomponio Leto, in a group of linked treatises written in the late s and early s.[506]

The entire work was written for the secondary level. The overall scope of the treatise corresponds to *Doctrinale*, dealing with individual parts of speech, syntax, prosody and construction:

[506] Grammars of Pomponio Leto are discussed by Ruysschaert ( ), – . See also Ruysschaert ( ); Zabughin (–), , – , – ; Percival ( ), – ; Rizzo ( ), – . Ruysschaert identified the following versions of Leto's grammatical texts: BAV Vat. Lat. , , , ; BML Ashb. and the incunable of preserved in MS collection as Reg. lat. (see *IGI*, n. : Venice,). BAV Vat. Lat. is described by Ruysschaert ( ), – . Ruysschaert sees five stages of Pomponio's grammatical work. The first is *Romulus*, of which the earliest version is BAV Vat. Lat. ; then comes *Fabius*, dedicated to Angelo Fasolo, bishop of Feltre, at the latest in ; then the metrical treatise, datable to before ; then the version contained in BAV Vat. Lat. , dedicated to Thomas James, castellan of Sant'Angelo, in spring , a reworking of *Romulus*, with a long historical introduction; finally the incunabular edition of , a resumé of all the preceding treatises. According to Ruysschaert, *Fabius* was written at the latest in – or – , but could also date from – or even – , at the beginning of his teaching. According to the dedicatory letter of *Fabius* to Fasolo, it was written to replace a barbarous Latin grammar which had recently become available in Rome; Ruysschaert has no secure solution to the enigma of whose grammar Leto is trying to replace here, but does suggest it might be a lost work of Valla's. Could it be Perotti's? Ruysschaert suggests the author may be dead, but this seems uncertain. Bursill-Hall ( ) gives a number of other grammatical manuscripts attributed to Leto not cited by Ruysschaert: Berlin Staatsbibliothek Preussch. Kulturbesitz MS Lat. O. ; Munich Staatsbibliothek clm. ; Venice Marciana lat. (.); Terni Biblioteca Comunale cod. .

The apparent reference to Pomponio's edition of Varro in the preface of *Romulus* (BML Ashb. , v:

Ipsa [Ipse MS] tua infoelix sum, pugnax [pugnas MS] Romule, lingua.
Ni iuvet inceptum Romula terra suum
Iamque palatini perierunt fulmine [fulmina MS] cives.
Incedit laceris Roma superba comis.
Est et averuncum [*sic*] omne mihi, sed gratulor uno;
Filia nunc tanti nuncupor esse ducis.
Aedidit in lucem me nuper Iulius et se
Commendat capiti, Romule dive, tuo)

which appeared in – (*IGI*, , , n. ; Hain ; *STC* , : Rome, Georg Lauer, with dedication to Bartolomeo Platina; BML copy: D'Elci) would seem to rule out earlier dates proposed by Ruysschaert.

I used BML Ashb. for Pomponio's grammatical texts. This Ashburnham manuscript is cited also by Manacorda ( ), , , but not identified as Pomponio's and considered as a pre-humanist grammar (see Ruysschaert ( ), n.).

BML Ashb. :

r– v: Treatise on parts of speech, entitled *Romulus*
r– v: Treatise on construction, entitled *Fabius*
r– v: Treatise on figures
r– r: Metric treatise

Despite its ostensible resemblance to *Ianua*, even *Romulus* is not actually an elementary morphology:[507] although it treats all eight parts of speech and includes full paradigms, nevertheless it also covers, like the first part of Perotti's *Rudimenta*, material normally treated in secondary grammar, such as heteroclyte nouns, comparatives and superlatives;[508] moreover, its length and detail show that Pomponio was writing for a more advanced readership than a mere beginning Latin class.

Nevertheless it is also clear that throughout this work Pomponio had children in mind. For example, in the preface to *Fabius* Pomponio declared that his work would please youth through its sweet and delicate flavours; if it should be o ensive to the learned, he asked them to bear in mind the di erence between writing for scholars and children.[509] Similarly, in the preface to the treatise on figures he declared that he had tried to adopt a tone and style which would be beneficial to boys' progress.[510]

Like all other humanist secondary grammars in the Quattrocento, Pomponio's treatises preserved some traditional elements. Not only did the overall scope of the treatise resemble the curriculum established by *Doctrinale*, but Pomponio intended a progression from morphology to syntax, reflecting the structure of elementary and grammatical education prevailing since the thirteenth century.[511] In *Romulus*, the treatise on the

507 Ruysschaert's ( ) description of *Romulus* as 'un manuel de lexicographie' ( ) is misleading: it is a treatise on the parts of speech, not a lexicon or a vocabulary treatise.

508 BML Ashb. , v– r.

509 BML Ashb. , v: Igitur quantum ad puerilem illam institutionem pertinere videtur tantum ex dictorum voluminibus accepisse satis est. Scio teneram etatem hoc veluti novis cibis potius delectari quam fastidire praesertim dulci quodam ac suavi sapore conditis [conditos MS]. Et si aliquid hic fuerit quod doctas et nimis eruditas aures o enderit, oro, iudices, operis mei parcite. Aliud enim est cum doctis, aliud cum pueris loqui. Illi gravitatem et pondera verborum desiderant. Hi lenitatem et iucunditatem ne fastiditi ab tanto quod queritis pondere abhorreant.

510 BML Ashb. , r–v: Ipse in praesentia tanquam accepto puero non ut possem copiosius scribam calamo scilicet meo verens [periens MS] ne puer quem e cio diligentem nimi[a] prolixitate se desperet. Cupiunt enim aures ille tenerrime non obtundi neque nimia indulgentia emolliri [...] Conor certe salvos esse singulos quosque qui se curae meae libenter permiserint.

511 BML Ashb. , r: Solent qui pueros ad nandum ducunt siccos cucumeres aut cucurbitas corpori supponere ut tutius in suma ac levi aqua manus ac pedes moveant festineque ludunt. Post securiores obdurato ore tumentibusque faucibus aquarum cumulos pectoribus rumpunt. Sic ingentes fluvios tranant nosque id imitantes pueritiam preceptori delegatam ab inclinatione ad coniunctionem vocum leviter traducimus veluti a rivulo ad flumen.

parts of speech, there are a number of similarities to *Ianua*. The individual sections preserve the same structure: definition, accidence, morphology (for declinable parts of speech). In treating nouns, the first full paradigm is given to *poeta*,[512] as in *Ianua*; similarly the basic exemplary verbs in both treatises are *amo*, *doceo*, *lego* and *audio*.[513] The section on verbs is divided into personal verbs, impersonal verbs, gerunds and supines,[514] resembling the pattern of Francesco da Buti's *latinum minus*.[515] The accidental categories in *Romulus* are mainly adapted and modified from *Ianua*.[516] In *Fabius*, the treatise on construction, Pomponio discusses only the syntax of the declinable parts of speech, following a tradition going back to *Doctrinale*.[517] His five verbal categories correspond to the traditional subdivision into active, passive, neuter, deponent and common verbs.[518] Pomponio also sometimes o ers invented examples in the conventional way.[519] Most significantly, the final treatise on prosody is in metre, corresponding to chapters and of *Doctrinale* on the same subject.[520]

However, it would be misleading to suggest that Pomponio's grammatical treatises were, in essence, conservative products from the same mould as the textbooks by Gaspare or Perotti; on the contrary, Pomponio obviously wanted to make a radical break from the school grammars composed up to his time by other humanists.[521] In *Romulus*, he followed neither Donatus's nor Priscian's order for the parts of speech:

Donatus	Priscian	Pomponio
Noun	Noun	Noun
Pronoun	Verb	Pronoun
Verb	Participle	Verb
Adverb	Pronoun	Participle
Participle	Preposition	Adverb
Conjunction	Adverb	Conjunction
Preposition	Interjection	Preposition
Interjection	Conjunction	Interjection

512 BML Ashb. , r. 513 BML Ashb. , v– v. 514 BML Ashb. , r– r.
515 See above, .
516 Cf. BML Ashb. , v, v, v, r, r, r, r, r, with Schmitt ( ), – .
517 v: De reliquarum [MS: reliquam] partium orationis collatione quae inclinari non patiuntur in *Romulo* diximus. 518 r.
519 E.g., (r) Olim multa verba quae nunc deponentis sunt comunis fuere. Communis est activi passivique, nota, ut populus veneratur Caesarem et veneratur Caesar a populo. (v) Ex his sum dativis confertur ut dicendi ornate est mihi studio. (v) Pronomina sic: ego Caesaris sum, tu vero pompeianae factionis es. 520 r .
521 For further discussion of Pomponio's innovations, see Rizzo ( ), – .

Nouns were not analysed in relation to declensions but rather mainly according to the ending of the nominative singular.[522] Divergence from the traditional medieval teaching structure was even more marked at the syntactical level in *Fabius*, which is mainly organized according to constructions with cases:[523] first nominative,[524] then genitive,[525] dative,[526] accusative[527] and ablative.[528] Its structure thus diverges from the traditional pattern, which was laid out according to constructions with various parts of speech and their sub-types: nouns, verbs, participles, gerunds, relatives, comparatives, superlatives, interrogatives, etc.[529] Pomponio also entirely abandons the concept of natural word order and the corresponding scholastic syntactical terminology, such as *ante se*, *post se*, *suppositum* and *appositum*. There are no mnemonic verses at all in Pomponio's discussion of syntax, nor is there any vernacular (nor indeed in any of Pomponio's grammatical treatises).[530] The section on figures represents an even more radical break with tradition. In the Italian prose treatises from Pietro da Isolella to Guarino, figures had been treated grammatically, that is, as excusable lapses in strict grammatical usage, with a concentration on figures of construction, usually eight in number.[531] But Pomponio treats figures as compositional ornaments, beginning with a series of stylistic maxims (cavenda semper obscuritas, vitanda ambiguitas, ne sit occultus sensus, vim rebus aliquando verborum humilitas a ert, verba nisi a erant decorem non sunt ab harchanis eruenda, etc.)[532] and then passing to a list of rhetorical colours, mainly placed under the heading of tropes (including metaphor, antonomasia, onomatopoeia, catachresis, allegory, enigma and hyperbole)[533] and schemata (including prosopopoeia, irony, parenthesis and repetition)[534] – none of which had normally been discussed in secondary grammatical treatises.[535]

Pomponio's humanist inclinations are clear too in the authorities that he cites. He entirely cast aside not only medieval authors, but even late antique grammarians such as Priscian and Donatus, who had been spared the condemnation even of Valla.[536] The authorities whom he cited by name (though not all at first hand) were entirely from the clas-

[522] BML Ashb. , r– v. [523] See Rizzo ( ), – . [524] BML Ashb. , v.
[525] BML Ashb. , r– v. [526] BML Ashb. , r– v. [527] BML Ashb. , v– r.
[528] BML Ashb. , v– r.
[529] See above, . This, however, does recall Alexander's and Tebaldo's approach: see above, – , – . [530] See Rizzo ( ), . [531] See above, .
[532] BML Ashb. , v– v. [533] BML Ashb. , v– r.
[534] BML Ashb. , r– v. [535] See above, . [536] Percival ( ), – .

sical period, including writers such as Tacitus,[537] Lucretius,[538] Caesar,[539] Cicero,[540] Martial,[541] Ovid,[542] Valerius Flaccus,[543] Vergil,[544] Celsus,[545] Propertius,[546] Statius,[547] Plautus,[548] the elder and younger Pliny,[549] Frontinus,[550] Columella,[551] Catullus,[552] Cato,[553] Silius Italicus,[554] Suetonius,[555] Hirtius,[556] Seneca,[557] Terence,[558] Horace,[559] Persius,[560] Sallust,[561] Livy[562] and Petronius,[563] and grammarians and scholars such as Probus,[564] Quintilian,[565] Terentius Scaurus,[566] Palaemon,[567] Varro,[568] Nigidius Figulus,[569] Aristarchus,[570] Accius,[571] Asconius Pedianus,[572] Asper,[573] Asinius Pollio,[574] Caper[575] and Pomponius Mela.[576]

Pomponio Leto's pretentious and self-promoting erudition and his radical rejection of previous pedagogic traditions enjoyed little success: his grammatical treatises survive in only a handful of manuscripts and a single incunabular edition.[577] Teachers and pupils must not only have been put o by his work's repellent tone of self-congratulation and his polemical attacks on other grammarians;[578] as textbooks, Pomponio's treatises were confusing and disorganized. There is no easy way to follow his discussion of nouns. The section begins with accidence, goes on to full declensions, proceeds to miscellaneous nominal types listed without discernible order, continues with comparatives and superlatives, and finally returns to accidence. The section on verbs is similarly chaotic,

[537] BML Ashb. , v, v.
[538] BML Ashb. , r, v, v, r, r, r, r, v, r, v, r, v, v, r, v, r, v, v.
[539] BML Ashb. , v, v, r, r.
[540] BML Ashb. , v, r, v, r, v, v, v, r, v, r, r, r, r, r, v, r, v, r, r, v, r, r, v, r, v, r, v, r, v, v.
[541] BML Ashb. , r, v, r, r. [542] BML Ashb. , v, v, r, v, v, r, v, r.
[543] BML Ashb. , v, v, r.
[544] BML Ashb. , r, v, r, v, v, r, r, v, r, v, r, v, v.
[545] BML Ashb. , r, v, r, v. [546] BML Ashb. , r.
[547] BML Ashb. , r, r. [548] BML Ashb. , v, v.
[549] BML Ashb. , v, r, v, r, v, r, v, v. [550] BML Ashb. , v, v.
[551] BML Ashb. , v, v, r, v, r, r, v, r, r.
[552] BML Ashb. , r, r, r. [553] BML Ashb. , v, v, v, v, r, v, v.
[554] BML Ashb. , v, r, v, v, v, v, r, r. [555] BML Ashb. , v.
[556] BML Ashb. , r. [557] BML Ashb. , v, v, r, r, v, v.
[558] BML Ashb. , r, r. [559] BML Ashb. , v. [560] BML Ashb. , r.
[561] BML Ashb. , r. [562] BML Ashb. , v, r. [563] BML Ashb. , r.
[564] BML Ashb. , r, v, r, r, r, v, v, r, v, v, v, v, v, r, v, r, v, r, v, r, v, v, r, v.
[565] BML Ashb. , r, v, r, v, r, v, v, r, r, v, r, r, v, v, r.
[566] BML Ashb. , r, r. [567] BML Ashb. , r, v, r.
[568] BML Ashb. , v, r, v, v, r, r, r, v, v, v, v, v, v.
[569] BML Ashb. , r, v, v. [570] BML Ashb. , r.
[571] BML Ashb. , r, v, v, r. [572] BML Ashb. , r, v, r.
[573] BML Ashb. , v, r. [574] BML Ashb. , v. [575] BML Ashb. , r.
[576] BML Ashb. , v. [577] See n. above. [578] BML Ashb. , r–v, r–v.

beginning with accidence, going on to derivatives, continuing with full paradigms, and then proceeding to impersonals, gerunds, supines and participles. His treatise on syntax is ostensibly organized according to case, but since he is not thereby able to discuss all relevant types of construction, he concludes with digressions on verbs enjoying more than one syntactical pattern, as well as on double accusatives, verbs without subjects or objects, ablative absolutes (not identified as such), gerunds and finally comparatives, appending a treatment of various miscellaneous constructions not previously considered.[579] In a similarly confused manner, the treatise on figures does not clearly define the di erence between tropes, schemata, barbarisms and solecisms. Pomponio rejected the traditional superstructure for secondary grammar, as well as the sources and methods used by previous Italian teachers, but, without a new comprehensive organization, the result was chaotic and confusing. It is ironic that Pomponio spurned Priscian, because, with his own philological bent, he was in one sense able to revive Priscian's discursive method – an approach which proved just as indigestible for pupils in the Renaissance as Priscian's had been for their predecessors in the middle ages.[580]

A work meant to make Priscian available at the secondary level, with the probable intention of o ering an alternative to various medieval secondary grammars, was the humanist Francesco Patrizi's epitome of the first sixteen books of the *Institutiones grammaticae*.[581] Patrizi's intentions are clear from the four verses appended to the end of the work.[582] There are a number of educational features in Patrizi's text. For example, he gives a clearer introduction to what will be treated in book than Priscian, who never actually said what the main subject of the book would be (i.e.

579 BML Ashb. , r– v.

580 Pomponio himself realized that his innovations were being resisted by what has been called the 'mercato scolastico': Rizzo ( ), – . This same conservatism obliged another humanist innovator (although one not so radical as Pomponio Leto), Sulpicio da Veroli, to reintroduce vernacular into the second edition of his grammar: Rizzo ( ), . On this grammar master, also known as Giovanni Sulpizio Verulano, see also Percival ( ), – .

581 Inc. Vox est aer tenuissimus ictus vel sonum sensibile aurium. I read this text in MSS BML Gaddi (XV^2), (XV^2, incomplete), and BRF (XV^2), where it ends with the normal epigram (v: see below, n.). BRF was sold by Lorenzo di Girolamo di Tingo to Ser Alessandro di Romigi Strozzi for lire on March : v.

582 BML Gaddi , v:

Cum legeris nostri compendia parva laboris
  Dicere non pudeat gratia[m] magna[m] tibi.
Nam quae vix poteras multis edicscere in annis
  Mensibus haec paucis meminisse potes.

the past perfect of the first and second conjugations).[583] Nor did Priscian give a clear idea of the order of topics: e.g. before actually discussing the formation of the perfect of first and second conjugations in book , he gave a general introduction on the kinds of changes that occur to every vowel and consonant (, – , Keil (–), , –) in forming the perfect, but he did not clearly signpost his path, failing to clarify what he was treating in this introductory section or what would follow: all this is added by Patrizi.[584] These may in fact be remnants of scholastic teaching and commenting methods, where the various sections of a work are shown and divided, recalling not classical, but medieval teaching techniques. Patrizi also gives a simplified, clearer version of Priscian's introduction to participles.[585] Despite these formal scholastic features, the work is still a genuine epitome of Priscian in the sense that no additional material is presented; the only changes seem to be in the presentation and clarification of the text, signposting its order in the medieval manner. Patrizi attempted a compromise between classical material and medieval teaching practice; as such his work seems to have satisfied few teachers or pupils in the fifteenth century, as is clear from its modest di usion,[586] showing once again the di culty encountered by the humanists in dislodging medieval grammarians from their dominant position in secondary education.

583 BML Gaddi, , v: In sequenti libro de preterito perfecto primae et secunde coniugationis tractabimus sed antequam incipiamus non alienum est rationem quorumdam verborum quae inequalem habent declinationem et de preterito imperfecto omnium coniugationum tractare. (Cf. Priscian, , (Keil (–), , .)

584 BML Gaddi , v: Nunc quia tam vocales quam consonantes aliquando in preteritis mutantur de eis antequam de preterito tractemus dicendum est.

585 Cf. Priscian, , (Keil (–), ,) with Patrizi, BML Gaddi , v.

586 Bursill-Hall ( ), , separates manuscripts with the same incipit as three di erent works, i.e., anonymous, Priscian *Institutiones maiores*, and Franciscus Patritius Senensis *De octo partibus orationis libellus*. Besides two Gaddi MSS, Avesani ( ), n. , mentions BAV Urb. Lat. , r– v, the second part of which, under the title *De quattuor partibus indeclinabilibus ex Prisciano compendium*, is also found in Vat. Ott. Lat. (see Mercati ( ),). On Urb. Lat. , see Stornajolo ( ), – , where the text (– v) has same inc. and expl., including final epigram. On the basis of Bursill-Hall ( ), other possible MSS of this text are: Basel Universitäts Bibliothek Cod. F. . , v– r (XVc.); Erfurt Wissenschaftliche Bibliothek der Stadt Cod. O. , v– v; BL Add. , – v (XVc.); Milan Ambrosiana H. inf., r– v; Bergamo Biblioteca Civica Cod. Delta . , r– (XVc.); Berlin Staatsbibliothek Preussischer Kulturbesitz Cod. Lat.Q. , – v (XVc.); Ferrara Biblioteca Comunale Cod. . , r– v (XVc.); Pisa Biblioteca Cateriniana Cod. , r– v (XVc.); Rome Biblioteca Corsiniana Cod. Rossi (.G.), – (XVc.); BNP Lat. , – v (XVc.: Patrizi named as author). These MSS have been checked against Passalacqua ( ) and are not listed there as texts of Priscian, so that they may actually be versions of Patrizi. BRF , which Bursill-Hall ( ), , lists with same incipit for r– v, under the title 'Epitome Prisciani', has nothing to do with Patrizi, given that the MS has the internal date of June (v).

Another secondary grammatical course with humanist a liations is preserved in a series of seven Florentine manuscripts[587] and five others outside Florence,[588] all dating from the second half of the fifteenth century. The compilation seems to constitute a full school-level grammatical syllabus, beginning with morphology of the parts of speech;[589] continuing with syntax;[590] going on to Guarino's heteroclyte nouns,[591] his orthography[592] and his *Carmina di erentialia*;[593] and ending with a brief section on verbal conjugations.[594] The course seems to have strong Florentine associations, given that seven manuscripts are now in Florence. According to Albinia de la Mare two further manuscripts are associated with the humanist scribe and bibliophile, Giorgio Antonio Vespucci (one written mainly in his hand[595] and the other corrected by him[596]), a fact which strengthens this Florentine connection; his copying and annotation, of course, might indicate authorship, or, at least, use in teaching his grammar pupils.[597] The only positive indication of date is a reference to in BNCF Magl. . .[598]

This course is interesting for a number of reasons. In the first place, it demonstrates that the linking of morphology and syntax was the invention of neither Perotti nor Pomponio Leto but was becoming common Italian practice in the second half of the fifteenth century. With the inclusion of three tractates by Guarino, it shows the attraction which grammatical treatises by humanists were beginning to command in the later Quattrocento. Humanist influence is clear too in the direct citations of classical authors, including Vergil,[599] Sallust,[600] Cicero,[601] Terence,[602]

587 BNCF Magl. . ; BRF , , ; and BNCF CS J. . contain fuller versions of treatises. BNCF Magl. . (acephalous) and Magl. . contain shortened versions, with the same material in almost the same order but ending with a section on cases and conjugations, omitting the Guarinian orthography, heteroclyte nouns and *Carmina di erentialia*. The shorter versions contain some but not all the classical quotations of longer versions. The fascicles of BNCF Magl. . are out of order: first should come r– v, then r– v and finally r . BRF has an internal date of March (, if it is Florentine): see De Robertis and Miriello ( ), .

588 Plimpton ; BL Burney ; BL Add. ; Venice Biblioteca Marciana Lat. ; Warsaw Biblioteka Narodowa Cod. Boz. . I have not seen the last two manuscripts, whose location and shelf-marks I have taken from Bursill-Hall ( ).

589 E.g., BRF , r– r. 590 BRF , r– v. 591 BRF , r– r.

592 BRF , v– r. Cf. Bodley Can. misc. , r–v.

593 BRF , r– r. Cf. Bodley Can. misc. , v– v. 594 BRF , v– r.

595 Plimpton . 596 BL Burney .

597 On his activities as a teacher and private tutor, see Ullman and Stadter ( ), ; de la Mare (b), and nn. – .

598 v: Ut nos sumus in anno ab incarnatione domini mellesimo quadringentesimo sexagesimo quinto, die vera [*sic*] XX^a^ aprilis.

599 BRF , r, r, r, v, r, v, v, r, v, r, r, v, r.

600 BRF , r, r. 601 BRF , r, v. 602 BRF , r, v, v, r, r.

Lucan[603] and Juvenal.[604] This compilation probably gives a good indication of the kind of grammatical training that sons of the Florentine patriciate were receiving in the second half of the fifteenth century. Finally, it shows that, despite the window-dressing provided by Guarino's treatises, the secondary grammar course remained profoundly conservative even in later fifteenth-century Florence. The morphology followed the pattern of *Ianua*, with the Priscianic order of the parts of speech (noun, verb, participle, pronoun, preposition, interjection, adverb, conjunction) and *Ianua*'s exemplary words (*poeta*, *amo*, *doceo*, *lego*, *audio*, etc.). As in Mancinelli's *Donatus melior*, vernacular translations are included with paradigms. The overall syllabus of the syntactical treatise is traditional.[605] There are the usual invented examples, lists of verbs in subclasses with vernacular equivalents and thematic translations; there is the traditional syntactical vocabulary (*ante se*, *post se*) and the implicit concept of natural word order. These treatises were still in use during the second half of the sixteenth century.[606] Indeed, governance according to the system of *ante se*, *post se* was still being employed in connection with these treatises in ,[607] when a series of 'Regole delli inpersonali che s'usano nella scuola di Giusto Buonamici da Volterra'[608] were appended to the end of the compilation.[609]

Traditional secondary grammars were still commonly being produced in Florence and elsewhere in Italy throughout the Quattrocento. One example comes from Filippo Casali, grammar teacher in Florence, Pistoia, Bologna and Volterra during the third quarter of the fifteenth century,[610] and now found in a manuscript datable to *c.* (BML Ashb.

603 BRF , r. 604 BRF , r.

605 Nominal declensions. Nominal types (substantive, adjectival, proper, appellative). Concordance (substantives, relatives, verbs). Verbal syntax: personal verbs: active verbs: unnamed species; passive verbs: unnamed species; neutral verbs: substantive, possessive, acquisitive, transitive, absolute, imperfect; neutral passive verbs; neutro-passive verbs; common verbs; deponent verbs: passive, active, possessive, acquisitive, e ective, absolute, imperfect; vocative verbs; impersonal verbs; familiar verbs (constructed with *volo*, *posso*, etc.); infinitives; gerunds; supines. Participles. Verbals. Derivative verbs. Relatives. Comparatives. Superlatives. Conjunctions. Figures. Nominal terminations. Heteroclyte nouns (Guarino). Guarino, *De orthographia*. Guarino, *Carmina di erentialia*. Verbal conjugations (formation, principal parts, etc.).

606 BNCF Magl. . , second front membrane flyleaf: Queste regole sono di Pandolfo di Pellegrino Cattani, che, se a sorte lui le perdesi et venisino a le mane di un'altro che lui sapia chi è el padrone; quando che lui le abia, adoparase quello che gli piace si ricordi di me che lo perse, fatta la scritta . 607 BRF , v.

608 BRF , r: see De Robertis and Miriello ( ), .

609 BRF , v: Exigunt [...] ante se genitivum et post infinitum; r: A fronte requirunt accusativum, a tergo genitivum [...] This fragmentary treatise covered impersonals, infinitives, gerunds and participles: v– r, inc. Impersonale verbum est.

610 Davies ( ), ; Battistini ( ).

), with the title 'Regule Magistri Philippi Casalensis ad discipulos' (r– v). This concise secondary grammar covers an entirely traditional syllabus. Personal verbs are divided into the usual five syntactical categories: active, passive, neutral, deponent and common, and into the normal six subcategories (called *maneries*) (r).[611] He employs the traditional syntactical vocabulary (*suppositum*, *persona vel res agens*, *ante se*, *post se*, *regere*) and relies on the the scholastic concepts of natural word order and governance. He gives vernacular equivalents of Latin grammatical forms. He also deals with thematic translation and problems in the conventional way. There is little indication of humanist influence in this treatise apart from an apparent rejection of a type of thematic construction proposed by fourteenth-century grammarians such as Francesco da Buti.[612]

An even more conservative secondary grammar, found in a manuscript dating from the second half of the fifteenth century (Bodley Can. Misc. , b verso– v), is entitled 'Regule Magistri Iohannis de Sancto Genesio'. The manuscript is apparently from the Veneto, judging from the vernacular found in one of its texts, but the provenance of this Giovanni da S. Genesio or Ginesio is unclear, given that there are a number of villages in various Italian regions with this name. The *Regule* provide a typically traditional secondary grammar course. The opening section on the parts of speech di ers from the introductory sections of the grammars by Perotti and Pomponio Leto in that it does not provide a full set of paradigms for the declinable parts of speech, but it may have served a similar function, providing revision of morphological material already covered by *Ianua*. The rest of the treatise is entirely conventional, with the usual scholastic syntactical vocabulary (*ante se*, *post se*, *ex natura*, *regere*, *persona agens/patiens*, *suppositum*, *antecedens*), verbs divided into classes with examples and vernacular equivalents, invented sentences and mnemonic verses. There is the normal thematic translation, including the kind of construction abhorred by Filippo Casali.[613] What is particularly interesting about this treatise is the context in which it occurs in the man-

611 The entire manuscript, containing a school-level grammatical and rhetorical anthology, was written by Giovanni di Salvaticcio de' Guidi and dated September ; the colophon is published by Kristeller (–), , .

612 r: *Tu medicato da docto medico non morrai*, tu curatus a docto medico non morieris; barbare tamen dicitur: tu cui mederi fuit doctum medicum. For Francesco da Buti's treatment, see Black (b), .

613 Bodley Can. misc. , r: el medico medicato Antonio se alegra, medicus quem mederi fuit Antonio gaudet. See above, n. .

uscript.[614] This represents a Guarinian type grammar course, beginning with *Ianua*, progressing to a set of secondary *regule* and finishing with *Doctrinale* – but without Guarino's own grammar. If it constitutes a course in existence before Guarino's *Regule* were published, then it further suggests the conventional context of his curriculum; if it was stimulated by his syllabus, then it indicates how his work tended to reinforce traditional teaching patterns. This grammar continued in use Tuscany during the sixteenth century, to judge from its *ex libris*.[615]

In Florentine libraries there are also a clutch of anonymous fifteenth-century secondary grammar treatises of the traditional type. In terms of content and format, they are indistinguishable from the Trecento predecessors. For example, BNCF Magl. . (Inc. Vocum alia litterata, alia inlicterata), written on reused parchment dating from the s and datable to the first half of the Quattrocento, is probably of Tuscan provenance (v: Tuscus florentinus, r: vado Florentiam). The overall scope resembles Trecento secondary manuals already discussed, although again the controlled structure of Francesco da Buti and Filippo di Naddo is wanting. There are copious mnemonic verses, including citations from *Doctrinale* (r) and *Graecismus* (r, v), and the usual syntactical focus is evident not only from the omnipresent thematic translations but also from the terminology (*suppositum*, *determinatio*, *ex parte ante*, *ex parte post*, *latinari*).[616]

Others include BRF , dating from the first half of the century;[617] BRF , dated January ;[618] Florence Biblioteca Moreniana Palagi , dated ;[619] and BNCF CS J. . [620] and BRF

[614] r– r: *Ianua*. v– v. Pseudo-Cato, *Disticha*. b verso– v: <Magister Iohannes de Sancto Genesio, Regule [grammaticales]> inc. Incipiunt regule Magistri Iohannis de Sancto Genesio. Partes orationis sunt octo [...] expl. Que figura est excusabilis apud autores et substinenda sed non immitanda. r– v: Alexander de Villadei, *Doctrinale*.

[615] r: di Batista Pazaglia; Iacopo Bertolini da Pistoia [both indicated by same XVIc. hand]; v: di Iacopo Bertolinii da Pistoia. Chi lo trovasse degnisi di renderlo.

[616] E.g. r: sciendum est quod in oratione sunt tria, scilicet suppositum, verbum et determinatio; r: ex parte ante [...] ex parte post; r: Si autem non reperiatur participium, tunc tripliciter possumus latinari.

[617] Inc. De verbis activis. Nota quod adesse verbi activi tria requiruntur.

[618] Inc. <G>ramatica est scientia recte loquendi recteque scribendi, origo, fundamentum omnium liberalium artium. r: Expl. Epilogus. Colligit epilogus predicta sub brevitate. Die gennai . Omnes in *Doctrinali* latius patent figurarum forme, capitulo ultimo etc. Quere ibi.

[619] Inc. Quatuor sunt partes gramatice, videlicet littera silaba dictio et oratio. r: Ego Ciprianus notarius de Sancto Miniate subscripsi, anno domini nostri Yesu Christi . Probably Florentine: see (r) Florentie, (v) Florentiam, (r) Florentinus.

[620] Acephalous. Inc. Ut prelibatum est, quo lucidius potero intimare decrevi. Quorum primum est nominis divisio non quidem completa sed que impresentiarum ad prefatum opusculum utilis ac

,[621] both datable to the second half of the Quattrocento. These manuals cover the conventional syllabus. All the treatises use mnemonic verses, invented examples and vernacular translations of Latin forms, including verbs under the normal subcategories with *volgare* equivalents; the standard syntactical vocabulary is also omnipresent, and all of them are thoroughly peppered with thematic translations. As had become typical in the fifteenth century, these anonymous treatises occasionally cite, in addition to invented examples, passages from classical authors:

BRF : Priscian, Vergil
BRF : Donatus, Priscian, Cicero, Ennius, Vergil
Moreniana Palagi : Priscian, Vergil
BNCF CS J. . : Donatus, Priscian

but medieval authorities are still quoted, e.g.

BRF : *Doctrinale*[622]
BRF : Theodulus.[623]

There are a number of partial or fragmentary grammatical treatises dating from the fifteenth century in Florentine libraries, and these too reflect conservative teaching patterns. One is a treatise on the syntax of verbs, found in three manuscripts: in BRF it is attributed to Maestro Albertino, whereas it is anonymous in BNCF Landau Fin. .[624] Maestro Albertino is more fully identified as coming from Monte-Latrone (a village in southern Tuscany near Arcidosso and about kilo-

footnote (*cont.*)
expediens esse constat. It possibly dates from , in view of the following date in an example: v: scripsi regulas anno domini millesimo quadringentesimo sexagesimo. Possibly Florentine: r: E signori di Firençe ànno sbanditi dua cittadini fuori del loro territorio.

621 Inc. Verbum est illud quod cum modis et temporibus est significativum agendi vel patiendi vel neutrius. r: Regole di Palla figliuolo di Bernardo Rucellai e degli amici (XVIc.).

622 r, v, r, v, r, r. 623 r.

624 BNCF Landau Fin. , r:
Quoniam constructio verborum a parte post videtur causari a genere verbi sciendum est quod quinque sunt principalia genera verborum, scilicet, activum, passivum, neutrum, comune et deponens. Verbum activum est illud quod desinit in o ut amo et format de se passivum in or ut amo addita r et fit amor. Et regit post se accusativum rei rationalis ut ego amo deum.

BRF , r:
Quoniam constructio verborum ex parte post videtur causa in genere verbi, sciendum est quod sunt principalia genera verborum secundum quod pertinet ad presens propositum scilicet activum passivum neutrum comune et deponens. Verbum activum est illud quod desinit in o et format de se passivum in or ut amor et reget post se accusativum rationalis ut ego amo deum.

metres northeast of Grosseto) in the third manuscript (BRF , r– v).[625] This text is an entirely traditional treatment of verbal construction. In the usual manner, Albertino gives lists of verbs under each subclass with vernacular equivalents; he employs the normal scholastic syntactical vocabulary (*regere*, *persona/res/agens/patiens*, *ex natura*, *ante se*, *post se*, *suppositum*, *appositum*); he invents his own examples; he provides mnemonic verses; he gives thematic translations. Another partial secondary grammar, this time apparently a fragment, is found in a manuscript datable to the first half of the fifteenth century (BRF , r– v); it too covers part of a traditional curriculum. This section has the usual syntactical vocabulary (*ex natura*) and thematic translations; typically for a fifteenth-century secondary grammar, there are a few citations of ancient and Christian authorities, including Priscian (r), Lucan (v) and the Bible (r). Another fragmentary secondary grammar (BNCF Magl. .) is interesting as evidence of the traditional curriculum taught to the sons of the Florentine élite in the fifteenth century and early sixteenth century, copied as it was by a member of the Soderini family,[626] and used by another member of the family in the early sixteenth century.[627] The text's curriculum follows the usual pattern. In the section on personal verbs, the subclasses are illustrated in the traditional way by lists of verbs with vernacular equivalents; there are mnemonic verses, as well as the usual syntactical vocabulary (*suppositum*, *appositum*, *regere*, *ex natura*, *a parte ante*, *post se*) and thematic translations. Nor were traditional secondary grammars the exclusive preserve of the Florentine élite in the fifteenth century. Such a text (BNCF Pal. n.) belonged to the Puccini family, who seem to have emigrated from Pistoia to Florence in the second half of fifteenth century: the first two sections of the manuscript were completed by the notary Bartolomeo Puccini da Pistoia on

625 Acephalous with following explicit:

BRF , v:	BNCF Landau Fin. , v:	BRF , v:
Et sic suo modo <dicendum> est de supino quia eodem modo construitur. Amen. Expliciunt notabilia Magistri Albert<ini> de Monte Latrone.	et sic suo dicendum est de supino quia eodem modo construitur. Amen.	Et sic suo modo dicendum est de supino quia eodem modo construitur. Expliciuntur verbalia Magistri Albertini Deo gratias amen.

626 v: Expliciunt regulae verborum personalium mei Pauli Luisii Ioannis de Soderinis. Incipiunt eiusdem regulae verborum impersonalium.

627 (Front flyleaf, recto) Iste liber est Ieronimi Soderini.

May , and then passed to his son Gabriele.[628] Parts – of this manuscript contain the 'Notabilia minora Magistri Macthie de Urbe Veteri',[629] which not only cover part of the standard secondary syllabus[630] but also have other traditional features such as vernacular translations of verbal lists, scholastic syntactical vocabulary (*ante se, ex natura, post se, regere, agens, patiens*), mnemonic verses and thematic translations. Indeed, this text adopts a format used by an earlier secondary grammarian from Lombardy, Giovanni da Soncino, who, like the above Mattia, organized his work in the manner of miscellaneous notabilia, introduced by the phrase 'Notandum est quod [...]'; in one manuscript this is referred to as 'notanda Magistri Iohannis de Soncino'.[631] This format of course embodies a fundamental feature of medieval Latin, namely the introduction of reported speech with *quod* rather than the infinitive;[632] indeed, this manner of presentation for a secondary grammar was entirely traditional in the Italian schoolroom, going back at least to the early thirteenth century and Bene da Firenze's *Summa*.[633]

628 v:

Signum mey Bartolomey Puccinj de <Pisto>rio notarii etc.
Hic liber est mei Bartolomey supradicti.
Completus fuit die Maiy.

Top line then altered to read: Signum mey Gabrielis Bartolomey de Puccinis de Florentia. Second line also altered to: Hic liber est mei Gabrielis Bartolomey supradicti.

629 Acephalous. Folios now out of order; correct order written in old numbering in upper right corner: = , = , = , = . Missing folio/folios between and , but order of topics as treated here seems to be: infinitives, gerunds, supines, case governance, adverbs, relatives, interrogatives. does not have an old number, but if the order of material follows that found in grammarians such as Francesco da Buti, then , which covers deponents and impersonals, should precede all the rest.

The treatise seems to be Florentine/Tuscan in origin or redaction, since florins are referred to as the standard currency. Tuscan geographical reference: (r) Serthianum [=Sarteano] distat a Senis triginta quatuor miliaribus.

630 See above, n. .

631 Thurot ( ), . I examined the following manuscripts with grammars attributed to Giovanni da Soncino: BNCF CS B. . , r– r (expl. ad presens dicta su ciant. Johannes de Soncino); BML Ashb. Append. (XVmid): see Kristeller (–), ,). I also looked at Bodley Can. misc. (XVmid), r– v (inc. Notandum est quod scientia potest accipi duobus modis; expl. O dolet o clamat gaudet o miratur et optat), attributed by Bursill-Hall ( ), , to Johannes de Soncino but I was able to find no attribution in the manuscript. BML Ashb. Append. consists of a series of grammatical notes arranged in alphabetical order according to verbs (augeo, audio, ago, etc.) but with other material inserted. It preserves the normal traditional content and terminology for a secondary prose *summa* (*suppositum, appositum*, mnemonic verses, *thema/si thema datur, ante se/post se, ex natura*, invented examples drawn from school life). The geographical locations cited are Venice, Bologna and Florence. This Giovanni da Soncino may be synonymous with a mid-Trecento grammarian who taught in Bologna: see Sabbadini ( ), , n. . Jensen ( ), – , , seems to assume that, because BNCF CS B. . is dated , the text attributed to Giovanni also dates from then. Two copies of his *Notabilia* were bought for two Venetian orphans in : Connell ( ), .

632 See Rizzo ( ), n. .

633 See BNCF CS B. . , r– r *passim*.

In the thoroughly traditional teaching climate of the fifteenth century, it is not surprising to find, moreover, that the prose *summe* of the thirteenth and fourteenth centuries continued in heavy use e.g. **Pietro da Isolella's *Summa*.**

BRF	First owned in XVc. by Messer Battista da Pisa,[634] whose son, Bindo, sold it to the Florentine, Pandolfo Pandolfini, in .[635]
Bodley Can. Misc.	Although copied apparently in the second half of Trecento, nevertheless it shows no signs of ownership until XVc., when many there are *ex libris* and probationes.[636]

Similarly **Filippo di Naddo**'s treatise continued in use during the fifteenth century and even later:

ASF Carte Bardi II. , r– v	One text in miscellany dated .
BML Ashb.	Datable to XV²; use by hand with humanist elements (r); ownership note by 'Antonius Nerius' (r) datable to XVIin.
BNCF CS G. . , –	Datable to XV¹.
BRF , r– r	Incomplete; datable to XVin.
BRF , r– v	Datable to XV¹.

634 v: Messer Batista da Pisa ebbe dì di dicenbre la prima peza del Digesto Vehio.

635 r: Questa Soma è di Pandolfo di Giannoço d'Agniolo di Filippo Pandolfini, conperata da Bindo di Ser Batista a ddì XXIII di febraio MCCCCXXXII.

636 (inside front cover) Rubius de Sansonibus debet dare [...] die XII marzii [...] Item [...] die III madii [...] N. Italian hand, XVc.; also the fact that this account record is in Latin suggests it is not Tuscan.
Ista suma est Ambroxii Thome et Johannis fratrum de Tabernis filiorum — [*erasum*] de Tabernis [an older ownership note is rubbed out and adapted]
v: Ista suma est mei Ambroxii et Iochannis? filiorum Domini? Iochannis?
Ista suma est mei <...> de <...> filii domini <...> qui bonus <...> qui santi?
r: Ista suma est mey <...>
abcd est

Francesco da Buti's *Regule* maintained their appeal in the fifteenth-century grammar classroom as well:

BML Med. Pal.	XV^{1}; used in schools of two Tuscan XVc. teachers, Benaccio da Poppi, communal grammarian in Volterra[637] and Taddeo of Pescia,[638] teacher in Volterra,[639] Florence,[640] Piombino and even Corsica[641] besides by a student living apparently in the Sapienza of Pistoia[642] in XV^{2}.[643]
Florence B. Moreniana Palagi	Datable to XIVex.; belonged to member of Florentine Corsi family studying in Pisa in XVc.[644]
BNCF CS B. . , r– r	Extract; completed by author's nephew Giovanni di Ser Jacopo *de Ceuli* on January .[645]
BRF	XV^{1}. See above, .
Bodley Lat. misc. e.	XV^{1}. See above, .

A final manuscript (BML Antinori , XV^{1}) is interesting in that it shows not only the use of Francesco's grammar in the second half of the fifteenth century but also the traditional educational context in which the work was still being read. The *ex libris* is of a friar, written in a fifteenth-century French hand.[646] The French friar also wrote a macaronic note in Italian and French, mentioning 'endare a Perouse' (v). All this may suggest that Frère Jacques was studying at the University of Perugia; he

637 (r) Iste liber est mei Giovannes Petri in iscola Magistri Bonacci: *Regule pisane.* v: Iste liber est mei Giovannis Petri de Vulterri[s] in iscola Magistri Bonacci. See Battistini ( ) – , ; Volterra Biblioteca Guarnacci MS (Persius, *Satires*), v: Iste liber est mei Iohannis Michaelis de civitate Vulterre manentis in schola mag. Benacci de Casentino.

638 r: Iste liber est mei Iovannis Petri de Vulterris in scola Magistri Taddei de Piscia.

639 Battistini ( ), – , – ; Battistini ( ), – .

640 Battistini ( ), – ; Park ( ), – ; Davies ( ), .

641 Battistini ( ), . 642 See Zanelli ( ), .

643 ': Iste liber est ad usum Fratris Brasi de Vulterris studentis in allocacionibus Pistorii commorantis.

644 Inside rear cover: Queste reghole sono pisan<e> e sono di Francesco Corsi in Pisa.

645 BNCF CS B. . , r– r. For abbreviated version of colophon containing this information, see Kristeller (–), I. ; see Alessio (a), n. .

646 v: Iste liber pertinet Fratri Iacobo Fabri eiusdem ordinis Sancti Augustini de Francia. There is another note on the same page, dated October . Ave marie. A dì doctobre mille . Another hand on this page wrote the following note: […] sum acturus in studio fortiter, videlicet in gramaticis atque rethoricis ut facilius possim habere et intelligere loycam atque philosophiam. Et sic de aliis scientiis ut tempora sequentia possim sacram scripturam […]

was certainly using Francesco da Buti's *Regule*, a work which, it was hoped, would enable it user to climb the traditional medieval educational hierarchy from grammar to rhetoric, and then to logic and philosophy, culminating in theology. Finally, another friar, identified only as 'Fr. G.' copied a further traditional Trecento grammar (BML Ashb.),[647] this time by Pietro da Asolo, in and ,[648] while some of the other items in this traditional compilation were also copied in by Domenico da Pinedello,[649] a village in the Veneto not far from Conegliano and Treviso, the two towns where Pietro spent most of his teaching career.[650]

An interesting example of how a traditional secondary grammar course could be assembled out of disparate elements in mid-Quattrocento Tuscany is provided by manuscript BNCF Landau Fin. , which consists of several principal elements.[651] One of the copyists, Gentile Pele da Colle, seems to have been the organizing force behind the compilation in , putting together for himself a miscellany which combined a traditional topical vocabulary, a secondary grammar consisting of texts by Albertino da Montelatrone and Francesco da Buti, and an orthography which is heavily reliant on Hugutio, as well as citing *Graecismus*, Priscian, Lucan, Ovid and Vergil.

It has been seen above how in the fifteenth century *Doctrinale* began to be used not only as a mine of mnemonics to reinforce the grammatical rules of the prose *summe* but also as a supplement to the thin grammar courses of teachers such as Guarino. The endorsement of this eminent humanist pedagogue could only have bolstered the status of this venerable work, and so it is hardly surprising to find that Italian copies of ***Doctrinale*** proliferated in the first half of the Quattrocento:

647 See above, . 648 r; v: Expliciunt infinita. Deo gratias. M. Fr.r G. . Amen.

649 v: Iste constructiones expelete fuerunt curentibus annis domini millesimo quatrincentessimo trigessimo quinto mensis augusti, per me Dominicum de Pinedello.

650 Gargan ( ), – .

651 ( ) r– r: Domenico Bandini, *Vocabula*. Inc. Incipiunt vocabula gramaticalia. Hic deus dei *iddio*.
( ) v: Anon. *De patronimicis*. Inc. Nota quod nomen patronomicum est duplex.
( ) r– v: [Magister Albertinus, *Verbalia*] Inc. Quoniam constructio verborum a parte post videtur causari a genere verbi.
( ) v– r: Anon. *De supinis* Inc. Nota quod sunt quedam verba activa que carent supinis.
( ) v– r: Anon. *De gerundis et supinis*. Inc. Nota quod infinitus est quidam modus latinandi.
( ) r: Anon. *De derivationibus*. Inc. Hasta derivatur ab isto nomine hastus/us/ui.
( ) r– v: Francesco da Buti, *Regule grammaticales*, acephalous. Expl. et hec de antitosi et figuris dicta su ciant. Amen. Expliciunt regule grammaticales secundum Magistrum Franciscum de Buti pisanum civem per me Gentilem Pele de Colle Valliselse sub annis domini M°CCCC°XXXX°VII° indictione VII^a^ die vero XX°VIII° mensis settembris.
( ) r– v: Anon. *De orthographia*. Inc. Incipit Ortogrophya iuxta ordinem alphabeti. A quandoque est littera quandoque prepositio.

BML AD	XVin. Fragmentary. Glossed lightly by copyist and later writer (XV²); copyist divides text into chapters, giving headings and usual examples of grammatical rules, besides citing Psalms (r) and Vergil (v).
BML Ashb. [652]	XV² signatures of 'Leonardus Veronensis/Bergomensis';[653] school-type annotations of at least half a dozen other XVc. readers.[654]
BML sup.	XV¹; r– v lightly glossed, mainly with WOM;[655] some analytical glosses (e.g. r: Alx = tertia declinatio); vernacular translations (e.g. r: significatio = *è la significatione*); see admonition accompanying vv. – indicating level of expected readership: Iuvenes studentes in grammatica debent scire.
BML Strozzi	XV¹, probably from Cortona;[656] lightly glossed, both interlinearly and marginally, mainly by copyist: examples, definitions, WOM (e.g. r), vocabulary di erences, exceptions; two references to ancient authorities (v: Priscian, Vergil).
BRF [657]	numerous XVc. glossators, including many brief annotations by puerile hands (e.g. r, r, r, v, r, r, v, v, r, r).
BRF	XV¹; various signatures;[658] *probationes* recalling *Ianua*;[659] school-type imprecation to return book to owner.[660] Light, mainly interlinear glossing, giving simple vocabulary paraphrases, explications and especially illustrative examples, with annotations often incorporating vernacular (e.g. r).
BNCF Landau Fin.	; see below.

It is also not di cult to find examples of *Doctrinale* manuscripts produced in the second half of the century:

652 For date and earlier use, see above, . 653 See above, n. .
654 See r, r, r, v, r, r, v– r, v, v, r, v, r– r.
655 On this practice as applied to literary authors, see below, .
656 Reused palimpsest parchment: r: Millesimo trecentesimo vigesimo <...>; r: Millesimo trecentesimo septuagesimo secundo <...> quondam Nuccii de Cortona; v: Cortone in domo <...> Ego Lodovicus quondam <...> de civitate Cortone <...> notarius <...>
657 For date and earlier use, see above, .
658 r: Io Frate Lionardo mi veni? el venerdì dopo l'ascenssione; v: Giovanni; Guaspar; questo libro è di Franceso; questo libro è di Domenico di Francesco.
659 v: Poeta, que pars est? Nomen. Quare? [...] Poeta, que pars est? Poeta, que pars est?
660 v: Si ni<...> ci lo truova, si lo renda per l'amor di dio.

BML AD	Fragmentary; light, occasional glosses (datable XV²) by various pupil-readers.
BML AD	, N. Italian.[661] Prepared as schoolbook, probably for the copyist's use: puerile admonitory colophon.[662] But little used: main glossing (r) illustrating text's rules; vernacular synonym (r).
BML sup.	XV². Interesting testimony to continued use in humanist context: in anthology containing humanist texts (Bruni, Barzizza, Landino), besides extracts from Seneca space was found for *Doctrinale*'s treatment of metrics (chapter , inc. Pandere proposui: r– v).
Florence B. Moreniana Moreni	XV². Virtually unglossed except for some interlinear vocabulary paraphrases (r) but copious school-type ownership marks, indicating Tuscan/Milanese possession.[663]
BRF , r– r	XV². Humanist context; not text but running commentary (incomplete) included in anthology containing a commentary on Terence and an oration by Donato Acciaiuoli.
Bodley Can. misc.	XV². In school anthology: see above, . Glossed by one/two Cinquecento hands.

Traditional expository commentary continued to be the norm in glossing and reading *Doctrinale* during the fifteenth century. One example is BNCF NA , which was copied and glossed by a Florentine Franciscan pupil in a Mantuan convent in , as revealed by an ownership note (front flyleaf recto).[664] The copyist's interlinear glossing

[661] r: Explectum est Doctrinale per me Johannem Petrum filium Magistri Petri fabri de Bagnono ad horam meredierum a. die mensis iulii et incepi a. die madii etc. Bagnono – Bagnolo near Brescia?

[662] r:

Si puer hoc sciret quantum doctrina valeret,
Numquam dormiret sed die nocteque studeret.
Si concederem, non rehaberem, si rehaberem,
Non tam cito. Si tam cito, non tam bonum.
Si tam bonum, perdam amicum.

[663] v: Iste *Doctrinalis* est mei Bastiani Magistri Petri de Laterina. Quis inveniet istum et non redet impiccatus erit. D.
r: Jacopo di Ser Andrea Banbocci
v: Questo libro è di Bastiano di Mona Diamente di Cristofano da Llaterina, che costò soldi Chi lo trova la [*sic*] renda.
Iste liber est mei Bastiani Tomasi Milane[n]sis.

[664] Istud *Doctrinale* est ad usum mei, videlicet Fratris Philippi de Florentia, ordinis minorum, quod ego manu mea scripsi in conventu Mantue A.D. .

normally consisted of paraphrase,[665] sometimes in the vernacular.[666] Much interlinear glossing is devoted to explanation and exemplification.[667] The marginal comment consists of the usual textual division, paraphrase and explanation, as for example, when discussing the construction of interrogatives (vv. –).[668] A somewhat later version of the text appears in BNCF Magl. . , written in humanist book hand about mid-century, and glossed by numerous school-type readers in the second half of the Quattrocento. Again, the interlinear glosses exemplify[669] or explain.[670] Often the marginal comments clarify di erences of meaning between similar words.[671] At times full declensions or conjugations are exemplified in the margins, e.g. *domus* (r) or *penus* (r); elsewhere, only summaries are provided.[672] On occasion the marginal comment explicates the rules given in verse, as for example when pointing out that nouns of the second declension ending in -er sometimes form the genitive in -eri (*pueri*), sometimes just in -ri (*magistri*).[673]

Even over the first century of printing, *Doctrinale* continued in unabated use by Italian teachers and pupils. Until , editions of the text were almost exclusively North Italian;[674] at least forty-six Italian editions of the work were issued,[675] half of these in Venice.[676] Although some of these Venetian editions would have been prepared for the ultra-

665 E.g.
pro et — id est qui legit hunc librum pueris id est scolaribus — reserabit id est manifestabit in propria lingua vulgariter
Atque legens pueris laica lingua reserabit. (v. , r)

666
id est presente — a questa opera — sia — la gratia — dello spiritu sancto
Presens huic operi sit gratia pneumatis almi. (v. , r)

667
id est nominativus — ut Eneas ut Lucas — ut Anchises — ut Egea Egina — nominativus
Cum rectus fit in as vel in es vel cum dat a grecus (v. , r)

668 v: Hic auctor docet quo ordine interrogativa debeant ordinari in constructione, et quatuor principaliter facit. Nam primo ponit doctrinam generalem de interrogativis. Secundo de adverbiis derivatis ab eis, ibi *hanc sua* [v.]. Tertio de isto interrogativo quis spetialiter ibi, *quis proprium* [v.]. Quarto de responsivis dat regulam, ibi *quesitam* [v.].

669 virgo — mare — tema (v)
O dabit e que vel a tibi declinatio terna (v.)

670 scilicet esse — nomen — tu — id est in una voce (r)
Id proprium dices quod non univoce res
Plures […] (vv. –)

671 E.g.: Municipium oppidum est recognoscens superiorem; municeps autem civis habitans in ipso. (v (v.))

672 crepo -as -pui; do das dedi; domo -as -domui; mico -as -micui; sto stas steti […] (v).

673 (v.) sed quod fit in er variamus. — r: Nam nomina terminata nominativo in er aliquando superant et aliquando non, ut infra videbis.

674 Reichling ( ), xlv. 675 Reichling ( ), ccxcv–ccciii. 676 Reichling ( ), xlv.

montane[677] and especially German market, nevertheless this cannot explain the *longue-durée* of *Doctrinale* among Italian publishers. The text was subjected to relentless attack in Northern Europe and especially in Germany during the first decades of the sixteenth century, with the result that it ceased to be used in schools there by about ;[678] the last German edition was produced in .[679] On the other hand, *Doctrinale* continued to be printed in North Italy, with a final series of editions coming out of Brescia beginning in and continuing until .[680] If *Doctrinale* were being printed in Italy primarily for Northern European and German use, it must be explained why there were no more indigenous German and so few other ultramontane editions after . The fact is that *Doctrinale*'s popularity in Italy grew, if anything, during the Quattrocento and sustained itself well into the Cinquecento. Out of a total of manuscripts,[681] Reichling lists twenty-three manuscripts now in Italian libraries;[682] on the other hand, out of a total printed editions,[683] were published in Italy.[684] Among all European countries, *Doctrinale* survived longest in Italy, the last printing occurring there in .[685]

677 Grendler ( ), .

678 Reichling ( ), xcviii; see also Heath ( ). Jensen (a), , speaks interestingly of 'the German tradition of a constructive dialogue with Alexander's *Doctrinale*. Perhaps that is why no edition of Alexander appeared in Germany after the s: by then the useful material found in Alexander had been absorbed in more modern textbooks.'

679 Reichling ( ), ciii. The only other ultramontane editions after this date are Paris and (Reichling ( ), ccci).

680 Reichling ( ), xlv–xlvi.

681 Reichling ( ), cxxi.

682 Reichling ( ), ccxci–ccxcii.

683 Reichling ( ), clxix.

684 Reichling, ccxcv–ccciii.

685 Reichling ( ), xlv–xlvi. Garin ( ), xxvi–xxvii, agreed that 'il *Doctrinale* di Alessandro de Villadei rimane' in XVc., citing Vittorino's purchase of it for his pupils. Although Battista Guarini recommended *Doctrinale* in his *De ordine docendi et discendi* of , Grendler (,) says that 'Renaissance students did not go on to medieval verse grammar such as the *Doctrinale*' maintaining that 'there is little evidence that Italian Latin schools used *Doctrinale* [...] after ' (Grendler ( ),), despite documentary indications in published sources to the contrary (e.g. in at Bassano, the grammar teacher was required to teach *Doctrinale* (Chiuppani ( ),), and the same was true at Pistoia in : Zanelli ( ), . In the grammar teacher at Sarzana declared he had given more than six lecture courses on *Doctrinale*: Mannucci ( ), . For copies in Venice and the Veneto throughout the century, see Connell ( ), , , . Reichling, in the introduction to his critical edition of *Doctrinale* ( ), had concluded on the basis of an admirably thorough study of the text's printing history that *Doctrinale* lasted more than fifty years into the sixteenth century (lxxxviii, xc). Grendler o ered the following comments in in response to my review article published in that year. 'Black asserts that "it is well known that manuals such as the *Doctrinale* [...] retained enormous popularity throughout the fifteenth century" [Black (c),]. Where is the evidence for this sweeping statement? I suspect that he is repeating an inaccurate commonplace based on an incomplete knowledge of the printing history of the *Doctrinale*. Reichling, the editor of the *Doctrinale*, listed fifteenth- and sixteenth-century printings; but only (%) were Italian imprints. Moreover, it is well known that major Italian publishers, especially those in Venice, sold their books all across

The vehement assaults on *Doctrinale* by Italian humanists are not testimony so much to a victorious campaign against barbarism as to a frustrated e ort to rid the schoolroom of a great medieval *bête noire*; their attempts to replace Alexander's poem with their own verse grammars was a tacit recognition of his longevity, and their ultimate failure to dislodge *Doctrinale* demonstrates not only the entrenched conservatism of the Italian Renaissance classroom but also of Alexander's practical superiority at the secondary level. When Valla wanted to expel *Doctrinale* from the humanist curriculum, he himself began to compose a thoroughly unclassical verse manual – a work which survived only as an obscure fragment.[686] In Antonio Mancinelli composed a metric grammar entitled *Spica*, which called on Alexander to return to his barbarous homeland together with his barbarisms.[687] *Carmen scholasticum*, a work similarly o ered in explicit competition with *Doctrinale*, was published *c.* by Pilade da Brescia, who, in order to bolster his campaign against Alexander, issued a direct philological assault the following year in the form of *Annotationes in Alexandrum de Villa Dei*.[688] Nevertheless, these e orts were in vain: only five months after the publication of Pilade's polemical commentary, his very own publisher issued a new edition of *Doctrinale*, calling it a useful work, while Aldo Manuzio, Venice's leading editor at the beginning of the Cinquecento, who, in his *Rudimenta grammatices* of , lamented his own youth misspent on Alexander's poem, could not prevent the publication of numerous editions of *Doctrinale* in his native city.[689] These Italian humanists were no more successful at dislodging Alexander from the classroom than their thirteenth-century precursor, John of Garland, whose interpolated, edited and corrected version of *Doctrinale* similarly failed to halt the progress of Alexander's original grammar.[690] The testimony of early German humanists – to the e ect that Alexander had already been banished from Italian schools by the beginning of the sixteenth century – cannot be taken literally: such misrepresentations of the Italian situation had their own polemical agenda, encouraged by wishful thinking

footnote (*cont.*)
Europe. In other words, the printing history of the *Doctrinale* suggests that the book was much used in Northern Europe and little used in Italy [...] The fact of the matter is that there is little evidence that Italian Latin schools used the *Doctrinale* [...] after ' (Grendler ( ), . He o ers the same argument in Grendler ( ), , n. .)

686 Rizzo and De Nonno ( ), – . Rizzo here definitively establishes the text's entirely serious purpose and authenticity, which had previously been questioned.

687 Reichling ( ), lxxxvii; Thurot ( ), .

688 Reichling ( ), lxxxvii–lxxxviii; Thurot ( ), .

689 Reichling ( ), lxxxviii–lxxxix.

690 Reichling ( ), liv–lvii.

and the far from disinterested claims of Italian humanist educators themselves.[691]

Graecismus too continued in school use during the fifteenth century, albeit perhaps without the enhanced cachet enjoyed by *Doctrinale.* A French thirteenth-century manuscript (BML CS)[692] had arrived in the Italian classroom by the turn of the Quattrocento, to judge from a couple of *probationes* (v: Jacob, fratres) of that period; it was in Florence by the second half of the century, when another annotation was made (see above,); and it continued in school use into the Cinquecento, when another annotator wrote 'Guarrinus' (r). Manuscripts of the text were still being prepared for glossing, as in the case of BNCF .. .[693] But among Quattrocento manuscripts of *Graecismus*, particularly interesting is BRF (XV^{1}).[694] The manuscript's vernacular glosses suggest a Venetian or Paduan provenance, but it soon travelled to Florence, passing, in the first half of the Quattrocento, through the da Panzano family into the ownership of Michele di Taddeo da Pontassieve.[695] The school context of the codex is beyond doubt, with numerous *probationes*,[696] as well as two alphabets (r), suggesting continued classroom use into the sixteenth century. The manuscript reveals two main types of glossing: copied marginal comment provided by the scribe(s) and more spontaneous interlinear glosses. All the glossing is normal school-type explication, beginning with a conventional *accessus*, which follows the normal fifteenth-century Aristotelian pattern of title, part of philosophy and causes. The reading level of the copyist(s) was basic, including word-order marks (r–v), grammatical terminology,[697] simple lexical synonyms,[698] vernacular equivalents,[699] and the missing letters of words abbreviated in the text

691 Reichling ( ), lxxxviii. Maaz ( ) deals briefly with some examples of late-medieval German use of *Doctrinale.* 692 See n. above.

693 v: Explicit Ebrardi *Grecismus* [...] Nomen scriptoris est Jacobus frater ordinis fratrum minorum, de conventu Forlivi, de civitate Janue, de illis de Montealto quantum ad nationem, die Ianuari.

694 Possibly one indicative water-mark (Briquet: letter S, n. a.). Text seems fragmentary at end: no sign of the last chapter on syntax.

695 v: Hic liber est mei Michaelis Taddei Simonis Dini de Ponte ad Sevem civis et notarius florentinus, qui liber habetur a Domino Rainaldo Mattei da Panzano, qui dedit mihi per ca(usam) hanc etc. 696 Especially r.

697 r: hec euphonia, -e, id est sonus bonus; hec tapinosis, -sis, id est perigrenatio; hec macrologia, -e, id est longus sermo.

698 r: parta = aquisita, constat = manifestum est, contra = id est per contrarium, inglorius = id est sine gloria.

699 r: vim = id est per forza; v: Abiurat patriam nunquam rediturus in illam = id est *zurare de no tronare mae in la soua patria.*

for metrical reasons.[700] A few interlinear glosses are not written by the copyist(s), but they are of an equally low level.[701] The copied marginalia are often vocabulary, normally accompanied by vernacular.[702] Often vocabulary lists are given for words mentioned in text, again with vernacular equivalents.[703] The marginalia also often provide explanation and definition.[704] One or two marginalia were not written by the scribe(s) nor were they copied from an exemplar, but again they o er the normal school-type grammatical fare.[705]

A number of miscellaneous grammatical topics often falling within the overall secondary grammatical curriculum were sometimes treated monographically in medieval and Renaissance Italy. One such topic consisted of synonyms/homonyms, the most famous treatment of which was Guarino's *Carmina di erentialia*, whose lexical contents have been well described by Keith Percival.[706] Like his other famous grammatical textbook, *Regule grammaticales*, *Carmina di erentialia* is not an original work. Its verse format belongs, of course, to the tradition of metrical textbooks going back to *Doctrinale* and *Graecismus*. Guarino was especially indebted to Evrard de Béthune, who not only provided the model for a school manual on lexicography but also furnished the specific source for much of the poem, which took many lines from *Graecismus* word for word.[707] It has been stated that what 'distinguishes Guarino's poem from works like the *Graecismus* is its brevity';[708] while it is true that *Carmina di erentialia* is far shorter than even the lexical sections alone of Evrard's work (chs. to), it would be misleading to suggest that conciseness in itself distinguished Guarino's verses from the traditional treatment of synonyms and homonyms. Indeed, two widely di used medieval treatments of the topics were the short treatises spuriously ascribed to Cicero as

700 graphia dia thastica
Orto. proso. dyasin. species tres gramatice sunt. (r)

701 de parto, -tis [*sic*] ex quinque et centum de nascor de dico de quiesco
Parsi quingenta natus dixitque quievi (r)

702 E.g.: hic punctus, -ti dictus a pupugi id est *el ponto che se fa in la pelle on ver in la carta on ver in del palpero*; hoc punctum, -ti dictum a punxi id est *el ponzere chi se fa con el scopelo on ver cum altra cosa.* (r)

703 v:
hec lis, -tis id est *l'atenzo*
hec glis, -tis id est *la napola*
[etc.]

704 E.g. r: Exallange est quando numerus singularis ponitur pro plurali ut naute complent naves armato millite ibi ponitur armato millite pro armatis militibus per exallanegem. Dicitur ab ex id est extra et alleos id est allienum et logos id est sermo quasi extra alienum sermonem.

705 E.g. Invenitur tamen in Tulio in colore de subiectione et est XVIII color: insuper grandi subiectione venitum est, etc. Iacet textus in ° rhetoricorum novorum. (r)

706 Percival ( ), . 707 See Percival ( ), – . 708 Percival ( ), .

Di erentiae[709] and *Synonyma*,[710] which also circulated in yet more abbreviated versions.[711] In fact, there is even a one-page *Di erentiae* in an early fifteenth-century grammatical miscellany which may have links with the Pisan grammarian Bartolomeo da S. Concordio,[712] who died in .[713] Nevertheless, it is also true that some pre-fifteenth century treatments of synonyms/homonyms could be far more wide-ranging than either Guarino's poem or the pseudo-Ciceronian treatises. For example, belonging to the same genre is a treatise divided into two parts, the first on nominal, the second on verbal, homonyms; both form parts of the same work, originally copied in the first half of the Duecento and then with the second part on verbal homonyms recopied at the end of the century or very beginning of the next. The work gives di erences and derivations of words in alphabetical order.[714]

Another secondary topic was orthography. It was di cult to be original in this field, too, in view of the long tradition of medieval orthographical textbooks. In Sabbadini demonstrated the similarities between humanist orthographies by Vittorino da Feltre and Cristoforo Scarpa and an anonymous later fourteenth-century treatise now found in BML Ashb. Append. , r– v, completed by the scribe Niccolino da Oppeano, near Verona, on May (v).[715] Even more eloquent of the medieval tradition's *longue-durée* is the fortune of pseudo-Phocas's orthography, a brief treatise mixing prose and verse,

709 Inc. [preface] Reperi autem etiam in antiquissimo codice libellum de di erentiis Ciceronis [...] inc. [text] Inter metum timorem et pavorem interest. I used following manuscripts: BRF (XV¹), r– v [inc. Inter aquam undam hoc interest]; BRF (XV²), r– v; Florence Biblioteca Marucelliana MS C.CCXCI (XV²), r– v; BNCF . (XV²), r– v.

710 Inc. [preface] Sinonimas M.T.C. diu frustra quaesitas tandem per Ser Coluccium Pieri honorabilem cancellarium inventas. Inc. [dedication] Cicero L. Veturio. Collegi ea quae pluribus modis dicerentur. Inc. [text] Abditum opertum abscondicum obscurum. I used the following manuscripts: BRF (XV¹), r– r; BRF (XV²), r– r; BRF (XV²), r– v; BRF (XV²), r– r; Florence Biblioteca Moreniana Moreni (XV²), r– r: Finis Ciceronis sinonimorum li(bri?) per Fratrem Baptistam ordinis Servorum Sancte Marie gramatice studendem [*sic*] (v); BML sup. (XVmid), r– r; BNCF . (XV²), r– r; BML Ashb. (*c.*), r– r.

711 E.g. *Di erentiae*: BNCF CS G. . (XV²), r– v; BML Gaddi (XVmid), r– r. On these texts, see Sabbadini ( ), ; Brugnoli ( ); Brugnoli ( ).

712 BRF (XV¹), r: inc. Di erentia est inter intendo et intelligo et vaco. On the same page begins Bartolomeo da S. Concordio's *Orthographia*: ( ) r– v: Incipit ortografia fratris Bartholomey de Concordia de Pisis ordinis predicatorum.

713 See Thurot ( ), – .

714 BML . , [ ] r– v: Inc. de nominum ac verborum nec non aliarum partium orationis di erentiis tractaturi de ipsis secundum ordinem abicedarum opipare {id est splendide} disseramus. [...] [ ] r– v: Inc. Dictis incidenter que dicenda erant de nominis de ernetiis, secundario vero quoniam verbum in ordine tractandi ponitur ut Priscianus de constructionibus tractans asserit.

715 See Sabbadini ( ), – .

composed before the thirteenth century;[716] borrowings from these mnemonics were made not only in the Duecento by Giovanni Balbi in *Catholicon* and Sion da Vercelli in *Novum Doctrinale* but also in the Quattrocento by Guarino, Vittorino and Scarpa, as well as by one Messer Niccolò di Ser Guido da Castelfranco in BRF and the anonymous adaptor of Guarino in BML Ashb. (v– r).[717] Sion da Vercelli wrote a verse orthography of his own too, starting from pseudo-Phocas's twenty verses and adding thirty-two more, probably mixing some original compositions with further borrowings.[718] Pseudo-Phocas's verses were accompanied by a prose commentary,[719] and this format was adopted possibly during the Trecento (and no later than : see the above-mentioned colophon) in the anonymous orthography of BML Ashb. Append. (r– v), as well as in the orthography by the humanist Cecco d'Ascoli,[720] both of whom commented on Sion da Vercelli's mnemonic verses. There is no question but that these spelling aids in verse format were widely used in schools: Sion's lines are accompanied by the usual classroom-type complaints about Priscian's prolixity,[721] and one version of his text is given a title explicitly referring to school use.[722] There are a number of other free-standing orthographies

716 Sabbadini ( ), , suggests 'avanti al sec. XIII, verso il XI', highlighting diphthongs 'ae' and 'oe', which were, according to the treatise, 'scribuntur sed non proferuntur', and which corresponded to spelling up to the earlier Duecento.

717 Sabbadini ( ), – . These verses also adapted in a Guarinian-type grammar copied by Ma eo Valaresso di Giorgio at Venice in : Segarizzi (– a), – .

718 Found in two MSS: BML Ashb. Append. , r– v, and Brescia Biblioteca Queriniana H. . ( ), v– v (the latter published by Beltrami (–), –). Discussion of this work by Capello ( ), , is inaccurate and confused: e.g. these two MSS contain the same mnemonic verses in the same order, and not just eighteen in common.

719 Sabbadini ( ), – . 720 Beltrami (–), – .

721 Beltrami (–), and n. , misunderstood the introduction of Ashb. Append. . He maintained that reference to 'prolixitatem primo traditam de hac (*scil.* orthographia) in maiori volumine' referred to the 'trattato ortografico, che sta nello stesso codice, f. A sgg.', but this must be an allusion to Priscian's treatment of orthography in the earlier books of the *Institutiones*, normally called *Priscianus maior*, explicitly criticized in a similar way in the Brescian MS:

Ashb. Append. , r (ed. Beltrami, –)	Querinano H. . , v (ed. Beltrami,)
Hic inferius quidam in Orthogrofiam versus causa vitandi prolixitatem primo traditam de hac in maiori volumine et memorie facilius retinendi, e Magistro Syon digno ac perito gramatice professore editi continentur […]	Quidam magister Simon propter prolixitatem orthographie Prisciani composuit ista carmina […]

722 BML Ashb. Append. , r: Incipit alius liber Orthogrofie qui legitur in scolis (cited by Beltrami (–),).

found in Florentine libraries,[723] but among these the best-known treatment is Barzizza's *De orthographia*, written about [724] and found in two Florentine manuscripts (BML Ashb. and).[725] It has been suggested that Barzizza's orthography was a particularly humanist work because of its rhetorical context,[726] as is made clear by its preface.[727] However, orthography had been associated in the middle ages not only

723 These include four treatises in BML Ashb. Append. : ( ) r– v, inc. Ad comunem scriptorum et lectorum utilitatem considerans. ( ) r– v: see above, . ( ) r– v, inc. Ut noticiam de orthogrofia habeamus breviter sciendum est, with colophon (v): Expliciunt volumina quatuor orthogrofie per diversos professores gramatice compillata et per me Nicholinum de Opp(ea)no exemplata. Sabbadini ( ), , said there were five treatises in this codex, possibly on the basis of this colophon, but I can find only three preceding it and a total of four. ( ) r– v, inc. Tractaturi de orthografia videamus quid sit orthogrofia et unde dicatur. Orthogrofia est pars gramatice. See Sabbadini ( ), – and above. This last text has the same incipit as Milan Biblioteca Ambrosiana Cod. N. sup., as cited by Bursill-Hall ( ), . The overall school context of the manuscript is clear from three roughly contemporary ownership marks on r, besides *probationes* on v– v, including alphabets (r), citation of first two lines of Boethius's *Consolation* (r) and immature drawings (v).
BNCF Magl. . (XVmid): r– v: inc. Vocum alia licterata alia inlicterata. Same incipit found in BNCF Magl. . : see Galante (–), ; and in BRF , r– v: Inc. Vocum alia literata alia inliterata.
BRF (XV¹): r– r: inc. Q[u]ocum alia litterata alia illiterata. expl. potest saltem in latinis dictionibus. Amen. Amen. Explicit utilis tractatus orthographie editus per Dominum Nicholaum Ser Guidonis de Castrofranco gramaticorum prestantissimum. Amen. See Sabbadini ( ), – . Cites mnemonic verses throughout, including three from *Doctrinale* (r). Apparently has same incipit as Magl. . , BNCF Magl. . and BRF .
BML AD (XVmid). r– v: Inc. Vocum alia litterata alia inlitterata. Vox litterata est illa que litteris scribi potest ut deus. This seems to have the same incipit as the above treatises. Repeated mnemonic verses. Cites *Doctrinale*, Priscian, *Graecismus*, Isidore. v (second front flyleaf): Est Hieronymi Miolti de Barga et amicorum. r: Di Girolamo di Maestro Franc. da Barga. Correct order of folios: , , , , , , , , , , , , .
Magl. . , r– r (XVmid), and BML sup. (XV²), v– v, have the same incipit.
BRF (XV¹), alphabetical orthography. r– v: Inc. A quandoque est littera, quandoque prepositio. Explicit in anno milleximo quadracintesimo vigessimo septimo die vigesima nona mensis decembris in vigesima secunda hora per me Jacobo [*sic*] Nicholai in terra Prati. Amen. Ibid.: Iste liber est mei — [*erasum*] de Prato scripto anno primo mei studi de mense decembris die hora septima nocturnis horis. This has been altered to: Iste liber est mei Petri Antonii Martini de Prato scripto anno de mense decembris . Includes copious mnemonics as well as citations of Lucan, Hugutio, Priscian, *Graecismus*, Sallust, *Doctrinale*.
BRF (XV¹), r: Carmina ortogrophie Magistri Johannis. Inc. A tum quibus componitur ab abs a separans. Expl. Compositum sic quoque difert. Attributed by Kristeller (–), . , . , to Tortelli.

724 On this treatise, see now Percival ( ), who cites relevant previous bibliography; for date, see – .

725 The copy in Ashb. (containing Filippo Casali's grammar course: see above, , and below,) is not listed by Bursill-Hall ( ) or Percival ( ) but is described by Kristeller (–), , . It occupies v– v. 726 Percival ( ), – .

727 BML Ashb. , r. See Percival ( ), , n. , quoting the passage from Venice Marciana Lat. . , r.

with grammar but also with rhetoric, as is apparent in the *Orthographia* by Maestro Parisio da Altedo, written in to improve the spelling among the notariate, a profession traditionally closely linked to the *ars dictaminis.*[728] Nor was Barzizza's tendency to appeal to ancient authorities in orthographical questions[729] unprecedented among medieval grammarians. For example, Parisio da Altedo cited Priscian more than thirty times in his orthography;[730] moreover, he was aware of archaic classical spelling[731] and he also cited Vergil.[732] Nor can the humanists be credited with novel brevity in the field of spelling, in view of the fact that short orthographies were commonplace in the medieval tradition. For example, there are the brief verse orthographies by pseudo-Phocas and Sion da Vercelli discussed above, or the *Orthographia* by the Pisan grammarian Bartolomeo da S. Concordìo (d.), which occupies only two folios,[733] or the treatise explicitly entitled *Orthographia parvis et*

728 BNCF NA (XV[1]), r–v: Incipit Ortagraphia Magistri Parisii de Altedo ad Baldum notarium amicum suum. <P>recordiali suo conpatri Baldo notario Parisius de Altedo salutem et desiderii sui partem. Rogatus a te quod in ortographia regulas aliquas compilarem, incertorum prius a ectuum fluctibus agitabar. Nam inter ansias rei scolastice tempestates, et mihi durum erat huiusmodi studio mentem advertere, at longe durius tue dilectionis nutibus, quoad fieri poterat, non parere. Sane tanto facilius me tua movere precamina quanto te, quem mihi fervens unit caritas, super hac re non sine causa noveram diutius studiosum. Ea quippe arti tue tabellionatui doctrine, cui dudum et ego deservio, est admodum oportuna [...] Datum penes armarium notarii kalendis maii anni millesimi ducentesimi nonagesimi septimi nativitatis dominice illabentis. There is an older MS (BNP Sorb.) identified by Thurot ( ), , where author is identified as 'de Altedo comitatus Bononie'. School context of this work is apparent from numerous citations of mnemonic verses; the text ends with a final summary in metric form (BNCF NA , v– v: inc. Vocalis prior a vocales transit in omnes. expl. M sed subtracta cui dic git proposita sunt) o ered to aid memorization, as is made explicit in the final prose paragraph (r):

Novissime autem quia nequit oculus dispersa locis variis nisi cum di cultate circumfer[enti]a mentis consistorio presentare, versus omnes supra suis locis expositos hoc loco in unum recolligendos d<u>xi et ad faciliorem memoriam finali methodo repetendos.

On Parisio di Benvenuto da Altedo, see Cavazza ( ), – ; Schiavetto (–).

729 See Percival ( ), .

730 BNCF NA , r, v, r, v, v, r, v, r, r, r, r, v, v, v, r, r, v, v, v, r, v, r, v, r, v, v, v, r, v.

731 BNCF NA , v: Et apud antiquissimos quotienscunque nd sequitur e in his verbis que a tertia coniugatione nascuntur loco e invenimus u scriptum ut faciundum legundum dividundum pro faciendum legendum dividendum

r: antiqui dicebant lubens pro libens pessumus pro pessimus

v: ut maius peius eius troia in quibus antiqui geminabant i dicentes maiius peiius

732 r–v:

Hec littera [sc. s] in metro apud vetustissimos plerunque vim suam amictit ut in Virgilii [Virgilio MS] libro:

Inter se coisse viros et discernere ferro.

733 BRF , r– v [XV[1]]: Bartolomeo da S. Concordìo, Orthographia, inc. Incipit ortografia fratris Bartholomey de Concordia de Pisis ordinis predicatorum. Post tractatum de dictionibus proferendis restat ut describendis aliquid breviter videamus de verbalibus. Found in BNP Lat. , v– r, inc. Incipit orthographia. Post tractatum de dictionibus. expl. Explicit orthogra-

utilis,[734] which is a thoroughly non-humanist text (albeit found in a manuscript dating from the s).

The force of tradition was prevalent in the teaching of formal grammar in the fifteenth-century Italian schoolroom, but there are some interesting instances of instruction which was fundamentally conservative but yet still willing to take on board innovations. One such example is an anonymous compendium on construction dated (Florence Biblioteca Marucelliana MS A.c.s.).[735] The author was a teacher evidently working near Florence, as is clear from the predominance of geographical references to the city;[736] it seems that he had some particular association with Castelfiorentino, which is the only smaller town repeatedly mentioned in the text.[737] The work's secondary grammar context is clear not only from the opening reference to *iuvenum ingenium*, but also from the repeated examples drawn from school life.[738] The compendium is divided into four subtractates, covering concordance, governance by case, governance by the eight parts of speech and impediments to construction; within each section, the time-honoured format of question and answer is adopted.

On the one hand, this is a highly traditional work: unusually for an Italian grammar manual, the text is even imbued with concepts and terminology from speculative and modistic grammar, usually more characteristic of North Europe. Thus, not only is there the usual traditional

fia fratris Bartholomei de Sancto Concordio Pisani ordinis fratrum predicatorum. See Thurot ( ), – ; Bursill-Hall ( ), . It is the same treatise: e.g.

BRF , r	Thurot ( ),
Omnia verbalia desinens [*sic*] in io debet scribi per illas litteras quas scribitur suppinum a quo descendit; unde, si in suppino sit t, et in verbali erit ut amatum amatio.	Omne verbale desinens in *io* debet scribi per illas litteras per quas scribitur supinum a quo descendit Unde si in supino sit *T*, et in verbali erit, ut *amatum*, *amatio.*

Found in Rome Bibl. Casanatense MS , r .: Manacorda ( ), ; Kaeppeli (–), , .

734 BRF , r– r, inc. Ortogrophia est ordinatio licterarum in silabis, not listed by Bursill-Hall ( ). For this MS see below, , .

735 r r: inc. Compendium regiminis et constructionis gramaticale ad iuvenum ingenium. expl. ob expletionem istius opusculi regularum gramaticalium, deo gratias, amen, anno . The codex is one of the Conventi Soppressi MSS now in the Marucelliana.

736 v: florentinus; r: civitas Florentie; v: studui Florentie; r: studui Florentie; vado Florentia[m]; r–v: venio Florentia; v: venio Florentie [*sic*], mansi tribus mensibus Florentia [*sic*].

737 r: Castrum Florentini; r: studui Castro Florentini. The rear flyleaf, apparently the original cover, is a fragment of a notarial act (XIVc.) from Castel Fiorentino.

738 v: quot sunt pueri in studio; r: doceo Petrum gramaticam; r: scolares student, unus gramaticam alter loicam; v, r: Petrus studens; r: currunt scolares; r: iste verberatur a magistro.

vocabulary found in grammarians such as Pietro da Isolella and Francesco da Buti (*appositum, suppositum, antecedens, regere, a parte ante, a parte post, transitio*) but the author also repeatedly discusses *modi significandi*; similarly, not only does the text cite the normal traditional authorities (Alexander, Donatus, Priscian, *Catholicon*, *Graecismus*) but, extraordinarily for an Italian secondary treatise, Northern European grammars infrequently encountered in Italy such as *Flores grammaticae* by Ludolphus de Lucho and the anonymous *Priscianus metricus*, not to mention northern grammarians such as Petrus Helias and 'Rubertus [Kilwardby]' and even the prominent thirteenth-century modal theorist, Michel de Marbais. In fact, one of the author's principal theses is that an understanding of modal theory is essential for a true grasp of construction and governance.[739] These comments must have been directed against the Italian grammatical tradition, in which little notice was taken of modal grammar; in fact, they have overtones of a rivalry and even animosity of academic a liation, suggesting perhaps that the author had studied in or perhaps was originally from Northern Europe.

On the other hand, as a teacher now working south of the Alps in the second half of the fifteenth century, the author of the Marucellian compendium felt the need to build bridges to Italian grammar teaching, and particularly, to humanism. Thus, he also repeatedly cited classical authors, and in particular Terence, and he took on board a significant amount of the latest avant-garde humanist approach, in particular, the work of Valla.[740] Thus, when discussing the use of ablatives and geni-

739 v: Quero primo utrum cognitio modorum significandi sit necessaria ad sciendum regimina et constructiones in gramatica [...] Dico quod sic [...] Patet ergo clare quod modi [MS: modus] significandi sunt causa regiminis et constructionis; contra, plures reperiuntur boni gramatici qui modorum significandi cognitionem ignorant [...] Licet sint boni gramatici usuales [...] tamen non sunt gramatici scientifici et perfetti, quia omnis [MS: omne] sciens cognoscit causam sui sed illi ignorant causam sui sciti. The hand of the copyist shows some possibly Northern European features, such as the constant use of the long final 's' and a -shaped 'et' with a vertical stroke curving to the left.

An earlier Italian grammarian who drew heavily on northern and indeed modistic traditions was Giovanni del Virgilio: see Alessio (b). His treatises, as reported by Alessio, range beyond limits of normal Italian secondary syllabus. For further indication of the penetration (albeit limited) of modistic theory in XVc. Italy, see Jensen ( ), – .

The XVc. Sicilian humanist Tommaso Schifaldo's modal grammar treatise was not a school-level work: see Kaster and Noakes ( ), – .

740 This early evidence of the modest penetration of Valla into Italian grammar schools is paralleled by passages for thematic translation made by one Acchino during , found in Bologna Bibl. Univers. MS , analysed by Tavoni ( ), who conclusively demonstrates that they are not the work of Valla himself. Further evidence comes from the *ricordanza* of Filippo Strozzi (ASF CStrozz. . , lxxxv recto) where his son Alfonso, a grammar pupil, is paid on March 'per leghaturo d'uno libro e miniatura di L° Valla'. However, Tavoni ( ), , is certainly right to emphasize the overall lack of influence of Valla's *Elegantiae* at the school level: 'e presumibile che la novità di struttura, l'oggettiva di coltà e la scarsa maneggevolezza del testo ne abbiano impedito una di usione scolastica capillare [...]'

tives of price, he conceded that the modists were more logical, but Valla more elegant.[741] It is not surprising that the author did not always take Valla's part, siding with Poggio, who had criticized Valla's understanding of gerunds.[742] Nevertheless, in the question of the second supine, the author of the compendium again gave credit to Valla's approach.[743]

741 r–v: Sed hic averte, ut dicit Laurentius de Vallo, qui [MS: quis] se fundat in dittis poetarum, cum ista regula iam ditta semper regunt accusativum [MS: accusativo] cum ablativo et numquam regunt alios genitivos preter istos scilicet tanti quanti minoris et pluris, et hoc quando isti genitivi per se sine substantivo [MS: substantivum] capiuntur, sed cum [MS: tunc] capiuntur cum [MS: con] substantivo debent poni in ablativo: exemplum ut quanti emisti, non aute[m] quanto emisti, sed quanto pretii emisti et non quanti pretii emisti. Sed tamen qui [MS: quia] argueret contra Laurentium de Vallo et diceret si ista verba habe[n]t modum di(cendi) per quem possunt regere isti quatuor genitivum dittorum [MS: dittos], quare pe[r] eundem modum [MS: modiis] dicendi non possunt regere alios genitivo[s], cum ibi eadem causa et idem efettus manere debet, nec valet motivum suum, quo arguit, poete non posuerunt, ergo non regunt, cum argumentum ab autoritate negative non valet. Dico quod artificialiter loquendo etiam potest regere alios genitivos sed magis eleganter qui [MS: quia] ut poete dicunt, et hoc vult Laurentius de Vallo.

742 r: De materia gerundiorum [...] est verbum ut patet per di nittionem [...] quidquid regit casum a parte ante est verbum, sed gerundia regunt casum a parte ante, scilicet acusativum, ergo sunt verba. Ex quo patet [quod] gerundia non sunt nomina neque participia, quia tales partes nullum regunt casum a parte ante. Contra participia; ergo non sunt verba. Antecedens probo p[er] Laurentium de Vallo in formam sic dicentem: Gerundia licet a participiis di erunt, tamen proprie inter participia numerari possunt, sicut suppina inter verba merito que parti(cipia) vocata sunt. Nam genera et casus habent in utroque numero, ex quo verba non sunt, sed participia. Ibi expresse dicit gerundia non esse verba [sed] participia. Dico quod licet Laurentius de Vallo multa verba [MS: verbo] dixerit de terminorum elegantia, tamen salva sua reverentia in ista materia gerundiorum multum errat, nec ratione ad istud suum dittum potest similiter et in aliis pluribus materiis sed in nudis poetarum dittis se fundat. Quorum quidam maxime nomine Pogius quandam invectivam contra istum Laurentium dedit in qua asserit [MS: abserit] Laurentium sua propria non intellexisse verba gerundiorum.

743 v– v: Quero [...] quot [MS: quod] sunt proprietates que comuniter [a]scribuntur ipsis participiis [...] secunda proprietas est [quod] omne participium sit derivatum a verbo [...] Contra, ultimum suppinum numquam debe[t] construi cum verbo significante [MS: significantem] motum de loco, ergo dictum est falsum. Antecedens probo per Laurentium de Vallo sic arguentem: omnis nostra latinitas pri[n]cipium habuit a Grecis et precipue a poetis. Sed in nulla poetria ultimum suppinum reperitur [MS: non reperitur] cum verbo significante [MS: verbum significantem] motum de loco, ergo utimum suppinum non potest construi cum verbo significante [MS: significantem] motum de loco. Dico quod secundum nostros comunes gramaticos negando consequentiam qui[a] locus ab autoritate negativa non valet etc. potest dici ad argumentum dictum quod maior est falsa, quia latinitas nostra magis summitur a proportione [MS: proportionem] modorum quam ab autoritate et dico ultra quod licet non sit actoritas in poetria, tamen autoritas probata Petre Helie, Alexandri et Floriste, Thomme et multorum aliorum nobis suficiunt [suficint MS], et ratio nos cogens, que sumitur [MS: summitur] a parte finis istorum suorum, ut dittum est supra nobis sufragatum. Nota diligenter quod licet ista dici potest sicut dictum est de ultimo suppino, qui[a] omnis gramatica hoc nunc habet, tamen rei veritate puto quod ultimum suppinum magis elegante[r] et proprie construitur cum [MS: con] nominibus adiettivis ut mirabili[s] visu [MS: vinsu], facile [MS: facere] dictu. De hoc probo, quod habet dictus Laurentius, quod nullus negat ipsum, quoniam antiqui gramatici et precipue poete usi sunt ultimo suppino, sicut et primo, sed cum primum suppinum sepe reperitur cum verbo significante motum ad locum et ultimum suppinum semper construitur cum nomine adiecttivo et non cum verbo significante [MS: verbum significantem] motum ad locum, ergo veresimile est quod ultimum suppinum debet construi cu[m] nominativo significante [MS: significantem] motum de loco. Maior istius rationis probatum [*sic*]: Nam Terrentius habet istas orationes de

The Marucellian compendium thus at least acknowledged the existence of humanist grammatical theory, nor was its author the only progressive working in Florence. In a miscellaneous manuscript (BML Antinori), compiled by the Florentine Lodovico Do between [744] and [745] and including religious tracts and medical recipes, there is also found a secondary grammar treatise.[746] The scope of this textbook is entirely traditional,[747] as is its grammatical terminology (*a parte post, causa e ciens/finalis/materialis /instrumentalis*), and it includes the normal mnemonic verses too. What is unusual about this treatise is its use of the vernacular. It not only provides the normal vernacular equivalents of Latin example words[748] and thematic translations[749] but also gives a vernacular table of contents[750] as well as some running headings in the *volgare*.[751] What is extraordinary is that this mid fifteenth-century treatise also o ers extended grammatical explanations in the vernacular, e.g. for

footnote (*cont.*) primo suo in *Andria* [...] Item de ultimo su[ppino] habet istas orationes in tertia commedia [...] Sed quibus non placet sic dicere forte responderet quod in predittis orationibus factu non esset ultima suppina si esset abl[a]tivi casus nominum quarte declinationis verbalium, quia ab isti[s] verbis adiettivis reguntur ex vi efettus cause materialis, in qua per sinodocham costructionis iterum reprobatur ad longum per Laurentium de Vallo. [744] See r. [745] See v.

746 v– v.

747 It touches on phonetics, nominal declensions and genders, orthography, derivative verbs, participles, gerunds, comparatives, superlatives, interrogatives, verbals, pronouns, partitives, conjunctions, figures, nominal accidence, nominal types (distributive, negative, infinite), prepositions, and prosody.

748 (v) Hec touroma -tis. *Li adornamenti sopra letto*, hoc mare -ris *il mare*, hoc sedile -lis *la chazzuola*, hic et hec virgo -nis *il maschio et femina vergine*, hoc lac -tis *il latte*, hic alco -cis *il pesciolino*, hic david davidis *davieti*, hic cimber -bri *il fiandresco*.

749 v: Egho servivi Petro tamen ipse odiat me. *Benché io abbia servito Piero niente di meno elgli m'odia.* Petrus servivit mihi sed Martinus odit mihi. *Piero à servito me ma Martino m'odia.*

750 v:

IIIº parte di gramaticha
VII gienerazione de' nomi
E nomi degli animali
V declinazione de' nomi
L'adizzioni che'npedischono il verbo principale
De' verbi inchoativi
De' verbi imitativi
De' participii
Chonsequentie et chonchomitanzie
[...]

751 r: *De' pronomini che ssono XV semplici*
r: *Del numero de' nomi*
v: *Della fighura secondo gramaticha*
r: *Del chaso del nome*

participles,[752] superlatives,[753] or nominal accidence.[754] The overall appearance of this treatise is macaronic; nevertheless, its quantity and particularly its use of the vernacular to explain Latin grammatical doctrines not only show the force of the *volgare* tradition in Florence but also point to a future time when the Italian language would provide the normal medium for Latin pedagogy and when the vernacular, not Latin, would predominate in the field of grammar.[755]

Another peculiarly macaronic grammar treatise from the later fifteenth century is found in manuscript BRF . This work is organized according to the normal progressive structure of the secondary syllabus.[756] What is not usual is that this material is presented not in terms of explanation or examples but rather in terms of thematic exercises for translation. Each of these topics (and their numerous subdivisions) is represented by a passage in the vernacular, which is then followed by its translation into Latin. The obvious purpose here was to provide practice in Latin prose composition at each of the various stages of the normal progressive syllabus. For example, the first passage to translate deals with the so-called first order of active verbs.[757] This is then

752 r: *E verbi attivi ànno due participii uno in* ans vel in ens *e formansi da preteriti inperfetti levato* bam *e agunto* ans *overo* ens fit amans et docens, *e l'altro* in tus *e formasi dal supino agiuntovi* rus fit amaturus et doturus, et *verbi passivi anche n'ànno due, l'uno in* tus *e l'altro in* dus *e lo in* tus *si forma dal supino agiuntovi* s *ed è fatto* amatus *e* doctus *e lo in* dus *si forma dal gienetivo del participio in* ans vel in ens *levato* tis *e agiuntovi* dus *e fatto* amandus et docendus, et *verbi neultri n'ànno due e non più cioè in* ans vel in ens et in rus et *formansi chome quelgli de' verbi activi detti di sopra. Et verbi deponenti ànno tre participii cioè in* ans vel in ens et in tus et in ens *cioè* sequens secuturus *e* sechutus *e formansi chome è detto di sopra de' verbi attivi e de' passivi et verbi chomuni n'ànno quattro cioè quelgli che ànno gli attivi et passivi et formansi nel medesimo modo, e sopradetti tutti participii non regghono inanzi a lloro niuno chaso e dopo se quel chaso ch'el verbo loro e il forte s'adoperano nelle consequenzie et conchomitanzie.*

Consequentia: magistro legente scolares adiscunt.

Conchomitantia temporis, *cioè quando in uno medesimo tempo si fanno due cose, cioè* Petro anbulante ad palatium transivit per forum. 753 r. 754 r–v.

755 See excellent discussion in Grendler ( ), – .

756 Beginning with active verbs, and going on to passives, neutral possessives, neutral acquisitives, neutral transitives, neutral e ectives, neutral absolutes, common verbs, deponents (including acquisitve, e ective), impersonals, gerunds, supines, participles, verbals, relatives, numerals, adverbs of time and place, patronymics, comparatives and superlatives, derivative verbs, figures, punctuation, and finally letter writing.

757 r–v:

Ex diferentiis primi ordinis activorum

Se ogni di tutti voi havessi portato e libri che voi udite a casa, e le vostre membra havessino patito gl'incommodi de le veglie che producono fructi tanto suavi, che tutti li huomini savi ne hanno voglia, e se almen che sia ne' dì di lavorare ne' vostri studii vi fussi consigliati o con maestro o con li amici che vi harebbono consigliato bene, e de' quali ciascheduno a qualunche di voi harebbe dato aiuto, e provisto a la utilità di tutti intorno a le buone lettere e buoni costumi, io per mia fe' non solamente vi harei voluto e vorrei bene e assai amato ma ancora per tutto

followed by a (less than literate) Latin translation.[758] In both these works, one is nearing the point at which the predominant language in teaching Latin would not be Latin but the vernacular – a development which would become pronounced in the sixteenth century.[759]

Another glimmer of innovation in the Quattrocento classroom was the occasional use of ancient grammatical texts little used during the Italian middle ages. An example is the *Ars de nomine et verbo* by the late ancient grammarian Phocas. This work, written as a school text for his pupils in Rome probably during the early fifth century, enjoyed a modest circulation and influence in Northern Europe during the middle ages, but hardly any at all in Italy (apart from an early copy made at Montecassino in the late eighth century and the use made by Lorenzo da Montecassino, abbot of Amalfi (d.), of Remigius of Auxerre's commentary on the *Ars de nomine et verbo*). After Poggio's recovery of the text at Fulda in , it became a fashionable work in Italian humanist circles: of the forty-one fifteenth-century manuscripts, almost all are Italian; a number are connected with prominent Italian patrons such as the Bembo, Montefeltro and Strozzi families; some can even be directly associated with humanists such as Poliziano, Pietro di Montagnana, Pietro Odi da Montopoli and Matteo Ronto. Some fifteenth-century copies reveal characteristic school use such as vernacular glossing (BAV Reg. Lat. and Vat. Lat.), and a gloss on one version makes an explicit reference to the teaching of Pietro Odi.[760] Of the Quattrocento versions in Florence, two are fair copies without an educational context,[761] but two others can be regarded as possible schoolbooks. BML AD , datable to the later fifteenth century, has no significant glosses but forms an anthology with the most popular school-level stylistic

footnote (*cont.*)
portato honore e riverenza, e benché siate giovanetti, come buono consigliatore non sarei mancato mai chieditori di consiglio [...]

758 v: Si quotidie vos omnes libros, quos auditis, domum tulissetis et membra vestra vigiliarum incommoda tulissent, quae fructus ferunt tam suaves ut omnes viri sapientes eos desiderent, et si in diebus saltem profestis in vestris studiis vel magistros vel amicos consuluissetis, qui bene vobis consuluissent, et ex quibus quisque quenque vestrum iuvisset, omniumque utilitati circa bonas litteras moresque consuluisset, ego medius fidius vos non solum dilexissem et diligerem valdeque amavissem verum etiam coluissem, et licet estis adulescentuli, ceu consultor bonus vobis nunquam consultoribus defuissem [...]

759 See above, . Growing predominance of vernacular as medium for teaching Latin in XVIc. is illustrated in Aonio Paleario's *Dialogo intitolato Il grammatico, overo delle false essercitazioni delle scuole*, published in , where he says that the grammarian must 'insegnare con la lingua che ha propria et che è commune a lui et a' scolari': cited by Avesani ( ), .

760 Preceding remarks are based on the excellent study by Jeudy ( ).

761 BML Ashb. (XV^2), r– r; BNCF Magl. . (XVmid), r– v.

manual of the later Quattrocento, Agostino Dati's *Elegantiolae.*[762] BML Gaddi , datable to the earlier or mid-fifteenth century, was copied by Alessandro Arrighi, probably a Florentine;[763] a school context is suggested by the vernacular *probationes* on the front parchment flyleaf or cover (r) as well as by a vocabulary list of Greek terms transliterated into Latin which follows the text (r–v). Despite this evidence of school-type activity, nevertheless, it would be misleading to emphasize the influence or di usion of Phocas's *Ars* in fifteenth-century schools, as is clear, for example, from its modest incunabular history.[764]

But despite these glimmers of change the Italian Quattrocento must remain, in the history of secondary grammar, a period of tradition and failed reform: the twelfth century invented the secondary verse grammar; the thirteenth century produced the secondary prose *summa*; the fourteenth century added the vernacular as a teaching method for secondary theoretical grammar; but the fifteenth century witnessed Guarino's conservatism, the ine ectual reform e orts of Sozomeno, Gaspare and Perotti, and the failed revolution of Pomponio, who, despite his radicalism, was unable completely to set aside tradition. Even in a negative sense the Quattrocento did not succeed in banishing medieval grammatical ignorance and barbarity – to repeat Valla's condemnation[765] – from the schoolroom: until at least the advent of printing Francesco da Buti and Pietro da Isolella continued in wide use; Papias, Hugutio and *Catholicon* happily survived the coming of the press; and all attempts to replace or correct *Doctrinale* failed in Italy until the mid-Cinquecento. It is a bizarre fact that, among all Western European countries, Alexander of Villedieu remained strongest in the very cradle

[762] See below, .

[763] Florentine provenance suggested by watermark, identified by Jeudy (,) as a variation of Briquet (Florence, –) and by ownership of Florentine Agnolo di Zanobi Gaddi as well as by reference to 'Cini di Firenze' (r). However, I have been unable to find a convincing candidate for the copyist 'Alexander Arigus' (v). If he belonged to the Florentine Arrighi family, apparently three possibilities exist: ( ) Alessandro di Jacopo di Francesco, b. March , d. , a figure of some political importance, who sat as a member of Dodici Buonuomini in , of Sedici Gonfalonieri in and of Signoria in ; ( ) Alessandro di Simone di Alessandro di Jacopo, b. ; ( ) Alessandro di Jacopo di Bernardo di Jacopo di Francesco, b. before , date of his father's death (BNCF Carte Passerini , r–v, r, r–v). The book is too early to have been copied by ( ) or ( ), and ( ) seems too old to have copied it as a grammar pupil, if it is true that the work first came to prominence in Italy as a result of Poggio's discovery in ; he would also seem to have been too prominent politically and socially for a teacher.

[764] See *IGI*, , – .

[765] See Percival ( ), – .

of humanism. Humanist teachers faced a real dilemma: they were repelled by the logical underpinning of the traditional approach to secondary grammar, and its reliance on barbarous Latin mnemonic verses and the vernacular. And yet these were practical solutions to the teaching of Latin composition to non-native speakers; a return to Priscian's discursive and philological methods, attempted by Pomponio Leto, was just as unsatisfactory in the fifteenth century as it had been in the early middle ages. In the history of grammatical education, what the Quattrocento created was not a series of tangible innovations – no genuinely new and successful methods or textbooks – but rather a revolutionary ideology: the aim was to replace scholastic linguistic terminology and theory, medieval verse grammars and prose *summe*, but humanist school grammarians did not yet know how or with what. In the Italian Quattrocento, the aspirations were high but the practical results few. As Sabbadini aptly declared: 'il medio evo era più facile biasimarlo nella teoria che sostituirlo nella pratica'.[766]

766 Sabbadini ( ), .

Latin authors in medieval and Renaissance Italian schools: the story of a canon

The study of the Latin authors was the principal activity of Roman grammar schools,[1] and this educational tradition was handed down to the middle ages.[2] Beginning in the high middle ages there was a tendency to distinguish two types of authors, major and minor,[3] as Conrad of Hirsau (*c.* –*c.*) suggests in his *Dialogus super auctores.*[4] Which authors Conrad considers to be major or minor becomes clearer from the context. As *minores* suitable for 'rudimentis parvulorum',[5] there are the grammarian Donatus, Cato (an anthology of philosophical *sententiae* in distichs and monostichs, dating from imperial Rome), Aesop (the late-antique collection of fables in prose) and Avianus (forty-two fables in distichs, written *c.*); next come the Christian poets Sedulius (the fifth-century writer of the *Paschale carmen*), Juvencus (the author of an hexameter life of Christ), Prosper of Aquitaine (who versified some *sententiae* of Augustine in the earlier fifth century) and Theodulus (an unknown author of a tenth-century eclogue contrasting paganism and Christianity). Conrad is not explicit about the *maiores*, but having treated the *minores*, he says, 'Veniamus nunc ad romanos auctores':[6] here he includes Arator (the sixth-century author of a hexametrical version of the Book of Acts), Prudentius (the outstanding early Christian poet, writing at the turn of the fifth century), Cicero, Sallust, Boethius, Lucan, Vergil and Horace; subsequently he also discusses Ovid, Juvenal, *Ilias latina* (a reduction of the *Iliad* to hexameters, made possibly in the first century by Baebius Italicus), Persius and Statius.[7] A similar

[1] Marrou ( ), – . [2] Riché ( ), .

[3] For this contemporary terminology, instead of the anachronistic *Libri catoniani*, I follow Avesani (b). On the minor authors, the fundamental work remains Avesani ( ).

[4] Conrad of Hirsau ( ), : 'a minoribus quibuscumque auctoribus inciperem et per hos ad maiores pervenirem et gradus auctorum inferiorum occasio mihi fierent in discendo superiorum'. [5] Conrad of Hirsau ( ), . [6] Conrad of Hirsau ( ), .

[7] Curtius ( ), , .

distribution of school authors appears in the *Ars lectoria* ( ) of Aimeric of Gâtinaux, whose golden and tin authors are thus roughly synonymous with Conrad's major and minor.[8]

This classification of school authors as *maiores* and *minores* persisted into the later middle ages and Renaissance. Hugh of Trimberg, in his *Registrum multorum auctorum* ( ), divided the authors into *ethici maiores* and *ethici minores*,[9] and in the *De recuperatione Terre Sancte* (–), Dubois wrote of the 'Puer cum audiet librum Cathonis et alios minutos actores',[10] while in at the University of Bologna Giovanni del Virgilio was appointed to teach 'versificaturam et poesim et magnos auctores, videlicet Virgilium, Statium, Luchanum et Ovidium'.[11] Giovanni Conversini da Ravenna, writing of his early school days in Bologna *c.* , grouped the minor authors together, distinguishing them from the elementary syllabus.[12] The statutes of the University of Perpignan (*c.*) used similar terminology.[13] In , an anthology was published at Pamplona with the title *Libros menores*, while in his *De optimo studio iuvenum*, published in , Heinrich Bebel likewise wrote of *minutiores auctores*.[14]

:

This canon of authors was by no means fixed: not only did certain authors rise and fall in popularity over the centuries, but there were even periods when the study of the great classics went into eclipse. In the Roman era there had been vacillation, too: under the late Republic, texts written by poet-masters such as Livius Andronicus and Ennius dominated, until, at the beginning of the Christian epoch, Vergil (even before his death) and other contemporary poets were introduced; in Rome, indeed, all the great poets were read at school in their own lifetimes, including Ovid, Statius and Lucan. At the end of the first century ,

[8] Curtius ( ), . [9] Avesani (b), . [10] Avesani (b), n.

[11] Rossi ( ), .

[12] *Rationarium vite*, extracted by Sabbadini ( ), ; Garin ( ), : 'Quippe cum essem ordinis secundi, cuntorum latina carmina notabilia antecedentium, Catonis preterea Prosperi, Boecii quidquid legeretur, complecti mente ac reddere compellebat.' I am grateful to Silvia Rizzo for clarifying the meaning of these lines. She suggests that the comma after 'Catonis' should actually follow 'antecedentium'; this would then give the following translation: 'when I was in the second class, he [sc. the teacher] made me memorize and recite the notable Latin verses from everything read before [i.e. the Psalter] and in addition whatever was lectured on of Cato, Prosper and Boethius'. Misconstrued by Sabbadini (, : 'Con che s'intende che Esopo, "Eva columba", "Tres leo naturas" e forse "Chartula nostra tibi" precedevano Catone, al quale seguivano Prospero e Boezio'). [13] Avesani (b), – . [14] Avesani (b), .

however, a new classicism, championed first by Quintilian, took root, centring the curriculum on the giants of earlier Latin literature: Vergil, Terence, Sallust and Cicero. These authors were as good as canonized by Arusianus Messius in his collection of *Exempla elocutionum ex Virgilio, Sallustio, Terentio, Cicerone digesta per litteras*, published in and cited as the *Quadriga Messii* by Cassiodorus.[15]

Similarly in Italian schools under the early barbarian kings, the status of the authors vacillated. On the one hand, the literary tradition of Roman grammatical study persisted in Italy until the end of the sixth century. A hundred years earlier in the secular schools of Ravenna, the future Christian poet Arator, destined for a legal career, was introduced to classical poets and prose-writers by a fellow student, Parthenius.[16] For his contemporary, Cassiodorus, grammar was the art of fine discourse derived from classical poets and authors.[17] Even in the later sixth century, after Italy had been ravaged first by the wars between the Ostrogoths and Byzantines and then by the Lombard invasions, the traditional study of the classical authors had not yet perished: Venantius Fortunatus's mastery of classical poetic technique was based on early grammar lessons in Ravenna which he enjoyed together with his friend Felix; even Pope Gregory the Great, famous for rejecting classical culture after his conversion,[18] had, as a member of the Roman senatorial aristocracy, enjoyed a formation based on the classical authors, one which continued to leave its mark on his writings. A last glimmer of the Italian literary tradition can be seen in the education of the mid seventh-century hagiographer, Jonas, whose education at Susa in northwest Italy provided him with a knowledge of Roman history, as well as of Christian and pagan poets.[19]

On the other hand, the growth of Italian monasticism in the fifth and sixth centuries began to o er an alternative to traditional secular Roman grammatical education. Figures such as Benedict of Nursia saw pagan and Christian culture as incompatible; according to his biographer, Gregory the Great, Benedict had hardly begun secular studies before abandoning them, terrified by the dangers which they posed. In early monastic schools, for example at Montecassino, reading material was no longer the classical authors but the Psalter and other biblical texts, monastic rules, works of the Church Fathers, and lives of the Fathers and of the martyrs.[20] Secular studies similarly were excluded in the

[15] Marrou ( ), – , . [16] Riché ( ), . [17] Cassiodorus ( ), , .

[18] See his declaration that the same mouth cannot utter praises of Jove and Christ (*Ep.* .), in Gregory the Great ( ), . [19] Riché ( ), , – , – , – , – .

[20] Riché ( ), , – .

nascent episcopal schools; the curriculum, limited to sacred literature, included the Scriptures, the Acts of Martyrs and the lives of saints.[21]

The exclusively Christian, rather than antique, style of education seems to have gained the upper hand in seventh-century Italy. At the monastery of Bobbio, founded in by the Irish monk, Columbanus, the early library was largely limited to religious works. These manuscripts are mostly palimpsests, written over pagan Latin and Arian texts; the scribes at Bobbio procured texts of Livy, Cicero and Plautus, which they proceeded to rub out, recopying Christian authors considered more appropriate for study. Nothing specific is known about Latin education among the Lombards in the seventh century, except that the claim for the existence of a law school at Pavia is groundless; the intellectual concerns of the court seem to have been mainly religious. Literary studies were weak in the city of Rome itself. Pope Agatho (d.) protested against the simplicity and limited knowledge of the Latin bishops, and among northern barbarians Rome enjoyed prestige more as a model of rite and liturgy than as a centre of Latin learning. The Lateran scriptorium was dormant: no manuscripts produced there in the seventh century have survived; on the other hand, its past treasures provided bibliophiles throughout the West such as Benedict Biscop with rich pickings, few, if any, of which were replaced.[22]

In the eighth century this predominantly Christian education continued to prevail in Italy. Lombard princes refounded or established monasteries, but these were, like their sixth-century ancestors, liturgical and ascetic centres; the education there was in *sacris litteris*. Even Montecassino, restored about after almost a century and a half's abandonment, was simply a school for monastic discipline; monks learned reading there, but its scriptorium did not begin to function until the second half of the century, books such as the Bible and the rule of St Benedict having to be imported from Rome. Paul the Deacon (b. *c.*), who came in , was the abbey's first monk educated in profane literature. Similarly, Latin literature seems to have been little cultivated in the city of Rome itself. Biographies of popes repeat the commonplace 'divinis scripturis eruditus, pro eruditione ecclesiasticae disciplinae'. Documents and texts issuing from the Lateran indicate the standard of studies: accurate but plain Latin, lacking inspiration from classical literature. Purchases and commissions for eighth-century Roman libraries substantiate the city's predominantly religious education: secular writ-

[21] Riché ( ), .   [22] Riché ( ), – , – , , , , – ; Riché ( ), .

ings from the city's ancient stocks are mentioned mainly for export.[23] In fact, the most important contribution of Italy to the early Carolingian Renaissance was the movement of books from great repositories, for example in Rome, Campania and Montecassino, to the North. In this ambience, prevailing in transalpine Europe as well as in Italy, the reproduction of classical texts dwindled to such an extent that the very survival of the pagan literary heritage of Rome was threatened.[24] This indi erence to classical literature persisted even into the ninth century. The anonymous *Versus de Verona*, composed shortly before , probably by a clerk of the cathedral, reveals the stylistic influence mainly of the Scriptures, the Fathers and of Christian poets, despite the presence in the Chapter library of numerous classical Latin texts.[25]

At the same time, literary studies had begun a slow revival in northwest Italy during the first half of the eighth century, when Bobbio's scriptorium began to produce secular works, and grammatical texts began to be written as palimpsests over books of the Bible. It seems that this revival is related to similar contemporary developments in the towns of Northern Italy, where an urban renewal took place in the eighth century. Recent scholarship has found no evidence for the continuity of autonomous lay schools from the sixth to the eighth centuries; with the collapse of antique educational institutions, the teaching of the urban laity seems to have passed into the hands of the church.[26] In contrast to the seventh century, however, there is now positive evidence for renewed study of the classical authors: an actual school text survives, Verona Biblioteca Capitolare MS ( ), dating from the second half of the eighth century and containing two stalwarts of the Latin secular curriculum, *Disticha Catonis* and Claudian's *De raptu Proserpinae*; it was also in early eighth-century North Italy, first in Cividale di Friuli and then in Pavia, that the future historian of the Lombards, Paul the Deacon, received his excellent education.[27] It is just possible that this north Italian literary revival had reached Rome by the end of the eighth century.[28]

It was in the ninth century that, after more than two hundred years of decline, a significant revival of the ancient literary curriculum based on a study of the classical authors was launched. The great Carolingian teachers and classical scholars – Alcuin, Theodulf of Orléans, Rabanus

[23] Riché ( ), – , – , – . [24] L. Reynolds ( ), xxi–xxiv, xxvii.
[25] Bullough ( ), .
[26] For recent assessments, see Riché ( ), – ; Petti Balbi ( ), n. ; Sasse Tateo ( ), and n. .
[27] Riché ( ), – , *passim*; Bullough ( ), – , *passim*; Riché ( ), – .
[28] Riché ( ), – , n. .

Maurus, Lupus of Ferrières, Remigius of Auxerre, Heiric of Auxerre, John Scottus Erigena, Walafrid Strabo, Einhard – were all northern European figures, but Italy too showed some distinction in the study of the Latin classical authors. There was insular influence at Bobbio, Verona, Milan and Fiesole; there was contact with the northern centres of Carolingian culture in Turin, Brescia and Verona. There were some notable teachers active in Italy, including the poet and bibliophile Pacificus of Verona and Hildemar of Civate, author of an educational manual *De recta legendi ratione*. Despite the Saracen invasions, Latin grammatical activity is also detectable in southern Italy during the ninth century: grammatical textbooks were composed by Bishop Ursus of Benevento and Hilderic of Montecassino (see above,), and the Neapolitan school produced two *littérateurs* at the very end of the ninth century: Eugenius Vulgarius and Auxilius of Naples. Sedulius Scottus presented Eberhard, marquis of Friuli and son-in-law of Louis the Pious, with a copy of Vegetius on the occasion of his son's birth.[29] All this provides only indirect evidence for the study of the Latin authors, but there is also positive proof in the form of manuscripts. Although the contribution here is far less than in northern centres such as Corbie, Reims, Tours, Fleury and Auxerre, there were still some school-level Latin authors copied in Italy during the ninth century: Bern MS (Horace, Ovid, Servius on Vergil), BNP lat. A (Lucan, Terence, Horace, Juvenal), BNP lat. (Horace) – not to mention other Latin literary texts normally read at a higher curricular level (Quintilian; Cicero's speeches, *Brutus*, *De divinatione*, *Disputationes tusculanae*; Livy; Seneca's letters, *De beneficiis*, *De clementia*). Indeed, the ninth-century North Italian monk and teacher, Hildemar of Civate, turned his back on the exclusively Christian education which had characterized Italian schools from the sixth to the eighth century: commenting on the passage in the Benedictine ruling calling for the establishment of solely monastic schools, he pointed out that there were also schools of liberal arts; moreover, he returned to the basic assumption of Augustinian Christian humanism, declaring that a foundation in Latin literary studies was required in order to gain a full understanding of Scripture.[30]

29 Riché ( ), – , , , , . This text, described as 'librum rei militaris', may be the one mentioned in his library inventory of , also including two copies of Fulgentius: Becker ( ), – . 30 L. Reynolds ( ), xxix–xxx; Riché ( ), , – .

:

It was in the tenth century that the withdrawal from the Latin classics, so pronounced in Italian schools during the Dark Ages, really came to an end.[31] At the turn of the century, the poem *O admirabile Veneris idolum* shows the influence of profane Latin poets, while the anonymous, possibly Veronese, author of *Gesta Berengarii imperatoris* demonstrated a reasonable knowledge of Vergil, Juvenal, Statius and *Ilias latina*, to the point of plagiarizing entire passages verbatim. This poet was clearly a teacher, addressing as he does his *iuvenes*; moreover, his poem was glossed in the standard school manner, with philological explanations of di cult allusions and references to classical authors including Horace, Juvenal, Cicero and Terence. Allusions to Vergil and to Livy are evident in the Modenese poem *O tu qui servas armis ista moenia*, and Ratherius of Lobbes (in Hainault), a life-long student of classical authors,[32] after becoming bishop of Verona, read Catullus and became acquainted with the first decade of Livy in the Chapter library, which he had copied by members of his clergy; he also knew the version there of Pliny's letters.[33] Stefano da Novara, a teacher in his native city as well as in Pavia and then in Würzburg, commented on Martianus Capella, a favoured text in Carolingian schools.[34] Nevertheless, not all tenth-century Italians were so well received north of the Alps. The mockery of Gunzo for latinity corrupted by vulgar Italian usage on arrival in St Gall is famous,[35] although there is evidence of direct acquaintance on his part with Ovid, Horace, *De inventione* and *Rhetorica ad Herennium*, if not with Terence. Greater knowledge of classical authors can be found in Gunzo's contemporary, Liutprand, bishop of Cremona, who also included rhetorical speeches invented according to the classical manner in his histories.[36] Italian teachers never reached the level of Gerbert of Aurillac, and yet Otto I took the opportunity of his conquests south of the Alps to send masters such as Stefano da Novara and Gunzo to Germany. Bobbio could claim an impressive library of more than five hundred manuscripts, including ancient texts, when Gerbert became abbot in . In the library of Cremona under Bishop Olderic contained a considerable number of works related to the study of classical authors,

[31] For subsequent material, I follow Bullough ( ), .

[32] Riché ( ), . [33] L. Reynolds ( ), , , . [34] Riché ( ), .

[35] Novati ( ), ; Taylor ( ), , – ; Bullough ( ), ; Riché ( ), .

[36] Bullough ( ), – .

including Priscian, Martianus Capella and Remigius of Auxerre,[37] as well as more elementary texts (Avianus, Arator, Prosper, Prudentius, Sedulius)[38] which would later be included among the *auctores minores.* Although most of Gerbert's career as an educator was spent at Reims, his brief stays in Bobbio and Rome may have encouraged the teaching of classical authors, including Vergil, Statius, Terence, Juvenal, Persius, Horace and Lucan, for which he was praised (credibly) by his biographer Richer of Reims.[39] The intensive copying of classical Latin authors, begun in ninth-century Italy, continued into the tenth century, producing newly uncovered texts as well as better versions of works already recovered.[40]

The study of classical Latin authors in earlier medieval Italy intensified during the eleventh century. The Lombard rhetorician Anselm of Besate presented himself as a new Vergil when dedicating his part-prose, part-verse *Rhetorimachia*, modelled on Martianus Capella and Boethius, to Emperor Henry III.[41] When the Lombard Guido, a teacher at Auxerre, died in , it was declared that grammar would grieve.[42] At Pomposa in the eleventh century copies were made of Seneca's *Tragedies* (BML .), and of Justinus;[43] its library catalogue of , listing books most of which had been recently copied,[44] mentions Seneca's *De beneficiis* and *De clementia*,[45] a decade of Livy, an historical/geographical anthology (including Orosius, Eutropius, the elder Pliny and Solinus) and Seneca's letters to Lucilius.[46] However, the greatest Italian monastic centre for the study of the Latin authors in the eleventh century was of course Montecassino, whose school, developing hand-in-hand with its scriptorium, showed an interest in Latin grammar, rhetoric, poetry and history;[47] here fundamental copies were made of Apuleius, Seneca, Tacitus, Varro, Cicero, Ovid, Justinus and Juvenal, and there is evidence for the presence of *Ilias latina* and Terence too.[48] Alfano, educated in his native city of Salerno and later its archbishop, had an acquaintance with the ancient Latin poets and a command of classical metre.[49] Immo, raised in the cathedral school of Worms with whose intensely classical circle he was associated, brought his enthusiasm for Latin authors to Arezzo where he became bishop in / .[50] Of his own classical edu-

[37] Riché ( ), , , , . [38] Becker ( ), – . [39] Riché ( ), , .
[40] L. Reynolds ( ), xxxi. [41] Riché ( ), , .
[42] Novati ( ), ; Taylor ( ), , .
[43] L. Reynolds ( ), , , ; see Mercati ( ), .
[44] Mercati ( ), . [45] L. Reynolds ( ), . [46] Mercati ( ), , , .
[47] Riché ( ), – . [48] L. Reynolds ( ), xxxiii, – , .
[49] Riché ( ), ; Haskins ( ), , . [50] Wieruszowski ( ), – .

cation in his native Ravenna, Peter Damian wrote expansively.[51] This is the period in which Italians from Lombard cities were satirized for spending large sums on a peripatetic grammatical education and for their intellectual *hauteur*, claiming to have houses filled with books; these grammarians were said to hold in contempt ultramontanes who, with a little Latin, believed themselves to be new Vergils.[52] The excesses to which Italian enthusiasm for classical Latin authors could perhaps extend in this period are evident from a famous episode narrated by the historian Radulfus Glaber:

In Ravenna someone called Vilgardo was possessed by an uncommon passion for the study of grammar; indeed, it has always been the custom of Italians to neglect other arts in pursuit of this subject. Swelled with pride by his knowledge of this art, he began to betray increasing signs of madness: one night, demons assuming the guise of the poets Vergil, Horace and Juvenal appeared to him; they feigned to thank him for the passion with which he studied what they had said in their books, as well as for preserving so happily their memory in the eyes of posterity. Moreover they promised that eventually he would partake of their glory. Corrupted by this diabolic delusion, he began to teach vehemently in a manner contrary to the holy faith, declaring that the words of the poets were to be believed in every respect. In the end he was judged a heretic and condemned by Peter, bishop of the city. This then led to the exposure throughout Italy of numerous followers of this pernicious doctrine, who themselves also succumbed to the sword or to the stake.[53]

Perhaps it was inevitable that this kind of enthusiasm for the classics would provoke a reaction. Just as the classicized Christian schools of late antiquity called forth the ascetic monasticism of the sixth century, so the Latinized educational tendencies of the tenth and eleventh centuries stimulated a call for reform in the eleventh century. Arnolfo of Milan, one of the leaders of the Patarene movement, declared that Cicero was not for him,[54] but the leader of the movement against secularized, Latinized and paganized education in the eleventh century was Peter Damian. He spoke as somebody who knew the enemy: he was one of the outstanding Latinists of his day, having been prepared for a legal career in North Italy with a thorough grammatical and rhetorical education, before renouncing the secular world at the age of twenty-eight in .
For him, the pupil entrusted to the grammarian could lose his soul in

[51] Taylor ( ), , : 'Olim mihi Tullius dulcescebat, blandiebantur carmina poetarum, philosophi verbis aureis insplendebant, et Sirenes usque in exitium dulces meum incantaverunt intellectum.' [52] Riché ( ), ; Taylor ( ), , .

[53] *PL* . ; Riché ( ), ; Bullough ( ), , ; Novati ( ), , ; Taylor ( ), , . [54] Riché ( ), .

explicating the pagan authors. He railed against the lies of Vergil, against the extravagant inventions of the poets, against the comic dramatists for exciting poisonous passions. He was horrified at the appearance in Italy of a Frenchman, 'eloquent like Cicero, a poet like Vergil' and yet 'leading such a life that the doors of the monastery were closed on him'. He called for a return to the monastic education of the days of St Benedict in the sixth century, when reading was limited to the sacred texts alone. Although he believed that, for the secular clergy, a Latin education was necessary in order produce capable preachers and to safeguard against heresy, he insisted that this was a means to an end, not an end in itself: 'The goal for whoever enters a grammar school, having mastered his art, is to leave again.'[55] After his conversion ('mea grammatica Christus est'[56]), Peter Damian's ferocious reaction shows the extent to which Latin pagan authors had penetrated Italian schools:

> Now let me speak with chagrin about those who follow after the rabble of the grammarians and who, abandoning spiritual studies, lust to learn the trifles of earthly art. Counting as little the Rule of Benedict they rejoice to apply themselves to the rules of Donatus. These, scorning the experience of ecclesiastical discipline, and panting after secular studies, what else do they seem to do but abandon the chaste spouse in the marriage bed of faith and descend to actresses and harlots?[57]

It is at this point that the manuscripts of Latin authors in Florentine libraries listed below in Appendix begin to provide concrete illustrations of the texts used to teach grammar in Italian schools.[58] Among these are two of the minor authors, the versification attributed to **Theobaldus** of the *Physiologus*,[59] and the poetry of **Sedulius**. A fragment of the former, used as a rear flyleaf, is an Italian manuscript dating from the turn of the twelfth century (BML sup. , ' r–v). This folio contains the beginning of the alphabet ('abcd'), written twice as *probationes pennae*, and it is interesting to see a puerile habit such as the writing of alphabets on a schoolbook already in use in the twelfth century.[60] The verses by Sedulius, classed as a minor author by Conrad of Hirsau[61] and frequently found in school anthologies,[62] were even copied by a group of

[55] Riché ( ), – . [56] *PL* . , cited by Taylor ( ), , ; Riché ( ), .
[57] *Opuscula varia, PL* . . Tr. Ross and McLaughlin ( ), – .
[58] In the following discussion, constituent elements which circulated independently before coming together to form composite manuscripts will be counted as separate items; manuscripts which were deliberately composite from the beginning or which were composite as a result of restoration will be counted as one item. [59] See Garin ( ), – ; Manitius (–), , – .
[60] Near the lower alphabet, the following *probationes* are also written in a XIIc. hand: ut g, ut genus.
[61] See above, . [62] Munk Olsen ( ), – , , .

schoolboys in a German manuscript of the tenth/eleventh century.[63] The example now in Florence (BML sin. , r– v), consisting of the *Paschale carmen* (r– v) together with the two *Hymni* (v– v) separated by the spurious *Epigramma* (r), dates from the eleventh century and was copied in Italy, possibly in Lombardy.[64] In the early years of its history, this manuscript reveals the normal signs of school reading, such as word-order marks and simple interlinear vocabulary equivalents (v: ast = set, v: sator = id est creator, r: piaret = id est purgaret, v: nitor = splendor, v: a ectaret = desideraret, v: trucidat = id est occidit, r: amnes = id est flumina, v: que = et, r: corripi = constringere).[65] Possibly Italian too is a manuscript of **Prosper**'s *Epigrammata* (BML Ashb.), dating from the late eleventh century or the turn of the twelfth; this manuscript contains simple interlinear vocabulary glossing of the school type (e.g. r: queunt = possunt, iussa = precepta, agens = faciens) as well as a little simple marginal paraphrase (see below,) written by a hand just slightly later than that of the copyist. Eleventh-century Italian manuscripts now found in Florence also include a text which would become the most popular school author in later medieval and Renaissance Italy: **Boethius**'s *Consolation of Philosophy*.[66] The first section of the manuscript (BML . , r– v) was written in southern Italy or Sicily in the second half of the eleventh century; moreover, it was annotated in a typical school manner by a contemporary hand, who not only included simple Latin lexical interlinear glosses[67] but also extracted sections of the commentary by the Carolingian teacher, Remigius of Auxerre for his marginal glosses;[68] in fact, Remigius's commentary would provide the source for a considerable number of school-level glossators in these Florentine manuscripts, beginning with this Laurentian codex and continuing into the early fifteenth century.[69] This practice of copying sections of large-scale commentaries for use in the margins of schoolbooks was a frequent teaching method in the middle ages;[70] moreover, the material selected

63 Munk Olsen ( ), – .

64 There is an early *probatio* or ownership mark (v), written by a hardly literate schoolboy, Guglielmo di Piero da Novara, and datable to XIIIc.: q(ui) legerit lib(er) Seduli Wulielm(us) Novariensis filiu(s) Petris / frater suos Averrardus.

65 WOM and interlinear glosses all appear to date from XIIc. Numerous XIIIc. *probationes* (v, original rear flyleaf), including mentions of 'pueri', 'magister' and 'scolaros [*sic*]' and two partial alphabets: 'abbcdefghiklm' and 'abcdefghiklmnopq'.

66 Black and Pomaro ( ); see below, .

67 Black and Pomaro ( ), , . For this characteristic school practice, see below, .

68 Black and Pomaro ( ), – , and see below, .

69 Black and Pomaro ( ), , and below, .

70 Black and Pomaro ( ), – , and below, .

from the Remigian commentaries by this glossator was typical of the school-level material normally borrowed from the great medieval commentators: simple pharaphrase or explication, geography, mythology, history, etymology and figures.[71]

The majority of eleventh-century school manuscripts found in Florentine libraries are texts of the major authors: **Horace**, **Ovid** and **Vergil**. An important testimony of Tuscan school study of the classical authors in this early period is BML Strozzi , a manuscript of **Vergil**'s *Opera omnia*, of which r– v represents the nucleus (comprising the end of the *Eclogues* and the beginning of the *Georgics*). This section of the manuscript, written in Tuscany, possibly even in the tenth century, is extensively glossed by the copyist himself. Another part of the same codex, r– v (containing the earlier books of the *Aeneid*), dates from the eleventh century; the hand seems possibly to derive from the same ambience but is marginally later than the first copyist's, and, again, this second scribe also extensively glossed this part of the codex. A third section of the manuscript, r– v, containing later sections of the *Aeneid* and also dating from the eleventh century, is a fragment of di erent provenance (also glossed heavily by its copyist), which was used by the restorer of the manuscript, working at the turn of the thirteenth century, who put together the three earlier fragments, filling in himself the gaps between them and writing over unclear or lost passages throughout; the Vergilian corpus was completed by yet another restorer, working in the Quattrocento. Another early example of a possible school manuscript is an *Aeneid* from central Italy, dating from the turn of the twelfth century (BML .), which was given short glosses by a hand contemporary with the text.[72] A third possible witness to early Italian school activity is a manuscript of **Horace**'s *Opera* (BRF), copied by at least three di erent hands, one of which seems to be eleventh century (r– v), the others possibly a little but not much later.[73] A fourth, definitely Italian school-type manuscript from this early period is a fragment of **Ovid**'s *Tristia* (BML San Marco , r– v) dating from the end of the eleventh century; in the past some doubts have been raised about its

[71] Black and Pomaro ( ), – , and below, .

[72] Extremely brief but numerous marginal annotations, indicated with symbols, given by a reader contemporaneous with the copyist and consisting of the simple philology (figures, metre, explication, paraphrase, grammar, geography, mythology, word order, Roman customs, rudimentary philosophical doctrine) characteristic of the school room, extend throughout first five books (to r).

[73] Ascribed to Italy by Munk Olsen (–), , – and Villa (–), , but could have Swiss/Austrian provenance: none of many early marginal glossators is clearly Italian and the final flyleaf is also not Italian.

Italian provenance,[74] but a later note of possession (v, end of the thirteenth century) leaves no doubt about the West Tuscan origins of the fragment.[75] This section of the manuscript, written by at least three hands, includes sparse contemporaneous interlinear glosses. A fifth definitely school-type manuscript, containing the *Metamorphoses*, possibly from central/southern Italy and dating from the turn of the twelfth century (BML San Marco), has light school-type interlinear vocabulary glosses, as well as occasional normally brief philological marginalia by a number of di erent hands dating from the period in which it was copied.

:

Literary and direct manuscript evidence, therefore, makes it clear that the Latin authors, both major and minor, were being read intensively in Italian schools in the eleventh century, and this kind of study continued over the next hundred years, as Italian and indeed European educational worlds underwent a vast expansion. This educational upsurge – not just at the levels which would eventually be transformed into universities but in the less advanced school sectors – is also demonstrated by the prodigious number of twelfth-century Italian schoolbooks surviving in Florentine libraries. Two of these codices contain texts of the minor authors. One is an anthology of the late-antique Christian poets, **Sedulius**, **Prosper** and **Arator** (BML CS); the manuscript is a composite, with the first section (r– v) occupied by Sedulius's *Hymni* (*PL* . –) and *Paschale carmen* (*PL* . – , –), the second (v– v) by Prosper's *Epigrammata* (r– v) and his spurious *Poema coniugis ad uxorem* (v– r), and by Arator's *Historia apostolica*, both parts being datable to the twelfth century. The first section was evidently written in central/southern Italy (to judge from the script), and the two sections were already joined together by the fourteenth century, as is clear from the final note (v): 'In isto volumine continentur Sedulius, Prosper, Arator, quaterni XII.' Typical school features of the manuscript are not only the occasional simple interlinear (e.g. r: sors = id est mors, sepulcrum = id est terra, terrigenae = nati terrae) and marginal (e.g. v: laberinthus est edificium inflexibus [sic] parietibus qui apud Cretam a

74 Munk Olsen (–), , : 'Allemagne (ou Italie)?'

75 Die XX mensis nov(em)bris B<....e>ne(m) qui dicitur <...>sthinus <?> Thomas<i> pignoraverunt d<...>am<...to> hunc librum pro III sol. pisano(rum) hac (con)<ditione> et pacto q(uod) <...> ad duos menses possit <...>ll<...> recoligere. Testes fuerunt Mag(iste)r Gratianus, Yustinus <...et> Cardutius.

Dedalo factus est) glosses to Sedulius (written by hands near contemporary with the copyist's) but also the appended grammatical fragment on r– v, containing elementary morphological material similar but not identical to that provided by *Ianua*.[76] Another twelfth-century manuscript of the school type, possibly written in central Italy, is BML Ashb. , containing a text of **Avianus**'s *Fabulae* with a few typically simple roughly contemporaneous lexical equivalents (e.g. v: Tytan = id est sol, r: amaris = acerbis, r: humilis = id est vilis spes, v: opaca = id est obscura).

The majority of Italian twelfth-century schoolbooks in Florentine libraries preserve texts of the classical Latin poets. Of these, the most popular author was **Lucan**:

Location	School-use
BML sin. [77]	Composite: see below for school use.[78]
BML .	Abundant interlinear and marginal glossing, mainly contemporaneous or shortly following production.[79]
BML .	WOM (copyist and contemporaries); r: Lucanus Magistri Andree.
BML .	Glossed by final copyist with lexical interlinear and philological marginalia (especially paraphrase) throughout; contemporary WOM (e.g. v, v, v).[80]

76 See above, .

77 Consisted originally of two distinct but contemporaneous Italian elements, both dating from earlier XIIc. Now made up of (a) r– v, r– v, r– v, r– r, the other of (b) v– v. Munk Olsen's description (– , . : 'S. XI²'. f.: 'f. – , – , – (f. – : compl., s. XII/XIII)') needs revision: ( ) section (a) is datable to the earlier XIIc., not the later XIc., and is contemporaneous with (b); ( ) section (b) was not a XII–XIIIc. completion of (a), but rather a fascicle from an independent text, as shown by erasures on v, v.

78 Section (a) was given typical school-level glosses in later XIIc., including WOM (especially r– r), simple lexical interlinear equivalents (e.g. r: tamen = licet, r: ex facili = id est leviter, r: quam = pro quantum) and rudimentary philological marginalia (e.g. r: Anibal dux Cartaginensium, r: Catilina Lentulus et Cetheus coniuraverunt se in rem publicam set deprehensi sunt a Cicerone consule, v: Silla Metridatem vicit set non ita in mortem illum conpulerit, v: iuxta Thebas quas Cadimus construxit). No indication that section (b) was used as a schoolbook until XIIIc., when it was given a full apparatus of WOM (e.g. r), interlinear lexical equivalents and marginal philology by a hand then proceeding to gloss the rest of the codex in the same way.

79 Passed into hands of pupil from Florentine cathedral school (XV²), who left no annotations but provided an ownership note: (r) Questo Luchano è di Bartolomeo di Giovanni di Baldo Buon<...> lanaiuolo di San Martino. Chi lo truo<va rendalo> al figliuolo chiamato Lorenzo da <...> alla schuola de' cherici di Santa Liperata.

80 Ownership note (Iv: Iste liber est mei Octaviani Ser Bartolomei) by immature hand (XV²), who seems never to have glossed text.

BML . [81]	Non-professional product of many di erent copyists.
BML . [82]	Near-contemporaneous glossing with continuous WOM, simple interlinear vocabulary paraphrases, simple philological marginalia, several di erent contemporary annotating hands.

Alongside Lucan comes **Horace**, whose works are found in seven twelfth-century Florentine school manuscripts:

BML Edili [83]	Contemporary interlinear and marginal school-type glosses.
BML .	Extensive marginal and interlinear glosses by several contemporaneous hands.
BML .	Extensive glossing to *Ars*, the satires and epistles by the copyist, by contemporaneous hand and by several slightly later hands (r); also a contemporaneous *accessus* to *Ars* (v).
BML .	r– v: heavily annotated by a number of nearly contemporaneous hands (WOM, simple synonyms); *accessus* to *Ars* (r).
BRF	Composite (r– v, r– v), both sections with simple lexical interlinear glosses by respective scribes.[84]
BRF	Heavily glossed, both interlinearly and marginally, by both copyists and by at least one contemporary reader.[85]

Almost as prevalent in the twelfth-century Italian schools were **Juvenal**'s satires:

[81] Provenance problematic: angular script, ultramontane-type abbrevations (e.g. et = ÷) suggest possible non-Italian provenance, but -shaped abbreviation for 'et' is the normal Italian type, approximating 'z' with shorter bottom horizontal stroke. This ambiguity is compounded by absence of contemporaneous glossing. Nevertheless, it was in intensive Italian use as a schoolbook from XIV¹ to XV¹, with omnipresent WOM, lexical interlinear glosses, many di erent contemporaneous glossing hands, simple philological marginalia and vernacular glosses (e.g. v: *per asotigliare* et *per innanimare*).

[82] Nucleus (r– v) datable to XIIc.

[83] Munk Olsen (–), . , ascribes MS to 'France ?', an attribution treated as definitive in Fabbri and Tacconi ( ), . However, there are no secure French elements here; moreover, contemporaneous glossing hand seems distinctly Italian.

[84] School XIVc. annotation (r): Nota puer bene.

[85] Signature of XVc. schoolboy: v: Iste liber est Aluysi Becheto fili quondam d<e> Jacobo, qui pargit ad scolas Magistri Rofini. Alvise (Luigi) Becchetti, a notable Sforza courtier and papal curialist (fl. –), was the son of prominent Milanese humanist and secretary, Giacomo Becchetto, who apparently died between and , with the last certain notice of him in : see *DBI*, . – . If Alvise was already an active Milanese diplomat in (ibid.), then Giacomo must have died soon after , since Alvise is hardly literate in this ownership note.

BML S.Marco	Heavily glossed before XIIIc.
BML .	Several contemporaneous glossators.
BML .	XIIc. interlinear school-type vocabulary glossing (as well as a few basic philological marginalia); typical XIIc. *accessus* (r–v).
BML .	Heavily glossed by several contemporaneous hands, both marginally and interlinearly.
BML Strozzi	A number of school-type glossators evidently working at the turn of the thirteenth century and perhaps a little later, including one whose hand seems possibly north Italian.[86]
BRF	Interlinear and some marginal glosses by two annotators, one contemporaneous with the copyist, the other slightly later.

Ovid is well represented among twelfth-century schoolbooks in Florentine libraries:

BML . [87]	Glossed from beginning to end by a number of near–contemporary hands.
BML .	Lightly glossed by one of its several copyists.[88]
BML S. Marco [89]	School-type glosses by a twelfth-century hand, including a simple grammatical annotation showing early influence in Italy of Northern European grammatical terminology.[90]

86 To judge from Gallic-type elongations and -shaped 'et' with vertical stroke leaning to right.

87 Possibly North Italian provenance, in view of Latin orthography (r: dissuaxionem, alliam; r: specialli; v: generalli; r: confuxa; r: responssionem) of glossator (XIV/XVc.); however, initial and final restorations were Florentine (– ,).

88 North Italian provenance suggested by earliest surviving note of possession, written in elongated *cancellaresca* script datable to XIII²: (v) Iste liber est Magistri Jacobi de <...> de Viglevano; qui est bonus puer d<ebet ...> Therefore Munk-Olsen's attribution to 'France' (– , ,) is doubtful. This instance suggests that angularity of script and use of abbreviations (e.g. et = ÷ and a vertical line over 'q' for 'qui' instead of 'q') normally associated with Northern Europe are inadequate indications of non-Italian provenance. Further indications of continued school use are the added Trecento colophon written by an immature hand (r: finito libro <...> qui me furat<ur ...>), besides (v) sketch of 'labe<rinthus>' and mention of 'Magistro Martino', both XIVc.

89 r– v, r–v, r– r, forming part of a subsequent composite codex.

90 r: quia nominativus pluralis regit nominativum singularem. See , above.

BML S. Marco	Contemporary simple philological interlinear and marginal annotations (e.g. see v– r).[91]
BML S. Marco	Glossed by three contemporaneous hands; WOM soon after the production of the text (r, r, r).[92]

Other classical Latin poets frequently read by medieval pupils are less well represented among school manuscripts preserved in Florentine libraries. After Lucan, Juvenal, Horace and Ovid, it is **Vergil** who appears most frequently:

BML Strozzi [93]	Extensive school-type annotation both before and by first restorer (turn of XIIIc.).
BML Strozzi [94]	Core section of *Aeneid* (r–v, r– v) glossed in normal school manner by several hands working in the earlier thirteenth century.
BNCF Magl. .	Glossed in typical school manner at time of production.

[91] Particularly interesting are the following grammatical exercises on changing cases of nouns and adverbs of place (v) by XIII^{2} Italian hand:

Romam Rotomagum Vernone[m] tendit Atenas;
Rus tendebat humum miliciamque domum.
Roma [*corr. ex* Romam] Rotomago Vernone redibat Atenis;
Rure [*corr. ex* rus] redibat humo miliciaque domo.
Roma Rotomago Vernone meabat Atenis;
Rure meabat humo miliciaque domo.
Rom(e) Rotomagi Vernone moratur Atenis;
Ruri [*corr. ex* Rure] moratur humi miliciaeque domi [*corr. ex* domo].

These correspond closely to some near-contemporary French verse-glosses on Horace (BNP lat.), besides to Ralph of Beauvais's *Verba preceptiva* (BL Add.): see S. Reynolds (a), .

[92] After initial glossing, no further signs of use in school context, although MS later passed through the hands of two grammar teachers, Filippo Pieruzzi and Giorgio Antonio Vespucci (for their teaching activities, see above, , and below,). For Pieruzzi's ownership, see erased ownership note (v: Liber mei Philippi Ser Ugolini Peruzii notarii); for Vespucci's interventions, see r– v and r, restored and copied by him (for Pieruzzi's and Vespucci's association, see Ullman and Stadter ( ),). MS not in XVc. catalogue of S. Marco, probably because it did not yet belong to the library, although it could be n. : 'Eiusdem [sc. Ovidii methamorphoseos] de sine titulo, in volumine parvo albo in membranis' (Ullman and Stadter ( ),); nevertheless, this MS not mentioned there, nor by de la Mare (b).

[93] First restorations (XII/XIIIc.) by Tuscan hand (r– v, r– v, r– v).

[94] Composite, with nucleus dating from XII/XIIIc. (r– v, r– v, r– v, r– v), restored and completed in late XIVc. v contains a not completely comprehensible note referring to a 'mariscalcum' dying in (obiit <...> MCCCLXXVIIII^{or} die februarii), a 'fidelem' soldier of 'Regina Johanna' (Giovanna I of Anjou, d.), whose own death and burial in the Neapolitan church of S. Chiara (hec extincta fuit i<n> fabrica clara deo) seems to be mentioned; not impossible, from graphic standpoint, to hypothesize a southern Italian, even Neapolitan, provenance, given that the hand of the restorer, a tiny Gothic script, has features

Persius is represented by one Italian manuscript from the turn of the thirteenth century (BRF),[95] in which there are interlinear and marginal glosses by the copyist, and similarly there is one later twelfth-century Italian manuscript of **Statius**'s *Achilleis* (BML sin. , r– v), already mentioned as forming a fortuitous composite with Sedulius and Claudian; here Statius is given the usual school-type mixture of interlinear and marginal glosses by the text's contemporaneous reviser (see r–v), as well as by the original copyist himself, who also provides an *accessus* (r). **Terence** too is found in two twelfth-century manuscripts:

BML CS (r– v)	Heavily glossed by hand contemporary with copyist; *accessus* written just slightly later (r–v).[96]
BML S. Marco	Heavily glossed, both interlinearly and marginally, by a hand slightly later than the copyist's.

In the middle ages and Renaissance, verse was regarded as particularly suitable for memorization,[97] and so it is not surprising that the favoured authors for school study were always the poets; nevertheless, by the eleventh century it is clear that prose-writers were also being widely read in the grammar schools, at least in northern Europe.[98] The Florentine evidence in consideration here suggests that prose began to be widely read in Italy at the school level in the twelfth century. Of particular importance in this regard was **Sallust**, already the favoured classical prose writer in northern schools:[99]

BML .	Copyist o ers extensive interlinear and marginal glosses and brief *accessus* (v) besides some lively glosses reflecting on episcopal life in XIIc. Italy (r, r).
BML inf. .[100]	XIIc. interlinear glossing evident at the beginning of the codex (e.g. r).
BRF	Glossed by number of hands contemporaneous with copyist.

footnote 94 (*cont.*)
calling to mind the *lettre batarde* of Angevin Italy. Prevalence of French graphic features in this Italian region might account for Gallic characteristics of one XIIIc. glossing hand, such as 'z' with a horizontal line through the diagonal stroke (v) and the general elongations of another (e.g. r, v, r).

95 On original rear flyleaf verso, *probationes* written in Italian notarial hand, XIII² (Nos Gregorius dei gratia sancte Aquilegen[sis], Nos Gregorius Sancte Sedis Aquileg[ensis]: Gregorius de Montelongo, bishop of Tripoli, patriarch of Aquileia –).

96 Ed. Alessio (a), – .

97 See above , and below, .

98 See Munk Olsen ( ), .

99 Munk Olsen ( ), , .

100 Composite of two independent sections, one with *BC* (r– v), other with *BJ* (v– r), both produced in central Italy (XIIc.).

Besides Sallust, the most important prose writer at the school level in the middle ages was **Cicero**, whose shorter moral treatises (*De amicitia, De senectute, De o ciis, Paradoxa stoicorum* and *Somnium Scipionis*) provided the most appropriate and popular reading matter:

Edili [101]	Copyist (also the principal glossator) an inexpert reader, frequently using WOM[102] and giving simple philological marginal glosses (e.g. biography of Cato[103] or fable of Orestes[104]) typical of school manuscripts; also included considerable vernacular interlinear glossing of southern Italian provenance.[105]
BML .	WOM (v, r, r).
BML . [106]	Copyist and/or reader's two marginal comments (v, r) are philological.
BML . [107]	Many of the typical features of a grammar-school text: letters written over words to show word order;[108] contemporary simple *accessus* outlining the work's *intentio, utilitas* and philosophical classification;[109] elementary glosses (Anibal rex cartaginensis,[110] Themistocles imperator grecus fuit[111]). Direct reference to school experience, with comment that ecclesiastical grandees tend to forget school friends: sicut fit de episcopis qui edlliguntur [*sic* for eliguntur] [et] spernunt veteres amicitias scolarium quos habuere.[112]

101 r– r: dating of manuscript and vernacular glosses confirmed by Gabriella Pomaro and Albinia de la Mare.

102 r, v, v, r, r, v, v, r.

103 r: Cato habuit quemdam senem amicum cum quo semper disputabat de senectute. v: Cum nuntiatum esset sibi in Africa existenti suum filium suum [sic] mortuum Rome, respond(it) ipse Cato nuntio satisfec(isse) filium nature quia mortalis erat.

104 v. 105 See below, – .

106 Composite: ( ) *De o ciis* (r– v), dating from XII/XIIIc.; ( ) *De amicitia* (r– v), slightly earlier (XII²). The copyist of ( ) apparently assembled composite, in view of his occasional annotations to the earlier section (v– r).

107 The marginal glosses, almost entirely contemporaneous, are mainly the work of the second copyist. Commentary almost completely philological, with no additional moral or ethical teachings – nearly all paraphrase.

108 BML . , r, r, r, v, r, r, r, v, v, r, v, v. See below, .

109 BML . , r: Est ergo Ciceronis in hoc opere materia amicitia [...] Intentio est auctoris de amicitia tractare, precepta quidem de ea dare de quibus veram a non vera posscimus [*sic pro* possimus] agnoscere et honestis modis excolere. Utilitas est quod per huius operis doctrinam sciemus amicitiam congruis modis excolere, utilitatem nobis parare et falsam et inhonestam evitare. Subponitur ethicae. Ostendit enim mores qui digni sint [...] See below. On this *accessus*, see Pellegrin ( ), , n. ; Munk Olsen (–), , .

110 BML . , r. 111 BML . , r.

112 BML . v: apparently the 'réclame contemporaine' mentioned by Munk Olsen (–), , (not actually on v).

:

At this point it may be interesting to summarize the findings hitherto of this survey of the Latin classics used as school authors in Florentine libraries:

Century	Cic.	Hor.	Juv.	Lucan	Ovid	Pers.	Sall.	Stat.	Ter.	Verg.	Total
XI											
XII											

These figures not only reflect and confirm the well-known expansion of education which took place in the twelfth century, but become particularly striking and significant if, by way of anticipation, the results for the thirteenth century are considered:

Century	Cic.	Hor.	Juv.	Lucan	Ovid	Pers.	Sall.	Stat.	Ter.	Verg.	Total
XIII											

What is clear here is nothing less than a collapse of the study of the ancient Roman classics in thirteenth-century Italy. This pattern, to some extent, mirrors the drop in overall numbers of classical manuscripts being produced in Europe as a whole in the thirteenth century,[113] but the extremity of the fall suggests that the shift away from the classics was particularly cataclysmic in Italian schools of the Duecento.

The status of the classics in the thirteenth century was a hotly debated historical controversy in the earlier twentieth century, but since then the question has been to some extent put to one side.[114] Nevertheless, the striking results of the present survey of schoolbooks in Florentine libraries make it imperative to reconsider the problem. It is perhaps most useful to begin with a series of well-known contemporary texts directly relevant to this question. Their author was Boncompagno da Signa (*c.* –*c.*), a renowned professor of rhetoric at the University of Bologna. First, Boncompagno declares that he had never imitated Cicero nor indeed ever lectured on him.[115] Then he goes on to reject his predecessors' methods of teaching the *ars dictaminis*, accusing them of too much reliance on the ancients: of the traditional five parts of the letter, only three were actually essential; if this was against the doctrine

113 See L. Reynolds ( ), xxvii, giving a drop of per cent in the overall number of manuscripts cited in the book (from to) between XIIc. and XIIIc.

114 As recognized by Bruni ( ), , in an important article reopening the question.

115 *Palma*, in Sutter ( ), ; see also .

of the ancients, then their teachings had been useless and damaging.[116] He derides the methods of writing letters before his day: masters had spent huge amounts of time adorning their epistles with vivid displays of verbiage and learned quotations from the authors, who were believed to provide the seal of approval for their literary productions.[117] He even criticizes Cicero's theory as inept and self-contradictory.[118] He says that he was reprimanded for rejecting the traditional practice of padding his prose with classical quotations (*proverbia*) and rarified terminology, complaining that he was derided for lacking a knowledge of Latin literature (*litteratura*),[119] and for drawing examples from the present day.[120] At the turn of the thirteenth century, the school of Orléans was particularly associated with the traditional study of the classical authors,[121] and Boncompagno accuses his academic opponents of too much indulgence in Aurelianism.[122]

These texts were first highlighted in by Louis Paetow in an influential published dissertation[123] citing them as evidence to support his thesis that classical studies su ered a momentous decline in the thirteenth century, especially in the nascent French and Italian universities. Paetow's hypothesis was accepted by his teacher, Haskins, in his famous work *The Renaissance of the Twelfth Century*,[124] while independently G. To anin sustained the same view in his *Storia del umanesimo*, in which he devoted the first volume, memorably entitled *Il secolo senza Roma*, to the thirteenth century.[125] Also apparently without knowledge of either Paetow's or To anin's work, Etienne Gilson, in his *Philosophie au Moyen Âge*, similarly dubbed the thirteenth century 'L'exil des belles-lettres'.[126] Paetow's thesis was first attacked by E. K. Rand in , arguing on the basis of French, English and German evidence, that, far from being on the wane, classicism in the thirteenth century was on the rise.[127] In Helene Wieruszowski joined the fray, looking at the Italian situation, which had not been considered by Rand.[128] Her conclusion was that

[116] *Palma*, in Sutter ( ), ; see also , . [117] *Rhetorica antiqua*, in Sutter ( ), .

[118] *Rhetorica novissima*, ed. Gaudenzi ( ), .

[119] *Rhetorica antiqua*, in Sutter ( ), , n. . [120] Ibid.

[121] Matthew of Vendôme, *Poetical formulary*, vv. – , cited by Paetow ( ), n. ; Geo rey of Vinsauf ( ), , vv. – ; sermon of to students of Toulouse, cited by Paetow ( ), n. . Alexander of Villedieu, in *Ecclesiale*, Prologue, accused the school of Orléans of being contaminated by classical authors: Thurot ( ), . See John of Garland, *Ars lectoria ecclesiae*, cited by Paetow ( ), n. . [122] Preface to *Liber X tabularum*, in Delisle ( ), .

[123] Paetow ( ). Paetow apparently developed his thesis in tandem with his teacher Haskins: see Haskins ( ), , . [124] Haskins ( ). [125] To anin ( )

[126] Gilson ( ), – . [127] Rand ( ); see also Rand ( ).

[128] Wieruszowski ( ), reprinted in Wieruszowski ( ).

Paetow had distorted the Italian evidence, just as he had done for Northern Europe: there was unbroken continuity of classical learning from the twelfth century in Italy all the way up to Italian Renaissance itself. For France, Paetow had cited many contemporary witnesses to the decline of classical studies, the most famous of which, of course, was Henri d'Andeli's *La bataille des VII. ars*, which Paetow himself later translated and edited.[129] Just as Rand had discounted contemporary testimony for Northern Europe, Wieruszowski did the same for Italy, marginalizing the texts by Boncompagno which have just been noted above.[130] Nevertheless, Wieruszowski's views did not win universal acceptance.[131] In a paper read in and published three years later,[132] Francesco Bruni reopened the debate in full with a treatment of Guido delle Colonne's *Historia destructionis Troiae* (begun in , completed in), where he highlights a disparaging attitude to the classical poets (Vergil, Ovid, Homer);[133] suggestive too is his reading of a *sententia* from the *Georgics* (, –), which, starting from Campana's insight that the line was not cited from the original text in the thirteenth century but rather from a reworking in *Pamphilus*, Bruni uses to suggest a distance from the classics in the thirteenth century.[134] He also points to some evidence regarding Guittone d'Arezzo's indi erence to the classics, based on readings of Dante's *De vulgari eloquentia* (, –) and *Inferno* . – (supported by Boccaccio[135]). Nevertheless, recent work by Gian Carlo Alessio and Claudia Villa seems to tend in the opposite direction, pointing to the 'continuità della scuola' and its basis in the study of the classical authors from the thirteenth to the fifteenth centuries.[136]

The problem with this controversy is that no new type of source material had been found to confirm one side or the other of this fundamental debate about the development of the Latin classical tradition after the twelfth century. On the one hand, Paetow was able to cite direct

[129] Paetow ( ). [130] Wieruszowski ( ), .

[131] Allesio and Villa ( ), n. : 'potrà constatarsi la discreta povertà di connettivo nelle testimonianze raccolte in favore della persistenza della "lectura" dagli sforzi meritori di H. Wieruszowski'. [132] Bruni ( ). [133] Bruni ( ), – .

[134] Bruni ( ), – . See Campana ( ), – .

[135] 'Guido ebbe a sdegno Virgilio e gli altri poeti': Boccaccio ( ), . See Bruni ( ), – , – .

[136] Alessio and Villa ( ), – . Nevertheless, they still seem undecided. In reworking their article ( ) in ( ), n. , they write: 'Non è ancora maturo il tempo per dare risposte fondate alla questione relativa allo spessore della presenza dei classici nella cutura del XIII secolo'; after this they go on to repeat their criticism of Wieruszowski (n. above). They also make tentative suggestions here about the di usion of Vergil in southern Italy (XIIIc.–XVc.), and an 'age of Lucan' (XIIc.–XIIIc.). But Alessio ( ), , , suggests decline of authors in Italian schools from *c.* , with revival after .

contemporary witnesses, while Bruni has been able to call forth indirect evidence; on the other, Rand and Wieruszowski could point to innumerable specific examples such as Dante, Lovati, Mussato or Geri d'Arezzo, all of whom obviously had exposure to ancient authors, while Villa and Alessio can make suggestive remarks about the classical orientation of Pier della Vigna, Pietro da Prezza, Albertano da Brescia, Guido delle Colonne or Rolandino da Padova.[137] It is clear, however, that neither impressionism nor reliance on narrative evidence can be definitive; moreover, continual recourse to great individuals and the intellectual élite can never elucidate the lower levels of culture and especially the ordinary school with its humdrum teachers and pupils. But now that the results of the present survey of grammar-school authors in Florentine libraries is available, the balance in the argument seems to be swinging, at least in the case of Italy, away from Wieruszowski and Rand and returning to Paetow and Haskins.

To move from figures to actual manuscripts, in the present survey of Italian schoolbooks in Florentine libraries there is one Duecento manuscript of **Horace** (BRF), datable to the middle of the century, consisting of two independent sections joined together at the end of the Quattrocento (between v and r) and containing the *Ars poetica* (r– r), the satires (r– v) and the epistles (r– v). A second Horace (BNCF Landau Fin.), straddling the thirteenth and fourteenth centuries, Florentine or Tuscan in provenance and containing the *Ars poetica* and the *Epistolae*, was given extensive interlinear glossing by a number of Trecento hands; this version is particularly interesting for its annotation, in which there is as much if not more vernacular than Latin – a fact suggesting how far down the curriculum the Latin classics could sometimes descend.[138] **Lucan** is also represented by two Italian thirteenth-century manuscripts. One, dating from the first half of the century (BRF), is glossed interlinearly by several contemporary or near-contemporary school-level readers: one hand, writing at the same time as the copyist, appears in the text on the first few folios, then again only on r; there are two further hands, dating from the later Duecento, the second of which writes a macaronic mixture of Latin and vernacular (see v). The other, dating from the second half of the century (BNCF Panciat.), was probably prepared as a schoolbook, given its low-quality production, although there do not seem to be any Duecento glosses; the virtually sole commentator, who dates from the Trecento, left the usual school-level combination of simple interlinear lexical equivalents and

[137] Alessio and Villa ( ), – . [138] See Black (b), – and below, .

basic marginal philology (history, mythology, geography, sketch-maps). **Ovid** is similarly represented by two Italian thirteenth-century manuscripts. One is a codex of the *Metamorphoses*, dating from the mid-Duecento and completed at the turn of the fourteenth century (BML .), with school-type glossing both before and after its restoration.[139] The other is a manuscript of his *Epistulae ex Ponto*, dating from the first half of the thirteenth century, possibly in northwest Italy (BML .), and glossed by a number of hands contemporary with the copyist's. There is also a school-level ***Aeneid***, datable to the end of thirteenth century and probably of Pisan provenance (BML .), which is substantially glossed by a hand contemporary with that of the copyist.[140] Among the prose-writers, there are two Italian copies of **Sallust**. One, dating from the second half of the Duecento (BML .), is without doubt a schoolbook: not only did the copyist prepare the text for grammatical glossing, with generous spacing between the lines and ample margins, but he also wrote an alphabet on the inside front flyleaf ( ), so indicating in the conventional fashion that he was preparing a text for the classroom.[141] The copyist provided throughout a typical school-level mixture of interlinear paraphrases and word-order marks (for the latter see below, n.) and of brief simple philological marginal comments (especially paraphrase and grammar); there is also another contemporaneous school-level glossator, who gives a few grammatical and philological marginalia.[142] The other Italian Sallust (BML Ashb.), a

[139] Two sections: A (r– v) and B (v– r). A is datable to XIIImid, and B to XIII/XIVc. B follows A without textual adjustment or alteration; so the most likely hypothesis is that B was a restoration to a pre-existing fragment. Decoration throughout is uniform, apparently added soon after restoration. As Anderson ( ), – , has shown, A was 'a virtual diplomatic copy' of Beneventan MS Naples Biblioteca Nazionale IV.F. (N) – not only the text but the glosses too; B had no relation to Naples MS. However, the correspondence between A and N is limited to text and interlinear glosses, as is clear from photographs published by Anderson; A's copyist provided generally brief marginal comments throughout his section not corresponding to N. These marginalia to A consist of simple, low-level comments (mythology, grammar, geography, figures) typical of schoolbooks (including one allusion to Vergil: v), and it seems not unreasonable to hypothesize that A's copyist added these for teaching or study purposes: they do not correspond either to Arnulf of Orléans's commentary (see Ghisalberti ( )) or to the so-called vulgate commentary (see Coulson ( ), –). For ownership note of Maestro Peregrino da Pisa, see below .

[140] This stupendously illuminated MS shows how a luxurious product could immediately descend to school use. Copyist's glosses are typical school fare, including WOM (see v) and simple lexical paraphrase (v cited below, n.), besides simple philological marginalia, including basic secondary-level grammar (see v).

[141] For this and similar alphabets, see below, n. .

[142] E.g. r: hec insomnia feminini generis numeri singularis significat vigiliam; neutris [*sic pro* neutri *vel fortasse* neutr<i gener>is] numeri pluralis sunt ea que videntur per somnium. Other glosses by this hand on v, r, v, r.

manuscript dating from the mid-thirteenth century, is particularly interesting for its extensive vernacular interlinear lexical glosses, which not only suggest a West Tuscan provenance but also a notably modest academic level;[143] the copyist, who was responsible for these interlinear annotations as well as numerous word-order marks,[144] also left a simple philological commentary in the margins.[145] Other authors, including Juvenal, Persius and Terence, who had been notable in the twelfth-century curriculum, now seem to have disappeared, but the most notable absence in the Duecento was Cicero: it is clear that during the thirteenth century the shorter moral treatises dropped out of the Italian grammar-school curriculum. In fact, it is di cult to find any Italian manuscripts at all containing *De amicitia, De senectute, Paradoxa stoicorum* or *De o ciis* which are clearly datable to the thirteenth century: this seems to hold true not only for Florentine libraries[146] but also for manuscripts so far described in *Les manuscrits classiques latins de la Bibliothèque Vaticane.*[147]

Notable figures such Thomas Aquinas, Salimbene of Parma, Brunetto Latini, Guittone of Arezzo, Iacopone of Todi, Dante, Pier della Vigna, Henry of Isernia, Rolandino of Padua, Giovanni da Viterbo, even Boncompagno himself, all displayed knowledge of classical authors. But it is seldom clear where or when this familiarity was acquired: an extraordinary figure such as Dante may have revealed considerable knowledge of the classics, but it cannot be assumed that this was based on a grounding at school. Paetow's critics are able to cite almost no direct school-related evidence apart from the anecdote discovered by Weiss that Geri d'Arezzo read Terence at school as a boy.[148] But since there is now available substantial positive evidence to the contrary explicitly associated with school activity, the thesis of a continuous reading of the Latin classics at the grammar-school level must be open to doubt: it seems that the study of classical authors in the classroom reached a bare minimum in thirteenth-century Italy, dwindling to a small fraction of the quantity studied in the previous period.

It must be wondered how this collapse of the classics in thirteenth-century Italian schools is to be explained. Fundamental here was the rise

[143] See below, . [144] See below, n. . [145] See below, n. , for some examples.

[146] BML Ashb. (*De inventione, Rhetorica ad Herennium, Paradoxa stoicorum*), datable to XIII/XIVc., but glosses to XIVc.

[147] Pellegrin (–). BAV Borg. Lat. , containing (r– r) *De senectute, De amicitia, Paradoxa stoicorum* and *De o ciis*, which despite this catalogue (. : 'Origine: italienne') is clearly French, for example using Z = et. L. Reynolds ( ), , , gives French provenance. Also eliminated were Chigi H. . (*Tusc., Orations, De or., Orat.*, : no school-type use) and Pal. Lat. (*De o* . XII^2, Ital., no school-type use, only one sophisticated XIVc. commentator; *De or., Orat.* XV^1).

[148] Wieruszowski ( ), . See Weiss ( ) , Appendix .

of the professional Italian universities concentrating on the study of the *ars dictaminis* and *notaria*, law and medicine. These put pressure on the grammar schools to streamline their curricula, focusing on practical and rapid learning of Latin and eliminating the redundant study of Latin literature, previously at the heart of the grammar syllabus. An indication of the spin-o on the school curriculum from the developments in Italian higher education comes in the renowned French text of the early thirteenth century, Henri d'Andeli's *La bataille des VII. ars*: among the forces ranged against grammar and the authors is rhetoric, marshalling many Lombard knights.[149] The Lombards following rhetoric rode together with dialectic, wounding many honest enemies from the authorial camp.[150] The authors are now abandoned in France; *artisti* and *canonisti* are removed from grammar's jurisdiction. Bretons and Germans still are under grammar's sway, but grammar would be throttled by the Lombards, given a chance.[151]

In place of the authors there now burgeoned practical manuals for the study of secondary Latin in thirteenth-century Italy, a genre which had hardly before existed south of the Alps (see above,). The thirteenth century saw the first great flowering of Italian grammatical studies; this was also a period in which many copies were made in Italy of Alexander's *Doctrinale* and Evrard's *Graecismus* (see below,). In some sense, the latter two works came to serve a dual purpose in thirteenth-century Italy: on the one hand, they reinforced previous grammatical knowledge, providing rules and lists in an easily memorized verse format; on the other, they provided a type of substitute for the study of the authors themselves, and were accordingly glossed repeatedly in the traditional school manner, as soon as they made their appearance in Italy.

Another substitute for the classical authors was late Latin literature, and in particular one text: **Boethius**'s *Consolation of Philosophy*. This was considered a particularly suitable replacement for the more cumbersome Latin poets and prose-writers, evidently because it provided a short and varied anthology of poetry and prose.[152] It is hardly surprising to find that, as early as the thirteenth century, there are as many school-level Italian manuscripts of Boethius in Florentine libraries as of any one classical Latin author. One manuscript dating from the second half of the Duecento in which one of the copyists provided an interesting thirteenth-century marginal commentary (BNCF CS J. .) is still funda-

149 Ed. Paetow ( ), , vv. – .
150 Ed. Paetow ( ), , vv. – , – .
151 Ed. Paetow ( ), , vv. – .
152 See below, .

mentally grammatical in character, although it also incorporates some more advanced material.[153] Another (Venetian in origin) was probably produced for the school-book market (BNCF CS J. .), given its codicological similarity in format to other late-medieval Italian Boethian school manuscripts, although there are no glosses datable before the fourteenth century.[154] The third Italian Boethius, of West Tuscan provenance (BNCF NA) and dating from the turn of the fourteenth century, is exactly the same type as the preceding codex: a school product without glosses datable earlier than the Trecento.[155] Besides Boethius, there were a few other later authors who may have substituted for the Latin classics. One of these was **Maximianus** (BRF), whose poetry was glossed in the school manner with simple philological interlinear and marginal annotations by the copyist. A second was the ancient school text, ***Ilias latina***, a copy of which (BRF .), dating from the first half of the thirteenth century and written as a palimpsest over eighth/ninth-century late uncial script, contains in the hand of the copyist simple interlinear vernacular glosses of southern Italian provenance as well as a typically puerile explicit, not to mention other typically school-boyish annotations in an unformed hand from the Duecento such as a prayer, an alphabet and rudimentary grammatical notes.[156] Another was **Henry of Settimello**'s neo-Ovidian/neo-Boethian *Elegia*, a school classic,[157] found in a manuscript of Italian, possibly Tuscan, provenance dating from the last quarter of the thirteenth century (BNCF Magl. . , r– v) together with a text of the twelfth-century comedy ***Pamphilus*** (r– v), a work like Vitalis of Blois's *Geta* sometimes used in schools. Another Italian manuscript dating from the very end of the Duecento and containing ***Physiologus*** and **Aesop** (BNCF Magl. .) is glossed in the school manner by two principal hands, both writing at about the same time as the copyist: the interlinear glosses consist of simple Latin paraphrase, word-order marks and vernacular equivalents; the marginalia consist of figures and grammatical explanation, and there is a short conventional *accessus* to Aesop (v). Finally, there is a manuscript, possibly west Tuscan, of the **pseudo-Boethian *De disciplina scolarium***, dating from the very end of the

[153] See Black and Pomaro ( ), – , – .

[154] See Black and Pomaro ( ), – , – . Two school *ex libris*: Black and Pomaro ( ), .

[155] See Black and Pomaro ( ), – .

[156] See below, , – , , .

[157] See Filippo Villani's comment: 'Hic libellus, cui titulus "Henriguettus" est, primam discentibus artem aptissimus, per scholas Italiae continuo frequentatur' (Villani ( ),). See Cremaschi (–); Monteverdi ( ), – ; Viscardi ( ), – .

century (BML sup.),[158] copiously glossed by the copyist (up to r) and another contemporaneous hand (up to); the interlinear lexical equivalents and marginal explication and paraphrase suggest a school context (notwithstanding three brief *sententiae* attributed to Cicero and Aristotle (v, r)).

: –

If the focus now moves from the thirteenth to the fourteenth century, it will become clear that a significant reaction has set in against the anti-classical tendencies which had emanated from the rise of the universities and the professionalizing and specialist developments characteristic of schools in the Duecento. This is first of all evident in the numbers of Italian school texts of classical authors which are now found in Florentine libraries:

Century	Cic.	Claud.	Hor.	Juven.	Lucan	Ovid	Pers.	Sall.	Sen. Trag.	Stat.	Ter.	Val. Max.	Verg.	Total
XIII														
XIV														

This upsurge of interest in the classics at school in the Trecento is confirmed by the testimony of archival documents relating to the teaching curriculum. There are the examples of Maestro Nofri di Giovanni da Poggitazzi,[159] who in was said to have been teaching Vergil and

158 See Black and Pomaro ( ), – .

159 de Angelis ( ), n. , seems to assume that there are two di erent Nofri, one from Siena and one from Poggitazzi, who appears in a MS of *Thebais*, XVin., Perugia Bibl. Com. C , v: 'ego Nofrius Iohannis de Pagitatio […]' In fact, there is only one Nofri di Giovanni, who was variously said to be from Florence, Poggitazzi, San Giovanni Valdarno and Siena, as is clear from following archival documents. On January , 'quidam magister Nofrius Johannis de Pogitatio comitatus Florentie de presenti docens gramaticam in civitate Senarum' was appointed to teach grammar in Colle Valdelsa (ASSColle , lxiii verso–lxiiii recto), working there until (ASSColle , xxxiiii recto–verso), when he went to teach in San Gimignano (ASSG NN , r–v, v, v, r). On September , Pistoia elected 'Magister Nofrius Johannis de Senis' (ASPistoia Provv. , r), then teaching in Colle Valdelsa (see note immediately following), as communal grammarian, an appointment which he refused, since he continued teaching in Colle (ASSColle , v, r, lxii verso–lxiii recto). On September , in a reappointment at Colle, he was referred to as 'Magister Honofrius Johannis de Florentia' (ASSColle , xxxviii verso). On August 'Magister Honofrius Johannis de Sancto Johanne Vallis Arni superioris' accepted appointment as communal grammarian in S. Gimignano (ASSG NN , r–v, v, v, r). This variation in nomenclature is comprehensible: San Giovanni Valdarno is only km. from Poggitazzi, and other itinerant figures were given di erent names according to their peregrinations: e.g. Benedetto Accolti was referred to variously as Messer Benedetto da Pontenano (his father's birthplace) or d'Arezzo (his own birthplace): Black ( ), *passim*.

Lucan in Colle Valdelsa,[160] and of Maestro Niccolò di Ser Duccio da Arezzo, grammar teacher in Florence, Pistoia, Castiglion Fiorentino and Arezzo, who required one pupil in to buy from him a copy of Lucan.[161] At Chioggia in the last decades of the fourteenth century the grammarian was appointed to teach 'volentibus audire tragedias Senecae, Virgilium, Lucanum, Terentium et similes poetas et auctores'.[162] In a Friulian exercise book datable to the second half of the fourteenth century, Ovid appears as one of the standard school authors.[163] The humanist Antonio da Rho asserted that in the s, when he wrote his *Apologia*, schoolboys everywhere were reading Lucan and Statius – authors whom he himself had read at school at the end of the Trecento.[164] Giovanni di Paolo Morelli implied that as a grammar-school boy in late fourteenth-century Florence he read Vergil and Seneca.[165] Of this type of document the earliest is apparently the appointment of Giovanni del Virgilio to teach Vergil, Statius, Lucan and

[160] Bacci ( ), . The correct date of the famous document referred to by Bacci is , not . Bacci assumed that the document could not be later than , the supposed year of death of Maestro Piero da Ovile da Siena, mentioned there as teaching grammar in Siena. Bacci took this information from Zdekauer ( ), – , who cites the necrology of San Domenico di Siena (Siena Bibl. Comunale degli Intronati cod. C. . , [r]) where Maestro Piero, called 'doctor grammatice summus', was recorded as having died on August . I checked the original necrology in Siena, only to find that there were in fact two grammarians named Piero, one dying on August , the other on August :
Siena Biblioteca Comunale degli Intronati MS C. . ,

r: [...] Anno domini M°CCC°XXXVI. Incepimus scribere in isto libro omnes defunctos quorum corpora sepulta sunt in loco fratrum predicatorum de Senis [...]

r: [ ] Magister Petrus doctor gramatice summus sepultus est die XVI augusti.

r: M°CCCLXXXIII. Magister Petrus magister gramatice sepultus est die XVIII augusti in claustro in sepulcro suo cum habitu ordinis.

Bacci's document was compiled by 'Johannes Ser Franceschi', Pistoiese ambassador sent to find a grammar teacher for his native city. In fact, there is a document dated October in the Archivio di Stato, Pistoia, appointing Maestro Nofri, one of the list's teachers, as grammarian in Pistoia, with the following note regarding the acceptance of the appointment: (ASPistoia Provv. , r–v) [...] placeat [...] electionem prefatam acceptare de cuius acceptatione vel renumptatione, quod absit, nobis placeat infra triduum a die presentationis presentium computandum per publicum instrumentum vel per proprias licteras exibendas per Ser Johannem Ser Francisci ambaxiadorem nostrum in hac parte ad vos propterea destinato redere certiores. (This mention of Ser Giovanni di Ser Francesco was overlooked by Zanelli ( ), – .) This information accords with the date of suggested by Zanelli ( ), , for the beginning of Nofri's teaching in Pistoia. These new documents prove not only that Bacci's document is datable to and not to , but also that Maestro Piero da Ovile died in , not in . Moreover, in Bacci's document Francesco da Buti is referred to as 'Maestro Francesco vecchio, poeta e doctore e ora canciellieri di Pisa', a description which hardly agrees with Francesco da Buti's date of birth ('intorno al ': Bausi ( ),) but which accords with , when Francesco da Buti was approaching sixty. [161] Black (d), . [162] Bellemo ( ), .

[163] Schia ni ( ), .

[164] Antonio da Rho ( ), . I am grateful to David Rutherford for this reference.

[165] Morelli ( ), .

Ovid in Bologna in ; the election was made by the commune of Bologna and there is no mention of the *Studium* or university.[166] Giovanni was simply appointed along with Bertolino Benincasa, the latter to teach rhetoric.[167] It would be misleading to argue that this appointment was therefore independent of the university, as Bologna was of course the seat of one of Europe's greatest *studia generalia*. On the other hand, the authors were not normally included in the university curriculum in Italy until the fifteenth century; Giovanni del Virgilio's activity here would constitute an uncharacteristic example in the Trecento, especially given that his teaching duties in Bologna were said to include rhetoric in a subsequent document.[168] It could be argued that, rather than a university-level appointment, his post at Bologna resembled the work of a communal grammar teacher and *auctorista*, who also taught the authors and rhetoric to more advanced pupils, like, for example, Nofri di Giovanni da Poggitazzi at Colle Valdelsa in , who 'leggie Vergilio, Lucano et tucti altori, rector[ic]a et anche lo Dante, a chi volesse udirlo'.[169] What is significant here is that these documents confirm the results of the census of grammar schoolbooks in Florentine libraries: the Latin authors were once again being taught widely in fourteenth-century Italy.

There is strong evidence that this activity was taking place at the school level in Trecento Italy. Fortunately, a considerable number of copies of Latin authors have been preserved which were actually been signed by pupils in fourteenth-century Italian schools. A commented text of Seneca's tragedies (BML sup.) was completed on August 'per me Jovannem Antonii [...] in scholis Magistri Antonii Ser Salvi de Sancto Geminiano' (r),[170] then teaching in his native city.[171] Another manuscript of Seneca datable to the last quarter of the century and produced near Florence (BML .) was written by Maestro Nofri di Giovanni da Poggitazzi,[172] the teacher in Colle Valdelsa, San Gimignano and Siena, and glossed by a pupil who wrote: 'Dicit Magister Nofrius quod Seneca dormitabat quando composuit istum finem

166 Albini ( ), x–xi. 167 Rossi ( ), – . 168 Lidonnici ( ), .

169 Bacci ( ), .

170 Full colophon published by Bandini (–), ., where subsequent ownership notes of Giovanni di Maestro Matteo di Ser Lori de' Fineschi da Radda and of Domenico di Niccolò de' Pollini on the same folio are transcribed.

171 ASSG NN , r–v (October), when he was appointed to teach for five years, beginning October .

172 v: scripte per Nofrium Johannis; Bandini (–), . publishes entire colophon. de Angelis ( ), n. , dates MS: 'XIV exeunte'.

carminis' (r). In a late fourteenth-century manuscript of Horace's *Ars poetica* and epistles, copied either in Florence or nearby (BML .), one owner, probably still during the Trecento, left the following note of possession: 'In schilis [*sic*] Magistri <...> gramatice loice ac r(hetorice); qui michi furatur vel reddat m(ihi) vel moriatur. Bartulus' (v). In a late twelfth-century manuscript of Lucan (BML .), an earlyish fourteenth-century hand rewrote the original text and cleaned all the parchment, including the numerous notes of possession at the end of the manuscript: one of these erased ownership notes was 'Iste Lucanus est <...e>lis <...> Magistri Andree', suggesting the usual formula 'morantis in scholis magistri'; previously the book seems to have belonged to Maestro Andrea himself, judging from another note on r: 'Lucanus Magistri Andree'. In another Lucan, this time copied in the thirteenth century (BRF), there are a number of erased notes of possession, one of which speaks of 'morantis in sc<...>' (v); these notes must go back to the fairly early Trecento, because they were covered by seven verses written in *cancelleresca* script, datable no later than the third quarter of the fourteenth century. In a manuscript of Ovid, copied at the end of the twelfth century (BML .), a note of possession on the final folio referring to Maestro Jacopo da Vigevano may even go back to the end of the thirteenth century.[173] A Sallust copied in the twelfth century (BML inf. .) was later owned by a lawyer called Ognibene *de Vedrotis*,[174] who left not only *ricordi* of his various professional activities in , and (v, v), including a period as a judicial rector in Pescia, but also this possible indication of his own schooldays: 'Require illud modicum istius primi libri in libro tuo *Apostilorum* domini dey, et principium secundi libri in *Donato* Magistri Guiçardi optimi professoris' (v).[175] There is also a clear North Italian, Lombard school Sallust in Florence (BML Ashb.), dating from the early fourteenth century and bearing the following late-Trecento note of possession: 'Est Marcholi de Pergamo qui legit in iscola Magistri <Bar>tolomei de Magna' (v).[176]

173 See above, n. .

174 v: Explicit liber Salustii D. Ugnibeni de Vedrotis iudicis.
v: vernacular *ricordo* telling of 'Alberto <...> per prexonero <...> de Venexia. Coreva <...> Dì d'avosto morì Messer Marxicio <...>'. The sense is unclear, as is the date, which, however, seems to contain CCC and an X; the language is without doubt Venetian. Hand is more cursive than Ognibene Vedrotti's Latin writing, but it may be the same writer; in that case, Ognibene was a judge of Venetian origin working as a foreign rector in Pescia.

175 This annotation, coming at end of the incomplete *BC* and acephalous *BJ*, indicates where to find the missing passages. On Guizardo da Bologna, see n. , below.

176 v: Marcolo identifies himself as son of 'Domini Michaelis de Pergamo'.

There are three other manuscripts now in Florence which possibly reveal school *ex libris* from the Trecento: BML . , a fourteenth-century Horace (v: Iste liber est <…?> scolaris Magistri Francisci gramatice professoris; iste liber est Giorgii Gheççi morantis in scolis Magistri Francisci doctoris gramatice ac loice); BRF , another Trecento Horace (v: Iste liber est Fagiani Ser Angeli morantis in iscolis Magistri Francisci); and BML . , a composite *Metamorphoses* copied in the thirteenth and at the turn of the fourteenth century (r: Liber Magistri Peregrini de Pisis).

It is di cult not to associate this upsurge of school interest in the Latin classics during the Trecento with pre-humanism and then with Petrarcan humanism itself. Nevertheless, it would be unconvincing to argue that such a wide-ranging and extensive phenomenon as this new di usion of the Latin authors throughout the schools of Italy could owe its origins wholly to a movement like early humanism, still limited to an avant-garde, however influential. What must be true, however, is that an undoubted change of educational fashion from the thirteenth century obviously encouraged, and was encouraged by, leading humanists from Lovato, Mussato and Geri up to Petrarch, Boccaccio and Salutati.

Among the fourteenth-century copies of school authors found prominently in Florentine libraries, two stalwarts of the medieval Italian classroom maintained a substantial presence: **Horace** and **Ovid**, the former almost always represented by an anthology consisting of the *Ars poetica* and the epistles:

BML .	Interlinear paraphrase glosses and brief marginalia in the school manner by two di erent hands datable to end of the Trecento (the first on v– r, and the second on r– r). Commissioned by Florentine Francesco Vannicelli in : see below, and n. , and and n. .
BML .	Most copious commentator (mainly r– r) was the copyist, with interventions all suggesting school-level use: ( ) simple lexical interlinear glossing;[177] ( ) free-standing brief literary/grammatical commentary on vv. – of *Ars* (r– r), including Aristotelian-type *accessus*[178] emphasizing Horace's activities as grammar teacher and text's educational purpose;[179] ( ) marginal commentary on *Ars* (r– v), literary and grammatical in character, repeating much material found in

[177] See below, . [178] See below, .

[179] r: […] Oratius in partibus suis studuit in istis gramaticalibus et his que pertinent ad gramaticam. Postmodum transtulit se in Greciam ubi studuit in artibus et in loycalibus precipue ut ipse dicit ad hoc ut cognosceret curvum a recto [*Epistvlae*.e . .]. Postea venit Romam et ibi longo tempore stetit cum quodam qui vocabatur Piso cuius filios instruxit et ipsis instructis cum non haberet certas regulas in arte poetica ipse ad eorum doctrinam fecit istum librum.

	preceding commentary.[180] Also other late fourteenth-century glosses, often by the 'Bartulus' mentioned above ( ) as subsequent owner; his interventions, concentrated between v and v, consisted mainly of simple lexical interlinear equivalents, including vernacular (e.g. v: fineris = id est *sia ornato*, v: alsit = *era fredo*, r: siculi = *ciciliani*, v: ylia = *i fianchi*, r: defers = *prolunghi*, v: oleam = *l'oliva*), as well as the beginning of a margin comment.[181] A third school-level reader glossed the rest of manuscript with usual interlinear simple lexical equivalents and some philological marginalia (figures, paraphrase, rhetorical structure, brief explication). Both the copyist and this third glossator, albeit still reading in school context, were more advanced than Bartulus, in view of the fact that both annotated entirely in Latin.[182]
BML .[183]	Extensive Trecento interlinear glossing, including word-order marks (v, v, v), alphabets (v, r), and copious vernacular synonyms.
BML .	Significant amount of fourteenth-century vernacular interlinear glossing;[184] also some typically school-level philological Trecento marginalia at the beginning of manuscript by several di erent hands (grammar, explication,[185] simple literary criticism,[186] mythology,[187] paraphrase).

[180] Cf. notes v with those r. All not taken from preceding commentary, e.g. (r) 'primo removet sex vicia [...]' not appearing on r. See below, , for this method of extracting from free-standing commentaries as the school method for marginal glossing.

[181] v: Hic revertitur adhuc Oratius a[d] colletionem et duo primo: apparently beginning of scholastic *divisio textus* (on which see below,)

[182] Another late Trecento owner, contemporaneous with Bartulus and also schoolboy (in view of immature hand and illiterate Latin), left the following ownership note, indicating his membership of a Florentine patrician family: (r) Iste liber est Iovannes Manni de Nobilibus de Florentia. P(re)suna [*sic pro* persona] [que] id invenit et non restituerit in mala morte periebit.

[183] Probably Bolognese, to judge from annotations of early XIVc. hand, including marginal note: O du[l]cis mater, hic est Bononia pate(r) (v). Soon passed into Tuscany, as suggested by interlinear vernacular glosses (r: *meçina* [*mezzina* for *vaso* is Tuscan]; see r: *e i giuochi e i bagni*), possibly made by Tuscan owner still writing in XIVc.; v: possibly end of *ex libris*: <?>glo da Prato, amen.

[184] Suggesting Tuscan provenance: e.g. r: cervicem = *uno collo*, equinam = *di cavallo*, undique = *d'ogni parte*, collatis = *raguaglati*, superne = *dalla parte di sopra*, vane = *vanamente*, cupressum = *l'arcipresso*, enatat = *nuota*.

[185] E.g. glossing *Ars poetica* :

v: Archilocus fuit quidam magister qui volebat accipere uxorem. Fuit locutus cum quodam viro qui vocabatur Liambe et [h]abebat filiam que vocabatur Nobe. Et dedit in uxorem et postea abstulit sibi. Ipse vero p(ro) magnam verecundiam [*sic*] quam [h]abuit de uxore sib[i] ablata de ipso composuit versus iambos. Ipso [*sic pro* Ipse] hoc audito quod de eo versus composuerat, <id>eo propriis manibus propter <e>u(m) se firmiter subfocavit.

Pseudo-Acron (–), , :
Iambicum metrum primus Archilocus invenit, quo usus est in Lycamben, quem persecutus est, quod ei Neobulen desponsatam iam filiam denegavit, in tantum, ut Lycambes iambos eius voluerit morte vitare; nam ad laqueum confugit.

[186] r: Di erentia est inter comediam et traiediam, quia commedia habet triste principium et letum finem, traiedia vero letum principium set tristem finem. [187] Footnote is overleaf.

BML .	Well glossed marginally and interlinearly by many Trecento hands, including one in particular, providing typical school-level Latin lexical annotations and brief philological marginalia.[188]
BML Strozzi	Abundant contemporaneous vernacular interlinear glossing and simple marginal philology.
BNCF CS J.VI.	Glossed principally by the copyist in typical school-level manner (mainly interlinear annotations and brief marginalia). Substantial mythological gloss on Atreus (v), dating from turn of XVc., is typical school fare.
BRF	Glossed during Trecento only and in typical school manner: simple interlinear lexical equivalents throughout, WOM (v, v), a little vernacular (v, r), simple philological marginalia consisting of mythology and especially paraphrase.
BRF	Primarily glossed by at least one contemporaneous hand, with typical school-level comments, consisting of lexical paraphrase and simple philological marginalia.
BRF	Glossed by a reader contemporaneous with copyist in typical school manner with mainly Latin (but also some vernacular) lexical equivalents.

The other standby of the curriculum to resume a leading position in the syllabus during in the Trecento was **Ovid**'s ***Metamorphoses***:

BML AD	Only slight possibly school use in XIVc. (r, r, v), although the first two books were given lexical/philological

187 Glossing *Ars poetica* :

r: Telephus fuit quidam rex qui venit in adiutorium Troianorum et vulneratus fuit ab Achille et non poterat evadere nisi iterum vulneratus esset ab eo et ivit ad Achillem et rogavit eum [ut] vulneraret iterum. Achilles vulneravit eum et ipse evasit.	Pseudo-Acron (–), , : <Telephus> Ab Achille vulneratus est et curatus.

188 Latter section (containing Horatian texts) was described as having been written 'in German Gothic book hand (XIII)' by Gehl ( ), and ( ), , a view corrected by Villa (–), ('Gotica libraria italiana'): the manuscript bears an Italian *ex libris*: (v) Iste liber est <Ser> Stefani Ser Francisci, deo gratias, besides Italian vernacular interlinear glosses, e.g. v: diu = *lungho*, recuset = *rifiutava*.

	marginalia in mid XVc. (r– r), and there was occasional further school-type activity at about the same time (e.g. v– r, v– v, v– r, v– v) until eventually there is a direct reference to a lecture course on Ovid, possibly in Verona, beginning on April .[189]
BML CS	Glossed by two XIVc. readers: one provided philological glosses of school type, also citing some other authors[190] – a practice common at school level;[191] the other provided, among normal school-type philological glosses, some allegorical mythologies[192] – again a common procedure among school readers.[193]
BML CS	Glossed mainly by the copyist himself overwhelmingly in the standard philological school manner, taking also three allegorical moralities from Giovanni del Virgilio (r, r).[194]
BML .[195]	The simple interlinear paraphrases, the philological marginalia (mainly paraphrase, explication) and the allegories borrowed from Giovanni del Virgilio, in which each transformation is

[189] r: Maistro Columbino V(er)oniso comenzò el *Metamorphoseos* a dì de aprillo ; Ma<i>stro Colonbino Veroniso comenzò el *Morphoseos* a dì aprillo .

[190] v: Ovid, *Fasti*; v: Claudian, Juvenal; r: Vergil, *Bucolics*; v: Ovid, *Heroides*, r: Lucan; Ovid, *Ars amatoria*.

[191] See below, and Appendix .

[192] r: Nota allegoriam dei descendentis pro salute humani generis [...]; r: nota quod moralis est ista fabula. Per Martem intelligendum est virum virtuosum et probus [*sic*] [...]; r: Nota quod ista mutatio Phebi [...] est moralis. Nam per Phebum intelligendum est virum sapientum [*sic*].

[193] See below, .

[194] See below, .

[195] The glossator, Nofri di Angelo da San Gimignano, undertook his work in at least two phases, one completed in , the other in (see de Angelis ( ), , n.). He was also communal grammar master in Colle Valdelsa between and and / (ASSColle , xxxiii recto; , xiiii recto, xliii verso, xlv recto, lviii verso–lx recto; , xxxvi recto; , v– v, r–v; , viiii verso–xi recto), besides : de Angelis ( ), n. , based on Coppi ( ), , who seems to give no relevant information here: 'In questo [anno sc.] mentre Don Onofrio d'Angelo Coppi Abbate dell'Abbazia di S. Baronto in quel di Pistoia, fu dal Pubblico chiamato per Professore d'eloquenza alla Patria, e con titoli molto decorosi al suo merito gli fu scritto, ed egli accettò tale incumbenza, siccome ancora fu chiamato da' Signori Colligiani. Questo mio Don Onofrio era un huomo dottissimo, e fece molte esposizioni a Persio, e a Giovenale [...]' In the other part of the book numbered separately under the title *Uomini illustri di S. Gimignano* ( ) he states: 'Viveva egli nel , nel qual tempo lo ritrovo Maestro d'Umanità a Colle quando spiegò la nuova Poetica di Gualfredo Inglese eruditissimo, facendoli le sue note, siccome le fece avanti nel a Persio [...]' In fact, he was elected communal grammar master for one year beginning November : ASSColle , xxviii verso–xxviiii recto. He served in San Miniato in and (ASSColle , r–v; , xi verso) and San Gimignano between and (ASSG NN , xxviii recto–verso).

	narrated and interpreted (see below,), must all have related directly to Nofri di Angelo da San Gimignano's work in the classroom.[196]
BML .	Glossed in an entirely standard school manner by the copyist, including simple lexical paraphrase and philological marginalia.

Another standby of the the curriculum somewhat less well represented among fourteenth-century schoolbooks now in Florence is **Lucan**:

BML CS	Collaborative school-level product copied by at least three hands and then glossed by yet at least another three, all of whom provide usual simple philological, historical and geographical marginalia, as well as standard simple lexical paraphrases and WOM.
BML .	Glossed by hand from end of XIVc. providing considerable quantity of vernacular commentary, extending to the margins, besides copious simple interlinear lexical annotations and simple philological marginalia typical of schoolroom.
BML .	Second copyist is the principal glossator who provides a school-level commentary, consisting of interlinear lexical paraphrases and extensive marginalia of literary/grammatical nature (r– v, r– v, r– r, v).
BNCF Panciat.	Glossed mainly by two contemporaneous hands with simple interlinear lexical equivalents and marginal philology (paraphrase, geography, mythology, cosmology, history, Roman customs, figures).

196 Apart from the glossator writing in , who is di erent from Nofri (indeed, criticizing Nofri's gloss on r), who expresses anti-Florentine sentiments and whose philologically critical comments are not those of a school-type reader, there is no further use of this MS. de Angelis ( ), , n. , publishes the glosses of the annotator, whom she interprets to be Nofri himself; the criticism of 'glosator iste' for confounding 'Ancona' and 'Ançi' refers, in her view, to another commentary which Nofri has at hand and which he has found to be inaccurate. But 'iste' would seem to refer to the gloss closest to the point at which the annotator is writing; de Angelis does not seem to note that the hand of the glossator is di erent from Nofri's (see for example the di erent type of -shaped 'et' used by each). The manuscript must have been out of Nofri's possession in . I could find no evidence in Coppi ( ), as seems to be suggested by de Angelis, that Nofri became 'priore canonice Castri Veteris' only in , as he signs himself on v, so that the book could have passed out of his hands before .

One author whose presence in the Duecento had dwindled to insignificance but who began to show slight signs of revival in the Trecento was **Vergil**:

BML Ashb.	Two glossators (XIV/XVc.), the principal providing heavy interlinear and brief marginal glosses, all typically philological in school manner, while the other gives rhetorical divisions of the speech opening *Aeneid* (v– r).[197]
BML .	Glossed by the copyist with the usual interlinear vocabulary equivalents and with marginalia devoted to paraphrase, summaries, headings and simple mythology.[198]
BML .	Usual mixture of almost entirely Latin interlinear synonyms together with simple marginal philology, written by two di erent contemporaneous hands, one of whom was the copyist.
BNCF .. (r– r)	Written by grammar teacher in Poppi for more than twenty years, Ser Santi di Biagio da Valiana;[199] annotations provide a few interlinear glosses and some philological marginalia – all appropriate classroom fare.
BNCF Pal.	Commentary looks possibly copied from schoolbook: simple philology, obvious paraphrase, basic grammar.

Just as striking as these reappearances of Horace's *Ars* and letters, the *Metamorphoses* and, to some extent, Vergil and Lucan's *Pharsalia* is the absence or only rare appearances of other former stalwarts of the curriculum during the Trecento. One of these is **Terence**, unrepresented in the Duecento and only present during the next century in the anthology made by Santi da Valiana just mentioned (BNCF ..); the versions of Terence's comedies (v– v), dated (r) and (v) are preceded by copied *accessus* and *argumenta* (r– v),[200] and Santi's entirely philological commentary is limited largely to v– r. Another author still thinly represented in the Trecento schoolroom was **Persius**:

[197] Common school exercise: see below, .

[198] One earlier Quattrocento school reader called 'Antonius' left the following *probatio* at end of text: (r) abcdef.Antonius.

[199] Billanovich ( ), – .

[200] Villa ( ), .

BML . (r– r)[201]	Second late Trecento glossator (see above,) provided school-type interlinear paraphrase glosses (r–v).
BML . [202]	No actual school use of the manuscript during XIVc., but one owner then (v: Iste liber esst Betonie clericus) was a child, to judge from the crude writing and from the immature sketch of a king which this *ex libris* accompanies.

These two examples hardly suggest heavy school use for Persius in the fourteenth century, and the same can be said for **Juvenal**, whose only appearance among Florentine school manuscripts is in the above-mentioned Vannicelli anthology of (BML . , r– r),[203] where the text of his satires remains unglossed. Similarly the only Trecento school-level **Sallust** now in Florence (BML Ashb.), mentioned above as signed by a pupil from Bergamo, is unglossed.[204] Finally, **Ovid**'s ***Heroides***, weakly represented up to the end of the Duecento, continued to languish in the Trecento, the only schoolbook in the present census being the well-known BML . , a copy datable to the second half of the century and owned by Messer Luca Buondelmonti, from whom it was purchased by Cosimo de' Medici for use at the school of Maestro Niccolò di Ser Duccio d'Arezzo.[205] Cosimo's glossing probably

201 In the anthology mentioned above ( ) commissioned in by Francesco Vannicelli: (r) Iste liber est <*deletum*> populi Sancti Felicis in platea, quem ipse fecit scribi anno domini MCCC°LXXX° de mense septembris. Deo gratias. Amen. Over erasure, 'Francisci Iohannis Vann<…>' is partially restored by XVIc. hand.

202 Executed in early XIVc., probably a copy of a considerably earlier heavily commented version, as suggested by problems evident in organizing glosses on the page (see v– r). An old prototype can also be inferred from the diphthong 'ae', not even yet written with cedilla (see r: Helenae). 203 See above n. for colophon with this information.

204 See above, . Other ownership notes (r: Iste liber est meii Andrioli de <…> Iste liber est mei Stefanini de Mediolano.) come from immature hands but seem to date from XVc.

205 See ownership note (v), published in part by Bandini (–), . ; same partial transcription republished by Hankins ( ), n. . de la Mare ( ), , gives a full transcription, of which she publishes a photograph (plate (b)): 'Iste liber est Cosme Iohannis de Medicis morantis ad scolas d. Magistri Nicholai de Aretio et eum Emi a d. lucha de bondalmontibus de Florentia. costitit uno flor(en)o s(olidi) octus videlicet.' The phrase 'costitit uno flor(en)o s(olidi) octus videlicet' seems not to make sense. These words appear to be a later addition, to judge from their following the flourish in the shape of a large ' ' or 'z' after 'de Florentia', which must have been the original end of the *ex libris*. The photograph is deceptive here: several re-examinations of the original have led me to the view that the letter at the end of 'octu' may not be an 's' but rather an ' ', possibly rewritten from an 'o', in which case the phrase would read literally 'costitit uno flor° soctu vz'; this would then be transcribed as 'costitit uno floreno s(olidis) octu, videlicet'. The problem remains that there is no spacing or punctuation among the letters 'soctu ', but de la Mare too inserts a word-break between 's' and 'octus'. (The word 'octus', meaning eight *asses*, a contraction of *octussis*, occurs only in the late grammarian Charisius and in any case would make no sense here.) According to the proposed possible reading, the cost of the book was one florin, eight *soldi*.

took place at the turn of the fifteenth century, when Niccolò di Ser Duccio was teaching in Florence: he was in fact given an o cial appointment by the Studio o cials for the academic year – .[206] All the annotation on the manuscript is typically grammar-school fare. The codex contains intermittent marginal comments in the hand of the copyist, possibly extracted in the normal school manner from a larger commentary on the text. After the scribe, the first reader of the book seems to be a tiny, fine cursive hand which provides frequent simple interlinear paraphrases (e.g. r) especially at the beginning of the work. There was also another early reader who provided a couple of marginalia on r. Both these preceded Cosimo de' Medici, who rewrote the latter marginal glossator's comments on r and wrote over the interlinear commentator's glosses on the same folio. Cosimo's glosses are not di cult to pick out, writing as he did with a distinctively dark ink. His interlinear glosses are typical simple lexical equivalents: e.g. (r) Lacedemona = Grecia, deserto = relicto, querenti = petenti, spatiosam = longam, leto = morte; his marginalia are the normal basic philology.[207] Roughly contemporaneous with Cosimo were several other glossators, one of whom amended his gloss on Laertes.[208]

The author whose absence from the grammar schoolroom in the Trecento is the most striking is **Cicero**; his shorter moral treatises had had, it has been seen, a significant place in the twelfth-century Italian curriculum but had vanished in the Duecento. These texts began again to be copied in Italy during the fourteenth century, but they seem not yet to have re-entered the schoolroom.[209] Their principal academic use

206 Gherardi ( ), .

207 E.g.

r: Penolope fuit filia Ycarii
Antilocus fuit filius Nestoris quem Paris interfecit.
Trilolomus fuit filius Erculis interfectus ab Ethore.
Pat(ro)colus fuit filius Meneaci interfectus ab Ethore.
v: Resus fuit rex Traice.
epitetum
v: Telemacus fuit filius Ulixis.
r: Anteas erat quidam mons a quo lignis ortis naves fiebant.
r: Traicus fuit Orfeus, repertor lire.
v: Pliasdis uxor Athamantis que habuit VII filias cum quibus omnibus concubuit Iupiter et eas mutavit in Gallinella[m] signum celeste.

208 Cosimo had written simply (v) 'Laertes fuit pater Ulixis'; the subsequent glossator added to the beginning 'hic tangitur mos antiquus' and to the end 'et filius consueverat claudere oculos patris post ipsius mortem', so that the whole gloss now reads:

Hic tangitur mos antiquus: Laertes fuit pater Ulixis et filius consueverat claudere oculos patris post ipsius mortem.

209 The following XIVc. Italian manuscripts of the shorter moral treatises have been examined and eliminated as schoolbooks. Florentine libraries: BML . , . . , inf. ; Strozzi , . BRF

in the fourteenth century seems to have been at the university level, to judge from one Florentine manuscript of *De o ciis* with the following colophon: 'Marci Tulii Ciceronis liber tertius et ultimus ad Marcum eius filium feliciter explicit per me Michaelem filium Domini Johannis de Mutina die iovis XII mensis decembris .'[210] This was apparently a university-level textbook, originally a large volume ruled in the customary fashion with double lines round a small central text and surrounded by a dense, all-embracing commentary. In this case, unfortunately, it is impossible to discover how *De o ciis* was studied, since the comment was scrubbed o the margins and is only faintly visible now under ultra-violet light,[211] but more can be said about another university-level text of *Paradoxa stoicorum*, dating from the turn of the fourteenth century.[212] Here the text forms the third part of an anthology with the Ciceronian rhetorical works, *De inventione* and *Rhetorica ad Herennium*; it seems that the numerous fourteenth-century students of rhetoric who left their copious glosses on this manuscript went on to read the *Paradoxa*, making grammatical (e.g. r, r), philological (r), rhetorical[213] and moral philosophical[214] comments on the text, suggesting that they were possibly following a course on rhetoric and moral philosophy, often studied in the early stages of the notarial or legal university syllabus.[215]

A particularly significant feature of the study of the authors in the Trecento was the introduction into the curriculum of texts never previously read in the classroom. The most important of these were the tragedies of Seneca. It is a curious feature of the medieval and Renaissance use of classical works that Seneca's moral treatises and letters seem to have been little read in Italian schools; no manuscript copies of these texts have

footnote (*cont.*)
, . BAV: Arch. S. Pietro H. ; Vat. Lat. ; Chigi, H. . . Catalogued as XIVc. but eliminated as XVc. and not apparently schoolbooks: Vat. Lat. (humanist script), (late Gothic script), (late Gothic script), (heavy late Gothic script); Ottob. Lat. (humanist script), (heavy, late Gothic script); Chigi H. . (widely spaced, late Gothic hands); Arch. S. Pietro H. (late Gothic script); Barb. Lat. (humanist script); Pal. Lat. (late Gothic script).

210 BML Edili , v. Reusing notarial parchment, dated (v) 'Millesimo trecentessimo trigessimo quinto'.

211 University-level commentary erased from r– r, r, r, r, v, r, r, r. Passed into ownership of Giorgio Antonio Vespucci in later XVc.: see v for his *ex libris* and v for his motto.

212 BML Ashb. .

213 BML Ashb. , r, where glossator provides *accessus*, emphasizing the power of rhetoric to lend probability to true statements, which otherwise would remain improbable and obscure.

214 BML Ashb. , v, r.

215 Kind of course o ered by Giovanni Travesio in later XIVc. at Pavia: see Rossi ( ), – ; Barzizza appointed to teach moral philosophy and rhetoric at Padua in : Panizza ( ), – ; Mercer ( ), , .

been found in Florence showing typical school usage[216] – a pattern which confirms the results of Munk Olsen's conclusions regarding the period before the thirteenth centuy.[217] Up to the end of the Duecento, **Seneca's tragedies** apparently remained unused in Italian grammar schools too, but suddenly in the Trecento they became favourites of the classroom, even overtaking Horace's *Ars* and letters as the most popular Latin classics. This of course mirrors the history of their transmission, which had been extremely limited before the thirteenth century but was stimulated by the work of the Paduans Lovati and Mussato and then by interest at Avignon, leading to Nicholas Trevet's commentary.[218]

BML AD	Glossed by several contemporaneous hands with usual school mixture of synonyms and philology, and a couple of citations of other authors (v, v: see Appendix).
BML CS	Glossed by several late XIVc. writers with normal interlinear paraphrases, marginal philology and some citations of other authors (v, v, r, r: see Appendix).
BML CS	Archetypal schoolbook, containing sporadic heavy interlinear paraphrase glossing (including a little vernacular), besides marginal glosses; two XIVc. hands most active as glossators are the copyist (see r, v, v, v) and the contemporaneous writer who particularly comments on *Oedipus* (v– v) but is also found elsewhere (v and r). Several good sketches (v, r, v) but one particularly crude drawing of Octavia with a nurse (v) must be the work of a child.[219]
BML sin.	Archetypical schoolbook, glossed by several near-contemporaneous hands, including the copyist,[220] who provide

216 Following manuscripts were examined and eliminated: BML AD , CS , Edili , , Med. Fies. , , , Pl. . , . , . , . , . , . , . , . , . , . , . . , . , . , . , . , . , . . , sup. , sup. , sup. , sup. , sup. , inf. , dxt. , sin. , San Marco , ; BNCF, . , CS J. . , J. . , J. . . Revealing are comments of Perotti in *Rudimenta grammatices* (Naples), n.n., recommending Seneca for post-grammatical education:

> Cavendum tamen est ne nimio brevitatis studio squalens et ieiunia et concisa ac plane sicca oratio fiat, qualis est Annei Senece, a cuius lectione adolescentes animo avertendi sunt. Nam pravum ac vitiosum dicendi modum imbibant, quanquam paulo post, quasi iactis iam fundamentis, idem auctor summo studio legendus sit, in quo magne alioquin virtutes fuerunt, multum ingenii, plurimum eruditionis, cum presertim sit vitiorum diligentissimus insectator.

217 Munk Olsen ( ), – . 218 L. Reynolds ( ), – ; Billanovich ( ), , .

219 Probably XVc., given that the caption identifying Octavia contains a 'ct' ligature characteristic of humanist script.

220 E.g. r: Tres sunt iudices infernales, scilicet Minos, Radamanthus et Eacus, quorum unus inquirit peccata, videlicet Minos; alter iudicat, scilicet Radamanthus; alter punit, scilicet Eacus. Unde dantur tales versus de predictis:

> Cognitor est veri Minos cogitque fateri,
> Veraque scruptanti[s] censura subest Radamanthy,
> Tu miseros punis ardentibus, Eace, prunis.

	normal school-level variety of simple lexical paraphrase and basic marginalia (etymology, figures, mythology) especially in second half of codex.[221]
BML .	From the school of Maestro Nofri di Giovanni da Poggitazzi (active in Tuscany *c.* to *c.*),[222] glossed by his pupil with usual school-type interlinear and marginal glosses, besides citing Vergil (v); several other roughly contemporary hands, one citing Seneca, Cicero's *De amicitia*, Augustine's *De civitate dei* (v– r), another Boccaccio (r), a third citing Vergil's *Aeneid*, pseudo-Seneca's *De moribus* and Boccaccio again (v);[223] also a partly verse guide to Roman dates written by a child with vulgarized Latin spelling.[224]

221 In XVc., used by Francesco Foraboschi, minorite friar at S. Croce in Florence: (v) Ad usum fuit Fratris Francisci de Foraboschis, qui pertinet armario florentini conventus Sancte Crucis ordinis minorum. Foraboschi was a pupil reading Boethius's *Consolation* in under Maestro Francesco *de Alverna* (BML sin. : see Black and Pomaro ( ),) but there do not seem to be any of his glosses surviving in this Seneca.

222 For some examples, see above, n. .

223 Citation of Boccaccio (v) is mentioned by Branca ( ), , evidently following Bandini (–), . . This contains a garbled *sententia*, which Branca deciphers to give a comprehensible version. Although when writing, Branca says he was unable to find this *sententia* in any of the usual reference works, it is now found in Schmidt ( ), n. a , referring to *Florilegium adagiorum et sentiarum latino-germanicum*, ed. Andreas Ritzius Sangallensis, Basle , .

Branca ( ) also observes that the passage on Diana (v) is perhaps from Boccaccio's *Genealogie deorum gentilium.* This reference to Diana is part of a list, partly etymological, of various goddesses, beginning not with Diana but with Proserpine: Prosperpina in inferno; Diana in silvis [...] Delia a Delo monte vel insula [...] This seems too generic to permit the identification of a source.

Branca apparently did not notice the following gloss, by another roughly contemporaneous hand, also citing Boccaccio. Here it is possible to find a genuine Boccaccian source.

Seneca, *Thyestes*	BML . , r	Boccaccio, *Genealogie*, . , in Boccaccio ( ), , .
puerone parcit? an scelus sceleri ingerit?	Qui puer nominatus fuit Arpagines secundum Dominum Johannem Bocacium alegantem Theodontium dicentem de hoc.	Tercium hunc puerum Theodontius dicit Arpagigem nuncupatum.

The explicit reference to Boccaccio here in Maestro Nofri's schoolroom confirms what has hitherto been asserted, on the basis of indirect evidence deriving from the famous search for a grammar teacher by the city of Pistoia in (Bacci ( )), that Maestro Nofri was an outstanding Tuscan teacher: his direct use of an up-to-date humanist text such as Boccaccio's *Genealogie*, besides the citations by his pupils of Vergil's *Aeneid* and Cicero's *De amicitia*, place Nofri di Giovanni in the avant-garde of the movement in education which would bring those texts back into vogue in XVc., after nearly two centuries of oblivion in the schoolroom.

A notable later gloss is the completion of the one already mentioned (see above, – and n.) alluding to Nofri's comment on Seneca's somnolence. At the end of this gloss ([...] quando composuit istum finem carminis: see above, –) a later XVc. hand added: cum ipse cacaret ut ait D(ominus) Marsilius. Could this be Ficino? There is no internal indication when this MS arrived in Florence.

224 v:

Sex nonas maius octuber iulius et mars

BML .	Glossed primarily by one contemporaneous hand with fairly simple interlinear paraphrases besides marginal summaries and metric analyses throughout; citations of other authors (see Appendix) do not contradict school context.
BML sup.	Signed by Giovanni di Antonio di Jacopo da Gambassi in the Valdelsa and recording teaching which he received in from Maestro Antonio di Ser Salvo da San Gimignano. This commentary comprises usual school fare, including *accessus* (r),[225] simple interlinear vocabulary glosses (sometimes in vernacular[226]) and entirely philological marginalia consisting mainly of paraphrase and explication; not untypically, other authors are cited (see Appendix) and only some of the tragedies are glossed (*Hercules furens*, end of *Medea*, *Agamemnon*, beginning of *Octavia*).
BML Strozzi	First glossed by a typical school reader, contemporary to the copyist, and then by another hand, who wrote that he had finished teaching the text on June .[227]
BML Strozzi	Glossed by several near-contemporaneous hands, providing consistent covering of interlinear glossing and brief philological marginalia throughout the manuscript, including simple paraphrase; brief citations of other authors (see Appendix) do not rule out school context.
BNCF Banco Rari	Became schoolbook quickly at the beginning of XVc.
BNCF NA	Mainly glossed by the copyist with usual simple interlinear paraphrase and marginal philology, besides citations of other authors (v– r: see Appendix).
BRF	Glossed first by the copyist (r– r) with commentary where simple interlinear vocabulary paraphrases, repetitive explanations of rhetorical figures (see v, r) and simple mythology suggest a school context – a hypothesis not necessarily contradicted by occasional citations of other authors (see Appendix).[228]

reliqui menses <h>abent quattuor nonas e<t> octo idus, et omnes alii dies calendas vocantur mensis sequentis. E<t> prima dies mensis vocatur calendas primo martii e<t> sic de ali<i>s.

For a set of verses beginning similarly, see Walther ( ), n. ; Bandini (–), . – .

225 Strictly speaking, a general introduction rather than either of the conventional types of *accessus* (i.e. type 'C' or Aristotelian variety: see below,). 226 See below, – .

227 v: Die mensis iunii M°CCCC°V° fuerunt perfecte legi has tragedias. Bandini's reading ('[…] fuerunt perfectae. Legi has tragoedias.': – , .) seems unjustified, given lack of spacing or punctuation.

228 See Roberti ( ), – , in particular, – . Roberti's hypothesis that hand R²'s glosses are directly based on Nicholas Trevet's commentary is unconvincing, given the absence of close linguistic parallels. Her arguments that hand R² is not Boccaccio seem definitive. For citations of other authors in schoolbooks (including Petrarch), see below, and Appendix .

An author also neglected in Italian schools before the fourteenth century was **Valerius Maximus**, who now became well established in the Trecento Italian classroom:

BML Edili	Written by Francisco di Ser Adamo da Farneta (in Casentino near Bibbiena), also copying mysogenistic *Dissuasio Valerii ad Rufinum* and thirty hexameters by grammar teacher in Poppi, Ser Santi di Biagio da Valiana,[229] encountered above ( ) as copyist of and commentator on Vergil and Terence and to be seen below ( ) as glossator of Statius. Seems possible that this manuscript, with occasional contemporaneous historical or philological marginalia and interlinear lexical paraphrases, was associated with Santi's teaching in Poppi. If so, then Ser Santi can be seen teaching a variety of classical authors (Vergil, Terence, Valerius Maximus, Statius) in Poppi's grammar school in the closing decades of XIVc.[230]
BML .	Glossed by at least two XIVc. hands with combination of simple grammatical paraphrase and basic philology (history, etymology, explication, definition), besides WOM (e.g. r).
BML .	Learned and personal commentary, apparently the work of a scholar called Andrea, born in ,[231] who visited Rome in ,[232] besides learned annotations by scribe; also extensive simple interlinear lexical paraphrases by various Trecento writers (e.g. v: quid = cur, v: Arcades = de Archadia). Given that the scribe and the humanist commentator also made some grammatical annotations of school type (v, v, r), it is possible that this text was being used simultaneously by a scholarly teacher or teachers and his or their pupils.[233]
BML Strozzi	Interlinear and marginal glossing on first few folios from school-type readers not long after production.

229 Entire poem published by Bandini (–), . , with slightly inadequate transcription of colophon (actually: Hos M(agister) Sancti gramatice Pupp(ii) profexor composuit ex gesti[s] indomiti cuiusdam Coraze canonarii in palatio Pupii).

230 Two other texts of Valerius Maximus with XIVc. school use are Arezzo Biblioteca civica MSS and .

231 v: Andreas natus est in MCCCt(ri)gesimo quarto die XXXVIIII^a^ de mense novembris, videlicet in vigilia Sancti Andree appostoli. Bandini (–), . mistranscribes date as 'MCCCigesimo quarto'. 232 For relevant glosses (v, v) see below, n. .

233 Extensive XIVc. and XVc. *probationes* (r–v).

Another school author little read in Italian schools up to the end of the Duecento but who became a favourite in the Trecento schoolroom was **Statius**, particularly as the writer of the ***Achilleis***:

BML .	Interlinear glosses of school type by the copyist throughout, besides school-level interlinear and marginal glosses (r– r) by a hand roughly contemporaneous with the copyist.[234]
BML .	Annotated by copyist with the usual simple interlinear vocabulary glossing besides brief philological marginalia (figures, mythology, geography, definitions, etymology, rhetorical structures, paraphrase, explication).
BML sup.	Annotated by copyist with simple interlinear vocabulary glosses, sometimes in vernacular, besides school-level marginalia (geography, mythology, rhetorical *topoi*, figures, definitions, explication).
BML sup.	Glossed by the copyist with usual mixture of interlinear paraphrase and philological marginalia (grammar, mythology, geography, explication), and some citations of other authors (see Appendix).
BNCF .. (r– r)	Contains only school-type philological comments on Statius.
BNCF NA (v– v)	Possibly passed through Domenico di Bandino's school in Bologna during s;[235] reveals normal school fare of simple lexical paraphrase and marginal philology (paraphrase, mythology, explication, figures) written by one late Trecento glossator.

Statius's other epic poem, ***Thebais***, although widely used in ultramontane schools, was little read in the Italian classroom;[236] there are only two Trecento manuscripts with a possible school context, and neither demonstrates entirely convincing classroom use:

234 v– r contain *Argumenta hexasticha*, published by Jeudy and Riou ( ), – ; they make use of this MS (–), following lead of Bandini (–), . , but there is also another version of *Argumentum primi libri*, written as a gloss at the top of r, inc. Raptor Alexa(n)de(r), by the marginal and interlinear glossator of r– r.

235 See Appendix , .

236 Eliminated: BML ., ., ., ., ., sin. ; San Marco ; Strozzi .

BNCF . .	Heavily annotated version, copied in Bologna by one 'Iannoctus' possibly in ,[237] which has some interlinear glossing too, sometimes simple; Giannozzo, who provided a conventional *accessus* (r) besides the ancient *argumenta*,[238] also made copious references to many other authors (see Appendix). Giannozzo also refers to Pietro da Moglio,[239] which might suggest that these glosses have some relation to his teaching in Bologna before his death in ;[240] nevertheless the scope of Giannozzo's learning and interests[241] transcends the normal grammar-school curriculum.
BNCF . .	Dated ; autograph of Franciscan Tedaldo della Casa, who did a little interlinear paraphrase glossing.

Another text new to the Italian classroom in the Trecento is **Claudian**'s ***De raptu Proserpinae***. One copy (BML sup.) has already been discussed above ( ), while another, a Tuscan if not actually Florentine product dating from the third quarter of the century (BML Ashb.), is glossed by several contemporaneous hands with simple interlinear paraphrases as well as brief philological marginalia. It is noteworthy that both *De raptu Proserpinae* and *Achilleis* appeared in school anthologies together with the minor authors; these texts had figured in the anachronistically named 'Libri Catoniani' of the earlier middle ages,[242] and it is not surprising to find them associated in the Trecento with the *auctores minores*, who themselves enjoyed a significant revival in the fourteenth century.[243] In fact, the standard position of the minor authors in the Trecento Italian school curriculum was highlighted by Giovanni Dominici, writing at the beginning of the next century but referring to teachers of *il buon tempo antico*: 'La prima cosa insegnavano era il salterio e dottrina sacra; e se gli mandavano più oltre, avevano

237 'Huchet' watermark, Briquet n. (Bologna), with following colophon: Explicit liber Statii Tebaydos, Bon(onie) die XX. augusti ᵉ indictionis. Iannoctus subscripsit. Since this hand is datable to XIVex., the only indiction which fits would be .

238 Each book preceded by *argumenta*, here called 'continentie': e.g. v: *Interea*. Iste est secundus liber Statii Thebaidos qui liber in .ᵒʳ capitula continetur; in primo continetur reditus Mercurii [...]; v: In isto ᵒ libro Statius aliter procedit, quia primo proponit, invocat et narrat.

239 r: Nota hic secundum aliquos capitulum debet incipi hic [at sed MS] sed secundum aliquos debet incipi ibi [...] Petrus de Muglo tenet quod incipiatur ibi etc.

240 Billanovich ( ), .

241 Includes long scientific gloss (v).

242 Boas ( ), – ; Munk Olsen ( ), . See Avesani (b).

243 An interesting document dating from June is mentioned by Gorrini ( ), , where a teacher from Alessandria called Alessandrino promised to teach Pietrino di Andalò da Chiavari to 'latinare' with all the verbs and figures of 'grammatica' (Latin), and to familiarize him, over a year, with Prosper, Cato, *Cartula* and Aesop (Gorrini's reading of 'Properzio' and 'Catullo' was demonstrated to be a mistranscription by Petti Balbi ( ), and Della Corte ( )).

moralità di Catone, fizioni d'Esopo, dottrina di Boezio, buona scienza di Prospero [...]'[244] The following table shows the results of the present survey of schoolbooks in Florentine libraries for the minor authors in the Trecento.

Text	Copies
Prosper of Aquitaine, *Epigrammata*	
Aesop, *Fabulae*	
Prudentius, *Dittochaeon*	
Henry of Settimello, *Elegia*	
Ilias latina	
Physiologus	
Vitalis of Blois, *Geta*	
Cartula	
Disticha Catonis	
Alain de Lille, *Anticlaudianus*	
Avianus, *Fabulae*	
Doctrina rudium	
Facetus	
John the Abbot, *Liber de septem viciis et virtutibus*	
Prudentius, *Psychomachia*	
Pseudo-Boethius, *De disciplina scolarium*	
Pseudo-Ovid, *De lumaca*	
Pseudo-Ovid, *De lupo monacho*	
Pseudo-Ovid, *De pulice*	
Theodulus, *Ecloga*	

[244] Ed. Garin ( ), .

It would be inappropriate to attach too much significance to the relative numbers of texts of these authors now found in Florentine libraries. It probably should be observed that the relatively high showing for Henry of Settimello can be related to his local Florentine origins, whereas the low representation of the *Disticha Catonis* is almost certainly due to its link with the elementary reading text, *Ianua*, which itself is preserved in few manuscripts before the fifteenth century.[245] These forty-six texts of the minor authors are preserved in twenty-two manuscripts – a fact which reflects the tendency of these shorter, more elementary texts to circulate in school-type anthologies.

Several fourteenth-century manuscripts of minor authors have already been mentioned as forming part of anthologies with classical Latin texts (BML . , . , sup. , BML Strozzi), and there are a number of other fourteenth-century school collections without the major authors:

Shelf-mark	Texts of minor authors	School use
ASF CStrozz. .	Henry of Settimello	Usual school-level philological marginalia (history, paraphrase, explication, mythology, figures); possible signed schoolbook: (v) Iste liber<…> Magistri (XIV), Iste liber <…> <s>co<l>is? M<a>g<istri>? <…>, rubbed-out alphabet.
BML AD	Avianus, pseudo-Ovid	Lightly glossed by various XIVc. hands with interlinear lexical paraphrases and marginal explications and figures.
BML AD [246]	Henry of Settimello, Cato, *Physiologus*, *Geta*, *Cartula*, *Facetus*, Prosper, *Psychomachia*, *Doctrina rudium*, Aesop, *Dittochaeon*, Geo rey of Vinsauf and Boethius	Almost certainly written by a novice and then passed into possession of Francesco Nelli, friend of Petrarch and Boccaccio, at end of the s. Notebook containing excerpts and incipits of school authors, besides other grammatical notes, *sententiae*, excerpts from Jacopo della Lana's commentary on Dante and from sermons of Remigio de' Girolami delivered in Santa Maria Novella.
BML AD	Aesop, *Dittochaeon*	Usual interlinear glossing of the school type.

[245] See above, , and below, Appendix .
[246] See Black and Pomaro ( ), – .

Shelf-mark	Texts of minor authors	School use
BML .	Henry of Settimello, John the Abbot, *Liber de septem viciis et septem virtutibus*	Fortuitous composite; both copyists responsible for most of the school-type interlinear and marginal glosses.[247]
BML .	Pseudo-Boethius	Unglossed but probably prepared as a schoolbook to receive interlinear and limited marginal annotations.
BML sup.	*Ilias latina*	Several glossators working contemporaneously with the scribe left usual school mixture of interlinear paraphrase and simple philological marginalia.
BML sup.	Prosper	Small quantity of vernacular interlinear glossing in a contemporaneous hand.[248]
BML Strozzi	Cato, Prosper, Aesop	Sporadic interlinear glosses, sometimes in vernacular (e.g. v). Intensive WOM to Aesop (v– r, v), written apparently by XIVc. hand, also adding *probationes* on v along with other XIIIc. or XIVc. writers.
BNCF . .	Prosper	Almost unglossed.
BNCF Landau Fin.	Prosper	Signed schoolbook from Friuli (r: Iste Prosper est mey[249] Joanis de Porpeto[250] qui vadit ad scolas Magistri Gulelmy[251] de Regio. Qui scripsit scribat, semper cum domino vivat. Deo gracias amen.); a few interlinear glosses in a vernacular attributable to northeast Italy.[252]

247 For simple interlinear glosses to John the Abbot here, see Klein ( ), n. .

248 See below, n. . The 'one marginal note on v' (Gehl ( ),) is not a gloss but rather a missing line of text (*PL* . : Si cor participis [...]) There are childish drawings of animals on r.

249 'Fratris' is written above the line between this and the following word in italicized hand (XV²).

250 Porpetto is a village near Udine.

251 Reading based on examination with ultraviolet light. In place of 'Gulelmy', Lazzi and Scarlino ( ), , , suggest 'Luigi', which certainly is not there; Roediger (–), , reads 'guglielmi'. However, 'Gulelmy' seems secure.

252 E.g. r: *cum divers colors*, istic = *in chest lu*. According to Lazzi and Scarlino ( ), ,), there are 'glosse esplicative interlineari a c. r in dialetto friulano', but they give no examples.

Shelf-mark	Texts of minor authors	School use
BNCF Panciat.	Prosper, Aesop, *Cartula*, *Dittochaeon*, *Physiologus*, *Geta*	Unglossed but archetypal school anthology.
BRF (r– r)	*Ilias latina*	Unglossed.
BRF (r– r)	Prosper	Almost entirely glossed with simple interlinear lexical paraphrases.
BRF	Aesop	A little interlinear glossing of the simple vocabulary type, sometimes in the vernacular.
BRF	Henry of Settimello	Glossed by the copyist, with interlinear glosses including WOM and simple marginalia including paraphrase, mythology, simple astronomy, etymology, geography.
BRF (r– v)	Aesop (fragment)	Unglossed.
BRF	Prosper	Some interlinear glossing roughly contemporaneous with the copyist and of Venetian provenance.

By far the most widely used schoolbook in the Trecento was neither a minor nor a major author, but rather **Boethius's *Consolation of Philosophy*.**[253] Among school authors in Trecento Italy, Boethius appears to have occupied a particularly prominent role. It has already been seen how Giovanni Dominici, writing at the very beginning of the Quattrocento, placed Boethius next to the minor authors as the standard fare of Italian schools in the good old days, and how Giovanni Conversini da Ravenna numbered Boethius among the authors which he learnt as a grammar-school boy in Bologna *c.* .[254] Of this text, indeed, there are twenty XIVc. school manuscripts in Florentine libraries, and eleven of these preserve ownership notes of pupils:[255]

253 For following material on Boethius, see Black and Pomaro ( ), *passim.*
254 See above, , . For further testimony to di usion of Boethius's *Consolation* in XIVc. schools, see Black and Pomaro ( ), – .
255 Black and Pomaro ( ), , , , , , , , , , .

BML Ashb.	Heavy interlinear marginal glosses by a number of indeterminate fourteenth- and fifteenth-century hands, as well as brief marginalia.[256]
BML CS	Glossed by numerous indeterminate XIVc. and XVc. hands.[257]
BML sin.	Extensive marginal and interlinear glosses by the copyist as well as light marginalia by another Trecento reader.[258]
BML sup.	Glossed extensively by two Trecento hands: ( ) the copyist; ( ) pupil of Maestro Francesco del Garbo.[259]
BML sup.	Glossed extensively by XIVc. copyist, although ownership mark dated .[260]
BNCF CS J. .	Indeterminate interlinear glosses from XIVc. and XVc. writers.[261]
BNCF CS J. . (r– v)	Copious indeterminate fourteenth- and fifteenth-century glosses.[262]
BRF	Not apparently glossed until the early Quattrocento.[263]
BRF	Not apparently glossed until the beginning of the Quattrocento.[264]
BRF	Despite school *ex libris*, virtually unglossed.[265]
BRF	Extensively glossed by a hand working at the very end of century.[266]

These manuscripts of Boethius signed by pupils in school are indistinguishable, apart from their *ex libris*, from those Trecento codices of the text without school signatures.

256 Black and Pomaro ( ), – , – .
257 Black and Pomaro ( ), , .
258 Black and Pomaro ( ), – , – .
259 Black and Pomaro ( ), – , – .
260 Black and Pomaro ( ), – , – .
261 Black and Pomaro ( ), – , – .
262 Black and Pomaro ( ), – , – .
263 Black and Pomaro ( ), – , – .
264 Black and Pomaro ( ), – , – .
265 Black and Pomaro ( ), – , – .
266 Black and Pomaro ( ), – , – .

BML dxt.	Anonymous Trecento glossator apparently had some connection with grammar-school education, either as a pupil or, more likely, as a teacher, as suggested by similarity of Latin glossing to other Boethius schoolbooks, including basic interlinear lexical equivalents and overall simple philological tenor of the marginalia; one of the few original contributions made as glossator was a rhyming mnemonic lexical couplet particularly characteristic of schoolbooks (r).[267]
BML .	Light interlinear glosses by copyist.[268]
BML .	Brief marginalia by several late hands.[269]
BML .	Interlinear and marginal glosses by two Trecento hands.[270]
BML Strozzi	Tiny amount of Trecento marginal and interlinear glossing.[271]
BNCF Magl. . (fragment)	Tiny amount of interlinear glossing, as well as *probationes* and a sketch probably by a child.[272]
BRF	Light marginal but extensive interlinear glossing from Trecento.[273]
BRF	One fairly extensive interlinear and marginal Trecento glossator.[274]
Florence Seminario Maggiore B. .	At least three fourteenth-century marginal and interlinear glossators.[275]

To sum up, it is clear that three di erent kinds of authors were extensively represented in the fourteenth-century curriculum: the *auctores minores*, Boethius's *Consolation of Philosophy* and the Latin classics. The most popular of the minor texts was clearly Prosper of Aquitaine's *Epigrammata*, but Aesop's fables, Prudentius's *Dittochaeon* and Henry of Settimello's elegy also achieved a notable presence. Boethius's *Consolation* became the single most popular piece of school literature in the Italian Trecento. Of the Latin classics, Horace's *Ars poetica* and letters and Ovid's *Metamorphoses* were the most widely read texts from the traditional

267 Black and Pomaro ( ), – , – .
268 Black and Pomaro ( ), – , .
269 Black and Pomaro ( ), – , – .
270 Black and Pomaro ( ), – , – .
271 Black and Pomaro ( ), – , – .
272 Black and Pomaro ( ), – , .
273 Black and Pomaro ( ), – , .
274 Black and Pomaro ( ), – , – .
275 Black and Pomaro ( ), – , – .

school authors, but a new best-seller, so to speak, was Seneca's tragedies. Another popular newcomer to the Italian schoolroom was Statius's *Achilleis.* Vergil was beginning to show slight signs of revival, and Lucan still maintained some presence. Juvenal, Persius and Terence were still languishing while Claudian's *De raptu Proserpinae* was beginning to make a showing. Among the prose-writers, Cicero's shorter moral treatises still remained unread and Sallust's showing was weak; here the new figure to be reckoned with was Valerius Maximus. All these texts received the same kind of traditional school-level glossing: interlinear vocabulary paraphrase and simple marginal philology.

:

The minor authors

The Quattrocento is usually regarded in the history of education as a period of radical change; it will be seen that there were important curriculum alterations in the study of authors in the fifteenth century, and yet equally striking are elements of continuity in the literary syllabus of Italian schools. The usual picture of the traditional curriculum's rapid displacement[276] is not substantiated by the survival of minor authors, as revealed in the present survey of manuscript textbooks in Florentine libraries.

Italian manuscripts containing minor authors in Florentine libraries	
Century	Copies
XI	
XII	
XIII	
XIV	
XV	

[276] Garin ( ), xxii: 'Il brusco mutare dei libri di testo è stato notato: gli *auctores octo* tendono a scomparire rapidamente dalla scuola italiana [...]'; Grendler ( ), – , : 'Italian pedagogues had e ected a curriculum revolution, one of the few in the history of Western education, in the relatively short time of about fifty years – to [...] They discarded the late medieval Latin curriculum of [...] morality poems [...]'

If anything, these figures suggest that the reading of the minor authors continued enthusiastically into the fifteenth century. A similar picture emerges if individual texts are considered:

Text	XIV Century	XV Century
Prosper of Aquitaine, *Epigrammata*		
Aesop, *Fabulae*		
Henry of Settimello, *Elegia*		
Prudentius, *Dittochaeon*		
Ilias latina		
Avianus, *Fabulae*		
Theobaldus, *Physiologus*		
Pseudo-Ovid, *De lumaca*		
Vitalis of Blois, *Geta*		
Cartula		
Disticha Catonis		
Theodulus, *Ecloga*		
Prudentius, *Psychomachia*		
Bonvesin da la Riva, *Vita scolastica*		
Pseudo-Boethius, *De disciplina scolarium*		
Richard of Venosa, *De nuptiis Paulini et Pollae*		
Pseudo-Jerome, *De contemptu mulierum*		
Facetus		
Martin of Braga, *Formula honestae vitae*		
John the Abbot, *Liber de septem viciis et septem virtutibus*		
Doctrina rudium		
Liber cerdonis		
Maximianus, *De senectute*		

Text	XIV Century	XV Century
Proba, *Centones virgiliani*		
Salutati, *Elegia*		
Salutati, *Fabula*		
Bernardo of Clairvaux, *Epistola de re familiari*		
Pseudo-Ovid, *De pulice*		
Pseudo-Ovid, *De lupo monacho*		
Alain de Lille, *Anticlaudianus*		
Total number of individual texts		

It is of course well known that the survival rate for manuscripts in the Quattrocento is higher than for previous centuries; nevertheless, the fact that there are twice as many fifteenth- as opposed to fourteenth-century texts of the minor authors is an eloquent refutation of the commonly believed assumption that the study of the traditional school texts declined in Italy with the coming of the fifteenth century. In fact, it will be seen that the number of surviving manuscript textbooks of the Latin classics in the fifteenth century had little more than doubled since the Trecento; this is further proof that, even under the influence of humanism, the minor authors were remarkably resilient in schools. It would be misguided to attach too much significance to the fluctuations of individual texts between the fourteenth and fifteenth centuries. Nevertheless, it is clear that Prosper, Aesop, Henry of Settimello, Prudentius (in the *Dittochaeon*), *Cartula*, Cato and Theobaldus maintained a significant following in both centuries; it is also noteworthy that *Ilias latina* and Bonvesin da la Riva achieved a new popularity in the Quattrocento. Texts such as *Doctrina rudium*, pseudo-Jerome, pseudo-Boethius, Vitalis of Blois's *Geta*, Prudentius's *Psychomachia* and the pseudo-Ovidian *De lumaca* seem to have remained marginal in the Italian classroom.

The following table summarizes the presence of fifteenth-century manuscripts containing minor authors in Florentine libraries:

ASF Bardi .	Cato, *Dittochaeon*, *Cartula*	Probably associated with the Florentine monastery of S. Salvatore di Settimo, possibly with the grammar school there; one text dated ; entire manuscript written by same anonymous hand.
BML CS	Aesop	Little glossed but used by German pupil, who expostulated (v), 'Wie stinkest du!'
BML .	Henry of Settimello	Copyist, using heavy late Gothic hand, added school-type lexical interlinear and marginal glosses (paraphrase, explication, mythology, legendary history, simple natural philosophy, grammar, figures, anecdotal philosophy, ancient and medieval history).
BML .	Statius *Achilleis*, Ovid *Heroides*, pseudo-Boethius	Colophons[277] reveal the copyist, Santi di Giovanni, as a grammar pupil in Siena in , possibly at the school of Maestro Nofri di Giovanni da Poggitazzi, a teacher with long Sienese association;[278] by Santi was living with the Tolomei, a leading Sienese noble family, probably as a private tutor while attending university. Santi glossed the entire MS in school manner; in marginal commentary to pseudo-Boethius, consisting mainly of grammar, mythology, paraphrase, literary identification (v– r) and elementary natural philosophy, he cited *Rhetorica ad Herennium*, Terence, Horace, Seneca.
BML .	Composite: ( ) Statius *Achilleis*, *Ilias latina*; ( ) Ovid *Ars amatoria*	( ) receives interlinear vocabulary glosses in Latin only and WOM (v) by various contemporaneous hands.

277 To Statius:

v: Explicit liber quintus et ultimus Statii Achilleydos. Deo gratias, die X^{a} aprilis , Senis in scolis Magisti Nofri. S(an)c(t)es scripsi;

To Ovid:

(r) Huius tibi deo mera reddatur gratia plena. Feliciter finitur a Sancte Johannis, cuius est et sit liber. XX die settembris MCCCCXV;

To pseudo-Boethius:

(r) Sub anno de mense giunii in domo Ghuidonis Tallomeorum Senis. Sanctes Johannis scripsi.

278 Bacci ( ), n. , hypothesized that this was Nofri di Angelo da S. Gimignano. This view is to be rejected, given that the latter was teaching in Prato from to : ASPCD , r.

BML sup.	Composite: ( ) *Ilias latina*, Salutati *Elegia*, *Physiologus*, Theodulus, Salutati *Fabula de vulpo et cancro*, Bernard of Clairvaux *Epistola de cura rei familiaris*, *Dittochaeon*, *Facetus*, *Psychomachia*, Giovanni Bonadrea *Ars dictaminis*, Avianus; ( ) Claudian *De raptu*	Assembled by Paolo Morelli, from a Florentine patrician family, still evidently a schoolboy;[279] ( ) lacks significant marginalia, although there is ample school-level simple lexical paraphrase, including vernacular.
BML Redi	Composite: ( ) Avianus, *Dittochaeon*; ( ) *Ilias latina*	Avianus only glossed by several hands contemporaneous to the copyist, providing simple lexical equivalents in Latin and vernacular[280] besides WOM (v).
BNCF ..	Boethius, *Dittochaeon* (both fragmentary)	The latter text was extensively glossed by the copyist in the same manner in which he glossed the first work.[281]
BNCF CS C. . [282]	*Physiologus*, *Dittochaeon*	Not strictly a reading text: it does not o er running texts of *Physiologus* and *Dittochaeon* with marginal/interlinear commentary but rather is a commentary

279 Paolo di Morello di Paolo di Bernardo (–), nephew of the renowned diarist: see Appendix . 280 E.g. r: tendit in urbis opes = anbulat *della cità in nelle richeççe.*

281 For the glosses to Boethius, see below, .

282 Gehl's description ( ), , needs revision. ( ) This MS is a normal scholastic commentary with lemmata; the overall character of the book is that of a continuous commentary, not a text accompanied by glosses. ( ) The manuscript is datable to XVc., rather than to XIVc. (Gehl). It is a composite consisting of two sections: . r– v (fascicles) and . r– v (fascicle). . was written by a late Gothic cursive hand with humanist features such as the ampersand and hence must be dated to XVc.; the writer of . seems to have supplied the final missing fascicle, also writing in late Gothic cursive hand. Writers of . and . probably were not working together, because they used paper with di erent water marks, the paper in . is slightly larger, and the layout of the text in each section is di erent. Nevertheless, . was subsequent to . because the copyist of . wrote the catchword for his final fascicle at the end of . (v). Therefore, both . and . are datable to XVc. (probably relatively early).

The use of the ampersand and its particular formation in this MS by the first writer suggests some kind of link to early Florentine humanist circles (in particular Niccoli and Corbinelli), although it is impossible to be more exact, despite the MS's provenance from the Badia (not noted by Blum ( )). On r there is an invocation to saints dated <M>cccliii, written by the same hand that left this erased note of possession below: Questo libro è di Nicholo <...> Amen. Ch'il truova et no' lo reda in su le force penda. Amen. This date, although far preceding the text's copying, is consistent with the handwriting of the ownership note and may indicate the beginning of a never-completed schoolbook, then used subsequently by writer of I. The other note of possession on this page (Iste liber est Simonecti Andree de <...>) is XVc.

		on the two texts with intermittent citations of them. Thus, e.g, only quatrains of *Dittochaeon* are cited in full (r– v), and are interspersed with copious commentary; the entire text of *Physiologus* is cited, but is dominated by long passages of intervening commentary. Nevertheless, a little evidence of school-type interlinear glossing by the first copyist (r: deo = id est soli; v: tempnis = pro contem[nis]; v: quod hic = quoniam est deus; r: quod = id est quia; r: quamlibet = qualis), as well as simple paraphrase and explicatory marginalia (e.g r: iemnans = dicitur enim quod iemnat xl diebus et xl noctibus); moreover, the first copyist also includes on flyleaf a list of nouns/adjectives and corresponding relative/interrogative pronouns (r) reminiscent of the secondary grammatical syllabus (e.g.: Florentinus lombardus cuias cuiatis) and including school-type vocabulary (boetista et priscianista). All this suggests some kind of school context.
BNCF CSJ. .	Henry of Settimello, *Ilias latina*, Vergil *Eclogues*, Statius *Achilleis*	Written at school of Maestro Antonio da Tivoli[283] in Bologna.[284] Henry glossed heavily by the copyist (Benedetto) with interlinear Latin simple lexical paraphrases and some grammatical marginalia; *Ilias latina* receives, besides similar interlinear annotation, copious marginal commentary, again by same scribe, consisting of usual school-level philology (history, mythology) and conventional accessus (r).
BNCF Landau Fin.	Statius *Achilleis*, *Cartula*, Alexander *Doctrinale* (fragmentary), Cato	Cooperative work of Antoniotto Morelli (–), son of diarist Giovanni di Paolo, Francesco di Francesco Ferantini (b.) and a third anonymous pupil.[285]

283 v: In nomine domini, amen. Anno domini millesimo CCCC° XL mense octobris die Sancti Luce ego Benedictus et frater meus Stephanus venimus ad scolas Magistri Antonii de Fornariis de Tibrir(e). Et alter frater meus Marioctus die X introitus Ian.

284 One copyist is the above Benedetto and the other is probably his brother Stefano; together with their other brother, Mariotto, they seem to have attended Maestro Antonio's school in Bologna, to judge from a payment record, also found on the same page: In primis habuit a nobis magister carlinos sex / Item in alia mano b(o)l(ognin)os XVIII.

285 See below, .

BNCF Magl. .[286]	*Ianua*, Cato, Theodulus, *Dittochaeon*, *Cartula*, *Physiologus*, Bonvesin, Aesop, pseudo-Jerome *De contemptu mulierum*	Only texts to receive significant glossing are Aesop, with a little interlinear and marginal annotations by several Quattrocento hands, and pseudo-Jerome, with r– r heavily glossed in the usual school manner: interlinear synonyms and philological marginalia giving explanations of mythological, historical and biblical characters, besides definitions.
BNCF Magl. .	Statius *Achilleis*, *Ilias latina*, Proba *Centones virgiliani*	The third text was written by and has *ex libris* of Torrigiano Bigliotti, a pupil at the school of Maestro Zanobi;[287] unglossed.
BNCF Magl. .	Cato, Prosper, *Ilias latina*, *Dittochaeon*, Bonvesin, *Dissuasio Valerii ad Rufinum*[288] pseudo-Boethius	Only a little philological interlinear and marginal commentary, almost entirely in hand of the copyist (v, v, r, v).
BNCF Magl. .	Bonvesin	Glossed by the copyist only with interlinear vocabulary equivalents, brief marginal explications/paraphrases.
BNCF Magl. .	(a) r– r: Bonvesin, Horace *Ars Epistolae*, Statius *Achilleis*; (b) r– v: *Ilias latina*	(a) Obvious schoolbook, although Bonvesin virtually unglossed; (b) some typical school-type glossing,[289] although composite element containing it does not consist of the normal collection of school texts, nor does it reveal the usual schoolbook appearance.
BNCF Magl. .	Statius *Achilleis*, *Ilias latina*, Henry of Settimello, Maximianus *De senectute*, humanist elegies by Porcello, Guarino, Niccolò Volpi da Vicenza	No glosses except on first text.

[286] Frequently misdated to XIVc. or even XIIIc.; numerous palaeographical analyses have confirmed that all three parts of this composite date from after $XV^{1/4}$: see Appendix , – below.

[287] r: Iste liber est Torrigiani Bigliotti, qui moratur scolis Magistri Zanobi p(ro)f(e)x(or)is.

[288] Also known as pseudo-Jerome *Epistola ad Rufinum* and pseudo-Jerome *De contemptu mulierum*: text in *PL* . – .

[289] v: Pars pro toto. Ulna est pars brachii et ponitur pro brachiis totis. v: Nota quod tres sunt parcae sive fate, quae ita dicuntur Croco Lachesis et Antropos. Unde versus: Croco colum baiulat, Lachesis trahit, Antropos occat. See below, , for this type of verse glossing.

BNCF Magl. .	*Dittochaeon*	Signed school manuscript;[290] only interlinear vocabulary glosses, in both Latin and the vernacular (r–v, v).
BRF	Prosper	Normal school mixture of light marginal philology (paraphrase, explication, structure) and interlinear lexical synonyms in Latin and vernacular.
BRF	*Doctrina rudium*, John the Abbot *Liber de septem viciis et septem virtutibus*, pseudo-Ovid *De lumaca*, *Ilias latina*, Martin of Braga *Formula honestae vitae*, Cicero *De senectute*, *De amicitia*, *Paradoxa stoicorum*	Unglossed.
BRF	Prosper, Aesop	Ample basic vocabulary equivalents, in Latin and Italian, but no noteworthy marginalia.
BRF	Prosper, *Dittochaeon*, Cato	No significant glosses.
BRF	*Dittochaeon*, *Geta*, *Physiologus*, *Doctrina rudium*	Usual simple interlinear vocabulary glosses to Prudentius (v– r), including vernacular.
BRF	*Psychomachia*, Vergil *Eclogues*, *Physiologus*	Extensive interlinear and marginal glosses to Vergil but only interlinear lexical paraphrases, including vernacular, to minor authors.
BRF	Bonvesin, *Cartula*	Interlinear vocabulary glosses in at least two hands, including the copyist's and the organizer of composite; glosses limited to first text.
BRF (r– v)	Avianus, *Dittochaeon*, *Geta*	Unglossed although prepared as schoolbook with space for interlinear and marginal annotations.
BRF	Cato, *Cartula*, *Dittochaeon*, *Physiologus*, Theodulus, Bonvesin, Prosper, Aesop	Occasional simple marginal paraphrase glosses and interlinear lexical equivalents, including vernacular, by several hands contemporaneous with scribe.

290 r: Iste liber est mei Benedicti Petri de Canbinis. Iste liber est mei Benedicti Petri de Kanbinis qui moratur in scolis Domini Baptiste de Vulterra. v: Questo libro è di Benedetto di Piero Chanbini. Ser Battista di Andrea Bisconti da Volterra taught grammar in Florence, – : Park ( ), – . Taught in Colle, – : ASSColle , r– r.

BRF	Cato, Aesop (composite)	A little sixteenth-century vernacular glossing in Cato (e.g. r: munus = *el dono, la sperientia*); Aesop reveals WOM contemporaneous with the copyist (r) and a little XVc. interlinear vernacular lexical glossing (e.g. r: lenit = *lusinga*, non est sincera = *non buona*).
BRF	Composite: ( ) (–) Aesop, *Physiologus*, where the anonymous copyist is replaced by Pietro di Angelo (r); (–) Theodulus, where Pietro di Angelo is the scribe; (–) Henry of Settimello, where hand could still be Pietro's.	Signed twice by Pietro di Angelo, pupil in the school of an anonymous teacher,[291] glossing of ( ) is low-level: simple interlinear vocabulary equivalents, in both Latin and Italian; ( ) contains numerous short marginalia of typical school variety: mythology, history, paraphrase, explication, figures.
BRF	Composite: ( ) Persius (fragmentary); ( ) *Ilias latina* (with five vernacular *terzine* occupying one of the final blank pages); ( ) *Liber cerdonis*[292]	Only first two texts glossed (heavily), receiving typically school-level mixture of paraphrase and grammatical/philological explication.
BRF [293]	*Dittochaeon*, Henry, Cicero *De amicitia*	Copied and signed at Monte Ulmo in Marche (near Ascoli Piceno) in the school of Maestro Giovanni da Monte Ulmo by an anonymous pupil from Mogliano, also in Marche (near Macerata), with heavy glosses in normal philological school manner (exegesis, history, mythology) to first two works.

291 v: Iste liber est Petri Angeli morantis in iscolis Magistri <…>; v: Iste liber est Petri Angeli.

292 For this text, see Walther ( ), n. .

293 Composite: ( ) – and ( ) – ; unclear whether there was some connection between two parts. ( ) contains Prudentius's *Dittochaeon*, anonymous *Orthographia parva et utilis* (r– r) followed by series of short texts (epistolary, edifying: r– r), Henry's *Elegia*, Cicero's *De amicitia*; ( ) contains Guarino's translation of Plutarch's *De liberis educandis* (here anonymous; not listed by Kristeller (–)). ( ) written by one hand, in late Gothic script; ( ) by another hand, using humanist script (mid-XVc.). ( ) with colophons: (r– v, Prudentius) Explicit liber Prudentii de columba, scriptus sub anno domini M° CCCC° XLV^{a}, scriptus a me — [*deletum*] de Moliano. In slightly darker ink the copyist added to the beginning of the colophon: in Monte Ulmo hora viexima prima diey, and below: addi martii. Above the erasure 'Jacobus Magistri Macthey' was added later. (r– v) Henry: Explicit Henricus cuy non f[u]it nullus a<m>icus. Finito libro referamus gratiam Christo. Scriptus est liber iste a me — [*deletum*] de Moliano sub doctrina Magistri Johannis Ricchi de Monte Ulmo. Anno domini M° CCCC° XL ^{a} VIII^{a} indicione ^{a} die ^{a} martii ora decima sectima. r– v, Cicero: explicit feliciter sub anno dominy M° CCCC° ° die ^{a} mensis sectembris. Deo gratias amen.

BRF (r– v)	Prosper	Unglossed but set out as a schoolbook, with wide spacing between lines and large lettering.

It is well known that fifteenth-century humanist educators railed against the barbarity of the minor authors.[294] Nevertheless, there is evidence that even humanist teachers continued to use the minor authors during the fifteenth century. An example comes from BNCF Magl. . , containing Ovid's *Epistulae ex Ponto* (r– r), Persius (r– r) and *Ilias latina* (r– r). It was copied by three hands, all using italic cursive script, but the glosses throughout are due only to the first scribe; the entire manuscript was a joint e ort, probably by a group of pupils attending a grammar school. Who their teacher was becomes clear from the colophon to the Ovidian text:

r: Finis. Explicit liber epistularum Ovidii de Ponto, quem legit Magister Gulielmus civis aretinus. Amen. Finis, ame[n].

Maestro Guglielmo di Giovanni da Bourges was one of the most prominent teachers in Arezzo in the mid fifteenth century;[295] his a liations to avant-garde humanism are clear from the fact that he was recommended for his post in Arezzo by Carlo Marsuppini[296] and that after Marsuppini's death he continued to enjoy the patronage of the Medici.[297] Besides working in Arezzo, he also taught in Castiglion Fiorentino, Città di Castello[298] and Sansepolcro[299] (–), but the manuscript was certainly a product of his activity in Florence: of the many signatures which appear on r, v and r–v, that of the Florentine 'Simone d'Antonio di Piero Allamanni' seems to be the hand of the third copyist. As for the date of the manuscript, palaeographic analysis suggests the s or s; this would coincide with documentary evidence, which places Guglielmo in Florence after [300] and before , when he went to teach in Castiglion Fiorentino.[301] A *terminus post quem* is provided by the reference to him as 'civis aretinus' in the colophon: he received Aretine citizenship some time between January and November .[302] His next period of residence and teaching in Florence was to ,[303] but that appears rather late for this

[294] Garin ( ), – . [295] Black (d) *ad indicem.* [296] Black (d), .
[297] Black (d), . [298] Jaitner-Hahner ( ), , – , , , – , – , .
[299] Black (d), . [300] Black (d), , . [301] See above, n. .
[302] On the former date he was mentioned in a notarial document as merely 'habitator in civitate Aretii' (Black (d),), while on the latter the Aretine commune addressed him as 'concivi nostro' (Black (d),). [303] Black (d), n. ; Davies ( ), – .

manuscript. What is significant here is that one of Maestro Guglielmo's pupils copied *Ilias latina* while another gave it a conventional set of school-type lexical interlinear glosses and simple philological glosses (paraphrase, mythology, ancient customs, etymology): this text of a minor author was clearly being used in an important humanist teacher's school in mid fifteenth-century Florence.

Another example is Antonio Mancinelli, one of the most famous humanist grammar masters of the later Quattrocento, who not only continued to use *Ianua*,[304] but also wrote a commentary on the opening of the *Disticha Catonis*. Moreover, there is in Florence a schoolbook signed in his school in Velletri, containing another of the minor texts, *Ilias latina* (BML AD , v).[305] Besides *Ilias latina* (r– v), this manuscript also contains a medieval text also sometimes used in schools,[306] Richard of Venosa's *De nuptiis Paulini et Pollae senum* (r– r), again with a signature suggesting Mancinelli's school (r).[307] As in other school books, the text is glossed by the copyist with simple Latin interlinear vocabulary synonyms, copiously in *Ilias latina*, less so in Richard's elegy. *Ilias latina* also receives typically a series of philological and grammatical marginalia, in which Ovid's *Remedia amoris* and *Tristia* are cited (v); Seneca and Juvenal are quoted with reference to the text by Richard (r).[308]

Similarly, Pietro Crinito, a favoured disciple of Poliziano's, continued to use the minor authors as a Latin teacher in Florence at the turn of the XVIc.[309] For Crinito this activity with the *auctores minores* was not always

304 Grendler ( ), .

305
T°lvwAmen Finis
Exscriptus per me Placentinum die martii , in
ludo Magistri Antonii Mancinelli Velietri.
Velitris, .
Hoc opus peractum fuit die aprilis .

306 Sometimes printed together with Henry of Settimello: Brunet ( ), , – . May have been more frequently used in northern schools: one printed edition refers to 'ludo' in Lyons. See also Chevalier ( ), . .

307
TÊlvwRiccardus
Iudix Riccardus tale peregit opus.
Finis. Amen.
Excriptum per me Placentinum Sancti Lariani de Praeneste die martii
Velitris.

308 Has series of *probationes*, drawings, ownership notes (r– v), some (r–v, v) XVIc., thus demonstrating continued use of minor authors in schools even then.

309 di Pierro ( ), : 'Nactus sum codicem perveterem a Cosmo Saxetto, in quo et Arator et Avianus et Prosperus et Beda [identified as BML . : de la Mare ( ),] … Ego non indignum sum opinatus ex Aviano aliquid percipere, qui Aesopi fabulas in latinum convertit, ne quid instituto operi desit. Die nov. .'

a welcome task.[310] Crinito also resented the time he had to spend on Henry of Settimello's elegy, which he also apparently used in teaching, as is suggested by his *Miscellanea* (BML . , r).[311] Nevertheless, Crinito acquired his own copies of minor authors, presumably for teaching purposes: thus he duly recorded the presence of both Bonvesin's *Vita scolastica* and *Ilias latina* in the table of contents which he appended to BNCF Magl. . , an anthology which he personally assembled.[312]

Boethius's Consolation of Philosophy

Documentary and literary evidence confirms not only the continued study of the minor authors in the fifteenth century but also of another standby of the Trecento classroom.[313] In fact, this survey confirms that Boethius's *Consolation* continued to be widely read in Quattrocento Italian schools, found as it is in ten XVc. school codices in Florentine libraries:

BML CS	At least four closely contemporary marginal glossators, all working in XV[1] and leaving a normal school-level combination of simple interlinear vocabulary equivalents, including a bit of vernacular, and marginal philology (paraphrase, explication, mythology, history, figures, simple natural philosophy).[314]
BML CS	Besides a variety of contemporaneous interlinear vocabulary glosses including vernacular, two marginal glossators: ( ) working not much after the copyist, makes extracts in the school manner from commentary by William of Conches, while ( ) writing XV/XVIc., gives metric analysis of each of the text's poems, based on commentary by Trevet.[315]

310 As he wrote after transcribing some verses from Prosper's *Epigrammata*: 'Non libuit plura excerpere, nam bonum tempus ludicris et nugis collocavi. Ego Petrus Crinitus V Nov. ' (di Pierro ( ),).

311 Ex libro Henrici [...] Explicit Henrici liber [...] Perlegi Henricum, in quo opere tempus perditum, quod carmen ineptum et plane britannicum, ex libro Car[o]li Benini. For the approximate date of this excerpting, see v: Exscripsi ego Petrus Crinitus Florentiae nonis aug. [...] See Bandini (–), . for partial transcription; Angeleri ( ), , gives garbled and inaccurate version of Bandini's entry, repeated by Ricciardi ( ), .

An example of traditional school authors probably coming from a Florentine humanist school is BNCF Magl. . , an anthology dated and containing *Achilleis*, *Ilias latina*, Henry of Settimello and Maximianus, besides pedagogic poetry by two famous humanist teachers, Guarino and Porcello: see above, . An example of minor authors used in an early humanist context is BNCF CS C. . : see above, – .

312 See Appendix below, . For evidence of persistence of minor authors in Roman schools in late XVc., see Rizzo ( ), – .

313 See above, .

314 Black and Pomaro ( ), – , – .

315 Black and Pomaro ( ), – , – ; see below, .

BML CS	Almost completely unglossed, although nearly identical in format to many other school copies of *Consolation*.[316]
BML CS	Substantial marginal commentary extracted by the copyist from William of Conches's *Glosae*, together with interlinear vocabulary glosses by several XVc. readers.[317]
BML .	Glossed interlinearly in the usual school fashion by the copyist and several other contemporaneous writers.[318]
BML .	Glossed by three hands working almost contemporaneously: ( ) provided marginal excerpts from Trevet's commentary; ( ), working together with ( ), provided a brief series of marginal glosses partly extracted from commentary by Remigius of Auxerre; all three also left a substantial set of interlinear vocabulary glosses, those of ( ) including a considerable quantity of vernacular synonyms in Bolognese dialect.[319]
BML .	Hand contemporaenous to the copyist's made extensive interlinear vocabulary glossing, including vernacular.[320]
BML .	Autograph of teacher and Dante commentator, Bartolomeo Nerucci, completed April while a pupil in the grammar school of Mattia Lupi in San Gimignano; he provided two types of commentary: as pupil, besides usual interlinear vocabulary equivalents, he copied Trevet's *accessus* and made extracts from his glosses, which he placed in margins beside the relevant passages of text; marginal commenting while at school limited to first three poems and two proses, and later in life, possibly over many years, he added the rest of his extensive marginal commentary, in which he cited a range of other authors and texts ranging beyond the normal grammar-school syllabus.[321]
BNCF . .	Glossed first by the copyist with a dense series of interlinear vocabulary synonyms, often in *volgare*, besides copious set of marginal paraphrases; the second glossator, writing contemporaneously, left another set of vocabulary equivalents, this time entirely in Latin, besides more marginal paraphrases, now often borrowed from Trevet.[322]
BRF	Almost completely unglossed apart from handful of interventions from the copyist and another contemporaneous writer, although clearly preserving normal schoolbook format.[323]

316 Black and Pomaro ( ), , . 317 Black and Pomaro ( ), , – .
318 Black and Pomaro ( ), – , – . 319 Black and Pomaro ( ), – , – .
320 Black and Pomaro ( ), – , – .
321 Black and Pomaro ( ), , – , – . 322 Black and Pomaro ( ), – , – .
323 Black and Pomaro ( ), – , – .

As with the minor authors, the humanists castigated Boethius. Valla regarded Boethius as personally responsible for the decadence of Latin: 'Boethius […] nos barbare loqui docuit';[324] it was di cult to recommend a school author 'whose age', wrote Scaliger, 'was barbarous; hence his prose was flawed'.[325] And yet his *Consolation* continued to be taught in humanist schools. One example is Bartolomeo Fonzio (–), tutor to various Florentine families including the Rinieri,[326] and probably the Sassetti[327] and Cattani di Diacceto,[328] as well as a teacher over many years at the Florentine Studio,[329] who left marginal glosses in a copy of the *Consolation* belonging to the Cattani di Diacceto family.[330] The annotations composed by Fonzio resemble the brief summaries of each section of the text which often appear in grammar-school copies,[331] a fact which suggests that they may have been intended for the use of his pupils. Niccolò Perotti, moreover, used Boethius's poems as teaching material.[332]

The Latin classics

Continuity thus seems to have been the hallmark of the lower levels of the literary syllabus of Italian grammar schools well into the Quattrocento: beginning with the minor authors, Italian pupils progressed, like their predecessors in the Trecento, to Boethius's *Consolation*. However, it cannot be said that tradition was the main feature of the upper strata of the literary syllabus in the fifteenth century; it would be misleading to argue that there was a complete rupture with the past, but it is clear that there was important innovation in the selection of the Latin classics for school reading:

Century	Cic.	Claud.	Hor.	Juven.	Lucan	Ovid	Pers.	Sall.	Sen. Trag.	Stat.	Ter.	Val. Max.	Verg.	Total
XIII														
XIV														
XV														

324 Cited from the *Elegantiae linguae latinae*, , (*Opera*, Basle,) by Gaeta ( ), .
325 Grafton ( ), .
326 Francesco di Bernardo Rinieri learnt Latin from Bartolomeo Fonzio in : ASF Corporazioni religiose soppresse dal governo francese . , v.
327 See de la Mare ( ), – , *passim*.
328 Black and Pomaro ( ), – .
329 Verde (–), , – .
330 Black and Pomaro ( ), – .
331 E.g. Black and Pomaro ( ), – , – .
332 See below, .

It will be seen that there were a number of authors who, on the one hand, had secured or maintained for themselves a strong place in the Trecento curriculum, but who now in the Quattrocento, on the other hand, failed to move beyond their earlier popularity; in view of the usually far better survival rate for manuscripts from the fifteenth century than for those from preceding centuries, it is clear that these authors must have su ered a relative, if not absolute, decline in favour at school during the Quattrocento.

Lucan, Claudian, Seneca the Tragedian

One author whose popularity in the schoolroom seems never to have regained the heights reached in the twelfth century was **Lucan**, who, having maintained a steady presence in the thirteenth and fourteenth centuries, now in the fifteenth failed to make a significant showing:

BML CS	Glossed mainly by one contemporaneous hand with usual school mixture of interlinear vocabulary paraphrases and simple marginal philology.
BNCF CS J. .	Normal schoolbook format consisting of widely spaced lines and large writing, with sole clear school use coming from contemporaneous glossator, leaving interlinear vocabulary synonyms and simple philological marginalia (r, r–v).[333]

Another author failing to build on his position gained in the Trecento was **Claudian**, whose *De raptu Proserpinae* is only found in two schoolbooks now in Florence, both from the earlier Quattrocento:

BML .	Completed by Bartolomeo di Giovanni, then a pupil at Mattia Lupi's school in Prato; notable for large quantity of vernacular glossing included by Bartolomeo in marginalia, o ering a macaronic mixture, doubtless reflecting Lupi's pragmatic teaching methods; otherwise normal school-type philology (paraphrase, explication, geography, mythology).
BML sup.	Full-scale school-level commentary consisting of interlinear WOM (v) and lexical paraphrase, including some vernacular, and marginal philology (explication, paraphrase, figures, grammar, rhetorical structure) besides *accessus*.[334]

[333] The marginalia by the scribe (r– v) are unaccompanied by interlinear glossing and show more critical facility than normal for a school reader: e.g. (v) Confundit hystoriam: nam dicit quosdam occisos a Mario qui caesi fuerant a Sylla.

[334] See below, ch. *passim*.

An author whose popularity declined not just relatively but even absolutely in the Quattrocento was **Seneca the Tragedian**, whose leading position in the Trecento appears to have collapsed during the next century:

BML AD	Work of well-known Pistoiese scribe, Tommaso Baldinotti (–), copied in at the age of ;[335] his own school-level glosses include references to Ovid's *Heroides* (v, r), *Papias* (v) and possibly Gerald of Wales (r); another hand, writing in more traditional Gothic style, adds citations of Lucan and Statius (r, r).[336]
BML Edili	A little school-type interlinear and marginal glossing, including reference to the allegoric meaning of the myth of Orpheus and Euridice as presented in Boethius's *Consolation* (v).
BML Rinuccini	Simple interlinear vocabulary paraphrases throughout by a number of di erent contemporaneous hands, besides occasional basic philological and grammatical brief marginalia.
BNCF Magl. . . (*Hercules furens*, fragment)	Copiously glossed by several hands (XV^1) with interlinear lexical equivalents and paraphrase and with simple marginal philology (figures, paraphrase, explication, mythology).
BNCF Magl. . . (*Octavia*, fragment)	Sparingly glossed by the copyist with rudimentary interlinear vocabulary and brief marginal paraphrase.

Valerius Maximus, Statius and Horace

Several authors seem to have held their own during the Quattrocento, without, nevertheless, demonstrating a striking or novel rise in popularity. One of these was **Valerius Maximus**:

335 On Baldinotti and this MS, see de la Mare ( ), , , .

336 Continued to be owned by the Baldinotti family in XVIc. (see v: Baldinoctus de Baldinoctis de Pistorio minimus iuris utriusque ex caritate posuit atque dicavit), but no sign of school use after mid XVc.

BML AD	School colophon by Piermatteo di Ser Nicola da Città di Castello,[337] who also composed extensive marginal commentary, citing many authors and texts (see Appendix). Obviously much was added over years of study and reading, but some of the simpler glosses (on Roman customs, figures, anecdotes, geography, *sententiae*, history, introductory rhetoric) may go back to Piermatteo's school days. Continued school use shown by the fact that Piermatteo lent it to his friend Filippo Tifernate, a pupil of Guarino's, correspondent of Poggio's and grammar teacher himself.[338]
BML CS	Apparently prepared for school use, with wide spacing between lines; a little interlinear and marginal glossing, often in vernacular and written by a couple of immature hands (XV/XVIc.).
BML .	Intermittent interlinear glossing over first folios and not many significant marginalia, apart from a couple of references to Pliny's *Natural History* and to Livy (r–v) and reference to some Greek verse translated by Guarino.[339] School context clear from the *ex libris* of unidentified adolescent.[340]

337 v: Scriptum fuit istud opus manu mei Permatthei Ser Niccole de Civitate Castelli cum gramaticalibus studiis cupide indulgebam. Deo gratias, anno domini MCCCCXVIII. Piermatteo worked as a notary in his native city, from to , but this manuscript seems to have been copied while away from home in Castel Durante near Urbino, between and . It has the following attached note (XVII or XVIIIc.): (r) Petrus Matthaeus, cuius grammaticales in Valerium Maximum labores hoc in codice continentur, patriam habuit Tifernum Tiberium [...] quod [...] nunc Civitas Castelli appellatur. Hic tabellionatus o cium [...] exercuit; pluraque ipsius instrumenta ab a. ad in tabulario civitatis asservantur, ubi se subscribit: Ego Piermatthaeus Ser Nicole Ser Marii etc. [...] Noster autem Petrus, turbato fortasse civitatis vel rerum suarum statu, a. in Brancalionum ditionibus ad Castrum Durantis se receperat, unde cum revocare voluerant priores civitatis, indicta poena centum florenorum auri, nisi mandatis pareret. Id constat ex litteris datis die novembris, quae in actis reformationum (pag.) in secretiore archivio exhibentur [...]

338 See Walser ( ), , , – ; Guarino (–), , – ; Poggio Bracciolini (–), , – , – . Filippo Tifernate returned the volume to Piermatteo with a letter attached (verso), speaking of his solace from reading Valerius: quoniam horum studiorum humanitatis me flagrantissimum nosti, ab iisque vi pestilentiae depulsus, in hoc Valerio tuo tamquam in amici sinu praecipue acquievi.

339 v: Guarinus.
Phebum de trypode rogitas, Miles[i]a proles,
Hunc tripodem addito cuius sapientia prima est.

340 r: Iste Valerius Maximus doctorum ac morabilium [*sic*] est doctissimi adoloscentis. There is a roughly contemporaneous signature on the same page: Libro di Misser Andrea d'Andolo fo de Misser Lucha. Later passed into possession of Pietro Vettori: r.

BML sup.	Bought by Ficino's grammar teacher, Luca Bernardi da San Gimignano, on May .[341] Bernardi made no annotations,[342] possibly because first quarter of text already given copious simple interlinear lexical glossing, besides normal school-level marginal paraphrase, history, geography and structural analysis, by the copyist, possibly himself a tutor or student *repetitore* living with a Bolognese family (see below,); this glossator made a slip possibly indicative of modest scholarly attainments.[343]
BRF	Learned commentary by the copyist, whose cultural level exceeded the limits of grammar school;[344] soon passed into the hands of a group of schoolboys from Viterbo who, possibly in , made a crude attempt to transliterate their names into Greek.[345]
BRF	Apparently prepared for school use, with wide spacing between lines; brief *accessus* and reference to Isidore of Seville (r).
BRF	Intermittent simple interlinear vocabulary equivalents in hand roughly contemporaneous with the copyist's (v– v, v, v– v, r, v); philological marginalia consist mainly of grammar (see v), history and paraphrase.

Another author showing a modest relative increase in popularity during the Quattrocento was **Statius**. The ***Achilleis*** regularly formed part of school anthologies with the minor authors and so a number of manuscripts have already been mentioned (BNCF Magl. . , BNCF Magl. . , BNCF Magl. . , BNCF CS J. . , BNCF

341 v: Iste liber est mei Luce Antonii de Sancto Geminiano, quem emi a quodam presbitero Sancti Laurentii de Florentia pro pretio florenorum quinque, a c(arta) , anno domini die maii. Bandini (–), . , corrects spelling here. Santi di Lorenzo was Ser Santi da Dicomano, a teacher active in Florence from – : see below – n. .

342 Except for orthographical/etymological marginal annotation: see below, , n. .

343 r: Hoc scribit Titus Livius primo *O ciorum* in capitulo de temperantia circa medium.

344 Cites Livy, Augustine, Ovid, Orosius, Jerome, 'Cronica annalium romanorum', Ambrose, Cicero, Solinus, Averroes, Sallust, Isidore, Vergil, Juvenal, Seneca, Aristotle, Boethius, Lucan, Vegetius, Hugutio, besides 'versus sepulcri Sardinapali' (r).

345 v: Viterbienses qui facultatem habeant ire, stare et morari in terris perfecti:
Nicola de Messer Alloysi
Rasino de Andrea de Ruzo de Rasinio
El pecorone
Lippo de Cornalova
Boccha
Malacencia
Jacovo de Marchangelo
El orto
Et Jacovo de Savina.
quin .

Landau Fin. , BML . , BML .); of these, the glosses of one (BML .) have already been discussed[346] and two others (BNCF Magl. . , BNCF Magl. . (r– v)) have no significant glosses, while BNCF CS J. . , BNCF Landau Fin. and BNCF Magl. . have the usual school mixture of interlinear lexical synonyms and marginal philology (including figures, definitions, paraphrase, mythology, geography). XVc. school manuscripts of ***Achilleis*** also include:

BML .	Commentary by Santi di Giovanni (see above,) consisting of interlinear vocabulary paraphrases, occasionally including vernacular, exegetic marginalia and – a common pedagogic technique in grammar schools – rhetorical analysis of a speech (here Thetis's to Neptune[347]); includes *accessus*.[348]
BML Strozzi	Hardly glossed marginally although has contemporaneous and later fifteenth-century interlinear paraphrase glosses, including vernacular.
BNCF ..	Belonged to Cesare Malvicini, schoolboy from Viterbo in [349] and containing *Achilleis* (r– v) glossed in normal school manner.
BRF C	Extensive interlinear and marginal commentary, mainly by copyist, notable for many rhetorical figures indicated.
BRF	Intensive vocabulary interlinear glossing (r–v, r–v); only one brief philological marginal annotation (v).

Statius's *Thebais*, a text which seems to have played little role in Italian schools albeit a favourite in the ultramontane classroom, is contained in two possible school-level copies:

346 See above, .

347 See below, n. . Santi proceeds to write in margins appropriately (v– r): narratio, petitio, conclusio.

348 r: Im presenti auctor Statius Sirculus Papiensis vult probare poeticho modo quod fatum est. Propter quod notandum quod Domitianus imperator filius Vespasiani imperatoris habebat intra se et suos sapientes unum dubium, videlicet, utrum esset fatum. Et ubicumque Domitianus sciebat esse hominem sapientem, mittebat tandem pro eo: sicut Statium esse sapientem hominem, misit pro eo. Statius accessit et eo, adunata multitudine hominum sapientum, disputaverit utrum fatum debeat retineri. Et tandem Statius maximis rationibus obtinuit quod fatum erat. Unde Statius ad huius probationem inducit Achillem cum non potuit evadere de troyano bello quia fatatum erat ei [...]. See Black and Pomaro ( ), – , for this MS.

349 r: . MCCCLXXIX. Hic liber est Caesaris Malvicini viterbensis. This same page contains some *probationes* written by Cesare.

BML Ashb.	Intensive interlinear and marginal commentary mainly by two earlier to mid fifteenth-century hands up to v, after which point one ceases to gloss; most of marginalia appear to consist of exegesis, mythology and paraphrase;[350] Ovid's *Tristia* cited (r).
BRF (r– v: fragment (. –))	Full set of school-type marginal and interlinear glosses.

Among Quattrocento grammar teachers there seems to have a sense of satiety, even boredom, with the classical literary heritage of the Trecento. They appear determined to do something new, even if they could not or would not entirely cast o tradition. This is nowhere clearer than in their use of **Horace**. He had been a great standby of the classroom since the early middle ages, but there are only a few fifteenth-century schoolbooks now in Florence.

BML CS	*Epistles*	Normal school-level commentary to Horace, limited to paraphrase, explication, figures, grammar, citation of some authors (e.g. r: Ovid).
BML CS	*Odes Epistles Carmen saeculare*	Has normal contemporaneous school-level glosses in hand of scribe, including extracts from pseudo-Acron commentary (v, r) and citations of Juvenal and *Aeneid* (r), but also a list of Florentine pupils of a teacher called 'Fulgentio Iotini', dating from XVIc.[351]

350 Glosses do not appear to bear relation to commentary by Lactantius Placidus.

351 v:
Scolari di Fulgentio Iotini:
Francesco Tomasini a di maggio II
Pietro Croce a di maggio
Bastiano dell'Alfieri a di maggio
Camillo Lotti a di maggio
Camillo Contucci a di giugno I
Bastiano di M. Paris a di giugno II
Camillo Giorgi a di giugno I
Marcantonio Menicucci a di giugno II
Giovambattista Cungi a di giugno II
Verginio Galletti a di giugno
Marco di Cione a di giugno I
Cristofano Guidalotti a di giugno
Arcangiolo Iubi a di giugno II
Giovanni Bartoli a di giugno

BML .	*Odes Epistles Carmen saeculare*	First half of manuscript is given usual simple interlinear/marginal glossing by several XVc. hands.
BML Rinuccini	*Ars Epistles Sermones Odes*	Copied and dated between and / by *ripetitore* (identified only as 'Do.') in the house of Dominus Andrea,[352] and extensively glossed by the copyist: *Ars* receives mainly usual school-level interlinear vocabulary paraphrases (but there are some philological marginalia), whereas letters receive full interlinear and marginal commentary, including *accessus* (r) and normal grammatical/philological annotations; satires and odes receive normal school-type glossing.
BNCF .. , r– v	*Ars*	Signed in by a schoolboy from Viterbo, with usual school-type glosses.[353]
BNCF Landau Fin.	*Odes Epodes Carmen saeculare*	First glossed at school level XV–XVIc. (r) and including boyish notes and *probationes* (v– v).
BNCF Magl. . (r– v)	*Ars Epistles*	Very lightly glossed.[354]
BNCF Palatino Baldovinetti	*Odes Ars*	*Odes* glossed by several contemporaneous hands with a mixture of figures, mythology, grammar, definition and vernacular, besides citations of Vergil, Priscian, Sallust.
BRF	*Epistles Carmen saeculare*	Considerable quantity of vernacular glossing from early Cinquecento.

Andrea Vardi a di giugno
Orsino Orsini a di giugno I
Giovambattista Pellegrini a di luglio
Fabiano [possibly corrected to Nerone] Galletti a [possibly crossed out] di giugno
Venantio Bartoli a di agosto

352 v: Explevi ego Do. hora XVI de die veneris M°CCCC°XXX° die XVIIII° mensis maii et in domo Domini Andree cum quo stabam tunc ad repetitionem et tempore Pape Martini quinti etc. r: Quinti Horatii Flacci epistolarum liber explicit perfectus a me Do. MCCCC°XXXI° tempore Eugenii Pape Quarti mense iulii die XXVI hora XIIII post sumptum prandium et in studiolo consueto nostro. r: Explicit liber sermonum Oratii Flacci venusini die XXVI ianuarii et hora quinta noctis in studiolo nostro consueto M°CCCC°XXXIII^a tempore Eugenii Pape Quarti. 'Dominus Andrea' may be Messer Andrea de' Pazzi, whose son Piero (b.), was of school age in . If manuscript is Florentine, then date mentioned in final colophon would be . MS completed XV^2 (v– v).

353 See above, . Also contains 'Commentum super Poetria Oratii' (r– v).

354 E.g. v: colligit = capit, ponit = deponit, inberbis = sine barba; r: palam = manifeste.

In terms of manuscript numbers, therefore, **Horace** shows stagnation with respect to the Trecento, but with regard to the choice of texts and their use, on the other hand, these Horatian schoolbooks begin to reflect the changing tastes characteristic of Quattrocento humanism. It has already been seen ( ) that in the Trecento the overwhelming preoccupation of the classroom had been with the *Ars poetica* and the *Epistulae*; now, however, there are a considerable number of school manuscripts which contain the *Odes*. There is also developing humanist interest evident in a composite manuscript, in which an early fourteenth-century copy of Geo rey of Vinsauf's *Poetria nova* is linked to a text of Horace's *Ars poetica*, datable to the first decade of the Quattrocento (BML Strozzi).[355] The entire manuscript is glossed by the copyist of Horace, o ering a stylistic/philological commentary and citing Aristotle's *Rhetoric*, Cicero's *De oratore*, Quintilian's *Institutio*, Servius's commentary on the *Aeneid*, Cicero's *De senectute*, Isidore's *Etymologies*, Vergil's *Aeneid*, Hugutio's *Magnae derivationes*, Ovid's *Metamorphoses* and Geo rey of Vinsauf's *Poetria nova*; the strictly literary range of the authors cited as well as the stylistic focus of the commentary (see r on the six vices of poetic style to be avoided, according to Horace) suggest an academic context near the end of the grammar curriculum, at the point of transition to the study of rhetoric. This unfortunately anonymous commentator is clearly linked to the early stages of Quattrocento humanism, with his reading of Quintilian and *De oratore*, but also remains with one foot, so to speak, in the Trecento world, with citations of Hugutio and Geo rey of Vinsauf. Finally, there is a manuscript of the *opera omnia* (BML AD), written at Perugia in by Alessandro di Iacopo *de Montebodio*,[356] who left numerous glosses throughout; this is entirely philological, but it is probably related to a school context, given the attention devoted to metrical analysis of the poems (e.g. v, r, v– v, v– r, r– v), and the *probationes*, including schoolboyish drawings and writing (v). It is notable that Perotti's treatise on Boethius's metres, to be mentioned below ( ), also included an analysis of Horace's versification, and it seems clear that metric study of diverse poetic forms was becoming a preoccupation of humanist grammar teachers in the Quattrocento.

355 For Emilian provenance and early ownership, see Appendix , below. Text of Geo rey of Vinsauf given school-type reading by several Trecento hands, including vernacular (see below, n.) and WOM (v); then glossed by hand providing free-standing commentary on *Ars poetica* (r– v) as well as by the copyist of Horace, both writing at beginning of XVc. and possibly working together.

356 r: Est mei Alexandri Iacobi de Montebodio scriptus mano mea Perusie .

Ovid, Persius, Juvenal, Terence, Vergil and Sallust

At this point it may be enlightening to consider a text which has often been linked to educational developments at the turn of the Quattrocento. In his *Regola del governo di cura familiare*, written between and , the Florentine preacher Giovanni Dominici voiced his opinion on the school curriculum.[357] Dominici says that the minor authors (Cato, Aesop, Prosper, Prudentius, *Physiologus*, Theodulus) had been the staple in the schools attended by his contemporaries' forefathers, but now children were reading Ovid's *Metamorphoses*, *Heroides*, *Ars amatoria* and other lascivious texts (presumably the *Amores* and *Remedia amoris*), Vergil and (Seneca's) tragedies. Dominici does not say that the classics had not been read by 'nostri antichi', nor that the minor authors and Boethius were no longer being read at school; what he suggests is that Ovid, Vergil and Seneca constituted a new addition to the curriculum. In fact, Dominici is relatively precise in reflecting the changing curriculum of schools at the turn of the fifteenth century. The present census confirms, in conformity with his declarations, that the minor authors and Boethius were staple features of the curriculum in both the Tre- and earlier Quattrocento. Moreover, Dominici's focus on Seneca's tragedies is born out by the preeminent place these works had assumed in the syllabus by the close of the Trecento. Even more revealing is his emphasis on the addition of Vergil and Ovid's *Heroides* and other amorous verses. Vergil had featured only marginally in the fourteenth-century curriculum, while the principal Ovidian text in the Trecento had been only the *Metamorphoses*, not the *Heroides*, *Ars amatoria*, *Amores* or *Remedia amoris*. It will be seen that these works would now assume the front ranks at the upper levels of the grammar curriculum in the fifteenth century, along with other classical poets previously neglected, such as Juvenal, Persius and Terence. What Dominici is signalling here is the shift in the choice of classical authors taught in the schoolroom coming in the wake of Quattrocento humanism. What this educational change meant above all was the addition of previously marginalized authors; others either maintained a respectable presence (*auctores minores*, Boethius, Horace, Statius, Valerius Maximus) or stagnated (Lucan, Claudian) or declined (Seneca). The influence of Quattrocento humanism on the classroom did not signify a rejection of former curriculum stalwarts nor indeed an unprecedented classicism; rather, it meant a change in fashion as to which classical texts were given prominence

[357] Ed. Garin ( ), . For English translation of first half of passage, see Gehl ( ), .

among the *auctores maiores*. It would be exaggerated to argue that Quattrocento humanism constituted a radical change such as occurred in the thirteenth century with the rise of scholasticism or in the fourteenth century with the reintroduction of the Latin classics into the grammar syllabus. There was clearly now a determination to do something new, but this represented above all a change in taste rather than a 'revolution in the schoolroom'.

Of the authors who showed a marked increase in popularity during the Quattrocento, **Ovid** was given the prime place by Dominici, and it can be confirmed that there was a striking shift in the Ovidian texts used at school in the fifteenth century. The ***Metamorphoses***, which had represented six of the seven Ovid schoolbooks in this survey for the Trecento, showed an absolute decline in favour, represented as they are by only five fifteenth-century schoolbooks:

BML CS	Glossed mainly by the principal copyist with school-type simple interlinear lexical equivalents and marginal paraphrases and *divisiones textus*; beginning of text restored by mid-XVc. writer leaving some marginal glosses, including two references to Pliny's *Natural Histories* (r).
BML .	Fully glossed by the copyist with dense interlinear lexical paraphrases (especially in middle books) and marginal exposition, paraphrase, history and mythology, besides a life of Ovid (r) and conventional *accessus* (r).[358]
BML .	Work of one 'Cubellus' (r), pupil at the Pratese grammar school of Mattia Lupi, who anonymously glossed the manuscript together with his acolyte, together producing commentary, consisting of usual philological marginalia (simple geography and natural philosophy, paraphrase, mythology, structure, figures, allegory (not by Giovanni del Virgilio)) and basic lexical interlinear synonyms, besides referring to Macrobius, *Graecismus*, the elder Pliny, Fulgentius, Seneca (Tragedian), Boccaccio.[359]
BML .	Principal glossator, writing towards mid-century and providing the usual school mixture of interlinear vocabulary and simple philological marginalia (figures, etymology, mythology, vocabulary, geography), besides some vernacular interventions and allegory; also interlinear glosses and some marginalia by copyist.

[358] Partly published by Allen ( ), , n. .

[359] r, r, v, v, v, r, v, v.

BML .	Work of two cooperating copyists: second left colophon[360] indicating that Gaspare, from Radda in Chianti, was working as *ripetitore* in household of the Florentine Canocchi family; possibly related to Lorenzo di Ser Niccolò da Radda, copyist of *Heroides* in (BNCF Magl. . : see below,). Gaspare left school-level simple lexical interlinear glosses over the first fifty folios; his fellow copyist made some school-type marginal annotations (especially v– r).

The *Metamorphoses* represent the traditional face of Ovid, but among those works hardly represented in the Italian curriculum before the fifteenth century, first place goes to the ***Heroides***, a text whose novel appearance in the curriculum at this time was signalled, as has been seen, by Dominici:

BML .	Came into possession of Mattia Lupi: general *accessus* complemented by individual prologues to each letter; contrast between conventional moralism of *accessus* and entirely philological content of running marginal commentary (grammar, geography, figures, mnemonic verses, explication, paraphrase, etymology); Seneca's tragedies, Ovid's *Remedia amoris* cited.
BML .	Cosimo de' Medici at the school of Maestro Niccolò d'Arezzo, possibly in the academic year – (mentioned above, –), provided, with fellow pupils, usual interlinear lexical paraphrases and marginal philology (figures, mythology, ancient customs, paraphrase), besides making one citation from Seneca's tragedies (r: see above, –).
BML .	Copied by 'Francischinum Cosii de Motta': for his entirely philological commentary (narrative, history, mythology, grammar, mnemonic verses, figures) he mixes classical and medieval sources indiscriminately (r, r: see Appendix).
BML .	By scribe Santi di Giovanni in probably at Nofri da Poggitazzi's Sienese school; besides conventional *accessus* (r), Santi di Giovanni also provided most of the letters with a short prologue, explaining circumstances of the epistle and Ovid's intention in writing; marginal commentary consists of usual philology, focusing especially on figures.

360 r: Explicit Ovidius Metamorfoseos, deo gratias, amen, amen. Hic liber est mei Gasparis Niccholai Petri de Radda et sum domi Andreae Dominici de Canochis. Et explevi eum <h>odie die veneris mensis otobris in ora vigesima prima, / / .

BML Strozzi	The copyist covered the text with heavy interlinear lexical glossing (including vernacular: e.g. r: sceleri = *peccato*), besides some simple philological marginalia towards beginning (r), grammatical comment (v: averbium dolentis heu; v: nota quod omnia nomina terminata in -osus significant plenitudinem), focusing especially on rhetorical figures (v, r, r, v, r, etc.)
BNCF .. , v– r (Sappho's letter)	Signed in by a schoolboy from Viterbo, see above, , ; glossed in usual school fashion.
BNCF Magl. . r– v (Sappho's letter)	In school-type anthology with grammatical texts treating several topics from secondary syllabus (diphthongs, genitive terminations, prosody, formation of preterites/supines, orthography, figures: see n. , below); hardly glossed.
BNCF Magl. .	Written by Lorenzo di Ser Niccolò da Radda in Chianti, *ripetitore* teaching in the household of Tommaso di Bartolo da Castelfiorentino in ,[361] providing conventional moralizing *accessus* to four letters (v, r, r, v), while running marginal commentary consists of mythology, narrative, figures and rhetorical analysis (v– r).
BRF (r– r, r– r: two versions of Sappho's letter)	First version has usual simple interlinear glosses and philological (geographical) marginalia.
BRF [362]	Lightly commented by several XVc. hands.

Yet more novel works by **Ovid** were sometimes added to the curriculum in the fifteenth century. One of these was the ***Epistulae ex Ponto***, already noted (above,) as having been used by Maestro Guglielmo da Bourges in his school, probably in Florence between and (BNCF Magl. .); the glosses of his pupil are of the usual simple interlinear lexical equivalents and basic philological marginalia, including some antiquarian information. Another was the ***Fasti***, found

361 r: Explicit liber *Epistolarum* Ovidii deo gratias, amen. Ego Laurentius Ser Niccholai de Radda scripxi finemque vidi MCCCCVII in domo Tommasii Bartholi de Castro Florentino die decimo setimo agusti.

362 Contemporaneous possession note: (r) Hic liber est Hioannis Karoli de Charradoris, qui vochatur <...>.

in two possible school manuscripts: one, datable to the third quarter of the century (BNCF Magl. .), was glossed interlinearly and marginally by the copyist, but there is also a childish hand who wrote 'et' above 'que' on v; the other, datable to the second half of the century (BML .), is annotated by the copyist, who provided a considerable commentary, consisting of interlinear lexical glosses and marginal geography, mythology and history, with the usual rhetorical analysis as well, particularly at the beginning of the text. Another text was the ***Remedia amoris***, also found in two schoolbooks in Florentine libraries: one, datable to the first half of the century and southern Italian in provenance (BRF), was given an intensive interlinear lexical glossing, including the vernacular, both by the copyist and another contemporaneous hand; the other, part of the above mentioned anthology ( ) containing grammatical texts, Ovid's letter from Sappho, Vergil and Sallust (BRF , r– r) and datable to the second half of the century, was the work of its owner, 'Ser Ieronimi Antonii de Guernacciis plebanus [*sic*] Saxe' (r), who may possibly have worked as a teacher in Volterra, given that Sassa is a village in the diocese of Volterra and the book later passed into the possession of 'Alesandri Benedicti de Richobaldis de Vulterris' (r), 'Domini Ioanis Batiste Vulterani Contugii' and the latter's brother 'Karoli de Vechiano' (r).[363] The latter manuscript, although obviously part of a school anthology, is virtually unglossed, as is another Ovidian text, the ***Ars amatoria***, dated , found similarly in a classroom collection already mentioned in connection with Statius's *Achilleis* and *Ilias latina* (BML .).[364] Another collection of Ovidian and pseudo-Ovidian texts (*Ars amatoria, Nux, Medicamina faciei, Amores* III. *[De somno], De virtutibus herbarum [De medicamine aurium]*) was copied by Filippo Pieruzzi, the noted bibliophile, towards the beginning of the century (BNCF Magl. .); he left a set of full glosses to the first text, although he also provided *accessus* to all but *Medicamina faciei* and *Pulex*. His commentary follows the pattern seen above (–) in several manuscripts of the *Heroides*: moralizing, particularly linked to material associated with the conventions of the *accessus*, soon gave way to philology (topography, geography, history, mythology, figures, explication, rhetorical structure) and quotation from other authors (Seneca's tragedies, Vergil's *Aeneid*). It is to be noted that Pieruzzi, after his retirement from the Florentine

[363] See De Robertis and Miriello ( ), . [364] See above, .

chancery, became a grammar teacher at the Badia a Settimo near Florence.[365]

Another author whose position was strikingly transformed in the Quattrocento schoolroom was **Persius**, who had shown a scant presence in previous centuries:

BML .	Glossed by several Quattrocento hands with typical school set of interlinear and marginal annotations.
BML .	Has at least one obvious school-level reader (see e.g. r–v), contemporary with copyist, who made simple interlinear and marginal annotations of lexical and philological variety throughout, citing Cicero's *Paradoxa* (r).
BML Rinuccini	Completed by *ripetitore* with complete interlinear and marginal commentary of normal classroom variety.
BNCF, Magl. .	May already transcend the limitations of the grammar school: copied by Giovannantonio Mazzi attending lectures of Florentine Messer Giovanni Lachi,[366] providing a full set of interlinear/marginal glosses; appended long free-standing commentary to Persius after glossed initial text. Marginalia appear high-level, citing and using Greek; may be more closely associated with lecturing on classical texts at university level by professors of *studia humanitatis* than with the humbler work of grammar teachers.
BNCF Magl. .	From Florentine school of Maestro Guglielmo da Bourges: see above – , – .
BRF	Discussed below ( ).
BRF	Discussed below ( ).
BRF (r– r)	Unglossed, but format with wide spacing between the lines, crude Gothic script and adequate margins for glossing gives appearance of book prepared for school use.
BRF	School-type interlinear and marginal glosses to fifth satire (r– v).
BRF	Usual school-type glossing.[367]

365 Calzolai ( ), ; Ullman and Stadter ( ), ; Vespasiano da Bisticci (–), . , .

366 v: Qui, tu lector, scripsit crede fuisse Ioannem, quem dii conservent secundum semper in orbe [...] Qui, tu lector, scripsit Mazzum fuisse putato. Hic liber Persius scriptus et auditus fuit ab Ioanne Antonio sub Domino Ioanne Lacho florentino , primo anno quo Florentiam appulit. See Galante (–), .

367 Except possibly for one marginal annotation, glossing lines 'gigni de nichilo nichil, in nichilum

Another author thinly represented in the thirteenth and fourteenth centuries but now notably renascent was Persius's fellow satirist, **Juvenal**:

BML CS	One reader, possibly an advanced pupil, made repeated lexical references to Giovanni Tortelli (r, v, v, v, r, v) and inserted occasional Greek words.[368]
BML CS	Completed by Lorenzo di Ser Niccolò on February ;[369] besides writing (ignorantly) upper-case Greek alphabet with corresponding names of letters transliterated above (v),[370] this pupil left some basic philological marginal (r– r, r, r– r, r) and simple interlinear (v– r, r– r: e.g. curvum = non rectum) glosses.
BML .	See above ( ).
BML .	The work of a *ripetitore* from Trino (near Vercelli), working for the Radicati di Brozolo family in Piedmont.[371] Contains simple lexical interlinear and philological marginal glosses by many hands, including brief bits of Greek; annotations peter out towards end.
BML Redi	Besides numerous *probationes pennae* (r– v, r, v), has some simple vocabulary glosses and occasional simple philological marginalia by various hands.
BML Redi	Heavily glossed marginally and interlinearly in philological manner (especially paraphrase, history) characteristic of schools; conventional *accessus*,[372] besides citations of Vergil and Cicero's *De oratore*.
BML Rinuccini	See above ( ); Juvenal here receives Aristotelian-type *accessus*: r.

nil posse reverti' (, –) concerning contradiction between philosophical theories of eternity and Christian idea of creation: see below, , n. . However, this was a theme which had itself found a place in school literature, given its appearance in school glosses to Boethius's *Consolation*: see e.g. Black and Pomaro ( ), .

368 Continued as schoolbook in early Cinquecento: see especially v– r, where early XVIc. immature hand makes extremely simple vocabulary glosses; same hand compiles brief Latin–vernacular vocabulary list on verso.

369 v: Iste liber est mei Laurentii Ser Nicholai, quem transcripsi de mea propria manu anno domini MCCCC°LXIIII° die mensis februarii dicti anni.

370 See below, .

371 v: die XXV februarii, expletus fuit liber iste per me Antonium de Pagliano de Tridino ad horas XVIII vel circha, videlicet in domo S. Domini Iohannis Iacobi de Broxulo ex comittibus Radicatus etc. Later passed into hands of owner (XV/XVI) from Mazzè, also in Piedmont: (inside rear cover) Hic liber est mei Bartolomei Petri Filitii de Mazaxio.

372 See below, .

BRF	One sophisticated reader (XV^{2}) and several earlier hands leaving school-level interlinear vocabulary glosses and basic philological marginalia.
BRF	Copied in large lettering with wide spacing between lines; several mid XVc. hands simultaneously made sporadic simple lexical interlinear glosses.
BRF	Hardly glossed except for r– v, where there are copious simple lexical paraphrases of the classroom type.
BRF	Several di erent hands making simple interlinear paraphrase glosses, besides a little vernacular (v), WOM (r), references to Jerome's letters (r) and Terence's *Adelphi* (r).
BRF	One main school-type glossing hand who, besides usual interlinear lexical equivalents, left several simple grammatical marginalia (e.g. v, r, v, etc.) besides references to Vergil's *Georgics* (v) and Terence (r).

A third author little encountered hitherto in this survey but with a striking appearance in the Quattrocento was **Terence**. The following manuscripts are datable to XV^{1}:

BML AD	Typical school-type interlinear and marginal glosses, including citation of Vergil (v), ample *probationes* (v– v, r– r) and the vernacular (e.g. r).
BML CS	Interlinear and marginal glossing of the philological school type by several writers and mainly by one contemporaneous with the copyist.
BML CS	Composite manuscript with XIIc. nucleus of three plays (r– v) completed in earlier XVc. by two scribes working together (r– r).[373] Later section shows limited but clear signs of school use: WOM (r, r), simple vocabulary equivalents (r: quam = pro quantum; r: in = contra, crimen = culpa; v: deos penates = domesticos), simple philological marginalia (eg. r: nota scibo futurum huius verbi scio -is; r: pistrilla id est furnus vel molendinum dicta a pistrio -is secundum Uguicionem).

373 v: illegible ownership note: Explicit *Phormio* Terrentii, et totus eius liber qui est meus <J…> florentini. This hand (XV^{1}) does not correspond to late Quattrocento *ex libris* found on original front and rear flyleaves: Florentii sacerdotis est iste liber; Florentii presbiteri liber iste est: see Alessio (a), . Florentine provenance of second section supported by list of Terentian comedies on v in hand reminiscent of Salutati's (see Ullman ( ),) making precocious use of ampersand and therefore to be associated with early development of humanist script in Florence: see Villa ( ), .

BML .	Glossed interlinearly and marginally by numerous contemporaneous, or slightly later, hands in typical school manner; couple of possibly more learned readers, working at same time, citing Priscian, Servius, Augustine, Horace, Cicero.
BML .	Annotated by the scribe with glosses typical of a schoolbook, including numerous indications of rhetorical commonplaces such as *captatio benivolentiae* (r–v, v, r, r, r), narrative summaries and arguments (e.g. v– v); conventional *accessus* (r–v).
BML .	School-type interlinear and philological marginal (figures, paraphrase) glosses mainly by copyist, although later immature writer bought book in and left some similar glosses together with *probationes pennae.*[374]
BNCF . .	Probably prepared as a textbook with wide spacing between lines; glossed by numerous hands with simple lexical interlinear and philological marginal annotations.
BRF	Various *probationes*, Greek alphabet and ownership mark of 'Antonio in Poppi de Pappiensis' (r–v).
BRF	Heavily used schoolbook, prepared for classroom use with wide spacing between lines, with many di erent interlinear and marginal glossators of school type; three principal school readers, both from the earlier part of the Quattrocento: one left conventional *accessus* citing Varro and Augustine, besides providing grammatical glosses with allusions to Hugutio, Isidore, Priscian (v, v, v, v, v, v, v); two others o ered grammatical annotations (v, v, r–v).

There are also three Terence schoolbooks datable to the middle of the century:

BML .	Although glossed heavily throughout by a scholarly reader citing Cicero (r), Varro (r), also contains some interlinear (including WOM: r) and marginal glosses by one or more immature hands (see e.g. r, r, r).
BNCF ..	r– v covered with school-type glosses; has drawings and other *probationes* (r– r, r, v); series of rudimentary vocabulary, grammatical/philological notes relating to Terentian comedy (v– v).

374 Bandini's (– , .) and Villa's (,) transcription of note of purchase (r) should be amended: Io comperai questo lhibro soldi c(ento) nel mille cinquec(ento) addì quartordic<i>, nel mille cinquec(ento) quaranta . Ownership note transcribed by Bandini (–), . ('in fine eadem manus adscripsit: Questo libro è di Giulio di Giovanni deg …') seems no longer extant.

BNCF Magl. Append. .	Extensive interlinear vernacular vocabulary equivalents by many di erent hands, continual WOM and philological marginalia (grammar, figures, paraphrase, mythology), including repeated citations of Priscian and Servius (v).

There are also six classroom-type Terences from the second half of the century:

BML Ashb.	Work of a student called Yvone Le Moel, a French clerk from diocese of Tréguier, indicating possession (writing in a French hand – probably Le Moel's – under the possible influence of Italian humanist script) on one of rear flyleaves.[375] Apparently studying or teaching while using book, to judge from school-level glosses (e.g. r– v, r–v); also passed through various other French hands in s, as indicated by various *probationes* and notarial exercises with date (v). This school-type work on the manuscript possibly took place in Italy, since there are glosses written towards end XVc. by an Italian hand in vernacular (r: habitasse = *habitavissi*, in patriam = *andrò*; v: illinc = *andrò*; v: odio = *malivolentia*), besides intense Latin interlinear glosses from XVIin. (v– v, v).[376]
BML CS	Lightly glossed interlinearly and marginally, besides including life of Terence 'excerpta de dictis D. F. Petrarche'.
BML .	Glossed only lightly in school manner but has *probationes pennae* throughout.
BML .	Possibly crude work of a pupil writing in heavy late-Gothic hand; intensive interlinear glossing of simple lexical variety by numerous di erent hands.
BNCF Panciat.	Light simple interlinear glossing throughout, besides various grammatical annotations and *probationes* dating from XV/XVIc.
BRF	Copied for own use by 'Francischo Iohannis sutoris' (v), with intermittent heavy lexical interlinear glosses and occasional philological marginalia, including some vernacular; continued in school use, to judge from number of signatures at the beginning and end of the codex.

However, among the Roman poets it was **Vergil** who, in the fifteenth century, first ascended to a primacy in the Latin schoolroom from which he was never to descend. Twelve Vergil schoolbooks date from the first half of the century:

375 v: Iste liber est Yvonis Le Moel clerici Trecorensis diocesis; iste liber est Yvome Lemoel clerici.

376 Passed to unidentified Jesuit college, XVIc.: (r) Coll. Agen. Soc. Jesu. Cat. Ins. Date on front flyleaf (Terentii A ri Comoedie), by late hand possibly from XVIIc., is unreliable.

BML Ashb.	*Eclogues* *Georgics*	Passed through the hands of several school owners (r, v), some in Florence; almost every word throughout glossed with synonym; the few marginalia are simple philology.
BML Ashb.	*Eclogues*	Copied by a scion of the Florentine patriciate, Andrea di Francesco Quaratesi, while a pupil in the grammar school of Ser Bartolomeo da Pratovecchio.[377]
BML Ashb.	*Eclogues* *Georgics*	Intermittent simple interlinear glosses.
BML Ashb.	*Eclogues* *Georgics*	Heavy interlinear/marginal annotations by various hands in first half of MS.
BML CS	*Aeneid*	Usual interlinear and marginal glosses of philological school type, besides allegorical interpretation of book .[378]
BML CS	*Aeneid*	Annotated by the copyist with interlinear lexical and grammatical marginal glosses: life of Vergil (r), citation of *Metamorphoses* (r) and references to *Georgics* and Varro's lost *Res divinae*, possibly cited via Augustine (r); certainly passed through hands of schoolboys: grammatical *probationes* written by an immature hand (v).
BML Edili	*Aeneid*	Typical school-type interlinear and marginal glossing, including many references to figures (see v– r for their definitions) and an allusion to Varro (v).
BML Rinuccini	*Aeneid*	Considerable quantity of interlinear Italian glossing (r– v), besides marginalia by two Quattrocento hands: one left a gloss on four elements (v) besides another giving Cicero's definition of orator (r), while the other cites Nonius Marcellus (v, v, v); all other marginal glosses are philological school type, except for some annotations copied by the scribe at the beginning.
BNCF CS J. .	*Georgics*	Associated with school in Bologna run by a teacher from Tivoli, with interlinear lexical and marginal paraphrase glosses; mentioned above ( ).

[377] r: Publii Virgilii Maronis *Buccholicorum* liber hic explicit, deo dante, scriptus per me Andream Francisci de Quaratensibus, dum in scolis reverendi preceptoris mei, Ser Bartolomei de Pratoveteri, moram trahebam nondum linquens gramatice documenta, sub anno domini ab incarnatione eiusdem MCCCCXXII et die XXVII martii, deo gratias, amen.

[378] See below Ch. , . Donated to Florentine convent of SS. Annunziata as gift of 'Domini Ludovici Martelli canonici florentini et conservatoris huius conventus , iunii' (r).

BRF	*Eclogues*	Usual school-type interlinear lexical annotations, including a little vernacular (r: procul = *discosto*), besides philological marginalia (figures, explication), mainly XV² hands.
BRF	*Aeneid*	Copious simple interlinear lexical glosses in several contemporaneous hands (r– v), written on the manuscript with a school-type format (large writing, wide spacing between the lines, ample but restricted margins).
BRF	*Aeneid*	Numerous intermittent lexical interlinear glosses by various hands: one, besides providing some allegorical interpretations (r–v, v), cited Cicero, Sallust, Horace, *Doctrinale* (contra *Doctrinale*: r), the elder Pliny, Lucretius, Apollonius of Rhodes's *Argonautica* (r).

There are also five school manuscripts of Vergil datable to the mid-Quattrocento, all copies of the *Bucolics* and *Georgics*:

BML CS	Extracts from *Georgics* (r– r) provided with philological glosses besides one allegorical/Christian interpretation (r).
BML .	Usual school-type glosses by the copyist and several later fifteenth-century hands, including the vernacular (r: exul = *sbandito*), rhetorical analysis,[379] low-level secondary grammar notes on verb forms with Italian translations.[380]
BML .	Possibly owned by humanist scribe Antonio Sinibaldi[381] with school-boyish interlinear and marginal glossing in various hands (v– r, r–v), besides various Florentine *probationes*,[382] including alphabets (v).[383]
BML .	Fairly intense school-type interlinear and marginal glosses in one main hand (v– r, r– r).

379 See below, , n. .

380 v:

Ego sum causa amandi. *Io sono per chagione d'amare.*
Tu is a[p?]tus amando. *Tu sse' per cagione d'amare.*
Illum est amandum. *Colui è per cagione d'amare.*
Supina sunt hec. *Supini sono questi: ego vado amatu. Io vo amare.*
Tu venis amatu. *Tu vieni d'amare.*

381 v: d'Antonio di Sinibaldi, on whom see de la Mare ( ), , – , where this MS does not seem to be mentioned.

382 v: Cosimo de' Medici et chompagni in Roma, Giovanni Beina, Georgi, Francesco Alamanni, Lorenzo de' Medici et chompagni deono dare al Francesco Alamanneschi.

383 Conceivably written by Antonio Sinibaldi, possibly as schoolboy.

BML sup.	Glossed mainly by the copyist: *Georgics* with interlinear synonyms over almost every word of the text, although in *Eclogues* similar glossing soon tails o ; both works annotated with usual marginal philology.[384]

From the second half of the Quattrocento there are six Vergil schoolbooks, of which two are copies of the *Aeneid*:

BML .	Interlinear/marginal philological glosses of school type (figures, mythology, biography) by various later XVc. hands; also includes some grammatical notes about parts of speech in catechistic form (v), obviously associated with school context.
BML sup.	Usual school type of interlinear/philological marginal glosses (figures, etymology, paraphrase, geography).

It is interesting to note that, among these Vergil schoolbooks, the texts normally did not circulate in the form of the *opera omnia* with the exception of BRF and in this case only a few folios were glossed in the school manner (r– v, r–v); there is also a copy of the *Eclogues* and *Aeneid* (BML Edili), which includes various signatures by members of the Marsuppini family from the early Cinquecento (r), and which has the usual school mixture of interlinear and marginal glosses by various hands, besides citations of Servius and Festus (v). The following are further XV² school-type copies of Vergil:

BNCF ..	*Georgics*	Copyist (identified in Greek only as Bartolomeo: v) provides the usual combination of interlinear vocabulary/marginal philology, including brief citations of Varro, Lucretius, Horace, Servius, Sallust (r, v, v, r, v, v).
BRF , r– r	*Georgics*	Numerous interlinear vocabulary glosses besides repeated indications of figures (v, v, v, r, r, v, r, v).

A last Vergil manuscript reveals a hybrid combination of texts and contexts. This version of the *Eclogues* (BML sup.), written in the first half of the century, has the usual interlinear vocabulary and marginal

384 Another mid-XVc. hand includes mythological, school-type mnemonic verses (r–v).

philological glosses (mainly figures). Besides Salutati's pseudo-Ovidian letter of Phyllis to Demophoon and the pseudo-Ciceronian *De sinonimis*, often used as a school text, it also includes a copy of *Doctrinale* (on the glossing of this particular text see above,). Moreover, it is possible that the manuscript came into the possession of a minor figure from the humanist world of Cosimian and Laurentian Florence. Bastiano Foresi was a notary who entered the Florentine chancery under Carlo Marsuppini and then served as principal assistant to Benedetto Accolti, later dedicating neo-Petrarchan poetry to Lorenzo as well as sharing musical interests with Ficino.[385] It appears that he added in his own hand the final pseudo-Ciceronian text to the manuscript, besides annotating Vergil with the usual school-type interlinear glosses. It might be wondered whether, after leaving the chancery following the death of Accolti, Foresi worked as a grammar teacher, using not only pseudo-Cicero and Vergil but also *Doctrinale*. Once more it can be seen here that avant-garde teaching of Latin in the later fifteenth century often occurred in a hybrid curricular context.[386]

Of the Roman historians, it was **Sallust** whose position was notably transformed in the Quattrocento Italian schoolroom:

BML .	*BC*[387] *BJ*	Glossed throughout by various contemporaneous hands, who provided an intermittent set of school-level simple interlinear paraphrases.
BNCF CS J. .	*BC BJ*	Possibly a joint e ort by various pupils, with extensive interlinear vocabulary glossing (r– r, v, v, v– r, v, r, v– r), besides basic marginal paraphrases at the beginning (r– v), including some simple rhetorical analysis typical of grammar-school texts.[388]
BNCF Panciat.	*BC BJ*	Occasional interlinear simple vocabulary glossing, besides typical school-level historical marginal comment.[389]

385 On Foresi and his handwriting, see Black ( ), – , , , , n, n, , n, – , , – , and de la Mare ( ), , – , , .

386 Continued as schoolbook in earlier XVIc., as apparent from following *probatio*: v: Questo libro sia scripto Giovanni di Piero di Guccio nel mille cinquecento vinta<?> et sia fatto bene el fat<?> suo. Other *probationes* by various XVc. and XVIc. boys: r, r–v.

387 For these abbreviations, see x–xii, above.

388 See below, n. .

389 r: *Lege sempronia*: Sempronius fuit quidam qui talem instituit legem ut quolibet anno duo consules eligerentur quorum unus custodiret Italiam, alter iret ad gentes divincendas rebelles.

BRF	*BC BJ*	Completed by Marino di Antonuccio da Turano, a *ripetitore* working in the household of Francesco di Giovanni di Nanni in Rieti on April .[390] Also contains a life of Sallust, *accessus* to *Catiline*, Bruni's *Isagogicon moralis disciplinae*, his *Epistola* (,)[391] and his translation of Basil's *Epistula ad adolescentes*, besides Guarino's translation of Plutarch's *De liberis educandis*, which has colophon indicating that Marino had moved from Rieti to Rome by October .[392] Marino was the principal glossator of Sallust, leaving simple interlinear paraphrases, densely in *Catiline* (including WOM: r), intermittently in *Jugurtha*; marginalia entirely philological glosses of usual school type (etymology, grammar, definition, Roman institutions, rhetorical analysis[393]).
BRF	*BC* (end) *BJ*	Belonged to several schoolboys, to judge from notes of possession, drawings, *probationes* (front flyleaf r–v, r, v), although manuscript remained unglossed.
BRF , r– r	*BC*	Almost entirely unglossed, but its format besides its inclusion in school anthology suggests that it was an unused textbook.
BRF	*BC BJ*	Explicitly prepared for schoolroom use at Florentine Badia a Settimo in .[394] Only the hand of Don Roberto appears in the manuscript's glosses, which consist of usual interlinear lexical synonyms/marginal philology (explication, definition, figures, grammar, simple rhetorical analysis); references to Hugutio (r), Cicero (r, v), Priscian (r).

390 r: Liber iste Salustii expletus est per me Marinum Antonutii de Turano, Reate in domo Francisci Iohannis Nannis sub a(nn)o d(omin)i M°C°C°C°C°LIII°, indictione prima, die vero VI° aprilis, hora vigesima pulsata, deo gratias, amen. See De Robertis and Miriello ( ), .

391 v– v: Inc. [N]on usque adeo me delectassent littere tue. This text omitted by De Robertis and Miriello ( ), – .

392 v: Plutarchus grece instituit; Guarrinus Veronensis in latinum e greco transtulit. Finis, Rome, , saecunda indictione, die XIX optobris, exscripsi ego Marinus Turanensis, deo gratias amen. See De Robertis and Miriello ( ), .

393 E.g. r: Oratio Catilinae ad milites que habet exordium, narrationem, confirmationem et conclusionem et est in genere deliberativo.

Texts and translations by Bruni and Guarino receive only a few interlinear and brief marginal glosses from Marino, insu cient to indicate use of these works directly in his grammatical studies.

394 r: Crispi Salustii *De bello Catellino et Iugurtino* liber feliciter explicit. Ego Dopnus Robertus Bonrius de Suchiellis, professus in monasterio Sancti Saulvatoris de Septimo scripsi hoc volumen ad laudem domini et omnium sanctorum et sanctarum et ad consolationem legentium et audientium, currentibus annis MCCCCLXVIIII. Inceptum fuit die vigesimo optavo ianuarii et fuit inn illo die festivitas Sancte Agnetis secundo. Expletum est <h>odie, scilicet a dì XVIII februarii ad horas vigesimas in anno supra. See De Robertis and Miriello ( ), .

BRF	*BC*	Glossed in the school manner with simple interlinear lexical synonyms and philological marginalia (figures, rhetorical structure); also includes *Jugurtha* and three Ciceronian orations but only the first text shows school use.

Cicero

Among the Latin prose-writers,[395] however, it was Cicero who finally assumed primacy in the Italian fifteenth-century grammar schoolroom. It is one of the achievements of the Italian Renaissance to have restored *De amicitia*, *De senectute*, *Paradoxa stoicorum*, *Somnium Scipionis* and *De o ciis* to the grammar-school curriculum, after two centuries of disuse. Now in the fifteenth century one again finds copies of these shorter moral treatises with typical school features such as alphabets at the conclusion or on the final folios;[396] *probationes pennae* in the vernacular, sometimes with childish contents (Francesco mio fratello, io vorei che tu mi mandasi una scarsella,[397] Detur pro pena scriptori pulcra puella,[398] scolares[399]) or in illiterate Latin (Deus in none tuo salum me fac);[400] references to the glossator's teacher;[401] childish ownership notes (questo libro è di Baroncino Baroncini; chi lo truova si lo renda);[402] puerile and illiterate verses (Adrisum multum potes congnoscere stultum./ Si prestabis non reabebis./ Si reabebis non tam bonum./ Se tam bonum non tam cito./ Se tam cito perdis amicus [*sic*]./ Omnia mea mecum porto.);[403] vernacular notes or glosses (imperio = *signoria*, Catone = *Censorino*,[404] itaque = *per la qual cosa*, ex quo = *per la qual cosa*,[405] *manza, la rason, la possanza, le zanze*[406]); glosses and notes referring to other standard works in the grammar-school curriculum[407] (v: Catholicon id est liber quidam ita dictus quia

[395] Caesar has been suggested as a pre-XVIc. school author, but without contemporary manuscript or other evidence, by Grendler ( ), . The manuscripts of his works in Florence reveal no school use; following codices examined and eliminated: BML . , . , . , . , . , . , . , . , . , . , . , . , . , inf. , sin. , Med. Fies. , CS , , , Ashb. ; BRF , , (XVc.: a few learned marginalia, but no school-type glossing); BNCF Landau Fin. ; BNCF Magl. . .

In view of the exiguous medieval commentary tradition (see Munk Olsen (–), , –), it is not surprising that Caesar was unused as a schoolbook before XVIc.: see Brown (a), – *passim*; Brown ( ), , – , *passim*. The principal XVc. commentated manuscript of Caesar seems to be BAV Reginensis lat. : see Brown (a), .

[396] ASF Carte Cerchi, , [ ] v, [ ] v; BRF , v.

[397] ASF Carte Cerchi, , [ ] v.

[398] BRF , v; see v: detur pro pena scriptori pulcra puella.

[399] BNCF Panciat. , v, r.

[400] ASF Carte Cerchi , [ ] v.

[401] BNCF Panciat. , r: see below, .

[402] BRF , v.

[403] BRF , v.

[404] BRF , r.

[405] BRF , v.

[406] BML Ashb. , v; see also BRF : arillus, -li est *lo vinaciuolo de l'uva* (v); talus, -li: *el dado grosso*, inde taxillus, -li: *el dado piccolo* (v); vulgare dictus parisitorum: id est *ghiotoncelli* (r).

[407] BML Ashb. .

universalis in tota gramatica, v: Secundum Uguzonem Secundum Papiam, r: Secundum K[a]tholicon et Magistrum Bene [da Firenze]); schoolboyish colophons (Finito libro isto frangamus ossa magistro);[408] simple Latin-vernacular vocabulary lists;[409] basic one-word equivalents of elementary vocabulary.[410]

In the fifteenth century, such copies of the shorter moral-philosophical treatises now abound, demonstrating the secure place which Cicero had regained in the curriculum.

ASF Carte Cerchi	*O*[411] *A S DT Orations*	A little interlinear paraphrase glossing at beginning of first two texts; school context clear from alphabets and *probationes* (< > v, < > v, < > v).
BML Ashb.	*S A P*	Work of two contemporary copyists, who shared annotation, including three *accessus* (r, r, r–v); interlinear glossses: often dense lexical paraphrases and one WOM (r); marginalia: usual paraphrase, explication, philology, definition; some citations of Vergil's *Aeneid*, Valerius Maximus, Cicero's *De o ciis*, Macrobius, Seneca, Aristotle, Quintilian.
BML Ashb.	*A S S S P*	The copyist provides, besides standard *accessus* to first text, sophisticated annotations with many Latin and some Greek authors cited; at the end of the manuscript, another writer provides typical school fare – Latin vocabulary notes/comments, citations of *Catholicon*, Hugutio, Papias, Bene da Firenze, some Latin–vernacular vocabulary equivalents (r– v).
BML Redi	*A S P*	Work of Lodovico, pupil of grammar teacher Giovanni da Roma;[412] glossed by the schoolboy copyist with usual mixture of interlinear lexicography and marginal philology; cites Sallust (r, v).[413]

[408] BRF , v.

[409] BML Ashb. , v: e.g. discedo, -dis, -ssi, -ssum: *per partirsi* [...] hec querela, -le: *la ramaricança*; hec mors, -tis: *la morte*; hec libitina, -ne: *la morte*; genitivo huius necis: *della morte* [...]

[410] BRF : see below, n. . [411] For these abbreviations, see x–xii, above.

[412] r: Explicit liber de amicitia M. T. Ciceronis intitulatus Lelius ad Aticum. Scriptum anno domini Eugenii MCCCCXXXIIII° per me Lodovicum de — [*deletum*]. r: M. T. C. Liber de senectute explicit. Ego Lodovicus scripsi amen. r: Exp[l]icit liber paradosse deo gratias. Ego Lodovicus scripsi. v: hoc opus est scritum dei gratia per me Lodovicum de — [*sic*] discipulus peritissimi Johannis de Roma vocatum [*sic*] gramatice peritissime doctum [*sic*]. Non solum hoc teneo sed omnes ydiomata tenent. Si tamen in hoc ero [*sic*], lectores mihi parcere quesso.

[413] No sign of other glossators in this MS, but by XVIc. it may have arrived in Tuscany, to judge from note (r) mentioning Micciano, name of two Tuscan villages (see Repetti (–), ,): A dì de dicenbre io Larione ivi a la pieve de Miciano, cch(e) dedi licenzia a Do. Jeronimo de Bagnaio, che ci missi Do(m). Bartolomeo de Signorello.

BML .	*A S P*	Little glossed; inclusion of traditional *accessus* to *De amicitia* (v– r), besides school-type ownership note,[414] followed by *sententiae*, suggests school context.
BML .	*A*	Usual simple lexical paraphrases by several contemporaneous hands; normal philological marginalia (structure, etymology, figures).
BNCF ..	*O*	Several di erent contemporaneous interlinear and philological (paraphrase) glossators.
BRF	*A S P*	Unglossed although obviously a schoolbook (anthology with minor authors).
BRF [415]	*A*	Two kinds of glossing: the first four folios, with hardly any interlinear annotation, receive sophisticated historical, philosophical, literary, rhetorical marginalia (including references to Cicero, Terence, Sallust, Boethius, Vergil, Seneca) clearly transcending normal school level; – , with intensive lexical interlinear glossing (including occasional vernacular) accompanying some simple philological marginalia (paraphrase, rhetorical colours), all typically schoolish.
BRF	*A*	Signed in school of Maestro Giovanni da Monte Ulmo in Marche by anonymous pupil from Mogliano, also in Marche; glossed with some brief rhetorical structural marginalia.
BRF	*O*	Usual interlinear lexical glosses by several contemporaneous hands (especially book); marginal annotations normal school-level philology and simple rhetoric, including brief references to *Rhetorica ad Herennium* (r) and Aristotle's *Ethics* (v).

414 r: Questo Tullio è di Tomaso di Barone di S(er?) Bartolomeo di Conte. <?>erai si llo renda et <?>llo troverà? renderà? una b(uo)na persona. Questo libro è di Tomaso. These notes are only partially legible under ultra-violet light. A *probatio* by same hand on inside front cover, alluding to the son of a prominent mid-century Florentine lawyer and statesman (Antonio di Messer Donato di Cocchi Ccocchi nostro amico), suggests Florentine provenance.

415 Subjected to a complicated process of collaboration, revision and reconstruction. The joint work of several writers, with the ultimate result that it consisted of four texts: *De amicitia*, *De senectute*, *Paradoxa stoicorum* and Bruni's translation of Basil's *Epistola*; physical restructuring of manuscript resulted in displacement of the original first folio of *Epistola* to the end of the original manuscript (r–v) and the recopying of that text's opening (r–v). Besides *De amicitia*, only the original beginning of *Epistola* (r–v) received any glossing, in that latter case a few simple interlinear paraphrase glosses in a couple of later XVc. hands possibly indicating the start of some school-level use, which, however, scarcely continued into rest of text (r). The incomplete text of *Rhetorica ad Herennium* (r– v) which finishes manuscript in present state was fortuitously added to the earlier book. The original final page of the manuscript (v) has XVc. *probationes pennae* typical of a schoolbook.

The above manuscripts are all datable to the first half of the Quattrocento, and the reading of Cicero's shorter moral treatises at the grammar-school level can be documented in the middle of the century too:

BML Ashb.	*A P*	Usual simple interlinear lexical glosses (r– v) together with a running guide to contents in margins; basic Latin-vernacular vocabulary list (v).[416]
BRF	*A*	Normal school-type commentary (paraphrase, definition, grammar, explication) (r– r).
BRF	*S A P*	Two contemporaneous glossators, including the copyist: usual mixture of interlinear lexical paraphrase/simple marginal philology (figures, etymology, geography, explication, Roman history, Roman institutions, grammar, rhetorical structure, mythology), besides a little vernacular (v, v); citations of Augustine's *City of God*, Valerius Maximus.
BRF	*O*	Three glossators: ( ) the copyist, with some philological marginalia (v, r, r, r, v, v); ( ) a later XVc. hand, with learned marginal commentary without interlinear glosses (r– r), referring to Plato, Didymus, Aristotle; ( ) possibly a school-level reader, who seems first to have copied the grammatical/philological commentary (citing a number of authors: see Appendix) in the margins of entire text and then gone back to begin adding elementary interlinear vocabulary equivalents, occupying only the first five folios (and r–v).
BRF	*O P S A*	Unglossed but clearly passed through schoolboy hands, to judge from *probationes* at end.
BRF	*S A P*	Unglossed, although passed through numerous school hands, to judge from the ownership marks/*probationes* (v– r, v– r, v, v).
BRF	*S A P SS*	Usual mixture of interlinear vocabulary (including the vernacular: r), besides occasional short marginalia (*notabilia*, paraphrase, figures).

416 Composite, with missing fascicles at end supplied by two hands writing not much later than the original copyist. First section contains several folios deriving from reused Italian parchment of an earlier poetic text, datable to later XIVc., probably itself a former schoolbook, to judge from remains of interlinear and marginal glosses.

BRF	*O*	Owned/glossed by Pietro Crinito,[417] with brief marginalia: *notabilia*, *sententiae*, occasional bits of philology (e.g. r: Romanum imperium potius patrocinium debebat nominari); may not relate to grammar teaching, but to an earlier school-level glossator with interlinear vocabulary glosses throughout, besides one simple philological marginalium, citing Isidore's *Etymologies* (r).

A number of school-type manuscripts containing Cicero's shorter moral treatises are datable to the second half of the Quattrocento:

BML Ashb.	*O*	Mixture of interlinear vocabulary paraphrases and quotations from authors (see Appendix), giving impression of pupil's collecting *sententiae*.[418]
BNCF Panciat. (r– r)	*A*	Explicit school context: (v) 'io sono andato a Pissa allo studio di <...>', while another hand wrote 'scolares <...>' below. Glosses to *De amicitia*: usual simple interlinear vocabulary equivalents/marginal philology, including marginal note, where pupil explicitly refers to his master's teaching.[419]
BRF	*O*	*De o ciis* has *accessus*, here anonymous, with life of Cicero.[420] This is Gasparino Barzizza's *praelectio* to *De o ciis*;[421] text hardly glossed but its proximity to Barzizza's explicitly pedagogic introduction may suggest intended school use which never took place.
BRF	*S A P*	Certainly passed into school hands XVI^1, to judge from ownership notes and *probationes*, including alphabet (r–v); no significant interlinear glossing, but simple philological/grammatical marginalia to *De amicitia*, including citation of Lucan (r), seem to suggest school-level reading.

417 Front flyleaf recto: Hic liber est mei Petri Criniti; rear flyleaf verso: Hic liber est mei Petri. See De Robertis and Miriello ( ), .

418 These particular glosses (r– v) are late, possibly dating from early Cinquecento.

419 r: Nota quod quando Scevola gravem sermonem cum gravi homine habuisset, tunc ineptum fuisset Tulio voluisse habere sermone<m> cum eo. Ideo dicit *et liceret*. Alii dicunt quod vult dicere numquam stetisse turpiter cum eo, quod tamen magister meus non sensit.

420 For incipit and explicit, see Appendix , n. .

421 On this text, see Pigman ( ), – ; Fera ( ), – .

BRF	*O*	Glossed in school manner, with interlinear vocabulary glosses and fairly regular marginalia; later passed into hands of Florentine lawyer and bureaucrat, Silvestro Aldobrandini (–),[422] who provided some philological glosses (r, r, r, r, v, v) besides notes on relatives/metric feet (v– r) possibly related to secondary grammatical study.
BRF	*SPASS*	v, v with su cient interlinear glossing to indicate possible school use of third text.
BRF	*SSSAP*	*Somnium/Paradoxa* provided with *notabilia* only; *De amicitia*, learned commentary, not accompanied by interlinear glossing, citing Gellius, Aristotle, Plutarch, younger Pliny, Cicero, Sallust, clearly transcending school level. *De senectute* annotated by the copyist (Florentine Bernardo d'Ambra) with simple interlinear vocabulary paraphrases, grammatical/philological marginalia (derivations, etymologies, definitions, simple rhetorical analysis, explication). Bernardo could not have been a schoolboy when glossing this text but there is possibly some kind of school context here, as glosses have didactic quality, with citations of Cicero's letters, Vergil, *De o ciis* (r).

There is a small amount of evidence that occasionally other Ciceronian texts were read at grammar schools in the fifteenth century, although their use constituted no more than a fraction of the interest devoted to the shorter moral treatises. One example was made known by Sabbadini, who found that Barzizza's emendations of ***De oratore*** were recorded in annotations to a manuscript of the text (BRF) by one of his pupils.[423] In fact, the annotations to the text referring to Barzizza were shared between the copyist and another glossator, both writing in the earlier fifteenth century and both making constant further references to their teacher: dixit Magister Guasper (v); secundum Guasparem sic exponentem (r); Guaspar (v); hic assignatur secundus liber secundum Magistrum Gasparinum (r); Gaspar (r). In view of these continual indications, it seems fair to assume that the entire commentary, as recorded by these two glossators, reflects Barzizza's teaching of *De oratore*, although there is a reference to another teacher at the

[422] r: Silvestri Aldobrandini et amicorum. See *DBI*, , – .

[423] r: Sed Gasparinus non putat esse Ciceronis [...] (r) Hoc supplet Gasparinus. Non tamen, ut proprio ex ore audivi [...] See Sabbadini ( ), . See Bandini (–), . – .

beginning of the manuscript's text of *Orator*.[424] Besides emendations and corrections to the text, the commentary provided citations of Valerius Maximus, Martianus Capella, Ovid and Cicero himself; the opening folios o er an analysis of the text's rhetorical structure, including the usual commonplaces of the *exordium*, and then the commentary moves on to paraphrase, explication, argumentative structure and philological explanation. The teaching does not seem to have always been at the exalted level of humanist textual emendation: at one point there is a reference to boys playing at odds and evens and to a race track near Rome.[425] One other manuscript, datable to the second half of the century and showing possible school-level reading of *De oratore* (BRF), has two commentators: the first (r– r, r), whose interlinear glosses are not simple synonyms but rather expand and expound the text and whose marginalia demonstrate wider philosophical interests as well as a knowledge of Greek, is obviously not working in a grammar-school context; the second (r– v), on the other hand, o ers simple interlinear lexical equivalents and basic marginal philology (explication, definition, grammar, history) typical of the classroom. There are also two manuscripts of ***Disputationes tusculanae*** which show possible grammar-school use in the fifteenth century. One, datable to the first half of the century (BRF) and glossed by several Quattrocento hands, o ers the usual school mixture of interlinear synonyms and philological marginalia (explication, paraphrase, definition, grammar, mythology), including one instance of the vernacular (v) and brief references to Varro, Valerius Maximus, Ovid, Cicero's oration *Pro Archia*, Pompeius Festus, Donatus and Servius. The other manuscript of the *Tusculan Disputations*, also datable to the first half of the century (BRF), is glossed by two readers at di erent levels: the first, contemporaneous with the copyist, seems to be a scholastically educated ecclesiastic who rails against contemporary morals and preaching, besides criticizing Cicero for his poor knowledge of Aristotle (r) and making references to the New Testament (v, r); the second commentator, working later in the century, provides copious interlinear vocabulary paraphrases (unlike the first glossator) and typically school-level marginal philology (simple rhetorical analysis, paraphrase, literary identification), besides adding a few Greek words (e.g. v). Another Ciceronian text, ***De finibus bonorum et malorum*** (together with the fragmentary ***Academics***), is found in a manuscript datable to the second half of the century and written in the school of the

424 v: Hic deficit principium tercii libri, ita continetur in illo Magistri Petri.
425 r: Ludebant cum illis lapillis sicut pueri *a par e chaf e a le Chapanelle.*

humanist Ognibene de' Bonisoli, probably in Vicenza (BML .),[426] although there was no actual sign of school reading in terms of interlinear glossing.[427] Finally, there are three manuscripts which show some possible school activity with Ciceronian orations in the fifteenth century. One is a manuscript of *De imperio Cn. Pompei*, datable between September and April , with a few interlinear paraphrase glosses and rhetorical marginalia (BRF). Another is a miscellany assembled by Nicodemo da Potremoli (BRF) and containing various orations, *Paradoxa Stoicorum* and *De amicitia*. The first oration against Catiline (r– v) includes a standard *accessus* (r), a few philological marginalia (definition, figures) and a handful of interlinear glosses, including a couple of vocabulary equivalents; the second *Catilinaria* (v– r) has a tiny amount of structural analysis (v) and one indication of a figure (r); the oration *In Vatinium* (r– v) has a few interlinear glosses, not usually giving simple vocabulary equivalents, while the few marginalia indicate figures and structure. Apart from the *accessus*, all this hardly suggests much school use for these orations, but the same is not true of two more traditional school texts: *Paradoxa* (v– v) has extensive interlinear glossing especially to the first half of the text (v– v) and marginalia indicating rhetorical structure; *De amicitia* (v– r) has similar interlinear annotations and philological marginalia (paraphrase, explication, Roman customs, history) as well as references to Valerius Maximus, Lucan, Boethius's *Consolation*, pseudo-Aristotle's *De pomo*, Eutropius and Seneca's letters to Lucilius. Moreover, there is one gloss which seems to reflect direct teaching.[428] This manuscript suggests that the teaching of Cicero was facilitated by the use of the traditional pedagogic texts, and the same conclusion is born out by a third school manuscript, datable to the middle of the century (BRF), containing Ciceronian and pseudo-Ciceronian orations (r– r) and Buonaccorso da Montemagno's *De nobilitate* (r– r), all unglossed, followed by a commentated version of Cicero's *De imperio Cn. Pompeii*, which is preceded by an *accessus* (r– v); at the end of the manuscript another contemporaneous hand wrote the beginning of Vitalis of Blois's *Geta et Birria*. This commentary was the work of a teacher, Antonio da Rena, as is clear from a note preceding the traditional *accessus*.[429] The

426 r: Absolvit Stephanus Borictius Omnibono schole.

427 One philological marginal comment, not written by the copyist (v).

428 v: Lelius premicit quid ipse sentiat de amicicia et quantum verbis venerabilibus commendet eam mente vostra diligenter considerate.

429 r: Contio edita per eloquentissimum virum Dominum Antonium de Arena, principem huius etatis preceptorum.

marginal commentary is of the usual school type, focusing on rhetorical structure, paraphrase, figures and explication, as well as citing Orosius, the younger Pliny and Livy, but it was clearly copied though not actually used by a pupil, given that there are no interlinear glosses throughout the entire text except once to give an alternative reading.

This is in fact a particularly interesting manuscript, further suggesting the hybrid character of humanist teaching in the fifteenth century. On the one hand, there was the avant-garde inclusion into the curriculum of Cicero's *De imperio*, a work which had never featured in the medieval syllabus; on the other, this same manuscript ends with an unglossed fragment of a minor author, Vitalis of Blois's *Geta* (v–   r), a work which was one of the stand-bys of the later medieval curriculum. The reintroduction of Cicero into the grammar schoolroom was a great achievement for fifteenth-century teachers, but it is clear that they found it more congenial and practicable to concentrate on texts which had once formed part of the medieval curriculum, albeit disused since the beginning of the Duecento; moreover, the teaching of Cicero, even his most avant-garde works, could take place in remarkably traditional contexts.

The late fifteenth century and the triumph of humanism

Of course, the introduction of printing during the last three decades of the Quattrocento had a great impact on the production of schoolbooks. It was not merely texts of an elementary reading and Latin manual such as *Ianua* and secondary grammars by Guarino and Perotti which were produced, as has already been seen, in large numbers by printers for the school market; copies of the Roman classics were obviously turned out in high quantity partly to satisfy the demands of teachers and pupils. In that sense, comparing the numbers of school manuscripts from the later with those from the earlier fifteenth century would be misleading, without making considerable qualitative allowance for the increasing numbers of printed schoolbooks in production and circulation towards the end of the century.

A move to put aside traditional features of the curriculum in the later fifteenth century, nevertheless, is clear in the case of Boethius's *Consolation*, a work whose popularity as a schoolbook was far from static in later medieval and Renaissance Italy. The following is a table showing the Florentine manuscripts according to date of copying:

Total manuscripts (counting each part of a composite as one item)
Manuscripts datable up to end of XIIc.
Manuscripts datable to XIIIc., XIII/XVc.
Manuscripts datable to XIVc., XIV/XVc.
Manuscripts datable to XV ¼–²⁄₄
Manuscripts datable to XVmid
Manuscripts datable after XVmid

In fact, of the five codices from the twelfth century or earlier, two are certainly not Italian and two others probably not; this data therefore suggests that Boethius was hardly used as an Italian schoolbook before the thirteenth century. After a slow start in the Duecento,[430] the text reached the climax of its favour in the schoolroom in the fourteenth century, maintaining a considerable presence still in the early fifteenth century, but then rapidly disappearing from use in the second half of the Quattrocento. The disappearance of the *Consolation* from the Italian schoolroom in the second half of the fifteenth century, as suggested by manuscript copies, is confirmed by its early printing history in Italy. There were only eight Italian,[431] as compared with fifty-six transalpine,[432] incunabular editions of the text. The copies of these Italian editions in Bodley and in the British Library show almost no possible school use in Italy.[433]

In fact, it seems to have been humanist censorship which removed Boethius from the curriculum. It has been seen above ( ) that Bartolomeo Fonzio used the *Consolation* in his Latin teaching. Nevertheless, he was already discontented with the pedagogic style adopted by his non-humanist predecessors and contemporaries. While the latter were content to repeat formulaic and inelegant summaries, sometimes derived from scholastic commentators such as Nicholas Trevet, Fonzio now composed his summaries afresh in humanist Latin, making heavy use of such classical stylistic features as indirect speech; he also abandoned the scholastic *divisiones textus* which had previously

[430] Dante's well-known reference to Boethius's *Consolation* as 'quello non conosciuto da molti libro di Boezio' in *Convivio* (, xii,), dating from the beginning of the Trecento, perhaps reflects limited Italian readership of text before XIVc.; alternatively, Dante could be referring to the lack of philosophical/theological understanding of the work in hands of Italian grammarians. Given all the evidence of Boethius's intensive use in Italian grammar schools in later middle ages, Dante's remark cannot be cited as evidence for limited penetration of *Consolation* into XIV/XVc. Italian culture.

[431] *GW* (*IGI*), (*IGI*), , (*IGI*), (*IGI*), (*IGI*), (*IGI*), (*IGI*). [432] *GW* , , – , – , – .

[433] See Black and Pomaro ( ), – .

characterized these exegetic summaries.[434] And yet, the chronology of the Florentine Boethius manuscripts, mentioned above, makes it clear that such adaptions as Fonzio had undertaken were insu cient to satisfy later generations of humanist teachers.

Not quite so dramatic, but still striking, was the eclipse of the minor authors in the second half of the fifteenth century. It has been seen that these traditional school texts were remarkably resilient in the first half of the Quattrocento, but during the second half of the century they undeniably went into decline.

Text	XV[1]	XVmid	XV[2]
Prosper of Aquitaine, *Epigrammata*			
Aesop, *Fabulae*			
Henry of Settimello, *Elegia*			
Prudentius, *Dittochaeon*			
Ilias latina			
Avianus, *Fabulae*			
Physiologus			
Pseudo-Ovid, *De lumaca*			
Vitalis of Blois, *Geta*			
Cartula			
Disticha Catonis			
Theodulus, *Ecloga*			
Prudentius, *Psychomachia*			
Bovesin da la Riva, *Vita scolastica*			
Pseudo-Boethius, *De disciplina scolarium*			
Richard of Venosa, *De nuptiis Paulini et Pollae*			
Pseudo-Jerome, *De contemptu mulierum*			
Facetus			
Doctrina rudium			

434 Black and Pomaro ( ), – .

Text	XV[1]	XVmid	XV[2]
Liber cerdonis			
Maximianus, *De senectute*			
Proba, *Centones virgiliani*			
Salutati, *Elegia*			
Salutati, *Fabula*			
Bernard of Clairvaux, *Epistola de re familiari*			
Martin of Braga, *Formula honestae vitae*			
John the Abbot, *Liber de septem viciis et septem virtutibus*			
Total number of individual texts			

These figures are consonant with the well-known fact that the standard anthology of the minor authors, the 'auctores octo', appeared only in thirty French incunabular editions.[435] It is clear that, as with Boethius's *Consolation*, the polemics of the Quattrocento humanists were having their e ects in Italy.[436]

Conclusion

The fifteenth century presents a complex picture of tradition and innovation in the study of Latin literature in the Italian schoolroom. Manuscript evidence suggests that the minor authors continued to thrive throughout the first half of the century; Boethius too remained heavily studied at least until the mid-Quattrocento. Classical Latin authors who had been staples of the Trecento curriculum such as Statius and Valerius Maximus continued in full use throughout the Quattrocento. On the other hand, there were strong forces of innovation as well. Authors not widely read at school in the fourteenth century, such as Persius, Terence, Juvenal and Sallust, now became curriculum heavyweights. To some extent, the fifteenth-century Renaissance in the schoolroom, as far as the Latin classics are concerned, represented a return to the twelfth-century Renaissance, when authors such as Juvenal and Sallust had been

[435] Goldschmidt ( ), ; Billanovich ( ), , n. ; Garin ( ), , n. .

[436] On these polemics in general, see Garin ( ), – ; Avesani ( ), ; pseudo-Boethius ( ), – .

curriculum luminaries. And yet the story was still more complex. In the fifteenth century, Vergil and especially Cicero assumed a preeminence in the syllabus such as they had never before enjoyed. New works, such as Ovid's *Heroides* and Horace's *Carmina*, previously little read in the classroom, achieved a sudden popularity.[437] There was also an important negative side to the Quattrocento renaissance of authors. A late Latin writer such as Boethius came under humanist censorship in the second half of the century, as did the traditional minor school authors. Moreover, there was also a significant disenchantment with many time-honoured curriculum stalwarts, a number of whom had been added to the syllabus in the Trecento: Seneca's *Tragedies*, Horace's *Ars poetica* and *Epistulae* and Lucan all su ered under the new Quattrocento broom. What is misleading is the attempt to place these significant fifteenth-century changes on a level of greater significance than any innovations which had occurred in the middle ages: in many ways, the rejection of the authors in the wake of thirteenth-century scholasticism, and their sudden return to the fore in the Trecento were more radical educational transformations. Moreover, it would be misleading to see the fifteenth-century Renaissance simply as a rejection of medievalism in favour of purer classicism. While humanist teachers did eventually purge the syllabus of late Latin texts such as Boethius's *Consolation* and the minor authors, they were also unenthusiastic about solid classical texts such as Seneca's *Tragedies*, Lucan's *Pharsalia* and Horace's *Ars poetica* and *Epistulae.* The fifteenth-century renaissance of school authors is perhaps better described as a major change of educational fashion rather than as a 'revolution in the schoolroom'.

[437] An interesting summary of authors read at Sarzana in is given by the grammar teacher there, Giovanni Meduseo, claiming that he had 'letto e leze le tre opere de Virgilio, Ovidio de le done chiamate de le epistole heroe, Sodulio, tulio de o cii, Cato et altre belle opere [...]': Mannucci ( ), . Another for Bellinzona in consisted of 'Salustio, Boetio, Ovidio, Apostolorum vita, Scolastica, Prospero, Esopo, Eva Columba, Terentio, Doctrinali Soma': Chiesi ( ), – . (The transcription of this list seems philologically incorrect; it possibly should read: 'Salustio, Boetio, Ovidio Epistolarum, Vita scolastica [...] Doctrinali, Soma'.) A third mentioning authors typically taught in XV^2 is found in a model letter written by the Piedmontese Augustinian, Gabriele Bucci da Carmagnola (*c.* –), as a guide to a teacher seeking employment: these included Aesop, *Doctrinale*, Terence, Juvenal, Ovid, Vergil, Boethius, Cicero (Nada Patrone ( ),). Such documentary material substantiates the hybrid picture of Quattrocento school authors disclosed by the present census.

Reading Latin authors in medieval and Renaissance Italian schools

In the preceding three chapters, this book's approach has been chronological, reflecting the significant developments in elementary and secondary education occurring in Italian schools from the twelfth to the fifteenth century. In this chapter, on the other hand, the treatment will be topical: the fact is that methods of reading and using school authors hardly changed over this long period. Simple philology (e.g. paraphrase, grammar, figures, word-order, geography, history, mythology, elementary rhetorical analysis) remained pupils' habitual fare. Even the use of the vernacular as an aid for learning Latin, after its introduction into Italian education during the Duecento, showed little significant development in succeeding centuries. Only in one or two marginal areas (for example, the new preoccupation with verse analysis in the fifteenth century) was there any sign of innovation in the approach to the authors.

Another important feature of school reading throughout this period is the overwhelming dominance of basic philology. Morals and philosophy make an occasional appearance, but invariably such comments are lost in an immense ocean of philological minutiae. There was no new preoccupation with the nitty-gritty of philology in the Italian Renaissance classroom: this had been the staple fare of medieval schools too.

:

The role of the vernacular

Although often well advanced in Latin, pupils reading the authors in the grammar schoolroom still glossed their texts in the vernacular, as is evident from a number of manuscripts signed by pupils in schools. One example is Giovanni di Antonio di Jacopo da Gambassi in the Valdelsa, whose version in (BML sup.) of the 'expositio' (r) by

Maestro Antonio di Ser Salvo da San Gimignano included vernacular equivalents of Latin vocabulary.[1] Among the twelve manuscripts of Boethius's *Consolation* found in Florentine libraries and signed by pupils, eleven contain vernacular glossing.[2] Most of the vernacular annotations in these Boethius manuscripts consist of simple vocabulary equivalents, but one glossator went further. In this mid fourteenth-century manuscript of Boethius's *Consolation* (BRF), a fifteenth-century glossator wrote entire explanatory phrases in Italian, most of the time between the lines but sometimes in the margins too.[3] Among signed schoolbooks from the fourteenth and fifteenth centuries, the most extensive vernacular annotation comes from the school of Mattia Lupi of San Gimignano while teaching in Prato. This copy of Claudian's *De raptu Proserpinae*, completed by his pupil Bartolomeo di Giovanni on November ,[4] gives many such glosses in Bartolomeo's hand in a mixture of Latin and Italian,[5] or in one or the other.[6]

Glosses such as those made in Mattia Lupi's classroom (mainly paraphrase, translation, geography and mythology) suggest a popular, low level of teaching, and it seems that, in studying the authors, teachers tended to resort to Italian when they were trying to explicate less advanced material. Thus, one generally finds the most copious vernacular glossing in manuscripts of the *auctores minores*.[7] There are also early examples.[8] The oldest instance of interlinear vernacular glossing in the present survey is found in a schoolboy copy of *Ilias latina*, datable to the

1 v: *schiere* vel sotietates equitum; r: attonita = *isbigottita*; v: mora = *indugio*. See v, r, r, v, r, r, v. Other examples of signed schoolbooks with vernacular glossses: BRF : cur = *perché*, preconem = *banditore*, tunicato = *toppato*, inique = *a malvagie*, vicus = *chiasso*, texta = *tessuta* (v, v, r, r, r, r); BML . : ch. , n. above; BML . , v, r: *nachosta, le risposste, con Cesere*; BML . , v: testa = *intessuta*; BRF , r: *ismostrare, ricordevole.*

2 Black and Pomaro ( ), – , , , , , – , – , , , – , , , , .

3 Black and Pomaro ( ), .

4 BML . , v: Ego Bartholomeus Iohannis scripxi hunc librum pro me quando morabar in iscolis Magistri Mathie de Sancto Geminiano castro comitatus Florentie, electi ad legendum gramaticam Prati, die duodecimo menssis novembris millesimo quadringenteximo tertio, amen, vel quarto secundum ordinem Pistoriensium.

5 r: for text, see Black (b), .

6 r: for text, see Black (b), . For extensive vernacular vocabulary glossing, both interlinear and marginal, in signed school copy from Bergamo of Theodulus and Bonvesin, dated and respectively, see Contini ( ), – .

7 BML sup. : r: data est = *si è data*, ut = *acciò*, v: obstrusa = *itorniata*; BRF , v: cura = *pensiero*; BML AD , e.g. v: succumberet = *socto entrasse*; BRF , v: *negli schogli*; BML sup. , r: orat = *pregia*, nata = *figuola*, heret = *agosta*, contemptus = *spregiato*; ibid. r: dimictere = *lasciate*, amissos = *perducti* (see v, r, v, v, r, r).

8 BML Magl. . , r: ingemit = *si duole*, lira = *e'liuto*; v: pluma = *piuma*, assidue = *crudele*, extinto = *amortuo*, plorato = *pangerò* (see r, v, r, v, v, v). BNCF Magl . , v: Hic macies maciei id est *magrezza*; r: tipicus = *figurato*, fugabis = *lacerai*, reprimit = *dicacia* (see r, v, v, r).

first half of the thirteenth century (BRF .), in which there are vernacular interlinear vocabulary equivalents of southern Italian provenance by the copyist.[9] This practice also went on outside Tuscany.[10] This method of annotating the minor authors continued to be practised widely in the fifteenth century,[11] sometimes almost every word being given a *volgare* equivalent:

anodato *il dosso* *diè* *tergum* *del servo* *alle batteture*
Annexus tergum dedit ut servile flagellus
perfecte stat *ancora* *el tempio* pro et *porta* ipsam rem *da essere honorata* *la colonna*
Perstat adhuc templumque rege(re) veneranda coluna
a noi pro et *si confa* *di tucte* *sanza parte* *vivere* *le bacteture*
Nosque decet cuntis imuens vivere fragris.[12]

El fiore e'l fructo si aquistano al favore risprende.
Flos et fructus emunt<ur>, hic nitet, ille sapit;
El fructo, si piace a te più che'l fiore, o tu, ekogh', e'l fiore
Si fructus plus flore placet fructum lege. Si flos [. . .][13]

It was not just signed schoolbooks which reveal vernacular glossing to Boethius's *Consolation.*[14] Out of the Boethius schoolbooks in Florence [15] contain vernacular glosses,[16] and of the manuscripts have several di erent commentators who have left glosses in the *volgare.*[17] Indeed, a number of glossators wrote extensive vernacular glosses extending beyond the space between the lines of text and into the margins.[18]

9 E.g. r: iniecit = *gettao*, orco = *allo'nferno*, bello = *per vattalia*, clarus = *novele*, implicitus = *legatu*, flevit = *planse*, auras = *le ventora*; v: dilaceratque comas = *scarsciavase le capellature*, tutus = *securu*; r: miseranda = *misericordevole*, cubile = *iacementu*, danaos = *li greci*, vulgus = *populaççu*, graium = *de li greci*, ager = *le carvonara*, sidera = *le stelle*, patefecerat = *avea manifestata*, proceres = *li prencipi*, invenit = *t(r)ovao*; v: pio reddit = *a lu pietosu*, devexit = *retornao*, protinus = *vivaccamente*, ferus = *lu crudele*, minis = *menacce*, inultum = non *vindicatu*, deserit = *avere laxate*; r: labor = *fatiga*, refers = *arrapporta*; v: decedit = *dao locu*, olimpo = *celu*, quietis = *reposu*. I am grateful to Teresa De Robertis for first referring me to this manuscript.

10 Venetian: BRF : *non vodaria* (r), and exigere = *reschodere* (v). Emilian: BML Strozzi , e.g. v: coma = *ramuscula.*

11 E.g. BRF : v: opulentia = *abondantia*, fractis = *rotte*, artat = *stringne*, exitus = *el fine*, BRF : r: gemina = *doppia*; v: sus = *el porco*, stolido = *paçço*; v: otia = *quieta* (see v, r).

12 BRF , r. 13 BRF , v.

14 Black and Pomaro ( ), –, –, , , , –, –, , –, .

15 Black and Pomaro ( ), –, –, –, , –, –, , , , –, , , , , –, –, , , –, , , –, , , , –, –, –, –, , –, –, , – . The only Florentine Boethius school manuscripts without vernacular glossing (BNCF Magl. . ; BRF ,) are almost entirely unglossed.

16 For vernacular glosses in Bodley manuscripts of *Consolation*, see Black and Pomaro ( ), , n. .

17 Black and Pomaro ( ), –, –, –, , –, –, , , , , –, – *passim*, –, , , –, –, –, , , , , –, , – .

18 Black and Pomaro ( ), , , , .

On the whole, minor and major authors were not collected together in anthologies, a pattern reflecting the di ering stages of the curriculum which they represented. Nevertheless, occasionally both classes of authors were included in anthologies, and it seems that pupils and teachers sometimes carried on the same form of glossing, including interlinear vernacular vocabulary notes, across this division of Latin school literature.[19] An anthology, including Statius's *Achilleidos*, *Ilias latina*, Claudian's *De raptu Proserpinae* and Alain de Lille's *Anticlaudianus* and dated (BML sup.), has extended vernacular marginal glosses to both Statius and *Ilias latina*.[20] Of the major authors, the poets were favoured in the study of grammar, but when studied at a more advanced

19 BML, Strozzi : *a meçina* (r), *purché* (v), *iocosa* (r), *pacifichi* (r), *mescolato, nella polpora* (v) (see r, v, r, v, r, v, r, v, r, v, v, r, r, r, r, v, v, v, r, r, v, r, v, r, v). BRF , r: *per logorare* (see v– v).

20 This type of vernacular marginal annotation is unusual in schoolbooks and in manuscripts of the Latin classics in general. A rare similar example is in a Lucan (BML .), glossed at nearly the same time, not in Umbria but in Liguria/Lombardy: see below, . In both cases, the comments are of a personal nature and do not reflect classroom context, although both were possibly written by teachers, to judge from their other glosses. Substantial vernacular marginal interventions with contents of more normal school type are found in a Claudian (BML . : see above,), while in a Boethius datable to XIVmid (BML dxt.) the principal glossator, almost certainly a teacher, added vernacular translations of the text and of William of Conches's commentary in margins (Black and Pomaro ( ), –).

In BML sup. , the glosses were written by the anonymous copyist, while working in Foligno in great poverty, so he declared in the colophon to Claudian, begging and thanking his friend Domenico di Duccio (also called Ocro), for liquid refreshment: see Bandini (–), . , where colophon and accompanying notes with this information are fully published. The vernacular glosses seem sometimes to reflect this glossator's distraught (and lascivious) mental state:

v [to *Achilleis* . –]: *Me é! Questa Deydamia aveva altra calda che di sole!*

r [to *Achilleis* .]: *Euchia.* Sunt instrumenta rotunda et intus sunt corde extense [...] et [...] mirabilem sonum reddunt. *Dediciamo [= Deduciamo] che sia tamburo. Bene era dolce melodia danzaresca a vergini regali.*

r [to *Achilleis* .]: Sic iste virgines Licomedis habent quandoque talem modum corizandi qualiter Lacene. Ille domine de Lacena solebant habere in cultura Diane, et quas mulieres plaudendos [*sic pro* plaudentes] inducit *Amyclis* id est suis civitatibus vel insulis. *A me pare che tutte le femine ballino e chiavino a uno modo, ma queste vergini non cantavano, elle no'. Che gente nulora dovevano essere a quel tempo!*

r [to *Achilleis* .]: Acchilles cum tubam audivit propter belli cupiditatem mulierum vestes decicit [...] *Intacte* id est valde tacte, quia lacerate per Achillem, vel *intacte* id est sine ullo tactu manuum, id est nullius manus appositione, sed quia laxaverat ideo ceciderunt. *Bene vestivano all'anticha*; ergo nudus remansit et sic manifestavit membrum genitale.

v [to *Achilleis* .]: *Adio bella hoste! Aspecta el torbo!*

v [to *Ilias latina* Interea toto Menelaus in agmine Trouum / querit Alexandrum ...]: *Così ci fussi stato io a 'fogaggine che non mi chiamarò.*

r: *E assai bella vendetta n'à fatta.*

The vernacular glosses here were noticed and partially published by de Angelis ( ), , n. ; on r above for 'nulora' she reads 'milota', but I have been unable to find a meaning for this latter word.

stage in the curriculum, they received less vernacular glossing than the minor authors.[21]

Nevertheless, some examples of vernacular annotations to the major poets can be found.[22] Apart from the schoolbook of Claudian from Mattia Lupi's school mentioned above,[23] the most extensive vernacular glossing to a classical poet is made on a Lucan, from the second half of the fourteenth century.[24] Here, the vernacular extends into the marginal commentary.[25] The oldest set of glosses in the *volgare* to a school major poet in the Florentine collections seems to be a twelfth-century Lucan (BML .), which has an extensive series of Duecento vernacular glosses.[26]

21 BML . : r: *dal greppetto.* BNCF Conv. Soppr. J. . : r: pannosa = *repezziata.* BML sup. : v: aspiret = *favoreggi,* solerti = *usato*; r: scapulas = *spalle,* strattus = *abattuto,* immixtus = *mesticate,* prosternit = *abatte,* phalanges = *le brigate*; v: macie = *per magrezza,* v: mostrum = *cosa maravilgliosa*; r: callidus = *malitioso*; r: labenti = *trascorsa*; v: clam = *nascose,* scissim = *spartitamente*; v: situ = *la stança*; r: ebur = *l'avorio*; v: texti = *del texuto*; r: liram = *liuto*; r: plectra = *liuto*; r: totam = *l'antrata.* BRF : r: *tolta*; v: coherce = *constrigne.*

22 BML . , v: vehemens = *frectoloso,* v: delirare = *sciocheggiare.* BNCF Landau Fin. : r: plerumque = *spesse volte,* purpureus = *di porpora, insieme seco sta, lo bosco,* ara Diane = *l'autare di Diana,* cur urceus exit = *perché lo vagello n'esce* (see r). BML . , v: *el dauno*; r: *il segno.* BRF , v: ceromatica = *unguentato.* BML sin. , r: flexit = *piegò*; v: pandit = *manifesta*; v: plebeia = *popolaçço*; v: clepit = *difende*; r: posteritas = *antichità.* BML . , r: *precetta*; v: *esca, della biada*; v: *così à parlato*; r: *schiatta.* BML . , r: *piegato, intorno al manico dello orciuolo.* BML Strozzi , r: tonsae = *fronzute.* BML . , r: *schogli.* BML Rinuccini : v: *à superato, un fiume*; r: *razza*; v: *prestamente passiamo.* BML . , r: Dicens sic: *Ella mi perdonarà bene, ma io non gittarò l'ossa de mia madre* etcet. r: hic oppidarius. *el castellano*; v: *da l'orscello, dal capeçale.* BML S. Marco , see r, r. BML S. Marco , v: humili cana = *la gelada*; r: *tanto.* BML CS , r: per ora = *per facia, pietre preciose,* crinis = *i capelli*; v: sydus = *stella*; v: prisco = *antico.*

23 BML . . 24 BML . .

25 r: *trombe, trombete, nacharete, corne e sinoleti*; v: *li fano cavaleri de novo como se Hanibal dovesse passar in Italia*; r: *a cavali magri va le mosche*; v: *volea sempre che la cossa andasse a brodeto*; r: vacillationes in undas, *vulgariter andava spesso a la banda*; v: vulgariter in lingua ianuensi: *scia, scia*; v: *li averiano bem bevudo de la vernaça de brancha da cornigia o d'um roçcese da Monterosso. Ancora credo che li averiano asagiato d'um vim de le cantine da Siena e del vim de Bergogna e de quel da San Porsan. Chi avesse fato una taverna a du bianchi o du agontani per petita e per foglieta o quatro soldi per bozzola o cinque soldini per grossa del vim trebiano su la Piaza de San Marco*; r: *La disperatione fa meter molti a l'ultimo pericolo, cotesto è vero, ma tu chi già tosto serai signor del mondo, meterti a l'aventura del mare, fai begli biene*; r: *como la canzone del Conte d'Armignach per Messer Iacomo dal Verme.* This reference to the defeat of the Florentine mercenary Jean d'Armagnac by Iacopo dal Verme at the battle of Alessandria in places the date of glossing shortly afterwards. The glossator seems to be an anti-Florentine, either from Liguria or Lombardy; see also below n. .

Some of these vernacular glosses seem to be textual translations or paraphrases: e.g.:

r: *Pensate chi sia pigro come voi a morte dare e ricevere.*	. : an similem vestri segnemque ad fata putastis?
Fare più cosse per morire che voi non fareste per difender Pompeio e' senatori.	. – : Pompei vobis minor est causaeque senatus/quam mihi mortis amor.
r: *Li cativi pigliano sempre la pegior parte*	. : degeneres trepidant animi peioraque versant.

26 This MS had some rudimentary school use during the thirteenth century, possibly in Tuscany, when several immature hands provided vernacular interlinear glossing (besides word-order

Before the fourteenth century, the principal classical prose writer for grammar pupils was Sallust. One important school manuscript of Sallust dates from the first half of the mid-thirteenth century (BML Ashb.), the glossing by the copyist of *mare nostrum* as *pisani maris* (r) and *nostro mari* as *pisano* (v) suggesting a provenance in western Tuscany. The copyist's crude writing is redolent of a vernacular, lay ambience, suggesting possibly a secular grammar pupil in the earlier thirteenth century. Accordingly, there is a great deal of vernacular vocabulary glossing.[27] Outside Tuscany before the fifteenth century another important manuscript,[28] dating from the twelfth century, has school-type glosses of all periods up to the early fifteenth century. This manuscript, which has some Venetian vernacular verses written on the rear flyleaf (v), may or may not be of Venetian provenance, because it is not clear when or how this flyleaf was added; similarly, the occasional vernacular glosses (e.g. v: *virtuoso*) are not clearly localized.

The other significant classical prose-writer in the medieval Italian classroom was Cicero. Most of the school-type glossing that occurred on Cicero in the twelfth or early thirteenth centuries was exclusively in Latin, but there is one important exception. This is an Italian manuscript of *De amicitia*, dating from the turn of the thirteenth century and glossed by the hand of the copyist,[29] a school-type reader, who included a considerable quantity of interlinear Italian of southern provenance.[30] Cicero's return to the classroom at the turn of the fifteenth century was accompanied by a small amount of vernacular glossing, although this

footnote (*cont.*) marks): v: veritus = *temuto*, WOM; v: conceptos = *adunati*; r ianitor = *portararo*; r: inmunem = *senza dono*; v: possessor = *posseditore*, rogum = *fuoco*, strue = *ordinamento*; r: decepit = *gannao*, e giem = *figura*, diurna = *contemporale*, funestas = *mortale*; v: WOM, simillima = *molto semiliata*, erigitur = *erizata*, habenas = *le retine*, prodere = *manefestare*; r: defunctos = *muorti*; v: WOM, tutele = *securanza*. See also v, r– v, v, r, r for similar glosses. The same group of glossators provided marginalia on r, where the missing line . was supplied and on v, where apparently a grammatical annotation was made ('scius inscius, gnarus et ignarus').

Vernacular glosses in English and French were frequently made in XIIIc. to *Doctrinale*, which assumed the status of an authorial text with the decline of the classics in that period: for examples, see Thurot ( ), – . Filippo Beroaldo the Elder had a propensity for vernacular explication of classical authors: see Mariotti ( ), and n. for further bibliography.

27 r: ut = *sichè*; r: scelestos = *scominicati*, facciosios = *discordiosi*; v: factiones = *per discordie*; v: casum = *avengemento*; r: conscientia delicti = *per la consacensa de peccato*, lege = *la lege*; v: socordia = *pigricia*; r: *descordie*; v: *usança*; r: dissensio = *departimento*; r: sollicitudinis = *rancure*, probra = *decorosa*; v: *villanesco, intemeroso*; v: *in alteça vel in alto*; r: obsides = *ostadici*; v: *cavallaresca battaia*. 28 BRF . 29 BML Edili . See above, .

30 E.g. v: *scomonecata, presentanza, adunatrice*; r: *ordinaremo, addemandare, iudicamenti*; v: *confortante*; v: indigeant = *abesonge*; v: intolerabilius = *non sostenebele*, sperni =*refudari*; r: *commova, tracta*; v: *conestringere*; v: *losengando*; v: *selvatebre*; r: *dissonore*; v: contumelie = *dissunuri*; v: *desertu*; r: comitas = *cortesia, losengamentu* (also on r, v); v: contio = *aringo*.

never reached the level found among the poets, either minor or major.[31]

Word order

Word order has always been a problem for learners of Latin as a second language. The most important technique used to overcome this di culty for inexpert readers was the use of word-order marks, placed between lines to indicate the logical sequence of words according to the pattern of the vernacular (*ordo naturalis*).[32] Thus, in a school manuscript of Aesop and *Physiologus* datable to the very end of the thirteenth century (BNCF Magl. .), a contemporaneous glossator wrote (r):

a c d e f

Cervus habere duas naturas atque figuras

b g h

Dicitur a physi[c]o cum docet, inde

Among the school manuscripts in Florentine libraries, this technique went back certainly to the turn of the twelfth century, as is clear from one glossator to a manuscript of Boethius's *Consolation*,[33] and probably represented a venerable practice even then.[34] In twelfth-century Italian schools, it was used to aid the reading of minor authors such as Sedulius,[35] classical poets such as Lucan,[36] and prose-writers such as Cicero.[37] There are examples from thirteenth-century Italian schools, as is evident in manuscripts of Horace[38] and Sallust.[39] Word-order marking continued to be done by Trecento Italian pupils, with examples

[31] See above, .

[32] William of Conches regarded the reconstruction of logical word order as a basic task of grammatical commentary: 'Necesse autem est in expositione ad suum naturalem ordinem dictiones reducere' (cited by Kneepkens ( ),). [33] Black and Pomaro ( ), .

[34] See Schmidt ( ), ; Reynolds ( ), – . [35] BML sin. , v, r– v.

[36] BML . , r– v, *passim*; . , v, v, v.

[37] BML . , v, r, r; . , r, r, r, v, r, r, r, v, v, r, v, v. This practice extended in the same period beyond Italy, as is clear from schoolbooks such as a northern European Horace datable to XIIc. (BML Strozzi), a XIIc. French Vergil with contemporaneous glossing (BML .) and a Lucan of similar date and provenance (BML .) again with word-order marks from the same period (e.g. r). [38] BRF , r, v, v, v, r–v.

[39] BML Ashb. , v, r, v; . , r, r, v, v, r, r, r, v, v, r, r, v, r. Also north of the Alps, as is clear from XIIIc. school manuscript of Boethius's *Consolation* (BRF): Black and Pomaro ( ), .

from school manuscripts of Henry of Settimello,[40] Horace,[41] Terence,[42] Vergil[43] and Boethius,[44] and was widespread throughout the Quattrocento in Italian schools, as is clear from manuscripts of Sallust,[45] Juvenal,[46] Horace,[47] Vergil,[48] Cicero[49] and Boethius.[50] It was not unusual for word-order marking to be made in one schoolbook over a number of centuries, as is clear from manuscripts of Boethius.[51] It sometimes pervades a single manuscript, as is clear from the glosses to Ovid in BML . [52] or to Boethius in BML Ashb. , BNCF CS J. . or BRF .[53] The word-order marks in this last manuscript are unusual, in that they are indicated by numbers as well as by letters. Out of Boethius school manuscripts in Florence, contain this elementary form of interlinear annotation,[54] and word-order marks are found in the fourteenth-century Italian school-level glosses to an Italian manuscript of the *Consolation* in the Bodleian Library, Oxford.[55]

Although most problems of word order were tackled through interlinear glossing, teachers and pupils sometimes had recourse to the fuller

40 BNCF Magl. . , v; see Gehl ( ), , and, for Prosper, .

41 BRF , v, v; , v, r; BML . , v, v, v.

42 BML CS , r, r. 43 BML . , v, r, v, v.

44 E.g. Black and Pomaro ( ), , , . 45 BRF , r. 46 BRF , r.

47 BRF : XIc. and XIIc. possibly Swiss/Austrian manuscript with late fifteenth-century Italian WOM. Certainly in Italy by later XVc., when it came into possession first of two Tuscan clerks: v: Hic liber mei est Francisci Christofori lucensis ordinis minorum. Nunc autem est Francisci de Bonagratiis quia ipse Franciscus ei donavit. r: Presbiteri Francisci Ser Filippi de Bonagratiis de Piscia. May already have arrived in Italy by end of XIIIc., when there is an annotation in XIIIc. hand, apparently Italian: (r) In nomine domini millesimo ducen(tesimo) nona<gesimo secundo> indictione quinta. Dominus Albertus fuit <...> (was the twelfth indiction, and the only fifth indiction in the s was .) 48 BNCF Magl. . , r.

49 BML Ashb. , r. For continued use of this technique in reading Cicero during later XVIc., see Grendler ( ), .

50 Black and Pomaro ( ), , , , . For this technique used in by Filippo Beroaldo the Elder in commenting on Statius's *Thebais*, see Mariotti ( ), (cited by Rizzo ( ), n.). 51 Black and Pomaro ( ), – , – , , .

52 WOM made during early phase of XIIc. and XIIIc. glossing found on almost every page of this MS. 53 See Black and Pomaro ( ), – , – , , .

54 Black and Pomaro ( ), – , , , , , , , , , – , , , – , .

55 Black and Pomaro ( ), , n. . Word-order marking was a habit which sometimes persisted after grammar school. In a XIIc. Italian manuscript of Cicero's *De inventione* and *Rhetorica ad Herennium* (BML .) the study was clearly university-level, to judge from the length and complexity of marginalia, but this XIVc. commentary was accompanied by WOM (v, r, r, r, r); similarly, in a XIIc. MS of Macrobius's commentary on *Somnium Scipionis* (BML . , v– v), a work usually associated with natural philosophy curriculum, there are occasional WOM. Scholars too sometimes did not shed this practice from school days: e.g., Tedaldo della Casa read Seneca's tragedies in , leaving WOM throughout entire book (BML sin.), while Boccaccio used this technique in reading *Appendix Vergiliana* (see Black ( ), –).

discussions made possible by marginal glosses, as is clear from an example of school-level glossators to Boethius's *Consolation*, where the commentator actually reorders the words of the text according to the normal pattern of the modern romance languages.[56] When more explanation was required, the pupil was often advised to search for the principal verb as the key to decoding the Latin word order.[57] Another method was to use the concepts of subject and predicate (*suppositum* and *appositum*).[58] Sometimes, however, both the principal verb and subject/predicate were highlighted to aid the struggling pupil.[59]

Interlinear Latin synonyms

Another characteristic feature of schoolbooks is the inclusion of synonyms for the simplest imaginable Latin words. An example of this practice is a manuscript of *Physiologus* and Aesop (BNCF Magl. .), datable to the end of Duecento, in which a glossator contemporaneous with the copyist wrote 'vero' = 'pro sed' (v), 'artus' = 'pro membra' (r) and 'sin' = 'pro set si' (v).[60] Of the Florentine school Boethius manuscripts, have this kind of simple, interlinear lexical glossing,[61] and most of the codices have numerous di erent hands leaving glosses of this nature.[62] Writing simple Latin synonyms above words of the text was a venerable practice in schoolbooks: the earliest glossator (XI^2) in the Florentine manuscripts of Boethius[63] does this type of glossing

[56] Black and Pomaro ( ), . Reordering introduced by phrase 'ordo est' was a standard method for restructuring syntax in antique scholia: see Rizzo ( ), n. .

[57] Black and Pomaro ( ), – . [58] Black and Pomaro ( ), , .

[59] Black and Pomaro ( ), , .

[60] See BML AD , r: Nam = pro quia; v: tamen = pro sed; r: preceps = velox, verum = pro sed (see r, r, v, r, r, r). BML . , v: cum = id est quando. BML . , v: rogo = id est quero, omnis = id est totus. BML CS , r: que = pro et. BML . , v: incola = habitator; v: possit = posset, in = contra (see r, r, v, v, v, r, v, v, r). BRF , r: videretur = manifestum est, adiumentum = auxilium, non modo = non solum, dissidentia = discordantia; v: primum = primo, Priamo = regi, quid = cur. BRF , r: post = postea, patere = manifesta esse; v: temperans = abstinens; r: sententia = opinio, aditus = ingressus, omnis = tota; v: proficisci = incipi; v: distribui = dividi, tueatur = conservet; r: parare = acquirere; v: tum = tunc; r: ait = dicit; v: que = et; v: calamitatis = miserie. BML sup. , v: formosum = pulcrum, ne = pro non, tantum = pro solum modo, assidue = sepius [etc.] BNCF Magl. . : r: facta = acta, prisca = antiqua, longe = valde, populatus = depredatus, ponto = mari; v, timuit = expavit, ponto = aqua.

[61] An exception is BRF (see Black and Pomaro ( ), –), a signed schoolbook: see Black and Pomaro ( ), .

[62] All Bodley Italian Boethius manuscripts have this type of simple interlinear lexical glossing: see Black and Pomaro ( ), , n. . [63] Black and Pomaro ( ), .

continuously, and examples can be detected in almost every subsequent century among these Boethius manuscripts;[64] indeed, this procedure is found in non-Italian as well as in Italian hands among the glossators of these codices.[65]

A variation whereby numerous synonyms in Latin are given for the words to be explained is found in the early fifteenth-century interlinear glosses written perhaps by the copyist of the Boethius manuscript, BML . .[66] This is a relatively unusual feature of schoolbooks,[67] and may indicate a teacher interested in vocabulary building; the school context is suggested by the usual repetitious explication of obvious and simple vocabulary. It is also interesting that a subsequent glossator of this same manuscript continued this individual form of interlinear annotation.[68]

It is hardly surprising that, out of the manuscripts in Florentine libraries which have been identified as schoolbooks in the present survey, only lacked this form of interlinear lexical annotation.[69] Of these unglossed schoolbooks, contained texts of the minor authors. This is hardly a coincidence. The minor authors were the first literary texts read by pupils after completing the reading course consisting of the alphabet/syllable sheet (*carta* or *tabula*), *salterio* and *Ianua*. It has already been observed that the method used to teach these elementary reading texts was based on phonetics and memory; it is no accident that there is hardly a gloss on any surviving manuscript of *Ianua*: the purpose of reading and studying this text was not so much comprehension as phonetic reading technique (*Donato per lo testo*) and memorization (*Donato per lo senno*). (See above, .) Comprehension began at the next stage of the grammar curriculum with the introduction of the minor authors. However, the move from uncomprehending phonetic reading and memorization to comprehension was a slow and gradual process. It is not surprising that vestiges of the old techniques based on phonetic reading and memorization without comprehension remained. These minor authors were still being used in the same way as the earlier texts of the reading curriculum; it is likely that much of the reading that

64 XIIIc.: Black and Pomaro ( ), , – .
XIVc.: Black and Pomaro ( ), –, , –, –, –, –, , –, , , , –, , –, , , , –, , .
XVc.: Black and Pomaro ( ), –, –, –, , –, , –, , , –, , –, , , –, , –, , , , , , , , , .

65 Black and Pomaro ( ), , .

66 Black and Pomaro ( ), – .

67 Occasional examples of other multiple-synonym glosses: Black and Pomaro ( ), , , , , , , .

68 Black and Pomaro ( ), .

69 BML Ashb. ; sin. , . , . , . , . , sup. . BNCF . ; Magl. . ; Panciat. . BRF , , , , , , , , , , .

occurred at the level of the minor authors began in this way and only gradually moved on to glossing and comprehension. By the time the pupil finished the minor authors and progressed to Boethius's *Consolation*, this type of reading based on phonetics and memory without comprehension seems largely to have ceased. It is no coincidence that the Boethius manuscripts in the present survey contain far more vernacular glossing than any other group of texts. In reading this text, simple comprehension and glossing seem to have been the paramount concerns, and so it is not surprising that teachers and pupils turned to the most basic form of understanding a foreign language: translation into the native tongue of the learner.

Grammatical analysis

Although less common than synonyms or word-order marks, there were also interlinear annotations focusing on grammatical analysis. A common school practice, for example, was to indicate the vocative case with an 'o' over nouns, as in a manuscript of Theodulus's *Eclogue* and Statius's *Achilleis*, datable to the end of the Trecento (BML .),[70] or in a manuscript of the *Achilleis* dated (BNCF Magl. .).[71]

Figures of speech were just as much a part of grammatical study in antiquity, the middle ages and the Renaissance as they were of rhetoric. These figures (often confusingly labelled rhetorical figures or colours) in fact showed permitted lapses of strict grammatical usage: hence they constituted the subject matter of the third part of Donatus's *Ars maior* (sometimes aptly named *Barbarismus* to suggest the breaking of rigorous grammatical rules). An understanding of figures was essential to a basic comprehension of texts, since the reader had to learn to make allowances for what amounted to poetic licence on the part of the author. Therefore even in simple literary texts such as the minor authors, obvious rhetorical figures had to be explained.[72] The practice of explaining the basic grammatical significance of figures of course was carried on in glosses to the major authors.[73] Poetic contractions were realized.[74] Understood subjects, verbs, antecedents and modified nouns

70 r: Phebe = O Apollo; v: Theti = O; r: Chiron = O; v: care puer = o; v: care = o.
71 r: Diva = o Caliope, Phebe = o.
72 BML . : r: proles = stirps et sumitur pro omnibus hominibus. See BML AD : r: Phebus = sol.
73 BML . : v: dies = sol. BML sup. , v: pecudes = id est homines virtuosi; r: omnis mundus = totus metonomia est. BRF , r: yronice.
74 BNCF Pal. , r: quis = quibus.

were written above the line.[75] Simple grammatical structures were explained.[76] One particular technique of grammatical analysis was the indication of subject and predicate by writing 'sup' (=*suppositum*) and 'ap' (=*appositum*) above the lines of text, as for example in some late Trecento glosses to Boethius, where in the text above 'Cresi' and again above 'Ciro' is written 'ap'.[77] This technique was used with particular intensity by one later Quattrocento Boethius reader, who throughout one manuscript continually wrote 'sup' and 'ap' above the lines.[78]

Whether the interlinear glossing consisted of providing vernacular equivalents, giving Latin synonyms, explaining word order, spelling out figures, realizing poetic contractions, explicating basic grammar or supplying understood words, it revealed a uniformly rudimentary level of comment.

:

Rhetorical figures

As with glosses between the lines, marginal notes consist overwhelmingly of basic points of philology. It has been seen already that grammatical and rhetorical figures constituted one of the most important features of the secondary theoretical grammar course, and so it is not surprising to find that one of the most characteristic types of marginalia in the schoolroom was the indication and explanation of figures. In the marginal glosses to the minor authors, a limited range of these, including synecdoche, tmesis, zeugma, metaphor and parenthesis, were annotated, but the most commonly indicated figure was *comparatio*. Usually these glosses were written in the margin without clarification,[79] but occasionally the

75 BML AD , r: quidam {homo}; r: Parvula {videlicet formica}. BML . , v: eo {veneno}, parentes {scilicet Adam et Eva}; r: que {sacra}, Ense {ipse Abel} cadit fratris (see r, v, r, v, v, r, v). BNCF Magl. . , r: quique = ille consultus, qui = ille. BNCF Magl. . , r: diva = Caliope, viri = Achillis, velis = tu Caliope, latentem = Achillem, comas = meas, tibi = Domitiano, pastor = Paris (see v). BML sup. , v: veniebat = ille Virgilius, solus = ipse Virgilius, tu = curas.

76 BNCF Magl. . , v: quod = id est quia. BML AD , v: capiare = pro capiaris; r: quid = pro aliquid; r: michi = a me, labore = cum. BML . , v: ipso = ente; r: tu = Domitiane; r: genitor = Neptune; r: qualis = talis ens. BNCF Magl. . , r: tu = Domitiane, qua = ea parte, vana = sunt. BML sup. , r: Alx = tertia declinatio; v: delitias = appositive, quid = pro aliquid, umbrosa = appositive, miserere = pro misereris, rapido = appositive.

77 Black and Pomaro ( ), . 78 Black and Pomaro ( ), .

79 ASF CStrozz. . , v, r; BNCF Magl. . , r; BML AD , v, r.

figurative meaning was explained, as in a gloss to Henry of Settimello[80] or in an annotation to Theodulus.[81] As the grammar pupil moved on to Boethius's *Consolation*, the range of figures was expanded to embrace hysteron proteron,[82] prosopopoeia,[83] paragoge,[84] anthypophora,[85] hypothesis,[86] circuitio,[87] epitheton,[88] prolepsis,[89] repetitio,[90] articulus,[91] irony,[92] praeoccupatio,[93] exclamatio,[94] tautology,[95] macrologia,[96] parabole,[97] hirmos,[98] epenthesis,[99] and metonymy,[100] but those already introduced in the minor authors were repeated, including comparatio,[101] synecdoche,[102] metaphor,[103] parenthesis,[104] hyperbaton[105] and tmesis.[106] Usually these figures were simply indicated in the margin without elaboration, but again, as in the minor authors, sometimes they were explained, as in the case of prosopopoeia, hypothesis and praeoccupatio. In marginalia to the major authors, further new figures were introduced, including tapinosis,[107] hyperbole,[108] litotes,[109] antiphrasis,[110] emphasis,[111] metathesis,[112] antiptosis,[113] apostropha,[114] occupatio,[115] transitio,[116] contentio,[117] contrarium,[118] sententia,[119] translatio,[120] confirmatio,[121] confutatio,[122] consequentia,[123] gradatio,[124] antitheton,[125] brevitas[126] and correption.[127] But the previous favourites did not go unmentioned, including synecdoche,[128] tmesis,[129] epitheton,[130] anthypophora,[131]

80 BRF , r: Methaforice loquitur, quia navis male vadit cum minus frangitur, sic mundus cum virtus receditur. 81 BML . , v: Babilon interpetratur confusio.
82 Black and Pomaro ( ), ; Bodley Can. lat. , r.
83 Black and Pomaro ( ), . 84 Black and Pomaro ( ), .
85 Black and Pomaro ( ), , , . 86 Black and Pomaro ( ), .
87 Black and Pomaro ( ), . 88 Black and Pomaro ( ), ; Bodley Can. lat. , r.
89 Black and Pomaro ( ), , , . 90 Black and Pomaro ( ), , .
91 Black and Pomaro ( ), .
92 Black and Pomaro ( ), , ; Bodley Can. lat. , r.
93 Black and Pomaro ( ), . 94 Black and Pomaro ( ), .
95 Black and Pomaro ( ), . 96 Black and Pomaro ( ), .
97 Black and Pomaro ( ), . 98 Black and Pomaro ( ), .
99 Bodley Can. lat. , r: *solvier* [, m. ,]: figura penthesis: adiunctio sillabe solvi.
100 Bodley Can. lat. , v. 101 Black and Pomaro ( ), , .
102 Black and Pomaro ( ), , , ; Bodley Can. lat. , v.
103 Black and Pomaro ( ), , , .
104 Black and Pomaro ( ), , , ; Bodley Can. lat. , r.
105 Black and Pomaro ( ), . 106 Bodley Can. lat. , r. 107 BML . , v.
108 BML . , r. 109 BML sup. , r. BRF , v. 110 BML sup. , r.
111 BRF , v. 112 BRF , r. 113 BRF , v.
114 BNCF Magl. . , r. 115 BML . , v. BRF , r.
116 BML AD , r. BRF , v. 117 BRF , v. 118 BRF , r.
119 BRF , r. 120 BRF , v. 121 BRF , v. 122 BRF , v.
123 BRF , r. 124 BRF , r. 125 BRF , r. 126 BRF , v.
127 BRF , v. 128 BML sup. , r. BRF , r, v.
129 BML . , v. 130 See above, for BML . , v.
131 BNCF Magl. . , v. BRF , r, r, v.

hysteron proteron,[132] metonymy,[133] praeoccupatio,[134] irony,[135] prolepsis,[136] repetitio[137] and especially parenthesis[138] and comparatio.[139] As for the minor authors and Boethius, the normal practice was simply to note these figures in the margins, but sometimes the glosses extended to explanation, as in cases of tapinosis,[140] metonymy,[141] litotes,[142] tmesis,[143] diaresis,[144] metalepsis,[145] parenthesis,[146] contrarium,[147] praeoccupatio,[148] metonymy,[149] synecdoche[150] and occupatio.[151]

Grammar

Marginal notes on technical points of grammar are rare in schoolbooks of the minor authors, but there are a few examples.[152] An early example

132 BRF , v, v. 133 BRF , r. 134 BRF , r.
135 BML CS , v. 136 BRF , v, v.
137 BML AD , v; BRF , v; BRF , r.
138 BML . , v, r, v, r, r, r. BML . , r, r. BML Strozzi , r, r, v. BML . , r, v, v. BML . , r, r.
139 BML sup. , v, r, v, r. BML . , r, r, v, r, r, r. BML sup. , r: facit comparationem inter Achillem et Apollinem; v: comperationem ponit inter congregationem animalium; v. BRF , r. BML . , r. BML Strozzi , r, v, v, r, r, r, r. BML . , r. BRF , r, r, r.
140 BML . , v, r: tapenosis est humiliatio magne rei.
141 BNCF Magl. . , v: secundum aliquos auctor hic utitur figura methomomia cum dicit est Eufrates, ponendo loca pro habitatoribus qui triumfum comitabantur.
142 BML sup. , r: lictote figura: minus dicit et plus facit.
143 BML sup. , v: figura que dicitur themesis id est transpositio literarum.
144 BML . , r: divisio sillabe est temesis quia dividitur ditio et est diaresis quando dividitur sillaba.
145 BML . , r: figura metalensis descriptio temporis cum denominatione rerum produttarum a tempore.
146 BML sup. , v: parentesis est interposit<i>o. BRF , v: parentasis sermonis interpositio.
147 BRF , r: color rethoricus qui dicitur contrarium quia dicit adsit et absit.
148 BRF , v: color rethoricus qui vocatur preocupatio quia dicit id quod promictit omictere.
149 BML Rinuccini , r: methonomia figura quia ponit id quod continet pro eo quod continetur, videlicet librum pro materia libri.
150 BRF , v: sinedoce quia ponitur pars pro toto [...] et est intellectio in rethorica; r: et est sinedoce quia ponitur continens pro contento.
151 BML . , r: hic est quidam color rethoricus qui appellatus est occupatio dicendo quod sum cito tradita regi tua culpa non est sed tua culpa est vel aliter quod sum tradita poscenti regi. Non est tua culpa quia rex sed culpa est quia cito vel aliter et melius quod sum cito tradita poscenti regi non est tua culpa quia rex, sed tua culpa est quia non repetis nec vendicas me.
152 BNCF Magl. . , v: Omnia nomina quarte declentionis faciunt dativum et ablativum plurales in ibus. BNCF Magl. . , r: ave veniens tibi dico, valeque recedens. Hoc verbum salve comprehendit aveque valeque. BML AD , r: Inter silere et tacere hoc interest: silet qui numquam cepit loqui; tacet qui loqui incepit. See BML . , r.

is an unfinished gloss from a copy of *Ilias latina*, made by a thirteenth-century schoolboy in Southern Italy.[153]

The grammatical focus became more intense when pupils moved from the minor authors to Boethius's *Consolation*. Some of their glosses involved grammatical topics already encountered at the level of the minor authors, such as etymology.[154] In fact, one etymological gloss on *biblus* is found repeated in similar form in three di erent school manuscripts.[155] Di erences between Latin words, always a preoccupation of grammar teachers, as can be seen in Guarino's well-known *Carmina di erentialia*, continued to interest teachers and pupils when moving from the minor authors to Boethius.[156] Another standard topic in Boethius manuscripts was orthography.[157] Accidence, in the sense defined in an introductory grammar text such as *Ianua*, was also glossed in school manuscripts of the *Consolation*.[158] The incipit of a well-circulated secondary Latin grammar, with five manuscripts now in Florence (Lictera est vox individua), is encountered once in a gloss to Boethius,[159] as is the terminology of northern speculative grammar.[160] Since the *Consolation* was an intermediate literary text in grammar schools,[161] it is not surprising to find that the most prevalent grammatical topic in these glosses was syntax, the main preoccupation of grammar study at the school level. Sometimes the comment involved relative pronouns and clauses,[162] sometimes sentence construction, focusing on the types of verbs,[163] but

[153] BRF . , r: Nota quod omnia nomina et p [breaks o here]. The same glossator wrote the following grammatical notes (v):

> Nota quod omnia nomina in sua vi non possunt regere aliquod in casum.
> Nota quod ubi averbium locale tribus modis ponitur in locutione: interrogative, ut ubi fuisti?; relative: ubi fuit Plato, ibi fuit Cato. Nota quod i[n]finiti verborum positi nominaliter possunt exiger[e] genitivum verbi gratia ut saitare tui placet michi et canere tui placet michi.

The contents of these notes fall within secondary grammatical curriculum, as developed in the course of XIIIc. (see above,). The focus on verbal syntax (*regere, exigere*) and on adverbs of location suggests the kind of teaching typical of XIIIc., as found e.g. in *Summa* of Pietro da Isolella (see above,); annotator's handwriting is certainly datable to XIIIc., but, given immature graphical formation, it is di cult to say how near in time he was to the MS's production. This glossator is the same schoolboy who wrote a prayer and alphabet (see below, n.) just above these grammatical notes. [154] Black and Pomaro ( ), , , .

[155] Black and Pomaro ( ), , , .

[156] Black and Pomaro ( ), , , , , , , .

[157] Black and Pomaro ( ), – .

[158] Black and Pomaro ( ), , ; Bodley Can. lat. , r: *Quidni* [, p. ,] est adverbium a ermandi sed ponitur interogative.

[159] Black and Pomaro ( ), ; see above, – .

[160] Black and Pomaro ( ), .

[161] Black and Pomaro ( ), – , summarized below, .

[162] Black and Pomaro ( ), , . [163] Black and Pomaro ( ), , , .

most of the time syntactical glossing on Boethius consisted of an analysis of subject and predicate (*suppositum* and *appositum*).[164]

Coming to the major authors, students continued to be preoccupied by some topics already annotated while reading the minor authors and Boethius, including etymology,[165] di erences,[166] accidence[167] and orthography.[168] Syntax was still commented on, but, unlike the school glossators on Boethius, with their focus on analysis of subject and predicate, those on the major authors are primarily concerned with verbal governance (*regere* or *regimen*) of constructions[169] although other aspects of verbal syntax were also noted.[170] The most influential ancient grammarians had a particular penchant for intricate problems of morphology, an interest which is reflected in school-level glosses to the Latin classics.[171]

Mnemonic verses

As has been seen, poets were preferred to prose-writers in the grammar curriculum because verse was regarded as more suitable for memorization.[172] This is clear not only from a gloss on *Doctrinale*, already men-

164 Black and Pomaro ( ), , – .

165 BRF , v, r, r, v, v, r, r, r, v, r: toga dicitur a tegendo; augurium dicitur a avium garritu; auspicium dicitur ab avium aspectu. proverbium quasi probatum verbum. solers solus in arte. viaticus id est victus qui in itinere ducitur seu apportatur. autumpnus auctus annus dicitur. encyclius dicitur ab eme quod est medium et ciclus quod est circulus quasi medius circulus. di undere in diversas partes fundere. sententia dicitur a sentio, -tis quasi mentis sentio. vehemens dicitur a veho, -is et mens. See BML . , r; BNCF Panciat. , r; BRF , r; BML AD , r; BRF , r; BRF , r.

166 BML . , v: simulare est ostendere quod non est; dissimulare est non ostendere quod est. See BML . , r; BRF , r; BML CS , r; BML . , r; BNCF Panciat. , r; BRF , r; BML . , r; BML . , r; BML . , r; BRF , r, v, v; BRF , r; BML Rinuccini , r; BML Edili , r.

167 BNCF Palatino Baldovinetti , v: Adverbium est desiderantis vel admirantis; BML . , r: nota hospita femina sed hic neutri generis.

168 BML sup. , r: aestimo scribitur per 'ae' diphthongon et per 's' litteram; dicitur enim ab aes, aeris et teneo, -nes. See BNCF . , . v, r.

169 BRF , v, v: Dicit Priscianus quinque verba neutra absoluta regere post se accusativum sue rei ut vixi vitam duram. Dicit Priscianus verba deponentia possexiva regere post se accusativum ut potitur comoda. Nota quod participium regit genetivum. See BML . , v; BML Ashb. , r. For XIIc. grammatical gloss in BML San Marco (r), see above, .

170 BRF , v: vocem activam pro passiva posuit sive gramaticha est antequa<m> quando dicit interpetrare. See BRF , v; BRF , v; BNCF Landau Fin. , r.

171 BML . , r: nomina namque greca <ter>minata in -es longum <ter>minant vocativum tam in -es quam in -e ut Ulixes vocativo o Ulixes. See BML . , v, r, v, v, r, v, r; BML Strozzi , r; BML sup. , r; BNCF Palatino Baldovinetti , r; BNCF . , v; BML . , v.

172 See above, , and in general Klopsch ( ), – ; Law (b), – ; Rizzo ( ), – .

tioned above[173] as well as from a fourteenth-century distich[174] but also from a similar view propounded by Battista Guarini in his *De ordine docendi et discendi.*[175] Sentiments along the same lines informed a comment on Geo rey of Vinsauf's *Poetria nova*, datable to the first decade of the fifteenth century (BML Strozzi , r).[176] In the middle ages there existed a pair of verses celebrating the usefulness of mnemonics.[177]

This belief in the value of verse not only influenced the choice of authors but also teaching methods. Mnemonic verses were used in the classroom to explain or reinforce grammatical points, as in a gloss to Aesop in a late Duecento manuscript.[178] The biography of authors could be taught through verse too, as in verses explaining the reasons for Lucan's failure to finish the *Pharsalia.*[179] Verses were a convenient way of summarizing the contents of school texts for easy recollection, as in some lines which were placed at the end of one fifteenth-century signed school manuscript of Statius's *Achilleis.*[180]

Teachers of Boethius's *Consolation* may have found short mnemonic verses useful too; for example, verse summaries are provided to books ,

[173] See above, n. .

[174] 'Delectat, breviat, retinetur firmius: istas / ob causas metrum gracius esse solet': cited by Klopsch ( ), and Rizzo ( ), n. . Giovanni Conversini da Ravenna was made to memorize and recite whatever he was taught from ps.Cato, Prosper and Boethius: see above, , n. .

[175] 'non inutilis erit is liber qui sub Alexandri nomine versibus habetur, [. . .] nam praeterquam quod omnia sumit a Prisciano, facilius etiam quae carminibus scripta sunt memoriae commendantur conservanturque': ed. Garin ( ), . Giovanni Sulpizio Verulano, writing in the preface to his treatise on nominal genders ( ), conceded that verse made for easier learning than prose, although he criticized *Doctrinale* as incomprehensible to pupils: Percival ( ), – ; Rizzo ( ), . Similarly Antonio Nebrija, in his secondary grammar (a work in Italian grammatical tradition: see Percival ( )), defended his use of mnemonic verse because it allowed boys to retain and hold in readiness minute bits of information: see Rico ( ), n. ; Rizzo ( ), .

[176] Dicit etiam Aristotelis ° *Rhetoricorum* quod metra facilius memorie commendantur his verbis propter quod et metra omnes memorantur magis quam non ligata. Numerus enim haberit quo mensuraretur.

[177] 'Metra iuvant animos, comprendunt plurima paucis, / Memoriam salvant: quae sunt tria grata legenti': cited by Sabbadini ( ), , quoting treatise *Exercitatio de arte metrica* by Bartolomeo da S. Concordio, who comments on these verses.

[178] BNCF Magl. . , v: Aver. dicatur coniuntio, dumque putatur, / Aver. demo<n>strans, ortans, ortans quoque querens, / Assimilantque negans monosillaba verba, / Preibunt adverbia demo<n>strandi ut en ecce. For orthography reinforced by verse, see *probatio* by German pupil below, , n. (BML CS).

[179] BL Harley (Goro d'Arezzo's commentary on Lucan), v: Ponimus hic metam: ne vituperate poetam, / Si finem posuit hic ubi non decuit / Qui, quia Neronem monstraverit esse leonem, / Illius gladium sentit ad exicium. / Appoligitici versus super incompleto Lucani fine.

[180] BNCF CS J. . , r: Primus semiferi matre<m> deducit ad antra, / Alter a virgineo Pelidem celat amictu, / Tertius occultas reserat Calcante latebras, / Armis ambiguum manifestat quartus Achillem, / Eacidem quintus narantem tradit Achivis.

and in BML . .[181] Three Florentine manuscripts preserve traditional verses on the three fates, also found in Nicholas Trevet's commentary.[182] Verses on the winds, present in Trevet's commentary too (but going back to glosses associated with William of Conches's commentary)[183] are cited in two manuscripts.[184] Verses describing the wheel of fortune, also partly found in Trevet (as well as in William of Conches's commentary), are given in two Florentine manuscripts.[185] There are also mnemonics evidently to aid recollection of the opening of book , m. .[186] However, the most widely disseminated verses found in schoolbooks of the *Consolation* provided a series of conveniently memorized summaries of the text; these are fully or partially found in seven di erent manuscripts.[187]

Ovid's *Heroides* was the text in connection with which there seems to have particularly heavy use of mnemonic verses. There are two manuscripts, both datable to the beginning of the fifteenth century (BML . and .), in which a few lines of metre, often with internal Leonine rhymes, are cited within the marginal commentary. Occasionally the source of these verses is given, as for example in a citation from *Graecismus*.[188] As in this case, the obvious purpose of the verses was to fix a point of grammar in the minds of the pupils.[189] However, most of these accompanying verses summarized or explicated the narrative of the relevant Ovidian verse epistle.[190] These mnemonics were apparently in general circulation, given that some are shared by both Laurentian manuscripts.[191]

181 Black and Pomaro ( ), , . 182 Black and Pomaro ( ), , n. .
183 Black and Pomaro ( ), , n. . 184 Black and Pomaro ( ), , .
185 Black and Pomaro ( ), , n. , , . According to Walther (–) n. , similar verses are found in BL Harley , v and Munich Staatsbibliothek , v.
186 Black and Pomaro ( ), , . 187 Black and Pomaro ( ), – .
188 BML . , r: Unde Grecismus: Corna gerit cornus. Pecudum sint cornus. / Cornu militis est quando properat sua bella gerendo; see v for another citation of *Graecismus*.
189 Similarly, BML . , v: Aspires horam, tibi tempus significabit; / Si non aspires, limbum dabit et regionem; BML . , r: Versus: Edo compono pario loquor et manifesto.
190 BML . : (Dido to Aeneas) r: Unde versus: Concubitu facto dolet h(ic) et tempore nacto. For Hermione's letter to Orestes, see r. BML . : (Briseis to Achilles) r: Unde versus: Briseis hortatur, se su<m>pta, pugnat Achilles, / Quam modo commendat Naso, nam casta remansit [...] Fert quoque vela dari nec premia Martis amari. For more examples see v, v, v, r, v, r, r, v, r, r, v, r, v, v, r, v, v, r, v, v, v, v.
191 BML . , v: Tandalides rapte, quod sunt fato, probat apte./ Matris capturam memorat quondam fore duram./ Penis seque sitam cupit Eacide fore metam. Variant readings according to BML . , r:

fate ate

vitam

Geography

Another important feature of the simple philology characterizing marginal glosses to school authors was an interest in geography. The geographical information conveyed in these texts was usually rudimentary,[192] although sometimes the geography was more specialized.[193] The focus of the comment was normally the etymology of place names[194] or the historical[195] or mythological associations[196] of the localities annotated. There was a strong interest in Roman topography,[197] which sometimes extended to the personal experience and taste of the commentator.[198] There was also an interest in the local geography beyond Italy.[199] There was even an occasional reference to classical geographical texts.[200]

History

Stronger than their interest in geography was the school commentators' preoccupation with history. Among glosses on the minor authors, the most famous historical personalities were occasionally noted, including Alexander the Great, Julius Caesar, Pompey, Brutus and Cassius,

192 BML sup. , v: Sunt tres partes mundi, scilicet, Europa, Africa et Asia, quarum Europa est minor et in illa sumus. BNCF CS J. . , r: Nilus est fluvius. BML . , v: Sparta est quedam civitas. See BML . , v; Bodley Can. lat. , r; BNCF Magl. . , r; BML sup. , v; Black and Pomaro ( ), , , , .

193 BML . , v: Malea est mons Grecie qui est ad similitudinem umbonis. See BML sup. , v; BML . , r; BML . , r; BML Ashb. , v; Black and Pomaro ( ), .

194 BML . , v: [Ianuam], civitas est a Ianuino nauta primo eius conditore nominata. BRF , v: Ariopagus erat contrata Athenis pro studentium habitationibus deputata ab ares virtus et pagos villa et inde Ariopagita. See BML CS , v; Black and Pomaro ( ), .

195 BML AD , r: *Olimpicum.* In Olimpico Monte in honore Iovis Olimpici certabant curili certamine. Roberti ( ), – : 'Tenedos est insula propter quam facta est guerra inter ianuenses et venetos. '. See BRF , v.

196 BNCF Magl. . , v: Trace erat insula proxima habitationi ubi stabat Chiron. See BML . , v; Black and Pomaro ( ), .

197 BNCF Magl. . , r: Erant templa duo, unum ad honorem Cupidinis, aliud ad honorem Veneris, consimilia et erat unum prope aliud, quorum marmores Romani portaverant de Troya ut facerent pulcra templa. BML . , v: Praxtellus, optimus in sculptura, fecit Rome caballos marmores, ipse et Phydias, qui adhuc hodie vocantur magni chaballi et est ibi scriptum opus Prextelli et opus Fidie [...] et hoc est contra cronicham Martini [sc. Poloni] ubi trattat de magnis caballis qui dicit eos fuisse phylosofos. See BML sup. , v.

198 BML . , v: Iste Fidias est, ut credo, ille idem qui fecit Rome magnos caballos marmores et duos ingentes viros ex marmore ubi scriptum est opus Fidie et opus Pranxiteli et hoc ibi vidi in anno domini et est opus mirabile.

199 Black and Pomaro ( ), n. , , .

200 BML AD , r: Caria regio, teste Pomponio M(ela) libro primo, in Syria propinqua Licie est. Habet adeo gentem pugnacem et bellorum avidam ut alienas guerras mercidibus querat. Cf. Pomponius Mela, *De chorographia*, . . – .

Marius, Nero, Arthur and Theodoric,[201] as well as famous historical events. The scope for historical comment was limited by the fictional content of most of the Latin poets, but there was some interest in ancient institutions and customs,[202] as well as ancient religion.[203]

Real scope for historical study came when grammar pupils turned to Boethius's *Consolation*, with its historical setting and its many historical allusions. There was now ample opportunity for reference to the history of Greece and the Near East;[204] here a favourite story was provided by Boethius's reference to Cyrus and Croesus (, p. ,).[205] But of course the greatest preoccupation of the commentators was with Roman history. Here there was some interest in the republic, including its birth[206] and its heroes.[207] Roman institutions and customs were also touched on by school-level commentators on Boethius.[208] But it was imperial history which most interested glossators of Boethius in the schoolroom[209] and in particular the salacious and vicious life of Nero.[210]

The Latin prose authors gave the grammar pupil an opportunity to deepen his knowledge of Roman history. Again, there was some annotation of non-Roman history.[211] But once more the primary focus was on Rome, especially now the history of the republic, which is hardly surprising, given that most of the texts used (Cicero, Sallust, Valerius Maximus) either originated during or dealt primarily with pre-imperial

201 BRF , v, v, r, v, r: Alexander rex Maced[on]um in tanta prosperitate fuit in bello quod totum mundum sub suo subiugavit imperio. Iulius imperator romanus tantam habuit prosperitatem in bello quod Pompeum et totum senatum subiugavit. Postea vero romanum imperium habuit et a Bruto et Cassio in — [*spatium*] de m(anib)us interfectus est. ¶Bucifal fuit equus Alexandri [...] ¶Marius iste Romanus fuit, qui multa bona et multa mala habuit, et Appollonius similiter, qui fuit de Tyro, multa naufragia, multas infirmitates habuit. ¶Arturus iste rex fuit Britanie qui singulis diebus expectat Asser et ipse numquam veniet. ¶Nero interfecit magistrum suum Senecam quia timebat eum.¶Theodoricus imperator illustrem virum scilicet Boetium iniuste dampnavit et apud Papiam in exilio posuit eum et mortuus est. See ASF CStrozz. . , v, r.

202 BML . , v: Hic tangitur mos antiquus [...] filius consueveret claudere oculos patris post ipsius mortem. BNCF Magl. . , r: Teatra erant loco [*sic*] circularia et rotundo [*sic*] ubi ludi celebrabantur.

203 BML . , r: Festa Bacci facta de triennio in triennium vel secundum alios ter quolibet anno. BML Rinuccini , v: Penetral est locus secretus in templo ad quod non licet nisi sacerdotibus templi accedere, et dicitur penetral a penetrando per antrifresim eo quo[d] non licet penetrari. See BML . , r.

204 Black and Pomaro ( ), n. , , , .

205 Black and Pomaro ( ), , .

206 Black and Pomaro ( ), .

207 Black and Pomaro ( ), n. , , , .

208 Black and Pomaro ( ), , .

209 Black and Pomaro ( ), , .

210 Black and Pomaro ( ), n. , – , .

211 BML . , v: Ligurgus fuit quidam Lacedimonicus sapientissimus et bonus. BRF , r: Alexandrum Phereum: nota quod iste Alexander non fuit Alexander Magnus filius Philippi sed fuit Phererorum populorum filius Antiochi regis Sirie de quo eademmet verba scribit Valerius [...] See BML AD , r; BML . , r; BML . , r, cited above, .

history,[212] although glossators to the major poets showed some interest in imperial history too.[213] There continued to be a strong interest in Roman institutions and customs,[214] including ancient religion.[215] There was now an interest in particular Roman laws undocumented in the study of the minor authors, Boethius and the classical poets and illustrating the more specialized level of study.[216] There was also a tendency now to relate the contemporary world to Roman history, as in some comparisons between twelfth-century ecclesiastical life and the Rome of Marius's day.[217] Previous practical experience was just as much a

[212] BRF , v: Marcus Portius Cato qui Sardineam subegit ubi ab Ennio litteris grecis istructus est consul celtiberos domuit ac ne rebellare possent litteras ad singulas civitates misit ut muros diruerent [...] Accusator assiduus malorum Cartaginem delendam censuit; post ottaginta annos filiam genuit. BRF , v: Cato autem rigidus et dictus est propter rigorem animi qui ad nichil tempore flecti potuit, de cuius rigiditate meminit Seneca in quadam epistola ad Lucillum que sic incipit: 'aliquis vir bonus', ubi cum suasisset Lucillo quod aliquem virum virtuosum observaret et sibi tanquam exemplum vivendi preponeret subiunxit, 'Elige itaque Catonem [...]' Iste Cato propter zelum [zelium MS] iustitie tante fuit auctoritatis, ut, in iudicanda causa que fuit inter Iulium Cesarem et Pompeium, Lucanus ipsum cum diis comparaverit libro primo [...] Qui cum turpe iudicaret servire Cesari invasori rei publice, se ipsum interfecit apud Uthicam, honestum iudicans post libertatem non vivere. Unde de eo dicit Seneca libro secundo *De senectute* [...] unde Valerius [...] See BML . , r; BRF , v; BRF , r–v; BRF , r; BRF , r; BRF , v; BML CS , r; BML . , r, cited above, .

[213] BML Strozzi , v, r: Dicit Suethonius quod Nero spoliavit omnia templa, simulcres et argento [*sic pro* argenta]. ¶Dicit Suethonius quod Nero in nulla re fuit dampnosior quam in edificatione domorum.

[214] BRF , r: Nota quod consuetudo Romanorum erat ut per novem dies unumquemque custodirent cum diversis istrumentis musicae cum quibus cantabant ne vivum sepellirent. Postea vero condiebant cum balsamo si dives erat. Si autem pauper ampullam unam ad caput et alias inter coxas ponebant ut esset immortalitatis signum. BML . , v: Erat mos Romanorum ut quandocumque ex uxore sua tres habuerant filios novo nuberent coniugi ut fuit de Martia Catonis que nupta est Hortensio. BRF , r: Viralis toga sumebatur in XV° anno vel sextodecimo. Virgilius autem togam anno decimo septimo sue etatis sumpsit. Erat enim vestis qua iuvenes ad mores senum conducebantur. See BML Ashb. , v, v, v, v, r; BML AD , v, v; BRF , r, r; BML . , v, r; BML . , v.

[215] BML . , r: Superstitio, id est, dampnum vel vana et superflua religio et observatio vel cultura ydolorum et dicitur a superstitionibus, id est, a senibus, quia multis annis superstites per etatem delirant et errant quadam superstitione nescientes que vetera colant vel dicitur a superstantibus, id est, a deis, scilicet, quando de deis non timenda timemus. See BML . , v.

[216] BML Ashb. , v: Lex Platica precipiebat ut si quis faceret contra rem publicam statim subieret capitalem sententiam. See BML Ashb. , v, r; BRF , v, r.

[217] BML . , r: ille clericus ostendit quod contempnat clericalem honorem qui luxuriose ducit vitam suam et ita faciebant Romani quia male vivebant, velut honorem habere etiam desiderarent et tantum ad ultimum petebant honorem licet essent luxuriosi et cum sint viciosi tantum <...> sunt vitiosi. BML . , r: Si aliquis clericus cum virtutum exibitione requirit episcopatum id est, illud quod est spirituale in episcopio <et> <of>ficium seculare ecllesiae, eo facto episcopo melior <esse de>beret quam prius esset versus proprium, <quia> in episcopo est regere posse et alia quae sunt in episcopatu quae sunt pluria [*sic*] quam sit illud ei proprium. Et ita dicit Marius Romanos debere facere. Si aliquis Romanus bonis moribus ad aliquam dignitatem tendebat habita dignitate melior deberet insistere ut ad totam rem publicam regendam posset pervenire quia maius [*sic*] est res publica quam ulla quaeque dignitas, quod non faciebant Romani quia priusquam habere<n>t honorem hostendebant se bonos sed habito honore fiebant luxuriosi, avari et similia.

prerequisite for twelfth-century bishops in Rome as it was for ancient generals such as Marius.[218] Similarly, there was an interest in more recent history evident at this level.[219] A particularly topical interest for glossators in the fourteenth century was the rise of Italian despotism.[220] With the occasional introduction into the grammar syllabus in the fifteenth century of *De oratore*, it is not surprising to find some discussion among the glossators to the theory of history writing.[221]

Mythology

If history was primarily a focus for school-level glossators to the Latin prose classics, the reverse was true of mythology, which is hardly encountered among authors such as Sallust, Valerius Maximus or Cicero[222] but is a constant topic for glossing to the poets, both minor and major. Among the *auctores minores*, the gods and goddesses were a major theme,[223] as were their

218 BML . , r: Sicut modo aliquis episcopus bene deberet scire illa quae sibi utilia sunt (sacrare ecclesiam, predicare populum) usu, id est discendo antequam sit episcopus, et hoc est *prius re atque usu* (*BJ* .).

219 BML sin. , v: Simile accidit Comiti Flandrrie bellanti contra regem Francie; simile accidit Manfredo filio Frederici; simile de Corradino. BML sin. , v: Simile exemplum de Sancto Ludovico rege Francorum qui soldano interroganti eum quid faceret ipsi soldano si teneret eum captivum, respondet quod decapitaret eum nisi vellet converti ad fidem. Soldanus autem dixit quod non faceret sic ei sed volebat de pecunia eius et ita rex redemit se.

220 BML inf. . , r: Ut sunt hodie tyrani. BML . , r: Non minorem patientiam diebus nostris audivi. Nam occupata civitate paduana vipere tyranide, dum per potestatem deprehenderetur quidam familiaris Domini Francisci iunioris de Carrara qui tratatum quemdam de readquirendo Paduam sciebat omnesque consentientes, dum in presentia potestatis foret, licentiam [e]scredendi in quamdam cameram petiit, simulans se necessitate corporis torquere, dumque ibi foret, timens in tormentis fortitudinem non habere, maluit vita privari quam conscios pandere, propter quod felicem eventum domini sui impediret, sicque propriis manibus gladio per guttura percussa vita famosissime se privarit, cuiusque nomen fuit [gloss breaks o here].

221 BML AD , r: Hystoria secondo libro *De oratore* est testis temporum, lux veritatis, vita memorie, magistra vite, numptia veritatis et dicitur historia ab hysteron g<rece>, id est videre vel cognoscere. BML Ashb. , v: Primum preceptum istoriographi est non dicere res falssas. Secundum preceptum istoriographi est non laudare aliquem propter amiciciam nec vituperet aliquem propter invidiam, sed vera narrare. Historiographus debet scribere regiones et suas circumstantias; debet etiam describere consilia ducum que precedent bella et que sint digna memoratu; debet etiam describere eventum et finem rei.

222 Minerva dicitur quasi minuens nervos quia Minerva appellatur sapientia et qui volunt e ci sapientes ita dant se ad studium ut macerimi e ciantur et ita minuuntur nervii [*sic*]: BRF , v.

223 BRF , v: Nomina septem planetorum: [Saturnus] quia frigidus est et metit flores et herbas. Mars deus belli et armorum. Sol est fons totius caloris. *Mercurius virgam* dicitur habere idem caduceum cum qua facit homines dormire. Juppiter in significatione aeris et ab ipso ere procedunt fulmina secundum phylosophos. Venus pluries est qui<a> sub eius domicilio plurtetates [*sic pro* plures voluptates?] fiunt et luxuriosi. Luna id est Diana quedam venatoris [*sic pro* venatrix?] est dicta et ideo dicitur habere sagiptas. BRF . , v: Pallas enim apparuerat ei in specie fratris dei Febi. See BRF , r.

o spring such as the giants[224] or the furies[225] or other fantastic creatures.[226] Relations between immortals and mortals were often touched upon,[227] and a favoured theme was always the Trojan War and its aftermath.[228]

For school-level glossators to the classical Latin poets, the children of the gods continued to attract interest[229] as did relations between gods and mortals,[230] and fantastic creatures such as the centaurs.[231] Glossators were also preoccupied by figures with divine powers such as Circes,[232] and especially Hercules.[233] Legendary history continued to

224 BRF , r: Tangit illud quod fabulose dictum est de gigantibus qui posu<e>runt montes super montes et volebant capere celum sed tamen Iuppiter eos fulminavit.

225 BRF , r: Alecto, Tesyphone et Megera tres furie infernales, quarum quelibet suam habet proprietatem, scilicet Alecto principium mali, alia perseveratio, tertia perficit.

226 BNCF Magl. . , v: <Chimer>a est animal habens capud leoninum et habens ventrem caprinum.

227 BRF , v: Licaon quidam tyrrampnus Archadie, Iovi humanas carnes proposuit ad manducandum. Iuppiter indignatus ipsum mutavit in lupum et ponitur pro ipso lupo in hoc loco. ASF CStrozz. . , r: Ysion fuit segretarius Iovis et voluit concubere cum Yunone uxore sua. Ista nubem interposuit. Iste habuit agere cum nube et nati sunt centauri et propter hoc delictum rotatur in inferno. BNCF Magl. . , v: Ticius fuit quidam vir qui voluit cognoscere Dominam Laconam sive Iunonem propter quod fuit precipitatus in infernum et habet istam penam quia duo vultures rosterçant cor suum et cum est rosterçatum iterum renovatur et semper istam penam habet. BNCF Magl. . , v: Tantarus fuit quidam homo qui interfecit filium per quod est laniatus et habet istam penam.

228 BNF Magl. . , r: I<n>t(er) greges fuerunt duo viri probissimi quorum unus vocatur Achilles, et alius vocatur Ector. BNF Magl. . , fol. r: Circes fuit quedam incantatrix que dum s<ocii Uli>xis ad partes aplicassent suis incant<ationibus> et mollitis potationibus ipsos fecit in <variis> animalibus converti. BRF . , r: [Atride =] Nomen regis patronomicum ubi Atrides dicitur qui fuit filius Atrei, [ad] cuius nomen provenerat Agam(em)n(on). At the end of the text (r) the same writer provided a list of those killed in Trojan Wars, citing Dares Phrygius: Qui troianorum quem grecorum occiderunt: Hector: Protesilaum Patroclum Merionem […] XV. Aeneas: Amphimachum Nereum. Alexander: Palameden Antilocum Aiacen Achillem […] Aiax telamonius et Alexander multis se vulneribus occidunt. Alexander in prelio moritur. Aiax telamonius in castris. Qui grecorum quem troianorum occiderunt de ducibus exceptis plebibus: Achilles: Eufremum Ipotoum Plebeum Asterium […] Neoptolemus: Pentisileam Priamum Polixenam. Ad tumulus [*sic*] patris Diomedes: Mesten? Xantipum Protenerem […] Hec Dareus mandavit litteris.

229 BML . , r: Castor fuit equorum domitor. BML . , r: Castor rapuit unam filiam Leucippi et Pollux aliam sororem.

230 BML . , r: Neptunus et Apollo […] dicuntur edificasse primam Troiam […] menibus auri, qua edificata Laumedon rex inficiatus est precium ob quod indignat<us> Neptunus inclinavit aquas ad […] littora Troie […] Rex Laumedon per suam audaciam non fecit bene custodiri mare unde multi se illum aggressi qui civitatem destruxer<unt>. BML . , v: [Ariadna] misit epistolam hanc in illo sed interim Baccus qui revertebatur de India quam subiugaverat eam sibi matrimonio copulavit et demum eamdem in signum convertit quod corona dicitur. See BML . , r; BML . , v; Roberti ( ), , , , (n.).

231 BNCF Magl. . , v: Ad radices Montis Pellei ubi Chironis erat antrum reverberat mare undas suas.

232 BML . , r: Incantationibus Circes, filia Forci que vocabatur Silla, conversa est in mostrum marinum quod vocatur Silla et pili vulve eius e ecti sunt canes latrantes.

233 BML CS , r: Olympicum certamen Hercules in honorem atavi materni Pelopis edidit quo singulo anni quaterni numerantur. Solinus. BML . , r: Caribdis uxor Cachi fuit quam Hercules proiecit in mari et conversa est in iocum periculosum sic dictum.

command the attention of commentators,[234] especially the Trojan War and its consequences.[235]

It was the metric sections of Boethius's *Consolation* which provided the greatest opportunities for mythological glossing of this text, although mythological annotation of the proses was not uncommon. Of some interest here were the gods themselves[236] and especially the fates, given the text's concern with the problem of providence and free will[237] but greater was the attraction of their children, such as the furies[238] and especially of Orpheus.[239] Relations between immortals and mortals continued to interest glossators[240] and especially fascinating here for grammar pupils and their teachers was the story of Midas.[241] The Trojan War was perhaps of lesser interest here[242] but Hercules continued to be a major attraction.[243]

Paraphrase

A particular feature of manuscript schoolbooks is marginal paraphrase. This normally takes the form of simple textual summaries.[244] A similar

234 BNCF Magl. . , r: Fuerunt enim duo fratres, scilicet, Tiestes et Atreus. Atreus habebat uxorem que vocabatur Gressa que, filocapta de Thiestis pulcritudine concubuit cum ea [*sic*] et filios ex eo genuit, de quo Atreus valde indignatus persecutus est fratrem, qui a regno aufugit et demum finxit eum reducere et pacificari cum eo et introduxit ipsum et filios suos in regnum, quo facto filios illos sui fratris interfecit et dedit ipsos patri ad comedendum; dicit quod ex tanto scelere sol indignatus vertit cursus suos in auroram. BNCF Magl. . , v: Tangit istoriam quod Jason Medeam duxit et demum ipsa demissa accepit Creusam. Quare Medea immisit ignem in palatio quando festum fiebat de Creusa in nu[p]tiis [MS. in nutiit] et combusta est Creusa et alii astantes. Postea filios proprios quos de Jasone conceperat interfecit. See BML CS , r; BML CS , r; BML . , r; Roberti ( ), , , (n.).

235 BML sup. , v: Aiax habebat scutum teptum septem coriis tauri. Nunc dicit quod ipse movebit menia Troie cum illo scuto. BML sup. , r: Proteselaus fuit primus homo qui intravit in tenitorium [*sic*] Troianorum et primus fuit mortuus. BNCF Magl. . , r: Ab Achille quando ipsum interfecerat ligavit ipsum ad caudam sui equi <et> iter circum muros Troye raptavit. BNCF Magl. . , v: Acchillem debere mori in bello troyano nisi balnearetur in istigia palude; ipsa balneavit totum nisi plantas pedum. BML . , r: Quadam vice debebant pugnare pro tota gente Paris et Menelaus [...] sed iste Pandarus fregit pactum sed secundum veritatem fuit Pollicanus. See BML sup. , r; BNCF Magl. . , v; BML . , r; BML . , r.

236 Black and Pomaro ( ), , .

237 Black and Pomaro ( ), .

238 Black and Pomaro ( ), .

239 Black and Pomaro ( ), , , .

240 Black and Pomaro ( ), , .

241 Black and Pomaro ( ), , .

242 Black and Pomaro ( ), .

243 Black and Pomaro ( ), , .

244 BML . , v– r: Hic describitur conquestio Teditidis in futurum [...] Hic describitur narratio ipsius Thetis ad ipsum Neptunum [...] Responsio ipsius Neptunni ad Tethim [...] [etc.] BRF , v: Hic incipi(un)t huius operis particularia, in quantum continetur descriptio phylosophye et eius multiplex correctio et alterna inter ipsam et hunc egrum collucutio. BNCF Magl. . , r, r, v, r: In parte ista facit vocationem ad dominum, dicens quod debet ipse venire ad succurrendum hominibus benignis, scilicet, sibi suo remo, id est, auxilio suo, ut una

technique could be used in more advanced texts, such as Ovid's *Ars amatoria*[245] or Cicero's *Disputationes tusculanae.*[246] Frequently employed in these schoolbooks was the scholastic *divisio textus*, whereby the sections and subsections of the text were subdivided numerically, as for example in a set of glosses to Henry of Settimello's elegy,[247] or in others to the same text.[248]

The most characteristic feature of the marginal glossing in school manuscripts of the *Consolation* is simple exposition or paraphrase: of the Boethius manuscripts in Florence[249] contain this type of simple exegetical marginal glossing,[250] and indeed the quantity of basic expository comment far exceeds all other types of glossing. Simple paraphrase was an enduring feature, as can be seen, for example, in later thirteenth-century glosses,[251] in early Trecento glosses,[252] in later fourteenth-century glosses[253] and in early fifteenth-century glosses.[254]

When the scholastic *divisio textus* began to be used in thirteenth-century schoolbooks, the tendency was simply to divide the text into numbered sections.[255] However, the procedure of dividing the text tended to become more complicated in the Trecento, as a system was introduced of numbering the textual citations, corresponding to the

navis, id est, iste liber transeat ad portus, id est, concedat sibi gratiam explere istum librum utiliter. [etc.]

245 BNCF Magl. . , r: Supra conclusit auctoritatem Apolinis; hic docet per exempla reducens exempla ad autoritatem Apollinis. ¶Superius auctor posuit precepta quod melius est occultare stupra amansiarum [*sic*] quam ea manifestare; hic per exempla probat.

246 BRF , r: In hac prima questione auctor intendit persuadere quod mors sit non metuenda, quia nedum non est mors malum set est bonum, quamquam peripatetici teneant quod mors sit malum necessarium, cum natura vellet hominem perpetuum esse. Et quia ens est bonum non ens non est bonum. Incipit sibi persuadere per quandam complexionem si mors est malum, alicui malum est. Si alicui aut mortuis aut morituris aut utrisque, quod neutris malum sit, nititur persuadere.

247 ASF CStrozz. . , r, v: In parte prima ponit multa generalia loca in <quibus> fiebant de eo ratiocinationes et (in) secunda dicit quod si ab istis commendaretur <...> autoribus quod eius fama bona non esset. [etc.]

248 BRF , v: Auctor in parte precedenti posuit suam miseriam et luctum in generali; in parte ista ponit a particulari et dividitur ista pars in quinque. Nam primo dicit quod omnia semina sunt ei nociva, id est, contraria scilicet helementa. Dicit quod omnes planete insidiantur ei subiungendo quod nesciet quid faciat. Tertio ait a priori patente cur non fuit alius tam infelix ut est ipse, subiungendo multos qui passi fuerant multas adversitates. Quarto ait quod magis dolet quia est in tam gravi miseria positus in patria sua quam si esset in aliena. Quinto notificat quod omnia tempora anni sunt ei contraria.

249 Black and Pomaro ( ), , , – , , –, , – , – , – , – , – , – , , –, –, –, –, –, –, , , , –, – .

250 For simple exposition or paraphrase in the Bodley Italian manuscripts of the *Consolation*, see Black and Pomaro ( ), n. .

251 Black and Pomaro ( ), – .

252 Black and Pomaro ( ), – .

253 Black and Pomaro ( ), – .

254 Black and Pomaro ( ), .

255 Black and Pomaro ( ), .

divisions of the paraphrase.[256] The beginning of the second division in the text was signalled by the phrase 'ibi secunda', written before the opening words of the section; there was never an 'ibi prima' because that section of the text was indicated by the gloss itself, which was written in the margin at the point where the entire text to be divided itself began. Sometimes the beginning of the text to be divided was indicated by a lemma in the commentary.[257] When textual divisions were extended beyond two sections, the same system of 'ibi secunda' was often expanded to 'ibi tertia', 'ibi quarta', etc.[258]

Full scholastic *divisio textus*, with subdivisions of sections and corresponding *lemmata*, was, of course, a procedure not limited in the classroom to annotating Boethius's *Consolation*.[259] This scholastic system continued in full force into the mid-fifteenth century, as is clear from glosses to the *Consolation*, written by a hand using a fine humanist script.[260] However, it seems that this scholastic system of textual division began to go out of favour with the rising influence of humanist teachers in the second half of the fifteenth century. This is clear, as seen above ( ), from the teaching activity of Bartolomeo Fonzio, the tutor to various Florentine families including the Rinieri,[261] and probably the Sassetti[262] and Cattani di Diacceto,[263] and lecturer over many years at the Florentine Studio,[264] who left marginal glosses in the *Consolation* belonging to the Cattani di Diacceto family. The annotations composed by Fonzio resemble the brief summaries of each section of the text often appearing in grammar-school copies.[265] It is clear, however, that Fonzio was already discontented (as seen above, –) with the style of teaching adopted by his non-humanist predecessors and contemporaries. While the latter were content to repeat formulaic and inelegant summaries, Fonzio now composed his textual resumés afresh in humanist Latin,

256 Black and Pomaro ( ), – . 257 Black and Pomaro ( ), .
258 Federici Vescovini ( ), ; Black and Pomaro ( ), – , , , – , , , – , .
259 BML sup. , r: *Inferni raptores*. Istud est proprie huius libri principium et dividitur liber iste in duas partes, scilicet in prohemium et tractatus, secunda ibi *dux Herebus*. Prima in duas. Nam primo ponit, secundo invocat, secunda ibi *dii quibus*. Prima in duas. Nam prima ponit brevem p(re)positionem [*sic*], secundo ostendit se spiratum spiritu fabeo [*sic*], secunda ibi *opressus removete*. Prima in duas: primo ostendit se spiratum [ab] Apolline, secundo comprobat hoc a signis, secunda ibi *iam mihi*. Prima in tot quod ponit signo partes patebunt in legendo. See BML CS , r, for a XV[1] *divisio textus* in Ovid's *Metamorphoses*.
260 Black and Pomaro ( ), – .
261 Francesco di Bernardo Rinieri learnt Latin from Bartolomeo Fonzio in : ASF Corporazioni religiose soppresse dal governo francese . , v.
262 See de la Mare ( ), – , *passim*. 263 Black and Pomaro ( ), .
264 Verde (–), . – . 265 Black and Pomaro ( ), – .

making heavy use of such classical stylistic features as indirect speech; he also abandoned the scholastic *divisiones textus* which had previously characterized these exegetic summaries.

Authorities

Most of the forms of glossing encountered hitherto were shared between the minor and major authors, but the practice of citing other authors in marginalia was largely limited to texts of the Latin classics used in schools. In Florentine libraries, in fact, there are only ten manuscripts of minor authors in which other texts are cited.

Text	*Author(s) cited*
BML . (Theodulus)	Genesis
ASF CStrozz. . (Henry of Settimello)	Seneca
BML AD (*Ilias latina*)	Ovid (*Remedia*, *Tristia*), Seneca, Juvenal
BML sup. (pseudo-Boethius)	Cicero, Aristotle
BML . (pseudo-Boethius)	*Rhetorica ad Herennium*, Terence, Horace, Seneca
BRF (Henry of Settimello)	Seneca, Vergil
BRF . (*Ilias latina*)	Dares Phrygius
BNCF Magl. . (Henry of Settimello)	Ovid
BNCF Landau Fin. (Cato)	Seneca, Vergil, Boethius *Consolation*, Ovid, Solomon
BML . (Henry of Settimello)	Bible

On the other hand, there are fifty-five manuscripts of minor authors in which no other authorities are cited. The absence of references to other texts in the glosses to the minor authors suggests a basic level of reading focused on simple comprehension: as pupils moved beyond the phonetic and mnemonic phase which characterized the reading of elementary texts such as the psalter and *Ianua*, the central concern became simple understanding, through lexical synonyms, word-order marking, grammatical analysis, figures and paraphrase. The next stage was a basic understanding of context – geographical, historical and mythological. All this was accomplished at the level of the minor authors. There was still little attempt to relate the text to the wider literary tradition, as represented by the writings of other authors.

This broader literary context came with the study of the major authors. Out of manuscripts in all, there are in which other authors are cited.[266] If the major and minor authors are considered together, the profile of the authorities cited gives the following results:

Authority	Number of MSS in which cited
Vergil	
Cicero (and ps.Cicero)	
Ovid	
Seneca (and pseudo-Seneca)	
Lucan	
Valerius Maximus	
Aristotle (and pseudo-Aristotle)	
Horace	
Isidore	
Sallust	
Servius	
Hugutio	
Boethius	
Augustine	
Livy	
Plato	
Terence	
Priscian	
Pliny the Elder	
Orosius	
Statius	
Varro	
Juvenal	
Petrarch	
Old Testament	
New Testament	
Suetonius	
Macrobius	
Martianus Capella	

[266] See Appendix .

Fulgentius
Dante
Festus
Vegetius
Papias
Eutropius
Jerome

What is striking about this list is its overwhelmingly literary/grammatical/philological character. Four of the top five authorities are primarily literary authors: Vergil, Cicero, Ovid and Lucan. Among the ten leading authorities, there is only one exclusively philosophical author: Aristotle. The top twenty include only four authors who could be considered principally as philosophers: Aristotle, Augustine, Plato and Seneca. The entire list includes only three authorities in theology: Boethius, Augustine and Jerome. Old and New Testaments are both near the bottom. Considering that this list comprises texts and glossators going back to the twelfth century, it is clear that the philological style of glossing often associated with Renaissance humanism was in fact a constant feature of Italian grammar education during the middle ages. Another important feature of the list is the almost total absence of scholastic philosophers and theologians: the only scholastic authority mentioned is Aristotle, who hardly dominates, given that he has only half the number of citations as either Vergil or Cicero.

The profile of the authorities cited among glossators to Boethius's *Consolation of Philosophy* [267] gives the following results:

Authority	Number of MSS in which cited
Old Testament	
Seneca (and pseudo-Seneca)	
Aristotle (and pseudo-Aristotle)	
Ovid	
Cicero (and pseudo-Cicero)	
Horace	
Lucan	
Augustine	
Plato	
Dante	
New Testament	

[267] See Black and Pomaro ( ), – .

Juvenal
Vergil
Valerius Maximus
Macrobius
Persius

Given the philosophical and theological subject matter of Boethius's text, it is not surprising to find a more prominent place for the Old Testament and for Aristotle than among the major authors, but again what is interesting is to discover such a strong showing for literary authorities: of the sixteen authors cited twice or more, ten were primarily literary figures (Ovid, Cicero, Horace, Lucan, Dante, Juvenal, Vergil, Valerius Maximus, Macrobius and Persius). What is more, there is again no sign of scholastic authorities other than Aristotle. These lists are clear testimony not only to the overwhelmingly philological character of grammar education in Italy in the middle ages and Renaissance, but also to the specialization of the curriculum which had occurred after the rise of scholasticism in the thirteenth century. Philosophical and theological learning, as represented by the scholastic authors, was removed from Italian grammar schools: grammatical and literary studies were relegated to the level of secondary education, while philosophical and theological study became the monopoly of the universities.

Introductory philosophy

Although the teaching of the authors in Italian secondary schools was thus overwhelmingly philological and grammatical, there was a limited role accorded to preparation for the subjects of higher education. Some attention, albeit highly circumscribed, was devoted at the school level to philosophy, natural science and even occasionally to theology; the intention of teachers may have been to familiarize pupils with a little of the subject matter that some of them might go on to meet at the university level. And yet it is important to emphasize that these higher disciplines were encountered in a superficial and unsystematic manner in the course of reading and glossing the authors at school: the occasional topics from philosophy, natural science and theology were introduced as part of an overall philological reading of texts; the approach was amateurish, with little or no technical vocabulary or terminology and few references to other philosophical authorities. Indeed, as has already been seen, there was an almost complete absence of references to scholastic authors, despite the fact that the glosses have a broad chronological range from the twelfth to the fifteenth century and often treat texts with explicitly philosophical contents.

The links between this elementary philosophical material and the overall philological/grammatical character of school glossing is apparent, for example, in the emphasis given to the history of philosophy: history, biography and historical anecdote played a central role in school-level marginalia and so it is not surprising to discover that the approach to philosophical topics in the grammar classroom was often historical. There was interest in the ancient philosophical sects,[268] in their etymology,[269] in their teachers[270] and in their biographies.[271] This historical interest of course extended to the basic doctrines of the ancient philosophical schools.[272] Of these the Stoics attracted particular notice,[273] but school glossators were also drawn to comment on the Epicureans, apparently because of their doctrine of pleasure, evidently fascinating however unacceptable.[274] Legendary philsophers and their doctrines interested commentators.[275] But the teachings of philosophical authorities whose legacy is preserved in their own writings are most extensively represented in school-level glosses, including Cicero,[276] Aristotle[277] and

268 BRF , r: Tres sunt septe philosophorum, scilicet stoica, peripatetica et academica. See Black and Pomaro ( ), . 269 Black and Pomaro ( ), .

270 Black and Pomaro ( ), .

271 BML AD , r: Aristotelis Nichomachi medici filius gente macedo patria straguritanus. Socratis tribus annis et Platonis XX discipulus. Alexandri Magni magister. Visit preter mortem Platonis annis XXIII, in totum vero annis LXIII. Composuit mille tractatus.

272 BRF , v: Stoici ponunt summum bonum in virtute tantum. Academici, Peripatetici ponunt summum bonum in bonis animi et corporis. Epicurei ponunt in voluptate. See BML Ashb. , r.

273 BRF , r: Haec est Stoicorum sententia qui dicunt rectam conscientiam et actionem bonorum, etiam sine aliis adiumentis, satis est ad bene beateque vivendum et ipsam virtutem esse pro remuneratione et premio quia virtus propter se ipsam expectenda. See BML Ashb. , v; BRF , r.

274 BML . , v: Sunt aliqui qui putant esse summum bonum voluptates ut Epycuri et hi virtutem destruunt. BML Pl. . , v: Epicurus dicebat voluptatem esse summum bonum, dolorem esse summum malum. See BML . , v, r; BRF , r.

275 BML AD , v: Xenocrates philosophus Platonis discipulus cuidam loquaci dixit, 'Multum audi, loquere pauca. Os enim unum et aures dua a natura accepimus.' Idem cum inter multos detratores taceret interrogatus cur solus sileret, 'Quia dixisse me', inquit, 'aliquando penituit, tacuisse numquam.' See BML Ashb. , r, r.

276 BRF , r: Idem libro quinto *De finibus*: Iustitie sunt, inquit, adiuncte pietas, bonitas, liberalitas, benignitas, comitas, queque sunt generis eiusdem, atque hec ita iustitie proprie sunt ut sint virtutum reliquarum comunia. See BML AD , v, r; BRF , r.

277 BML Ashb. , r: Amicicia est, secundum Aristotilem, mutua benivolentia in compaxis, non latens rationem eius qui diligitur et non propter se ipsum. Et nota quod tres sunt gradus amicicie. Est amicicia que est propter utile, secunda propter delectabile, tertia propter honestum. See BML AD , v; Black and Pomaro ( ), .

Plato,[278] whom one glossator cites as, according to Augustine, semi-divine and preferred by the gods themselves.[279]

There is occasionally general discussion of the structure of philosophy and learning[280] and even a little metaphysics and theology.[281] A notable amount of the philosophical glossing – such as it is – can be loosely classified as *moralia.* This included standard topics such as the divisions of moral philosophy,[282] the active and contemplative lives.[283] Frequently discussed themes in moral or political philosophy appear, such as liberty,[284] sensual desire,[285] death,[286] wisdom,[287]

278 BRF , v: Hic nota singularem Platonis opinionem de anima. Dicit enim quod anime in orizonte trinitatis creantur plene scientiis et virtutibus sed post unionem ipsarum ad corpus mole et corporis gravitate omnium penitus obliviscuntur et est orizon infimus gradus intelligentiarum. Unde secundum poeticam fictionem anima plena omnibus bonis descendens per Saturnum deponit eternitatem et assumit mortalitatem. Deinde descendens per Iovem deponit bonitatem et assumit maliciam. Deinde per Martem transitum faciens deponit mansuetudinem et accipit iracundiam et irascibelitatem. Deinde per solem transiens deponit divinitatem et assumit humanitatem. Descendens autem per Venerem deponit castitatem et assumit immundiciam. Deinde descendens per Mercurium perdit veritatem et recipit falsitatem, et descendens per Lunam perdit levitatem et assumit gravitatem. Et deinde sic virtutibus spoliata et viciis obscurata iungitur corpori et oportet ut sic spolietur quia purissima corpori non posset iungi. Deinde vero anima deificata a corpore separata rediens ad deum per omnia illa loca deponit singula vicia in singulis illis locis assumpta et resumit ibi prius dimissas virtutes in descensu. See BML Ashb. , v; BML . , v; Black and Pomaro ( ), .

279 BML AD , r: Dicit Augustinus libro secundo capitulo XII *De civitate dei* loquens de Platone: Putavi philosophum Platonem inter semideos commemorandum sed ego etiam diis ipsis preferendum non dubito.

280 BRF , r: Philosophia triples est, scilicet, naturalis, moralis et rationalis.

281 BRF , r: Isti tales philosofi, implicando contradictionem, teneba<n>t quod ex nichilo nil potest gingi et sic aliquid formale non potest reverti ad nichilion et hoc est contra fidem, scilicet quod mundus, quem ex nichilo deus fecit, non potest reverti ad nichilum quia in veritate deus ex nichilo creavit et ad nichilum reducet ipsum mundum et talis disputatio sepe inter istos philoso<fos> fiebat et sunt dialectici. See BML . , r.

282 BML . , r: Moralis philosophia dicitur in partes, scilicet in polyticam que dicitur a polys quod est civitas, nam de regimine civitatum tractat. Et in monosticam que dicitur a monos quod est unus, nam de se ipso curam habere instituit. Et in iconomicam que dicitur — [gap in text], nam curam rerum familiarum tenere monet. See BML . , v.

283 BRF , r: Triplex est vivendi genus, scilicet vita attiva, vita contemplativa, vita mixta. Vita attiva regum est, contemplativa philosophorum, mixta cum utroque ut Tulius vixit. See BRF , v; Black and Pomaro ( ), .

284 BML . , v: Duplex est libertas: una sub domino et ista est ficta; alia sine domino et ista est vera. Qui habet libertatem fictam et querit veram aliquando perdit utramque quia dominus aufert sibi et forte vitam. Melius ergo habere fictam quam nullam.

This gloss, written in the later Trecento possibly in Liguria or Lombardy, is an interesting ideological comment on the response to Visconti territorial expansionism. For writer's anti-Florentine sentiments, see above, n. .

285 BML AD , r: Et est sensus sicut semper appetere facit hominem cupidum et quodamodo infelicem quia infelicitas non est aliud quam voluntas et anime nostre inquietatio. Ita nichil plus appetere facit hominem beatum quia voluntas sua est in quiete.

286 See BRF , r, cited above, n. .

287 BRF , v: Nota non esse sapientis viri privatum commodum publico bono anteponere nec etiam debere ipsum virtutis intermissionem facere ullo casu si constantie nomen habere cupit.

law,[288] poverty,[289] glory,[290] fortune[291] and happiness.[292] But the major focus of the moral philosophical comments in the marginalia to schoolbooks concerned virtue and the virtues.[293]

Just as important as ethics, if not actually predominant, was the interest in natural science. Attention was given to topics in biology, including the bodily humours,[294] sleep,[295] vision[296] and plants, their powers and products.[297] There was also interest in physics, including discussions of the elements,[298] and motion and change.[299] Mathematics was touched on qualitatively, with glosses on geometry,[300] and time and chronology.[301] There was interest in astronomy and astrology, with discussions of the heavens and the planets.[302] Attention was also given to psychology and the relation between body and soul.[303] Finally, the school glossators even occasionally ranged into discussions of cosmology, attempting to show how the soul, the earth with its elements and the heavens are interrelated with divine creation.[304]

288 BRF , v: Lex est nervus in civitate: sicut enim nervi substinent corpus ita leges regunt civitatem. See BRF , v.

289 BML AD , v: Facit pulcerimam commendationem paupertatis et optimam legentibus persuasionem quatenus velint sequi antiquorum vestigia non conquerendo de paupertate. Est enim considerandus e ectus istorum qui in infima paupertate constituti pervenerint ad tantos gradus dignitatum appretiantes solam virtutem.

290 BRF , v: Gloria est frequens de aliquo fama cum laude.

291 BML inf. . , v: Quid est fortuna? Fortuna nichil alliud est quam eventus rerum.

292 Black and Pomaro ( ), .

293 BRF , v: Humana natura non potius regitur forte quam virtute quia animus dux vite mortalium vel dicunt quod potius regitur forte quam virtute sed falsum quia animus dux. BRF , r: Quid est honestas? Est vite finis. In quot partibus dividitur? In quatuor partes: iustitiam, temperantiam, fortitudinem, prudentiam. See BML . , r, v; BML AD , v; BML . , v; BML Edili , r.

294 BML . , r: Quattuor scilicet humores dominantes in humano corpore, scilicet sanghunei, flematici, collerci et malenconnaci.

295 BML . , v: Dicit secundus philosophus quod sompnus est ymago mortis.

296 Black and Pomaro ( ), .

297 BML . , r: Vinum est aqua putrefatta in vite propter potentiam solis. See Black and Pomaro ( ), . 298 Black and Pomaro ( ), . 299 Black and Pomaro ( ), .

300 BRF , r: Quadrangulus dicit quia quatuor angulos habet, scilicet orientem, occidentem, meridiem et septentrionem.

301 BML . , r: Nota quod Deus divisit mundum in quatuor etates, scilicet auream, argenteam, heream et feream. Qualis est di erentia inter metalla, talis fuit inter illas etates.

302 BML . , v: [Saturnus] dicitur esse prior tempore et maior et non habuisse patrem, unde quia est primus plan<e>tarum incipiendo a superiore et perficit cursum suum in XXX annis. See BRF . , r and Black and Pomaro ( ), – , , , .

303 BRF , r: Homo ex elementis et quinta exentia componitur, corpus ex elementis, anima ex quinta essentia. See Black and Pomaro ( ), , .

304 BML Rinuccini , v: Dixit *terq<ue> quater beatos* quia voluit hostendere beatos anima et corpore, scilicet cum dixit *terque* hoc ideo quia tres putabant animas et prout est invisibilis ut [in] arboribus, sensibilis ut in bestiis, rationabilis ut in hominibus, et omnes iste tres anime simul in hominibus sunt. Ideo dixit ter. Dixit *quater*, hoc ideo ut tangeret felicitatem corporis. Nam IIIIor elementa prout est ignis aer aqua e<t> terra absque quibus corpus recte nutriri non potest. Et ideo quater dixit. See Black and Pomaro ( ), .

Introductory rhetorical analysis

Just as teachers wanted to give their pupils a taste of various philosophical topics at the school level, so they also sometimes provided them with a brief sample of rhetoric, a discipline likewise studied normally after leaving secondary education. Again, as in the introduction to philosophy, rhetoric was touched on in a cursory and superficial fashion when reading the school authors; what the pupil might have gained from this type of commentary was a basic familiarity with rhetorical terminology.

Some attention was given to the genres into which rhetoric was divided by classical theorists.[305] Just as much interest was shown in the standard divisions of the speech.[306] Sometimes a shortened version of the parts of the oration is found.[307] The individual parts of the oration were also sometimes noted. The statement of facts or *narratio* was usually simply indicated in the margin without further elaboration,[308] although it was summarized on one occasion,[309] and on another the glossator pointed out that the *narratio* had verisimilitude, one of its three essential attributes according to classical theory.[310] The *divisio* or outline of the case was also occasionally mentioned briefly.[311] But more attention was paid to the proof (*confirmatio*) and refutation (*confutatio*). Sometimes these were simply noted,[312] but there was also a tendency to identify the type of arguments used.[313] Sometimes the standard arguments (*loci communes*)

305 BRF , r: Tres sunt genera causarum, auto<r> est ipse Cicero in *Arte nova*, scilicet demostrativum, deliberativum et iudiciale. Demostrativum versatur et collocatur in campo martio; deliberativum collocatur in genere deliberativo, id est in senatu; iudiciale genus et collocatum in foro, id est apud iudices.

306 BML Ashb. , v– r: exordium, naratio, divisio, confirmatio, confutatio, conclusio. BML . , v: Oratio Ayacis Thelamoni in qua primo ponit exordium, secundo narrationem, tertio confirmaciones et refutaciones et quarto conclusionem. BML . , v: Hic ponit orationem Tetidis auctor ad Nectunum esse, quam quattuor facit, quia primo ponit exordium captando benivolentiam ab auditoris persona, secundo narrationem, tertio petitionem, quarto conclusionem.

307 BML . , r: hic describitur narratio, ponit peitionem, ponit confirmationem. For BML . , v– r, see above, , n. .

308 BRF , v; BML sup. , v; BRF , r; BRF , v; BNCF Landau Fin. , v.

309 BNCF Landau Fin. , r: Narratio in qua explicat quid factum est a Mitridate ab illo tempore in posterum in quo recessit L. Silla et L. Murena.

310 BRF , r: verisimiliter narrat quia dignitates personarum a ert. See *Rhetorica ad Herennium*, . .

311 BRF , v: exponit divisionem; BRF , v, v: prima pars divisionis [...] secunda ibi [...] tertia ibi [...] quarta ibi [...] quinta ibi [...] pars secunda divisionis [...]

312 BRF , r, r; BRF , r; BRF , v, r, r, r; BRF , r, r; BML . , v.

313 BNCF Magl. . , r, v, v, v: argomentatio modo ab iure; argomentatio modo ad imposibilitatem; modo ab imposibili argomentatur; argumentatur modo ad utramquem partem; modo argumentatur ad partem contrariam; respondet quod verum est; iterum argumentatur ad imposibilitatem. BML . , v: argumentum sumptum a natura, argumentum necessarium, argumentum comodum.

of the proof or refutation could simply be mentioned generically[314] but they could also be more explicitly indicated.[315] Other standard arguments mentioned are shifting the guilt,[316] or argument from authority.[317] The five-part structure of an argument (*propositio, ratio, rationis confirmatio, exornatio, conplexio*)[318] is also mentioned.[319]

This stress on argument in proof and refutation may represent the new influence on teachers of the revival in the fourteenth and fifteenth centuries of the *Rhetorica ad Herennium*, in which this topic is given particular emphasis,[320] but there are also conservative features of rhetoric as treated in glosses to schoolbooks. One example in this connection is the rhetorical *divisio causarum*, which was on one occasion conflated with the scholastic *divisio textus*, resulting in a hybrid mixture of traditional and innovatory elements; interestingly, this scholastic form of analysis was applied to Cicero's oration, *De imperio Cn. Pompei*, a text which had not been read at the school level before the fifteenth century.[321] Another aspect of these school glosses suggestive of the traditional *ars dictaminis* is the substitution of *petitio* for the *confirmatio/confutatio* of classical theory,[322] and the summarial treatment of the *conclusio*.[323]

The commonest conservative feature of the simple rhetorical analysis found in glosses to schoolbooks was the prominent place given to the *exordium* or introduction. In a classical textbook such as *Rhetorica ad Herennium*, this topic was given a brief treatment (. –), whereas in the medieval *ars dictaminis*, greater emphasis was given to the *exordium* than to the other classical parts of the discourse, extensively treated in ancient

[314] BNCF Landau Fin. , v: Hic Cicero confirmat per locum communem.

[315] BRF , v, v: Primo enim arguit ab honestate quia superius de gloria romana [...] Tot nunc validioribus argumentis confirmat [...] ab utilitate [...] Hic arguit ab utilitate rei publice per partem fortitudinis [...] Hic ostendit partem illam tute utilitatis esse considerandum que pertinet ad consilium sive dolum et simul miscet partes prudentie cum ostendit commoda incomodi vicualium. Cf. *Rhetorica ad Herennium*, . . See BRF , v: per honestum a partibus iusticiae que est pars recti. Cf. *Rhetorica ad Herennium*, . .

[316] BML Strozzi , v: utitur argumento rethorico, scilicet translatio criminis.

[317] BRF , r: arguit ab autoritate. Cf. *Rhetorica ad Herennium*, . , .

[318] *Rhetorica ad Herennium*, . , . .

[319] BRF , v: dividitur in quinque partes argumentationis: primo ponit propositionem, secundo rationem, tertio rationis confirmationem, quarto exortationem, quinto complexionem.

[320] *Rhetorica ad Herennium*, . .

[321] BNCF Landau Fin. , v: *Divisio*. In qua divisione Cicero ostendit quid sit narraturus et primo pollicitur se dicturum de genere belli, ° de ipsius magnitudine, ° de imperatore eligendo, iby ª quoniam de belli genere dixi nunc de magnitudine belli dicam, yby ª restat ut de imperatore ad id bellum eligendo.

[322] BML . , v– r; BML . , r. Cf. Francesco da Buti, in Bodley Lat. misc. e. , r–v.

[323] BRF , v, r, v: epiloga<t> nunc, concludit nunc autor, nunc concludit epilogam [...] in duas partes; nunc manifestat hanc causam. Cf. Francesco da Buti, in Bodley Lat. misc. e. , v.

theory but now rapidly passed over.[324] The two kinds of introduction found in classical theory (direct opening or *principium*, and the subtle approach or *insinuatio*) are mentioned,[325] as is the classical doctrine of the four types (*genera*) of cases (*honestum, turpe, dubium, humile*).[326] The purpose of the exordium was to render the audience 'docilem, benivolum, adtentum' (*Ad Herennium*, .)[327] and in school glosses some attention was paid to ensuring listeners 'ut adtentos, ut dociles' (*Ad Herennium*, .).[328] But in the *ars dictaminis* the doctrine of 'captatio benivolentie' was a special priority,[329] and so it is not surprising to find this concept highlighted.[330] To ensure goodwill from the audience, classical theory recommended 'discussing our own person, the person of our adversaries, that of our hearers, and the facts themselves',[331] doctrines echoed in school glosses.[332] To secure goodwill 'ab nostra persona', it was recommended that 'nostrum o cium sine adrogantia laudabimus, atque [...] quales fuerimus [...] in amicos' (*Ad Herennium*, .), a doctrine echoed in school glosses.[333] Notable here was the famous *topos humilis*, favoured not only in classical theory but also in medieval practice[334] and echoed in school glosses.[335] Other specific recommendations for *captatio benivolentie* with reference to audience or adversaries are also encountered.[336] School

324 Typical is the treatment found in Francesco da Buti's *ars dictaminis*, where the non-classical greeting (*salutatio*) and classical *exordium* are extensively discussed, whereas the remaining parts (*narratio, petitio, conclusio*) are given only a cursory mention: see BRF , v ; Bodley lat. misc. e. , v– v (*narratio, petitio, conclusio*) but r– v (*exordium*).

325 BRF , r: Dicit Tullius in *Rethoricis* quod rethori<ca> cum exordio habet duos species, principium et insinuationem. Cf. *Rhetorica ad Herennium*, . .

326 BRF , r: Exordium: genus causae dubium. Cf. *Rhetorica ad Herennium*, . .

327 BNCF Landau Fin. , r: facit auditores dociles, actentos et benivolos; BNCF CS J. . , v: cum dicit, 'de coniuratione Catelline', addit nos dociles, cum dicit 'verissime potero', benivolos, 'absolvam paucis', intentos. Cf. *Bellum Catilinae*, . – .

328 BML . , r: Rethorice loquitur: di [*sic*] minoribus rebus magna promictit ut et levem materiam sublevet et auditorem atentum faciat. Cf. *Rhetorica ad Herennium*, . : 'Adtentos habebimus si pollicebimur nos de rebus magnis [...] verba facturos [...]' See BML Strozzi , r. BNCF . , .r. BRF , r, v; , v; , v.

329 See e.g. Francesco da Buti's treatment in Bodley Lat. misc. e. , r .

330 BRF , v: Benivolentie captatio, animam sibi benivolam reddit. BNCF Magl. . , r: captat benivolentiam. See BNCF Magl. . , r; Magl. . , r. BRF , r– v; , v, ; , r. BML . , r, v, v, r, r, r.

331 Tr. Caplan ( ), .

332 BML . , v: captando benivolentiam ab auditoris persona. BRF , r: eleganter benivolentiam captat et ab oratoris et auditorum persona et a rebus ipsis. See BRF , r. BNCF Landau Fin. , r. BML . , v.

333 BRF , r: a persona sua benivolentiam captat cum o cium suum extollat sine arrogantia monstrando qualiter fuit in amicos. See BRF , v.

334 Curtius ( ), .

335 BNCF Landau Fin. , r: Hoc exordium captat benivolentiam a modestia dicentis.

336 BML . , v: benivolenciam [...] captat deducendo adversarium ad contempcionem. Cf. *Rhetorica ad Herennium*, . . See BRF , r.

glossators occasionally even contradicted the teachings normally found in classical theory when identifying *captationes benivolentie* in their authors.[337]

Introductory and accompanying material

Probationes pennae, drawings and colophons

A characteristic feature of schoolbooks was the presence of additional written material. Sometimes this consisted of schoolboyish scribbling, often extensive and now given the inappropriately respectable Latin label of *probationes pennae.*[338] Often such *probationes* included Latin alphabets, sometimes concluding with abbreviation signs for 'et', the prefix 'cum-' or 'con-' or for the termination '-rum', so linking the texts of school authors with earlier elementary reading manuals, the *tavola* or *carta* and *salterio,* which in a similar way began normally with this type of alphabet:[339]

abcd
abcd[340]
abcdefghiklmnopqrstuxyz[341]
AAaAaAAbB
ccddeeeeeee
fgghhij
KLmmnnpppqr[342]
aabbccdde[343]
abcddefghijklmmnopqrrsstuxyç et con[344]
Abcdefghik
lmmnopqrstu
xxyç [sn.] [sn.]
[345]

Aabcd
abcdefg[346]

[337] BRF , v: Repetitio est ad maiorem benivolentiam. But cf. *Rhetorica ad Herennium,* . : 'exordium [...] vitiosum est quod [...] nimium longum est [...]'

[338] BML sup. , 'r; BML Rinuccini , v; BML . , v; BRF , v; BNCF Panciat. , v– v (n.n.); BML Ashb. , v; BML . , v; BRF , v– r, v– r, v; BRF , v, r, rear cover; BML AD , r– v; ASF CStrozz. . , v (Gehl ( ),); BML Strozzi , v– v; BNCF Panciat. , front flyleaves; BML San Marco , r.

[339] See above, n. .

[340] BML sup. , 'r.

[341] BRF . , v (XIIIc. annotation). A possible link with the psalter was the following prayer written by the same hand just above the alphabet: Deus i[n] nomine tuo salvum me fac et in virtute tua.

[342] BRF , v.

[343] BML . , v.

[344] BML . , r.

[345] BML . , r.

[346] BRF , v (XIIIc. annotator).

AabcdefghiklmnooppQqrRssttuuxz
aaaabcdefghilmnopqrstuxyz[347]
abcdefghiij <…> [348]
Aabcdefghikllmnopqrstuxyz[349]
Aabcdefghiklmnopqrstuxz et con rum[350]
Aabcdefghiklmnoprsstuxyz & con rum
Aabcdeefghklm[351]
a.b.c.d.e.f.g.h.i.k.l.m.n.o.p.[352]

After Greek began to be taught in the fifteenth century, Greek alphabets (sometimes ignorantly written) were occasionally included as well, sometimes with names of letters spelled out in Latin:[353]

Alpha Vita Gamma […]
[…]

A further sign of elementary Greek teaching was the crude transliteration into Greek in one manuscript of six schoolboys' names.[354]

Schoolboys were not reluctant to draw in their books, as is clear from sketches of animals (fish and a bird,[355] a horned animal's head in profile[356]), of acquaintances ('Sanese be o'[357]) or just faces,[358] heads[359] or a three-quarter profile.[360] There is a drawing of the devil corresponding to the text 'diabolus';[361] among objects sketched, notable is a musical instrument which appears to be a lute.[362] Sometimes the drawings serve as illustrations of the text, as for example one depicting Agamemnon with a nurse and Octavia;[363] particularly noteworthy is a drawing of the wheel of fortune to illustrate Boethius's *Consolation*,[364] resembling closely

[347] BML Ashb. , r. [348] BML sin. , r. [349] BRF , r.
[350] ASF Carte Cerchi , < > v. [351] ASF Carte Cerchi , < > v.
[352] BML . , inside front flyleaf, XIII^2 copyist. See above, n. , for other alphabets written by XIIIc. hands in BML sin. (Sedulius, XIc.), v.
[353] BML CS , v. The schoolboy copyist who wrote this alphabet neither knew how to write Greek letters nor their correct names. See BML sup. , r. In BML . , r, Greek alphabet written with names of letters written above; Greek diphthongs transliterated in Latin, and another attempted Greek alphabet. [354] BRF , v: see above, .
[355] BML Strozzi , v, v, r. [356] BML Edili , 'r.
[357] BML San Marco , v. Same hand filled this page with other sketches and wrote various names and dates: Ugolino di Vieri, Piero Chapponi, Giovanni Rucellai e chompagni <…>, anno domini MCCCC°LXL, Sono banchiere (et) chompa(gni) in Monpelieri di Francia, Mess(er)e Donato di Niccholò di Coccho-Donati, Cosimo di Giovanni di Bicci de' Medici (et) chompagni deono dare a Alamanno Salviati (et) chompagni, Francesco Mannelli e chompagni < …>
[358] BRF , r, r; BRF , v, v, r, r, v, r, r, r, r, v.
[359] BRF , r; BML Edili , 'r. [360] BML Edili , 'r. [361] BRF , v.
[362] BML . , v. [363] BML CS , v; see v, r, r, v.
[364] BML . , v, illustrated in Black and Pomaro ( ), pl. .

an illumination found in a manuscript of *Carmina Burana*,[365] not to mention a series of illustrations to the *Aeneid* with captions.[366] Sexual fantasies were not always far from the minds of schoolboys, as is evident in one capital 'M' which is turned into the shape of a female torso.[367]

Adolescent infatuation could also be expressed in traditionally symbolic form, as when a heart was sketched, pierced with an arrow, on either end of which were written the initials 'PGF' and 'APADD'.[368] This schoolboyish a ection was not always directed to members of the opposite sex, as is clear from these words recorded by one boy about another called Pollio.[369] More mundane was the concern of boys not to lose their books, as expressed by ownership notes, sometimes conveying violent or morbid admonitions to or curses upon wayward borrowers.[370] Particularly appropriate to the school ambience, where personal property was far from secure, were sententious verses (written in less than correct Latin).[371] The concern with property was not limited to books in these *probationes*.[372] Some verses accompanying schoolbooks had a more academic aim, however elementary their mnemonic purpose might be.[373] Sometimes

365 *Carmina Burana* ( ), table .

366 BML Strozzi , v: Amans Dido se combussit; v: Quando navigium Enee combustum fuit; v: Eneas dormiens, ymago Anchisei; v: Quando Venus fecit orationem ad Neptunum; v: Pali<nu>rus demersus in mare a deo sonni. Sunt equidem quidam dicentes ipsum fuisse submersum ab Enea. 367 BML . , r. 368 BRF , v.

369 BML . , r: La virtù et la diligientia toa si è tanta, Pollio mio suavisimo, che zertamente non dubito de avere da ti quello che el mio cor dimanda, inperoché la industria toa si è tanta che chome io ò dito [*sic pro* dato] non dubito de aver.

370 BRF , front flyleaf recto: Redde mihi librum quicumque inveneris istum. Nam referam grates semper, amice, tibi. BML sin. , v: Iste Lucanus est Felini Domini Barbaci <...> Quis me invenitur [*sic*] vel redat vel moriatur. BML Ashb. , r: Qeusta [*sic*] *Bocoli* et di Zanobi di Ser Bastiano; c[h]i la trova la re[n]da perché farà poco guadag[n]o questo lascito Zanobi. C[h]i lo vo vedere, lo gardi. BRF , inside front cover: Quest libriccino è ne di Papi da Ierello da Filichaia. Chi llo achatta lo renda e guardilo da man di fancugli e d'al(tr)>e. BRF , r–v, ownership notes dated November : Questo libro sia de mi Tomaso Morando. Se mai se perdesse me sia rese [*sic pro* reso]. Questo libro serà mio fin cha vivo e non più. Questo libro sia di mi Thomaso Montocalvo. Se mai se perdesse ché alcuno lo acatasse et non el volesse rendere, da le force se de enda. For slightly di erent transcriptions, see De Robertis and Miriello ( ), . BML AD , r: Qui mihi furatur vel reddatur vel moriatur / Et talem mortem quod suspendatur ad furcum. Black and Pomaro ( ), : 'Quis mihi furatur vel redat vel moriatur'. For similar admonitory *ex libris* in BML . , see above, . BRF , v: Finito libro isto frangamus ossa magistro. / Amen. / Finito libro isto referamus gra(tiam) Christo. / Qui mihi furatur vel reddat vel moriatur. / Qui mihi furatur tribus lignis asotiatur. / Iste liber est mei Andree Tomasi de Minerbectis. Amen. Amen. For a slightly di erent transcription, see De Robertis and Miriello ( ), .

371 See BRF , v, cited above, .

372 ASF Carte Cerchi , < > v: see above, .

373 BNCF Magl. . , r: Sex nonaas maius ottober iulius et mars, / Quatuor at reliqui tenet ydus quilibet octo / Omnes preter eas veteres dissere calendas. For a similar set of mnemonics, see BML . , v, cited above, – , n. .

these accompanying mnemonics served to help foreign students remember Italian orthography.[374] One particular pupil was of German origin, as is revealed by another of his *probationes* in the same manuscript.[375]

At times pupils served as copyists of their own schoolbooks, and their colophons could reflect a lack of confidence, often justified, in their graphic or linguistic competence. Sometimes pupil-scribes could evince pious emotions when completing their graphic tasks.[376] But at other times their feelings could hardly be described as spiritual: 'let a pretty girl be given to the writer for his trouble'.[377] Sometimes they were kindly disposed to their teachers after completing their academic work,[378] but not always ('the book having been finished, let the teacher's bones be broken').[379]

Accessus

School authors were frequently accompanied by introductory matter, usually known as *accessus*, which often summarized for the reader the author's biography, his motives for writing, the work's title and genre and a basic argument of the text. The technique of prefacing detailed textual study of literary works with biographical and generic background material can be traced to antiquity. A renowned teacher such as Servius began his commentary on the *Aeneid* by prescribing an introduction consisting of the author's life, the work's title, its genre, the author's intention and the number and order of the books; a similar scheme was recommended by another great Roman teacher, Donatus, and Boethius suggested a procedure along the same lines, enjoining the teacher to indicate as well the branch of philosophy to which the work belonged. Boethius was the first to use the term *accessus* to describe these prefaces to authors; the other name which he gave to these introductions (*didascalia*) more explicitly conveys the educational purposes for which they were normally intended.[380]

The school authors in Florentine libraries contain many prefatory

374 BML CS , v: Ytalice ÿsopus sic scribe. / Si nescis orthographiam stude. / Non s vice x nec x pro s pone. / Tibi sit Exopus, in quoquo ysopus. 375 See above, .

376 BRF , v: Finito libro isto reddamus gratiam Christo. ASF Carte Cerchi , < > v: Deus in none tuo salum me fac et in virtute tua iudica me.

377 BRF , v: Detur pro pena scriptori pulcra puella. BRF , v: Detur pro penna scriptori pulcra puela. 378 BRF . , r (XIII[1] copyist): Finito libro pisces deferte magistro.

379 BNCF CS J. . , r: Finito libro rumpantur ossa magistro. For a similar colophon in BRF , v, see above, .

380 On *accessus*, see Quain ( ); Hunt ( ), – ; Minnis and Scott ( ), – ; Curtius ( ), ; Huygens ( ); Spallone ( ), – .

accessus.[381] The conventions of these introductions obliged teachers to consider the author's intention[382] as well as the work's philosophical classification.[383] The fact that few school texts were actually works of philosophy caused teachers few problems. It was taken for granted that reading Latin literature was morally uplifting, and so, when addressing the question to what part of philosophy the work belonged, it was natural to reply: ethics.[384] For the same reasons, when considering the author's intentions in writing, it was normal to declare that these were moral, with the aim of encouraging virtue and discouraging vice.[385] Of course, these highly conventionalized *accessus* did not necessarily mean that teachers intended to give running moral interpretations to the works of literature they were about to teach. In fact, the opposite usually transpired: having got through the moral conventions of the *accessus* and so fulfilled any formal requirement of providing good morals in the classroom, teachers then felt free to turn to their real business: teaching Latin in a philological manner. Moralizing *accessus* were an ideal way to pay lip-service to the moralistic aims of education, which teachers felt under

381 BML . , v; BNCF Magl. . , r, v, r, r, v; BNCF Magl. . , v; BNCF Magl. . , v; BNCF Magl. . , r; BML . , r; BML . , r, r, v, r, v, r, r, v, r, v, r, r, v, r, r, v; BML . , r; BML . , r, r, v, v, r, v, v, v, r; BML . , r– v, r; BML Edili , v; BML . , v; BML Rinuccini , r, r; BML Ashb. , r– r; BML . , ; BML . , v, r, v; BML . , r; BRF , r; BRF , v, v; BML Strozzi , r–v; BML . , r–v; BML . , r–v; BRF , r; BNCF . , r– v *passim*; BML . , v; BNCF . , front flyleaf verso, r; BML sup. , r; BML . , r; BML AD , r– r; BNCF CS J. . , r; BNCF Magl. . , v; BML Strozzi , r; BRF , r; BML . , v– r; BML Ashb. , v; BRF , v; BNCF Landau Fin. , r; BML Ashb. , r; BML Ashb. , r; BML Ashb. , r– r; BML . , r; BML . , r– v; BML . , v; BML . , v; BNCF Landau Fin. , r; BML CS , r; BNCF CS J. . , r– r; Florence Biblioteca del Seminario Maggiore B. . , r; BML CS , r; BML . , r–v, r; BML . , r; BML dxt. , r– r; BML Strozzi , verso; BML . , r–v; BML . sup. , r; BML Redi , r, r; BML Redi , r; BML . , r.

382 BNCF Magl. . , r, v, r, r, v; BNCF Magl. . , v, v, r; BML . , r, r, r, v, r, v, r, r, v, r, v, r, r, v, r, r, v; BML . , r, r, v, v, r, v, v, v, r; BML Rinuccini , r, r; BML . , v; BML . , v, r, v; BRF , r; BRF , v, v; BML Strozzi , r; BML . , v; BML AD , r– r; BNCF CS J. . , r; BNCF Magl. . , v; BML Ashb. , v; BRF , r; BNCF Landau Fin. , r; BML Ashb. , r; BML Ashb. , r–v; BML . , v; BNCF CS J. . , v, r; BML CS , v (see Alessio (a),); BML . , r.

383 BML . , v; BML . , r; BML . , r; BML . , r; BML . , v; BML . , v; BNCF . , r; BML AD , r– r; BNCF CS J. . , r; BML Ashb. , r, r; BRF , r, v– r (see Fera ed. ( ), ,); BML . , v; BNCF CS J. . , r; BNCF Magl. . , v; BML . , r. 384 See preceding note.

385 E.g. BML Rinuccini , r: Autor in hoc opere virtutes operam vel materiam habet id est utile et honestum que re vera omnes virtutes complectuntur [...] Ibi enim vitiis extirpatis more boni agricole consequenter in hoc opere virtutes superseminavit. Primum enim est vitia extirpare et statim sequitur virtutes superseminare. See BML . , v, v.

no obligation to make into a reality in the classroom. A universal feature of all Florentine schoolbooks containing *accessus* is the gulf between their moralizing programmes and the philological character of the subsequent glosses and commentaries.

The Roman authors receiving *accessus* in Florentine schoolbooks are Ovid, Horace, Juvenal, Terence, Sallust, Statius, Seneca, Cicero, Lucan, Vergil and Boethius; the minor authors with *accessus* in this group of manuscripts are the *Disticha Catonis*, *Doctrina rudium*, *Ilias latina*, *Aesop* and Prosper of Acquitaine's *Epigrammata*; a work related to the school curriculum which was provided twice with *accessus* was Geo rey of Vinsauf's *Poetria nova.* A number of these texts were long works, sometimes consisting of numerous books or individual poems, letters or plays; nevertheless the normal procedure was to provide a single *accessus* to the entire work. But on one occasion, Horace's *Epistulae* were given individual treatments, focusing on Horace's particular intention in each case.[386] This kind of treatment was applied consistently to the *Heroides*, which, whenever they received *accessus*, were also provided with introductions to individual poems.[387] It is not di cult to understand why Ovid was given this particular attention. The focus of the individual *accessus* was usually Ovid's intention in writing, and so the opportunity was seized to assert the author's moral purpose, condemning the particular forms of immoral behaviour recounted in the poems, which were o ered up accordingly as future deterrents from such conduct.[388] This justified the reading of such salacious literature in the classroom and vindicated the philological methods which teachers and pupils would adopt in studying the texts; the moral formalities having been despatched before the actual reading began, pupils were now free to take the same kind of literary and grammatical approach to these lascivious texts which they were used to in reading less risqué material by Statius, Vergil, Lucan or Horace.

Sometimes these *accessus* reflected fashions which had prevailed up to

386 BML Rinuccini , r. For similar individual treatment of Horace, Terence and Ovid, see BML . , r– v; BNCF .. , r– v *passim*; BNCF Magl. . , v, v, r.

387 BNCF Magl. . , r, v, r, r, v; BML . , r, r, v, r, v, r, r, v, r, v, r, r, v, r, r, v; BML . , r, r, v, v, r, v, v, v, r.

388 E.g. BNCF Magl. . , r, v: Intentio autoris est commendare mulieres castum amorem servantes [...] Intentio autoris est commendare Ypernestram de legiptimo amore et quia manus suas sanguine fratris et mariti nollat maculare et quia pro marito suo talem penam patiebatur [...] See ibid. r, r, v.

BML . , r, r, v, v, r, v, v, v, r: Intentio sua est trattando [...] stultum et illicitum amore[m] reprehendere et corrigere et legittimum commendare [...] utilitas est scire aderere ligittimo amori, stultum et illicitum spernere. Cui parti filosofie? Etice quia pertinet ad mores hominum et secundum mores hominum loquitur [...] [etc.]

the twelfth century, classified by R. W. Hunt as 'type C' (*titulus, materia, intentio, modus, utilitas, cui parti philosphiae supponitur*); at other times, they assumed the format of the 'Aristotelian prologue' (*causa e ciens, causa materialis, causa formalis, causa finalis*) which had come to prominence in the course of the thirteenth century.[389] What is interesting is that there seems not to have been a general tendency for the Aristotelian prologue to supplant 'type C' in the thirteenth and fourteenth centuries, nor indeed for the latter to stage a resurgence under the influence of humanism in the Quattrocento. If there is a pattern to be detected, it perhaps depends on particular authors. The Roman classics, heavily read in the classroom up to and including the twelfth century, tended to cling to the 'type C' prologue, which had constituted their traditional accompanying material. There are a few Aristotelian prologues to the traditional authors,[390] but, in contrast, many more manuscripts which include the traditional 'type C' prologue, ranging over the entire period from the twelfth to the fifteenth centuries.[391] On the other hand, texts without an established place in the traditional twelfth-century Italian schoolroom (such as Boethius's *Consolation*, which entered the grammar curriculum in Italy mainly at the turn of the fourteenth century, or those texts newly composed in the Duecento, such as Geo rey of Vinsauf's *Poetria nova*) seem to have been more amenable to the Aristotelian prologue, fully established with the rise of scholasticism in the thirteenth century. Both *accessus* to manuscripts of the *Poetria nova* are of the Aristotelian type,[392] and out of the seven clearly definable *accessus* to Boethius's *Consolation* found among Florentine schoolbooks, five are of the Aristotelian type,[393] and the remaining two are non-Italian products, dating from the twelfth

389 See Minnis and Scott ( ), – .

390 BNCF . , r; BML Rinuccini , r; BML . , v; BML . , r; BML . , r; BML . , r; BML Ashb. , r; BML Redi , r; BML Ashb. , r; BML Redi , r; BML Ashb. , r–v; BRF , r; BML sup. , r; BRF , r– r.

391 BML . , v; BNCF Magl. . , r, v, r, r, v; BNCF Magl. . , v; BNCF Magl. . , v; BNCF Magl. . , r; BML . , r, r, r, v, r, v, r, r, v, r, v, r, r, v, r, r, v; BML . , r, r, v, v, r, v, v, v, r; BML . , r– v, r; BML Edili , v; BML . , v; BML Rinuccini , r; BML Ashb. , r– r; BML . , ; BML . , v, r, v; BRF , r; BRF , v; BML Strozzi , r; BML . , r–v; BML . , r–v; BNCF .. , r– v *passim*; BML . , v; BNCF . , front flyleaf verso; BML . , r; BML AD , r– r; BNCF CS J. . , r; BNCF Magl. . , v; BML . , v– r; BML Ashb. , v; BRF , r; BNCF Landau Fin. , r; BML Ashb. , r; BML Ashb. , r, v; BRF , r– r; BML . , v; BML . , r– v; BML . , v; BML . , v; BNCF Landau Fin. , r; BML CS , r; BNCF CS J. . , r; BML CS , r; BML Strozzi , verso; BML Redi , r.

392 BML Strozzi , r; BRF , r.

393 Black and Pomaro ( ), – , , – , – , .

century and found in a schoolbook imported to Italy probably from France,[394] where Boethius had been an established school author in the twelfth century.

Metric analysis

One innovatory feature of the grammar-school curriculum in the Quattrocento was the analysis of metres in the ancient Roman poets. Before the fifteenth century, it is di cult to find discussion in school commentaries of metric types or scansion. But in the Quattrocento a new interest in verse analysis appears. This is evident, for example, from glosses on Horace's *Odes*, as is suggested by comments of a Perugian school-level glossator writing in .[395] This interest was continued by a subsequent glossator who added the metrical scheme at the beginning of each of the later odes.[396] Similarly, verse analysis began to be added to glosses on Seneca's tragedies at the end of the fourteenth century,[397] and an interest in metre is also evident in glosses on Vergil's *Aeneid*.[398] Comments on metres even occur in a prose text such as Cicero's *Orator*.[399]

This new interest in metric analysis during the Quattrocento is most evident in school-level glosses to Boethius's *Consolation*. Whereas the marginal annotations in the fourteenth century are primarily philological and exegetic, in the Quattrocento they become increasingly concerned with metric analysis.[400] In fact, by the end of the fifteenth century, it is

394 Black and Pomaro ( ), .

395 BML AD , v: . . *Iam satis*. Hec oda est discolos tetrastophos: discolos quia duas metri varietates in se continet, thetrastophos quia a quarto versu fit metri replicatio; tres primi versus similes sunt. Saphonici ab inventore, a Saphone videlicet, et constant ex quinque pedibus: primo trocheo, secundo spondeo, tertio dactilo, duobus ultimis trocheis sive ultimo spondeo sive trocheo. See ibid. r. [396] v– r, v, r, r– v.

397 BML . , r, r, v, r, etc.

398 BRF , v: Versus spondiacus et in quinto non fit caesura. Scanditur enim sic: tu nil. lene. asquem. dardani. oam. chise.

399 BRF , v: Detailed notes, definitions, diagrams of poetic metres, including dactilus, iambus, paeon.

400 Black and Pomaro ( ), , – , , – , , – , – , – , , , , . For metrical glosses provided by XVmid glossator to Bodley Can. lat. , see Black and Pomaro ( ), , n. , where similar glossing in Bodley Lat. Class. d. , hand (XV[1] or XVmid) is compared with Trevet's commentary (Bodley Rawl. G.).

It is di cult to find a pre-XVc. Italian glossator providing this type of commentary: see Black and Pomaro ( ), , for some non-Italian XIIIc. metric glosses; Black and Pomaro ( ), – , for metrical glosses extracted from Trevet's and Guglielmo da Cortemilia's commentaries by XIVmid Italian glossator; Black and Pomaro ( ), , for two metric glosses made by an Italian hand, XIVex.

not easy to find any kind of marginal glossing to Boethius other than metrical analysis: the two latest glossators in Florentine manuscripts, writing either at the end of the fifteenth century or in the early Cinquecento,[401] both provide only or principally metric analysis. Bartolomeo Fonzio too followed newer fashions by indicating the metric types in the margins of the copy which he probably annotated for his private pupils.[402]

In harmony with this fifteenth-century Italian preoccupation with Boethius's metres was the appearance of the first new treatise since the time of Lupus of Ferrières: Niccolò Perotti's *Epistola de generibus metrorum quibus Horatius Flaccus et Severinus Boetius usi sunt ad Helium Perottum fratrem*.[403] Perotti's treatise had a didactic aim, intended for his young brother, described as an *adolescens* engaged in humanist studies like Perotti himself ('qui iisdem quibus ipse studiis deditus'), who desired to be instructed by his older brother.[404] It was obviously because of the diversity of metres found in Horace's *Odes* and Boethius's *Consolation* that these two works were particulary singled out as the subjects of verse analysis in Quattrocento schools, and the appearance of Perotti's work confirms a fashion for the study of verse types in this period.

The interest shown by Perotti in metric study suggests humanist influence in this new pedagogic fashion and this is confirmed by the verse sections of the *Consolation*, which attracted far greater admiration from the humanists than the proses: Erasmus even had doubts whether they were by the same writer.[405] Henricus Loritius similarly declared that in the *Consolation* 'longe maiorem gratiam habet carmen quam jejuna illa prosa'.[406] Giraldi spoke of Boethius's 'miraculous ability to compose verse',[407] which was also admired by Patrizi,[408] while Scaliger wrote that 'his poetic diversions are clearly splendid. Their elegance and gravity are unsurpassed; the frequency with which "sententiae" occur has not robbed them of charm, nor has their pointed quality stolen their purity. Indeed, I feel that few are comparable to him.'[409] In his *Discorsi del poema eroico*, Tasso placed Boethius on the highest level of the poetic hierarchy, alongside other philosopher–poets such as Parmenides, Empedocles, Lucretius and Dante and ahead of Homer and Vergil.[410]

401 Black and Pomaro ( ), – , . 402 Black and Pomaro ( ), – .

403 I used the Venice edition (*Hoc in volumine haec continentur. Francisci Manturantii Perusini de componendis carminibus opusculum Nicolai Perotti Sypontini de generibus metrorum. Ejusdem de Horatii Flacci ac Severini Boetii metris. Omniboni Vicentini de arte metrica libellus. Servii Maurii honorati grammatici centimetrum*). See Peiper ( ), xxiv; Panizza ( ), . 404 Diii <recto>.

405 Grafton ( ), . 406 Cited by Panizza ( ), . 407 Grafton ( ), .

408 Grafton ( ), , n. . 409 Grafton ( ), . 410 Panizza ( ), – .

Although it might seem ironic that the main inspiration for this analysis of Boethius's verses in the age of humanism was the scholastic commentary *par excellence* by Nicholas Trevet,[411] nevertheless it is significant that it was only in the fifteenth century that Italian school commentators began to turn to his metric glosses. Trevet's commentary had been circulating widely in Italy during the fourteenth century and was already being extracted in the Italian grammar schoolroom. It is evident that the growth of humanism began to have its first e ect on the Boethius commentary tradition with the new interest in metrics apparent in Italy mainly from the turn of the fifteenth century.[412]

Sententiae

The compilation of an armoury of *sententiae* (maxims) was another characteristic activity of the Italian grammar school. Pupils or teachers often used spare pages or fascicles in manuscripts to collect quotations to be used as *sententiae* in their own writing or teaching. One example is an early fourteenth-century miscellany, possibly compiled by a pupil called 'Curradinus Domini Chianni'[413] whose father is recorded there as having died in ;[414] this book's educational a liations are clear from a list of the traditional school *auctores minores*,[415] two of which are provided with standard school-level *accessus*.[416] The compiler of this *zibaldone* also

411 See Gibson and Smith ( ), . For a discussion of the medieval sources of this verse analysis, see Black and Pomaro ( ), – .

412 It is possible that the revaluation of Boethius as a poet was related to the humanist reinterpretation of philosophy's expulsion of the muses in book , p. . It is clear that a number of late-medieval Italian writers such as Giovannino da Mantova ( ) or the anonymous medical adversary of Petrarch's *Invectiva contra medicum*, had seen this passage as an outright rejection of poetry; Italian humanists, such as Mussato, Petrarch, Boccaccio and Salutati, on the other hand, counter-attacked saying that Boethius meant to reject only some kinds of less worthy poetry. These polemics in the fourteenth and fifteenth century seem to have led to a reassertion of the merits of poetry in general; implicit may also have been a reappraisal of Boethius's particular value as a poet, although this does not seem to have occurred explicitly until the sixteenth century: see Panizza ( ), – , *passim*.

413 BML AD , r

414 BML AD , v: Obiit genitor MCCC° XVII° in nocte sancti Martini [...]

415 BML AD , r– r.

416 BML AD , r– r: Prohemii Catonis. Ista est materia Catonis. Materia Catonis talis est. Quia dicitur Cato romanus fuisse sed qui vel cuius contemporaneus fuit nescimus. Verumtamen legimus duos esse homines quorum quilibet vocabatur Cato sive Catus, quia Cato sive Catus dicitur a caveo, -es. Unde dicitur uticensis et alius censerinus et neuter istorum sapiens fuit. Quidam dicit quod nec unus nec alius composuit hoc opus sed dicit quod Salominis fuit. Vidit autor quam plurimos homines a via recta deviare volens eos ad equitatis viam reducere etcetera. In principio istius libri quatuor sunt requirenda, scilicet materia, intentio, utilitas et cui parti phylosophie supponatur, et quid sit libri titulus [...] Proemii Quinque Clavium. Ista est materia Quinque Clavium [...]

included a collection of *Sententiae sanctorum* (r– r) and *Sententiae Salomonis* (r– r), as well as a selection of quotations from Henry of Settimello's *Elegy*[417] and from Boethius's *Consolation.*[418] Another example (BML Ashb.) describes the grammar course of one teacher, Maestro Filippo Casali, who taught for many years in Pistoia, Florence, Volterra and Bologna in the second half of the fifteenth century.[419] Besides containing his secondary-level course on Latin syntax and a group of invented model letters written by him, this manuscript also includes a long series of *sententiae* from a wide range of classical and Christian authors (r– r). Similarly, there is a revealing series of Florentine grammatical compilations, preserved in five Florentine manuscripts and five others outside Florence, all dating from the second half of the fifteenth century.[420] The compilation in the five Florentine manuscripts seems relatively uniform for a grammatical anthology, in general constituting a full school-level grammatical course of study. At the end of the strictly grammatical section of the compilation, the manuscript goes on to give the text of twenty-eight very short familiar letters of Cicero,[421] and a couple by Pliny.[422] The compilation ends with a series of *sententiae* drawn from the Bible, the Church Fathers and various Latin classical authors.[423] Another example is by Niccolò Paleario, who was grammar teacher in Tivoli in [424] and had connections with the Accademia Pomponiana,[425] and who compiled a *zibaldone* associated with his teaching, including a Greek alphabet with phonetic pronunciations and Latin equivalents, grammatical questions and answers, pseudo-Phocas's orthography, a text of Cato's *Disticha* and a collection of his own model letters; this collection also contains a miscellaneous anthology of *sententiae*[426] and a commentary on Cato's *Distichs*, in which the marginal glosses are predominantly *sententiae* drawn from classical authors (Pliny, Seneca, Hesiod, Columella, Ovid, Propertius, Juvenal, Plautus, Cicero, Horace, Aristotle, Vergil, Sallust, Terence and Lucan) as well as from the Bible.[427] Finally, there is a school-type miscellany, compiled by Francesco de' Medici in – (BRF), containing a heavily glossed text of Horace's satires, grammatical notes on the use of 'interest' as an impersonal verb and a collection of model extracts from

[417] Black and Pomaro ( ), .
[418] Black and Pomaro ( ), . See BRF , r– v; BML Gaddi , v– r, v.
[419] See above, – . [420] See above, – . [421] BRF , r– r.
[422] BRF , r. [423] BRF , v– r.
[424] BML Ashb. , r: Finis laus deo. Tibure die aprilis . Scriptum est hoc per me Nicolaum Angeli de Palearis tunc litterarum ludi magistrum civitatis Tiburis.
[425] Avesani ( ), . [426] BML Ashb. , r– r. [427] BML Ashb. , v– v.

Cicero's letters; this *zibaldone* also includes an anthology of *sententiae* on justice collected mainly from biblical sources[428] and a collection of proverbs compiled by one Nicolaus Angelus Bucinensis.[429]

Sententiae were not only amassed at school in the various types of notebooks illustrated above. Pupils and teachers also took the opportunity while glossing their literary texts to extend their command of *sententiae*. In Florentine Boethius manuscripts the most explicit example of this kind of activity was the glossing of Valentino di Antonio da Suessa Aurunca at the grammar school in Teano of Maestro Tomo, possibly to be identified with the Tomo da Suessa Aurunca active in the Florentine Studio perhaps as a grammar teacher in the academic year – .[430] In his signed copy of Boethius, Valentino's glossing consisted almost entirely of a long series of *sententiae*, from classical authors such as Seneca, pseudo-Seneca, Cicero, Sallust, Vergil, Aristotle, Ovid, Valerius Maximus, Horace, Lucan, Juvenal; from the New Testament; from Christian authors such as Prosper, Walter of Châtillon, Isidore of Seville, Augustine, Henry of Settimello, Richard of Venosa; and from recent Italian writers including Dante and Petrarch.[431]

Other school authors in which *sententiae* were collected during glossing included *auctores minores* such as Prudentius,[432] Henry of Settimello,[433] pseudo-Boethius,[434] pseudo-Cato,[435] Prosper,[436] and Richard of Venosa;[437] classical Roman poets such as Horace,[438] Juvenal[439] and Vergil;[440] and Roman prose-writers such as Valerius Maximus[441] and

428 BRF , v. 429 BRF , r– v. 430 Park ( ), .

431 Black and Pomaro ( ), – ; see , – .

432 BRF , r: Res vivas scilicet agnum sacrificatum per Abel per quem nostra anima inteligitur et significatur et terrena id est res terre sicut spicas grani v<a>cuas quas sacrificavit Cayn.

433 BRF , r: Unde Seneca sic ait: [...] nec ulli prestat velorum fortuna fidem.

434 BML sup. , v: Prudentia est bonarum rerum bonarumque scientia secundum Tulium. Iustitia est habitus cum comuni utilitate servata suam cuique tribuens dignitatem secundum Tulium. See r, v.

435 BNCF Magl. . , v: Post inimicitias iram meminisse malorum est.

436 BML . , r: Disce, disce, puer, dum tempus habes.

437 BML AD , r: Unde Seneca: Dum morata veniat iuvenis dotata est satis. Unde Iuvenalis: Non deest virtuti locus.

438 BML CS , v: Pauper non est cui parva su ciunt et per abstinentiam vivit sanus sed ille cui multa non su ciunt et propter gulam semper est egrotus.

439 BML San Marco , r: Nemo propheta sine honore nisi in patria sua.

440 BRF , v: Sedendo enim et quiescendo anima fit prudentior, ut inquit philosophus. r: Melius est innocentibus succurere quam nocentium delicta punire. See v, r.

441 BML . , v: (IX, iv, ext.) Avarus divitias non possidet sed a divitiis possidetur. BML AD , v: Aristotiles: Amicus est alter ego. Amicorum est idem velle et nolle. Tullius: Talis est sine amicis homo quale est corpus sine anima. Ovidius: Non minor est virtus quam querere pacta tueri. Salomon: In adversitate cognoscitur amicus et non absconditur inimicus.

Sallust.[442] But it is hardly surprising to find that the authors who attracted the most *sententiae* among their glosses were the two most famous Roman moralists, Seneca[443] and Cicero.[444]

It is important not to misconstrue the role of *sententiae* in the grammar-school curriculum. *Sententiae* appearing as glosses in school manuscripts normally represented only a tiny part of an overall philological and grammatical commentary: for example, the *sententiae* noted to the copy of Seneca's tragedies in BNCF Banco Rari constituted a minute fraction of the anonymous early fifteenth-century annotator's entire glossing, which was otherwise of the normal philological type; another instance is *expositio* made by Antonio di Ser Salvo at his grammar school in San Gimignano, as recorded by his pupil Giovanni di Antonio da Gambassi in (BML sup.), where again *sententiae* represented the smallest proportion of the teaching o ered. A second consideration is that, although it was obviously taken for granted that pupils compiling a collection of *sententiae* would be morally uplifted by their edifying contents, there was a more practical purpose in this activity too. *Sententia* was an essential building-block of Latin prose composition. It functioned most concretely as a rhetorical figure which, like others such as antithesis, apostrophe or interrogation (rhetorical question), served to embellish prose style. In fact, it was explicitly recognized in one Florentine schoolbook that *sententia* was a figure of speech.[445] As was stated in *Rhetorica ad Herennium*, 'Cum [sententiae] ita interponentur, multum adferent ornamenti' (,). On a more general level, the process of converting ideas, arguments and plans into words was linked to the process of finding *sententiae*: again as was stated in *Rhetorica ad Herennium*, 'Elocutio [i.e. expression] est idoneorum verborum et sententiarum ad inventionem adcommodatio' (,). The collection of *sententiae*

442 BRF , r: Omnis superfluitas turpitudo est. Nota quod quando animus est plenus malis artibus non potest unquam ab is<t>is removeri.

443 BML . , v: Tulius O tiorum. Leviora enim sunt ea que repentino aliquo motu acadunt quam ea que meditata et preparata inferruntur. r: Omnes bene vivendi virtutes a<tque> rationes in virtute sunt collocande. T(ullius). Dignitas forme deflorescit aut morbo aut vetustate. T(ullius). BNCF Banco Rari , r: Nota in adversitatibus virtutem magnam esse, non esse sub dolore nec debere a tramite rationis discedere. See r, v, r, v, r, v, v, r, r. See BML sup. , v, r, v; BML Edili , v; BML Strozzi , , v, v; Roberti ( ), ; BRF , r; BNCF Landau Fin. , v.

444 BRF , r: Veritas est origo unionis bonitatis magnitutdinis et aliorum princi<piorum> [...] naturalium. See BML Ashb. , r, r, r, v. BML Ashb. , v. BRF , v.

445 BNCF Landau Fin. , v: Hic Cicero confirmat per locum communem vel per colorem rectoricum qui dicitur sententia.

was not only a moral activity: much Latin prose writing consisted of stringing together series of *pulchrae sententiae*, and it was for that reason, as much as for any edifying purpose, that schoolboys were made to collect armouries of these maxims. The moral dimension of collecting *sententiae* was taken for granted; the reality of what schoolboys were doing when compiling collections of maxims was providing themselves with the building-blocks of Latin prose.

Allegory

Further indication of the limited scope for moral instruction in the Italian classroom is the role of allegorical teaching: to judge from the marginal glosses of textbooks preserved in Florentine libraries, allegory played only a small part as an educational tool at the grammar-school level.

Allegorical glosses are notable primarily in three authors: Boethius, Vergil and Ovid. Occasionally one of the Boethian verses is given a Christian interpretation.[446] Sometimes a passage from one of the proses is interpreted allegorically.[447] But for the most part teachers provided allegorical interpretations to the mythological poems, as for example the natural objects a ected by Orpheus's song,[448] the tale of Ulysses and Circe,[449] or the dog of hell, Cerberus.[450]

Although Vergil's *Bucolics* are occasionally given an allegorical significance,[451] it is the *Aeneid* that is the more usual subject for allegory. Sometimes book receives this kind of reading,[452] as does book ,[453] but more often it is book and particularly Aeneas's descent into hell.[454] This type of reading can even have a philosophical flavour.[455] But in general such allegorical interpretations are rare, as in the last example,

446 Black and Pomaro ( ), .

447 Black and Pomaro ( ), .

448 Black and Pomaro ( ), .

449 Black and Pomaro ( ), .

450 Black and Pomaro ( ), .

451 BML Strozzi , r– r; BML . , r: hic respondet Titire qui allegorice sumitur pro Virgilio.

452 BRF , r, v, v; BML Strozzi , r, v, v.

453 BML Strozzi , r: Allegoria: in generali tractat de largitate contra avaritiam et in hoc libro septimo.

454 BML Strozzi , r; BNCF Magl. . , r, v, v; BML Strozzi , r, v, r, v.

455 BML CS , r: Novem significat circulos quibus terra circumcingitur. Nam Stix est terra. Dicit Plato in quodam libro quod virtutes latent in his terris suburte [*sic*] a vitiis. Nam mala dominantur, ire, insydie et ita talia, et iure[?] in hac vita latent virtutes et impediunt mala ne ad orriginem transeamus.

where the rest of the glosses by this particular glossator are entirely philological.

The author most frequently subjected to allegory in the schoolbooks in Florentine libraries is Ovid, and the work in question is regularly his *Metamorphoses*. Occasionally a Christian interpretation is encountered.[456] Otherwise the allegories are of the normal moral type.[457] Although a few schoolbooks are replete with these moral allegories,[458] the more usual pattern is to find a few allegories swimming in a sea of literal mythological comment.[459]

:
’ *CONSOLATION*

The glossing of these Florentine school manuscripts was basic. As great works of literature, the reading texts used in the classroom at the intermediate and more advanced levels – Boethius's *Consolation* and the Roman prose and poetic classics – had been the subject of numerous learned ancient and medieval commentaries; it must be wondered whether this tradition had much impact on these school manuscripts, especially in view of the elementary nature of their glossing.

Some sign of borrowing from established commentaries is evident in the glosses of the *auctores maiores*. A fourteenth-century fragment of the *Aeneid* . – (BNCF Pal.), based on a school-level manuscript to judge from the simplicity of its interlinear glossing[460] has a citation of Servius's commentary on line .[461] Another example comes from a

[456] BML CS , r, cited above, n. ; BML AD , v, commenting on .– : Nota primo placandus est deus et postea omnia prospere cedunt, iusta illud: primo querite regnum dei et omnia aditientur vobis [Luke :]. For a biblical allegory, see n. , above.

[457] BML CS , r: Nota quod moralis est ista fabula. Per Martem intelligendum est virum virtuosum et probus [*sic*] [...] r: Nota quod ista mutatio Phebi [...] est moralis. Nam per Phebum intelligendum est virum sapientem [*sic*]. See BML . , r.

[458] BML . , v: In ista parte Ovidius descendit ad aliam trasmutationem que est de mutatione lapidum in homines et ostendit quod non su cit ad mundi facinora punienda quod unus solus homo puniatur sed sententia sua est quod quilibet patiatur penam de pecato suo. Similar allegories on v, v– v *passim*.

[459] The following examples seem to be the only allegorical glosses encountered in BML . : v, v, v, r, r, r, r–v. For two similarly isolated allegories, see BML CS , r, r.

[460] E.g. r: pandite = aperite et manifestate, manus = id est acies, rates = id est naves, una = id est simul, insignibus = id est nobilibus.

[461] BNCF Pal. , r:

BNCF Pal. , r:	Servius
Cosa secundum Servium civitas Tuscie fuit et deberet declinari hec cosa, -e	Cosas civitas Cusciae quae numero dicitur singulari

Source: Servius, Rome, *c.* [*IGI* , Hain * , BNCF shelf mark: B. .], v.

school copy of Horace's odes, where a number of the glosses are extracted from the commentary by pseudo-Acron.[462]

But among the *auctores maiores* there is particularly notable borrowing from medieval commentaries in the case of the *Metamorphoses*. A well-known example is the version of this text prepared at the turn of the fifteenth century by Don Nofri di Angelo da San Gimignano, schoolmaster in Colle Valdelsa, San Gimignano and Prato.[463] Nofri copied the prose and verse mythologies composed by Giovanni del Virgilio for every transformation in the first seven books of the text and placed them at the foot of the relevant page.[464] The del Virgilian allegories provided a fecund source for schoolmasters in the fourteenth and fifteenth centuries.[465]

To understand how and to what extent pupils and masters used existing commentary material in glossing their texts, it is particularly useful to examine the glossing of one important school author. Boethius's *Consolation of Philosophy* was both a key textbook in Italian grammar schools from the thirteenth to the fifteenth century and the subject of a

462

BML CS , v– r.	Pseudo-Acron (–), , : Tamquam ad totius
[. .] Tanquam ad totius pagi vel regionis pertineret infamiam si ager famosus fuisset morte domini.	pagi idest ad totius regionis pertineret infamiam, si famosus ager morte domini fuisset.
[. .] Spetiem pro genere posuit. Colchos enim Scythie civitas est, ex qua Medea fuit venenis et magica potens.	, : Specialem provinciam posuit pro generali crimine. Colchos enim Scythiae civitas est, ex qua Medea fuit venenis et magica potens.
[. .] Bosphoros ponti sunt fauces ubi propter angustias assidua naufragia sunt. Nomen dicitur accepisse quia inde in bovem Io mutata transierit.	, : Bosphoros enim Ponti sunt fauces, ubi propter angustias adsidua naufragia sunt. Nomen dicitur accepisse, quod inde in bovem Io mutata transierit.
[. .] Furvae id est nigrae unde et furta putant dicta quia obscuro tempore committuntur.	, : Alii volunt furvae nigrae positum, unde et furta putant dicta, quod committuntur obscuro.
[. .] Eachus Achillis avus qui pro iustitiae bono etiam apud inferos iudicium meruisse perhibetur, unde Iuvenalis: Quas torqueat umbras Eachus.	, : Aecus, Achillis avus, qui pro iustitiae bono etiam aput inferos iudicium meruisse perhibetur, unde Iuvenalis: Quas torqueat umbras/Aeacus.
[. .] Alceus poeta lyricus fuit a quo metrum alcaicum dictum est.	, : Nomen poetae lyrici, a quo et metrum Alcaicum dicum est.

For examples of a more remote relationship to pseudo-Acron, see BML . , v– r, discussed above, , n. .

463 BML . .

464 Ghisalberti ( ), – ; de Angelis ( ); Alessio (b). Last allegory (r): Vigesimaquinta transmutatio est de bellua de Themis et de cane Cefali. [...] Et sic expliciunt moralitates septimi libri. Cf. Ghisalberti ( ), .

465 BML CS : fol r: Allegoria quinte transmutationis gigantum [...]; Sexta allegoria transmutationis Licaon ... r: Tertia transmutatio est mundi in quatuor etates [...]; cf. Ghisalberti ( ), – . BML . : (Lb. I all.): Nature dominus cupientis adesse [...] Cf. Ghisalberti ( ), . BML . : a few metric allegories are inserted only in books and : v, v– r, v, r–v.

long and powerful commentary tradition, in which the preeminent figures were the Carolingian teacher Remigius of Auxerre, the twelfth-century philosopher William of Conches and the scholastic Nicholas Trevet.[466] However, school pupils and teachers did not use full commentaries: the great medieval commentaries on Boethius were substantial works, and so school-level glossators were perforce highly selective in what they extracted. It has been seen that simple philology was the overwhelming focus of their glossing in general, and so it is not surprising that they chose to excerpt from the commentaries this same kind of basic philological material. Here the most prevalent type of gloss was paraphrase or explication; school glossators also extracted from the great commentaries large quantities of geography, mythology, history, definition or etymology, figures, simple rhetorical analysis, elementary natural philosophy, simple logic, elementary history of philosophy and basic allegory.

The *Consolation of Philosophy* appears to have been a transitional text, read normally between the minor and major authors. Its position in the later medieval Italian grammar curriculum can also shed light on the problem of why this text was used so widely as a schoolbook. Pupils reading the minor authors had been exposed almost entirely to verse; while the *auctores maiores* also included many metric texts, at this higher level pupils were also introduced to important prose-writers, such as Sallust, Valerius Maximus and, in the fifteenth century, Cicero. In this respect, Boethius's *Consolation*, with its alternating metres and proses, o ered an unusual combination, one which had special advantages for a school reader hitherto almost exclusively familiar with poetry: it provided an ideal link between the poetic *auctores minores* and the less familiar prose discourse to be encountered in major authors such as Sallust and Cicero.

The way in which pupils and teachers read and annotated the *Consolation* also helps to explain why this text achieved such popularity in the Italian schoolroom. In fact, their form of reading and glossing, without altering the text itself, actually changed the nature of the text, transforming it into an eminently suitable schoolbook. On the level of interlinear glossing, indeed, Boethius school manuscripts show a

466 This section summarizes some of the conclusions of Black and Pomaro ( ). Limitations of space have prevented a fuller discussion and documentation here of the use of the medieval commentary tradition in Italian grammar schools; for an extensive treatment of this topic with particular reference to Boethius's *Consolation*, the reader is referred to the above-mentioned book.

rudimentary style of comment, including basic interlinear lexical glossing, word-order marks and simple marginal exposition and paraphrase. Boethian marginal annotations cover geography, mythology, history, simple grammatical analysis and terminology (sometimes citing school manuals such as *Doctrinale* or *Poetria nova*), simple definition and etymology, figures and colours, elementary rhetorical analysis, elementary natural philosophy, simple logic, elementary philosophical terminology and anecdotal history of philosophy, and simple allegory.

According to Garin, 'Boezio [...] ancora resiste come testo di morale al principio del ' ',[467] but, in view of the simplicity of *Consolation*'s school annotation, it must be wondered whether and to what extent this text served to teach moral philosophy, or philosophy at all. In fact, more than two-thirds of Florentine Boethius school manuscripts contain no philosophical, ethical or theological commentary. When philosophical, moral or even theological glossing occasionally occurs it is not presented in depth or with any regularity but forms part of an overall grammatical/philological commentary. Given the lack of philosophical interest in the text in later medieval Italy, therefore, it would be untenable to argue that its widespread use in early Renaissance schools was the result of its moralistic contents. It is a subject of continuing scholarly debate whether humanism brought in its train an enhanced preoccupation with morals in the classroom;[468] in view of how the *Consolation* was read and glossed in schools, it is clear at least that Renaissance teachers and pupils did not significantly look to Boethius for moral inspiration and guidance.

Boethius's *Consolation* had in fact become the subject of a new type of reading in later medieval and Renaissance Italy. Earlier in the middle ages, Boethius, like other authors, had formed part of a broad, universal curriculum embracing a broad spectrum of subjects; commentators such as Remigius of Auxerre had used the text as a jumping-o point to discuss a range of disciplines in considerable depth: grammar, rhetoric, philology, geography, mythology, biblical criticism, all branches of philosophy, science and theology. In the twelfth century, the breadth of discussion remained but there was even greater interest now in the text as a stimulus for philosophical and scientific discussion, as is clear, for example, from William of Conches's commentary. This catholic approach to the text was continued and expanded by a later medieval Northern commentator such as Nicholas Trevet, but when the *Consolation* became a fundamental text in Italian grammar schools, the

[467] Garin ( ), xxvi. [468] See above, .

focus of reading changed. As a result of the rise of the universities in Italy, with their concentration on and growing monopoly of higher professional education, the preliminary grammar or Latin curriculum also became compartmentalized, entrusted to specialist grammar teachers. Their role was to provide competence in Latin; philosophical, moral, rhetorical and scientific training, as well as professional preparation in law, medicine or theology, was left to the universities and *studia*. In view of this curricular and institutional specialization in later medieval Italy, it is understandable why Boethius's *Consolation* was read almost exclusively as a grammatical and philological work in Italian grammar schools. Since the work had no place in the university curriculum, it was inevitable, when the text was adopted as a standard grammatical author in Italy at the end of the thirteenth century, that this would be the approach of teachers and pupils.

In fact, the simple philological reading of Boethius in later medieval and Renaissance Italy offers a solution to the paradox of the *Consolation* in the late medieval Italian grammar-school room: how could such a demanding text, whose difficulties were reinforced by an extensive and profound medieval commentary tradition, have been read by schoolboys still mastering basic Latin? It is understandable why the text had not been adopted earlier for widespread use in Italian monastic and ecclesiastical schools of the earlier middle ages. Before the thirteenth century, the text would have entered into a comprehensive and unspecialized curriculum extending from the rudiments of reading and writing all the way to metaphysics and theology. This catholic curriculum was reflected in the wide-ranging commentary, for example, of a teacher such as William of Conches. In this context, it was unthinkable that the philosophical, scientific and theological dimensions of the *Consolation* could have been ignored. With the rise of specialized grammar schools in later medieval Italy, on the other hand, a new context for the reading of Boethius emerged. In line with their more limited role as exclusively Latin teachers, grammar masters pre-digested, truncated and reduced the text and its accompanying commentary tradition to the level of basic philology. From this point of view, the *Consolation* was an eminently suitable choice. The text – read according to their criteria of selection – offered exposure to basic facts about history, geography, mythology and natural science, besides providing copious illustrations of rudimentary grammatical and rhetorical principles. Given its evident intermediate position in the curriculum and its unusual combination of verse and prose, it offered an ideal link between the entirely poetic *auctores minores* and the less familiar prose discourse to be encountered in major authors such as Sallust and Cicero. Later medieval Italian grammar teachers no longer saw the text as an embodiment of profound philosophical, scientific, metaphysical and theological ideas; for them, instead, the *Consolation* represented a useful anthology of verse and prose. If modern preconceptions are put to one side, Boethius emerges, in a late medieval Italian context, as an exemplary schoolbook. Without actually changing a word of the text itself, teachers and pupils in fourteenth- and fifteenth-century Italy fundamentally altered the character of the work from what it had represented in the earlier middle ages and, indeed, from how it appears to modern readers.

Rhetoric and style in the school grammar syllabus

In the three preceding chapters, an attempt has been made to analyse the secondary grammar curriculum in Italian schools during the middle ages and earlier Renaissance. The emphasis has been on identifying the constituent elements of the syllabus: formal grammar rules, vocabularies, composition exercises, mnemonic verses, synonyms/homonyms, orthographies, minor and major authors. It is well established that there was a progression from the *auctores minores* to the *maiores*, but otherwise it is not always evident in what order the rest of the curriculum was presented.

Fortunately, some insight into the manner and order in which the theoretical, practical and literary elements of the grammar syllabus were integrated in early fifteenth-century Florence is o ered by a schoolbook now preserved as manuscript BNCF Landau Fin. . This paper codex, the work of a group of Florentine schoolboys, contains four texts (Statius's *Achilleis* (r– r), *Cartula* (r– r), *Disticha Catonis* (v– v) and the opening two books of Alexander of Villedieu's *Doctrinale* (v– v)), followed by a series of grammatical exercises (r– r, r– r). The first thirteen folios were written by a young member of the Florentine élite, Antoniotto di Giovanni di Paolo Morelli (hand A), who left his note of possession on the inside back cover (I'): 'Iste liber est mei Antoniotti Johannis Pauli de Morellis.' An unidentified hand (B) finished the text of *Achilleis* (–), and then another Florentine youth, Francesco di Francesco Ferantini (C), took over the copying of *Cartula*, *Disticha Catonis* and the first lines of *Doctrinale* (vv. – : up to r, line), leaving two colophons.[1] Thereafter (B) completed the rest of book of *Doctrinale*

[1] r: Exp<li>cit liber Cha<r>tule Beati Bernardi, deo gratias amen. Istud par Cartule sunt Francisci de Ferrantin<is>. r: Explicit liber Catonis deo gratias amen. Qui scrissit iscribat semper cum domino vivat, vivat in cielis semper cum domino felix. Iste libe<r> est Francisci Ferantin<i>.

(r, l. to v), and the remainder of the codex was almost entirely copied by a second unidentified hand (D). The manuscript carries throughout a series of dates progressing from to , usually placed in the upper margin of each page; these were written by (D), who acted as the overall organizer of the book, sometimes renumbering previous paginations or indicating catchwords even in the parts not written by him (v, v, v, v).

Hand (A) of the manuscript is identifiable with Antoniotto Morelli, the second son of the famous diarist, Giovanni di Paolo Morelli. Antoniotto was born on December , which would make him fifteen at the time that he copied Statius's *Achilleis*, dated in BNCF Landau Fin. .[2] Hand (C) is to be identified with Francesco di Francesco Ferantini, the youngest member of a household of four brothers; he was twenty-seven in ,[3] making him thirteen in , when he copied *Cartula*, *Disticha Catonis* and *Doctrinale* in BNCF Landau Fin. . Their grammar teacher at the time was called Ser Santi, as revealed by a colophon preserved within the manuscript.[4] This teacher was Ser Santi del fu Domenico d'Arezzo, documented as teaching grammar in Florence in ;[5] he also is possibly the teacher mentioned as having a school in Orsanmichele in a Florentine manuscript of Boethius's *Consolation* (BML Ashb.),[6] a text in fact which plays a prominent part in the curriculum evident in Landau . It is clear that the manuscript represents a collaborative e ort of various school pupils, working contemporaneously: the same watermark (a mountain) is found in the sections copied by Antoniotto, Francesco and (D); as a copyist (B) collaborated with both Antoniotto and Francesco; Antoniotto copied fives lines in (D)'s section (v, lines –); Antoniotto and (D) provided glosses to Francesco's section (v, v, r); Antoniotto's note of possession occurs at the end of the section copied by (D); and besides Antoniotto's and Francesco's, there is a series of notes of possession /

2 BNCF Carte Passerini bis, v– r. He died on July : ibid. In the Catasto (ASF Catasto , r– v, *portata* of Giovanni di Pagolo Morelli), Antoniotto is not mentioned in Giovanni Morelli's list of *bocche* (r) and therefore is confirmed as dead.

3 ASF Catasto , v: Bocche. Piero di Francesco Ferantini d'eta d'anni . Giovanni Ferantini d'eta d'ani <...> Alessandro Ferantini d'eta d'anni . Francesco Ferantini d'eta d'anni . The Ferantini were a moderately prosperous middle-ranking Florentine family, with total *valsente* in the Catasto of , florins, just less than half of Giovanni di Paolo Morelli's (, florins).

4 v: Deo gratias amen. Et non fecimus ulterius quia a? sse passus fuit magisster noster qui vochabatur Ser Santes, magisster valde inteligens i<n> filosofia in loicha et in gramaticha etc.

5 Cf. Black (d), . See ASF Catasto , v– r, his tax return.

6 Cf. Black and Pomaro ( ), .

probationes written by another Florentine schoolboy, Matteo Caccini,[7] as well as one of a possible relative[8] whose name also appears written twice.[9]

The material covered in was entirely literary and consisted of a mixture of major and minor authors, resembling the selection often found in school anthologies, where Statius's *Achilleis* was frequently combined with texts of the *auctores minores* (see above,). In reading Statius, Antoniotto Morelli made the usual simple interlinear paraphrases and explication, with the same type of material found in his rare brief marginalia. Francesco Ferantini made no annotations in his text of *Cartula*, but he glossed *Disticha Cathonis* with occasional simple interlinear paraphrases and explications; to this latter text he provided a few marginalia, which consisted not only of this same kind of philological material but of simple grammar as well; he also cited Seneca, Vergil, Boethius's *Consolation*, Ovid and Solomon.

If the schoolwork of in Ser Santi's school consisted entirely of reading relatively simple traditional school texts from both the minor and major authors, the next year the work became more varied. The first task was reading the first two books of *Doctrinale*, which were devoted to the formation of the five nominal declensions, patronymics, Greek and Hebrew nouns, pronouns, and heteroclyte and other irregular nouns. Here Francesco Ferantini provided the usual type of glossing already observed for *Doctrinale* (see above, ,), in the form of interlinear explications (r, v. : rettis = nominativis, quartus = accusativus), examples (r, v. : ut Andreas, ut Anchises, ut musa), rare appearances of the vernacular (v: consul, *el consolo*) and occasional brief explicatory marginalia. But the type of work changed when hand (D) took over the copying. Now there began a number of thematic translations, similar to those already highlighted in Bartolo Mancini's exercise book from the school of Domenico di Bandino in Florence some thirty years earlier. (See above, .) These constituted a series of vernacular passages, each followed by a literal Latin translation; every one was numbered in the left margin, the remaining work for consisting of sixty-one such

[7] r: Matteo d'Antonio di Giovanni di Domenicho di Matteo Chaccini in Firenze. v: M<atteo> d'Antonio di Giovanni di Domen<icho> Chaccini in Firenze. r: Matteo d'Antonio di Giovanni di Domenicho di Matteo Chaccini in Firenze.

[8] r: Antonio di Simone di Giovani di Domenicho di Matteo Chaccini.

[9] r: Antonio di Simone di Giovanni di Pietro di Filippo, Antonio di Simone di Giovanni di Pietro di Filippo. These hands do not appear in body of manuscript, nor that of another signatory ('Salamone di Charlo degli Strozzi'), written above Antoniotto's ownership note on I' in a hand datable to mid / later Quattrocento.

themes to translate (r– v). These translations were also grouped according to topics, indicated as centred titles preceding the passages. The topics for focused almost entirely on verbs, and roughly corresponded to the earlier verbal topics of the secondary grammar syllabus as found, for example, in Francesco da Buti's *Regule*, beginning at the end of the sections on verbs classified according to syntactical patterns (neuter, common, etc.) and moving on to impersonal verbs, infinitives, participles and derivative verbs. An example of this thematic translation can be found in a passage which appears under the heading of impersonal verbs of the passive voice.[10]

In the work continued with further thematic translations of derivative verbs (inchoative, meditative, frequentative, desiderative), but then the focus shifted, as in secondary grammars, to types of nouns (verbals and relatives (indefinite adjectives considered to be nouns and classified as relatives)) (r– r). The formal succession of numbered passages to translate was soon interrupted, however, by an intervening miscellaneous section (v– v). This consisted of grammatical definitions[11] and other theoretical material, interspersed with short thematic translations (not numbered or in topical order) and Latin/vernacular vocabulary lists, organized in topics like those by Goro d'Arezzo and Domenico di Bandino already encountered above (see). This material seems possibly to have o ered revision of subjects already covered earlier in the curriculum, as well as looking forward. There then follows an entirely new section, consisting of several short fictitious vernacular letters and corresponding Latin translations (r– v). Up to this point the work for in Ser Santi's school seems to have been entirely theoretical, but some idea of the year's reading matter is provided by the next item: vocabulary taken from Boethius's *Consolation*, entitled 'Ista sunt vochabula scritta a Boetio etc.' and consisting of a

10 r:

De impersonalibus passive vocis

Elgl'è stato letto e riletto da noi et no è mai stata trovata la storia de' Troiani, in nella quale, benché fossino socchorsi da molti amici, idi' el sa chome in quella battalgla si morì da' nobili et da' prencipi, da' quali si sarebe tornato alle lor familgle volentieri, se fosse stato concieduto dal llo aspro chaso.

Lettum et relettum fuit a nobis et nunqua[m] inventa fuit storia Troianorum, in qua, quamvis ipsis suchurretur a multis amicis, deus scit, sicut in illo bello a nobulibus et a principi[bu]s a quibus reditum fuisset a[d] suas familias libenter, si concessum fuisset ab asp[r]o chasu.

11 E.g. r– r: Quid est nomen? [...] verbum [...] participium [...] pronomen [...] preposi<ti>o [...] averbium [...] interietio [...] coniuntio [...] species [...] genus [...] numerus [...] fighura [...] chasus [...] declinatio [...] comperatio [...] nomen reciprochum [...] gramaticha [...] ars [...] littera [...] silaba [...] scientia [...] dittio [...] oratio [...] proprium nomen [...] nomen appellativum [...] nomen substantivum [...] nomen adiettivum [...] studium [...] dittamen [...] materia [...] interpetratio [...] claves sapientie [...] artes liberales [...]

running list of Latin words with vernacular translations for all of book (r– v). When this list ends, the numbered translations begin again, going from to . The topics now consist of types of nouns (numerals, weights, quantities, possessives, gentiles and patrials, patronymics), again corresponding roughly to the later stages of the formal secondary grammar curriculum found, for example, in Francesco da Buti's textbook. At this point it seems, as suggested by the colophon on v mentioned above (n.), that Ser Santi stopped teaching this group of boys. With Ser Santi's departure, the numbered thematic translations ceased, but the year was completed with another miscellaneous mixture of brief thematic translations, Latin/vernacular vocabulary and grammar notes (r– v). The next year, , continued with the same type of miscellaneous material (r– r), concluding with a section on homonyms, in the form of a Latin vocabulary list with vernacular equivalents, organized by grouping together identically or similarly spelled words with di erent meanings (r– r). These *Di erentiae* correspond to the works by pseudo-Cicero and Guarino discussed above (–); they normally seem to have come near the end of the theoretical secondary curriculum, as is suggested by the late placing of Guarino's *Carmina di erentialia* in the series of Florentine grammar treatises associated with Giorgio Antonio Vespucci which have been discussed above (see).

Thus, it seems that, in this Italian grammar school, literary reading (in the form of minor and initial major authors, as well as Boethius's *Consolation*) was interspersed with formal grammatical study (not only in the guise of *Doctrinale* but also in the form of an unidentified textbook which probably provided the theoretical context for the progressive series of themes); accompanying all this, especially after the reading of the minor authors, was a growing concentration on translation from vernacular into Latin. The mixture of translation, rules of construction and the epistolary composition seems to have been typical of Quattrocento grammar schools, as is clear from a letter of Guarino's in to another grammar teacher, Martino Rizzoni, once his pupil; his advice was to accustom his eldest pupil, Lodovico, to letter writing, to thematic composition and the rules of grammatical construction.[12]

It is interesting that one of the exercises given by Ser Santi to his group of Florentine pupils was the translation of letters from the *volgare* into Latin. This was a foretaste of the kind of work that the pupils would be doing at the next stage of their education. In BNCF Landau Fin. ,

[12] 'Ludovicum iam epistulis consuefacias interque themata constructionum regulas permisce [...]': Guarino (–), , , cited by Grendler ( ), and Garin ( ), .

these letters were translated in a literal fashion, just like the thematic translations made throughout grammar school.[13] The translation of letters from the vernacular into Latin would be the focus of the initial stylistic and rhetorical education of pupils in Italian schools, but at this next level the emphasis would no longer be on the literal rendering of vernacular into Latin. With their introduction to rhetoric, pupils would have to begin to learn how to give their Latin prose composition the elegance which was lacking in their earlier strictly grammatical e orts (although in the case of the above anonymous Florentine pupil of Ser Santi, one wonders – in view of his appalling Latin grammar – whether he was or ever would be suitable for promotion to the higher level of rhetorical study).

In Roman antiquity there were two distinct levels of post-elementary education: secondary schools were under the charge of a *grammaticus*,[14] whereas the only institution of higher education known in the ancient Latin world was the rhetorical school, headed by a *rhetor*.[15] Grammar and rhetoric were regarded as two separate subjects. Quintilian saw the particular *métier* of the grammar master as 'recte loquendi scientiam' (.iv.). The key word here was *recte*: the emphasis in grammar was on correct expression. Rhetoric, in contrast, Quintilian defined as the 'bene dicendi scientiam' (.xv.):[16] here the crucial term was *bene*; the focus in rhetoric was on e ective expression. The contrast was between using language, on the one hand, without error and, on the other, for compelling communication. This fundamental distinction between the two subjects persisted into late antiquity. For example, in Martianus Capella's allegorical *De nuptiis Philologiae et Mercurii* (*c.* –), where a separate book was devoted to each, Grammar appears as an old, grey-haired woman, carrying a casket of ebony that contains surgical implements to

[13] E.g.:

r: Hec [e]pisstula dirigitur ad que[m]dam [*sic*] puellam: *O dolcissima Venere, per la chui influentia la quale genera nelgli uomini a fargli venire et sentire e primi disiri per li per li* [sic] *quali a mettere in persichutione, io disspiaratamente di voi m'inamorai, non movendomi altro se no gli atti achosstumati, e quali molto si confano, a' vesstri occhi più atti a volere disiderare onessta che altra chosa* [...]

v: O dulcissima Venus, per chuius influentiam que in [h]ominibus generatur, eos faciendo venire ad chongnoscendum primas chupiditates amoris quas in persecutione mittere, desperate de vobis filocepi, non movendo me nisi attus morigeratos, q[u]os multum decet vestris ochulis attioribus, volendo desiderare magis honesstatem quam aliud [...]

[14] Marrou ( ), – . [15] Marrou ( ), – .

[16] Defined in same terms: .xiv. ; .xv. .

remove children's grammatical mistakes, whereas Rhetoric strides forth as a splendidly beautiful and tall lady, dressed in a gown decorated with figures of speech.[17]

Such distinctions persisted in the middle ages. The famous thirteenth-century gloss on *Doctrinale* known as *Admirantes* distinguished explicitly between rhetoric, which sought to move, and grammar, which was limited to literal meaning.[18] This meant that the skilled Latinist, according to the same text, was able to use two levels of style, one simple and grammatical suited to the masses, the other ornamented and rhetorical for the learned.[19] This led to the distinction, made at the beginning of the thirteenth century, between types of word order: one natural and suited to grammatical expression, the other artificial and appropriate to rhetoric.[20] According to one fourteenth-century manuscript, when carrying out the work of the grammarian, such as commenting on texts, *ordo naturalis* was used; on the other hand, for *dictamen* (i.e. rhetoric) *ordo artificialis* was appropriate.[21] The same type of distinction between the disciplines of rhetoric and grammar persisted into the fifteenth century, as is clear from a gloss in the school-level grammar course of Filippo Casali, grammar teacher in Tuscany and Bologna in the third quarter of the century.[22]

Even in antiquity, nevertheless, there could already be found some interpenetration and merging of the two disciplines. Quintilian, who himself deplored this amalgamation, observed that in his day *rhetores* tended to disdain preparatory work, whereas *grammatici* wanted to move

[17] Curtius ( ), – .

[18] Thurot ( ), : 'Sermocinalis scientia dividitur in hunc modum. Sermo est ordinatus ad movendum aut ad significandum [...] rethorica [...] per sermonis eloquentiam movetur iudex ad partem propriam nutriendam et partem adversam deprimendam. Si ordinetur ad significandum, sic est gramatica.'

[19] Thurot ( ), : 'quantum ad figurativas locutiones est ut sapientibus et provectis sapientes et provecti, figurativis locutionibus mediantibus, suos exprimant a ectus et intellectus per plenarias sententias et profundas. Nam peritus gramaticus sibi duplex preparat instrumentum, unum, quo utitur ad plures, ut est sermo simpliciter congruus, et aliud, quo utitur ad sapientes, ut est sermo figurativus.'

[20] Thurot ( ), : 'Scias itaque quod duplex est ordo, scilicet naturalis et artificialis. Naturalis ordo est, quando nominativus cum determinatione sua precedit et verbum sequitur cum sua, ut *ego amo te*. Artificialis ordo vel dispositio est, quando partes proprie transponuntur et pulcrius ordinantur, ut *Petrum sincera dilectione prosequor et amplector*.' For a good discussion of distinction, see Mengaldo ( ).

[21] Thurot ( ), : 'In constructione duplex est ordo, naturalis videlicet et aritficialis. Naturalis est ille qui pertinet ad expositionem, quando nominativus cum determinatione sua precedit et verbum sequitur cum sua, ut *ego amo te*. Artificialis ordo vel compositio est illa que pertinet ad dictationem, quando partes pulcrius disponuntur; que sic a Tullio definitur: Compositio artificialis est constructio equaliter polita.'

[22] BML Ashb. , r: gramaticus loquitur, rhetoricus eloquitur, id est ornate loquitur.

into higher levels of study; the result was that the first stages of rhetoric were coming to constitute the end of the grammar curriculum (.i. –). In later antiquity, it became increasingly common for the *grammaticus* also to teach rhetoric;[23] teachers were becoming fewer, and there was a tendency to confuse the secondary and higher curricula.[24] For Alcuin in the early middle ages, grammar and rhetoric constituted a seamless garment: 'The authors' books [the preserve of the grammarian] ought to be read, and their words well impressed upon our memory. If someone has fashioned his style upon theirs, he cannot but express himself with refinement, however much he might try to the contrary.'[25] Gerbert of Aurillac also saw an indissoluble link between the teaching of grammar and rhetoric.[26] With the growing specialization of education in the twelfth century, the old boundaries between grammar and rhetoric tended to be resurrected. In Italy, rhetoric was transformed into the *ars dictaminis*, which became, beginning in the thirteenth century, primarily a university-level subject, whereas, with the rise of private and communal schools, grammar normally descended to the pre-university level. Nevertheless, given the assimilation, beginning in antiquity and reinforced in the early middle ages, of the two disciplines, it is not surprising to find that the first stages of rhetoric often found their way into the end of the grammar syllabus in medieval and Renaissance Italy.

:

An early example of the penetration of rhetoric into the grammar syllabus in Italian schools is provided by Pietro da Isolella's *Summa*, probably datable, as seen above ( ), to the second half of the thirteenth century. This school-level grammar textbook also contains a short chapter on rhetoric, called 'De dictamine in soluta oratione',[27] which, as is evident from its title, o ers an introduction to the then fashionable *ars dictaminis*: in addition to furnishing a definition of *dictamen*, this brief section of the text mentions the letter and its constituent parts (*salutatio*, *exordium*, *narratio*, *petitio* and *conclusio*), as well as the di erent types of

[23] Riché ( ), . [24] Riché ( ), .

[25] *De rhetorica*, , ed. Halm ( ), . Translation by Howell ( ), (corrected). See Riché ( ), . [26] Richer ( ), , . See Riché ( ), .

[27] Ed. Fierville ( ), – , who follows text of MS of Bibliothèque Muncipale de Laon. He also publishes corresponding chapter in BNP MS lat. , presenting substantial divergences from Laon MS and which is closer to one of Pietro's main sources, the Provençal grammarian Sponcius. See Fierville ( ), n. , – and – .

phrases, clauses and sentences (*coma*, *colum*, *periodus*, *subdistinctio*, *clausula*), besides touching on punctuation (*punctum*) and cadential rhythm (*cursus*) – all of which were principal concerns of theorists and teachers of *ars dictaminis*.[28] This material is handled only summarily by Pietro, whose purpose here can hardly have been other than to provide a foretaste of a subject to be encountered later in the educational hierarchy. Such generalities were probably of little immediate practical use to school pupils, but nevertheless in this chapter there was one topic which received a little more detailed attention: this was the subject of style. Here Pietro seems to leave the realm of platitudes and enter a more realistic and utilitarian world when discussing stylistic shortcomings and in particular faults of expression: some of these are simply formulaic repetitions of the well-known passage from *Rhetorica ad Herennium* (.), echoing the warning there against consecutive vowels (e.g. 'mala aula amat crimen'), overuse of a particular letter (e.g. 'soleas in sola non sacras faciebat suas'), repetition of the same word (e.g. 'cuius rationis ratio non extat rationi, non est ratio probare fidem rationi'), recurrence of the same ending (e.g. 'infantes stantes, lacrimantes, vociferantes'), dislocation of words ('nulla mulierum est vir'), and overly long periods. Nevertheless, other stylistic faults are not found in pseudo-Cicero and perhaps reflect more immediate problems encountered by teachers in the work of their pupils, such as juxtaposition of undi erentiated words (e.g. 'celebre studium maxime proficiat'), too many long words (e.g. 'ex celebritate studiorum magnam commoditatem sapientes consequantur'), use of metre or rhyme in prose,[29] following a word ending in 'm' by one beginning with a vowel (e.g. 'animam anxiam amo' or 'bonum agnum eum'), or two sibilant sounds at the end and beginning of successive words (e.g. 'ex sorte', 'ars studiorum' or 'rex Xerxes'); in fact, in listing these supplementary faults, Pietro refers to the views of 'moderni doctores'.

The order of chapters in Pietro da Isolella's *Summa* varies considerably among manuscripts, and so there is no indication of the point in the school Latin curriculum at which thirteenth-century pupils were first introduced to rhetoric and *dictamen*. Nevertheless, in one manuscript the above-mentioned chapter 'De dictamine in soluta oratione' occurs at the end of the treatise,[30] and by the fourteenth century it seems that introductory rhetoric had come to represent a normal complement to the

28 On the contents of *ars dictaminis*, see Murphy ( ), – ; Faulhaber ( ); Haskins ( ), – *passim*; Banker (a) and (b); Polak ( ); Kristeller (a), .
29 Mentioned in Guido Fava's *Summa dictaminis*: see Faulhaber ( ), .
30 BNP Lat. : see Fierville ( ), xv.

secondary grammar syllabus – a pattern suggested by a number of manuscripts containing Francesco da Buti's *Regule grammaticales.* In these copies Francesco's secondary grammar is followed by a set of *Regule* rethorice,[31] a work intended by Francesco for school use, as is clear from the preface, where he distinguishes between his textbook for children (*rudes*) and complete *dictamen* treatises by learned authorities.[32] Francesco chose his words carefully here: when speaking in terms of compilation and omission, he was implying that he had taken this text from fuller treatises on rhetoric and *dictamen,* and in fact his *Regule rethorice* o er almost entirely an abbreviated version of *Rhetorica ad Herennium*'s fourth book, supplemented by conventional material found in Italian *artes dictaminis.* Thus, Francesco states that his aim is to provide a guide to polished prose composition (*exquisitum dictamen*), which is achieved by three means: elegance, arrangement and appropriate ornament (*elegantia, compositio, ornatus*).[33] Here he is summarizing the formulation in *Rhetorica ad Herennium,* . . Francesco devotes no more than a few lines to elegance, which he defines as purity of Latin and clarity of explanation, again a repetition of *Rhetorica ad Herennium,* . ,[34] and he then quickly moves through his second topic, *compositio,* which consists of a brief discussion of phrases, sentences, clauses and their punctuation as well as cadential rhythm (*cursus*)[35] – all standard topics in *dictamen* treatises.[36] The treatment here again is summarial, representing a formulaic synopsis of the traditional handling of these themes;[37] similarly cursory and conventional is Francesco's short paragraph on stylistic faults, repeating the classic passage in *Rhetorica ad Herennium* (.) with one addition, which reiterates a fault also highlighted by Pietro da Isolella ('m' at the end of

[31] Alessio (a), – , n. , lists eight MSS giving *Regule rethorice* as appendix to his *Regule grammaticales.* I read the text in BRF , v– v, and Bodley Lat. misc. e. , r . According to Banker (a), , Francesco's rhetorical treatise was written *c.* ; he cites BRF , n. .

[32] Bodley Lat. misc. e. , r: Quoniam facultas recthorice sine arte potest di cillime doceri, igitur ad eius doctrinam et artem penitus capescendam quedam introductoria sub breviloquio compilemus, obmissis aliis que ad erudiendum rudes minime necessaria reputamus, cum ea querentibus per documenta doctorum illustrium patefiant. Cf. BRF , v.

[33] Bodley Lat. misc. e. , r: Sciendum est quod tria in omni exquisito dictamine requiruntur, scilicet elegantia, compositio et ornatus. Cf. BRF , v. This recalls Pietro da Isolella's formulation (ed. Fierville ( ),), itself a revision of *Rhetorica ad Herennium,* . . See Giovanni del Virgilio's *Dictamen,* ed. Kristeller ( ), . Francesco later substitutes *dignitas* for *ornatus* (Bodley Lat. misc. e. , v: Unde de tertia parte scilicet de dignitate videndum est), so following formulation in *Rhetorica ad Herennium,* . ; Pietro da Isolella (ed. Fierville ( ),) and Giovanni del Virgilio (ed. Kristeller ( ),) both use *dignitas.*

[34] Bodley Lat. misc. e. , r. Cf. BRF , v– r. Also found in Giovanni del Virgilio, ed. Kristeller ( ), . [35] Bodley Lat misc. e. , v– r. [36] See above, – .

[37] See e.g. Giovanni del Virgilio, ed. Kristeller ( ), – .

a word followed by a vowel at the beginning of the next).[38] The longest section of Francesco's *Regule rethorice* is his treatment of rhetorical colours,[39] which, echoing *Rhetorica ad Herennium*, he defines in terms of style.[40] Once again it is no surprise to discover that this entire section is taken from *Rhetorica ad Herennium*: for example, the first colour, *repetitio*, is handled identically.[41] *Rhetorica ad Herennium* similarly provides the source from which Francesco extracts the rest of his treatment of rhetorical colours,[42] and it is therefore not unexpected to find that the remainder of Francesco da Buti's school-level Latin course consists of material drawn from conventional treatments of the *ars dictaminis*. In several manuscripts, his *Regule rethorice* are followed by a *Tractatus epistolarum*,[43] a work similarly intended for school pupils, as is clear once more from the preface.[44] This text o ers a standard but relatively brief treatment of the parts of the letter according to the medieval doctrine of *dictamen*, concentrating, as was usual, primarily on the first two sections, that is, the salutation and the exordium, and giving only a brief mention to the narration, the petition and the conclusion.[45]

Like Pietro da Isolella's chapter on *dictamen*, Francesco da Buti's treatment of rhetoric and epistolography is thus almost entirely derivative: both texts represent compendia of existing theoretical material, whether from *Rhetorica ad Herennium* or from existing *dictamen* literature. Abbreviation represents the main way in which these works have been adapted to the particular needs of school pupils, and so it is not surprising to find that, in comparison with his widely di used and influential

38 Cf. Bodley Lat. misc. e. , v and Pietro da Isolella, ed. Fierville ( ), .

39 Bodley Lat. misc. e. , v– r.

40 Francesco da Buti, Bodley Lat. misc. e. , v: dignitas est enim que orationem exornat et pulcra varietate distinguit. Hec enim in verborum et sententiarum exornationes distinguitur. Verborum exornatio est que in ipsius sermonis insignita verborum continetur perpolicione. Sententiarum exornatio est que non in verbis sed in ipsis rebus quandam habet dignitatem. Cf. *Rhetorica ad Herennium*, . .

41 Francesco da Buti, Bodley Lat. misc. e. , v: Repetitio enim est cum ab eodem verbo continenter in rebus similibus et diversis principia sumuntur hoc modo: vobis istud actribuendum est, vobis gratia est habenda, vobis res ista est honori. Cf. *Rhetorica ad Herennium*, . .

42 Cf. Bodley Lat. misc. e. , v– r and *Rhetorica ad Herennium*, . – .

43 Bodley Lat. misc. e. , r– v; BRF , v (fragmentary at end).

44 Bodley Lat. misc. e. , r: Quoniam dictamen tripliciter dividitur, nam aliud prosaicum, aliud rictimicum et aliud metricum, et prosaicum quatrupliter dividitur, scilicet in istorias, privilegiam, contractus et epistolas, cum hec omnia explanamenta requirent non parvam temporis quantitatem, solum de epistolari dictamine presentis intentionis est utilitati rudium. Cf. BRF , v.

45 E.g. Guido Fava's treatment of the *salutatio* is eight times the total length of his discussion of the *exordium*, *narratio* and *petitio*, while the latter two are handled in a single paragraph; he does not even mention the *conclusio*: see Faulhaber ( ), – . According to Banker (a), , commentators were most interested in Giovanni di Bonandrea's treatment of the *salutatio* and *exordium*.

Regule grammaticales, Francesco da Buti's rhetorical and epistolary rules enjoyed a more limited circulation.[46] The same cannot be said of another later medieval school-level work on rhetoric: among Italian manuscript schoolbook collections it would be di cult to overlook the powerful presence of **Geoffrey of Vinsauf's *Poetria nova***, a verse treatise on rhetoric composed between and .[47] In Florence, for example, there are at least eleven manuscripts of this work, all of them probable or certain schoolbooks:

Shelf-mark	Date	Provenance	School use
BML AD	XVin.	Italy	Copied and glossed by a number of contemporary hands in usual school manner, including some interlinear vernacular.
BML CS (v– r)	XVmid	Italy	Copiously glossed by scribe.
BML Strozzi	XIV¹	Emilia	Glossed extensively in Trecento, also by two XVc. copyists of Horace (see above and Appendix below,), all possibly working in a school context.
BML Strozzi	XV¹	Florence[48]	Unglossed schoolbook containing *probationes* (v– v) and Latin verses written by immature hand (r) besides rubbed-out notes of possession (v).
BNCF CS J. .	–	Italy	Given full and interesting commentary by copyist,[49] including some vernacular.

46 For manuscripts, see above, n. .

47 Geo rey of Vinsauf ( ), ed. Faral. For date, see Geo rey of Vinsauf ( ), – . According to John Conley, who was preparing a critical edition in , there are more than MSS: see Gallo ( ), . For the work's place in nine medieval Italian libraries, see Manacorda ( ), – ; for further MSS preserved in Italian libraries, see Manacorda ( ), – . *Poetria nova* was a principal focus for the teaching activities of two Italian pre-humanists, Guizzardo da Bologna, who taught there from to , and Pace da Ferrara, who worked at the Paduan Studio in the early fourteenth century. Both left important commentaries on Geo rey's text: see Woods ( ) and ( ); Stadter ( ). For the commentary by Bartolomeo da San Concordio da Pisa (d.), see Manacorda ( ), Wilmart ( ) and Woods ( ). For the text's extensive manuscript circulation in fifteenth-century Italy, see Woods ( ).

48 Written by two hands reusing Trecento Florentine notarial parchment.

49 Part of *accessus* quoted by Corradi ( ), , n. . The early commentary by Bartolomeo da S. Concordio (d.) is preserved in Rome Bibl. Casanatense MS : see Manacorda ( ); Kaepelli (–), , .

Shelf-mark	Date	Provenance	School use
BNCF Panciat.	XVmid	Florence[50]	Copious *probationes* on two front flyleaves; immature hand wrote alphabets (v, v); Latin/ vernacular vocabulary list (r) written by only glossator, providing usual school-type simple interlinear paraphrase and basic philological marginalia including vernacular (r: hoc opus/*il bisogno*), besides citing Vergil's *Aeneid* (v), Donatus (v), Priscian (r).
BRF	– [51]	Italy	Marginal commentary (up to v) by hand contemporaneous with copyist, besides occasional interlinear glosses by various hands; school ownership note[52] and puerile drawing of a crenellated tower (v).
BRF [53]	XIV^{1}	Tuscany/ Angevin Naples[54]	Substantial marginal commentary by copyist and interlinear glosses by slightly later hands, alphabet (v).
BRF	XV^{1}	Italy	Copyist: heavy Gothic hand, providing most of glosses; school ownership note. Names of pupil and teacher written over previously erased names: book previously owned by anonymous pupil from Florentine parish of S. Felicita.[55]

50 Reusing parchment of Florentine *ricordanza* (v: Ridolfi e compagni; r: Gherardi; v: Gianni di Bartolo di Messer Iachopo de' Bardi; v: di Firenze <…> ricordo che <…>; r: Guidotti), dating from : see r, where date is legible; v: MCCCXXX.

51 *Probatio* (v): Amen. Anno ab eiadem [*sic*] incarnationis millximo trecenteximo sexageximo nono.

52 v: Iste liber est Antonii <Arnaldi> morantis in scholis <Magistri Spiliati>. Amen. To be identified with Maestro Spigliato di Cenne da Firenze, a teacher working in Florence and Prato in the early s (ASPCD , v, r–v, r, r–v, r, v, r–v, r–v). Names 'Arnaldi' and 'Magistri Spiliati' are written over earlier names. The name beneath Maestro Spigliato's is no longer legible, but 'fighinensis' is decipherable, indicating some connection with an earlier pupil or teacher from Figline.

53 Gehl ( ), (XIII^{2}). At end: Iste liber est Johannis olim Ser Francisci Guadagni de Romena, deo gratias, amen (v), written in *cancelleresca* hand (XIV^{1}).

54 See two letters from Angevin court appended to end of treatise (v, v).

55 v: Iste liber est Alexandri Ser Nicholai populi Sancte Felicitatis ultra Arnum, morantis in scholis Magistri Antonii <de Garbo?> doctoris gramatice. Transcription published by Gehl ( ), , requires emendation, as is clear from photograph, .

Shelf-mark	Date	Provenance	School use
BRF (r– v)	XVin.	Italy	Glossed on first folio and beginning of second with normal school-type interlinear and marginal glosses.
BRF (r– v: fragment)	XVmid	Italy	Copious low-level interlinear vernacular glossing and simple marginal philology.

Poetic composition was not a principal activity in Italian grammar schools during the later middle ages, and so it may seem paradoxical that a treatise ostensibly on the writing of verse achieved such a wide following among Italian teachers and pupils. Geo rey of Vinsauf may have intended his work as a new poetics to replace Horace's *Ars poetica*, a work often referred to as his *Poetria*,[56] but in Italian schools *Poetria nova* was used primarily to teach prose composition.[57] This is immediately clear from the text's glosses, which exemplify Geo rey's theoretical points in prose.[58] Similarly in the glosses it is normally stated that Geo rey was

56 Curtius ( ), .

57 It is normally assumed that *Poetria nova* was used in the middle ages as a guide to writing poetry: e.g. Gallo ( ), – : 'We have to ask ourselves how we are to understand the doctrines of the *Poetria nova.* We must not consider them simply as establishing procedures which every right-thinking medieval poet strove to follow'; : 'The medieval *poetriae* may have laid down preceptive principles for the poet to follow.' Parr ( ), – : 'The vogue for using metrical form as the most e ective means of communication lies behind the literary prescriptions of the thirteenth and fourteenth centuries [...] This common craze for verse-form created a need for versified manuals on the theory of poetic. The need was met among others by Geo rey of Vinsauf [...] By the end of the twelfth century the great interest in versification produced a series of works setting forth the poetic doctrines of the time. They were little more than manuals or exercise books intended to provide practical assistance to the would-be poet.' Nims ( ), – : '[...] Geo rey of Vinsauf [...] in writing his new *ars poetica*, hoped to [...] o er precepts for the poet-in-training; scope for practice, in the form of model exercises [...] the twelfth- and thirteenth-century *artes poeticae* [...] represent [...] the training in expression of most of the poets of western Europe from the thirteenth century through the Renaissance'.

58 E.g. BNCF CS J. . , r: Interpretatio fit cum dico: scientia hominem nobilitat et decorat, quoniam idem dico, sed muto verba. Et idem: hoc nos magnificat et exaltat. Ista verba portant idem sed mutata sunt per hunc colorem. v: conduplicatio di ert [...] ab interpretatione, quia [...] posita proprietate alicuius rei removetur obiectum eiusdem, ut: ista iuventutis est et non facit senilis. Interpretatio enim per diversa verba eandem sententiam ponit, ut: sapientia nos decorat et honorat. ¶Parudigma est dictum [h]ortantis vel de[h]ortantis, cum exemplo ait: tam fortiter ruit apud Yponem Scipio quam Atice Cato. ¶De comparatione [...] dicitur quod fit dupliciter, aperte et occulte. Aperte per tria signa: per magis, minus et eque. Per magis sic: Qui furtum committit vita corporis est privandus; ergo multo magis qui sacrilegium commisit ultimo supplicio est tradendus. Per minus sic: qui sacrilegium committunt veniam promerentur; ergo multo magis qui furtum faciunt debent veniam promereri. Per eque sic: Catellina[m] labefacientem [MS: labefaciantem] rem publicam Cicero interfecit; vos consules Gracium eque subvertentem publicam rem minime occidisti[s].

imitiating Cicero, with the implication that, like the latter, he was o ering guidance in prose composition.[59] Moreover, the recipient of Geo rey's advice is sometimes said in the glosses to be a *dictator*, i.e. a prose writer.[60] This substitution of prose for metre (and vice versa), typical of medieval stylistics,[61] was based on the notion of *ordo artificialis*: as is made clear in a passage by William of Conches,[62] the authors' poetry and prose were both prone to artful manipulation, and so it was implicit that they were both subject to the same rules of deconstruction (accomplished by the grammarian, who, through commentary, restored the logical or natural word order to artificial discourse, whether poetry or prose) or construction (carried out by the rhetorician, who, for the sake of art, elevated natural language into elegant discourse, again either poetry or prose).[63]

Poetria nova is ostensibly a treatise covering all five traditional parts of rhetoric (invention, disposition, diction, memory and delivery), but its focus is evident from the space allotted to the various sections: out of a total length of , verses, invention is only one among several topics rapidly passed over in the general introduction (vv. –); the two succeeding stylistic themes, on the other hand, occupy the body of the treatise, with vv. – and – dedicated to *dispositio* and *elocutio* respectively; in contrast, the remaining two topics receive less than a hundred lines each, with memory treated in vv. – and delivery in vv. – . Both Pietro da Isolella's and Francesco da Buti's school-level treatments of dictamen showed some emphasis on style,[64] but *Poetria nova* went much further: Geo rey of Vinsauf in fact wrote a manual of style rather than a full-blown textbook on rhetoric, as is confirmed by comparison with classical rhetorical treatises, where the emphasis had been on invention: according to *Rhetorica ad Herennium*, invention was the most di cult part of rhetoric (.), while Cicero in

[59] E.g. BML Strozzi , v: Tullius quem autor iste imitatur [. . .] v: autor exemplificavit secundum ordinem Tullii [. . .] ¶prima pars dividitur in partes quinque secundum quod significatio ut dicit Tullius potest fieri quinque modis [. . .]

[60] E.g. see BNCF CS J. . , v, cited below, n. .

[61] See Curtius ( ), – .

[62] 'Omnes auctores vel metrice vel prosaice vel mixtim scribunt. Ut autem necesse est, naturalis ordo dictionum lege metri mutatur. Cum naturalis ordo exigit nominativum preponi in oratione, verbum sequi, deinde obliquum casum, adverbium verbo aderere et similia, aliquando propter tempora et pedes metri ordo ille mutatur, ut hic [...] Necesse autem est in expositione ad suum naturalem ordinem dictiones reducere; quod sine sciencia construendi facile fieri non potest. Qui vero prosaice scribunt, ordinem naturalem similiter mutant, quippe sunt dictiones que post quasdam male, post alias bene sonant. Qui autem arte et non casu scribunt, prius scienciam diligunt; deinde quot modis illa sentencia potest significari, aspiciunt; postea pulcriora verba ad hoc faciendum ponunt considerantes quo ordine illa verba prolata melius sonabunt.' (Cited by Kneepkens ( ), –)

[63] See also Mengaldo ( ).

[64] See above, .

De inventione called it 'princeps [...] omnium partium' (.). In contrast, *Poetria nova*'s treatment of invention was limited to a few generalities and platitudes: plan thoroughly before writing (vv. –); choose the appropriate material for the beginning, middle and end (vv. –); take care lest any single part should blemish the whole (vv. –); start honestly, continue strenuously and solemnly, finish honourably (vv. –). In fact, the stress on style in this text was well appreciated in the later middle ages. The early fourteenth-century copyist of BML Strozzi provided a set of rubrics which highlight the overriding stylistic emphasis of the work.[65] In the Italian medieval and Renaissance classroom, Geo rey of Vinsauf thus provided a manual on prose style in verse format for easier memorization; in fact, it represented the rhetorical/stylistic counterpart to Alexander of Villedieu's verse grammar, *Doctrinale*.

Poetria nova's treatment of style begins with the distinction between natural and artificial word order.[66] Although natural word order may have been thought appropriate for purely grammatical study, it is now considered sterile, and the artful approach is regarded as more productive.[67] Abandoning thus the natural accuracy learned at the secondary grammatical level, the pupil now acquires a capacity for artistic expression. In this connection, Geo rey recommends several ways of varying natural word order: by beginning the sentence with the end or the middle of the natural word order; and by introducing a proverb or an example, at the beginning, middle or end of the sentence (vv. –).[68] He then proceeds to illustrate how to amplify or fill out simple sentences, recommending duplication (vv. –), circumlocution (vv. –), comparison (vv. –), exclamation (vv. –), personification (vv. –), digression (vv. –), description (vv. –) and juxtaposition (vv. –); for abbreviation, on the other hand, he recommends innuendo (*emphasis*), staccato expression (*articulus*), ablative absolutes, omission of conjunctions (asyndeton) and fusion into a single proposition of several statements (vv. –). Nevertheless, amplification and abbreviation are only the beginnings of ornate style; moving from natural to artificial expression also requires colour.[69] This is achieved in the first place (vv. –) through metaphorical language, such as

65 v: De inventione. r: De dispositione. v: De elocutione. r: De memoria. r: De pronuntiatione. 66 Vv. – .

67 On distinction between *ordo naturalis* and *artificialis*, see also Scaglione ( ), .

68 Guido Fava makes the same distinction between natural and artificial word order, declaring that the latter is 'illa compositio que pertinet ad dictationem, quando partes pulcrius disponuntur', o ering some of the same suggestions as Geo rey: Faulhaber ( ), – . This further confirms that Geo rey's treatise was applied to prose composition in Italy. 69 Vv. – .

attributing human qualities to things and vice versa; figurative treatment of verbs, adjectives and nouns; and use of particular tropes (e.g. metaphor, onomatopoeia, antonomasia, allegory, metonymy, hyperbole, synecdoche, catachresis, hyperbaton). Secondly, discourse is given colour through figures of speech (vv. –) (e.g. rhetorical questions (*interrogatio*) or ending words similarly (*similiter disinens*)) or of thought (vv. –) (e.g. understatement (*diminutio*) or imagined dialogue (*sermoncinatio*)). Thirdly, sentences are rendered more colourful by employing the doctrine of conversion (vv. –), that is, by changing one part of speech or grammatical form into another: verbs into nouns (e.g., *ex hac re doleo* = *ex hoc fonte mihi manat dolor*), adjectives into nouns (e.g., *candidus est vultus* = *illuminat ora candor*), one nominal case into another (e.g., *ego rem sceleratam consilio feci* = *consilium scelerata manus produxit in actum*), or indeclinable into declinable parts of speech (e.g., *huc veniet* = *hic locus admittet venientem*). Fourthly, colour can be achieved by using grammatical relations between words (vv. –), e.g. between nouns (*es Cato mente, Tullius ore, Paris facie, Pirrusque vigore*) or between adjectives and oblique cases (*avarus plenus opum, vaccus virtutum, avidissima rerum, prodigus alterius parcus rerumque suarum*). Finally, Geo rey completes his discussion of style (vv. –) by urging care in the choice of words, by warning against various stylistic faults (such as juxtaposition of vowels among two or more words; repetition of the same letters, words or final syllables; sentences of excessive length; or forced metaphors)[70] and by recommending good judgement, a sensitive ear and attention to usage.

It is clear from Geo rey's text that the work at this new, rhetorical/stylistic level of school education involved kinds of exercises similar to those already encountered at the earlier secondary grammatical stage. Again the key term here is *thema*, but this now becomes the grammatically correct but plain Latin passage to which the pupil must apply his art; the theme is given in natural Latin order and wording, and it has to be rendered elegant and artificial.[71] For example, one way is to begin at the end. Geo rey recommends that the opening of the theme according to natural word order should, so to speak, wait outside, letting the end enter first; nature puts the end of the sentence in last place but art raises it to the highest position.[72] Similarly, the middle of the theme provides

[70] Repeating sometimes points made in *Rhetorica ad Herennium*, . .

[71] This procedure of elaborating a plain *thema* was also at heart of *ars dictaminis*: e.g., Guido Fava distinguishes between the letter's *thema* or subject and its *materia* ('plena et artificiosa verborum ordinatio ex hiis que in themate assumantur'): Faulhaber ( ), .

[72] Vv. – .

an opening potentially as elegant and artificial as the end.[73] If the natural word order of the theme is to remain unaltered, then another path to art o ered by Geo rey is to eschew the theme's mundane and particular wording and recast the beginning as a general proverb (*sententia*); using this approach, it is possible to open with the beginning, middle or end of the theme.[74]

Thus thematic composition was the practical focus of the rhetorical level of school Latin education, just as it was at the secondary level; the theme remained the passage assigned to the pupil, whose task now, however, was no longer to render the theme into grammatically correct but naturally ordered Latin, but rather to turn the latter into artful and elegant prose. In fact, the stylistic emphasis at this stage of school education is also clear from glosses made to manuscripts of *Poetria nova* now found in Florentine libraries. For example, the Trecento copyist and principal glossator of BNCF CS J. . not only highlights the principal stylistic assumptions and features of the work, including the division of the second part of rhetoric (*dispositio*) into natural and artificial order[75] as well as rhetorical thematic composition,[76] but also adds further explanation of the various stylistic devices recommended by Geo rey to embellish plain Latin prose, as for example in the discussion of circumlocution.[77] Similarly, in the rubrication made by the copyist of BML Strozzi , invention, memory and delivery are passed over with single headings (see above, n.) but disposition and diction are subdivided in

73 Vv. – . 74 Vv. – .

75 r:

dispositio seu ordo { naturalis / artificialis

76 r: dicto qualiter summendum sit principium a fine et a medio, nunc dicitur qualiter summendum est a proverbio et tale principium alterum a precedentibus. Et debet ita fieri proverbium, quod generale sit et nichil contineat speciale, et quasi superbum et altum stet super thema datum, et nichil dicat de themate sed pertineat ad illud, ut si dicam: Devotus servus et fidelis domino suo non desinit obedire; quod considerans Habraam filium suum Ysahac Ch(rist)o voluit ymolare. Ecce thema.

77 v: Nunc determinat de sermone ampliandi materiam, que est circuitio sive circumlocutio. Que a Donato dicitur peryfrasis, a peri, quod est circum, et frasis, ferre, id est, circumlatio vel circumlocutio. Que fit aut ordinande rei causa que pulcrior est, aut colende rei causa que turpis est. Et dividitur hec pars in duas. In prima tradit doctrinam de circuitione; in secunda docet circuitionem fieri tripliciter, ibi *cum triplici claustro*. Fit autem primo circumlocutio cum loco nominis ponitur descriptio eius, ut prudentia Scipionis loco eius quod Scipio; secundo, loco verbi cum ponitur obiectio, ut bellando superavit pro eo quod est vicit; tertio de utroque quod per predictam partem ponit, scilicet, quando variatur nomen et verbum similiter. Prudentia Scipionis (primus modus) bellando superavit (secundus modus). Dicere poteram, Scipio superavit, sed unicuique additur per circumlocutionem: prudentia Scipionis bellando superavit (tertius modus).

detail.[78] In fact, one glossator even refers to the process of thematic composition in reference to *Poetria nova*.[79]

:

Francesco da Buti's complete grammar course ended with epistolography, and in the fifteenth century too the writing of letters continued to be the final practical task of grammar curricula. It has been seen above that Francesco's secondary grammar rules continued in heavy use during the fifteenth century,[80] and in fact at least two manuscripts containing not only his *Regule grammaticales* but also his *Regule rethorice* and *Tractatus epistolarum* date from the Quattrocento (BRF and Bodley Lat. misc. e.). A similar example of a traditional set of secondary

78

De dispositione
    De ordine
        Ordo artificialis crescit in octo modos
            Principium a fine ruptum
            A medio
            Proverbium a principio, medio et fine
            Exemplum
            Epylogus
        Ordo naturalis
        Artificiale
            Principium a fine
            A medio
            Proverbium ad principium
            Ad medium
            Ad finem
            Exemplum ad principium
            Ad medium
            Ad finem
            [...]
    De elocutione
        De inanimato ad animatum
        De animato ad inanimatum
        De urbana transsumptione
        Repugnantia in verbis
        Verbum proprie et improprie sumptum
        Quibus modis dictio transsummatur
        De adiectivo
        De fixo nominativo
        [...]

79 BNCF CS J. . , v: Hic docet auctor quod dictator ad faciendum predicta non debet esse nimium festinus. Unde si quis blanditor det thema et petat rem sine mora, dictator debet petere spatium et consulere mentem suam et dicere illi, 'Tu es nimium preceps.'

80 See above, .

grammar rules ending with an epistolography is provided by BML Ashb. , a manuscript copied in a heavy late Gothic hand datable to the second half of the fifteenth century. Here the prefatory treatise is not Francesco da Buti's *Regule grammaticales* but rather the secondary grammar by his Trecento Tuscan predecessor, Filippo di Naddo. After the close of Filippo's *Regule*, as indicated by the phrase on r 'Expliciunt regule Magistri Philippi', there follows without break a brief treatise entitled 'De pulcritudine vel ornatu epistolarum'; it is unclear whether or not the copyist was suggesting that this epistolography was also by Filippo di Naddo, since there is no colophon or attribution at the end (v);[81] there is no doubt that the treatise is Italian in origin, given that there are repeated references to place names in Italy (e.g. Bologna, Florence, Parma, Padua). Nevertheless, this brief work is the kind of traditional epistolary treatise that Filippo di Naddo might have written, couched as it is in the conventional terminology of *ars dictaminis* (e.g. *dictamen, dictator, punctum*, etc.). The text is divided into two sections: the first focuses on faults to be avoided in letter writing; the second, introduced by the title 'De regulis occurrentibus in dictamine' (v), concentrates on a number of miscellaneous grammatical and stylistic principles in epistolography. Most of the general points in both sections are illustrated by examples. Thus, the author allows the intervention of a genitive between a preposition and its object[82] but not otherwise.[83] The author abhors separation of closely related grammatical units by verbal phrases,[84] a practice not even allowed under any pretext of stylistic ornament,[85] because the adjective 'vestre' is rendered unclear by excessive separation from its noun.[86] The author's stylistic concerns come to the fore when he proceeds to recommend variation in the position of the verb.[87] In general, good style requires a relative without a conjunc-

81 Inc. De pulcritudine vel ornatu epistolarum. Nota quod prepositio potest removeri [...] Expl. ut duxi vostre gratie supplicandum vel consulendum.

82 r–v: Nota quod prepositio potest removeri a suo casu proprie mediante genitivo, ut 'De Guidonis bonitate confido.'

83 v: Non tamen bene diceretur, 'Bonitate loquor de Guidonis.'

84 v: Item verborum transpositio turpis et incongrua fugiatur, ut ibi: 'Omnis caput habet homo.'

85 v: Non enim alicuius ornatus pretestum est deformis transpositio facienda, ut si dicam, 'Vestre de servitiis mihi fratris quantascumque possum gratiarum actiones uberes et inmensas refero bonitati.'

86 v: Vides qualiter hoc adiectivum vestre confunditur ex nimia distantia sustantivi.

87 v– r: Item ad summam pertinet venustatem ut quotiens potest fieri, sententie gravitate servata, quod nominativi et obliqui sequantur et verba nunc primum, nunc medium, nunc ultimum locum debeant possidere. Exemplum: Labuntur in nimiam egestatem divitie temporales.

tion to precede its antecedent.[88] It is good style too for a relative immediately to follow its verb.[89] Other topics considered are stylistic and grammatical problems with antecedents, participles, proper nouns, personal pronouns, verbs of sending, the polite plural pronoun (*vos*), relatives and particular verbs (*retorquere, extorquere, redundare, duxi*). All these subjects are treated with examples, but there are a couple of general, unexemplified precepts. One is that brevity is always desired in letter writing,[90] while another is that usage is paramount.[91] This treatise is interesting for a number of reasons: in the first place, it shows the continued survival of traditional *dictamen* and epistolography in Italian schools well into the second half of the fifteenth century; secondly, in view of its position in the manuscript immediately following Filippo di Naddo's *Regule*, the text confirms that stylistic refinement and epistolography continued to be the normal complement to secondary grammar in the fifteenth century, just as they had been in the fourteenth; thirdly, the tractate, with its mixture of grammar and rhetoric, suggests the natural kind of progression which took place between the two disciplines in medieval and Renaissance Italian schools.

A similarly conventional stylistic aid came from the pen of Stefano Fieschi of Soncino, a pupil of Barzizza's and schoolmaster in Ragusa during the s and s. His *De prosynonymis* or *Synonyma sententiarum*, written in Venice about , is a guide to elaborating thematic translations from the vernacular: the work, written explicitly for schoolboys ('pueri et adolescentes'), goes through the parts of the letter, beginning with the exordium and giving simple vernacular sentences which are then progressively rendered into more and more ornate Latin.[92] This of course is the kind of variety taught in a traditional manual such as Geo rey of Vinsauf's *Poetria nova*.[93] The sentences he gives have nothing

88 r: Item ad p<u>lcritudinem et ornatum dignoscitur pertinere ut relativum coniunctione non indigens suum preveniat antecedens. Exemplum: Qui penitentiam non egerit in presenti, pecatori venia negabitur in futuro.

89 r: Item ad magnam pertinet venustatem ut relativum, nullo mediante, iuxta suum verbum ponatur. Exemplum: In errorem non de facili labitur qui metitur rerum exitus sapienter.

90 r: Nota quod in dictamine debes esse brevis et non obscurus. Brevitas est in qua nullum nisi necessarium verbum assumitur.

91 v: Item nota quod non debet aliquis calupniari locutionem illam quam usus et consuetudo probavit.

92 On this work, see Grendler ( ), – ; Mazzuconi ( ). There is an incomplete anonymous version of the beginning of this treatise (inc. Cum superiora verborum sinonima) in BNCF Magl. . , v– v, not listed by Mazzuconi ( ) or Bursill-Hall ( ).

93 See above, .

to do with classical Latin prose,[94] nor does he make any reference to ancient Roman literary texts.[95] The closest that the work comes to the antique revival is the repeated insertion of the name Cicero into his invented sentences.[96] Fieschi's work enjoyed a vogue in the fifteenth century, preserved as it is in more than twenty manuscripts and thirty-eight incunabular editions.[97]

Fieschi's allusions to Cicero, however superficial, were nonetheless indicative of changing educational tastes at the stylistic level in the mid-Quattrocento, and, in fact, epistolography as the final topic of the grammar syllabus was also handled in a more up-to-date fashion during the Quattrocento. Cicero's letters had been almost unknown in the middle ages and so were never used in the medieval classroom, but in the fifteenth century they began to be employed as stylistic models in Italian schools. With regard to Latin composition, as distinct from reading Latin texts (*lactinare* as opposed to *auctores audire*), it has been seen that the grammar-school curriculum involved a graduated progress from the composition of short phrases or passages up to the composition of an entire letter. It seems to have been at this final stage of the grammar curriculum that Cicero's letters, rediscovered by Petrarch and Salutati in the fourteenth century, were used in the fifteenth-century schoolroom.

Their place at the end of the grammar curriculum is suggested by the interesting series of Florentine grammatical compilations possibly associated with Giorgio Antonio Vespucci, already discussed above with regard to secondary grammar.[98] In general, this compilation seems to constitute a full school-level grammatical course of study, after which it goes on to give the text of twenty-eight extremely short familiar letters of Cicero,[99] and a couple by Pliny.[100] The compilation closes with a series of *sententiae* drawn from the Bible, the Church Fathers and various Latin classical authors.[101] It seems that the Ciceronian letters are placed at the end of the treatise for stylistic inspiration in epistolography, which, as has been seen above, was the traditional end of the school grammar course; because of their brevity and their proximity to a mnemonic text, Guarino's *Carmina di erentialia*,[102] as well as to the *sententiae*, these Cicero

94 See examples provided by Grendler ( ), – , including such phrases as 'in te amando', 'nostram benevolentiae coniunctionem sempiternam', 'nostram amicitiae a nitatem immortalitati conservari'.

95 Grendler ( ), . See Mazzuconi ( ), – , for limitations of Fieschi's acquaintance with classical authors, possibly not extending beyond Cicero and Terence.

96 Grendler ( ), .

97 Mazzuconi ( ), – ; Grendler ( ), .

98 See above, .

99 BRF r– r.

100 BRF r–v.

101 BRF v– r.

102 See above, .

letters were obviously intended for memorization by the pupil. Memorization of his letters for stylistic improvement, indeed, was enjoined by Battista Guarini: 'In Ciceronis epistulis declamabunt, ex quibus stili tum elegantiam tum facilitatem et sermonis puritatem ac scientiarum gravitatem adipiscentur; quas si memoriae mandaverint mirificos postea fructus in scribendi promptitudine percipient.'[103] Giorgio Valagussa also recommended that the brief extracts from Cicero's letters which he published in his compendium (see below, –) should be memorized as a quick route to Ciceronian style.[104]

This group of Ciceronian letters can be related to the model letters traditionally associated with the *ars dictaminis*, a custom continued in the fifteenth century with such compilations as Barzizza's *Litterae ad exercitationem accommodatae* or Giovan Mario Filelfo's *Novum Epistolarium seu ars scribendi epistulas.*[105] Similarly, Filippo Casali's grammar course, as preserved in BML Ashb. , also contains a group of model letters.[106] It is well known that various florilegia from Cicero's letters were compiled, probably for school use, including Giorgio Valagussa's *In flosculis epistolarum Ciceronis vernacula interpretatio* and Giovanni Gabriele's *Ciceronis clausulae ex epistolis familiaribus excerptis.*[107]

Cicero's letters also provided another kind of stylistic exercise in the fifteenth-century grammar schoolroom. It has been seen above that fourteenth- and fifteenth-century grammarians illustrated various syntactical points by reference to vernacular sentences which are then provided with Latin translations. This reflects the schoolroom practice of *themata*, which, as has been seen above, were vernacular passages assigned to pupils for Latin translation.[108] What is significant for the history of Cicero's use in the Renaissance classroom is that manuscripts of his familiar letters can be found preceded by such vernacular translations. One manuscript of this type contains twelve such letters by Cicero, as well as five by Leonardo Bruni, similarly prefaced by vernacular translations.[109] This manuscript seems to have belonged to Battista, the -year-old son of the papal secretary, Pietro Lunense, largely compiled at the time of the former's enforced residence in Viterbo during an outbreak of

[103] *De ordine docendi et discendi*, ed. Garin ( ), .

[104] Resta ( ) : 'Te quoque pro viribus exhortor, ut memoriae hoc compendium mandes: nam brevi tantum dicendi ornatum in te confluere, ut tum et ipse miraberis, ne nisi Ciceronem ipsum in concionem omni in loco, omni epistula e undere videberis [...]'

[105] Bracke ( ), – .

[106] r– v. As befitting model letters, they are all without dates, places or even addressees, except for the first letter. [107] Bracke ( ), [108] See above, .

[109] BML sup. , r– r.

plague in Rome during the summer of ;[110] it is clearly a schoolbook associated with the *studia humanitatis*, which, so Battista declares, he himself was then pursuing.[111] Not only does it contain miscellaneous philological information useful to a beginning classicist,[112] as well as a text of Cicero's *Somnium Scipionis,* glossed in the usual schoolish elementary philological manner,[113] but also metrical analyses of verses by Boethius,[114] whose poems in *De consolatione philosophiae*, as has been seen above, were frequently studied in this way in fifteenth-century schools.[115] This manuscript bears various signatures or *probationes* typical of a schoolbook, including one with a reference to a gratuity (*lo vanto*)[116] normally given to schoolmasters on various religious holidays. It is to be presumed that a pupil such as Battista Lunense practised his Latin prose composition by translating the vernacular text given first in the manuscript, and then comparing the results with Cicero's original. This procedure is confirmed by the Lombard humanist, Giorgio Valagussa, whose *In flosculis epistolarum Ciceronis vernacula interpretatio* (also entitled *Elegantiae Ciceronianae*)[117] was composed while working as a teacher at the Sforza court in Milan, probably in the later s.[118] This work, intended for school use,[119] consisted of extracts from Cicero's letters, preceded by vernacular translations.[120] Valagussa's preface suggests that pupils were

110 Parroni ( ), – .

111 Parroni ( ), : 'Cum humanitatis studia quibus omnem operam praestare decreveram Romae aeris intemperie interrupta essent, meque Viterbii nullis impeditum negociis haberem [...]'

112 BML sup. , r: Significatio litterarum antiquarum et abbreviature antique que reperiuntur in epistolis prescriptis. r: Debent omnia poni in eo casu et proferri in quo posite sunt dictiones ad quas referuntur ut M. Cicero Marcus Cicero, ut M. Ciceroni Imp. Marco Ciceroni imperatori [...]

113 BML sup. , r: legio a legendo quia meliores legebantur milites; tribunus dicitur a triba quia populus romanus in tribus partibus dividebat[ur]; migrare cum tota familia ire [...]; v: legatus quem hodie dicimus comissarius [*sic*], sine quo nec bellum nec pacem dux tractare quibat. 114 BML sup. , r– r. 115 See above, .

116 BML sup. , v. This meaning of *vanto* does not appear in Tommaseo and Bellini (–), . , . *Vanto* was a standard educational term in XVc., meaning the 'mancia' given by pupils at various religious holidays (Easter, Christmas, Santa Maria Candelaia, Ognisanti) to teachers. For example, according to *ricordi* kept for heirs of Francesco Pecori, on January reference was made to 'S. cinque [. . .] dati a Dino [di] Francesco per dare il vanto al m° dell'abacho per lla chandellaia': ASF Dono Panciatichi Patrimonio Pecori , right.

117 On this work, see Resta ( ), – ; Grendler ( ), – ; Bracke ( ), .

118 Printed at Venice *c.* , republished *c.* ; other editions: Venice , (Resta ( ), n.).

119 See preface: 'ut [. . .] his meis quoque tirunculis, qui in praesentia in nostra Achademia militant, opitularer atque eorum studiis hac mea nova excogitatione aliquid emolumenti brevi a errem' (Resta ( ),).

120 It is curious that Resta ( ), , gives the impression that vernacular translations followed Latin here, since it is clear from the photograph he publishes opposite that vernacular precedes Latin.

meant to practise on these various Ciceronian passages, evidently rendering them in the traditional thematic manner from vernacular into Latin, so that, when faced with having to write real letters, they would not recoil from the required struggle.[121] Manuscript evidence makes clear that this practice using dual-language Ciceronian letters continued into the sixteenth century.[122] The stylistic use of Cicero's letters in fifteenth-century schools is also suggested by their distinctive appearance in manuscripts. Unlike his shorter moral treatises, they are rarely glossed,[123] and this contrast is all the more telling when the unglossed letters appear in the same manuscript[124] together with texts traditionally subject to *lectura* – such as Horace's satires,[125] heavily glossed for example in a version copied by Francesco de' Medici in ,[126] who, as a pupil, begs the forbearance of his readers: 'Que cernis, lector, scripsit discipulus ipse Franciscus; parcas barbara signa [que] leges.'[127] In the sixteenth century, there is explicit testimony from a prominent teacher regarding the use of translation back into Latin by pupils from vernacular versions of Cicero's letters, so that they could thereby see, through comparison, the extent to which they had erroneously diverged from Cicero's model.[128]

The importance of Cicero as a model for epistolography in Italian Renaissance schools is underlined in one of the most widely circulated grammar manuals of the fifteenth century. In his treatment of letter writing in *Rudimenta grammatices*,[129] Niccolò Perotti singles out Cicero as the unique paradigm for teachers and pupils alike; Ciceronian vocabulary and even entire phrases should not only be imitated but indeed purloined (*furentur*) by pupils, who should be wholly nurtured, so to speak, on his milk.[130]

121 Resta ( ), : 'Hi [sc. tirunculi nostrae achademiae] enim etiam simulacro pugnae sese exercent, ut deinde in vero certamine non perhorrescant.' Another example of vernacular translations preceding Cicero's Latin letters is found in BNCF Magl. . , v– r, r– r (XVmid). 122 BNCF Magl. . (*Epistolae familiares*).

123 BNCF Magl. . , compiled for *pueris* in ; BML inf. : readers, one learned, the other school-level, latter of whom hardly glosses, while former's glosses are too sophisticated and learned for school; BML . ; BRF . 124 BRF , r– r.

125 BRF , r– v.

126 BRF , r: Hec sunt quedam epistole Ciceronis ex toto volumine electe et scripte fuere a Francisco Medice in anno MCXV tertio nonas octobris. 127 BRF , r.

128 Aonio Paleario, as cited by Avesani ( ), : 'farla ridurre in lingua latina et confrontarla con quella di Marco Tullio e mostrare loro in che habbiano errato'.

129 For this work as textbook of secondary grammar, see above, .

130 Perotti, *Rudimenta*, Naples , n.n.: Quis maxime preponendus est quem studeant adolescentes imitari? Marcus Cicero. Hic in omni dicendi genere omnium optimus fuit. Hunc solum preceptores legant. Hunc discipuli imitentur, nec modo verba eius hauriant sed eciam clausulas, quin eciam partes ipsas epistolarum interdum furentur et suis inserant. Ita enim fiet ut, succo Ciceronis quasi lacte nutriti, veri illius imitatores evadant.

Perotti was distinctly in line with current Quattrocento educational fashions in his advocacy of Cicero as the one and only suitable model for letter writing, and yet there are a number of traditional features in his treatment of epistolography too. Thus, the section on letter writing comes at the end of the grammar course, so following a pattern well established in the fourteenth century by teachers such as Francesco da Buti and possibly Filippo di Naddo.[131] Perotti also employs catechetical form throughout the treatise on epistolography, following the traditional format for educational texts established by Donatus in late antiquity and continued during the middle ages in *Ianua*. Moreover, as in Francesco da Buti's and Pietro da Isolella's treatments,[132] the tractate is closely associated with a discussion of punctuation,[133] thus recalling the traditional organization of *artes dictaminis*;[134] the preoccupations of the *dictatores* are also recalled when Perotti discusses, in a section entitled 'Quomodo exordiende sunt epistole', the salutation of the letter.[135] Particularly indicative of Perotti's links with Italian pedagogic traditions is his repeated use of passages from vernacular letters to be translated into Latin.[136] In one sense, the entire treatise on epistolography is a discussion of how to translate a whole letter, phrase by phrase, from the vernacular into Latin; indeed, at the end of the tractate Perotti gives the full text of the letter which he has gradually been rendering into elegant Latin. This recalls not only dual-language collections of model letters of thirteenth- and fourteenth-century *dettatori* such as Guido Fava and Pietro de' Boattieri,[137] but also the thirteenth-century collections of model *exordia*, letters and speeches in both Latin and Italian by Guido Fava.[138] In fact, Perotti was by no means the only avant-garde humanist with connections to these particular traditional methods; indeed, Wouter Bracke has recently published a short series of dual-language letters, with the Latin text following the vernacular version, a collection which seems to have emanated from Pomponio Leto's school in

[131] See above, , – . [132] See above, .
[133]

De punctis quibus oratio distinguitur

Quot sunt puncti quibus impresentiarum utimur? Novem: suspensivus, colus, coma, periodus [...]

De componendis epistolis

[134] See e.g. Faulhaber ( ), .
[135] See Faulhaber ( ), ; Fierville ( ), , , – ; Francesco da Buti, in BRF , .
[136] Quomodo eleganter dicimus: Io ho recevuta la tua lettera? [...] Quomodo latine et eleganter dicimus: de la quale lettera io ho preso gran piacere? [...] Quomodo eleganter dicimus: perché da la decta lettera io ho facilmente compreso che tu sey sano e che tu non solamente mi voi bene ma me ami grandemente [etc.] [137] Zaccagnini ( ). [138] Faulhaber ( ), – .

Rome.[139] A similar dual-language work was Francesco Filelfo's *Exercitatiunculae*, consisting of of his letters preceded by vernacular translation, and published in at least four incunables.[140] A further link with traditional practice is Perotti's inclusion near the beginning of the treatise of a discussion of stylistic faults in epistolography, so recalling the treatments of Pietro da Isolella, Francesco da Buti and Filippo di Naddo.[141]

However, the work most similar to Perotti's treatment of style is Geo rey of Vinsauf's *Poetria nova*. It is di cult not to be struck by the resemblance between Geo rey's discussion of variation in word order to achieve greater elegance[142] and the treatment in Perotti's epistolography.[143] Just as in *Poetria nova*, in fact, much of Perotti's epistolography consists of listing alternative and more elegant ways of phrasing simple Latin statements.[144]

Perotti's handling of epistolary stylistics may thus be similar in outline and shape to discussions in traditional *dictamen* treatises, and yet there is a fundamental di erence which distinguishes him here as a humanist. The treatments of Geo rey and Perotti depend on a fundamental distinction between simple and grammatical style, on the one hand, and elegant and elaborated style, on the other; however, Geo rey's artificial language is formed by various devices such as word-order manipulation and rhetorical figures which are not necessarily regulated by reference to antique models and standards; although partly derived from ancient sources, Geo rey's artificial discourse becomes in the end an abstract system. Perotti, on the other hand, sees elegance more concretely in terms of classical imitation and usage: his reference to Cicero as a model and his repeated rejections of so-called barbaric practices show that for

139 Bracke ( ), – . 140 Quaquarelli ( ), . 141 See above, , , .

142 See above, .

143 [...] modus compositionis in epistolis servatur ut verbum frequenter in fine clausule coll[oc]es hoc modo: ego te commendare non cesso. Quod longe pulcherius est quam si diceretur: ego non cesso te commendare. Et spem maximam habeo, potius quam, habeo maximam spem. Ipse interdum tamen in medio ponitur, ut spem habeo maximam. Interdum in principio, ut scripsit ad me Cesar.

Similar emphasis on rearranging word order to achieve greater eloquence – again recalling Geo rey of Vinsauf – was practised in Guarino's school, where ornate composition ('ornate componere') was seen particularly in placing the verb at end of sentence ('ut oratio plerunque verbo claudatur'): see Sabbadini ( ), .

144 E.g. *Io ho recevuta la tua lettera.* Multis id modis dici potest: Accipi letteras tuas. Accipi abs te litteras. Reddite mihi fuerunt littere tue. Reddite mihi fuerunt abs te littere. Reddidit mihi Helius Perottus litteras tuas. Accepi quasdam e Helio Perotto. Dedisti litteras. Accepi epistolam quam escripsisti. E Tusculano reddita mihi est epistola tua. Attulit mihi Helius Perottus epistolam tuam.

him an elegant style is no longer a series of abstract artifices but rather a type of prose which approximates to the actual epistolary language of the ancients. Although in the handling of secondary grammar, Perotti can with some justification be considered to have been repackaging a used product,[145] here in his treatment of epistolary stylistics he was in fact doing just the opposite, putting new wine into old bottles.

Thus, Perotti may include a treatment of the salutation, a topic at the forefront of the *ars dictaminis*, but his actual discussion of this subject specifically rejects three aspects of medieval epistolary practice as barbaric and non-classical: the placing of the name of the recipient before that of the sender, if the former were an important personage; the use of titles before the name of the addressee; and the use of the polite plural.[146] In the same way, Perotti discusses faults of epistolary style, as in the *ars dictaminis*, but a number of the defects that he mentions were actual practices recommended in a work such as *Poetria nova*, such as *circumlocutio* (v.) and *asyndeton* (vv. –). Perotti also rejects several contemporary phrases as non-classical and barbaric, such as *lator presentium*, o ering in this instance Cicero's usage as a counter-example;[147] *quod* instead of an infinitive construction;[148] *indulgentia* rather than *venia*;[149] and *licentia*, in this case accusing contemporary grammar teach-

145 See above, .

146 Quomodo exordiende sunt epistole? […] Cuius nomen preponitur? Scribentisne an eius ad quem scribit? Scribentis, eciam [si] ad pontificem maximum sive regem aut imperatorem scribat homo infimus […] Cavendum preterea est ne numquam dominus, honoris causa, nominibus propriis preponatur, ut Domino Pyrrho et Domino Vuernero. Barbara est enim ea locutio et nuper inventa. Non hoc Latini, non Greci veteres fecerunt. Potest tamen addi nomen dignitatis sive magistratus potest post proprium nomen, ut si ita scripseris: Sixto pontifici maximo […] Illud eciam summo studio fugiendum est ne ad unum scribens plurativo numero utaris. In quem errorem omnes fere nostre etatis homines incurrunt, putantes se magis honorare eum ad quem scribunt si barbare loquantur […]

147 Retulit tibi Helius Perottus litteras quas michi abs te attulerat. In quo notandum est retulit esse, non refert. Ubi omnes fere nostre etatis errant, dicentes lator presentium, in quo non modo barbare loquuntur sed eciam falso. Non enim lator est, nec cum scribuntur littere nec cum leguntur, sed cum scribuntur, laturus est; cum leguntur, attulit. Inspiciendum autem a nobis est tempus quo leguntur, non quo scribuntur. Cum igitur literas legit, is ad quem scripsimus non feruntur sed iam relate sunt littere. Itaque retulit dicendum est, non refert, ut Cicero ad Valerium.

148 […] notandum est quod, ex ea que per subiunctivum verbum cum constructione quod dici possunt, longe elegantius sine quod infinitum dicitur. Verbi gratia: *Io so che tu legi* – scio quod tu legis – scio te legere. *Io ho conosciuto che tu me ami* – perspexi quod tu amas me – perspexi te amare me vel me amari abs te […]

149 Dare veniam, estne quod dicimus indulgere an aliud significat? Longe hec diversa sunt. Imperiti capiunt indulgenciam pro venia, ut indulgenciam et remissionem pecatorum tuorum tribuat tibi omnipotens et misericors dominus. Sed hoc barbare non latine dicitur. Indulgere enim est concedere et cum quadam quasi suavitate permittere, ut indulgent gule, indulgent ventri. Quintilianus: mollis illa educatio quam indulgenciam vocamus. Non ergo indulgentia pro venia

ers of particular barbarity.[150] Perotti is also critical of contemporary writers' failure to distinguish between *abstinentia* and *continentia*,[151] and he is especially scathing over the barbarity of modern religious usage.[152]

Perotti's treatment of stylistics, coming as it did at the end of his best-selling *Rudimenta grammatices*, achieved an extensive circulation in the later fifteenth century,[153] but there was another manual of Latin style which may have attained even greater popularity. This was the *Isagogicus libellus* by the Sienese humanist, Agostino Dati, a work which came generally to be called *Elegantiolae*. This short treatise, first published in Cologne in by Ulrich Zell and then soon afterwards in at Ferrara by André Belfort,[154] received at least a further incunabular

accipienda est, nec dicendum est, eo Romam pro indulgentia sed eo Romam ad impetrandum veniam vel gratia impetrande venie. Sed e contrario, veniam aliquando quasi pro indulgentia ponitur, ut da mihi hanc veniam, hoc est, indulge mihi et concede aut permitte mihi quasi veniam daturus postquam id fecero et cum venia tua ibo, hoc est, dabis mihi veniam si ibo.

150 [...] imperiti dicunt cum licentia. In qua re errant omnes fere grammatice preceptores, pro bonis litteris docentes discipulos suos barbariem. Idcirco diligenter notandus est hic locus. *El maestro de la schola ha dato licentia a li soy scholari.* Non est dicendum, ludi magister dedit licentiam discipulis suis. Licentia enim est libertas quedam potius ad male agendum, et dicitur a verbo licet, hoc est cum licet quicquid libet. Sed ludi magister dimisit discipulos suos, vel ludi magister indulsit dixcipulis suis ut abirent [...]

151 Tamen hec duo vocabula aliquando apud scriptores indi erenter capiuntur, que res quendam nostra etate virum doctissimum traxit in errorem, ut in expositione eorum verborum longe a veritate discesserit.

152 Sciendum est non absurde vocari a nostris conventus religiosorum, ut puta conventus minorum, conventus hermitarum. Verum id vocabulum non domum sive habitaculum significat, ut vulgus sentit, sed ipsam conventionem et congregationem religiosorum, hoc est, ipsos religiosos, ut ego habui orationem in conventu religiosorum hominum, hoc est, in congregatione et quasi corona religiosorum. Quod significatum habet ecclesia apud Grecos, sed ignari homines, quemadmodum nomen conventus transtulerunt ad habitacula religiosorum virorum, ita nomen ecclesie, quod contionem significat, ad templa. Templum enim sive edes sacra in singulare dicitur locus deo dicatus, non ecclesia, sed errant in hoc ut in aliis plerisque. Quippe claustrum barbare dicunt pro atrio, sacristiam pro sacrario, beneficium pro sacerdotio, de iure patrio pro gentilitio, observantiam pro observatione, missam pro sacrifitio, confiteor pro audio confessiones, confessorem pro auditore confitentium, indulgentia pro venia [...]

153 For further discussion of Perotti's epistolography, and especially its relationship with *De componendis epistolis* spuriously attributed to Lorenzo Valla and with Valla's *Elegantiae*, see Alessio ( ), who discusses traditional and innovative features of humanist epistolography with reference to many texts.

154 I shall refer here to latter edition, unfoliated and opening with title: De variis loquendi figuris sive de modo dictandi. Ad andream civem senensem Isagogius libellus feliciter Incipit. and closing with the following imprint (r n.n.): Expliciunt elegantiae parve domini augustini dathi Senensis. Impraesse ferrarie die dicimanona Octobris. M.CCCC.LXXI.

Impressi Andreas hoc opus: cui francia nomen
Traddit: at civis ferrariensis ego.
Herculeo felix ferraria tuta manebat
Numine: perfectus cum liber iste fuit.

I examined the following manuscripts of *Elegantiolae*: BML AD (XV²); BNCF Magl. . (XV²), Magl. . (XV²: fragmentary), Magl. . (XV²), BRF (XV²).

printings and many more during the sixteenth century;[155] its popularity was such that one scholar has been led to write that 'le *Elegantiolae* ebbero un successo editoriale, superiore a quello di qualsiasi altro manuale scolastico italiano del Quattrocento'.[156]

Dati begins with a reference to contemporary methods of achieving Latin elegance. The reading and imitation of Cicero had now become central to the teaching of Latin style in the fifteenth century, and Dati agrees that immersion in the study of Cicero will yield some profit for an aspiring Latinist.[157] His use of the words *pauca* and *proximius* here is significant: an authoritative model such as Cicero will go only so far. Rules are needed, but the trouble is that they are not hard and fast.[158] As in other arts, the fundamental principle of variety defies precise regulation; moreover, rules are always problematic because art must never seem artful.[159] Nevertheless, Dati declares himself willing to jot down a few points which may prove generally, if not always, useful.[160]

Dati's allusions to Cicero and Quintilian mark the *Elegantiolae* from the start as an avant-garde textbook, but it would be wrong to overlook the traditional features of this work. In fact, the *Elegantiolae* have a striking overall resemblance to Geo rey of Vinsauf's *Poetria nova.* Both texts are overwhelmingly preoccupied with teaching stylistic elegance. Like Geo rey's distinction between natural and artificial style,[161] Dati begins his treatment by contrasting grammatical and oratorical style.[162] Both

155 Viti ( ), ; Jensen (b), , n. .

156 Viti ( ), . It is a common misconception that Dati's work was an imitation (Bolgar ( ), ,) or epitome (Jensen ( ) n. and (a)) of Valla's *Elegantiae*, possibly deriving from the later title ascribed to it by publishers.

157 r: Credimus iamdudum a plerisque viris etiam disertissimis persuasi tum demum artem quempiam in dicendo non nullam adipisci, si veterum atque eruditorum secttans vestigia optima sibi quisque semper ad imitandum proposuerit. Neque enim qui diutius in Ciceronis lectione versatus sit, non esse in dicendo et ornatus et copiosus poterit [...] lectitanti igitur Ciceronis volumina, quem eloquentie parentem merito appellaverim, pauca anotatione digna visa sunt. Quibus si utamur [...] ad eloquentium orationem proximius accedemus.

158 r–v: Sed tamen id in primis quisque admonendus sit, quod rhetor diligentissimus et insignis orator Fabius Quintilianus de orationis partibus dicere consuevit: neque enim leges oratorum quadam veluti inmutabili necessitate constitute, nec rogationibus, ut idem dicebat, plebis vestitis.

159 v: Sancta sunt ista praecepta, sed, uti in statuis picturis poematis ceterisque, itaque in exornanda quoque eloquentis viri oratione, semper decoris venustatis habuit varietas [*sic*]. Atque quod dici solet cavendum tenendumque illud est ante omnia: ne ars ulla dicendi, si fieri potest, esse videatur.

160 v: Hoc igitur iacto fundamento, perpauca deinceps scribam, amice suavissime, quae, si non semper, ut plurimum tamen hiis rationibus tibi servanda erunt.

161 See above, .

162 v: Plerumque enim qui oratoriae artis floribus ac faleratis, ut aiunt, student verbis contra tritam vulgatamque gramaticorum consuetudinem [...] coeptant [...]

start where grammar leaves o : Geo rey's point of departure is natural style, whereas Dati's is the terminology for the parts of the sentence developed by contemporary (medieval) grammarians.[163] Just as the purpose of Geo rey's work is to convert natural into artificial style, so Dati's aim is to turn the inelegant language of contemporary grammarians into eloquent prose. Geo rey, as has been seen, makes continual reference to natural and artificial language, and Dati too distinguishes throughout between grammatical and rhetorical standards.[164] Geo rey had written from the point of view of the rhetorician, sco ng at the inelegance of so-called natural Latin, which he derided as sterile in contrast to the fertility of the artificial style (vv. – : see above,), and Dati too ridicules grammatical style, not only calling it, as has already been seen (see above, n.), trite and vulgar, but also referring to 'multi ignari litterarum etiam grammaticae artis expertes' (r–v). Moreover, like Geo rey (see above,) Dati begins his treatment with word order, suggesting, as in *Poetria nova*, that it is more elegant to abandon the natural sequence of subject–verb–predicate.[165] In elegant writing, the predicate comes first, followed by the subject and then the verb.[166] Even if another element is placed after the *appositum*, it too should come at the beginning.[167] As in *Poetria nova*, variety is paramount,[168] not only in phrases but also in individual words.[169]

In terms of external purpose and general orientation, therefore, Dati's work closely resembles Geo rey of Vinsauf's textbook; in fact, the place occupied by the *Elegantiolae*, taking as its point of departure the end of the

[163] v– r: Scis plenam orationem constare tribus partibus quod suppositum, ut eorum ipsorum vocabulis utar, quod verbum, quod appositum vocant.

[164] E.g. r: Licet tam grammatice quam oratorie genitivos quorumcumque casualium cum possessivis quocumque casu prolatis coniungere [...]

[165] r: Dicunt igittur grammatici: Scipio Aphricanus delevit Carthaginem. Ornatioris vero eloquii homines converso potius utantur ordine: Carthaginem Scipio Aphricanus delevit. Illi [sc. grammatici]: Marcus Cicero utitur familiariter Pulio Lentulo; hii [sc. oratores] vero: Publio Lentulo Marcus Cicero familiariter utitur.

[166] r: Quibus plane exemplis patere arbitror: appositum primum in oratione, suppositum medium, novissimum vero locum verbum tenere.

[167] r: Sed etsi quid pro gramaticorum more post appositum situm erit, id initio orationis poni solet. Cuius rei exempla subnectam: Scipio Emilianus evertit Numantiam urbem opulentissimam Hyspaniae; Hyspaniae opulentissimam urbem Numantiam Scipio Emilianus evertit. Non ignoras esse multa genera epistolarum; epistolarum genera multa esse non ignoras [...] Multaque consimili ratione. Appositum igitur plerumque principio ponitur, suppositum medio, fine verbum [...]

[168] v: Optimum factu fuerit, ne his aut modis orationis aut verbis utamur, ut initio diximus. Varia plurimum probatur oratio, et si eruditis quibusdam flosculis aspergitur, ut pro mori, diem obire [...] Et item pro vivere, vitam agere, degere aetatem.

[169] v– r: Et quod de variis orationis modis dicimus, id // ipsum de singulis partibus orationis intelligendum est, ut pro oro rogo praecor obsecro, pro quasi poene fere ferme.

grammar syllabus, is precisely the same as in a traditional medieval work such as *Poetria nova*. However, the internal content of Dati's manual is completely di erent from Geo rey of Vinsauf's treatment of stylistics: just as with Perotti, Dati abandons the medieval abstract definition of ornate style, substituting in its place the practice and usage of the Roman classics. Similarly, for both Dati and Perotti, Cicero emerges as the supreme example for prose style, cited in the *Elegantiolae* four times more than any other author (see below, n.). Perotti had warned against a spare and dry style, citing Seneca as a model to be avoided,[170] and Dati too admonished his readers with similar vocabulary.[171] Perotti had criticized modern grammar teachers,[172] and, as has already been seen, this was a constant theme in Dati's work too; indeed, he suggests that some are 'ignari litterarum' (v), ridiculing 'paedagogicam opinionem' (v). As with Perotti, this criticism of contemporary practice extends beyond grammarians, when Dati not only censures jurists for their misuse of the term *usurpatio*,[173] but also teachers of *dictamen* for confusing epistolography and oratory.[174] Finally, another point of contact between the *Elegantiolae* and Perotti's epistolography is that Dati devotes considerable attention to stylistic issues of particular relevance to letter writing, for example, certain adverbs,[175] especially those ending in 'i',[176] and verbs such as *devincio*,[177] or *peto*.[178] Indeed, the end of the treatise is devoted entirely to epistolary salutations (v– r) and dating formulae (r– v).[179]

Despite its external resemblances to *Poetria nova* and the viewpoint and contents shared with Perotti's epistolography, there is little doubt that

170 See above, , n. . Both Perotti and Dati apparently follow Quintilian's lead here: see *Institutio oratoria*, .i. – . This rejection of Seneca as a prose model became commonplace in the later Renaissance: see Grendler ( ), .

171 r: Nam et horridiora crebrius consectati, ipsi quoque aridi ieiunii inculti fiant, necesse est.

172 See above, – .

173 r: Usurpatio et usurpare non ita intelligi debent sicut iurisconsulti utuntur, sed usurpationem oratores frequentem usum vocant et usurpare habere in frequenti usu.

174 v: eorum praeceptiones, qui easdem et epistolis et orationibus partes tribuunt, quorum penitus eripiendus est error.

175 r: Quaedam adverbia sunt quae epistolis quam maxime congruunt, sicut prope diem quamprimum percito [*corr. ex* procito] confestim. Et item postridie [...]

176 v: Multa adverbia in i exeuntia etiam in ipsis epistolis pulcherrima sunt. Sed haec in primis: ruri vesperi belli domi.

177 r: Devincio verbum tum pulcherrimum, tum praecipue epistolis congruit. Significat devincio obligo, et devinctus est obligatus.

178 v: Peto te hanc rem, ornatius nec minus latine dici potest quam peto hanc rem a te, et id pulcherrimum Cicero in epistolis consuevit.

179 r–v: Quamobrem, si qua iam reliqua sunt, paucis // expediamus. Nam quum proficiendis epistolis haec potissimum attingerimus, si salvationis formulam et kalendarum iduum nonarumque observationem patefecerim, iure huic parvo instituto finem ac modum statuerim.

Dati was attempting to break new ground in the *Elegantiolae*. Perotti was still strongly linked to traditional practices with his near-total identification of stylistics and letter writing, but this is no longer the case with Dati: despite the fact that his treatise ends with a discussion of epistolary salutations and dates, the great bulk of the text is about prose style in general. Moreover, Perotti still makes use of thematic translation from the vernacular, recalling the practices both of traditional secondary grammar and of *dictamen*, but Dati explicitly eschews the *volgare*,[180] and, indeed, the vernacular makes not the slightest appearance in the *Elegantiolae*. It would be incorrect to regard Dati's work as a type of florilegia of passages from the Latin classics;[181] in fact, direct quotation makes up only a part of the *Elegantiolae*, whose contents consist of general points of Latin usage, copiously illustrated by Dati's own examples as well as ones that he is able to find in classical authors. Nevertheless, Dati goes much further than Perotti had done in his citation of classical texts, including passages not only from Cicero but also from authors such as Vergil, Terence, the younger Pliny, Sallust, Livy and Caesar, as well as citations from grammarians such as Nonius Marcellus, Pompeius Festus, Servius and Priscian. Particularly suggestive are Dati's several references to Aulus Gellius's *Attic Nights*.[182] This ancient grammatical and literary miscellany seems possibly to have provided Dati with a model for the structure of his *Elegantiolae*, which, like Gellius's text, follows no logical or topical pattern, but simply moves at random from point to point. Here Dati firmly put to one side the medieval logically structured pedagogic tradition, adhered to for example by Geo rey of Vinsauf, whose *Poetria nova* is organized rigorously according to the five

180 r: vulgarium sermonem aspernati, ad eloquentium orationem proximius accedemus.
181 See Viti ( ), .
182 Number of named citations of classical writers in *Elegantiolae*:

Author	Citations
Cicero	
Terence	
Gellius	
Vergil	
Nonius Marcellus	
Priscian	
Servius	
Pliny	
Sallust	
Caesar	
Varro	
Donatus	
Livy	
Pompeius Festus	

divisions of rhetoric; even Perotti had adopted an overall schematic structure for his epistolography, which goes through an entire letter in order, beginning with the salutation and ending with dating. Dati, on the other hand, adopts Gellius's miscellaneous organization; in this sense, he aligns himself with the humanist avant-garde such as Valla, Tortelli and the Perotti of the *Cornucopia* (not of the *Rudimenta grammatices*). *Elegantiolae* was in fact an attempt to bring the material and format of humanist philology down to the level of the schoolroom. It is a great testimony to Dati's abilities as a teacher and communicator that his work achieved such success in the last quarter of the fifteenth century: he accomplished the kind of breakthrough in stylistics which Pomponio Leto had so signally failed to realize in the field of secondary grammar.

Dati's distinction between his treatise and the writings of grammarians confirms the point at which stylistics were treated in the school curriculum. The *Elegantiolae* presume a full knowledge of basic Latin grammar; for example, Dati takes for granted that his readers will have a full syntactical grasp of an advanced conjunction such as *quin*.[183] In treating this conjunction, Dati's role is to clarify its stylistic force.[184] In Quattrocento Italy, it is clear that grammar was learned first, almost entirely divorced from stylistics and rhetoric. Grammar, as has been seen above, continued to be taught almost entirely according to conventional methods and in line with traditional standards. Once this basic grammar was mastered, the pupil's Latin was then gradually purified at the end of the syllabus through the study of stylistics and introductory rhetoric. This distinction found expression first in the contrast between *auctorista* and *grammaticus*, and then between *humanista* and *grammaticus*, which developed from the fourteenth to the sixteenth centuries.[185] This curriculum structure explains why humanism entered so little into the syllabus at the grammatical level, even in the schools of humanist teachers such as Guarino, Barzizza or Perotti: one first learned Latin grammatically and only thereafter stylistically. This two-staged process followed medieval precedents, based on the distinction between natural and artificial language,[186] and it was no doubt thought also to recall ancient teaching

183 r–v: 'Quin' particula quomodo vel increpet vel exhortetur, quomodo item conformetur et quomodo interroget, satis exploratum est.

184 r–v: Sed nos ea pulcherrime utimur: non possum quin admirer [...] significat enim, fere non possum me continere ut non admirer [...]

185 See above, .

186 Dante explicitly signalled this kind of division as characteristic of contemporary educational practice, pointing in *De vulgari eloquentia* (.) to four levels of style ('insipidus, sapidus, venustus, excelsus') and assigning the first grade ('insipidus'), equivalent of Geo rey of Vinsauf's *ordo naturalis*, to school children: 'gradus [...] insipidus qui est rudium, ut Petrus amat multum dominam

practice, where the division between the teaching of grammar and rhetoric is at the forefront of a work such as Quintilian's *Institutio*.[187] The di erence was that, in antiquity, only one language was being taught, but now during the Renaissance in e ect two languages were involved: first the pupil learned medieval Latin from the grammarians and then classicized Latin from the humanists. Humanists themselves thus wore two hats, as can clearly be seen in the case of Guarino and Perotti. When the twenty-year-old Battista Lunense said he was pursuing the *studia humanitatis* in ,[188] he was signalling that he was now transcending the work of mere grammarians. It is no accident that at the end of the fifteenth century, a linguistic distinction emerged between *grammatici*, meaning classical philologists, and *grammatistae*, signifying lowly grammar teachers: in terms of the school curriculum, the *studia humanitatis* were now separate from mere *grammatica*, each becoming the preserve of its own particular class of teachers.[189]

Bertam'. See Mengaldo [ ]. Similarly Guido Fava declared that *constructio naturalis* (e.g. 'ego amo te') was used for school-level teaching, but *constructio artificialis* for elegant composition or *dictamen*: see Sabbadini ( ), .

187 See esp. .i. .

188 See above, n. .

189 See above, – . The contrasting fortunes of *Doctrinale* and *Poetria nova* in the wake of printing underline the di erences between the grammatical and rhetorical levels in Italian Renaissance schools. *Poetria nova* went rapidly out of fashion at the end of the fifteenth century, failing to be printed before (Woods ( ),). In part, this must have been the e ect of the new broom wielded by humanist editors and teachers, resulting in the sharp decline of the minor authors and Boethius's *Consolation* in the last quarter of the Quattrocento: see above, . More specifically, it is clear that *Poetria nova* was now supplanted by up-to-date Ciceronian manuals from Dati and Perotti. *Oratio naturalis* remained unchanged in the age of humanism, whereas *oratio artificialis* now became largely identified with Ciceronianism: *Doctrinale* was just as relevant at the end of the fifteenth century as in the thirteenth and fourteenth, whereas *Poetria nova* was now obsolete.

Conclusion

The real revolutionaries in the history of Italian medieval and Renaissance school education would appear to be the Northern European grammarians and philosophers who reshaped the theory of language in the twelfth century, together with the thirteenth-century French and Italian teachers who brought this new logical approach to Latin down to the level of the classroom. Like true radicals, masters such as Alexander of Villedieu were extremists, not only opposing the heritage of theoretical grammar as inherited from Roman antiquity but also the reliance on direct study of the Latin classics that had dominated schools since the close of the Dark Ages. Inevitably, there was counter-revolution, though this was not so much the achievement of famous fifteenth-century humanist pedagogues as of their less celebrated predecessors, the grammarians of the Trecento.

The educational momentum inherited by the fifteenth-century Renaissance from the later middle ages was considerable. The system of teaching elementary reading through phonetics as applied to a written text, followed by memorization, had evolved over many centuries; the streamlining of this technique which occurred in the thirteenth and fourteenth centuries made possible an explosion of literacy among the Italian urban population. The extensive penetration of the vernacular into Latin education, not as a system for learning to read, but rather as a tool to simplify the understanding of Latin texts and to ease the learning of Latin composition, facilitated the burgeoning of the Latin-educated professional classes which is such a promiment feature of Italian civic life from the thirteenth to the fifteenth centuries.

These achievements of the later middle ages left humanists of the fifteenth century with restricted opportunities for manoeuvre in the classroom. They did not even try to interfere with the tools and methods of mass literacy: *tabula/carta*, psalter and *Ianua* remained the universal apparatus of elementary education throughout the fifteenth century.

Purists such as Pomponio Leto despised the use of the vernacular in schools, but his more pragmatic colleagues such as Guarino and Perotti realized that it was a lost cause to try and expunge the Italian language from the Latin classroom. Similarly, humanists may have found the scholastic logical approach to Latin syntax and composition distasteful, but without a practical alternative they had no choice but to continue in the footsteps of their medieval forerunners. The same was true of mnemonic verses: it was easier to vilify Alexander of Villedieu than to find a replacement for his *Doctrinale*. The main success enjoyed by the humanists at the lower levels of the Latin curriculum was in expelling the traditional school authors and Boethius's *Consolation*. But even here conservative inertia was potent, and it was only in the last decades of the fifteenth century that they began to rid the classroom of these medieval *bêtes noires*.

It was at the upper levels of the grammar syllabus that the humanists were able to operate to greater e ect. Here their crusade for the revival of the Latin classics had a firm foundation inherited from the Trecento. The way was prepared for their restoration of Cicero, Vergil, Terence, Juvenal and Persius by the fourteenth-century resurrection of Seneca the tragedian, Valerius Maximus and Statius, as well as by the Trecento reinforcement of Horace, Lucan and Ovid. Their reform of Latin stylistics too was given a head start by the medieval division of discourse into natural and artificial language. With his *Poetria nova*, Geo rey of Vinsauf had carved out an ideal niche for Ciceronian manuals by Agostino Dati and Perotti.

What is sometimes overlooked about Renaissance humanists – particularly as school masters – is their essential pragmatism and flexibility. In many ways, the educational system of the middle ages was admirably suited to their needs. As teachers, humanists were able to enjoy many benefits from a medieval heritage which allowed the spread of widespread literacy among the urban masses as well as basic Latinity for the professional classes. The traditional curriculum structure even o ered a distinct level at the end of the syllabus for reform of Latin prose along Ciceronian lines. The medieval system provided humanists with an opportunity for a favoured posture – one-upmanship, enabling them to claim superiority over humble grammar teachers, from whom they sought an ever increasing distance. The division of the grammatical profession into *grammatici* and *auctoristi*, initiated during the Trecento, allowed humanists gradually to gain freedom from the burden of instructing young children and to concentrate their energies on the preferred activity of teaching the classical authors and Ciceronian stylistics.

It is misleading to take humanists' criticisms of the medieval heritage out of their ideological context. In Italy, these attacks were made not so much as a manifesto of a root-and-branch educational reform but rather as a platform for professional advancement, to secure a place for themselves at the higher levels of the educational hierarchy. Humanists shared a common background with humble grammar masters and even humbler elementary teachers: all these occupations were descended from the unitary grammar schools of the earlier middle ages, when there was no institutional, professional or curriculum division among the activities of teaching reading, basic Latinity and advanced stylistics and literature. With the increasing specialization of learning in the later middle ages and earlier Renaissance, it was imperative for humanists to seize the educational high ground. As Kristeller so e ectively demonstrated,[1] similar polemics from them against Aristotelian scholastics and against medieval philosophy and theology in general were not an attempt to reform the entire university syllabus along humanist lines but rather to win a respected place for their profession in the educational world and in society at large. The same is true of assaults by humanists on traditional grammar: they had no serious intention of replacing the medieval heritage; instead, their aim was to secure a privileged position within the grammatical hierarchy as inherited from the middle ages.

[1] Kristeller (b).

BL Harley : the earliest known manuscript of Ianua

BL Harley [1] is a parchment codex, *inc.* Incipit Donatus gramatice artis. Poeta que pars ortionis est? Nomen. Quare [...] It has been examined by Albinia de la Mare, who writes, 'The script is certainly Germanic – S. German, Austrian or, I suppose, Swiss, s. XII². Certainly *not* Italian.'[2] However the text contained in this Germanic manuscript seems almost certainly to be Italian in origin, as suggested by the post-antique geographical place names mentioned, all of which are Italian (Milan, Alatri (r); Pavia, Milan, Fiesole, Pisa, Italy (v); Pavia, Italy, Bologna (r)). This means that the text of *Ianua* was circulating in Italy for some time before the second half of the twelfth century, by which time it had already reached Germanic localities. An Italian provenance from no later than the earlier XIIc. is also confirmed by the use made of *Ianua* by the Italian grammarian Paolo da Camaldoli in his own elementary grammar, entitled *Donatus,*[3] itself datable to the later XIIc.[4]

Harley provides a full text of *Ianua,* even beginning with the usual 'Incipit Donatus gramatice artis', and so it must be wondered why this text has not previously been identified. The answer is that, unlike most other versions of *Ianua,* it does not begin with the verse prologue, *inc.* Ianua sum rudibus primam cupientibus artem. Another feature which perhaps discouraged identification as *Ianua* is Harley 's length: unlike other versions, which average about to folios (e.g. BNP MS lat. , r– r or BNCF Magl. . , r– v), the *Ianua* text in Harley consists of folios.

Harley includes virtually all the material contained in the version of *Ianua* transcribed in part by Schmitt (itself a typical incunabular edition published at Pavia in); e.g.:

[1] Acquired on January for Edward Harley by Nathaniel Noel, bookseller employed by Harley to buy manuscripts chiefly on the Continent: Wright ( ), , , . No indication where or from whom Noel bought the manuscript. [2] Private communication.

[3] Sivo (a), – . [4] Sivo (a), – .

Harley	Schmitt ( )
r: Poeta, que pars orationis est? Nomen. Quare? Quia significat substantiam et qualitatem […] Nomin<i> quot accidunt? Quinque. Que? Species, genus, numerus, figura, casus. Cuius speciei? Derivative. Unde derivatur? A poesis. Vel primitive. Quare? Quia nullo derivatur.	: Poeta quae pars est? nomen est. quare est nomen? quia significat substantiam et qualitatem […] Nomini quot accidunt? quinque. quae? species genus numerus figura et casus. Cuius speciei? primitivae. quare? quia a nullo derivatur. Cuius speciei? derivativae. quare? quia derivatur a poesis.
r: Nominativo hic poeta. Genitivo huius poete. Dativo huic poete. Accusativo hunc poetam. Vocativo o poeta. Ablativo ab hoc poeta. Et pluraliter nominativo hii poete. Genitivo horum poetarum. Dativo his poetis. Accusativo hos poetas. Vocativo o poete. Ablativo ab his poetis.	: Nominativo hic poeta. Genitivo huius poetae. Dativo huic poetae. Accusativo hunc poetam. Vocativo o poeta. Ablativo ab hoc poeta. Et pluraliter nominativo hi poetae. Genitivo horum poetarum. Dativo his poetis. Accusativo hos poetas. Vocativo o poetae. Ablativo ab his poetis.
r: Bene, que pars orationis est? Adverbium. Quare? Quia stat iuxta verbum et semper nititur verbo […] Adverbio quod accidunt? Tria. Que? Species figura et significatio […]	: Tunc quae pars est? adverbium est. quare est adverbium? quia stat iuxta verbum et semper nititur verbo. Adverbio quot accidunt? tria. quae? species significatio et figura […]
r: Heu, que pars orationis est? Interiectio. Quare? Quia interiacet ceteris partibus orationis […] Interiectioni quod accidunt? Unum. Quid? Significatio tantum […][5]	Heu quae pars est? interiectio est. quare est interiectio? quia interiacet aliis partibus orationis. Interiectioni quot accidunt? unum. quid? significatio tantum […]

Nevertheless, Harley also has a considerable amount of additional grammatical material not found in later versions of *Ianua*. Some of this material includes definitions of the categories of accidence for the parts of speech, given in catechetical form. Thus, Harley contains the following accidental definitions and etymologies not found in other versions of *Ianua* for the noun, e.g.:

Quod est species? Elementaris compositio per quam habetur primitivi vel derivativi proprii vel appellativi discretio. Unde dicitur species? A specificando, id est a dividendo, eo quod unum dividat ab alio[6]

and for the verb:

[5] Cf. also v, r, r, v, v, v, r, v, r, v, v, v, r, r with Schmitt ( ), – .
[6] BL Harley , r; see v, r.

Quid est genus in verbo? Terminatio in o vel in or cum significatione actionis vel passionis vel utriusque.[7]

There is also an extended catechism and classification of the types of derivative verbs unique to this version of *Ianua*.[8] Just as for nouns, there is a discussion of the formation of composite verbs not found in other versions of *Ianua*.[9] Similarly peculiar to this text of *Ianua* is the full parsing of verbs for which a full conjugation is given, as for example in the case of *amo* and *amor*.[10] There is also a full introductory catechism for the impersonal verb *licet* not included in other *Ianua* texts.[11] Also not found in other *Ianua* versions are catechisms for the past participle (*lectus*), future participle (*lecturus*) and the gerund (*legendus*), besides questions and answers about the number of participial genders and cases.[12] Rules and exceptions regarding the derivation of participles are similarly found only in this version.[13] Besides questions and answers on the numbers of pronominal persons and cases,[14] unique to this manuscript are also more extended discussions of demonstrative pronouns,[15] derivative pronouns,[16] and composite pronouns.[17] Questions and answers about numbers of adverbial figures and significations are also unique to this manuscript,[18] but particularly extensive is a discussion of adverbs of place, particular to this version too.[19] Further elaboration of copulative conjunctions is also unique to this version,[20] as is an additional note on causal conjunctions.[21]

As a schoolbook, *Ianua* appears with wide variations among manuscripts and early printed versions, school masters freely adapting the text according to their own needs and preferences. Nevertheless, Harley stands out as a particularly copious treatise. Schmitt has shown that *Ianua* is mainly a reworking of material from Priscian into an elementary catechism, in the manner of Donatus's *Ars minor*,[22] and some of the additional material not found in other *Ianua* versions consists of further extracts from Priscian; e.g.,

7 BL Harley , r; cf. v, v, r. 8 BL Harley , v– r.
9 BL Harley , v.
10 BL Harley , r, v. The same preliminary parsing is undertaken for doceo (v), doceor (v), lego (r), legor (r), audio (r), audior (v– r). There are shorter introductory classifications for penitet (r: penitet verbum inpersonale coniugationis secunde), sum (v: sum verbum anomalum substantivum generis nullius), fero (r: fero verbum activum coniugationis nullius), volo (v), edo (r), gratulor (r), gaudeo (r), fio (v), possum (r), ferio (r), memini (v). 11 BL Harley , v. 12 BL Harley , r.
13 BL Harley , v– r. 14 BL Harley , r. 15 BL Harley , v.
16 BL Harley , v. 17 BL Harley , v. 18 BL Harley , r.
19 BL Harley , v– r. 20 BL Harley , v– r. 21 BL Harley , r.
22 Schmitt ( ), .

Harley	Priscian, *Insitutiones grammaticarum,* V (Keil (–), ,)
v: Quid est numerus? Forma dictionis que discretionem quantitatis facere potest.	Numerus est dictionis forma, quae discretionem quantitatits facere potest.[23]

[23] Cf. also BL Harley , v– r, r, r–v, v– r, v, v with Priscian, *Institutiones*, – (Keil (–), , –), (Keil (–), , –), – (Keil (–), , –), – (Keil (–), , –), (Keil (–), ,), (Keil (–), ,). Also similar treatments of the second (r–v), third (r– v), fourth (v) and fifth (v– r) declensions are not found in other versions of *Ianua* and are likewise taken from Priscian. Cf. also BL Harley , v with Priscian, *Institutiones*, – (Keil (–), , –). There are similar rules and exceptions for the four other conjugations on r– r, v– r and v– r, similarly drawn from Priscian.

A handlist of manuscripts of Ianua[1]

MS location and shelfmark (in rough chrono-logical order)	Folios containing *Ianua*	Folios containing *Disticha Catonis*	Type of script	Provenance of copyist	Date
BL Harley 2	r– v	Not included	Caroline	Germanic, text is Italian	XII^{2}
BNP lat. 3	r– r	Not included	Early Gothic	Northern France, probably Paris	*c.* –
ASU Frammenti 4	r– v	Not included	Gothic	Italy	XIIIc.

[1] Gabriella Pomaro is particularly insistent about the dating of *Ianua* manuscripts (apart from Harley, Paris and Strozzi) to XVc. One problem with previous attempts to date *Ianua* is that the character of script employed has not always been assessed, as is clear for example from the egregiously early datings of BNF Magl. . to anywhere from the eleventh (!) to the fourteenth century, when, in fact, the script is clearly Gothic, and late Gothic at that. Another problem has been the tendency to overlook the persistence (indeed, prevalence) of Gothic script in XVc. and even XVIc.: it has sometimes been assumed that Gothic script means a XIVc. manuscript.

[2] Bursill-Hall ( ), ; Black (e), – .

[3] Bursill-Hall ( ), ; Sivo (a), , , , , , , , , , , , , ; Fierville ( ), – ; Delisle ( ), ; Thurot ( ), ; Pellegrin ( ), , n. ; Schmitt ( ), ; Black (a), – ; Black (e), – , , .

[4] Scalon ( ), and plate This book contains a catalogue of mainly notarial fragments, which include five fragments of *Ianua.* I have been unable to examine any of these manuscripts personally, and so I reproduce here the details of this catalogue. Because of the fragmentary nature of the manuscripts, it is impossible to tell whether they represent copious versions of *Ianua* similar to Harley and Strozzi , or abbreviated versions similar to Magl. . .

ASU Frammenti 5	r–v	v	Gothic	Italy	XIIIc.
ASU Frammenti 6	r–v	Not included	Gothic	Italy	XIII/ XIVc.
BML Strozzi 7	r– v	v– v	Gothic	Italian	XIVin.
ASU Frammenti 8	r–v	Not included	Gothic	German (?)	XIV^2–XV^1
ASU Frammenti 9	r–v	Not included	Gothic	Italian	XV^1
BNCF Magl. . 10	r– v	v– r	Gothic	Italian	XVc., after $XV^{1/4}$
BRF 11	r– v	r– v	Mercantesca, with some humanist elements	Florentine, owned by Papi di Ierello da Filicaia, Tomaso da Filicaia and Bastiano di Agustino da San Godenzo	XV^2 (Papi da Filicaia died in : BNCF Poligrafo Gargani)

5 Scalon ( ), , plate . . Scalon's transcription of the end of *Ianua* requires correction. On the basis of the photograph reproduced as plate , instead of 'quecumque, a quibus, a quibuscunque (!), quaque. Deo gratias.', the transcription should read: quecumque, a(blativo) a quibus, a quibuscunque quaque[?]. Deo gratias. This is the same paradigm as found in Harley , r: Nominativo quicumque [...] d(ativo) quibuscumque, a(ccusativo) quoscumque quascumque quecumque, a(blativo) a quibuscumque. On the basis of the photograph, the reading of the final word 'quaque' is highly uncertain, and in any case makes no sense in terms of the paradigm.

6 Scalon ( ), – .

7 Boas and Botschuyver ( ), lxii, lxx; Bursill-Hall ( ), ; Gehl ( ), – ; Bandini (–), . ; Black (a), – ; Black (b), – ; Gehl ( ), , , , – ; Black (e), – *passim.*

8 Scalon ( ), – .

9 Scalon ( ), .

10 Schmitt ( ), – , *passim*; Grendler ( ), , ; Bursill-Hall ( ), ; Garin ( ), ; Gehl ( ), – ; Galante (–), – ; Sanford ( ), ; Fava ( ), ; Sivo (a), – ; Black (a), – *passim*; Black (b), – ; Gehl ( ), , , , , , , ; Black (e), – *passim.*

11 Bursill-Hall ( ), ; Black (b), , n.

Brescia Biblioteca Queriniana cod. B. . [12]	r– v	r– v	Gothic	Italian	XVmid
BML Med. Pal. [13]	r– v	v– v	Humanist script	Italian, probably Florentine	XV²
Berlin Staatsbibliothek cod. lat. qu. (formerly Phillips)[14]	r– v	r– v	Heavy Gothic bookhand, with humanist elements	Southern Italy	XV²
Milan Biblioteca Trivulziana n. [15]	r– r (beginning of text missing)	r– r	Humanist bookhand	Milan, written for Massimiliano Sforza	
Modena Biblioteca Estense MS Alpha U. . (lat.)[16]	r– v	r– v	Gothic, with some humanist elements	Ferrara (Jacobus de Sancta Agnete de Ferraria: copyist)	XVc., perhaps XV¹
Modena Biblioteca Estense MS Alpha O. . (lat.)[17]	r– r	r– v	Heavy, rigid Gothic, without humanist elements	Italian	XV¹, but possibly later
Rome Biblioteca Casanatense MS [18]	r– v	r– r	Gothic	Not Italian, possibly German	

[12] Bursill-Hall ( ), ; Sivo (a), ; Beltrami ( ), – , n. .
[13] Bandini (–) . ; Bursill-Hall ( ), ; Sivo (a), ; Black (b), .
[14] Schmitt ( ), ; Bursill-Hall ( ), ; Sivo (a), .
[15] Transcribed, with reproduced facsimile, in Bologna ( ), – ; Bursill-Hall ( ), ; Sivo (a), ; Schmitt ( ), – . [16] Bursill-Hall ( ), ; Sivo (a), .
[17] Bursill-Hall ( ), ; Sivo (a), .
[18] *Catalogo dei manoscritti della Biblioteca Casanatense* ( ), , – ; Bursill-Hall ( ), ; Sivo (a), .

BAV Ottob. lat. [19]	r– v	r– v	Gothic	Italian, possibly northern	XVIc.
Montecassino Biblioteca dell'Abbazia cod. TT[20]	pp. – (*Ianua sum rudibus* prologue not included)	Not included (fragmentary at end)	*Lettre batarde*	Apparently French, but possibly southern Italian	XVc.
Venice Biblioteca Marciana cod. lat. (.)[21]	r– v	r– v(n.n.)	Gothic	Italian	XVc., not early
Venice Biblioteca Marciana cod. lat. (Z)[22]	r– r	r– v	Gothic	Italian	XV[1]
BAV Chigi L. . [23]	– v	Not included	Humanist italic	Italian	XV[2/4]
New York Columbia University Plimpton [24]	r– r	r– v	Gothic	Italian	XVc., not early
Vienna Österreichische Nationalbibliothek cod. [25]	r– r	r– v	Humanist bookhand	Milan, for Giangaleazzo Sforza	XV[2], finished according to Schmitt ( ),

[19] Bursill-Hall ( ), ; Sivo (a), .
[20] Inguanez (–), , pt and , ; Bursill-Hall ( ), .
[21] Bursill-Hall ( ), ; Zorzanello (–), , ; Grendler ( ), .
[22] Schmitt ( ), ; Bursill-Hall ( ), ; Sivo (a), ; Zorzanello (–), , .
[23] Bursill-Hall ( ), ; Sivo (a), .
[24] Plimpton ( ), – , n. ; Ives ( ), ; de Ricci and Wilson ( ), ; Grendler ( ), , ; Bursill-Hall ( ), .
[25] *Tabulae* (–), MS ; Schmitt ( ), ; Bursill-Hall ( ), ; Sivo (a), .

Vienna Österreichische Nationalbibliothek, cod. [26]	r– v	v– r	Gothic	Italian, probably north	XV^2
El Escorial Biblioteca Real Cod. S. . [27]	r– v	r– r	Gothic, influenced by the printed book	Italian	s or s
Bodley Can. misc. [28]	r– v	Not included	Gothic	Italian	XVmid or $XV^{3/4}$
Bodey Can. misc. [29]	– r	v– v	Gothic	Veneto	XV^2
Padua Biblioteca del Seminario cod. [30]	r– v	v– v	Gothic	Veneto, copied by *Iohannes de Sibinicho, frater*	Completed April
Padua Biblioteca Universitaria cod. [31]	r– v	v– v	Humanist italic, with Gothic elements	Italian	XV^2
BNP lat. [32]	r–v (fragment of beginning)	Not present	Gothic	Italian	XV^2
BNP lat. [33]	r– r	r– r	Humanist bookhand with Gothic elements	Italian	XV^2

26 *Tabulae* (–), MS ; Schmitt ( ), ; Bursill-Hall ( ), ; Sivo (a), .
27 Antolín ( ), , ; Schmitt ( ), ; Bursill-Hall ( ), ; Sivo (a), .
28 Coxe ( ), ; Bursill-Hall ( ), .
29 Coxe ( ), ; Bursill-Hall ( ), .
30 Donello ( ), ; Bursill-Hall ( ), . See Kristeller (–), , .
31 Bursill-Hall ( ), .
32 Lauer ( ), ; Bursill-Hall ( ), .
33 Delisle ( ), n. ; Bursill-Hall ( ),

New Haven Yale University Library Marston MS [34]	r– r	r– v	Gothic	Italy, north-east?	XVmid (before)[35]
ASF Carte Bardi .	v– r	r– v	Gothic	Florence, convent of S. Salvatore di Settimo	All one hand: XV²; other texts dated (r)

[34] Faye and Bond ( ), .

[35] v: Tome d'Algreza dee dar a mi Beti per uno saldo fato cum lui a dì de mazo ; monta in suma L. S. D. .

Witt ( ) has argued in favour of the vernacular as a medium for teaching reading in early Renaissance Florence, putting forward three possible pieces of concrete evidence. Firstly, he notes that some vernacular versions of the Latin classics 'appear in manuscripts as if they were used for teaching purposes, with the text in the middle and commentaries and notes in the wide margins or between the lines' (–). Secondly, he says that 'Florentine vernacular verses on the ABCs ascribed to a certain Guidotto exist for the fourteenth century, suggesting a direct link with instruction in the *tavola*' ( ). Thirdly, he points to a collection of vernacular texts (BML Gaddi) which 'served as a vernacular parallel to short Latin texts such as the *Disticha [Catonis]* and *Dittochaeon* [on these school texts, see above] used at the grammar school level' ( ).

I remain unconvinced. Firstly, translated commentaries sometimes accompanied Latin texts (e.g. excerpts from William of Conches's commentary on Boethius were translated and copied into the margins of BML dxt. : see Black and Pomaro ( ), ,) but the translations do not seem to have been used for teaching (see Black and Pomaro ( ), n.). Commentaries were mechanically translated along with texts from commentated Latin versions (see e.g. BRF (translation of Henry of Settimello, *Elegia*) v) but this kind of vernacular mechanical translation of texts does not indicate teaching or a school context, any more than the mechanical copying of Latin commentaries. Secondly, Maestro Guidotto's alphabetic rhyming couplets (for another ms. not mentioned by Witt, see BNCF II.II. , r-v) call to mind the opposite of reading in the vernacular: oral, not written, teaching of the alphabet (a type of alphabetic nursery rhyming). Thirdly, as Witt acknowledges, the text of BML Gaddi cannot itself be a schoolbook, given that it is written in *mercantesca* script (hardly found in schoolbooks) and is an unused copy; he goes on to speculate that there is 'a strong probability that the *Gadd.* represents *volgare* collections which were so used and subsequently disappeared from wear and tear' ( ). However, the assumption that this book was the work of schoolboys is uncertain: the owners are not identified as attending schools, and the hand of the copyist recalls not a school context but the vernacular ambience of devotional codices from the mid-fourteenth century (not Witt's XV¹).

Manuscripts of Tebaldo's Regule

A further description of Tebaldo's *Regule* is included here because it is a XIIIc. Italian grammar enjoying a noteworthy dissemination but one which has hitherto failed to attract scholarly attention.

This text, with the incipit 'In presenti opusculo rudium utilitati volens intendere', is found in the following manuscripts:[1]

Location	Shelf mark	Folios	Date, provenance	Bibliography
Aquila Biblioteca provinciale	J.	r– r	XVc.	Bursill-Hall ( ), ; Kristeller (–), .
*BML Strozzi		v– r	XIVin., central Italy	Boas and Botschuyver ( ), lxii, lxx; Bursill-Hall ( ), ; Gehl ( ), – ; Bandini (–), . ; Black (a), – ; Black (b), – ; Gehl ( ), , , , – ; Black (e), – *passim.*

[1] Manuscripts marked with an asterisk have been examined personally; details regarding others have been taken from catalogues cited.

Appendix III

Location	Shelf mark	Folios	Date, provenance	Bibliography
*BML AD		v– r	XIV^2, Italy, not apparently Tuscany	Bursill-Hall ( ), ; Gehl ( ), – ; Black (b), ; Gibson and Smith ( ), –
*BL Add.		r– r	XIII^2,[2] Italy	*List* ( ), ; Bursill-Hall ( ), ; Gehl ( ), – .
London Dr Brian Lawn Medieval and Renaissance Manuscripts		r– r	XIVc.	Kristeller (–), . b.
New York Columbia University Library Lodge MSS		r– v	XIII–XIVc.	Kristeller (–), . .

[2] Two sections:

(a) r– r. Small, delicate Gothic hand, using often old-fashioned angular g with diagonal line from right to left going below bottom loop. No other antique features. Gothic crossed t; i sometimes dotted: XIII^2.

(b) r– v. Much more simplified, larger, rounded script: XIV^2.

Kindly inspected for me by Albinia de la Mare, who wrote on . . : 'The first part seems s. XIII^2 but not late in this period I think. The second part does indeed seem to be s. XIV^2.' Gehl ( ), accepts dating of XIVc. found in *List* ( ), . Gibson and Smith ( ), , date r– r as XIVc. and r– v as XIIIc., in my view inexplicably. Contents:

( ) r– v pseudo-Cato, *Distichs.*

( ) r– v [Tebaldo, *Regule* and additional material: see below, –] inc. In presenti opusculo rudium utilitati volens. r expl. tibi sunt communia lector. Deo gratias. Amen. v Inc. Nota quod VI sunt adverbia localia. expl. v Ubi fuisti in Monte Pensulano vel apud Montem Pensulanum vel prope.

( ) r– v Prosper, *Epigrammata* and *Poema coniugis*

( ) r– r Boethius, *Consolation*, incomplete at end

( ) r– v Aesop, *Fabulae*

r: Colle. Agen. Socie.t Jesu Cata. inscrip. (XVII, XVIII c.)

A very few marginal glosses, a very few interlinear to Boethius.

Obvious schoolbook. Schoolboy drawings: v, v (*Iustitia*, holding sword and balance).

The version of Tebaldo's *Regulae* here is shorter than in BML AD . Former goes up only to constructions with accusative, breaking o in the middle of the sections on accusatives with verbs.

Manuscripts of Tebaldo's Regule

Location	Shelf mark	Folios	Date, provenance	Bibliography
Rome Biblioteca Angelica		r– v[3]	XVc.	Bursill-Hall ( ), ; Narducci ( ), .
Venice Biblioteca Marciana lat.	(.)	r– v	XIII–XIVc.	Zorzanello (–), . (with incipit); Kristeller (–), . (incipit not confirmed); Bursill-Hall ( ), .
Udine Biblioteca comunale fondo principale		r– r	XIVc.	Bursill-Hall ( ), ; not confirmed by Mazzatinti (–), , , but confirmed by Sabbadini ( ), .

3 Bursill-Hall ( ), , gives incipit as ‘Substantivum nomen est illud cui preponitur unum articulare tantum’, which corresponds to the second paragraph of the text: see BML AD , v: Substantivum nomen est illud cui preponitur unum articulare tantum. Narducci ( ), , gives the incipit as ‘in presenti opusculo rudium utilitatem volens intendere’.

Appendix III

In the following manuscripts, the treatise with the above incipit ( ) is listed by Bursill-Hall, but not confirmed by other sources.

Library	Shelf mark	Folios	Date, provenance	Bibliography
Aquila Biblioteca provinciale	K.	r– v	XVc.	Bursill-Hall ( ), . Only partly confirmed by Kristeller (–), . : 'Regule magistri Theobaldi' (without incipit).
Assisi Biblioteca comunale		r– r	XIII–XIVc.	Bursill-Hall ( ), . Not confirmed by Mazzatinti (–), . : 'Regulae Magistri Thebaldi, principio illegibile, fin: causa finalis. Expliciunt regule magistri Thebaldi senensis. (–). Note grammaticali (–).' Phrase 'causa finalis' apparently not in BML AD .
Bern Bürgerbiblio-thek		v– v	XIII–XIVc.	Bursill-Hall ( ), ; not confirmed in Hagen ( ), .

Manuscripts of Tebaldo's Regule

Library	Shelf mark	Folios	Date, provenance	Bibliography
Naples Biblioteca Nazionale	V.C.	r– r	, Corphoi	Bursill-Hall ( ), ; not confirmed by Kristeller, (–), , , who gives di erent incipit.

A *terminus ante quem* for the treatise is o ered by its preservation in one manuscript datable to the second half of the thirteenth century (BL Add.), and a *terminus post quem* is provided by two references in the text to *Graecismus*, written in .[4] The treatise may possibly be the work of one of two Sienese grammarians active in XIII². In manuscript of Assisi Biblioteca Comunale, possibly the same text is ascribed to Maestro Tebaldo: Expliciunt regule magistri Thebaldi senensis (see above,). There are two grammarians known to have lived in Siena during XIII²: Tebaldo di Orlandino, Sienese citizen and *maestro di grammatica*, was active between and [5] while another, Maestro Tebaldo di Jacopo, also a Sienese citizen, made his will in bequeathing several grammatical works, including 'Alisander super Prisciano minore [...] Priscianum meum maiorem et minorem et unum scriptum super minorem [...] unum doctrinale et regulas magistri Boni.'[6]

Tebaldo's *Regule* are followed in two manuscripts by other short grammatical texts:

BML AD	BML Strozzi
(a) r– v: inc. Cuilibet verbo impersonali debet fieri suppositio per nominativum [...] expl. Gerundia habent or casus scilicet	(a) r– r: inc. Cuilibet verbo impersonali debet fieri suppositio per nominativum [...] expl. Gerundia habent casus, scilicet

[4] BML AD , r: Item construitur genitivus cum prepoxitione per *Grecismum*, ut:
tenus crurum pendent palcare a mento.
r: Regitur etiam ablativus ab hiis prepositionibus: a.ab.abs.cum.coram. etc. sed loco ablativi per *Grecismum* recipiunt genitivum ut
tenus crurum pendet paleare a mento

[5] Cecchini and Prunai ( ), – , .

[6] Apparently Bene da Firenze: see above, ; Cecchini and Prunai ( ), – .

nominativum genitivum accusativum et ablativum […] Suppina habent duos casus accusativum et ablativum […] resolvitur sic, ut vado lectum, id est ad legendum. Explicit. Expliciunt regule.	nominativum genitivum accusativum et ablativum; supino [*sic*] habet duos casus: facit accusativum ablativum. Explicit primus tractatus Magistri Tebaldi.
(b) v– r: inc. Exigentia casuum tractaturi primo de constructione nominativo […] expl. iste leo est fortior solito id est plus solito […] vel iste laudat librum suum plus debito laudare. Explicit.	(b) r– r. inc. Exigentia casuum tracta[n]tium primo de constructione nominativi […] expl. iste est fortior solito id est fortior plus sex solito.
(c) v– v: Figura est intransitiva dictionum adiunctio […] expl. apparet hic esse servus domini pauperis. Expliciunt regule Magistri Bartholomei. Deo gratias.	(c) r– r: inc. Figura est transitiva dictionum adiunctio […] expl. proparet hic esse servus domini pauperis.
(d) v– r: inc. Localium adverbiorum or sunt species […] expl. usque quadragesimam usque nativitatem domini. Expliciunt regule fulgitive. Deo gratias. Amen.	(d) r– r: inc. localium adverborum or sunt species […] expl. potest responderi per ista adverbia […] sinistrorsum et similia […] unde petit regimen cum verbo stat sine motu. Expliciunt regule fulgitive deo gratias. Amen.

These texts may also follow the treatise in Venice Biblioteca Marciana lat. (.): according to the indications in Zorzanello (–), . this MS seems to have the same incipit for this material as BML AD and Strozzi : inc. Quilibet verbo impersonali ['Quilibet' is possibly a mistranscription here of 'Cuilibet']. Similarly, in BL Add. , there is overlap of material too:

BL Add.	BML AD
v: Nota quod sunt adverbia localia	v: Localium adverbiorum or sunt
v: Ubi fuisti in Monte Pensulano vel apud Montem Pensulanum vel prope	v: ad Montem Pesulanum
	r: versus Monte[m] Pesulanum

The authorship of these treatises is only partly specified: (a) is attributed to Tebaldo in BML Strozzi , whereas (b) is ascribed to Maestro Bartolomeo in BML AD . I can see no foundation for Bursill-Hall's identification of the latter as 'Bartholomeus de Lodi [*sic pro* Laude]', accepted by Gehl ( ), .

(a) is a treatise on verbal syntax and the formation from verbs of gerunds, supines and participles. (b) is a treatise on the construction of cases with nouns. (c) is a treatise on figures of construction. (d) is a treatise on adverbs and interrogatives of place. These all were standard topics found in the secondary grammar syllabus in the thirteenth century (see e.g. Pietro da Isolella's *Summa* above,) and would have gone some way to broadening Tebaldo's monographic scope into a more generalized secondary treatise.

The title of (d) ('Regule fulgitive') is puzzling. Perhaps some idea of its sense can be inferred from comparison with another short treatise, this time in verse, found in BML AD , v– r, entitled 'Regule fugitive Magistri Sissami', inc. Qua per ubi vel quo loco quero sive per unde, expl. At si ponatur constructio non vitiatur. Deo gratias amen amen. Expliciunt regule fugitive Magistri Sissami; Mathiolus scrixit, quem dominus benedixit. Maestro Sissamo's *Regule fugitive* similarly deal with words of place (adverbs, interrogatives, nouns, prepositions). *Fulgitive/fugitive* evidently signified either fleeting, in the sense of easily forgettable, or resplendent, meaning that they made pupils shine: see above, n. , where annotations giving these definitions in BRF are transcribed.

Handlist of manuscripts of school authors produced in Italy and now found in Florentine libraries

In the Italian middle ages and Renaissance, the increasing specialization of education led to the emergence of types of schoolbooks which tended to become not only distinctive themselves but also to di er from university teaching manuals (linked to the *studium* curriculum of rhetoric, law, philosophy, medicine and theology), as well as from elementary reading texts, theoretical grammar treatises or indeed from other types of medieval and Renaissance manuscript literature. Of course, such boundaries were not rigid. For example, it was not unknown for anthologies of school authors, especially the *auctores minores*, to include elementary theoretical grammar tracts.[1] Nevertheless, surviving manuscript copies, as well as other contemporary evidence such as curriculum outlines and appointment documents, bear witness to an identifiable genre of school authors.

Medieval and Renaissance Florence o ers particularly fertile ground for the investigation of school manuscripts; today's great Florentine libraries – the Medicea Laurenziana, Riccardiana and Nazionale Centrale – can boast hundreds of schoolbooks among their vast manuscript collections.

The following census is based on an examination of , manuscripts carried out mainly over two years (–); as a result, it has been possible to identify manuscripts as suitable for inclusion as school authors used in grammar schools in the period up to the end of the fifteenth century. At the end of the handlist, there follows a summarial list of all excluded manuscripts.

The potentially random survival of manuscripts is a di culty for any survey of the influence and readership of classical and medieval texts, but there has been an attempt to obviate that problem ( ) by choosing, in Florence, one of the world's major manuscript centres, with large collections from varied sources (monastic, ecclesiastical, private families

[1] E.g. see below ASF Carte Bardi . ; BML AD , CS , sup. , Strozzi ; BNCF Landau Fin. , Magl. . , Magl. . , Panciat. ; BRF , , , , , , .

and owners and individual scholars); ( ) by supplementing and controlling the results through selective examination of other collections, for example by studying all the Italian manuscripts of the *Consolation of Philosophy* in the Bodleian Library, Oxford[2] and in the Biblioteca Statale of Lucca,[3] as well as manuscripts of Cicero's moral treatises in the Biblioteca Apostolica Vaticana so far described in Pellegrin (–).[4]

Particular problems regarding the survival of some types of schoolbooks will not, it is hoped, substantially a ect this study. It is necessary to distinguish between, on the one hand, schoolbooks whose texts subsequently became obsolete in the schoolroom (e.g. *Ianua*, psalter, minor authors) and which, usually subsequently discarded, now can have a poor survival rate; and schoolbooks containing classical works, on the other hand, which have maintained themselves, because subsequent generations have continued to value their texts. There would be many fewer Caroline or Gothic manuscripts of Latin classical texts if school use had significantly led to their loss. With regard to the distorting e ect of greater fifteenth-century survival, this does not seem to have been operative, for example, with manuscripts of Boethius's *Consolation*, whose greatest numbers appear in the fourteenth, rather than the fifteenth, century.[5]

Two other scholars have assisted in compiling this handlist. I myself carried out preliminary examination of inventories, with the assistance of Jane Black, who was my research assistant during the academic year – . The next stage of the research was a rapid examination of manuscripts selected from inventories with a view to detecting signs of school use; here, I shouldered most of the burden, but I was greatly assisted by Jane Black, who examined an enormous number of microfilms of fifteenth-century manuscripts in the Biblioteca Medicea Laurenziana, as well as Quattrocento manuscripts directly in the Biblioteche Riccardiana and Nazionale Centrale, during the spring and summer of .

However, my greatest debt here is to Gabriella Pomaro, who worked on this project as my research assistant for a year from January to December . My background as an historian rather than as a palaeographer created significant problems with regard to the dating and localization of literary manuscripts. In fact, without the assistance of

[2] These are: Can. lat. , , , (omitted by Gibson and Smith ( )), , D'Orville , Lat. class. d. , Laud. Lat. , Rawlinson G. (also described in unpublished edition of Trevet (not used by Gibson and Smith ( )), xxi, made by Silk, who used it as one of his eight base manuscripts). [3] See Black and Pomaro ( ), – .

[4] See above, , n. . [5] See above, , ,

one of Italy's foremost palaeographers in the person of Gabriella Pomaro, the present scope of this work, ranging from the turn of the eleventh to the end of the fifteenth century, would have been inconceivable. The greatest di culty was determining the date and provenance of pre-fifteenth century manuscripts. Only an expert palaeographer with years of experience in cataloguing and describing manuscripts is normally qualified to determine whether, for example, a twelfth-century manuscript written in a Caroline hand is of Italian or French or even German origin. Moreover, Gothic script survived long beyond the introduction and spread of humanist bookhand at the beginning of the fifteenth century; again, an expert such as Gabriella Pomaro is in the best position to ferret out the many fifteenth-century Gothic schoolbooks which have been misdated because they were written in a conservative script. Thus, the next phase of research was for Gabriella Pomaro to examine and describe briefly pre-fifteenth-century manuscripts selected as possible schoolbooks on the basis of the inventories and preliminary examination; she also examined problematic or di cult fifteenth-century manuscripts. Finally, I myself then read the glosses and examined the condition of the manuscripts, to make a final decision (normally in consultation with Gabriella Pomaro) with regard to inclusion in the following handlist. I began this work of detailed study of manuscript glosses in and completed it at the end of , while this book was being written; during these six years, I have been privileged to continue working closely with Gabriella Pomaro, as a consultant, as a research associate for our collaborative project from to on school authors in Florentine libraries and as a co-author of our related book, *Boethius's* Consolation of Philosophy *in Italian Medieval and Renaissance Education. Schoolbooks and their glosses in Florentine manuscripts*, which was published by Società Internazionale per lo Studio del Medioevo Latino at the Florentine Certosa in . Finally, during the summer and autumn of and the winter of , I personally checked once again on site in Florence all manuscripts included in this handlist. I myself have made the final decision about inclusion in or exclusion from this handlist, and I alone take full responsibility for any errors or misinterpretations found therein.

For the purposes of identification as schoolbooks, there are two distinct types of manuscripts. In the first place, there is a substantial group of manuscripts actually signed by pupils at school. A well-known example of a signed schoolbook is BML . , a copy of Ovid's *Heroides* which contains this note of ownership: Iste liber est Cosme Iohannis de Medicis morantis ad scolas D. Magistri Nicholai de

Aretio.[6] Out of the , manuscripts considered for our census, I have found manuscripts (or per cent of the schoolbooks in the census) with similar explicit notes of ownership by school pupils.[7]

This group of signed manuscripts is crucial, not only because they provide the core of this study, but because, by analysing their format and contents, it has been possible to identify a group of further school manuscripts in which either such notes of possession have been erased or otherwise disappeared or which never contained any such indication of ownership. The fact is that the practice of signing schoolbooks explicitly as a pupil began in Italy only at the beginning of the fourteenth century; nevertheless, schools obviously existed before and the majority of pupils even in the fourteenth and fifteenth centuries seem never to have bothered to indicate their ownership of their books. By analysing the typical features of the core group of signed schoolbooks, I am confident of having been in a position to identify the remaining group of unsigned schoolbooks.

Of course, apart from an explicit signature, there is no absolute criterion for proving a manuscript to have been a schoolbook. Nevertheless, by finding a number of the salient characteristics of a signed schoolbook in another manuscript, it is possible to make a relatively secure identification. The most important of these typical features of a schoolbook are:

( ) extremely simple interlinear glossing, giving one-to-one paraphrase synonyms of elementary Latin vocabulary, particularly of words (such as 'que=et') whose meaning probably only a pupil would need to recall;

( ) *probationes pennae* in the manuscript, particularly exercises in writing the Latin or sometimes the Greek alphabet;

( ) cheap writing materials, such as reused or repaired parchment or low-quality paper;

( ) interlinear glossing by several di erent contemporary hands studying the same section of the manuscript at roughly the same time, so indicating the joint or collective use of a manuscript typical of a school;

( ) elementary word-order marks, usually indicated with letters of the

6 For this ownership note, see above, n. .

7 BML AD , , ; Ashb. , , ; CS , ; Edili ; sin. , sin. , . , . , . , . , . , . , . , . , . , . , . , . , . , . , . , . , . , . , inf. . , sup. , sup. , sup. , sup. , sup. ; Redi ; Rinuccini ; Strozzi . BNCF . . , . . ; CS J. . , J. . , J. . ; Landau , ; Magl. . , . , . , . , . ; NA ; Panciat. . BRF , , , , , , , , , , .

alphabet but sometimes with arabic numerals, written above individual words of the text;

( ) vernacular interlinear glosses, which usually indicate an elementary reader who does not yet know equivalent Latin synonyms;

( ) marginal glosses reflecting the main elements of curriculum of the theoretical grammar-school course;

( ) texts grouped in anthologies which are known to have been collections of school authors on the basis of contemporary *curricula auctorum* and syllabus outlines;

( ) marginal glosses limited to relatively brief entries, since school books tended not to have the all-embracing glossing of university-level manuscripts, where the text was often overwhelmed by the quantity of the glosses and o ered primarily an opportunity for the commentator to expound his own learning and thoughts;

( ) copying or glossing by an unformed hand, probably that of a school pupil.

It is to be emphasized that no one or even several such criteria is a necessary proof of school use; in the end, the experience and expert knowledge of the researchers is paramount.

In selecting schoolbooks, I have included all manuscripts which, in my view, were associated with a school context. This includes books used not only by pupils but also by teachers. Mention of a classical author alone usually indicates that the manuscript contains his normal *opera omnia*, e.g. Sallust = *Bellum Catilinae* and *Bellum Iugurthinum*. For other abbreviations see x–xii, above.

FLORENCE, ARCHIVIO DI STATO

Shelf-mark	Text(s)	Date	Provenance	Page(s) above
Carte Bardi .	Cato, Prudentius *D, Cartula*[8]	*c.*	Florence	
Carte Cerchi	Cicero*O A S DT Orations*, pseudo-Cicero and pseudo-Sallust *Orations*	XV[1]	Probably Florence	
CStrozz. .	Henry	XIV[1]	Florence[9]	

[8] Also contains *Ianua* and grammar texts: see above, n. , n. , and Appendix , . [9] Probatio (XIV): v: Priores artium et vexillifer.

FLORENCE, BIBLIOTECA DEL SEMINARIO MAGGIORE

B. .	Boethius	XIV[1]	Tuscany	

FLORENCE, BIBLIOTECA MEDICEA LAURENZIANA

	Terence	XV[1]	Florence[10]	
[11]	Avianus, pseudo-Ovid *De lumaca et lombardo De pulice De lupo monaco*	XIV[3/4]	Italy	
	Seneca (fragment)[12]	XIV (late)	Italy	
	Seneca		Pistoia	
	Ilias latina, Richard of Venosa *De nuptiis Paulini et Pollae senum*	,	Velletri	
	Horace		Perugia	
	Ovid *Met.*	XIVmid	N. Italy	
	Val. Max.		Castel Durante (Urbino)	
	Aesop, Prudentius *D*, Prosper[13]	XIV[2]	Italy, not apparently Tuscan	

10 r: Iste liber est mei Fratris Alexandri Blasii Ihonanis Marcii de Scarperia scarperiensis; v: Luigi Bartolini utebatur.

11 Gehl ( ), , excludes this manuscript from his Trecento census as 'XV', but it is written in a well-formed *scrittura cancelleresca*, datable to XIV[3/4].

12 *Hercules furens*, – .

13 Also contains grammatical texts: see above, – and Appendix , , – .

	Sallust	XIIImid	W. Tuscany	–
	Prosper	XIex. or XI–XIIc.	Italy	
	Vergil *A*	[14]	Italy, possibly Tuscany	
	Vergil *E G*	XV[1]	Florence	
	Vergil *E*	March	Florence	
	Vergil *E G*	XV[1]	Italy	
	Boethius	XIV[1]	Florence	
	Sallust *BC*	XIV[1]	Lombardy	,
	Vergil *E G*	XV[1]	Italy	
	Cicero *A P*	XVmid	Italy, possibly Tuscany	
	Cicero *O*	XV[2]	Italy	
	Claudian	XIV[3/4]	Tuscany, possibly Florence	
	Statius *T*	*c.* s	Italy	
	Cicero *S A P*	XV[1]	Italy	
	Terence	XV[3/4]	France or Italy	
	Avianus	XIIc.	C. Italy	
	Cicero *A S SS P*	XVin.	Italy	

[14] Colophon (v) has been rewritten: Explicit duodecimus et ultimus liber Virgilii Eneidos <deo gratia>s amen. M°CCC°XVIII. But dating is consistent with the manuscript's Gothic script, still showing signs of vertically straight stroking characteristic of XIIIc. writing; copyist has strong predilection for archaic straight 'd'.

	Terence	XVin.	Italy	
	Lucan	XV[1]	Prato[15]	
	Ovid *Met.*	XIV$^{3/4}$	Tuscany, probably Florence	
	Boethius	XV$^{1/4}$	Lombardy	
	Val. Max.	XVmid	Italy	
	Ovid *Met.*	XV[1]	Italy	
	Sedulius; Prosper, Arator[16]	XIIc.	Central/ Southern Italy; Italy	–
	Boethius	XVmid	Italy	
	Boethius	XV[1]	Italy	
	Vergil *A*	July [17]	Monte- pulciano	
	Ovid *Met.*	XIVex.	Italy	
	Horace *E*, Seneca *Epistulae morales* (selection), Vergil *G*, Geo rey	XVmid	Italy	'
	Juvenal[18]	XV[2]	Probably Florence	
	Horace *O E CS*	XVmid	Probably Florence	

15 v: Expletus est iste liber per me — [*deletum*] de Prato V iunii.

16 Also contains grammatical fragment: see above, .

17 r: Explicit liber *Eneydorum* Virgilii Maronis quem explevi et finem imposui die vigesimo primo iulii anno millesimo quatuorcenteximo trigesimo nono indictione secunda in terra Montispuliciani, tempore regiminis et potestarie nobilis et expectabilis viri Francisci Nicolai Andree del Benino pro magnifico populo et comuni Florentie potestatis dicti loci, deo gratias amen. Filippus Augusti de Montecastello notarius.

18 Composite, with fragment of Persius added at end and written by di erent contemporaneous hand; this latter section (r– v) shows no sign of school use.

	Juvenal	February /	Possibly Florence	
	Lucan	s	Italy	
	Seneca	s or s	Florence	
	Terence	XIIc.; XV^1	Italy; Florence	;
	Terence	February / [19]	Possibly Poppi[20]	
	Boethius	XIV^2	Probably Tuscany	
	Boethius	XV^1	Italy	
	Seneca		Perugia?[21]	
	Vergil *A*	August [22]	Florence[23]	
	Aesop	XV^1	Italy	

	Val. Max.	December	Probably in exile from Poppi[24]	
	Seneca	XV^1	Italy	
	Horace	XIIc.	Italy	
	Vergil *E A*	XV^2	Tuscany	
	Vergil *A*	XV^1	Probably Florence[25]	
26	Cicero *A*	XII–XIIIc.	Italy	, –

19 r: Vos valete et pandite. Ego Caliopus recensui. Publii Terentii Afri poete *Phormio* explicit foeliciter. Finitus Kal. Februarii M°CCCC°LXXIII°.

20 XV^2 ownership note: v: Terentius iste est mei <Michel?>is Ser Angeli de Lapucciis de Puppio et amicorum suorum. Et Torelli eius filio [*corr. ex* Torello; <Michel?>is *deletum, substitutum* Jac]. XVIin. ownership note: r: H<ic liber> est Torelli Jacobi de Lapucciis et <…>; XVImid ownership note: r: Ego. Mag. Sebasti(anu)s Salu<st>ius de Castro S. <…>

21 v: scripta a me Francisco et expleta A.D. MCCCLXXXVII, ind. XI^a et die XXVII° novembris, in quo tempore Papa Urbanus Sextus in civitate Perusii suam residentiam faciebat.

22 v: die V agusti M°.CCCC°.VI.

23 Reusing Florentine notarial parchment: e.g. v: populus florentinus; r: comunitas Flor.

24 As suggested by colophon (correctly transcribed by Bandini (–), . –); reusing notarial parchment from Pratovecchio and Poppi datable to XIVmid.

25 See catalogue entry by Angela Dillon and Anna Fantoni in Fabbri and Tacconi ( ), – .

26 *De amicitia* (r– r) fortuitously combined with other non-school texts: see Bandini (–), . – .

dxt.	Boethius	XIVmid	Tuscany	
sin.	Lucan	XII[1]	Italy, possibly Southern[27]	
sin.	Seneca	XIVex.	Florence[28]	
sin.	Sedulius;[29] Statius *A*	XI; XII[2]	Italy, possibly Lombardy; Italy	;
sin.	Boethius	XIVmid	Tuscany	
.	Claudian	November	Prato	
.	Henry	XV[1] [30]	Italy, probably not Florence	
.	Horace	XIIex.	Italy	
. [31]	Horace *AP E*; Juvenal; Persius		Florence	,
.	Horace	XIIex.	Italy	
.	Horace	XII–XIIIc.	Italy	
.	Horace *O E CS*	XV[1]	Italy	
. [32]	Horace *AP E*	XIV[4/4]	Florence	–
.	Horace *AP E*	XIVin.	Probably Bologna	
.	Horace *AP E*	XIVmid	Tuscany	

[27] Early XIVc. hand wrote note on v indicating pawning of this book for seven *soldi*, where name '<...> Bartolomei Johannis de Branditia <...>' [= Brindisi] appears.

[28] Reusing Florentine notarial parchment dated (see r).

[29] Contains non-Italian version of Claudian's *De raptu*.

[30] Gehl ( ), : 'XIVex.'

[31] Commissioned February by Florentine Francesco di Giovanni Vannicelli of parish of San Felice in Piazza: see above, n. , for revision of colophon in Bandini (–), . . See de la Mare ( ), ; since MS copied in Florence, the date must be *ab incarnatione* and so there seems no need for ' /? ' (de la Mare ( ),). Later owner: Cosimo de' Medici (see autograph *ex libris* on r, r and r, latter two first transcribed by Bandini (–), . , first by de la Mare ( ),). Gabriella Pomaro agrees with de la Mare's attribution of marginal gloss on v, l. up to Cosimo: see de la Mare ( ), .

[32] On palimpsest parchment from Florentine vernacular *ricordanza* dating from late Duecento (see v: MCCLXXXII): used for r– v and r– v; some other reused parchment comes from Trecento notarial records: (v) compangni<a> di Calimala.

.	Juvenal, Persius	XV[1]	Italy	–
.	Juvenal	XII[2]	Italy	
.	Juvenal	February	Piedmont	
.	Juvenal	XII[1]	Italy	
.	Juvenal	XII[2]	Italy	
.	Henry (extracts)	Nonis aug.	Florence	
. [33]	Lucan	XIV[2]	Liguria/ Lombardy[34]	
.	Lucan	XIIc.	Tuscany, possibly Florence	
.	Lucan	XII[1]	Italy	
. [35]	Lucan	s or s	Italy	
.	Lucan	XIIc.	Prob. Tuscan	
.	Lucan	XIIex.	Italy? France?	
.	Lucan	XIIc.	Italy	
.	Ovid *Met.*	?[36]	Italy	
.	Ovid *Met.*	XV[1]	Prato	

33 Has earlier Quattrocento restoration, adding text from . to end (r– v).

34 Explicit reference to Genoese *volgare* (v: see above,) as well as to historical events in Ligurian/Lombard area in suggests Genoese/Lombard provenance.

35 Two copyists (respectively writing r– v, r– v and r– v). r–v and r–v are late restorations, possibly by one of Bandini's copyists. Analysis of fascicles and watermarks has shown that final two folios were not restorations, but rather a change of scribe. v: after 'Explicit liber Lucani' there follows, in late XVIc. hand, 'Scripsit Jo. Victorius die VI ottobris an. domini . Laus deo.' This date is impossible, given handwriting of the two scribes, both using late-Trecento cursive *bastarda*. MS later belonged to Pietro Vettori (v: Liber Petri Victorii et amicorum n°), but attribution of copying to Giovanni Vettori may, like the date, be antiquarian fantasy. Pietro Vettori glossed r– r, v.

36 Dating on r (millesimo CCCC° °), interpreted by Bandini (–) . as 'mill.CCCC. .', cannot mean , given the fully developed humanist script employed; possibly the scribe was copying an older colophon, but the reading of 'millesimo quadrigentesimo sexagesimo' would accord well with the script used.

.	Ovid *Met.*	XIIImid, XIII–XIVc.	C. Italy, possibly Tuscany	,
.	Ovid *Met.*	XVin.	Arezzo/ Casentino[37]	
.	Ovid *Met.*	October	Florence	
.	Ovid *Met.*	$XII^{3/4}$	Italy, possibly North	
.	Ovid *Met.*	XIIex.	N. Italy	
.	Ovid *Met.*	XIVex.	Colle Valdelsa/S. Gimignano or nearby	–
.	Ovid *Met.*	XIV^{2}	Possibly Bologna or N. Italy[38]	
.	Ovid *Fasti*	XV^{2}	Italy	
.	Ovid *Her.*	XVin.	Probably Tuscany	
.	Ovid *Her.*	XIV^{2}	Tuscany, presumably Florence	– ,
.	Ovid *Her.*	XVin.	Probably Florence or nearby	
.	Seneca	$XIV^{4/4}$	near Florence	
.	Seneca	September	Venice[39]	

37 Reusing Aretine or Casentinese notarial parchment.

38 On basis of some watermarks, identifiable with Briquet n. .

39 Bandini (–), . , fully transcribes the colophon giving this information (v), besides the note, written by 'Martinus' (read 'Martinus subscripsit', not Bandini's 'scripsit') at foot of that page giving number of written folios in manuscript, and subsequent ownership note of 'Presbiteri Angeli rectoris S. Remigii de Florentia' (v). However, he does not publish this later *ex libris* (r: Emi hunc librum ego Xanthius Laurentii de Decomano a Francisco biblyopola die mensis octobris), showing that the book came into ownership of the Florentine grammar teacher Santi da Dicomano: on his grammar teaching in Florence in and then from

.	Persius	XIV[1]	S. Italy, possibly Naples[40]	
.	Persius	XV[1]	Italy	
. [41]	Prosper, Horace *AP E*	XIVin., XIV[1]	Italy	
.	Statius *A*, Ovid *Her.*, Pseudo-Boethius	April , September ,	Siena	, ,
.	Statius *A*[42]	XIV[4/4]	Italy	
. [43]	Statius *A*, *Ilias latina*; Ovid *AA*		Florence	
.	Terence	XV[1 44]	Italy	
.	Terence	October [45]	Possibly Reggio Emilia	

footnote (*cont.*)
to his death in , see Verde (–), , , , – *passim*; , – . For his earlier teaching in Florence between and , see Davies ( ), – . Although Santi da Dicomano taught grammar for many years in Florence, there is little indication that he used this copy of Seneca for teaching purposes. Sporadic brief XV[2] marginalia throughout do not seem to be in his handwriting, although there is a generic similarity.

40 Southern Italian provenance suggested by other Trecento *probationes* (v: Iste vero est Rasolv<?... > napolitanus bacellarius in medisina, napolitanus est), and by adolescent drawing there of two women, one a crowned queen, possibly Giovanna I or II of Anjou, accompanied by partially rubbed out caption reading at end 'di Agiu'.

41 Fortuitously composite anthology, with text of Prosper incomplete, missing chapters and (*PL* . – and –); the first seem to correspond to loss of one folio at beginning of a fascicle, but the second come after a blank page (v).

42 Contains Salutati's pseudo-Ovidian *Conquestio Phyllidis.*

43 Commissioned by Macingo di Gioachino Macinghi: (r) Iste liber scripsit Ser Antonius de Mercatello pro Macignio Ioachini de Macignis anno domini < : *deletum*> . Bandini (–), . , reads erroneously: 'An. Domini MCCCCXVIII'. This copyist wrote only the second section, the first having been written by di erent contemporaneous hand. Entire MS may have been commissioned by Macinghi, in view of his family arms appearing in both sections, which both have similar initial decoration (r, r). Certainly joined together soon after production, to judge from similarities between sections.

44 Villa's dating (, : XIV[1]) seems impossible: the book was a joint e ort of five scribes, with changes on v, v, v, v; the first scribe made continual late Gothic use of -shaped 'r' at beginning of words, while the second and third introduced the humanist lower-case 'g', and the fourth and fifth, the ampersand.

45 v: Hisce Terentii poete disertissimi commediis propria manu Gabrielis de Donelis civis notariique Regini finis deo dante fuit impositus, anno domini MCCCCXXXVI prima die octobris. Also note of visit by Emperor Frederick III to Geneva in October : (v) Imperator

.	Terence	XV¹	Italy	
.	Terence	XV²	Italy	
.	Terence	XVmid	Italy	
.	Terence	XV² [46]	Not Tuscany[47]	
. [48]	Theodulus; Statius *A*	XIV–XVc.	Italy	
.	Vergil *A*	XI–XIIc.	C. Italy	
.	Vergil *A*	XIIIex.	Italy, probably Pisa	
.	Vergil *A*	XV²	Italy	
. [49]	Vergil *A*	XIV–XVc.	Florence[50]	
.	Vergil *E*	XIVex.	Italy	
.	Vergil *E G*	XVmid	Florence[51]	
.	Vergil *E G*	XVmid	Florence	
.	Vergil *E G*	XVmid	Italy	

Federicus de Haustria venit Gebenas die XXIII octobris MCCCCXLII et fuit receptus honorifice ab ill. duce Sabudie qui erat cum regina, sorore sua coniuge et natis et nobilibus patrie et recesit die XXVII^a eiusdem. According to Villa ( ), , the MS belonged to Martin Le Franc, secretary to antipope Felix V and canon of Lausanne; eventually came into possession of Francesco Sassetti: see de la Mare ( ), .

46 Dating by Villa ( ), ('XIV²') seems a century too early, given the continual use of -shaped 'r's at beginnings of words, and the late date of glossators (XV²–XVI).

47 Last original page (v) reveals thematic translation (XVI) with some non-Tuscan elements, e.g.: *Lo s<c>ulare che ama gli studi delle buone letere desprexa ogni fatica a ciò aquisti le letere le quali m<a>i surano aquista sesa grande sudore.* Discipulus quem amat studis bonas literas spernit laborem ut aquires literas que nemeo assurat [*sic pro* nemo assumet?] sine magno sudor[e]. Abundant interlinear vernacular glosses.

48 Gehl ( ), ('XV').

49 Bandini thought the manuscript written perhaps by Boccaccio (– , .), suggestion repeated by Alessio ( ), , but the copyist's handwriting seems to have no resemblance to Boccaccio's; in any case, it would have been unusual for Boccaccio to have re-used such recent notarial parchment.

50 Reusing Florentine parchment dating between and (see r).

51 Several signatures and *probationes* on rear flyleaf (v: Giovambaptista di Bernardo Nassi, io Nicholaio di S(er?) Zanobi, al nome di dio a dì detto Fl. larghi, Dominus Lucha Lachi, Zanobi di Lucha, Zanobi di Lucha Lachi) contemporaneous with production and revealing Florentine provenance. Soon passed to monastery of S. Salvatore di Settimo: (r) Hic liber est monasterii Sancti Salvatoris de Septimo (XVIin.).

.	Val. Max.	XIVmid	Near Florence[52]	
.	Val. Max.	XVmid	Italy, not Tuscany[53]	
.	Val. Max.	s/ s	Florence[54]	
.	Sallust	XV^1	Italy, possibly Florence[55]	
.	Sallust	XIII^2	Italy	
.	Sallust *BJ*	XIIc.	Italy	
.	Cicero *De finibus bonorum et malorum, Academici*	XV^2	Probably Vicenza	
.	Cicero *O P* (fragment)	XIIex.	Italy	
.	Cicero *O A*	XII–XIII, XII^2	Italy	
.	Cicero *A*	XII^2	Italy	
.	Cicero *A S P*	XV^1	Probably Florence	
.	Cicero *A*	XV^1	Italy	
.	Henry; John the Abbot	XIV (late); XIV (late)[56]	Florence?;[57] Italy	

52 Re-using Trecento ecclesiastical parchment from various parishes near Florence.

53 See love note between two boys on r of this MS (see below, , n.), written in non-Tuscan vernacular contemporaneous with book's production.

54 Re-using parchment from Florentine private vernacular *ricordanze* (XIV/XVc.), with references (r) to 'fiorini', (v) to Florentine Ardinghelli family, (v) to 'MCCLXXXVIIII', and (r) to Florentine Mozzi family (Noi Messer Tommaso e Messer Vanni de' Mozzi e compagni <...>) Further confirmation of local Florentine origins is following the gloss by the scribe: (v) Regio picena est illa que hodie vocatur pistoriensis. Picena dicebatur a quodam castro iusta Pistorium existente quod adhuc hodie vocatur *Peteccio* vulgariter.

55 In possession of Florentine Capponi family by XV^2: (r) Antonius Capponus. Bandini's transcription (–), . , adds extra 'i' after 'n' in surname.

56 Description by Gehl ( ), – , is problematic: both sections of manuscript do not seem to date from 'XIV^1' but rather from end of century, as is clear from widely spaced script and frequent appearances of -shaped 'r's at beginning of words; (late) Quattrocento restoration did not consist of only 'fols. , , and ' but rather of , , , , , , , and . Klein ( ), , also dates the MS's second section to XIV^1.

57 Re-using apparently Florentine documentary parchment.

.	Boethius	$XV^{1/4}$	Italy	
.	Boethius	$XIV^{2/4}$	Florence	
.	Boethius	XVin.	Bologna	
.	Boethius	XIV^{1}; XV^{1}	Italy	
.	Boethius	$XIV^{4/4}$	Possibly N. Italy	
.	Boethius		Prato	
.	Boethius	XI^{2}	S. Italy	
.	Pseudo-Boethius	XIVmid	Italy	
inf. .	Sallust	XIIc.	C. Italy	
sup.	*Physiologus* (fragment)	XI–XIIc.	Italy	
sup.	Boethius	XIVin.	Florence or nearby	
sup.	Boethius	$XIV^{3/4}$	Probably S. Italy	
sup.	Val. Max.[58]	March [59]	Bologna	
sup.	Pseudo-Boethius	XIIIex.	Possibly W. Tuscany	–
sup.	*Ilias latina*	*c.* [60]	Florence[61]	

58 For humanist texts in MS, see Bandini (–), . – .

59 r: Valerii Maximi *Factorum dictorumque memorabilium* ad Tiberium Caesarem liber decimus et ultimus feliciter explicit. Bononie in domo de Bonazolis transcripsi. Scriptus per me Andream Ugolini de Vichio. Hoc opus exstat , die martii expletus est. Bandini (–), . , corrects the colophon's Latin.

60 Dated by one glossator (r). For slightly later ownership note of Giovanni Bottingori da Pistoia (v), see Bandini (–), . , also transcribing subsequent ownership note of Agnolo Gaddi .

61 Re-using Florentine notarial parchment (see v, v).

sup.	*Ilias latina*, *Physiologus*, Theodulus, Bernard of Clairvaux *Epistola de cura rei familiaris*,[62] Prudentius *D*, *Facetus*, Prudentius *P*, Avianus, Bonvesin (fragment),[63] *Cartula* (fragment); Claudian[64]	XVin.	Florence	

62 r– v; for text, see *PL* . – . Gehl ( ), , omits this text, erroneously replacing it with *Cartula*. 63 Five lines of opening of this text (r) not mentioned by Gehl ( ), – .

64 Also contains Salutati's *Conquestio Phyllidis* and *Fabula de vulpo et cancro*, Giovanni Bonandrea's *Brevis introductio ad dictamen*. Composite: – r (all texts except Claudian) are by one, – v by another, contemporaneous hand. The sections were put together by Paolo di Morello Morelli, who wrote a table of contents for the whole volume (with titles mainly indicated by incipits) on v, together with ownership note:

Iste liber est Pauli Morelli de' Morelli.

Isti sunt libri qui continentur in isto volumine et nomina eorum infra descripta sunt hic, ut patet:

P(rim)o: Homero

o: Lesa

o: Tras leo

o: L'apistula di Sancto Bernardo

o: Eva columba

o: Faceto

o: Senex fidelis

o: Bononia natus

o: Rustica deflenti

o: Inventa secuit.

Paolo's poor Latin spelling, macaronic language and immature handwriting indicate that he compiled this list and hence the MS as a whole in his school days. The only chronologically relevant member of the Morelli family with his name and patronymic is Paolo di Morello di Paolo di Bernardo Morelli, born February . (See BNCF Carte Passerini bis, v– r.) Therefore, it seems likely that the MS was assembled in latter half of the first decade of Quattrocento. This extra-graphical information accords well with an independent palaeographical analysis made by Gabriella Pomaro, who dated the two sections as roughly contemporaneous and written XVin. Gehl's attempt ( ), – , to see more than one hand copying – is problematic, as is clear from consistent features of the script throughout this section (e.g. lowercase 'g' with bottom stroke protruding to right). His description of the contents (( ), : ' – *Ilias latina* v [Coluccio Salutati], *Elegia*') needs revision; Bandini (–) . had made it clear that the fascicles were out of order, so that, in its present state, Salutati's *Conquestio Phyllidis* is actually on r– v, with *Ilias latina* surrounding it on r– r and r– r. Texts on r–v (Bonvesin (fragment) and *Cartula* (fragment)) were not written by either of the principal copyists; they have the appearance of *probationes* by adolescent hand(s) and, to judge from the writing, they were probably added after Paolo Morelli assembled the volume and made his table of contents.

sup.	Vergil *E G*	XVmid	Italy	
sup.	Vergil *A*	Between and [65]	Florence	
sup.	Seneca	August	S. Gimignano	
sup.	Statius *A*	XIVex.	Tuscany, possibly Florence[66]	
sup.	Statius *A*; *Ilias latina*; Claudian; Alain de Lille *Anticlaudianus*	June	Foligno	
sup.	Prosper	XIV^{2} [67]	Probably Pisa[68]	
sup.	Vergil *E*[69]	XV^{1}	Probably Florence	

65 v: Fuit absolutum hoc opus die domenico quarto nonas novembris hora IIª Florentie, inceptum quidem scribi de anno , laus deo.

66 Re-using Tuscan and possibly Florentine parchment.

67 Gehl ( ), : 'XIV/XV'.

68 See vernacular prayer to virgin (v), in copyist's hand: *Vergine madre figlia del tu' figlio, guarda Pisa tua e me in buona pace, e qual si governa socto il mio artiglio, e se ci avesse alcum pensier fallace, provedi si ne l'eterno consiglio, che laude n'abia il tu' figliuol verace.* May have arrived in Florence by the end of the century, as is possibly suggested ('r) by the following erased Trecento ownership note: Questo <...> è di <Neri?> de' G<uas?[coni?]> figliuolo di Messer <...> Chi l<o ...> lo metta <...>

69 Written on paper, containing: ( ) r– v: *Doctrinale*; ( ) r– r: Salutati *Conquestio Phyllidis*, ( ) r– v: Vergil *Eclogues*; ( ) r– r: pseudo-Cicero *De synonymis*. ( ) to ( ) are written by same late Gothic hand, using variety of graphic styles; ( ) is written in semi-Italic chancery cursive script, possibly by Bastiano Foresi: see above, . See Gehl ( ), .

	Juvenal	XV²	Probably S. Gimignano[70]	
	Cicero *A S P*		Italy, possibly in or near Rome[71]	
	Avianus, Prudentius *D*; *Ilias latina*[72]	XV²; October [73]	N. Italy[74]	
	Juvenal	XVmid	Italy	

	Seneca	XV¹	Possibly Siena[75]	
	Persius, Juvenal, Horace *AP E S O* (incomplete)	– /	Possibly Florence	, –
	Vergil *A*	XV¹	Probably Tuscany[76]	

70 r: Hieronimus de Marsilis de Sancto Geminiano scripsit. From about the same time is *ex libris* (r): Questo libro è di Mariano di Nicholo di Premerano. Hic liber est mei Mariani Nicholai de Premeranis et amicorum. Primerano was a common name in San Gimignano: see Vincenzio Coppi, *Annali della terra di San Gimignano*, in Coppi ( ), , and *Huomini illustri da S. Gimignano*, in Coppi ( ), , , , , , . Another roughly contemporaneous ownership mark: Lodovicho da Maradi amen (r).

71 By XVIc. may have arrived in Tuscany: see n. above.

72 Fortuitously combined with various other brief Latin and vernacular texts, written by later XVc. hand and outside school context: for these texts, see BML catalogue in MS by F. Del Furia, , v– r.

73 v: Explicit liber Homeri Deo gratias. M°CCCC°LXXVI. A dì di optobre [changed from 'setembre'].

74 See interlinear vernacular glosses: (r) *lasare le bruture*; (v) *fu facto un puoco induxio*. Both parts probably came from the same ambience, to judge from similar colophons and dates of provenance.

75 In view of early Piccolomini *ex libris*: (v) Iste liber est <...> de Picolominibus / suorum de Picholominibus [immature hand].

76 Possibly written on paper produced at Colle Valdelsa in (Briquet) and owned by Antonio di Felice del Becchato (see r, r, r, r).

	Ovid *Met.*[77]	XIex.; XII^1	W. Tuscany	– ,
	Ovid *Met.*	XI–XIIc.	Central/ Southern Italy	
	Juvenal	XII^1	Italy	
	Ovid *Her.*	XII–XIIIc.	Italy, possibly northern	
	Ovid *Met.*	XII–XIIIc.	Italy	
	Terence	XII^1	C. Italy	

	Boethius	XIV$^{4/4}$	Probably N. Italy, possibly Ferrara	
	Val. Max.	August[78]	Probably near Florence	
	Ianua,[79] Cato, Prosper, Aesop[80]	XIV$^{1/4}$	Italy	
	Vergil	Xc. or X–XIc.; XIc.; XII–XIIIc.; XVc.	Tuscany	,
	Vergil	XII–XIIIc.	S. Italy (Naples)	
	Horace *AP E*; Prudentius *D*	XIVex.	Tuscany or near Florence	
	Ovid *Her.*	[81]	Siena	

77 Also contains *Tristiae, Medicamina faciei femineae* and pseudo-Ovidian *Nux.*

78 For colophon, see Bandini (–), . .

79 See above, and Appendix , .

80 Also contains grammatical texts: Appendix .

81 r: Ego B<...> Nannis de Senis scripsi hunc librum in millesimo CCCC° XV anno, et in quaterdecimo die mensis settembris perfeci in vigesima hora et cet., amen. May have later passed to a relative: (v) Iste liber est mei Ioannis Ser Antonii Nannis.

	Juvenal	XII^{1} (restored XII^{2}, XII–XIIIc., XV^{2})	Italy, possibly northern	
	Statius *A*	XV^{1}[82]	Tuscany, probably Florence[83]	
	Seneca	XIVex.	Italy	
	Seneca	s or s	Italy	
	Geo rey; Horace *AP*	XIV^{1}; XVin.	Emilia-Romagna[84]	,

82 Probably early XVc. copy of original dated . Graphic style makes dating of unlikely: widely spaced and simplified Gothic script, besides strong presence of final straight 's's (under the evident influence of humanist script), supports the hypothesis that the colophon (v: Ego Ser Guaspar Ser Francisci Masini hunc librum s[c]ribere feci anno domini ab eius incarnatione millesimo trecentesimo optavo quinto indictione nona) reproduced an earlier copy. A further point in favour of this view is the fact that MS and colophon were written by same hand, whereas the sense of the colophon suggests that Ser Guaspare Masini had the book commissioned from the copyist, then subscribing the text in his own hand.

83 Re-using Tuscan parchment. Ser Guaspare di Ser Francesco Masini, active at end of Trecento, was a Florentine notary, son of another Florentine notary, Francesco, notary of the Signoria four times between and : see Ciabani ( ), , . Passed into ownership of Florentines Simone and Antonio Canigiani in XV^{2}: see r, 'v.

84 At end of XIVc. came into the possession of 'Evangeliste Ser Angeli de Mutiliana' (v), today Mutigliano near Forlì. Emilian origins may perhaps be confirmed by note on its wooden cover: Anno domini M°.CCC°.LXXXXIIII die XXVI mensis septembris. Ego M(en)gatius (com)modavi cum consensu Evangeliste Ovidium *Metamorphoseos* Domino Bernardo Ser Bartolomei de Caxalibus. Maestro Filippo di Maestro Matteo Casali, grammar teacher, was of Bolognese origins: Zanelli ( ), ; Battistini ( ); and BML Ashb. , r (Optimae aepistolae Magistri Philippi bononiensis civisque pistoriensis, r: Regule Magistri Philippi Casalensis ad discipulos.) Casali was a common family name in Romagna and especially Bologna.

FLORENCE, BIBLIOTECA NAZIONALE CENTRALE

. .	Statius *T*		Bologna	
. .	Statius *T*		Italy	
. .	Cicero *O*	XV^{1}	Italy	
. .	Terence	XV^{1}	Italy	
. .[85]	Prosper	$XIV^{3/4-4/4}$	Italy	
. .	Statius *A*, Vergil *G*, Terence	[86] –	Statius in Caprese (near Pieve Santo Stefano); others probably in or near Poppi	,
. .	Boethius, Prudentius *D*	$XV^{1/4}$	Veneto, possibly Padua	,
. [87] .	Horace *AP*, Ovid *Epistola Saphonis*, Statius *A*	XV^{2}	Possibly Viterbo	, ,
. .	Vergil *G*	XV^{2}	Italy	
. .	Terence	XVmid	Possibly Prato[88]	

85 Gehl ( ), , excludes this MS as 'Ital' meaning 'Written in Italy but almost surely not in Tuscany'; although illuminated figure (r) seems ostensibly to suggest Bolognese provenance, given the illumination's coloration (showing similarity to Aretine liturgical codices), Tuscan provenance cannot be ruled out, especially in view of the note (v) indicating that the MS was originally bought from Marchese Antonio Albergotti of Arezzo before being purchased for the then Biblioteca Magliabechiana in .

86 Billanovich ( ), , publishes the date of Statius as 'MCCCLXV' instead of MCCCLXXV: see r.

87 For ownership note by Cesare Malvicini da Viterbo, dated , see above, . Contains *Copa* from the *Appendix Vergiliana*, epitaphs of Vergil, pseudo-Ciceronian *Di erentiae* (r– v) and *Synonyma* (r– r), some Latin vocabulary notes (v– v), some brief humanist texts, and collection of unannotated quotations and *sententiae* from Latin authors (r– r).

88 See v– r for series of mainly vernacular epistolary salutations and invocations, mentioning various Pratesi.

	Seneca	XIV–XVc.	Umbria?[89]	

C. .	*Physiologus*, Prudentius *D*	XV[1]	Florence	
J. .	Lucan	XV[2]	Italy	
J. .	Sallust	XV[1]	Italy	
J. .	Horace *AP E*, Geo rey	*c.* –	Italy	,
J. .	Henry, *Ilias latina*, Vergil *E*, Statius *A*	*c.*	Bologna	, ,
J. .	Boethius	XIVex.	Probably Florence	
J. .	Boethius	XIII[4/4]; XIV[1]	Veneto, probably Venice	,
J. .	Boethius	XIII[2]	Italy	–

	Horace *O Epo. CS*	XVmid	Italy	
	Prosper[90]	XIVex.	Friuli	

89 Formerly . . . v: Ego Agabetus propria manu schripsi vel ego Iovanides s(ive) Vanide Fannensis.

90 Contents: r– v, r– v: Prosper, *Epigrammata* (*PL* . –), preceded by preface, part prose and part verse: inc. Iste Prosper fuit equitanicus vir. expl. venerit, hoc promat carmine leta fides. Text: inc. Innocentia dei vera est. expl. perdit adepta tepens.

v– v, r: pseudo-Prosper, *Poema conjugis ad uxorem* (*PL* . –), inc. Age iam precor mearum [...] expl. duos spiritus unus alat. Explicit liber Prosperi. Deo gratias amen.

NB: These two texts presented as one here as well as in other schoolbooks: e.g. BNCF . . (same preface, same texts without break, same closing: (v) Explicit liber prosperi deo gratias. Amen.); BNCF Magl. . , r– v (Explicit liber Prosperi. Deo gratias.); BML AD , r– r (Explicit liber Prosperi. Deo gratias. Amen.); BML sup. , r– r; BML Strozzi , v– r; BNCF Panciat. , r– r (Explicit liber Beati Prosperi. Deo gratias), which is acephalous, opening with 'Eternus vere solus', poem in *PL*, as Morpurgo (–), , notes.

[91]	Horace *AP E*	XIII–XIVc.	Florence or Tuscany	
	Statius *A*, *Cartula*, Cato[92]	–	Florence	, , –

.	Ovid *Epistola Sapphonis*[93]	XVmid	Florence[94]	
.	Theodulus, Prudentius *D*, *Cartula*, *Physiologus*, Bonvesin, Aesop, pseudo-Jerome *De contemptu mulierum*[95]	$XV^{2/4}$	Italy	

Folios here are out of order. should follow , then ; between v and r, there is a gap beginning with last line of poem of and ending with penultimate line of prose of : this corresponds to folios of the volume which have been lost; proses of and are omitted on v; should follow ; on v prose of is omitted; between v and r there is a gap beginning with second line of prose of and ending with last two lines of prose of ; on r prose of omitted, and on v proses of and omitted.

91 Lazzi and Scarlino ( ), , date codex 'Sec. XIV, metà', but that seems too late, given XIIIc. elements in script and the explicit formula written in *scrittura cancelleresca* (r).

92 Also contains *Doctrinale* and Latin composition exercises: see above, n. and .

93 All one humanist cursive script except for rear flyleaf (r), written by XV[2] current hand. Mixed school-type, humanist anthology. For humanist elements, see Galante (–), – ; Mazzatinti (–), , . School elements are:

r: On diphthongs, inc. Diphthongi sunt quatuor apud latinos.

r– v: On genitive terminations. Inc. Incipit de terminatione genitivi. Terminata in A masculina vel feminina faciunt genitivum addita e.

r– v: Ovid, *Epistola Sapphonis*

r– r: On prosody, inc. Omnes pedes quibus versus conficiuntur aut sunt duarum aut trium aut quatuor syllabarum.

r– r: fragment on formation of preterites and supines, acephalous apparently: inc. Si in o non purum verba desinent. Expl. Lucano in primo Letalis ambitus urbi. Finis.

r– v: orthography, inc. Vocum alia licterata alia inlicterata. Expl. Y autem solummodo in dictionibus peregrinis utimur. Finis. Also found in BNCF Magl. . : see Galante (–), . See above, n. .

r– v: On figures, from Donatus – (Keil – , ,) Inc. Barbarismus est una pars orationis vitiosa.

94 Signatures (r–v), all datable to XV[2]: Sante <...> Jacopo <...>; Hic liber est Laurentii de Marcho de Quona; di Ruberto di Giovanni di Stefano Corsini; Hic liber est Roberti Iohannis Stephani de Corsinis; Roberti Johannis de Corsinis.

95 Begins with *Ianua* and *Disticha Catonis*: see ch. , , and Appendix , n. , above. See Gehl ( ), – , and ( ), , who dates the MS to XIIIc. and XIII/XIVc.

. [96]	*Physiologus*, Aesop	XIIIex.	Italy, probably Tuscan or even Florentine	
. .	Seneca *Hercules furens* (fragment)	XVin.	Italy	
. .	Seneca *Octavia* (fragment)	XV^{1}	Italy	
.	Ovid and pseudo-Ovid *AA*, *Nux*, *Medicamina faciei*, *Amores* (.), *De virtutibus herbarum (De medicamine aurium)*, *Pulex*	XV$^{1/4}$	Florence	–
.	Vergil *A*	XIIc.	Italy	
.	Boethius (fragment)		Padua or nearby	
.	Ovid *Fasti*	XV$^{3/4}$	Italy, prob. Florence	
.	Ovid *Her.*		Castel-fiorentino	
.	Statius *A*, *Ilias latina*, Proba *Centones virgiliani*	*c.*	Florence	
. [97]	Cato, Prosper, *Ilias latina*, Prudentius *D*, Bonvesin, *Dissuasio Valerii ad Rufinum*, Pseudo-Boethius	XV^{1}	Italy	

96 Gehl ( ), (XIIIc.).

97 This is presumably the MS meant by Gehl ( ), when citing 'Magliabecchi , ' on : BNCF Magl. . no longer exists, having been transferred to the Fondo Principale (. .); it is a vernacular MS. For a description of BNCF Magl. . , see Black and Pomaro ( ), – .

. [98]	Bonvesin	XV^{1}	Italy	
. [99]	Horace *AP E*; Bonvesin, Statius *A*; *Ilias latina*	September ;[100] XV$^{2/4}$; XV$^{3/4}$	Italy, possibly Florence; Castiglion Fiorentino[101]	, ,
.	Statius *A*, *Ilias latina*, Henry, Maximianus *De senectute*[102]	October ( )– March [103]	Italy, probably Florence	,
.	Persius		Florence	
.	*Pamphilus*, Henry[104]	XIII$^{4/4}$	Italy, probably Tuscany[105]	

98 Gehl ( ), (XIV^{2}).

99 Fortuitous composite, assembled by Pietro Crinito (r: Pet. Criniti et amicorum), who wrote table of contents on (n.n.) and numbered folios throughout the volume accordingly. Contents have been for the most part described by Galante (–), – , with some additions by Kristeller (–), , : neither mentions ownership note and role of Crinito. Crinito assembled MS from several elements. The possible school texts are contained in two sections: ( ) – , copied by Geminiano di Ser Bartolo, with Horace finished on September (v: see below, n.) and the rest finished presumably not long afterwards, as the entire section reveals the same page layout and graphic style. ( ) – were written by one Angelo in Castiglion Fiorentino, with internal date of completion of March (X kal. aprilis , presumably *ab incarnatione*: see n. below); it is unclear how many of texts in this section are included under this date. The rest of the manuscript was assembled from several di erent sources and hands, all XV^{2}.

100 v: Iste liber scriptus fuit a me Geminiano Ser Bartoli decimo nono die mensis septembris et sub ora tertia et sub annis domini MCCCC.^{mo}XX ^{vo}. See Galante (–), .

101 v: Explicit liber Homeri de bello troiano amen finis. Ego Angelus explevi hunc librum nonis may in Castilione Florentino ad primam noctis horam. Qui scripsit hunc librum ducatur im paradisum. Angeli finis. v: Est finis. Virgilii P. Maronis Bucolica finaliter expliciunt. t°lvw finis. Explevi hunc librum kalendis aprilis* die dominico. [*die XXXI martii: *deletum*] Text of *Ilias latina* straddles two fascicles, and so must have been written before text of Vergil: therefore *Ilias latina* must have been completed no later than the previous year; continuity of graphic style and layout suggests a date of completion for *Ilias latina* not long before Vergil. See Galante (–), , for partial transcriptions of colophons.

102 Also contains two Latin poems by Giannantonio Porcello (v): 'Laurina ad Saxum adulescentem' (Bertalot ( ) n.), here entitled 'Laurina Saxo adoloscenti perpulcro hec pauca', and 'Lauris Etruria Cinisio adulescenti' (Bertalot ( ), n.), here entitled 'Lauris Cinesio puero formoso hec etiam pauca'; Guarino's *Alda* (Bertalot ( ), n.) on v– r, here anonymous; and on r– r 'Elegia Nic. Vulpis Vicentini' (Bertalot ( ), n.), here anonymous. This manuscript with its humanist poetry is not listed by Kristeller (–) nor by Bertalot ( ).

103 v: Explicit liber Statii *Achilleidos* die ottavo octobris; v: Explicit liber Galli die vigeximo secundo mensis febrarii; r: Expleto hoc libro die mensis marzi .

104 These texts, all written by one hand, were fortuitously combined on r– v with *Summa poenitentiae*, inc. Quoniam circa confessiones animarum (see Bloomfield ( ), – , where this version (XIII–XIVc., incomplete) is not mentioned), and on r– r with various Latin verses (not found in Walther ( ) or Bertalot ( )) (XV^{2}).

105 See vernacular glosses, above, n. .

.	Ovid *Epistulae ex Ponto*, Persius, *Ilias latina*[106]	c.	Florence	– , –
.	Prudentius *D*	XVmid	Italy	

.	Terence	XVmid	Italy	

	Boethius	XIII–XIVc.	W. Tuscany, possibly Lucca	
	Statius *A*[107]	XIV^{2}	Italy, possibly Bologna	
	Seneca *Hercules furens* (fragment)	XIVmid	Italy	

(r)	Vergil *A* (X –)	XIV$^{4/4}$	Pisa[108]	, –

–

	Horace *O;* Horace *AP*	XV^{2}; XVIin.	Italy	

106 Also contains Marsuppini's elegy on death of Bruni.

107 Copied by same scribe is *Rhetorica ad Herennium* (r– v). A principal glossing hand which annotates throughout the pseudo-Ciceronian text indicates that he was a pupil of Domenico di Bandino: Egregius doctor Magister Dominicus de Aritio disputabit cras XX^{a} hora in scolis suis (v). This teaching activity seems to have taken place in Bologna: Domenico di Bandino's pupil paid for a 'lecticam' in 'bolononinis', besides a 'capiciale et cultram pro quatuor bononenis' (v). Domenico di Bandino taught *Rhetorica ad Herennium* in Bologna during the s (see Hankey ( ),); although Domenico's full commentary on this text has never been found (Hankey ( ),), nevertheless an indication of his teaching of *Rhetorica ad Herennium* can probably be found in the marginalia made by this glossator.

108 Copied into a chronicle of Pisa, because it deals with the origins of Pisa (v. : Hos parere iubent Alfea ab origine Pise).

	Prosper, Aesop, *Cartula*, Prudentius *D*, *Physiologus*, Vitalis of Blois *Geta*[109]	XIVmid	Italy[110]	
	Lucan	XIII^2	Italy	–
	Lucan	–	Italy	
	Cicero *A*[111]	September 112	Italy	
	Sallust	XV^2	Italy, possibly Florence	
	Terence	XV^2	Italy, probably Florence[113]	

109 Also contains two grammatical works by Goro d'Arezzo, *Vocabula* and *Regule parve*: see above, , – and Gehl ( ), – .

110 Passed into Florentine Gherardi and Valori families by later XVc: (r (n.n.)) Hic liber mei Filippi Bartholommei Filippi de Valoribus et amicorum eius; (r) hic liber est Filippi Bartolomei Filippi de Valoribus Florentie; (v) iste liber est nobilis Bernardi Francisci de de [*sic*] Gherardis civis nobilis florentinus [*sic*]. Gehl's reference ( ), , to an ownership note by 'Bernardo di Filippo Valori', unmentioned in this MS, seems to be a mistaken reference to Bernardo Gherardi.

111 Also contains unglossed texts of Cicero's *Paradoxa*, Plutarch's *De liberis educandis* in Guarino's translation, pseudo-Jerome's *De o ciis liberorum erga parentes*, Cicero's *De senectute* and various Ciceronian familiar letters.

112 r: Finis est anno domini MºCCCCºLX xiª settembris. Melchior Valgimiliensis Mº s(ubscripsit) B. R. Reading in Morpurgo *et al.* (–), , (MCCCCLXXI) cannot be correct, given the 'a' suprascript; alternative reading would be MCCCCLXX iª, but this seems unlikely because xiª is on the next line, and the 'a' suprascript is written above both the 'x' and the 'i'. None of the indictions of or correspond to a reading of MCCCCLX xiª [indictione]. The best solution seems to be 'xiª [die] settembris'.

113 r, ownership note, written in late XVc. hand: 'Baccii Valorii kt mà See Morpurgo *et al.* (–), , .

Appendix IV

FLORENCE, BIBLIOTECA RICCARDIANA

[114]	*Ilias latina* (r– r)[115]	XIVex.	Italy	
	Boethius	XIVmid	Italy	
[116]	Prosper	XVmid	Italy	
	Doctrina rudium, John the Abbot, pseudo-Ovid *De lumaca*, *Ilias latina*, Martin of Braga *Formula honestae vitae*, Cicero *A S P*	$XV^{2/4}$	Italy	,
	Prosper, Aesop	XVin.[117]	Florence[118]	
[119]	Prosper, Prudentius *D*, Cato; Vergil *E* (I only)	XVmid; XVIc.	Florence	

114 Cf. De Robertis and Miriello ( ), (XV^1); Gehl ( ), excludes this manuscript as 'XV', but the small Gothic writing could well date from end of XIVc.

115 Also contains grammatical texts, fortuitously combined with *Ilias latina*: see above, n. , , n. , – n. .

116 Gehl ( ), , dates this 'XIV', also writing, 'Ownership marks v indicate early monastic provenance'; but annotations there (Iste Prosper est fratrum Sancti Donati de Scopeto, di Sancto Donato in Scopeto) are written in a hand with humanist features, datable to XV^2.

117 Gehl ( ), : 'XIV'; however, straight 'd's and frequent failure to form counterbalanced curves suggest XVc. dating, also supported by reference to in *probationes*: see below, n. .

118 Florentine provenance clear from *probationes*: r: Simo(n) Giovannis Tommasi Florentie Filippii; in same hand mention of besides payment record: Giovanni di Tommaso <...> trecento d'oro, pagammo per loro Giovanni di Simone di Francesco e compagni setaiuoli <...> furono per due balle di panni di trenta Fl. l'uno. Another hand: [...] allochamo M° Giovanni Quaratesi in Firenze [...]

119 Work of the first owner, Andrea di Tommaso Minerbetti; then passed to his son; remained in family during XVIc., coming into possession first of Messer Tommaso Minerbetti, then of Bernardo Minerbetti, who added Vergil's first eclogue. v: Iste liber est mei Andree Tonasi de Minebectis; v: Iste liber est mei Tomae? Andree? de Minerbectis; v: Scripsit n(omina) propria s(ua) manu D. Tomas Minerbectus eques; r: Scripsit manu propria Bernardectus Minerbectus. For slightly di erent transcriptions, see De Robertis and Miriello ( ), – , who do not clarify that Vergil's eclogue (r– v) was written by Bernardo Minerbetti probably in early XVIc., so that their overall dating ('sec. XV metà') applies only to section written by Andrea Minerbetti (r– v).

[120]	Prudentius *D*, Vitalis of Blois *Geta*, *Physiologus*, *Doctrina rudium*; Prosper	XV[1]; XIV[1]	Italy	,
	Prudentius *P*, Vergil *E*, *Physiologus*[121]	XV[1]	Florence	,
	Bonvesin, *Cartula*	XV[1] [122]	Probably Florence[123]	
	Vergil	November [124]	Italy	
	Vergil *A*	XV[1]	Italy	
	Val. Max.	XV[1]	Italy, possibly Viterbo	
	Val. Max.	XV[1]	Italy	
[125]	Cicero *De oratore Orator*	XV[1]	Italy	
	Cicero *DT*	XV[1]	Italy, possibly Florence	
	Cicero *DT*	XV[1]	Italy	

[120] Gehl ( ), , dates first section XIV[2]; however, broad, widely spaced script, with frequent -shaped 'r's, suggest XVc. He implies there were two scribes in this first part, whereas there are three, all contemporary: one for Prudentius, another for *Geta* and *Physiologus*, third for *Doctrina rudium*.

[121] Also contains Filippo di Naddo's *Regule* and Albertino da Monte-Latrone's *Verbalia*: see above, n. , – , .

[122] Gehl ( ), , dates second section (*Cartula*) XIVex., but it is XVc.: consistent humanist features, such as Caroline 'g's (e.g. r, l. up).

[123] Ownership note (r), datable to mid-Quattrocento, nearly contemporaneous with copying of both sections of composite: Iste liber est Marci Hioannis Neri de Chambis cives florentinus. See Gehl ( ), .

[124] v: Explicit liber Virgilii *Eneidos* die XXV novembris M°CCCC°LXIIII°. See De Robertis and Miriello ( ), .

[125] See De Robertis and Miriello ( ), , where texts are not correctly listed; they state r– v contain *De oratore*, which ends on v, where acephalous version of *Orator* begins, ending on v. On references to Barzizza here, see Sabbadini ( ), ; Rizzo ( ), , , .

	Cicero *A*[126]	XVmid	Italy	
	Seneca	XIV^{2}	Italy	
	Terence	XV^{1}	Italy	
	Valerius Maximus	XVmid	Italy, possibly Florence	
	Lucan	XIII^{1}	Italy	
	Ovid *RA*	XV^{1}	S. Italy	
	Boethius	XV$^{2/4}$	Florence	
	Boethius	XIVex.	Arezzo	
	Cicero *O*[127]	XV$^{3/4}$	Italy	
	Cicero *SAPSS*	XVmid	Italy	
	Cicero *De oratore*	XV^{2}	Italy	
	Cicero *O*	XVmid	Italy	
	Cicero *S A P*	September [128]	Venice	
	Avianus, Prudentius *D*, Vitalis of Blois *Geta*[129]	XV^{1}	Italy	
	Cicero *A*	XV^{1}	Italy	
[130]	Cicero *O P S A*	XVmid	Italy	

126 Also contains Cicero *Orations*, Bruni *De studiis et litteris*, Plautus *Menaechmi*, Cicero *De amicitia*, Bruni *Orations* and papal privilege ( ), all unglossed (except for some summarial marginalia to last text by copyist).

127 Also contains Bruni's translation of Basil's *Epistula ad adolescentes* and two letters by Traversari. Prefaced to *De o ciis* is Barzizza's *praelectio* to *De o ciis*, here anonymous, r– r: inc. Incipit vita Marci Tulii Ciceronis. <E>t si inter summas occupationes. expl. quam ad M. filium de omni o ciorum genere Cicero scripsit accessus fiat etcetera. Incipit given by Kristeller (–), , . For an edition of this text, see Fera ( ), – ; Pigman ( ), – : neither lists this MS.

128 Dated and September and copied in Venice by Fra Bartolomeo da Verona: for dated colophons, see De Robertis and Miriello ( ), .

129 Fortuitous composite with works by Cicero, Ficino, Timoteo Ma ei and a Florentine o cial missive. 130 See De Robertis and Miriello ( ), .

	Cicero *S A P*	XVmid	Italy, probably Florence	
	Cicero *A S P SS* (beginning)	XVmid	Italy	
	Cicero *O*	XVmid	Italy, probably Florence	
	Cicero *O*[131]	XV^2	Italy, probably Florence	
	Horace	XIc. (r– v), XIIc.	Switzerland/ Austria? or Italy?	
	Horace *A E*	XIV^1	N. Italy	
	Horace *A S E*	XII–XIIIc.	Central Italy	
	Horace *A S E*	XIIImid	Italy	
132	Horace *A E*	XIV^2	Italy	
133	Horace *E*	XIV^2	Italy	
	Horace	XII–XIIIc.[134]	Italy	
135	Horace *E CS*	XV^2	Italy	
	Sallust	XIIc.	Italy	
	Cicero *SPASS*	XV^2	Italy	
136	Sallust	April	Rieti	
	Sallust	XV^2	Florence	

131 Also contains pseudo-Seneca *De quattuor virtutibus* (unglossed), grammatical notes (written by owner Silvestro Aldobrandini), and two prose passages, one vernacular, other Latin, latter in Aldobrandini's hand (v).

132 Later passed into ownership of Francesco Altobianco degli Alberti and Landino: (r) Iste liber est Francisci Altoblanci de Albertis de Florentia; posuit hoc manu propria V novenbris MCCCC° XXXIII. Hunc librum ego Landinus a Franco Altobianco dono accepi die augusti . Landino added marginalia, often erudite (citing e.g. Ovid's *Fasti* on r) but no interlinear glosses; apparently no glossing by Francesco.

133 Contains *Epistles*, .i. to end. Because just the first lines are missing, it must originally have formed part of larger anthology, probably with *Ars poetica*.

134 r–v and r– r are two separate XVc. restorations.

135 See De Robertis and Miriello ( ), .

136 See De Robertis and Miriello ( ), – .

	Ovid *RA*, Ovid *Epistola Saphonis* (copies), Vergil *G*, Sallust *BC*[137]	XV²	Tuscany, possibly Volterra	, ,
138	Aesop	XIVex.	Italy	
	Juvenal, Persius	XV¹	Italy, possibly Florence	,
	Juvenal	XV¹	Italy	
	Juvenal	XIImid	Italy	
139	Terence	December	Italy	
	Juvenal, Persius	XVmid	Italy, possibly Florence	,
140	Persius	XV¹	Italy	
141	Cato, *Cartula*, Prudentius *D*, *Physiologus*, Theodulus, Bonvesin, Prosper, Aesop[142]	XV¹	Florence	
143	Cato, Aesop	XV¹	Italy	
	Boethius	XIVmid	Florence or nearby	
	Boethius	XIVmid	probably Florence or nearby	
	Boethius	XIV–XVc.	Florence or nearby	

137 Also contains secondary grammatical anthology: see above, n. , n. .
138 See Gehl ( ), . 139 See De Robertis and Miriello ( ), .
140 Fortuitously joined to anthology of Latin texts, described by De Robertis and Miriello ( ), – , where Persius is not mentioned. 141 See Gehl ( ), – (XIV²).
142 Also contains Filippo di Naddo *Regule grammaticales*: see above, n. , .
143 Gehl ( ), : XIV², but both parts of composite are written in widely spaced late Gothic script typical of XVc.

[144]	Sallust		Florence (Badia a Settimo)	
	Cicero and pseudo-Cicero *Orations*, Vitalis of Blois, *Geta et Birria* (beginning)[145]	XVmid	Italy	
	Ovid *Her.*	XVmid	Florence	
	Persius	XII–XIIIc.	Italy	
[146]	Cicero *SS S A P*	, [147]	Florence	
[148]	Aesop, *Physiologus*, Theodulus, Henry	$XV^{1/4}$	Florence	
[149]	Henry	XIVex.	Tuscan	

[144] See De Robertis and Miriello ( ), – . Also contains two brief logical texts, written by scribe Don Roberto, filling blank folios of final fascicle, r– v.

[145] Also contains Buonaccorso da Montemagno's *De nobilitate.*

[146] See De Robertis and Miriello ( ), .

[147] Copied by Florentine Bernardo di Ser Francesco d'Ambra, completing first text on December , second on March , third on August and fourth on September . De Robertis and Miriello ( ), , transcribe relevant colophons, but give wrong corresponding date for 'septimo kalendas ottobrias': September, not 'ottobre '.

[148] Gehl ( ), – : XIV[1], but hands of the copyists of this deliberately organized composite are all late Gothic, with -shaped 'r's at beginning of words and wide spacing. Some are written on palimpsest parchment dating from the s (r: anno M. tregent(esim)o trige <...>) making this early dating unlikely. Last text shows influence of humanist script, with frequent straight final 's's beginning on v.

[149] Gehl ( ), – ; De Robertis and Miriello, (manuscript only cited); Cremaschi ( ) (manuscript R), . recto (n.n.): Iste liber est mei Gorgius [*sic*] Ser Amerigi de Vespucci<s>; verso: Iste liber est mei Ser Amerigi Stasii de Vespuccis; v: Iste liber est Anibaldi Ser Johannis de Piscia. Amen. Anibaldus. r: Iste liber est Anibaldi Ser Johannis. Iste liber est mei Ser Amerigi Stasii de Vespuccis de Florentia. Some of these ownership notes published with errors of Latin grammar and transcription in Gehl ( ), . Not cited by de la Mare (b or). Giorgio Antonio Vespucci's signature here must go back to his first years of learning to read and write: it does not correspond to any other writing style used by him; there are mistakes in Latin; the handwriting is distinctly childish; and Henry of Settimello was normally read as schoolbook. Handwriting of Anibaldo di Ser Giovanni da Pescia is datable to XVc.; his note of possession must refer to ownership before it passed to the Vespucci. Signatures indicate that it was owned first by Giorgio Antonio's father, Ser Amerigo di Stagio Vespucci (–), before coming into his own possession.

150	Cicero *Three orations, P A*[151]	XV^{1}	N. Italy (Lombardy)	
	Cicero *De imperio Cn. Pompei*, Persius, Statius *T* (vv. –)[152]	September – April 153	Italy	, ,
	Sallust, Cicero *Three orations*[154]	155	Città di Castello/ Tuscany[156]	
.	*Ilias latina*	XIII^{1}	S. Italy	
C	Statius *A*	XV^{1}	Tuscan, prob. Florentine[157]	
	Maximianus[158]	XIII	Italy	
159	Aesop (fragment)	XIV (late)	Italy	
	Juvenal	XV^{2}	Italy	
	Juvenal	XV$^{1/mid}$	Italy, prob. Florence	
	Persius, *Ilias latina*; *Liber cerdonis*[160]	XV^{1}; XV^{2}	Italy	,

150 See De Robertis and Miriello ( ), – , for partial description of the entire manuscript besides further bibliography.

151 Also contains other works sometimes associated with education, e.g. Plutarch's *De liberis educandis*, tr. Guarino; Bruni's *De studiis et litteris*; Barzizza's *Epistolae ad exercitationem editae*: none is glossed.

152 Also contains Guarino's *Carmina di erentialia*, r– v.

153 See De Robertis and Miriello ( ), . Persius has internal date ( ) on upper margin of v. These texts included in anthology of classical / humanist poetry, vernacular rhymes and other miscellaneous writings.

154 For other texts, see De Robertis and Miriello ( ), .

155 For dated colophon, see De Robertis and Miriello ( ), .

156 Written by Pistoiese notary, working for Florentine *podestà* in Città di Castello; therefore it may have been taken back to Tuscany.

157 Palimpsest over parchment sheets coming from account book with florin as currency.

158 Forms part of fortuitous composite with Horace's letters; this text, datable to XII–XIIIc., is not Italian (possibly German?). Few marginal Italian Quattrocento annotations to Horace, and none to Maximianus. No common glossing hand between two texts.

159 See Gehl ( ), (XIV^{2}). A miscellany assembled XVIIIc., also containing fragment of Filippo di Naddo's *Regule*: see above, n. , n. .

160 Also contains some vernacular *terzine* (r) and other vernacular verses (r–v). First and second texts written by same hand (XV^{1}) but working in two distant periods in life and identifying himself as 'Petrus Franciscus' (r), while other section copied by hand clearly XV^{2}.

	Prudentius *D*, Henry; Cicero *A*[161]	;	Marches of Ancona (Monte Ulmo)	,
	Cicero *O*, Geo rey, Statius *A*[162]	XV$^{1/4}$	Italy	, ,
	Vergil *A*	XV^{1}	Italy	
	Boethius	XIVmid	Probably N. Italy	

161 Also contains anonymous *Orthographia parvis et utilis* (r– r), inc. Ortogrophia est ordinatio licterarum in silabis (see above, –), not listed by Bursill-Hall ( ) and Guarino's translation of Plutarch's *De liberis educandis* (r– r), not listed by Kristeller (–).

162 A large anthology, of which earliest element is Sallust (r– r), begun by notarial hand (r– r) and then completed by less current Gothic hand, leaving this colophon: Explicit liber Salustii *De jugurtino bello* seu etiam *Catellinario*, deo gratias. Amen. Qui scripxit scribat semper, cum domino vivat, vivat in celis <Basilius de Sancto Genesio> in nomine felix. Expletus et completus in terra Montis Ulmi sub anno domini M°III^{c}LXXXXIII° indictione prima tempore Domini Bonifatii pape noni <de: *deletum*> die penultimo mensis maii. Basilio da S. Genesio then proceeded to read both Sallustian texts, leaving regular Latin / vernacular glosses, revealing him as mature reader without apparent school connections. Subsequently, another group of texts added to this core: Cicero's *De o ciis* (r– r) followed by traditional epitaphs of Cicero by twelve sages (r– r), Geo rey of Vinsauf's *Poetria nova* (r– v) and Statius's *Achilleis* (r– v). These texts were written by several di erent hands, datable to XVin. and working together, as these folios all share same water mark (large R). To this group of texts, series of humanist compositions and translations (by Petrarch and Poggio), pair of Malatesta letters besides Cicero's *Somnium Scipionis* were added after (the date of several of them: see v, v) at end of the original fascicles (all with the same R-shaped watermark) and ending on v. Another group of humanist texts (by Salutati and Bruni) occupy succeeding folios (up to v), all with less distinctive mountain-shaped watermark. The following Sallust texts, v– r contain letter to Rodolfo da Camerino (dated) and extract from Livy on Cicero's death. Original front flyleaf verso has anonymous (XIVc.) list 'omnium meorum librorum <...tatus> Perusii:

In primis Tullius de o tiis
It(em) unum Valerium
It(em) unum par Tragediarum
It(em) unum Bononienatum
It(em) unum librum Auctorit(atum)
It(em) unum Doctrinale
<...> Tullii
It(em) Tullius Recthoricorum
It(em) unum librum legis
It(em) unum Terrentium
It(em) unum Boetium
It(em) unum P(ri)sianum
It(em) unum quaternum M(agistri) Salimben(is)
It(em) unum bastardellum cum certis sententiis
It(em) unum libellum in arte rhetorice
It(em) unum quaternum
It(em) unum librum notabiliorum
It(em) robrice omnium librorum regum.'

Only the first three texts (*De o ciis*, *Poetria nova*, *Achilleis*) show signs of school use.

	Prosper, Geo rey (fragment)[163]	$XV^{3/4}$; XVmid	Italy	,
	Terence	XV^{1}	Italy	
164	Prosper	XIV^{2}	Venice	

MANUSCRIPTS EXAMINED AND EXCLUDED

,

Carte Cerchi ; Carte Strozziane . ; Manoscritti ; Ospedale di S. Matteo .

,

AD , , , , , , , , , , , , , , , ,
, , , , , , , , , , , , , , ,
, , , , , , , , , , , , ; Antinori
, , , , ; Ashb. , , , , , , , , , , , ,
, , , , , , , , , , , , , , ,
, , , , , , , , *, , , , , ,
, , , , , , , , , , , ,
, , , , , , , ; Ashb. Appendice ,
; Biscioni ; CS , , , , , , , , , , , , , ,
, , , , , , , , , , , , , , , , ,
, , , , , , , , , , , , , , ,
, , , , , , , , , , , , , , ,
; Edili , , , , , , , , , , , , ,
, , , , , , ; Gaddi , , , , , , ,
, , ; Med. Fies. , , , , ; Med. Pal. , , , ,

[163] Apparently fortuitous composite, containing fragmentary secondary grammar: see above, .

[164] Gehl ( ) publishes a 'descriptive census of elementary and intermediate Latin reading books written in Tuscany in the late thirteenth and fourteenth centuries' ( ). However, he did not consult or cite twelve manuscripts of traditional school authors in Florentine libraries (BRF ; BNCF .. ; BML sin. ; BML . sup. ; BRF ; BML sup. ; BML sup. ; BML Ashb. ; BML Ashb. ; BML Redi ; BNCF Magl. . ; BML . ; BRF) besides three manuscripts of Geo rey of Vinsauf's *Poetria nova* (BRF ; BML Strozzi ; BML AD); he also did not consult or cite out of a total of school manuscripts of Boethius's *Consolation* in Florentine libraries (BML . ; BNCF .. ; BRF ; BRF ; BNCF CS J. . ; BML sin. ; BRF ; BML sup. ; BML CS ; BML . ; BML . ; BML Ashb. ; BML Edili ; BML . ; BML Strozzi ; BML . ; BML . ; BML sup. ; BNCF CS J. . ; BML CS ; BNCF ..).

, ; Pl. . , . , . , dxt. , sin. , sin. , . , sin. , sin. , sin. , sin. , sin. , sin. , dxt. , sin. , sin. , . , . , sin. , sin. , sin. , sin. , sin. , sin. , sin. , . , . , . , . , . , sin. , sin. , inf. , inf. , inf. , inf. , inf. , inf. , sup. , sup. , sup. , sup. , inf. , inf. , sup. , sup. , sup. , sup. , sup. , sup. , sup. , sup. , sup. , sup. , sup. , sup. , sup. , sup. , sup. , sup. , sup. . , sup. , sup. , sup. , sup. , sup. , sup. , sup. , sup. , inf. , inf. , inf. , inf. , inf. , sup. . , sup. . , sup. . , sup. , sup. , sup. , sup. , sup. , sup. , sup. , sup. , sup. , sup. . , sup. . , sup. . , sup. . , sup. , sup. ; Redi , , , , , , , ; Rinuccini , , , , , , ; San Marco , ; Segni ; Strozzi , .

,

A.c.s. , B. . , C. , C. , C. , C. .

,

Moreni ; Palagi ,

,

. , ., . . ,. . ,. . ,. . ,. . , . , . . ,. . . ,
. , . . ,. . ,. . , . . ,. . , . . ,. . ,.
. , . . , . . ,. . ,. . , . . , . . , . . ,.
. ,. . ,. . ,. . ,. . ,. . ,. . , . ,
. , . , . , . , . , . , . ,
. , . , . ; Banco Rari , , ; Capponi (Vincenzo)
; CS A. . , A. . , A. . , A. . , B. . ,
B. . , C. . , C. . , C. . , C. . , E. . ,
G. . , G. . , G. . , G. . , J. . , J. . , J. . , J. . , J. . ,
J. . , J. . , J. . , J. . , J. . , J. . , J. . , J. . , J. . , J. . , J. . ,
J. . , J. . , J. . , J. . , J. . , J. . , J. . , J. . , J. . , J. . ,
J. . ; Landau Fin. , , , , , , , , , , ,
; Magl. . , . , . , . , . , . , . , . , . , . *bis*, . , . ,
. , . , . , . , . , . , . , . , . , . ,
. , . , . , . , . , . , . , . , . , . ,
. , . , . , . , . , . , . , . , . , . ,
. , . , . , . , . , . , . , . , . , . ,
. , . , . , . , . , . ; Magl. Append.
. , . , . , striscia ; NA , , , , ,
, , , , , , , , ; Palatino , , ,
n. ; Panciatichi , , , , ; Rossi Cassigoli

,

, , , , , , , , , , , , , , , ,
, , , , , , , , , , , , , , ,
, , , , , , , , , , , , , , ,
, , , , , , , , , , , , , , ,
, , , , , , , , , , , , , , ,
, , , , , , , , , , , , , , ,
, , , , , , , , , , , , , , ,

, , , , , , , , , , , , , , ,
, , , , , , , , , , , , , , , ,
, , , , , , , , , , , , , , ,
, , , , , , , , , , , ,
, , , , , , , , , , , ,
, , , , , , , , ,

Theoretical grammar manuscripts in Florentine libraries examined and included or eliminated as Italian school grammars

MANUSCRIPTS INCLUDED AS ITALIAN SCHOOL GRAMMARS

,

Carte Bardi . ; CStrozz. . ; Manoscritti ; Ospedale S. Matteo .

,

AD , , , , , , ; Antinori , ; Ashb. [2], , , , , , , ; Ashb. Append. , ; CS ; Gaddi , , , ; Med. Pal. , ; Pl. . , . , . , . ,[1] sup. , sup. ; Strozzi , , , .

,

A.c.s. , C. .

,

Moreni ; Palagi , .

,

. . , . . , . . ; CS B. . , G. . , G. . , J. . , J. . , J. . , J. . , J. . ; Landau Fin. , ; Magl. . , . , . , . , . , . , . , . , . , . , . , . , . , . ; NA , ; Palat. n. ; Panciat. .

,

, .

1 4/4, v– v. Possible school-level treatise on diminutives, giving clear and simple rules on their formation and citing Sallust, Juvenal and Cicero. Inc. Diminutivum est quod diminution-em sui primitivi absolute demostrat. Bursill-Hall ( ), , gives a slightly inaccurate incipit.

MANUSCRIPTS ELIMINATED AS ITALIAN SCHOOL GRAMMARS

,

Ashb. , , , , ; Gaddi ; Pl. . , . , sin. , sin. , . , . , . , . , . , . , . ; San Marco .

,

C. .

,

. ; CS A. . , B. . , C. . ,[2] G. . , G. . , J. . , J. . , J. . ; Magl. . , . , . , . *bis*, . , . , . , . ; Magl. Append. striscia ; NA ; Panciatichi .

, , , , , .

[2] This MS, written by XVc. French hand, was identified by Bursill-Hall ( ), , as containing 'Petrus Stroza, Rosarium gramaticae', on – , 'Inc: In omni idiomate grammatica doceri potest. Nota quod verbum transitivum a parte post dependet per modum receptibilis . . .' However, this description needs almost complete revision. Firstly, the correct incipit is: In omni ydyomate gramatica docere potest nos recte loqui. Secondly, the treatise here has nothing to do with Pietro Strozzi, a grammar teacher working in at Naples. Pietro Strozzi taught a text entitled *Rosarium grammatice* to a pupil called 'Joannes Marcus' from Parma, who finished transcribing the latter text on July in that year. All this information is contained in the colophon of this latter text, now found in BNP N. Acq. , as noted on , n. by Thurot ( ), who also gave some extracts and a general description. This Paris MS, as described by Thurot, has nothing in common with the Florentine MS except for the title, which was a generic name for a collection, sometimes grammatical (see e.g. Domenico di Bandino's *Rosarium* found in BN Marciana MS lat. (.): see Zorzanello (–), II, –), and for an identification in BNCF CS C. . , r by a XVIc. or XVIIc. hand as 'Grammatica M. Petri'. (There is no similar contemporaneous attribution in BNCF CS C. . ; it must derive from fact that the second half of this MS contains *Summa de arte dicendi* edita a Magistro Petro de la Hezardiere: v.) Bursill-Hall seems to have conflated the description of BNP N. Acq. , which has the incipit of fol. (Nota quod verbum transitivum a parte post dependet per modum receptibilis) with the incipit of BNCF CS C. . . In fact, BNCF CS C. . is the text of a Latin grammar not from Italy but rather from France, as is clear from its many French geographical references (v– v: Secanam, Franciam, Montem Pessulanum, Avinionem, Trecas, Gebennas, Ludino, Lotaro, Vigena, Ausono, Monte Aureo, Rothomam, Rodano, Rothomago, Suessione). This MS is cited as an Italian grammar by Jensen ( ), , .

Authorities cited explicitly in manuscripts of major school authors in Florentine libraries[1]

Shelf-mark	Author(s) cited
AD	Vergil
AD	Hugutio, Vergil
AD	Gerald of Wales, Lucan, Ovid (*Her.*), Papias, Statius
AD	Luke
AD	Aristotle, Augustine (*De civitate dei*), Benvenuto da Imola (*Romuleon*), Boethius (*Cons.*), Cicero (*De oratore*, *O*, *De inventione*, *A*, *Philippicae*, *P*, *In Verrem*, *S*), Dante, Eutropius, Frontinus, Horace, Isidore, Justinus, Livy, Lucan, Macrobius, Martianus Capella, Orosius, Ovid (*Fasti*, *RA*, *Met.*), Petrarch, Pliny (*Naturalis historia*), Plutarch, Pomponius Mela, Sallust, Servius, Seneca (*De ira*, *De beneficiis*, *Epistulae*), Solomon, Suetonius, Vergil (*G*, *A*)
Ashb.	Augustine, Cicero (*Academica*), Horace, Hugutio, Isidore, Seneca, Servius, Sallust
Ashb.	Aristotle, Gellius, Sallust, Seneca, Terence, Tibullus, Vergil
Ashb.	Ovid (*Tristia*)
Ashb.	Aristotle, Cicero (*O*), Macrobius, Quintilian, Seneca, Valerius Maximus, Vergil (*A*)

[1] Authors are cited generically in the MS unless otherwise indicated.

Authorities cited by major school authors

Shelf-mark	Author(s) cited
Ashb.	Bene da Firenze, Giovanni da Genova (*Catholicon*), Hugutio, Papias
CS	Augustine (*De civitate dei*)
CS	Claudian, Juvenal, Lucan, Ovid (*Fasti*, *Her.*, *AA*), Plato, Vergil
CS	Pliny the elder
CS	Plato
CS	Ovid
CS	Giovanni Tortelli
CS	Juvenal, Vergil (*A*)
CS	Boethius (*Cons.*), Ovid (*Her.*), Statius (*Thebais*), Vergil
CS	Vergil (*A*), Isidore, Ovid (*Fasti*)
CS	Hugutio
CS	Ovid (*Met.*), Varro (apud Aug.?), Vergil (*G*)
Edili	Boethius (*Cons.*)
Edili	Festus, Servius
Edili	Varro
.	Plato
.	Aesop, Cicero (*O*), Terence
.	Cicero (*O*)
.	Pliny the Elder, Ptolemy, Strabo
.	Papias, Vergil
.	Boethius, Petrarch, Valerius Maximus
.	Seneca, Valerius Maximus
.	Seneca, Valerius Maximus
.	Boccaccio, Evrard de Béthune (*Graecismus*), Fulgentius, Lucan, Macrobius, Pliny (*Naturalis historia*), Seneca (*Tragoediae*)

Shelf-mark	Author(s) cited
.	Vergil
.	Vergil
.	Ovid (*RA*), Seneca (*Tragoediae*)
.	Seneca (*Tragoediae*)
.	Alexander of Villedieu (*Doctrinale*), Evrard de Béthune (*Graecismus*), Ovid (*Met.*), Seneca (*Tragoediae*), Vergil (*A*)
.	Augustine (*De civitate dei*), Boccaccio, Cicero (*A*), pseudo-Seneca (*De moribus*), Vergil (*A*)
.	Alexander (?), Aristotle, Boethius, Cicero, Dante, Fulgentius, Gerald of Wales, Isidore, Josephus, Ovid (*Met.*, *Her.*), Suetonius, Vergil (*A*)
.	Cicero (*P*)
.	Augustine, Cicero, Horace, Priscian, Servius
.	Horace (*AP*), Lucan, Ovid, Sallust, Statius
.	Lucan, Ovid, Seneca, Valerius Maximus
.	Ovid (*Her.*)
.	Guarino, Livy, Pliny (*Naturalis historia*)
.	Aristotle (*Nicomachean Ethics*), Augustine (*De civitate dei*), Boethius (*Cons.*), Cicero (*O*, *De divinatione*, *A*, *P*, *DT*), Festus, Frontinus, Hugutio, Lucan, Orosius, Sallust, Vergil (*A*)
.	Lucan, Q. C. Rufus, Valerius Maximus, Vergil
.	Cato, Cicero (*DT*), Horace, Isidore, Juvenal, Lucan, Ovid (*Met.*, *Fasti*), Martial, New Testament, Seneca (*Epistulae*, *Tragoediae*, *De beneficiis*), Solomon

Authorities cited by major school authors

Shelf-mark	Author(s) cited
.	Nonius Marcellus
.	Aristotle, Augustine, Hugutio, Livy, Orosius, Sallust, Seneca (*Tragoediae*), Servius, Terence, Valerius Maximus
.	Plato
inf. .	Cicero (*De inventione*), Gregory the Great, Vegetius
sup.	Livy
sup.	Servius
sup.	Alain de Lille, Aristotle, Boethius (*Cons.*), Horace, Isidore, Ovid (*Met.*), Petrarch, *Rhetorica ad Herennium*, Vergil (*A*)
sup.	Horace, Ovid (*Her.*), Statius, Vegetius, Vergil (*G*)
Redi	Cicero (*S*), Sallust
Redi	Cicero (*De oratore*), Vergil
Rinuccini	Nonius Marcellus
S. Marco	Alain de Lille
Strozzi	Livy
Strozzi	Aristotle, Eutropius, Lucan, Ovid, Suetonius
Strozzi	Cicero (*De oratore*, *S*), Geo rey of Vinsauf, Hugutio, Isidore, Ovid (*Met.*), Quintilian, Seneca, Servius, Terence, Vergil

Shelf-mark	Author(s) cited
.	Boethius (*Cons.*), Cicero (*Rhetorica* (unclear which text), *O*), Dares Phrygius, Fulgentius, Horace, Hugutio, Isidore, Lucan, Martianus Capella, New Testament, Orosius, Ovid (*Met.*, *Epistulae ex Ponto*), Petrarch, Petrus Helias, Pietro da Moglio, Priscian, Seneca, Solomon, Statius (*A*), Valerius Maximus, Vergil (*A*)
. .	Horace, Lucretius, Sallust, Servius, Varro
Banco Rari	Aristotle (*Politics*), Suetonius, Vergil
Magl. .	Horace, Seneca (*Tragoediae*), Vergil (*A*)
Magl. .	Ovid
Magl. .	Cicero (*Epistulae*), Dante, Donatus, Plato, Vergil (*G*)
Magl. Append. .	Priscian, Servius
NA	Lucan, Ovid (*Her.*, *Met.*), Vergil
Palatino	Servius
Palat. Baldovinetti	Priscian, Sallust, Vergil
Panciat.	Cicero (*SS*)

Authorities cited by major school authors

Shelf-mark	Author(s) cited
	Ambrose, Aristotle, Augustine (*De civitate dei*, *Epistulae*), Averroes, Boethius (*Cons.*), Cicero (*DT*, *De oratore*), Hugutio, Isidore, Jerome (*Epistulae*), Juvenal, Livy, Lucan, Orosius, Ovid (*Her.*), Plato, Sallust, Seneca (*De beneficiis*, *Epistulae*), Solinus, Vergil (*A*), Vegetius
	Isidore
	Barzizza, Cicero, Martianus Capella, Ovid, Plato, *Rhetorica ad Herennium*, Valerius Maximus
	Cicero (*Pro Archia*, *De finibus benorum et malorum*), Donatus, Festus, Horace, Ovid, Servius, Valerius Maximus, Varro
	New Testament, Valerius Maximus
	Cicero (*O*), Hugutio, Ovid (*Met.*), Justinus, Petrarch, Seneca, Statius
	Vergil (*A*)
	Livy, Seneca
	Augustine (*De civitate dei*), Valerius Maximus
	Aristotle (*Nicomachean Ethics*), Benvenuto da Imola, Cicero, Gregory the Great, Isidore, Jerome, Lucan, *Rhetorica ad Herennium*, New Testament, Sallust, Seneca (*Epistulae*), Servius, Terence, Valerius Maximus, Vergil (*G*)
	Livy, Lucan, Valerius Maximus
	Isidore
	Ovid (*Her.*)
	Priscian
	Cicero, Hugutio, Priscian
	Livy, Orosius, Pliny the Younger

Shelf-mark	Author(s) cited
	Cicero (*Epistulae*, *O*), Vergil
	Pseudo-Aristotle (*De pomo*), Boethius (*Cons.*), Eutropius, Lucan, Seneca and pseudo-Seneca (*Epistulae*, *De senectute*), Valerius Maximus
	Jerome (*Epistulae*), Terence
	Terence, Vergil (*G*)
	Aristotle (*Nicomachean Ethics*), *Rhetorica ad Herennium*
	Alexander of Villedieu (*Doctrinale*), Apollonius (*Argonautica*), Cato, Cicero, Horace, Lucretius, Plato, Pliny (*Naturalis historia*), Sallust
	Augustine, Hugutio, Isidore, Priscian, Varro (in *De civitate dei*)

Bibliography

Acron (pseudo) (–), *Scholia in Horatium*, ed. O. Keller, Leipzig

Albini, G., ed. ( ), [Dante Alighieri] *Le egloghe*, Florence

Alessio, G. (a), 'Hec Franciscus de Buiti', *IMU*, , –

(b), 'I trattati grammaticali di Giovanni del Virgilio', *IMU*, , –

( ), ed., *Bene Florentini Candelabrum*, Padua

( ), 'Le istituzioni scolastiche e l'insegnamento', in *Aspetti della letteratura latina nel secolo XIII*, ed. C. Leonardi and G. Orlandi, Perugia and Florence, –

( ), 'Medioevo: tradizione manoscritta', *Enciclopedia virgiliana*, , – , Rome

( ), 'Il "De componendis epistolis" di Niccolò Perotti', *RPL*, , –

( ), 'Edizioni medievali', in *Lo spazio letterario del medioevo. . Il medioevo latino*, ed. G. Cavallo, C. Leonardi and E. Menestò, Rome, : *La ricezione del testo*, –

Alessio, G. and Villa, C. ( ), 'Per *Inferno* I, – ', in *Vestigia. Studi in onore di Giuseppe Billanovich*, Rome, , –

( ), 'Il nuovo fascino degli autori antichi tra i secoli XII e XIV', in *Lo spazio letterario di Roma antica*, ed. G. Cavallo, P. Fedeli and A. Giardina, : *La ricezione del testo*, – , Rome

( ), 'Per *Inferno* . – ', in *Dante e la 'Bella scola' della poesia*, Ravenna

Alexandre-Bidon, Danièle ( ), 'La lettre volée. Apprendre à lire [...] au Moyen Âge', *Annales*, , –

Allen, J. ( ), 'Commentary as criticism', in *Acta Conventus neo-latini lovaniensis*, Leuven and Munich, –

Alton, E. ( ), 'The wanderings of a manuscript of Ovid's *Fasti*', *Hermathena*, , –

Amati, Amato (– ?), *Dizionario corografico dell'Italia*, Milan

Amelli, A., ed. ( ), *Ars Donati quam Paulus Diaconus exposuit*, Montecassino

Anderson, W. ( ), 'Studies on the Naples MS IV F ', *Illinois Classical Studies*, , –

Angeleri, C. ( ), 'Contributi biografici su l'umanista P. Crinito', *Rivista degli archivi toscani*, , –

Antolín, G. ( ), *Catálogo de los códices latinos de la Real Biblioteca del Escorial*, , Madrid

Antonio da Rho ( ), *Apologia. Orazioni*, ed. G. Lombardi, Rome
Avesani, Rino (a), 'Leggesi che cinque sono le chiavi della sapienza', *Rivista di cultura classica e medioevale*, , –
(b), 'Il primo ritmo per la morte del grammatico Ambrogio e il cosiddetto "Liber Catonianus"', *SM*, ser. , , –
( ), *Quattro miscellanee medioevali e umanistiche*, Rome
( ), 'Epaeneticorum ad Pium II Pont. Max. libri V', in D. Ma ei, ed., *Enea Silvio Piccolomini Papa Pio II*, Siena, –
( ), 'La professione dell'*umanista* nel Cinquecento', *IMU*, , –
( ), 'Appunti per la storia dello "Studium Urbis" nel Quattrocento', in *Roma e lo Studium urbis*, Rome, –
Bacci, O. ( ), 'Maestri di grammatica in Valdelsa nel secolo XIV', *MSV*, , –
Baebius Italicus ( ), *Ilias latina*, ed. Marco Sca ai, Bologna
Baldelli, Ignazio ( ), 'Glossario latino–reatino del Cantalicio', *Atti dell'Accademia toscana di scienze e lettere La Colombaria*, , –
( ), 'L'edizione dei glossari latino–volgari dal secolo XIII al XV', in *Atti dell'VIII Congresso internazionale di studi romanzi*, , – , Florence
Bandini, A. (–), *Catalogus codicum latinorum Bibliothecae Mediceae Laurentianae* [...] Florence
(–), *Bibliotecae Leopoldinae sive supplementi ad catalogum* [...] *Bibliotecae Laurentianae* [...] Florence
Banker, James (a), 'The *Ars dictaminis* and rhetorical textbooks', *Medievalia et humanistica*, ns, , –
(b), 'Giovanni di Bonandrea', *Manuscripta*, , –
Barsanti, P. ( ), *Il pubblico insegnamento in Lucca*, Lucca
Bartoccetti, Vittorio ( ), 'Scolari e maestri a Fano nel ' ', *Studia picena*, , –
Battaglia, S. (–), *Grande dizionario della lingua italiana*, Turin
Battistini, M. ( ), *Filippo da Bologna maestro di grammatica a Volterra*, Bologna
( ), *Il pubblico insegnamento in Volterra*, Volterra
( ), 'Taddeo da Pescia, maestro di grammatica del sec. XV', *Bullettino storico pistoiese*, , –
Bausi, Francesco ( ), s.v. Fava, Guido, in *DBI*, , –
( ), s.v. Francesco da Buti, in *DBI*, , –
Bec, Christian ( ), *Les livres des Florentins*, Florence
Becker, G. ( ), *Catalogi bibliotecarum antiqui*, Bonn
Bellemo, V. ( ), 'L'insegnamento e la cultura in Chioggia', *Archivio veneto*, ns, , – ; , –
Belloni, Gino and Pozza, Marco ( ), *Sei testi veneti antichi*, Rome
Beltrami, A. ( ), 'Index codicum classicorum latinorum qui in Byblioteca Quiriniana adservantur', *Studi italiani di filologia classica*, , –
(–), 'L'ortografia latina di maestro Syon', *SM*, , –
Bene da Firenze ( ), s.v., in *DBI*, , –
Berengo, M. ( ), *Nobili e mercanti nella Lucca del Cinquecento*, Turin

Bernicoli, Silvio ( ), 'Maestri e scuole letterarie in Ravenna nel secolo XIV', *Felix Ravenna*, , –

Bersano, Arturo ( ), 'Le antiche scuole del comune di Vercelli', *Bollettino storico bibliografico subalpino*, , –

Bertalot, Ludwig ( ), *Initia humanistica latina* [...]*Band I: Poesie*, Tübingen

Bertanza, E. and Dalla Santa, G. ( ), *Documenti per la storia della cultura in Venezia*, , Venice

Bertoni, G. ( ), 'Note e correzioni all'antico testo piemontese dei "Parlamenti ed Epistole"', *Romania*, , – ,

Bertoni, Giulio and Vicini, Emilio (–), 'Gli studi di grammatica e la rinascenza a Modena', *Atti e memorie della R. Deputazione di storia patria per le province modenesi*, ser. , , –

Biasuz, Giuseppe ( ), 'Giovanni Conversino da Ravenna, maestro di grammatica a Belluno', *Archivio storico di Belluno, Feltre e Cadore*, , –

Billanovich, G. ( ), *Restauri boccacceschi*, Rome

( ), *I primi umanisti e le tradizioni dei classici latini*, Freiburg

( ), 'Leon Battista Alberti, il *Graecismus* e la *Chartula*', *Lingua nostra*, , –

( ), 'Giovanni del Virgilio, Pietro da Moglio, Francesco da Fiano', *IMU*, , –

( ), 'Auctorista, humanista, orator', *Rivista di cultura classica e medioevale*, , –

Black, Robert ( ), *Benedetto Accolti and the Florentine Renaissance*, Cambridge

(a), 'An unknown thirteenth-century manuscript of *Ianua*', in *Church and Chronicle in the Middle Ages*, ed. I. Wood and G. Loud, London, –

(b), 'The curriculum of Italian elementary and grammar schools, – ', in *The Shapes of Knowledge*, ed. D. Kelley and R. Popkin, Dordrecht, –

(c), 'Italian Renaissance education: changing perspectives and continuing controversies', *JHI*, , –

(d), 'Reply to Paul Grendler', *JHI*, , –

( ), 'Florence', in *The Renaissance in National Context*, ed. R. Porter and M. Teich, Cambridge, –

(a), 'Cicero in the curriculum of Italian Renaissance grammar schools', *Ciceroniana*, ns, , –

(b), 'The vernacular and the teaching of Latin in thirteenth- and fourteenth century Italy', *SM*, ser. , , –

(c), 'New light on Machiavelli's education', in *Niccolò Machiavelli, politico, storico, letterato*, ed. J. Marchand, Rome, –

ed. (d), *Studio e scuola in Arezzo durante il medioevo e il Rinascimento*, Arezzo

(e), '*Ianua* and elementary education in Italy and northern Europe in the later middle ages', in *Italia ed Europa nella linguistica del rinascimento*, , ed. M. Tavoni, Modena, –

( ), 'Boccaccio, reader of the *Appendix Vergiliana*', in *Gli zibaldoni di Boccaccio*, ed. C. Cazalé Bérard and M. Picone, Florence, –

Black, Robert and Pomaro, Gabriella ( ), *Boethius's* Consolation of Philosophy *in Italian Medieval and Renaissance Education. Schoolbooks and their Glosses in Florentine Manuscripts*, Florence

Bloomfield, M. ( ) *et al.*, *Incipits of Latin Works on the Virtues and Vices*, Cambridge, Mass.

Blum, R. ( ), *La biblioteca della Badia Fiorentina e i codici di Antonio Corbinelli*, Vatican City

Boas, M. ( ), 'De librorum Catonianorum historia atque compositione', *Mnemosyne*, ns, , –

Boas, Marcus and Botschuyver, Heinrich Johann, ed. ( ), *Disticha Catonis*, Amsterdam.

Boccaccio, Giovanni ( ), *Genealogie deorum gentilium*, ed. V. Romano, Bari

( ), *Esposizioni sopra la Comedia di Dante*, ed. G. Padoan, Milan

Boethius (pseudo) ( ), *De disciplina scolarium*, ed. Olga Weijers, Leiden

Bolgar, R. ( ), *The Classical Heritage*, Cambridge

( ), 'Classical reading in Renaissance schools', *Durham Research Review*, , –

Bologna, G., ed. ( ) *Libri per una educazione rinascimentale*, Milan

Bonvesin da la Riva ( ), *De magnalibus urbis Mediolani*, ed. F. Novati, *Bullettino dell'Istituto storico italiano*, , –

( ), *Vita scholastica*, ed. E. Franceschini, Padua

Borracini Verducci, R. ( ), 'La scuola pubblica a Recanati nel sec. XV', *Università di Macerata. Annali della facoltà di lettere e filosofia*, , –

Bracke, W. ( ), *Fare la epistola nella Roma del Quattrocento*, Rome

Branca, Vittore ( ), 'Una sentenza attribuita al Boccaccio', in his *Tradizione delle opere di Giovanni Boccaccio*, Rome,

Brown, Virginia (a), 'Caesar, Gaius Iulius' in *Catalogus translationum et commentariorum*, , ed. F. Cranz, Washington, –

(b), 'Lupus of Ferrières on the metres of Boethius', in *Latin Script and Letters A.D.* – , ed. J. O'Meara and B. Naumann, Leiden, –

( ), 'Latin manuscripts of Caesar's *Gallic War*', in *Palaeographica diplomatica et archivistica*, Rome, –

Brugnoli, Giorgio ( ), *Studi sulle di erentiae verborum*, Rome

( ), 'I synonyma Ciceronis', in *Atti del I° Congresso internazionale di studi ciceroniani*, , –

Brunet, Jacques ( ), *Manuel du libraire*, Paris

Bruni, Francesco ( ), 'Boncompagno da Signa, Guido delle Colonne, Jean de Meung: metamorfosi dei classici nel Duecento', in *Retorica e poetica tra i secoli XII e XIV*, ed. C. Leonardi and E. Menestò, Perugia, –

Bullough, Donald ( ), 'Le scuole cattedrali e la cultura dell'Italia settentrionale prima dei comuni', in *Vescovi e diocesi in Italia nel medioevo*, Padua, –

Burckhardt, J. ( ), *The Civilization of the Renaissance in Italy*, London

Bursill-Hall, Geo rey ( ), 'Teaching grammars of the middle ages', *Historiographia linguistica*, , –

( ), *A Census of Medieval Latin Grammatical Manuscripts*, Stuttgart

Calzolai, C. ( ), *La storia della Badia a Settimo*, Florence

Cambridge History of Renaissance Philosophy ( ), ed. C. Schmitt, Q. Skinner and E. Kessler, with the assistance of J. Kraye, Cambridge

Campana, A. ( ), 'The origin of the word "humanist"', *JWCI*, , –

( ), 'La citazione del *Pamphilus*', in *Atti del Convegno internazionale di studi accursiani*, , – , Milan

Cantalicio, Giovambattista ( ), [*Canones brevissimi grammatices et metrices*] Rome (BL shelfmark: .d. .)

Capello, Giuseppe ( ), 'Maestro Manfredo e Maestro Sion grammatici vercellesi del Duecento', *Aevum*, , –

Caplan, H., ed. and tr. ( ) *Rhetorica ad Herennium*, London

Cappellino, M. ( ), 'Note su maestri e scuole vercellesi nel secolo XIII', in *Vercelli nel secolo XIII*, – , Vercelli

Carmina Burana ( ), ed. A. Hilka and O. Schumann, , Heidelberg

Cassiodorus ( ), *Institutiones*, ed. R. Mynors, Oxford

Catalogo dei manoscritti della Biblioteca Casanatense ( ), , Rome

Cavazza, Francesco ( ), *Le scuole dell'antico Studio di Bologna*, Milan

Cecchetti, B. ( ), 'Libri, scuole, maestri, sussidii allo studio in Venezia', *Archivio veneto*, , , –

Cecchini, G. and Prunai, G., ed. ( ), *Chartularium Studii Senensis*, Siena

Cervani, Roberta ( ), 'La pubblicazione di grammatiche e glossari mediolatini e lo studio della cultura medievale', *Cultura e scuola*, ( ), –

( ), 'Considerazioni sulla di usione dei testi grammaticali: la tradizione di Donato, Prisciano, Papias', *Bullettino dell'Istituto storico italiano per il medio evo*, , –

ed. ( ), *Papiae Ars grammatica*, Bologna

Cesarini Martinelli, Lucia ( ), 'Sozomeno maestro e filologo', *Interpres*, , –

Chambers, D. ( ), 'Studium Urbis and *Gabella Studii*: The University of Rome in the fifteenth century', in *Cultural Aspects of the Italian Renaissance*, ed. C. Clough, Manchester, –

Cherubini, G. ( ), *Signori, contadini, borghesi*, Florence

Chevalier, U. ( ), *Répertoire des sources historiques du moyen âge*, Paris

Chiesi, Giuseppe ( ), 'Donatum et Catonem legere. La scuola comunale a Bellinzona nel Quattrocento', *Quellen und Forschungen aus italienischen Archiven und Bibliotheken*, , –

Chiuppani, Giovanni ( ), 'Storia di una scuola di grammatica dal medio evo fino al seicento (Bassano)', *Nuovo archivio veneto*, ns, ( ), – , –

Ciabani, R. ( ), *Le famiglie di Firenze*, Florence

Cipolla, C. ( ), 'Nuove congetture e nuovi documenti, intorno a maestro Taddeo del Branca', *GSLI*, , –

Città e servizi sociali nell'Italia dei secoli XII–XV ( ), Pistoia

Clark, Martin ( ), *Modern Italy*, London

Clogan, Paul ( ), 'Literary genres in a medieval textbook', *Medievalia et humanistica*, ns , –

I codici Ashburnhamiani ( ), , Rome

Colini-Baldeschi, Luigi ( ), 'L'insegnamento pubblico a Macerata', *Rivista delle biblioteche e degli archivi*, , –

( ), 'La cultura della Marca d'Ancona e i suoi rapporti con Bologna', *Atti e memorie della R. Deputazione di storia patria per le Marche*, ser. , , –

Connell, Susan ( ), 'Books and their owners in Venice – ', *JWCI*, , –

Conrad of Hirsau ( ), *Dialogus super auctores*, in Huygens ( )

Contini, Gianfranco ( ), 'Reliquie volgari dalla scuola bergamasca dell'umanesimo', *L'Italia dialettale*, , –

Coppi, Giovanni ( ), *Annali, memorie ed huomini illustri di Sangimignano*, Florence

Corradi, Augusto ( ), 'Notizie sui professori di latinità nello Studio di Bologna', *Documenti e studi pubblicati per cura della R. Deputazione di Storia Patria per le province di Romagna*, , –

Coulson, Frank ( ), 'Vulgate commentary on Ovid's *Metamorphoses*', *Mediaevalia*, , –

( ), 'Bibliographical update and *corrigenda minora* to Munari's catalogues of the manuscripts of Ovid's *Metamorphoses*', *Manuscripta*, , –

Courcelle, Pierre ( ), *La Consolation de philosophie dans la tradition littéraire*, Paris

Coxe, H. ( ), *Catalogi codicum manuscriptorum Bibliothecae Bodleianae pars tertia codices graecos et latinos canonicianos complectens*, Oxford

Cremaschi, Giovanni (–), 'Enrico da Settimello e la sua elegia', *Atti dell'Istituto veneto di scienze, lettere ed arti, classe di scienze morali e lettere*, , –

Curtius, E. ( ), *European Literature and the Latin Middle Ages*, tr. W. Trask, New York

Davies, J. ( ), *Florence and its University during the Early Renaissance*, Leiden

de Angelis, Violetta, ed. ( ), *Papiae Elementarium littera 'A'*, , Milan

( ), 'Magna questio preposita coram Dante et Domino Francisco Petrarca', *Studi petrarcheschi*, ns, , –

Debenedetti, Santorre (–), 'Sui più antichi "doctores puerorum" a Firenze', *SM*, , –

de la Mare, A. (a), 'The shop of a Florentine "cartolaio" in ', in *Studi o erti a Roberto Ridolfi*, ed. B. Biagiarelli and D. Rhodes, Florence, –

(b), *The Handwriting of the Italian Humanists*, , Oxford

( ), 'The library of Francesco Sassetti', in *Cultural Aspects of the Italian Renaissance*, ed. C. Clough, Manchester, –

( ), 'New research on humanistic scribes in Florence', in *Miniatura fiorentina del Rinascimento – *, ed. A. Garzelli, , – , Florence

( ), 'Cosimo and his books', in *Cosimo il Vecchio de' Medici*, ed. F. Ames-Lewis, London, –

Delisle, L. ( ), *Inventaire des manuscrits conservés à la Bibliothèque impériale sous les nos – du fonds latin*, Paris

( ), 'Les écoles d'Orléans au douzième et au treizième siècle', *Annuaire-Bulletin de la Société de l'histoire de France*, , –

( ), 'Inventaire des manuscrits latins de la Sorbonne conservés à la Bibliothèque Impériale [...] – ', *Bibliothèque de l'école des chartes*, , –

della Corte, Francesco ( ), 'Prospero d'Aquitania in un documento notarile genovese del ', *SM*, ser. , , –

de Ricci, Seymour and Wilson, W. ( ), *Census of Medieval and Renaissance Manuscripts in the United States and Canada*, New York

De Robertis, T. and Miriello, R. ( ), *I manoscritti datati della Biblioteca Riccardiana di Firenze*, : MSS – , Florence

( ), *I manoscritti datati della Biblioteca Riccardiana di Firenze*, : MSS – , Florence

de Stefano, Antonino ( ), 'Una nuova grammatica latino-italiana del sec. XIII', *Revue de langues romanes*, , –

di Pierro, Carmine ( ), 'Zibaldoni autografi di A. Poliziano', *GSLI*, , –

Donello, A., Florio, G. and Giovè, N., *et al.* ( ) ed., *I manoscritti della Biblioteca del Seminario vescovile di Padova*, Florence

Dorati da Empoli, M. ( ), 'I lettori dello Studio e i maestri di grammatica a Roma', *Rassegna degli archivi di stato*, , –

Ducci, Edda ( ), *Un saggio di pedagogia medievale: Il 'De disciplina scholarium' dello Pseudo-Boezio*, Turin

Egbert von Lüttich ( ), *Fecunda ratis*, ed. E. Voigt, Halle

Enrico da Settimello ( ), *Elegia*, ed. Giovanni Cremaschi, Bergamo

Fabbri, Lorenzo and Tacconi, Maria ( ), *I libri del Duomo di Firenze*, Florence

Faulhaber, Charles ( ), '*Summa dictaminis* of Guido Faba', in *Medieval Eloquence*, ed. J. Murphy, Berkeley, –

Fava, D. ( ), *La Biblioteca Nazionale Centrale di Firenze*, Milan

Faye, C. and Bond, W. ( ) *Supplement to the Census of Medieval and Renaissance Manuscripts in the United States and Canada*, New York

Federici Vescovini, G. ( ), 'Due commenti inediti del XIV secolo al "De consolatione philosophiae" di Boezio', *Rivista critica di storia della filosofia*, , , –

Feo, Michele, ed. ( ), *Codici latini del Petrarca nelle biblioteche fiorentine*, Florence,

Fera, V. ( ), 'Un proemio al "De o ciis" tra Filelfo e Barzizza', *Giornale italiano di filologia*, ns, ( ), –

Ferguson, W. ( ), *The Renaissance in Historical Thought*, Cambridge, Mass.

Fierville, Ch., ed. ( ), *Une grammaire latine inédite du XIIIe siècle*, Paris

Frati, Lodovico ( ), *Pietro da Moglio e il suo commento a Boezio*, Modena

Fredborg, K. ( ), 'The dependence of Petrus Helias' *Summa super Priscianum* on William of Conches' *Glose super Priscianum*', *Cahiers de l'institut du moyen-âge grec et latin*, , –

Frova, Carla ( ), *Istruzione e educazione nel medioevo*, Turin

( ), 'La scuola nella città tardomedievale: un impegno pedagogico e organizzativo', in *La città in Italia e in Germania nel medioevo*, ed. R. Elze and G. Fasoli, Bologna, –

( ), 'Le scuole municipali all'epoca delle università', in *Vocabulaire des écoles et des méthodes d'enseignement au moyen âge,* Turnhout, –

( ), 'Per una storia delle istituzioni scolastiche nel territorio piemontese in età medievale', in *Economia, società e cultura nel Piemonte bassomedievale*, Turin, –

Gabotto, F. ( ), *Lo stato Sabaudo da Amadeo VIII a Emanuele Filiberto, III: La cultura e la vita in Piemonte nel Rinascimento,* Turin

Gaeta, F. ( ), *Lorenzo Valla. Filologia e storia nell'umanesimo italiano*, Naples

Galante, L. (–), 'Index codicum classicorum latinorum qui Florentiae in Bybliotheca Magliabechiana adservantur', *Studi italiani di filologia classica,* , – ; , –

Gallo, E. ( ), '*Poetria nova* of Geo rey of Vinsauf', in J. Murphy, ed., *Medieval Eloquence*, Berkeley, –

Garbini, Paolo ( ), 'Sulla "Vita scolastica" di Bonvesin da la Riva', *SM*, ser. , , –

Gardenal, Gianna (a), 'Aspetti e problemi dello studio grammaticale nel medioevo: Giovanni da Pigna, maestro veronese del sec. XIII', *Quaderni veneti*, , –

(b), 'Alcune osservazioni in margine alla "constructio" nelle grammatiche medioevali', in *Terzo quaderno veronese di filologia lingua e letteratura italiana*, ed. Gilberto Lonardi, Verona, –

Gargan, Luciano ( ), 'Giovanni Conversini e la cultura letteraria a Treviso', *IMU*, , –

( ), 'Due biblioteche private padovane del Trecento', *Quaderni per la storia dell'Università di Padova*, , –

( ), 'Un maestro di grammatica a Padova e a Feltre nel secondo Trecento', *Quaderni per la storia dell'Università di Padova*, , –

Garin, E., ed. ( ), *Prosatori latini del Quattrocento,* Milan

( ), *L'educazione umanistica in Italia*, nd edn, Bari

( ), *L'educazione in Europa (–)*, Bari

ed. ( ), *Il pensiero pedagogico dello umanesimo*, Florence

( ), *Italian Humanism*, tr. P. Munz, Oxford

( ), 'Guarino Veronese e la cultura a Ferrara', in his *Ritratti di umanisti*, Florence, –

Gasca Queirazza, Giuliano ( ), *Documenti di antico volgare in Piemonte. Fascicolo III: Frammenti vari da una miscellanea grammaticale di Biella*, Turin

( ), 'Le glosse al *Dottrinale* di Mayfredo di Belmonte', *Studi piemontesi*, . (March), –

Gaudenzi, A., ed. ( ), *Parlamenti ed epistole di Guido Fava* in *I suoni, le forme e le parole dell'odierno dialetto di Bologna*, Turin, –

ed. ( ), Boncompagno da Signa, *Rethorica novissima*, in *Bibliotheca juridica medii aevi*,

( ), 'Sulla cronologia delle opere dei dettatori bolognesi da Boncompagno a Bene di Lucca', *Bullettino dell'Istituto storico italiano*, , –

Gehl, P. ( ), 'Latin readers in fourteenth-century Florence', *Scrittura e civiltà*, , –

( ), *A Moral Art. Grammar, society, and culture in Trecento Florence*, Ithaca

Gentile, G. ( ), *I problemi della scolastica e il pensiero italiano*, Bari

( ), 'La concezione umanistica del mondo', *Nuova antologia*, , –

( ), *Il pensiero italiano del Rinascimento*, in his *Opere*, Florence

Geo rey of Vinsauf ( ), *Poetria nova*, ed. E. Faral, in *Les arts poétiques du XII*[e] *et du XIII*[e] *siècle*, Paris, –

Gherardi, A., ed. ( ), *Statuti della università e studio fiorentino*, Florence

Ghisalberti, F. ( ), 'Giovanni del Virgilio espositore delle "Metamorphosi"', *Giornale dantesco*, ns, , a. , –

( ), 'Arnolfo d'Orléans, un cultore di Ovidio nel secolo XII', *Memorie del R. Istituto lombardo*, classe scienze morali e storiche, ser. , ( ), –

Gibson, Margaret, ed. ( ), *Boethius. His Life, Thought and Influence*, Oxford

Gibson, Margaret and Smith, Lesley, ed. ( ), *Codices Boethiani: a conspectus of manuscripts of the works of Boethius*. I. *Great Britain and the Republic of Ireland*, London

Gilson, Etienne ( ), *La philosophie au moyen âge*, Paris

Goldschmidt, E. ( ), *Medieval Texts and their First Appearance in Print*, London

Gombrich, E. ( ), *In Search of Cultural History*, Oxford

Gorrini, Giacomo (–), 'L'istruzione elementare in Genova durante il medio evo', *Giornale storico e letterario della Liguria*, ns, , – ; , –

Graesse ( ) *et al.*, *Orbis latinus. Lexikon lateinischer geographischer Namen des Mittelalters und der Neuzeit*, Braunschweig

Grafton, A. ( ), 'Boethius in the Renaissance', in Gibson ( ), –

Grafton, A. and Jardine, L. ( ), 'Humanism and the school of Guarino', *Past and Present*, , –

( ), *From Humanism to the Humanities: Education and the Liberal Arts in Fifteenth- and Sixteenth-Century Europe*, London

Gregory the Great ( ), *Gregorii I papae registrum epistolarum*, ed. L. Hartmann, in *Monumenta Germaniae historica*, Berlin

Grendler, Paul ( ), 'The concept of humanist in Cinquecento Italy', in *Renaissance Studies in Honor of Hans Baron*, ed. A. Molho and J. Tedeschi, Florence, –

( ), 'The schools of Christian doctrine in sixteenth-century Italy', *Church History*, , –

( ), *Schooling in Renaissance Italy*, Baltimore

( ), 'Reply to Robert Black', *JHI*, , –

( ) *Books and Schools in the Italian Renaissance*, Great Yarmouth, Norfolk

Guarino Veronese (–), *Epistolario*, ed. Remigio Sabbadini, Venice

Hagen, H. ( ), *Catalogus codicum bernensium*, Berne

Halm, C. ( ), *Rhetores latini minores*, Leipzig

Hankey, A. ( ) s.v. Bandini, Domenico, in *DBI*, , Rome, –

Hankins, J. ( ), 'Cosimo de' Medici as a patron of humanistic literature', in *Cosimo 'il vecchio' de' Medici*, – , ed. F. Ames-Lewis, Oxford, –

Haskins, Charles ( ), 'A list of text-books from the close of the twelfth century', *Harvard Studies in Classical Philology*, , –

( ), *The Renaissance of the Twelfth Century*, Cambridge, Mass.

( ), *Studies in Mediaeval Culture*, Oxford

Heath, Terence ( ), 'Logical grammar, grammatical logic and humanism in three German universities', *Studies in the Renaissance*, , –

Heinimann, S. ( ), 'Zur Geschichte der grammatischen Terminologie im Mittelalter', *Zeitschrift für romanische Philologie*, , –

Hildebrandt, M. ( ), *The External School in Carolingian Society*, Leiden

Holtz, Louis ( ), *Donat et la tradition de l'enseignement grammatical*, Paris

Hooker, P. ( ), 'Elementary education in Renaissance Italy', M.Phil. thesis, Warburg Institute, University of London

Howell, W. ( ), *The Rhetoric of Alcuin and Charlemagne*, Princeton

Hunt, R. ( ), 'The introductions to the "artes" in the twelfth century', in *Studia mediaevalia in honorem* [...]*R. J. Martin*, Bruges, –

Hunt, R. ( ), 'Hugutio and Petrus Helias', in his *The History of Grammar in the Middle Ages*, ed. G. Bursill-Hall, Amsterdam, – (first published in *Medieval and Renaissance Studies*, ( ), –)

Huntsman, Je rey ( ), 'Grammar', in *The Seven Liberal Arts in the Middle Ages*, ed. D. Wagner, Bloomington, –

Hurlbut, S. ( ), 'A forerunner of Alexander de Villa-Dei', *Speculum*, , –

Huygens, R. ( ), ed. *Accessus ad Auctores. Bernard d'Utrecht. Conrad d'Hirsau. Dialogus super auctores*, Leiden

Inama, V. (–), 'Una scuola di grammatica in Cles nel secolo XIV', *Archivio trentino*, , –

Inguanez, M. (–), ed. *Codicum casinensium manuscriptorum catalogus*, Montecassino

Ives, S. ( ), 'Corrigenda and addenda to the descriptions of the Plimpton manuscripts as recorded in the De Ricci *Census*', *Speculum*, , –

Jaitner-Hahner, U. ( ), 'Die ö entliche Schule in Città di Castello vom . Jahrhundert bis zur Ankunft der Jesuiten ', *Quellen und Forschungen aus italienischen Archiven und Bibliotheken*, , –

Jensen, Kristian ( ), *Rhetorical Philosophy and Philosophical Grammar. Julius Caesar Scaliger's Theory of Language*, Munich

(a), 'Humanist Latin grammars in Germany and their Italian background', in *Italia ed Europa nella linguistica del Rinascimento*, ed. Mirko Tavoni, , – , Modena

(b), 'The humanist reform of Latin and Latin teaching', in *The Cambridge Companion to Renaissance Humanism*, ed. Jill Kraye, – , Cambridge

Jeudy, Colette ( ), 'L'*Ars de nomine et verbo* de Phocas', *Viator*, , –

Jeudy, Colette and Riou, Yves-François ( ), 'L'*Achilléide* de Stace au moyen âge', *Revue d'histoire des textes*, , –

Kaeppeli, T. (–), *Scriptores ordinis praedicatorum medii aevi*, Rome (completed E. Panella)

Kaster, Robert and Noakes, Susan ( ), 'Tommaso Schifaldo's *Libellus de indagationibus grammaticis*', *Humanistica lovaniensia*, , –

Keil, Heinrich, ed. (–), *Grammatici latini*, Leipzig

Kessler, E. ( ), 'De significatione verborum. Spätscholastische Sprachtheorie und humanistische Grammatik', *RPL*, , –

Klapisch-Zuber, Christiane ( ), 'Le chiavi fiorentine di barbablù: l'apprendimento della lettura a Firenze nel XV secolo', *Quaderni storici*, , –

Klein, Heinz-Willi, ed. ( ) 'Johannis abbatis *Liber de VII viciis et VII virtutibus*', *Mittellateinisches Jahrbuch*, , –

Klopsch, P. ( ), *Einfürung in die Dichtungslehren des lateinischen Mittelalter*, Darmstadt

Kneepkens, C. ( ), 'Master Guido and his view on government: on twelfth century linguistic thought', *Vivarium*, , –

( ), '*Ordo naturalis* and *ordo artificialis*', *in Vocabulary of Teaching and Research between Middle Ages and Renaissance*, ed. Olga Weijers, Turnhout –

Kohl, B. ( ), s.v. Conversini, Giovanni, in *DBI*, , –

Kristeller, P. ( ), 'Un'"Ars dictaminis" di Giovanni del Virgilio', *IMU*, –

(–), *Iter italicum*, London and Leiden

(a), *Renaissance Thought and its Sources*, ed. M. Mooney, New York

(b), 'Humanism and scholasticism in the Italian Renaissance', in Kristeller (a), –

( ), 'Niccolò Perotti ed i suoi contributi alla storia dell'Umanesimo', in his *Studies in Renaissance Thought and Letters*, , Rome, –

Lauer, P., ed. ( ), *Bibliothèque Nationale. Catalogue général des manuscrits latins*, , Paris

Law, Vivien ( ), 'The first foreign-language grammars', *The Incorporated Linguist*, , –

( ), 'Linguistics in the earlier middle ages: the insular and Carolingian grammarians', *Transactions of the Philological Society*, –

(a), 'Late Latin grammars in the early middle ages', *Historiographia linguistica*, , –

(b), 'Panorama della grammatica normativa nel tredicesimo secolo', in *Aspetti della letteratura latina nel secolo XIII*, ed. C. Leonardi and G. Orlandi, Perugia and Florence, –

Lazzi, G. and Scarlino, M. ( ), *I manoscritti Landau Finaly della Biblioteca Nazionale Centrale di Firenze*, Milan

Lentini, Anselmo ( ), *Ilderico e la sua 'Ars grammatica'*, Montecassino

Liburnio, Nicolò ( ), *Le tre fontane*, Venice

Lidonnici, E. ( ), 'La corrispondenza poetica di Giovanni del Virgilio con Dante e il Mussato, e le postille di Giovanni Boccaccio', *Giornale dantesco*, , –

List of Additions to the Manuscripts in the British Museum [...] – ( ), London

Lucchi, Piero ( ), 'La santacroce, il salterio e il babuino: libri per imparare a leggere nel primo secolo della stampa', *Quaderni storici*, , –

Maaz, Wolfgang ( ), 'Zur rezeption des Alexander de Villadei im . Jahrhundert', *Mittellateinisches Jahrbuch*, , –

MacGregor, A. ( ), 'The manuscripts of Seneca's tragedies: a handlist', in *Aufstieg und Niedergang der römischen Welt.* [...] *II: Principat*, ed. H. Temporini and W. Haase, . , – , Berlin and New York

McGregor, James ( ), 'Ovid at school', *Classical Folia*, , –

McManamon, John ( ), *Pierpaolo Vergerio the Elder*, Tempe, Arizona

Manacorda, Giuseppe ( ), 'Un testo scolastico di grammatica del sec. XII in uso nel basso Piemonte', *Giornale storico e letterario della Liguria*, , –

(–), 'Un testo di grammatica latino–veneta del sec. XIII', *Atti della R. Accademia di Scienza di Torino*, , –

( ), *Storia della scuola in Italia. Il medio evo*, Milan Palermo and Naples

(– ,), 'Libri scolastici del Medio evo e del Rinascimento', *La bibliofilia*, (–), – ; ( ), –

( ), 'Fra Bartolomeo da S. Concordio grammatico e la fortuna di Gaufredo di Vinsauf in Italia', in *Raccolta di studi di storia e critica letteraria dedicata a F. Flamini da' suoi discepoli*, – , Pisa

Manitius, Maximilianus (–), *Geschichte der lateinischen Literatur des Mittelalters*, Munich

Mannucci, Francesco ( ), 'I primordi del pubblico insegnamento in Sarzana', *Giornale storico della Lunigiana*, , –

Marchesi, Concetto ( ), 'Due grammatici latini del medioevo', *Bulletino della società filologica romana*, ( ), –

Marigo, A. ( ), *I codici manoscritti delle* Derivationes *di Uguccione Pisano: saggio d'inventario bibliografico con appendice sui codici del* Catholicon *di Giovanni da Genova*, Rome

Mariotti, Italo ( ), 'Lezioni di Beroaldo il Vecchio sulla *Tebaide*', in *Tradizione classica e letteratura umanistica*, ed. R. Cardini *et al.*, Rome, –

Marrou, H. ( ), *A History of Education in Antiquity*, tr. G. Lamb, New York

Martini, G. ( ) *La bottega di un cartolaio fiorentino della seconda metà del Quattrocento*, Florence

Massa, A. ( ), 'Documenti e notizie per la storia dell'istruzione in Genova', *Giornale storico e letterario della Liguria*, , – , –

Mazza, A. ( ) 'L'inventario della "parva libraria" di Santo Spirito e la biblioteca del Boccaccio', *IMU*, , –

Mazzatinti, Giuseppe (–) *et al.*, *Inventari dei manoscritti delle biblioteche d'Italia*, Forlì and elsewhere

Mazzei, Lapo ( ), *Lettere di un notaio a un mercante del secolo XIV*, ed. C. Guasti, Florence

Mazzi, Curzio ( ), 'Cartiere, tipografie e maestri di grammatica in Valdelsa', *MSV*, , –

Mazzuconi, Daniela ( ), 'Stefano Fieschi da Soncino: un allievo di Gasparino Barzizza', *IMU*, , –

Mengaldo, Pier Vincenzo ( ) s.v. *constructio* in *Enciclopedia dantesca*, Rome, –

Mercati, G. ( ), 'Il catalogo della biblioteca di Pomposa', in his *Opere minori*, , Vatican City
( ), *Codici latini Pico Grimani Pio*, Vatican City
Mercer, R. ( ), *The Teaching of Gasparino Barzizza*, London
Milanesi, C., ed. ( ) 'Memorie di Ser Cristofano di Galgano Guidini da Siena', *ASI*, ser. , . , –
Milde, Wolfgang ( ), 'Zur Druckhäufigkeit von Niccolò Perottis *Cornucopiae* und *Rudimenta grammatices* im . und . Jahrhundert', *RPL*, , –
Minio-Paluello, L. ( ), *Education in Fascist Italy*, London
Minnis, A., ed. ( ), *Chaucer's* Boece *and the Medieval Tradition of Boethius*, Cambridge
Minnis, A. and Scott, A., ed. ( ), *Medieval Literary Theory and Criticism*, Oxford
Montiverdi, A. ( ), s.v. Arrigo da Settimello, in *DBI*, , –
Morelli, Camillo ( ), 'I trattati di grammatica e retorica del cod. casanatense ', *Rendiconti della R. Accademia dei lincei. Classe di scienze morali, storiche e filologiche*, ser. , , –
Morelli, Giovanni ( ), *Ricordi*, ed. V. Branca, Florence
Morici, Medardo ( ), 'Giambattista Valentini detto il "Cantalicio" a San Gimignano', *MSV*, , –
Morpurgo, S. (–) *et al.*, *Catalogo dei manoscritti panciatichiani della Biblioteca Nazionale Centrale di Firenze*, Rome
Mostra di manoscritti, documenti e edizioni. VI centenario della morte di Giovanni Boccaccio ( ), Certaldo
Munari, Franco ( ), *Catalogue of the* MSS *of Ovid's* Metamorphoses, London
( ), 'Secondo supplemento al catalogo dei manoscritti delle *Metamorfosi* ovidiane', in *Studia florentina A. Ronconi sexagenario oblata*, Rome, –
Munk Olsen, Birger (–), *L'étude des auteurs classiques latins au XI*[e] *et XII*[e] *siècles*, Paris
(–), 'La popularité des textes classiques entre le IXe et le XIIe siècle', *Revue d'histoire des textes*, – , –
( ), *I classici nel canone scolastico altomedievale*, Spoleto
Murphy, James ( ), *Rhetoric in the Middle Ages*, Berkeley
( ), 'The teaching of Latin as a second language in the th century', *Historiographia linguistica*, , –
Nada Patrone, A. ( ), '"Super providendo bonum et su cientem magistrum scholarum". L'organizzazione scolastica delle città nel tardo medioevo', in *Città e servizi sociali nell'Italia dei secoli XII–XV*, Pistoia, –
( ), *Vivere nella scuola. Insegnare e apprendere nel Piemonte del tardo medioevo*, Turin
Narducci, E. ( ), *Catalogus codicum manuscriptorum praeter graecos et orientales in Bibliotheca Angelica* [...] *de Urbe*, Rome
Nauta, Lodi, ed. ( ), *Guillelmi de Conchis Glosae super Boetium*, Turnhout
Neudecker, Karl Julius ( ), *Das* Doctrinale *des Alexanders de Villa Dei und der lateinische Unterricht während des späteren Mittelalters in Deutschland*, Pirna
Nims, Margaret, tr. ( ), Poetria nova *of Geo rey of Vinsauf*, Toronto

Novati, Francesco ( ), *La giovinezza di Coluccio Salutati*, Turin
( ), 'Due grammatici pisani del sec. XIV: Ser Francesco Merolla da Vico e Ser Francesco di Bartolo da Buti', *MSV*, , –
( ), 'Inventario di una libreria fiorentina del primo Quattrocento', *Bollettino della Società bibliografica italiana*, , –
( ), *L'influsso del pensiero latino sopra la civiltà italiana del medio evo*, Milan
Ortalli, Gherardo ( ), *Scuole, maestri e istruzione di base tra Medioevo e Rinascimento Il caso veneziano*, Vicenza (revised edition ( ): *Scuole e maestri tra medioevo e rinascimento. Il caso veneziano*, Bologna)
( ), 'L'istruzione', in *Storia di Venezia dalle origini alla caduta della Serenissima*, ed. G. Arnaldi, G. Cracco and A. Tenenti, Rome, –
Ottaviano, C. ( ), *Un brano inedito della 'Philosophia' di Guglielmo di Conches*, Naples
Paetow, Louis ( ), *The Arts Course at Medieval Universities with Special Reference to Grammar and Rhetoric*, Champaign, Ill.
ed. ( ), *The Battle of the Seven Arts. A French poem by Henri d'Andeli*, Berkeley
Pampaloni, G. ( ), 'La vita cittadina', in *Storia di Prato*, Prato, , –
Panizza, L. ( ), 'Gasparino Barzizza's commentaries on Seneca's letters', *Traditio*, , –
( ), 'Italian humanists and Boethius: was Philosophy for or against Poetry?', in *New Perspectives on Renaissance Thought. Essays in the History of Science, Education and Philosophy*, ed. J. Henry and S. Hutton, London, –
Paoli, C. ( ), *I codici Ashburnhamiani della R. Biblioteca Mediceo-Laurenziana di Firenze*, . , Rome
Park, K. ( ), 'The readers at the Florentine Studio', *Rinascimento*, ser. , , –
Parr, R., tr. ( ), *Geo rey of Vinsauf. Documentum de modo et arte dictandi et versificandi*, Milwaukee
Parroni, Piergiorgio ( ), 'Il cod. Oliv. di Marziale e il suo copista Battista Lunense', *Studia oliveriana*, , – (pagination of o print)
Pasqui, U. ( ), *Documenti per la storia della città di Arezzo nel medio evo*, , Florence
Passalacqua, Marina ( ), *I codici di Prisciano*, Rome
Pecori, Luigi ( ), *Storia della terra di San Gimignano*, Florence
Peiper, R., ed. ( ), *Anicii Manlii Severini Boetii Philosophiae Consolationis Libri Quinque*, Leipzig
Pellegrin, Elizabeth ( ), *La bibliothèque des Visconti et des Sforza ducs de Milan au XVe siècle*, Paris
( ), 'Quelques "accessus" au "De amicitia" de Cicéron', in *Homages à André Boutemy*, Brussels, –
ed. (–), *Les manuscrits classiques latins de la Bibliothèque Vaticane*, . , Paris
Percival, W. ( ), 'The historical sources of Guarino's *Regulae grammaticales*: a reconsideration of Sabbadini's evidence', in G. Tarugi, ed., *Civiltà dell'umanesimo*, Florence, –
( ), 'The grammatical tradition and the rise of the vernaculars', *Current Trends in Linguistics*, , –

( ), 'Renaissance grammar: rebellion or evolution?', in *Interrogativi dell'umanesimo*, ed. G. Tarugi, , – , Florence

(a), 'Textual problems in the Latin grammar of Guarino Veronese', *RPL*, , –

(b), 'The *Artis grammaticae opusculum* of Bartolomeo Sulmonese', *Renaissance Quarterly*, , –

( ), 'The place of the *Rudimenta grammatices* in the history of Latin grammar', *RPL*, , –

( ), 'On Priscian's syntactic theory: the medieval perspective', in *Papers in the History of Linguistics*, ed. H. Aarsle , L. Kelly and H. Niederehe. (Amsterdam Studies in the Theory and History of Linguistic Science, ser. ,), Amsterdam and Philadelphia, –

( ), 'A hitherto unpublished medieval grammatical fragment on Latin syntax and syntactic figures', in *De ortu grammaticae: Studies in Medieval Grammar and Linguistic Theory in Memory of Jan Pinborg*, ed. G. Bursill-Hall, S. Ebbesen and K. Koerner, Amsterdam Studies in the Theory and History of Linguistic Sciences, ser. . vol. , Amsterdam and Philadelphia, –

( ), 'The *Orthographia* of Gasparino Barzizza', *Annali dell'Istituto universitario orientale di Napoli*, , –

( ), 'A working edition of the *Carmina di erentialia* by Guarino Veronese', *RPL*, , –

( ), 'Italian a liations of Nebrija's Latin grammar', in *Italia ed Europa nella linguistica del Rinascimento*, ed. Mirko Tavoni, , Modena, –

Percival, W. and Pascal, Paul ( ), 'The Latin poems of Bartolomeo Sulmonese', in *Roma humanistica. Studia in hon. Rev[i] adm. Dni Dni Iosaei Ruysschaert collegit et edidit Iosephus IJsewijn*, Leuven, –

Petrarca, Francesco (–), *Le familiari*, ed. V. Rossi, Florence

Petti Balbi, Giovanna ( ), *L'insegnamento nella Liguria medievale. Scuole, maestri, libri*, Genoa

( ), 'Istitutzioni cittadine e servizi sociali nell'Italia centro-settentrionale tra XIII e XV secolo', in *Città e servizi sociali nell'Italia dei secoli XII–XV*, Pistoia, –

Pigman, G. ( ), 'Barzizza's studies of Cicero', *Rinascimento*, ns, , –

Pinborg, Jan ( ), *Remigius, Schleswig . A Latin Grammar in Facsimile Edition with a Postscript*, Copenhagen

Plimpton, G. ( ), 'Grammatical manuscripts and early printed grammars in the Plimpton Library', *Transactions and Proceedings of the American Philological Association*, , –

Pochat, Götz ( ), 'Eine datierte Boethius-Miniatur in der Laurenziana', *Mitteilungen des Kunsthistorischen Instituts in Florenz*, , –

Poggio Bracciolini (–), *Epistolae*, ed. Helene Harth, Florence

Polak, Emil ( ), *A Textual Study of Jacques de Dinant's 'Summa dictaminis'*, Geneva

Poliziano, Angelo ( ), *Opera*, Lyons

( ), *Prose volgari inedite e poesie latine e greche edite e inedite*, ed. I. del Lungo, Florence

( ), *Le Selve e la Strega, Prolusioni nello Studio fiorentino (–)*, ed. I. del Lungo, Florence

Professione, A. and Vignono, I. ( ), *Inventario dei manoscritti della Biblioteca Capitolare di Ivrea*, Alba

Quain, E. ( ), 'The medieval *accessus ad auctores*', *Traditio*, , –

Quaquarelli, L. ( ), 'Felice Feliciano nel suo epistolario', *Lettere italiane*, , –

Rand, E. ( ), 'The classics in the thirteenth century', *Speculum*, , –

( ), 'A friend of the classics in the times of St Thomas Aquinas', in *Mélanges Mandonnet*, , Paris, –

La règle du maître ( ), ed. Adalbert de Vogüé, Paris

Reichling, Dietrich ( ), ed. *Das Doctrinale des Alexander de Villa-Dei*, Berlin

Reilly, Leo, ed. ( ) *Petrus Helias Summa super Priscianum*, Toronto

Renouard, P. ( ), *Bibliographie des impressions et des oeuvres de Josse Badius Ascensius*, Paris

Repetti, E. (–), *Dizionario geografico–fisico–storico della Toscana*, Florence

Resta, Gianvito ( ), *Georgio Valagussa, umanista del Quattrocento*, Padua

Reynolds, B., ed. ( ), *The Cambridge Italian Dictionary*, , Cambridge

Reynolds, L. ( ), *The Medieval Tradition of Seneca's Letters*, London

ed. ( ), *Texts and Transmission*, Oxford,

Reynolds, Suzanne ( ), 'Ad auctorum expositionem: syntactic theory and interpretative practice in the twelfth century', *Histoire Epistémologie Langage*, ( ), –

(a), 'Glossing Horace: using the classics in the medieval classroom', in *Medieval Manuscripts of the Latin Classics*, ed. C. Chavannes-Mazel and M. Smith, Los Altos Hills, –

(b), *Medieval Reading: Grammar, Rhetoric and the Classical Text*, Cambridge

Ricciardi, R. ( ), s.v. Del Riccio Baldi, Pietro, in *DBI*, , –

Riché, P. ( ), 'Le Psautier, livre de lecture élémentaire d'après les vies des saints mérovingiens', in *Etudes mérovingienns*, Paris, –

( ), *Education and Culture in the Barbarian West Sixth through Eighth Centuries*, tr. J. Contreni, Columbia, South Carolina

(–), 'Apprendre à lire et à ecrire dans le haut Moyen Age', *Bulletin des antiquaires de France*, –

( ), *Écoles et enseignement dans le haut moyen âge de la fin du ve siècle au milieu du xie siècle*, Paris

( ), 'Les écoles en Italie avant les universités', in *Luoghi e metodi d'insegnamento nell'Italia medioevale (secoli XII–XIV)*, ed. L. Gargan and O. Limone, – , Galatina

( ), 'Le vocabulaire des écoles carolingiennes', in *Vocabulaire des écoles et des méthodes d'enseignement au moyen âge*, ed. O. Weijers, Turnhout, –

Richer, ( ), *Histoire de France*, ed. R. Latouche, II, Paris

Rico, F. ( ), *Nebrija frente a los bárbaros*, Salamanca

Rizzo, Silvia ( ), *Il lessico filologico degli umanisti*, Rome

( ), 'Il latino nell'umanesimo', in *Letteratura italiana*, ed. Alberto Asor Rosa, , –

( ), 'Petrarca, il latino e il volgare', *Quaderni petrarcheschi*, , –

( ), 'Sulla terminologia dell'insegnamento grammaticale nelle scuole umanistiche', in *Vocabulary of Teaching and Research between Middle Ages and Renaissance*, ed. Olga Weijers, Turnhout, –

( ), 'L'insegnamento del latino nelle scuole umanistiche', in *Italia ed Europa nella linguistica del Rinascimento*, ed. Mirko Tavoni, , Modena, –

( ), 'Il Valla e il progetto di un nuovo *Doctrinale*', – in S. Rizzo and M. De Nonno, 'In margine a una recente edizione di versi grammaticali del Valla', in *Filologia umanistica per Gianvito Resta*, ed. V. Fera and G. Ferraù, , Padua, –

Roberti, Luciana ( ), 'Il commento medioevale alle tragedie di Seneca nel codice riccardiano ', in *Quaderni dell'Istituto di lingua e letteratura latina.* Università degli Studi di Roma, Facoltà di Magistero, Rome, –

Robey, D. ( ), 'Humanism and education in the early Quattrocento: the *De ingenuis moribus* of P. P. Vergerio', *Bibliothèque d'humanisme et renaissance*, , –

Roediger, F. (–), *Catalogue des livres manuscrits et imprimés composant la bibliothèque de M. Horace de Landau*, Florence

Ronchini, A., ed. ( ), *Statuta communis Parmae ab anno MCCLXVI ad annum circiter MCCCIV*, Parma

Ross, J. ( ), 'Venetian schools and teachers fourteenth to early sixteenth century: a survey and a study of Giovanni Battista Egnazio', *Renaissance Quarterly*, , –

Ross, J. and McLaughlin, M., ed. ( ), *The Portable Medieval Reader*, London

Rossi, V. ( ), 'Un grammatico cremonese a Pavia nella prima età del Rinascimento', *Bollettino della Società pavese di storia patria*, , –

( ), *Dal rinasimento al risorgimento*, Florence

Rubinstein, Nicolai ( ), 'A grammar teacher's autobiography: Giovanni Conversini's *Rationarium vite*', *Renaissance Studies*, , –

Ruysschaert, J. ( ), 'Les manuels de grammaire latine composés par Pomponio Leto', *Scriptorium*, , –

ed. ( ), *Codices vaticani latini. Codices* – , Vatican City

( ), 'A propos des trois premières grammaires latines de Pomponio Leto', *Scriptorium*, , –

Sabbadini, R. ( ), 'Lettere e orazioni edite e inedite di Gasparino Barzizza', *Archivio storico lombardo*, , – , – , –

( ), *Studi di Gasparino Barzizza su Quintiliano e Cicerone*, Livorno

( ), *Vita di Guarino Veronese*, Genoa

( ), *La scuola e gli studi di Guarino Guarini Veronese*, Catania

( ), 'Versi grammaticali di Lorenzo Valla', *La biblioteca delle scuole italiane*, ser. , , –

( ), 'L'ortografia latina di Foca', *Rivista di filologia e d'istruzione classica*, –

( ), 'Dei metodi nell'insegnamento della sintassi latina: considerazioni didattiche e storiche', *Rivista di filologia e d'istruzione classica*, , –

( ), 'Frammento di grammatica latino-bergamasca', *SM*, , –

( ), 'Elementi nazionali nella teoria grammaticale dei Romani', *Studi italiani di filologia classica*, , –
( ), *Il metodo degli umanisti*, Florence
( ), *Giovanni da Ravenna, insigne figura d'umanista (–)*, Como
( ), *Storia e critica di testi latini*, nd edn, ed. E. and M. Billanovich, Padua
Saitta, G. ( ), *L'educazione dell'umanesimo in Italia*, Venice
Salvioni, Carlo ( ), review of Gaudenzi ( ), *Giornale storico della letteratura italiana*, , –
Sanford, E. ( ), 'The use of classical Latin authors in the *libri manuales*', *Transactions and Proceedings of the American Philological Association*, , –
Sasse Tateo, B. ( ), 'Forme dell'organizzazione scolastica nell'Italia dei comuni', *ASI*, , –
Savino, G. ( ), 'Leggere e scrivere nell'età comunale', *Incontri pistoiesi di storia arte cultura*, , Pistoia
Scaglione, A. ( ), 'The humanist as scholar and Politian's conception of the *grammaticus*', *Studies in the Renaissance*, , –
( ), *The Classical Theory of Composition from its Origin to the Present*, Chapel Hill
Scalon, C. ( ), *Libri scuole e cultura nel Friuli medioevale*, Padua
Scarcia Piacentini, Paola (–), *Saggio di un censimento dei manoscritti contenenti il testo di Persio*, Rome
Schia ni, Alfredo ( ), 'Frammenti grammaticali latino-friulani del secolo XIV', *Rivista della Società filologica friulana*, , – , –
( ), 'Esercizi di versione dal volgare friulano in latino nel secolo XIV in una scuola notarile cividalese', *Rivista della Società filologica friulana*, –
Schiavetto, F. (–), 'Parisio de Altedo, notaio bolognese del XIII secolo', *Il carrobbio. Tradizioni problemi immagini dell'Emilia Romagna*, – , –
Schmidt, P., ed. ( ), *Proverbia sententiaeque latinitatis medii ac recentioris aevi*, ns, , Göttingen
( ), 'Vom Epos zur Prosa. Prosaversionen lateinischer Dichtung', in *Kontinuität und Transformation der Antike im Mittelalter*, ed. W. Erzgräber, Sigmaringen, –
Schmitt, W. ( ), 'Die Ianua (Donatus)', *Beiträge zur Inkunabelkunde*, ser. , , –
Schullian, Dorothy ( ), 'A revised list of manuscripts of Valerius Maximus', in *Miscellanea Augusto Campana*, , – , Padua
Segarizzi, Arnaldo (– a), 'Una grammatica latina del secolo XV', *Atti del R. Istituto veneto di scienze, lettere ed arti*, . , –
(– b), 'Cenni sulle scuole pubbliche a Venezia', *Atti del R. Istitutto veneto di scienze, lettere ed arti*, , –
Silk, E. ( ), ed., *Saeculi noni auctoris in Boetii 'Consolationem philosophiae' commentarius*, Rome
Sivo, Vito ( ), 'Studi sui trattati grammaticali mediolatini', *Quaderni medievali*, , –
( ), 'Ricerche sulla tradizione grammaticale mediolatina', *Annali della Facoltà di lettere e filosofia, Università degli Studi di Bari*, , –

ed., (a), *Il* Donatus *di Paolo Camaldolese*, Spoleto
(b), 'Nuovi studi sui tratti grammaticali mediolatini', *Quaderni medievali*, , –
Souter, A. ( ), *A Glossary of Later Latin*, Oxford
Spallone, Maddalena ( ), 'I percorsi medievali del testo: "accessus", commentari, florilegi', in *Lo spazio letterario di Roma antica*, ed. G. Cavallo, P. Fedeli and A. Giardina, : *La ricezione del testo*, – , Rome
Spaventa, B. ( ), *Rinascimento, riforma, controriforma*, Naples
Specht, F. ( ), *Geschichte des Unterrichtswesens in Deutschland von den ältesten Zeiten bis zur Mitte des dreizehnten Jahrhunderts*, Stuttgart
Stadter, P. ( ), 'Planudes, Plutarch, and Pace of Ferrara', *IMU*, , –
Stornajolo, C. ( ), *Codices urbinates latini*, , Vatican City
Sutter, C. ( ), *Aus Leben und Schriften des Magisters Boncompagno*, Freiburg im Breisgau and Leipzig
Stussi, Alfredo ( ), 'Esercizi di traduzione trevigiani del secolo XIV', *L'Italia dialettale*, , –
Tabulae codicum manu scriptorum [. . .] in Biblioteca Palatina Vindobonensi asservatorum (–), Vienna
Tavoni, Mirko ( ), *Latino, grammatica, volgare*, Padua
( ), 'La linguistica rinascimentale. . L'Europa occidentale', in *Storia della linguistica*, ed. G. Lepschy, Bologna, –
Taylor, Henry ( ), *The Mediaeval Mind*, London
Terracini, B. ( ), 'Appunti sui "Parlamenti ed Epistole" in antico dialetto piemontese', *Romania*, , –
Thurot, Charles ( ), *Notices et extraits de divers manuscrits latins pour servir à l'histoire des doctrines grammaticale au moyen âge*, Paris
To anin, G. ( ), *Storia dell'umanesimo dal XIII al XVI secolo*, Città di Castello (second edition: ( ) *Storia dell'umanesimo*, Bologna)
Tolson, J. ed., ( ), *The* Summa *of Petrus Helias on Priscianus Minor* (with an introduction by Margaret Gibson), in *Cahiers de l'Institut du moyen-âge grec et latin*, –
Tommaseo, N. and Bellini, B. (–), *Dizionario della lingua italiana*, Turin and elsewhere
Ullman, B. ( ), *The Humanism of Coluccio Salutati*, Padua
Ullman, B. and Stadter, P. ( ), *The Public Library of Renaissance Florence*, Padua
Verde, Armando (–), *Lo studio fiorentino*, Florence
( ), 'Libri tra le pareti domestiche', *Memorie domenicane*, ns, , –
Vespasiano da Bisticci (–), *Le vite*, ed. A. Greco, Florence
Vicini, Emilio ( ), 'Le "Letture Pubbliche" in Modena nei secoli XV-XVII', *Rassegna per la storia della Università di Modena e della cultura superiore modenese*, , –
Vidmanová-Schmidtová, A., ed. ( ), *Quinque claves sapientiae. Incerti auctoris, Rudium doctrina. Bonvicini de Ripa, Vita scolastica*, Leipzig
Villa, Claudia ( ), 'Un'ipotesi per l'epistola a Cangrande', *IMU*, , –

( ), *La 'lectura Terentii'*, : *Da Ildemaro a Francesco Petrarca*, Padua
(–), 'I manoscritti di Orazio', *Aevum*, , – ; , – ; , –
( ), 'Censimento dei codici di Orazio', in *Orazio Enciclopedia oraziana*, , –
Villani, Filippo, ( ), ed. G. Galletti, *Liber de civitatis Florentiae famosis civibus*, Florence
Villani, Giovanni ( ), *Cronica*, ed. F. Dragomanni, Florence
Viscardi, A. ( ), 'La scuola medievale e la tradizione scolastica classica', *SM*, ns, , –
( ), 'Lettura degli *auctores* moderni nelle scuole medievali di grammatica', in *Studi in onore di Angelo Monteverdi*, Modena, –
Viti, Paolo ( ), s.v. Dati, Agostino, in *DBI*, , –
Walser, E. ( ), *Poggius florentinus*, Leipzig and Berlin
Walther, Hans (–), *Proverbia sententiaeque latinitatis medii aevi*, Göttingen
( ), *Initia Carminum ac Versuum Medii Aevi Posterioris Latinorum*, Göttingen
Weiss, Roberto ( ), *Il primo secolo dell'umanesimo*, Rome
Wieruszowski, Helene ( ), 'Arezzo as a center of learning and letters in the thirteenth century', *Traditio*, , – (reprinted in Wieuszowski ( ), –)
( ), 'Rhetoric and the classics in Italian education of the thirteenth century', *Studia Gratiana*, , – (reprinted in Wieuszowski ( ), –)
( ), *Politics and Culture in Medieval Spain and Italy*, Rome
Wilmart, A. ( ), 'L'art poétique de Geo roi de Vinsauf et les commentaires de Barthélemy de Pise', *Revue bénédectine*, , –
Witt, Ronald ( ), *Hercules at the Crossroads: The Life, Works, and Thought of Coluccio Salutati*, Durham, NC
( ), 'Whad did Giovannino read and write? Literacy in early Renaissance Florence', *I Tatti Studies*, ,
Woods, M. ( ), 'Poetic digression and the interpretation of medieval literary texts', in *Acta Conventus neo-latini sanctandreani*, ed. I. MacFarlane, Medieval and Renaissance Texts and Studies, , Binghampton, NY, –
( ), 'An unfashionable rhetoric in the fifteenth century', *Quarterly Journal of Speech*, , –
( ), 'A medieval rhetoric goes to school – and to the University: the commentaries on the *Poetria nova*', *Rhetorica*, , –
Wright, C. ( ), *Fontes Harleiani*, London
Wrobel, J., ed. ( ), Eberhardi Bethuniensis, *Graecismus*, Breslau
Zabughin, V. (–) *Giulio Pomponio Leto. Saggio critico*, Rome and Grottaferrata
Zaccagnini, Guido (a), 'Le epistole in latino e in volgare di Pietro de' Boattieri', *Studi e memorie per la storia dell'Università di Bologna*, , –
(b), 'L'insegnamento privato a Bologna e altrove nei secc. XIII e XIV', *Atti e memorie della R. Deputazione di storia patria per le province di Romagna*, ser. , , –

( ), 'Lettori e scolari della Marca d'Ancona allo Studio di Bologna dal sec. XIII al XV', *Atti e memorie della R. Deputazione di storia patria per le Marche*, ser. , , –

( ), 'I grammatici e l'uso del volgare eloquio a Bologna nel secolo XIII', *Studi e memorie per la storia dell'Università di Bologna*, , –

Zanazzo, G. ( ), 'Lo statuto dei medici di Vicenza nell'anno ', *Nuovo archivio veneto*, ser. ,

Zanelli, A. ( ), *Del pubblico insegnamento in Pistoia dal XIV al XVI secolo*, Rome

Zdekauer, L. ( ), *Lo Studio di Siena nel Rinascimento*, Milan

Zorzanello, P. (–), *Catalogo dei codici latini della Biblioteca Nazionale Marciana di Venezia non compresi nel catalogo di G. Valentinelli*, Trezzano

Index of manuscripts

NB: Manuscripts excluded in the lists on – and above are not included in this index.
§ = not seen personally

General index

Authors of secondary works and twentieth-century writers have not been included; mythological and legendary figures and literary characters have also been excluded. Only names of obscure persons have been identified (insofar as it has been possible to relate them to a school context). Names left in italics have not been modernized from their form in manuscript sources.

General index

General index

General index

General index

General index

General index